To the Student:

A helpful supplemental learning aid for this textbook is available through your college bookstore:

> * *Student Guide* by Dudley W. Curry consists of detailed chapter review outlines, objective tests, exercises, problems, and solutions.

If this supplement is not in stock, ask the bookstore manager to order it for you.

Prentice-Hall Series in Accounting

Charles T. Horngren, Editor

AUDITING: AN INTEGRATED APPROACH, 3/E
Arens/Loebbecke
INTERMEDIATE ACCOUNTING
Danos/Imhoff
FINANCIAL STATEMENT ANALYSIS
Foster
FINANCIAL ACCOUNTING: PRINCIPLES AND ISSUES, 2/E
Granof
INTRODUCTION TO FINANCIAL ACCOUNTING, 2/E
Horngren
INTRODUCTION TO MANAGEMENT ACCOUNTING, 6/E
Horngren
COST ACCOUNTING: A MANAGERIAL EMPHASIS, 5/E
Horngren
CPA PROBLEMS AND APPROACHES TO SOLUTIONS, 5/E
VOLUMES I & II
Horngren/Leer
KOHLER'S DICTIONARY FOR ACCOUNTANTS, 6/E
Cooper/Ijiri
ADVANCED MANAGEMENT ACCOUNTING
Kaplan
FUND ACCOUNTING: THEORY AND PRACTICE, 2/E
Lynn/Freeman
A NEW INTRODUCTION TO FINANCIAL ACCOUNTING, 2/E
May/Mueller/Williams
AUDITING PRINCIPLES, 5/E
Stettler
BUDGETING, 4/E
Welsch

Introduction to
MANAGEMENT
ACCOUNTING

Charles T. Horngren

Ph.D., C.P.A.
Stanford University

6th Edition

Introduction to
MANAGEMENT
ACCOUNTING

Prentice-Hall, Inc., Englewood Cliffs, New Jersey 07632

Library of Congress Cataloging in Publication Data

HORNGREN, CHARLES T.
    Introduction to management accounting.

    Bibliography: p.
    Includes index.
    1. Managerial accounting.   2. Cost accounting.
I. Title.
HF5635.H814   1981   658.1'511   80-265838
ISBN-0-13-487836-1

Editorial/production supervision by Rick Laveglia
Interior and cover design by Janet Schmid
Cover photograph: New York, N.Y. © Michael Melford, Peter Arnold, Inc.
Manufacturing buyer: Raymond Keating

*Material from the Certificate in Management Accounting Examination, Copyright © 1973–83 by
the National Association of Accountants, is reprinted and/or adapted with permission.*

Printed in the United States of America

10   9   8   7   6   5   4   3   2

ISBN 0-13-487836-1

Prentice-Hall International, Inc., *London*

Prentice-Hall of Australia Pty. Limited, *Sydney*

Editora Prentice-Hall do Brasil, Ltda., *Rio de Janeiro*

Prentice-Hall Canada Inc., *Toronto*

Prentice-Hall of India Private Limited, *New Delhi*

Prentice-Hall of Japan, Inc., *Tokyo*

Prentice-Hall of Southeast Asia Pte. Ltd., *Singapore*

Whitehall Books Limited, *Wellington, New Zealand*

to Joan, Scott, Mary, Susie, Cathy

Charles T. Horngren is the Edmund W. Littlefield Professor of Accounting at Stanford University. A graduate of Marquette University, he received his MBA from Harvard University and his Ph.D. from the University of Chicago. He is also a recipient of an honorary DBA from Marquette University.

A Certified Public Accountant, Horngren served on the Accounting Principles Board for six years, the Financial Accounting Standards Board Advisory Council for five years, and the Council of the American Institute of Certified Public Accountants for three years. He is currently serving as a trustee of the Financial Accounting Foundation.

A member of the American Accounting Association, Horngren has been its President and its Director of Research. He received the Outstanding Accounting Educator Award in 1973 when the association initiated an annual series of such awards.

The California Certified Public Accountants Foundation gave Horngren its Faculty Excellence Award in 1975 and its Distinguished Professor Award in 1983. He is the first person to have received both awards.

Professor Horngren is also a member of the National Association of Accountants, where he was on its research planning committee for three years. He is a member of the Board of Regents, Institute of Management Accounting, which administers the Certified Management Accountant examinations.

Horngren is the author of three other books published by Prentice-Hall: *Cost Accounting: A Managerial Emphasis,* Fifth Edition, 1982; *Introduction to Financial Accounting,* Second Edition, 1984; and *CPA Problems and Approaches to Solutions,* Fifth Edition, 1979 (with J. A. Leer)

Charles T. Horngren is the Consulting Editor for the Prentice-Hall Series in Accounting.

CONTENTS

PART TWO Accounting for Planning and Control

14 JOB-COSTING AND OVERHEAD APPLICATION   417

15 OVERHEAD APPLICATION: DIRECT
AND ABSORPTION COSTING   446

PART FIVE Quantitative Methods

16 INFLUENCES OF QUANTITATIVE TECHNIQUES
ON MANAGEMENT ACCOUNTING   479

CONTENTS

PART SIX Basic Financial Accounting for Managers

20 DIFFICULTIES IN MEASURING NET INCOME 635

PART SEVEN Appendixes

APPENDIX A: RECOMMENDED READINGS 673

APPENDIX B: FUNDAMENTALS OF COMPOUND INTEREST AND THE USE OF PRESENT-VALUE TABLES 675

APPENDIX C: GLOSSARY 682

INDEX 697

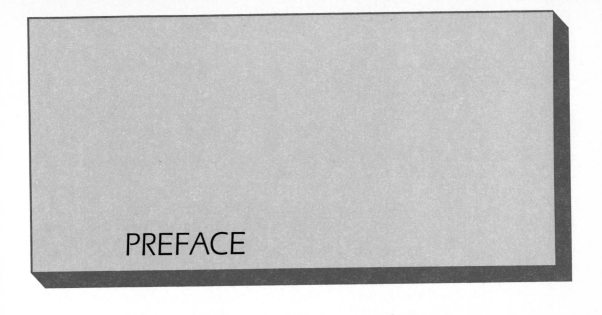

PREFACE

Introduction to Management Accounting is the second member of a matched pair of books that provides full coverage of the essentials of financial and managerial accounting. The first book is *Introduction to Financial Accounting*. In combination, the pair can be used throughout two semesters or three quarters of introductory accounting.

This book is an introduction to internal accounting—most often called *management accounting*. It deals with important topics that all students of management and business should study. The book is written primarily for students who have had one or two terms of basic accounting.

It is also appropriate for continuing educational programs of varying lengths in which the students have had no formal training in accounting. My twin goals have been to choose relevant subject matter and to present it clearly.

The major change in this edition is the inclusion in each chapter's assignment materials of additional short exercises and problems that cover the basic ideas in a straightforward way. More than ever, this is a basic book aimed at a reader who has a minimal background in accounting, if any.

This book attempts a balanced, flexible approach. For example, it deals as much with not-for-profit, retail, wholesale, selling, and administrative situations as it does with manufacturing. The fundamental accounting concepts and techniques for planning and control are applicable to all types and functions of organizations, not just to manufacturing. This more general approach makes it easier for the student to relate the book's examples and problems to his or her particular interests. Moreover, many valuable concepts (for example, master budgets) are more easily grasped if they are not complicated by intricate manufacturing situations.

Stress is on planning and control, not on product costing for purposes of inventory valuation and income determination. This approach, which excludes the troublesome but unimportant complications introduced by changes in inventory levels, simplifies the presentation of planning and control techniques in the classroom. Instead of the simultaneous discussion of costs for control and for product costing found in most texts, this text concentrates on planning and control without dwelling on product costing at all until Chapter 13. At that point, process costing, job costing, and the implications of overhead application for product costing may be considered in perspective and in relation to management policy decisions regarding the "best" inventory valuation method.

A chapter-by-chapter description of the new features and changes in this edition is given in the front section of the instructor's manual. Significant changes include the following:

1. As mentioned earlier, more straightforward, easier assignment material has been introduced, covering the nuts and bolts of each chapter. For example, consider Problems 2–9, 2–10, 2–15, 2–16; 3–22 through 3–26; 5–16 through 5–21; 6–15, 6–16, 6–17; 14–16 through 14–19; and 14–22 through 14–24. Simultaneously, the general nature of the assignment material, which has been a key to the popularity of preceding editions, has been retained. There is enough variety and flexibility so that instructors can tailor their courses to their students.

2. More emphasis on product costing. For example, a new chapter on process costing contains three separable parts for those instructors who desire to cover the topic either lightly or in depth.

3. A heavily revised chapter on job costing that focuses on basic journal entries and shows how overhead is applied to products.

4. A new presentation of the master budget and its preparation, including step-by-step examples and several short exercises in the assignment material.

5. The chapter on flexible budgets and standards has been divided into two separable parts.

6. A new chapter on capital budgeting and the effects of income taxes, including the impact of the Accelerated Cost Recovery System. Clearer and expanded presentation of how inflation affects capital budgeting.

7. Expansion of coverage of financial accounting, including financial ratios and inventory valuation issues, along with a statement of changes in financial position that focuses on cash as well as working capital.

8. More divisions of chapters into major distinctive parts to increase flexibility in using the book.

9. New sections "Highlights to Remember" and "Accounting Vocabulary."

10. Insertion of more "Summary Problems for Your Review" in the middle of chapters.

11. More cross-referencing by specific page numbers (instead of merely chapter numbers or exhibit numbers).

12. The student guide (by Dudley W. Curry), a supplement that parallels the textbook chapters, contains numerous changes and additions in the self-test and practice exercises, especially the multiple-choice items in quantitative form ("mini problems").

13. The chapter-by-chapter test bank (by Henry W. Collier), available free to adopters, has been revised and considerably expanded, both in the softcover version and in the computerized option that facilitates the construction of the tailor-made exams in volume.

In my opinion, the first nine chapters provide the foundation of the field of management accounting. These nine chapters may be amplified by assigning the subsequent chapters in the given order, or by inserting them after the earlier chapters as desired. Such insertion may be achieved without disrupting the readers' flow of thought. The most obvious candidates for insertion are indicated below:

Chapters   1   2   3   4   5   6   7   8   9 → 10–20

                ↑   ↑   ↑   ↑

              17   14   11   15

              18   (or 13 and 14) 12

              19

              20

If some of the basics of financial accounting are to be included in a course in management accounting, any or all of the financial accounting chapters (17–20) may be undertaken anytime. (For example, to provide a change of pace, I have even used such chapters in the midst of a course.)

Instructors tend to disagree markedly about the sequence of topics in a course in management accounting. Criticisms of *any* sequence in a textbook are inevitable. Consequently, this book tries to provide a modular approach that permits hopping and skipping back and forth with minimal inconvenience. In a nutshell, my rationale is to provide a loosely constrained sequence to facilitate diverse approaches to teaching. Content is of primary importance; sequence is secondary.

Teaching is highly personal and is heavily influenced by the backgrounds and interests of assorted students in miscellaneous settings. To satisfy this audience, a book must be a pliable tool, not a straitjacket.

As the author, I prefer to assign the chapters in the sequence provided in the book. But I am not enslaved by the sequence. Through the years, I have assigned an assortment of sequences, depending on the readers' backgrounds.

Part One, "Focus on Decision Making," provides a bedrock introduction, so I assign it in its entirety. Sometimes I assign Chapter 17 immediately after Chapter 1, particularly if the readers have little or no background in financial accounting. Moreover, if there is time in the course for students to become more familiar with product costing, I frequently assign Chapter 14 immediately after Chapter 3. Furthermore, there is much logical appeal to studying the chapters on capital budgeting (Chapters 11 and 12) immediately after the chapters on relevant costs (Chapters 4 and 5). However, tradition has prevented my placing such chapters there, plus the fact that capital budgeting is often amply covered in other courses. In addition, the master budget is often covered in finance courses, so Chapter 6 is frequently skipped in courses in accounting.

Part Two, "Accounting for Planning and Control," emphasizes the attention-directing functions of accounting. I often assign Chapter 15 immediately after Chapter 7 because it stresses the product-costing aspects of standard costs, whereas Chapter 7 focuses on the control aspects.

Parts Three, Four, and Five cover capital budgeting, product costing, and quantitative methods, respectively. In particular, the coverage of product costing has been expanded, especially the fundamentals of process and job costing. All of these topics are important. However, the decision to study them will depend on the teacher's preferences, the other courses in the curriculum, and the students' previous course.

Part Six introduces, interprets, and appraises basic financial accounting. These chapters form a unified package that covers all elementary financial accounting in capsule form with heavy stress on interpretation and uses and, except in Chapter 17, with little attention given to the accumulation of the information. In my view, a major objective of basic financial accounting should be to equip the student with enough fundamental concepts and terminology so that he or she can reasonably comprehend any industrial corporate annual report.

Chapters 17–20 may be skipped entirely or may be used in a variety of ways:

1. In courses or executive programs where the students have *no* accounting background but where the main emphasis is on management rather than financial accounting
2. In courses where the chapters may be used as a quick review by students who have had some financial accounting previously
3. In courses where one or two of Chapters 17–20 may be chosen to remedy weaknesses or gaps in the background of the students

Chapters 17–20 need not be used in total, page by page or topic by topic. Teachers are free to pick and choose those topics (particularly in Chapters 19 and 20) that seem most suitable for their students.

On the other hand, some teachers may want to use these chapters to teach the fundamentals of financial accounting to students with no prior background in accounting. Classroom testing has shown that such teaching can be done successfully, provided that the homework material is chosen carefully.

The front of the solutions manual contains several alternate detailed assignment schedules and ample additional recommendations to teachers regarding how best to use this book.

ACKNOWLEDGMENTS

I have received ideas, assistance, miscellaneous critiques, and assorted assignment material in conversations and by mail from many students and professors. Each has my gratitude, but the list is too long to enumerate here.

Professor Dudley W. Curry (Southern Methodist University) has my special thanks for offering many helpful suggestions and for preparing the student guide that is available as supplementary material.

Henry W. Collier (Florida Atlantic University) has my appreciation for preparing the test bank material.

I am also especially grateful to Jonathan Schiff for his preparation of Instructor Resource Outlines, available to adopters upon request.

The following professors supplied helpful reviews of the previous edition or drafts of this edition: Robert S. Adden, Metwalli B. Amer, Bobbe Barnes, James T. Bristol, David M. Buehlmann, Ron Burrows, Jim F. Cook, David B. Croll, William F. Crum, Keith B. Ehrenreich, William Ferrara, John Harris, Jean Karlhuber, Dee Kleespie, Melissa Martinson, Wiley S. Mitchell, Allen Schulden, Jan L. Sweeney, Srinivasan Umapathy, Alton Wheelock, and Robert W. Williamson.

Elsie Young has my special appreciation for her cheerful and skillful typing and related help. Lynnette Haxton, Dana Derebery, and Douglas Price have my gratitude for ably performing assorted editorial chores. Elizabeth J. Ritter deserves recognition for her flawless typing of the solutions manual.

My thanks to the American Institute of Certified Public Accountants (problem material designated as CPA), the National Association of Accountants (NAA), the Society of Management Accountants of Canada (SMA), and the Institute of Management Accounting (CMA) for their generous permission to use some of their problems and to quote from their publications.

And, finally, my thanks to Jack Ochs, Rick Laveglia, Janet Schmid, and Elinor Paige at Prentice-Hall.

Comments from users are welcome.

CHARLES T. HORNGREN

Introduction to
MANAGEMENT
ACCOUNTING

1

PERSPECTIVE: SCOREKEEPING, ATTENTION DIRECTING, AND PROBLEM SOLVING

Learning Objectives

Learning objectives will be found at the beginning of each chapter. These objectives specify some of the important knowledge and skills you should have after completing your study of the chapter and your solving of the assignment material:

1. List the three major means and ends of an accounting system.
2. Name the basic functions of a management planning and control system and identify the main accounting activities that relate to these functions.
3. Identify the three main characteristics of service organizations that distinguish them from manufacturing organizations.
4. Distinguish between the line and staff roles in an organization.
5. Contrast the functions of controllers and treasurers.
6. Describe the two major themes of this book: cost-benefit and behavioral implications.
7. Identify the major distinctions between management accounting and financial accounting.

The main purpose of this chapter is to gain an overall view of the accountant's role in an organization. We shall see that the accountant must fulfill three jobs simultaneously: scorekeeping, attention directing, and problem solving.

WHY STUDY ACCOUNTING?

Accounting is a very important subject. This opinion is widely shared, as shown by eleven hundred responses to a questionnaire sent to academicians and managers in 1979 by the American Assembly of Collegiate Schools of Business. Here are the top three courses ranked in terms of how much time and effort should be spent by students on each one of them:

	RANKED BY MANAGERS	RANKED BY PROFESSORS
Accounting	1	2
Finance	2	3
Economics	3	1

Because accounting is so pervasive, an understanding of its usefulness—and its limitations—is desirable for all managers in all types of organizations. Company presidents, production managers, public accountants, hospital administrators, controllers, school administrators, sales managers, and politicians are better equipped to perform their duties when they have a reasonable grasp of accounting data.

The study of management accounting can be especially fruitful because it helps us see through the eyes of those who are subject to accounting measures of performance and who often depend heavily on accounting data for guidance in decision making. There is no escaping the linkage of accounting and management, so the study of management accounting will help you regardless of whether you become a manager or an accountant, or whether you will work in retailing, manufacturing, health care, public management, or other activity.

Many production, marketing, and government executives are stronger managers when they have a solid understanding of accounting. Moreover, their performance and their rewards are often determined by how accounting measurements are made, so they have a natural self-interest in gaining knowledge about accounting.

The more that managers know about accounting, the better able they are to plan and control the operations of their organization and its subunits. Managers will be handicapped in dealing with both inside and outside parties if their comprehension of accounting is sketchy or confused. Therefore the learning of accounting is almost always a wise investment.

APPLICABILITY TO NONPROFIT ORGANIZATIONS

This book is aimed at a variety of readers, including students who aspire to become either managers or professional accountants. The major focus will be on profit-seeking organizations. However, the fundamental ideas also apply to not-for-profit organizations. In addition, managers of the latter typically have personal investments in profit-seeking organizations or must interact with businesses in some way.

Managers and accountants in various settings such as hospitals, universities, and government agencies have much in common with their counterparts in profit-seeking organizations. There is money to be raised and spent. There are budgets to be prepared and control systems to be designed and implemented. There is an obligation to use resources wisely. If used intelligently, accounting contributes to efficient operations. The strengthening of the accounting system was a mandatory condition imposed by the federal government in saving New York City from bankruptcy.

The overlap of government and business is everywhere. Government administrators and politicians are much better equipped to deal with problems inside and outside their organizations if they understand accounting. For example, a knowledge of accounting is crucial for decisions regarding research contracts, defense contracts, and loan guarantees. Keep in mind that decisions about loan guarantees have been made with respect to tiny businesses (for instance, through the Small Business Administration) as well as large businesses such as Lockheed and Chrysler.

MEANS AND ENDS OF AN ACCOUNTING SYSTEM

An *accounting system* is a formal means of gathering data to *aid* and *coordinate* collective decisions in light of the overall goals or objectives of an organization. The accounting system is the major quantitative information system in almost every organization. An effective accounting system provides information for three broad purposes or ends: (1) internal reporting to managers, for use in planning and controlling routine operations; (2) internal reporting to managers, for use in strategic planning, that is, the making of special decisions and the formulating of overall policies and long-range plans; and (3) external reporting to stockholders, government, and other outside parties.

Both management (internal parties) and external parties share an interest in all three important purposes, but the emphases of financial accounting and of management (internal) accounting differ. **Financial accounting** has mainly been concerned with the third purpose and has traditionally been oriented toward the historical, stewardship aspects of external reporting.[1] The distinguishing feature of management accounting is its emphasis on the planning and control purposes. **Management accounting** is the process of identification, measurement, accumulation, analysis, preparation, interpretation, and communication of information that assists executives in fulfilling organizational objectives.

[1] For a book-length presentation of the subject, see Charles T. Horngren, *Introduction to Financial Accounting* (Englewood Cliffs, N.J.: Prentice-Hall), the companion to this textbook. For an expanded definition of management accounting, see *Management Accounting*, April 1983, p. 65.

What means do accounting systems use to fulfill the ends? Accounting data can be classified and reclassified in countless ways. A helpful overall classification was proposed in a research study of seven large companies with geographically dispersed operations:

☐ By observation of the actual decision-making process, specific types of data needs were identified at particular organizational levels—the vice-presidential level, the level of the factory manager, and the level of the factory head [foreman], for example—each involving quite distinct problems of communication for the accounting department.[2]

The research team found that three types of information, each serving as different means, often at various management levels, raise and help to answer three basic questions:

1. *Scorecard questions:* Am I doing well or badly?
2. *Attention-directing questions:* Which problems should I look into?
3. *Problem-solving questions:* Of the several ways of doing the job, which is the best?

The scorecard and attention-directing uses of data are closely related. The same data may serve a scorecard function for a foreman and an attention-directing function for the foreman's superior. For example, many accounting systems provide performance reports in which actual results are compared with previously determined budgets or standards. Such a performance report often helps to answer scorecard questions and attention-directing questions simultaneously. Furthermore, the actual results collected serve not only control purposes but also the traditional needs of financial accounting, which is chiefly concerned with the answering of scorecard questions. This collection, classification, and reporting of data is the task that dominates day-to-day accounting.

Problem-solving data may be used in long-range planning and in making special, nonrecurring decisions, such as whether to make or buy parts, replace an X-ray machine, or add or drop a product. These decisions often require expert advice from specialists such as industrial engineers, budgetary accountants, and statisticians.

In sum, the accountant's task of supplying information has three facets:

1. SCOREKEEPING. The accumulation of data. This aspect of accounting enables both internal and external parties to evaluate organizational performance and position.

2. ATTENTION DIRECTING. The reporting and interpreting of information that helps managers to focus on operating problems, imperfections, inefficiencies, and opportunities. This aspect of accounting helps managers to concern themselves with important aspects of operations promptly enough for effective action either through perceptive planning or through astute day-to-day supervision. Attention directing is commonly associated with current planning and control and with the analysis and investigation of recurring routine internal-accounting reports.

[2] H. A. Simon, *Administrative Behavior*, 2nd ed. (New York: Macmillan), p. 20.

3. **PROBLEM SOLVING.** This aspect of accounting involves the concise quantification of the relative merits of possible courses of action, often with recommendations as to the best procedure. Problem solving is commonly associated with nonrecurring decisions, situations that require special accounting analyses of reports.

The above distinctions sometimes overlap or merge. Consequently, it is often difficult to pinpoint a particular accounting task as being scorekeeping, attention directing, or problem solving. Nevertheless, attempts to make these distinctions provide insight into the objectives and tasks of both accountants and managers. Exhibit 1-1 recapitulates the relationships just described. Above all, accounting systems are the means, and better decisions are the ends.

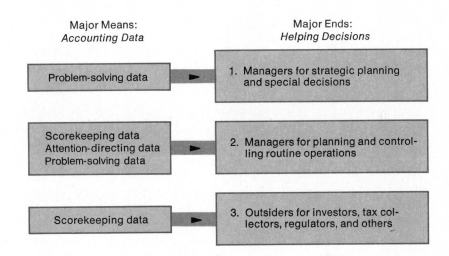

EXHIBIT 1-1

Means and Ends of an Accounting System

THE MANAGEMENT PROCESS AND ACCOUNTING

❑ Nature of Planning and Controlling

The nucleus of the management process is decision making, the purposeful choosing among a set of alternative courses of action in light of some objective. These decisions range from the routine (making daily production schedules) to the nonroutine (launching a new product line).

Decision making underlies the commonly encountered twofold division of the management process into (1) planning and (2) control. The left side of Exhibit 1-2 clearly demonstrates the planning and control cycle of current operations. **Planning** (the top box) means deciding on objectives and the means for their attainment. It provides the answers to two questions: What is desired? and When and how is it to be accomplished? **Controlling** (the two boxes labeled "Action" and "Evaluation" immediately below) means implementation of plans and the use of feedback so that objectives are optimally attained. The feedback loop is the central facet of any concept of control, and timely, systematic measurement is the chief means of providing useful feedback. Planning and controlling are so inter-

Perspective: Scorekeeping, Attention Directing, and Problem Solving

5

EXHIBIT
1-2

Accounting
Framework
for Planning
and Control

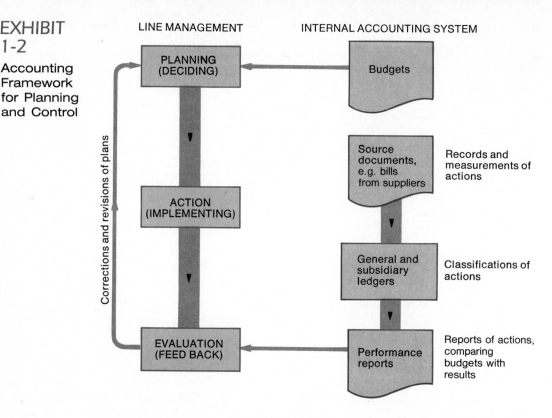

LINE MANAGEMENT

INTERNAL ACCOUNTING SYSTEM

PLANNING
(DECIDING)

Budgets

Corrections and revisions of plans

ACTION
(IMPLEMENTING)

Source
documents,
e.g. bills
from suppliers

Records and
measurements of
actions

General and
subsidiary
ledgers

Classifications of
actions

EVALUATION
(FEED BACK)

Performance
reports

Reports of actions,
comparing
budgets with
results

twined that it seems artificial to draw rigid lines of separation between them; yet at times we will find it useful to concentrate on one or the other phase of the planning-control cycle.

❏ Management by Exception

The right side of Exhibit 1-2 shows that accounting formalizes plans by expressing them in the language of figures as **budgets.** Accounting formalizes control as **performance reports** (the last box), which provide feedback by comparing results with plans and by highlighting **variances** (i.e., deviations from plans).

Exhibit 1-3 shows the form of a simple performance report for a law firm. Such reports spur investigation of exceptions. Operations are then brought into conformity with the plans, or the plans are revised. This is an example of management by exception.

Management by exception means that the executive's attention and effort are concentrated on the significant deviations from expected results and that the information system highlights the areas most in need of investigation. Management should not ordinarily be concerned with results that conform closely to plans. However, well-conceived plans should incorporate enough discretion or flexibility so that the manager may feel free to pursue any unforeseen opportunities. In other words, the definition of control does not mean that managers should blindly cling to a preexisting plan when unfolding events indicate the desirability of actions that were not authorized specifically in the original plan.

EXHIBIT 1-3

Performance Report				
	BUDGETED AMOUNTS	ACTUAL AMOUNTS	DEVIATIONS OR VARIANCES	EXPLANATION
Revenue from fees	xxx	xxx	xx	—
Various expenses	xxx	xxx	xx	—
Net income	xxx	xxx	xx	—

☐ Illustration of the Budget and the Performance Report

An assembly department constructs electric fans. The assembly of the parts and the installation of the electric motor are basically hand operations. Each fan is inspected before being transferred to the painting department. In light of the present sales forecast, a production schedule of 4,000 window fans and 6,000 table fans is planned for the coming month. Cost classifications are shown in Exhibit 1-4, the Assembly Department Budget.

The operating plan, which is crystallized in the form of a department budget for the coming month, is prepared in conferences attended by the foreman, the foreman's supervisor, and an accountant. Each of the costs subject to the foreman's control is scrutinized. Its average amount for the past few months is often used as a guide, especially if past performance has been reasonably efficient. However, the budget is a *forecast* of costs. Each cost is projected in light of trends, price changes, alterations in product mix, specifications, labor methods, and changes in production volume from month to month. The budget is then formulated, and it becomes the foreman's target for the month.

As actual factory costs are incurred during the month, the accounting department collects them and classifies them by departments. At the end of the month (or perhaps weekly, or even daily, for such key items as materials or assembly labor), the accounting department prepares an Assembly Department Performance Report (Exhibit 1-5). In practice, this report may be very detailed and contain explanations of variances from the budget.

EXHIBIT 1-4

Perspective:
Scorekeeping,
Attention
Directing, and
Problem
Solving

Assembly Department Budget For the Month Ended March 31, 19X1	
Material (detailed by type: metal stampings, motors, etc.)	$ 38,000
Assembly labor (detailed by job classification, number of workers, etc.)	73,000
Other labor (foremen, inspectors)	12,000
Utilities, maintenance, etc.	7,500
Supplies (small tools, lubricants, etc.)	2,500
Total	$133,000

EXHIBIT
1-5

Assembly Department Performance Report For the Month Ended March 31, 19X1			
	BUDGET	ACTUAL	VARIANCE
Material (detailed by type: metal stampings, motors, etc.)	$ 38,000	$ 39,000	$1,000 U
Assembly labor (detailed by job classification, number of workers, etc.)	73,000	74,300	1,300 U
Other labor (foremen, inspectors)	12,000	11,200	800 F
Utilities, maintenance, etc.	7,500	7,400	100 F
Supplies (small tools, lubricants, etc.)	2,500	2,600	100 U
Total	$133,000	$134,500	$1,500 U

U = Unfavorable.
F = Favorable.

The foreman and his[3] superiors use this report to help appraise performance. The spotlight is cast on the variances—the deviations from the budget. It is through management's investigation of these variances that better ways of doing things are discovered. The budget is an aid to planning; the performance report is the tool that aids controlling. The accounting system thus helps to direct managerial attention to the exceptions. Exhibit 1-2 shows that accounting does *not* do the controlling. Controlling consists of actions performed by the managers and their subordinates and of the evaluation that follows actions. Accounting assists the managerial control function by providing prompt measurements of actions and by systematically pinpointing trouble spots. This management-by-exception approach frees managers from needless concern with those phases of operations that are adhering to plans.

MANAGEMENT ACCOUNTING AND SERVICE ORGANIZATIONS

The basic ideas of management accounting were developed in manufacturing organizations. However, they have evolved so that they are applicable to all types of organizations, including service organizations. Service organizations or industries are defined in various ways. For our purposes, they are organizations that produce a service rather than a tangible good. Examples are public accounting firms, law firms, management consultants, real estate firms, transportation companies, banks, insurance companies, and hotels. Almost all nonprofit or not-for-profit organizations[4] are service industries. Examples are hospitals, schools, libraries, museums, and a department of forestry.

[3] For conciseness, "he" and "his" are often used in this book rather than "he or she" or "his or hers" or "person." If you prefer, substitute "she" or "hers" where appropriate. Incidentally, the assignment material frequently refers to women in a variety of management roles.

[4] *Not-for-profit* is more accurately descriptive of these organizations, but it is more awkward than *nonprofit*, which will be used henceforth for brevity.

The characteristics of service organizations include the following:

1. *Labor is intensive.* For example, the highest costs in schools and law firms are wages, salaries, and payroll-related costs, not the costs relating to the use of machinery, equipment, and extensive physical facilities.
2. *Output is usually difficult to define.* For example, the output of a university might be defined as the number of degrees granted, but many critics would maintain that the real output is "what is contained in the students' brains." In such a manner the output of schools and hospitals is often idealized; attempts to measure output are often considered immoral.
3. *Major inputs and outputs cannot be stored.* For example, although raw materials and store merchandise may be stored, a hotel's available labor force and rooms are either used or unused as the day expires.

Many activities of nonprofit organizations are little different from those of business organizations, as these two excerpts illustrate:

☐ Many colleges have begun turning over their facilities to virtually anyone with a check. Southern Methodist University and dozens of other schools are putting their staff and facilities to work over the summer. Rentals of dormitory rooms will bring in over $1 million for SMU this summer.[5]

☐ The success of the King Tut-inspired reproductions spotlights the push that many museums are making into the retail arena. Now, with Christmas approaching, once-stuffy institutions are busily advertising their wares in shops, mail-order catalogs, and tie-ins with leading department stores.[6]

In this book, references are made to service industry applications as the various management accounting techniques are discussed. A major generalization is worth mentioning at the outset. Simplicity is the watchword for installation of systems in service industries and nonprofit organizations, especially in the health industry, where highly paid professionals such as physicians barely bother with a written medical record, much less a time card. In fact, simplicity is a fine watchword for the design of any accounting system. Complexity tends to generate data-gathering and data-interpreting costs that often exceed prospective benefits. Simplicity is sometimes referred to as KISS (which means keep it simple, stupid).

ROLE OF THE ACCOUNTANT IN THE ORGANIZATION

☐ Line and Staff Authority

The organization chart in Exhibit 1-6 portrays how many manufacturing companies are divided into subunits. In particular, consider the distinction between **line** and **staff authority.** Most organizations specify certain activities as their basic mission, such as the production and sale of goods or services. All subunits of the organization that are *directly* responsible for conducting these basic activities are called *line* departments. The others are

[5] "Ivory Towers for Rent," *Newsweek,* August 9, 1982, p. 62.

[6] "Museums Find a New Patron: The Retail Market," *Business Week,* October 24, 1979, p. 135.

EXHIBIT 1-6 Partial Organization Chart of a Manufacturing Company

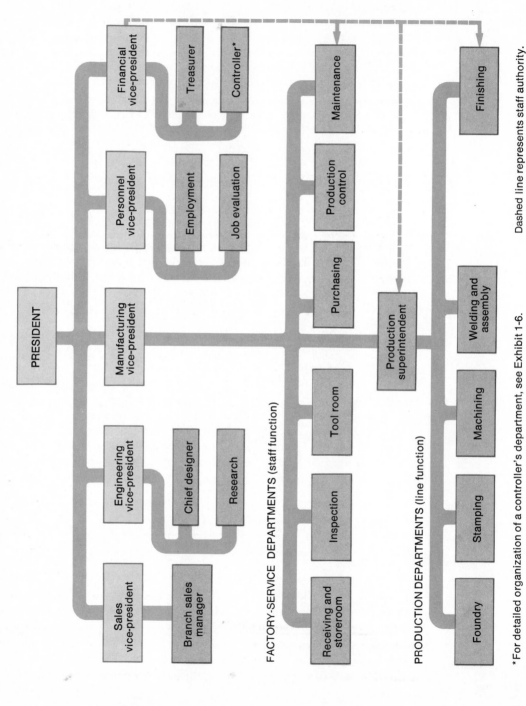

FACTORY-SERVICE DEPARTMENTS (staff function)

PRODUCTION DEPARTMENTS (line function)

Dashed line represents staff authority.

*For detailed organization of a controller's department, see Exhibit 1-6.

10

called *staff* departments because their principal task is to support or service the line departments. Thus staff activities are *indirectly* related to the basic activities of the organization. For instance, Exhibit 1-6 shows a series of factory-service departments that perform the staff functions of supporting the line functions carried on by the production departments.

The controller fills a staff role, in contrast to the line roles of sales and production executives. The accounting department has responsibility for providing other managers with specialized service, including advice and help in budgeting, analyzing variances, pricing, and the making of special decisions. The accounting department does not exercise direct authority over line departments: Its authority to prescribe uniform accounting and reporting methods is delegated to the controller by top-line management. The uniform accounting procedure is authorized by the company president and is installed for him by the controller. When the controller prescribes the line department's role in supplying accounting information, he is not speaking as the controller, a staff person; he is speaking for top-line management.

Theoretically, the controller's decisions regarding the best accounting procedures to be followed by line people are transmitted to the president. In turn, the president communicates these procedures through a manual of instructions, which comes down through the line chain of command to all people affected by the procedures. In practice, however, the daily work of the controller, and his face-to-face relationships with the production manager or foreman, may require him to direct how production records should be kept or how work tickets should be completed. The controller usually holds delegated authority from top-line management over such matters.

Exhibit 1-7 shows how a controller's department may be organized. In particular, note the distinctions between the scorekeeping, attention-directing, and problem-solving roles. Unless some internal accountants are given the latter two roles as their primary responsibilities, the scorekeeping tasks tend to be too dominating and the system less responsive to facilitating management's decision making.

❏ The Controller

The title of controller is applied to various accounting positions, the stature and duties of which vary from company to company. In some firms the controller is little more than a glorified bookkeeper who compiles data, primarily for external reporting purposes. In General Electric the controller is a key executive who aids managerial planning and control in over 160 company subdivisions. In most firms the controller has a status somewhere between these two extremes. For example, his opinion on the tax implications of certain management decisions may be carefully weighed, yet his opinion on other aspects of these decisions may not be sought. In this book, **controller** (sometimes called **comptroller,** derived from the French *compte,* for "account") means the chief management accounting executive. We have already seen that the modern controller does not do any controlling in terms of line authority except over his own department. Yet the modern concept of controllership maintains that, in a special sense, the controller *does* control: By reporting and interpreting relevant data, the

Perspective:
Scorekeeping,
Attention
Directing, and
Problem
Solving

11

EXHIBIT 1-7
Organization Chart of a Controller's Department

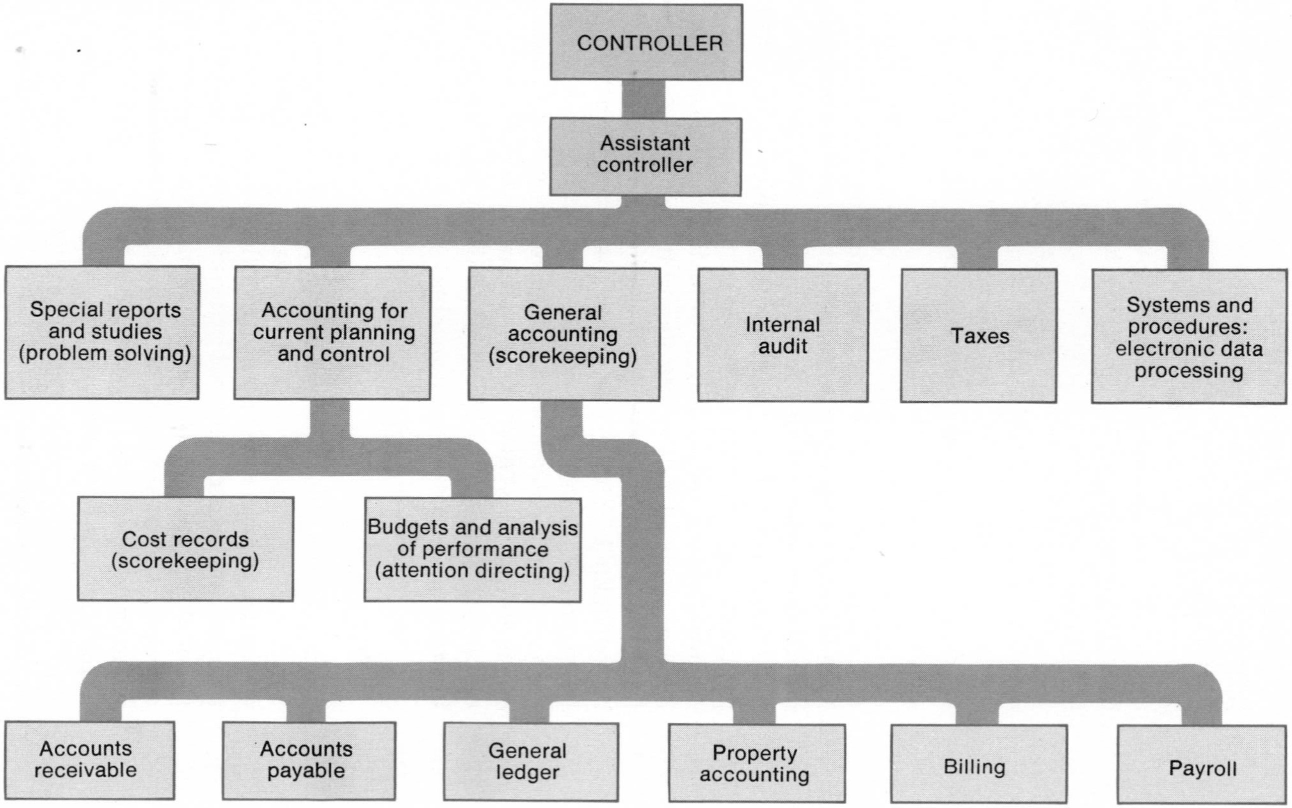

controller exerts a force or influence or projects an attitude that impels management toward logical decisions that are consistent with objectives.

Distinctions Between Controller and Treasurer

Many people confuse the offices of controller and treasurer. The Financial Executives Institute, an association of corporate treasurers and controllers, distinguishes their functions as follows:

CONTROLLERSHIP	TREASURERSHIP
1. Planning for control	1. Provision of capital
2. Reporting and interpreting	2. Investor relations
3. Evaluating and consulting	3. Short-term financing
4. Tax administration	4. Banking and custody
5. Government reporting	5. Credits and collections
6. Protection of assets	6. Investments
7. Economic appraisal	7. Insurance

Note how management accounting is the controller's primary *means* of implementing the first three functions of controllership.

We shall not dwell at length on the treasurer's functions. As the seven points indicate, the treasurer is concerned mainly with financial, as distinguished from operating, problems. The exact division of various accounting and financial duties obviously varies from company to company.

The controller has been compared to the ship's navigator. The navigator, with the help of his specialized training, assists the captain. Without the navigator, the ship may flounder on reefs or miss its destination entirely, but the captain exerts his right to command. The navigator guides and informs the captain as to how well the ship is being steered. This navigator role is especially evident in points 1 through 3 of the seven functions.

TWO MAJOR THEMES

We have already seen that management accounting is concerned with how accounting systems help collective decisions. This book emphasizes two major themes or philosophies or problems regarding the design of these systems: (a) cost-benefit and (b) behavioral implications. Both will briefly be described now; and because of their importance, both will also be mentioned often in succeeding chapters.

Cost-Benefit Theme

The **cost-benefit theme** (or call it a philosophy or state of mind if you prefer) is our fundamental approach to choosing among accounting systems and accounting methods. It will dominate this book. Systems and methods are economic goods that are available at various costs. Which system does a manager want to buy? A simple file drawer for amassing receipts and canceled checks? An elaborate budgeting system based on computerized descriptive models of the organization and its subunits? Or something in between?

Of course, the answer depends on the buyer's perceptions of the expected incremental (additional) benefits in relation to the incremental costs. For example, a hospital administrator may contemplate the installation of a TECHNICON computerized system for controlling hospital operations. Such a system uses a single document of original entry for automatic accumulation of data for financial records, medical records, costs by departments, nurse staffing requirements, drug administration, billings for patients, revenue generated by physicians, and so forth. This system will lead to more efficiency, less waste, and fewer errors. But the system costs $14 million. Thus the system is not good or bad by itself. It must meet the tests of the economics of information—its value must exceed its cost.

Steak and butter may be "good buys" for many people at 50¢ per pound, but they may become "bad buys" at $5 per pound. Similarly, a particular accounting system may be a wise investment in the eyes of the buyer if it will generate a sufficiently better collective set of decisions to justify its added cost. However, an existing accounting system is only *one* source of information for decision making. In many organizations it may be more economical to gather data by one-shot special efforts than by having a ponderous system that repetitively gathers data that are rarely used.

The cost-benefit theme provides innate appeal to both the hardheaded manager and the theoretician. Managers have been employing the cost-benefit test for years, even though they may not have expressed it as such. Instead, they may have referred to the theme as "having to be practical" despite what theory may say. But the cost-benefit theme has an exceedingly rich underlying theory of information economics.[7] It is good theory that can supply the missing rationale for many management practices.

❏ Behavioral Theme

Financial accounting is often looked upon as being a cold, objective discipline. But management accounting is not; it is wrapped up in behavioral ramifications. The buyer of an accounting system should be concerned with how it will affect the decisions (behavior) of the affected managers. Earlier we saw how budgets and performance reports may play a key role in helping management. Emphasis on the future is a major feature of management accounting, whereas it is not as prominent in financial accounting. Budgets are the chief devices for compelling and disciplining management planning. Without budgets, planning may not get the front-and-center focus that it usually deserves.

The performance reports that are so widely used to judge decisions, subunits, and managers have enormous influence on the behavior of the affected individuals. Performance reports not only provide feedback to improve future economic decisions but may also provide desirable or undesirable motivation. The choices of the content, format, timing, and distri-

[7] See J. Demski, *Information Analysis*, 2nd ed. (Reading, Mass.: Addison-Wesley, 1980).

bution of performance reports are heavily influenced by their probable impact on motivation.

In a nutshell, management accounting can best be understood by using a cost-benefit theme coupled with an awareness of the importance of behavioral effects. Even more than financial accounting, management accounting spills over into related disciplines, such as economics, the decision sciences, and the behavioral sciences.

MANAGEMENT ACCOUNTING AND FINANCIAL ACCOUNTING

☐ Freedom of Choice

Financial accounting and management accounting would be better labeled as external accounting and internal accounting, respectively. "Financial accounting" emphasizes the preparation of reports of an organization for external users such as banks and the investing public. "Management accounting" emphasizes the preparation of reports of an organization for its internal users such as company presidents, college deans, and head physicians.

Keep in mind that the same basic accounting system compiles the fundamental data for both financial accounting and management accounting. Furthermore, external forces (for example, income tax authorities and regulatory bodies, such as the United States Securities and Exchange Commission and the California Health Facility Commission) often limit management's choices of accounting methods. Organizations frequently limp along with a system that has been developed in response to the legal requirements imposed by external parties. In short, many existing systems are primarily oriented toward external rather than internal users.

Consider our cost-benefit theme that accounting systems are commodities like steak or butter. As just noted, generally accepted accounting standards or principles affect both internal and external accounting. However, change in internal accounting is not inhibited by generally accepted financial accounting standards. The managers who buy an internal accounting system can have anything their hearts desire—as long as they are willing to pay the price. For instance, for its own management purpose, a hospital, a manufacturer, or a university can account for its assets on the basis of *current values*, as measured by estimates of replacement costs. No outside agency can prohibit such accounting.

There are no "generally accepted management accounting principles" that forbid particular measurements. Indeed, the cost-benefit theme refrains from stating that any given accounting is bad or good. Instead, the theme says that any accounting system or method (no matter how crazy it appears at first glance) is desirable as long as it brings incremental benefits in excess of its incremental costs.

Of course, satisfying internal demands for data (as well as external demands) means that organizations may have to keep more than one set of records. At least in the United States, there is nothing immoral or unethical

Perspective:
Scorekeeping,
Attention
Directing, and
Problem
Solving

15

about having many simultaneous sets of books—but they are expensive. The cost-benefit test says that their perceived increases in benefits must exceed their perceived increases in costs. Ultimately, benefits are measured by whether better collective decisions are forthcoming in the form of increased net cost savings or profit (or, in the case of many nonprofit institutions, in the form of increased quality or quantity of service rendered for each dollar spent).

The major distinctions between management accounting and financial accounting are briefly enumerated in Exhibit 1-8. These points will be amplified in succeeding chapters.

❏ Effects of Regulation

The accounting reports to government agencies such as the Internal Revenue Service and the Securities and Exchange Commission are reports to outside parties. Hence such reports have usually been classified as subparts of financial accounting. Nevertheless, the proliferation of government regulation has definitely affected the design of internal accounting systems. Governmental agencies have broad powers, with the force of law, to subpoena any internal document deemed necessary.

An illustration of the effects of government regulation is the requirement that universities and defense contractors allocate costs to government contracts in specified ways or risk failure to get reimbursed.

The most noteworthy illustration is probably the **Foreign Corrupt Practices Act,** which was passed by the U.S. Congress in 1977. The title is misleading because the act's provisions pertain to the internal control systems of *all* publicly held companies, *even if they conduct no business outside the United States.* The act contains not only specific prohibitions against bribery and other corrupt practices but also requirements (a) for maintaining accounting records in reasonable detail and accuracy and (b) for maintaining an appropriate system of internal accounting controls.

The largest impact of the act has been the mandatory documentation of internal control by *management* rather than only by *outside auditors.* To help management, internal auditing staffs have been markedly increased. Internal auditors help review and evaluate systems with regard to minimizing errors, fraud, and waste. More important, many internal auditing staffs have a primary responsibility for conducting **management audits,** which concentrate on reviewing and evaluating managers' actions to see whether top management's operating policies are being implemented. Incidentally, management audits are not confined to profit-seeking organizations. The General Accounting Office (GAO) of the U.S. federal government conducts these audits on a massive scale. Moreover, in 1977 a public accounting firm did a management audit of the city of New York.

The overall impact of government regulation is very controversial. Many managers insist that the extra costs of compliance far exceed any possible benefits. One benefit is that operating managers, now more than ever, must become more intimately familiar with their accounting systems. The resulting changes in the systems sometimes provide stronger controls and more informative reports. In short, outside forces may have more influence on management accounting than appears at first glance.

EXHIBIT 1-8

Distinctions Between Management Accounting and Financial Accounting

	MANAGEMENT ACCOUNTING	FINANCIAL ACCOUNTING
1. Primary users	Organization managers at various levels	Organization managers and outside parties such as investors and government agencies
2. Freedom of choice	No constraints other than costs in relation to benefits of improved management decisions	Constrained by generally accepted accounting principles (GAAP)
3. Behavioral implications	Concern about how measurements and reports will influence managers' daily behavior	Concern about how to measure and communicate economic phenomena. Behavioral impact is secondary
4. Time focus	Future orientation: formal use of budgets as well as historical records. Example: 19X3 **budget** versus 19X3 **actual** performance	Past orientation: historical evaluation. Example: 19X3 **actual** versus 19X2 **actual** performance
5. Time span	Flexible, varying from hourly to ten or fifteen years	Less flexible. Usually one year or one quarter
6. Reports	Detailed reports: concern about details of parts of the entity, products, departments, territories, etc.	Summary reports: concern primarily with entity as a whole
7. Delineation of activities	Field is less sharply defined. Heavier use of economics, decision sciences, and behavioral sciences	Field is more sharply defined. Lighter use of related disciplines

❑ Career Opportunities

Accounting deals with all facets of a complex organization. It provides an excellent opportunity for gaining broad knowledge. Senior accountants or controllers in a corporation are sometimes picked as production or marketing executives. Why? Because they may have impressed other executives as having acquired general management skills. Accounting cuts across all management functions, including purchasing, manufacturing, wholesaling, retailing, and a variety of marketing and transportation activities. A number of recent surveys have indicated that more chief executive officers began their careers in an accounting position than in any other area such as marketing, production, or engineering.

In 1979 Korn/Ferry International, an executive recruiting firm, conducted a survey of thirty-six hundred senior-level executives (excluding presidents) working in several hundred of the largest companies in the United States. The composite executive began in accounting or finance and still believes that to be the "fast track" to the top. In particular, there is a dominance of accountants near the peak of the corporate pyramid.

High inflation and persistent economic recession have also accelerated the prominence of accounting as a major route to high-level responsibilities. Former controllers have risen to the top of such mammoth companies as General Motors, FMC, Fruehauf, and Pfizer. *Business Week* (August 15, 1982, p. 84) pointed out that controllers

☐ . . . are now getting involved with the operating side of the company, where they give advice and influence production, marketing, and investment decisions as well as corporate planning. Moreover, many controllers who have not made it to the top have won ready access to top management. . . . Probably the main reason the controller is getting the ear of top management these days is that he or she is virtually the only person familiar with all the working parts of the company.

☐ Certified Management Accountant

A prominent feature of the field of financial accounting is the use of outside auditors to give assurance about the reliability of the financial information being supplied by managers. These external auditors are called **Certified Public Accountants** in the United States and Chartered Accountants in many other English-speaking nations. The major U.S. professional association in the private sector that regulates the quality of outside auditors is the American Institute of Certified Public Accountants (AICPA).

The largest association of management accountants in the United States is the **National Association of Accountants** (NAA). The rise of the field of management accounting led the NAA in 1972 to establish the Institute of Management Accounting. The institute administers a program leading to the Certificate in Management Accounting (CMA).[8] The objectives of the program are threefold:

1. To establish management accounting as a recognized profession by identifying the role of the management accountant and the underlying body of knowledge, and by outlining a course of study by which such knowledge can be acquired.
2. To foster higher educational standards in the field of management accounting.
3. To establish an objective measure of an individual's knowledge and competence in the field of management accounting.

The highlight of the program is a qualifying examination covering five parts: (1) economics and business finance, (2) organization and behavior, (3) public reporting, (4) periodic reporting for internal and external purposes, and (5) decision analysis, including modeling and information systems. The CMA designation is gaining increased stature in the management community as a credential parallel to the CPA.

[8] Information can be obtained from the Institute, 570 City Center Building, Ann Arbor, Michigan 48104.

Summary

An understanding of the overall purposes of the accounting system provides perspective for the study of the usefulness of accounting to management. The accounting system of the future is likely to be a multiple-purpose system with a highly selective reporting scheme. It will be highly integrated and will serve three main purposes: (1) routine reporting to management, primarily for planning and controlling current operations (scorekeeping and attention directing); (2) special reporting to management, primarily for long-range planning and non-recurring decisions (problem solving); and (3) routine reporting on financial results, oriented primarily for external parties (scorekeeping). The first two purposes are the distinguishing characteristics of management accounting, which would be better called internal accounting.

Internal accounting is interwoven with management itself. Accounting is a service function. Internal accounting is not management as ordinarily conceived, but it helps management do a better job.

Summary
Problems For Your Review

(Try to solve these problems before examining the solutions that follow.)

❏ Problem One

The scorekeeping, attention-directing, and problem-solving duties of the accountant have been described in this chapter and elsewhere in literature. The accountant's usefulness to management is said to be directly influenced by how good an attention director and problem solver he or she is.

Evaluate this contention by specifically relating the accountant's duties to the duties of operating management.

❏ Problem Two

Using the organization charts in this chapter (Exhibits 1-6 and 1-7), answer the following questions.

1. Do the following have line or staff authority over the machine foreman: maintenance foreman, manufacturing vice-president, production superintendent, purchasing agent, storekeeper, personnel vice-president, president, chief budgetary accountant, chief internal auditor?

2. What is the general role of service departments in an organization? How are they distinguished from operating or production departments?

3. Does the controller have line or staff authority over the cost accountants? The accounts receivable clerks?

4. What is probably the *major duty* (scorekeeping, attention directing, or problem solving) of the following:

   1. Payroll clerk
   2. Accounts receivable clerk
   3. Cost record clerk

   4. Head of general accounting
   5. Head of taxes
   6. Head of internal auditing

Perspective:
Scorekeeping,
Attention
Directing, and
Problem
Solving

19

7. Budgetary accountant
8. Cost analyst
9. Head of special reports and studies

10. Head of accounting for planning
    and control
11. Controller

❑ Solution to Problem One

Operating managers may have to be good scorekeepers, but their major duties are to concentrate on the day-to-day problems that most need attention, to make longer-range plans, and to arrive at special decisions. Accordingly, because managers are concerned mainly with attention directing and problem solving, they will obtain the most benefit from the alert internal accountant who is a useful attention director and problem solver.

❑ Solution to Problem Two

1. The only executives having line authority over the machining foreman are the president, the manufacturing vice-president, and the production superintendent.
2. A typical company's major purpose is to produce and sell goods or services. Unless a department is directly concerned with producing or selling, it is called a service or staff department. Service departments exist only to help the production and sales departments with their major tasks: the efficient production and sale of goods or services.
3. The controller has line authority over all members of his own department, all those shown in the controller's organization chart (Exhibit 1-7, p. 12).
4. The major duty of the first five—through the head of taxes—is typically scorekeeping. Attention directing is probably the major duty of the next three. Problem solving is probably the primary duty of the head of special reports and studies. The head of accounting for planning and control and the controller should be concerned with all three duties: scorekeeping, attention directing, and problem solving. However, there is a perpetual danger that day-to-day pressures will emphasize scorekeeping. Therefore accountants and managers should constantly see that attention directing and problem solving are also stressed. Otherwise the major management benefits of an accounting system may be lost.

Highlights to Remember

This section will be found at the end of each chapter. It briefly recapitulates some key ideas, suggestions, comments, or terms that might otherwise be overlooked or misunderstood.

1. This book will stress two major themes: cost-benefit and behavioral implications. The choice of a system or method should be based on weighing the value of the system against its cost. This weighing entails making predictions of how individuals will collectively behave under one system versus another. Therefore the behavioral impact of alternatives is given ample attention throughout this book.
2. Nearly all managers are stronger managers when they attain an understanding of management accounting. Furthermore, their performance and their rewards are often heavily affected by how accounting measurements are made. Consequently, regardless of the size or goals of their organization, managers have a natural self-interest in learning about accounting.

Accounting Vocabulary

This section will usually immediately precede the "Assignment Material" for each chapter. Vocabulary is an extremely important and often troublesome phase of the learning process. A fuzzy understanding of terms hampers the learning of concepts and the ability to solve accounting problems.

Before proceeding to the assignment material or to the next chapter, be sure you understand the following words or terms. Their meaning is explained in the chapter and also in the Glossary at the end of this book:

Attention directing; budget; Certified Management Accountant; Certified Public Accountant; comptroller; controller; controlling; cost-benefit theme; financial accounting; Foreign Corrupt Practices Act; line authority; management accounting; management audit; management by exception; National Association of Accountants; performance report; planning; problem solving; scorekeeping; source document; staff authority; variance.

Assignment Material

The assignment material for each chapter is divided into two groups: *fundamental* and *additional*. The first group consists of carefully designed, relatively straightforward material aimed at conveying the essential concepts and techniques of the particular chapter. These assignments provide a solid introduction to the major concepts of accounting for management control.

The second group of assignment material in each chapter should not be regarded as being inferior to the fundamental group. Many of these problems can be substituted for ones in the fundamental group.

Fundamental Assignment Material

1–1. Role of the accountant in the organization: line and staff functions.

1. Of the following, who have line authority over a cost record clerk: budgetary accountant; head of accounting for current planning and control; head of general accounting; controller; storekeeper; production superintendent; manufacturing vice-president; president; production control chief?
2. Of the following, who have line authority over an assembler: stamping foreman; assembly foreman; production superintendent; production control chief; storekeeper; manufacturing vice-president; engineering vice-president; president; controller; budgetary accountant; cost record clerk?

1–2. Scorekeeping, attention directing, and problem solving. For each of the following, identify the function the accountant is performing—i.e., scorekeeping, attention directing, or problem solving. *Also state* whether the departments mentioned are service or production departments.

1. Processing the weekly payroll for the repair and maintenance department
2. Explaining the welding foreman's performance report
3. Analyzing the costs of several different ways to blend raw materials in the foundry
4. Tallying sales, by branches, for the sales vice-president
5. Analyzing, for the president, the impact on net income of a contemplated new product
6. Interpreting why a branch did not meet its sales quota
7. Interpreting variances on a post office supervisor's performance report
8. Preparing the budget for research and development
9. Preparing journal entries for depreciation on the personnel manager's office equipment
10. Preparing a customer's monthly statement

Perspective:
Scorekeeping,
Attention
Directing, and
Problem
Solving

21

Additional Assignment Material

1–3. Give three examples of service organizations.

1–4. "Additional government regulation assists the development of management accounting systems." Do you agree? Explain.

1–5. Distinguish between the American Institute of CPAs and the National Association of Accountants.

1–6. What two major themes will be emphasized in succeeding chapters?

1–7. "The Foreign Corrupt Practices Act applies to bribes paid outside the United States." Do you agree? Explain.

1–8. "The accounting system is intertwined with operating management. Business operations would be a hopeless tangle without the paper work that is so often regarded with disdain." Do you agree? Explain, giving examples.

1–9. What are the three broad purposes of an accounting system?

1–10. "The emphases of financial accounting and management accounting differ." Explain.

1–11. Distinguish between scorekeeping, attention directing, and problem solving.

1–12. Give examples of special nonrecurring decisions and of long-range planning.

1–13. Briefly describe the probable business information system of the future.

1–14. "Planning is much more vital than control." Do you agree? Explain.

1–15. Distinguish between a source document, a subsidiary ledger, and a general ledger.

1–16. Distinguish between a budget, a performance report, and a variance.

1–17. "Management by exception means abdicating management responsibility for planning and control." Do you agree? Explain.

1–18. "Good accounting provides automatic control of operations." Do you agree? Explain.

1–19. Distinguish between line and staff authority.

1–20. "The controller does control in a special sense." Explain.

1–21. "The importance of accurate source documents cannot be overemphasized." Explain.

1–22. Organization chart. Draw an organization chart for a single-factory company with the following personnel. Which represent factory service departments? Production departments?

Punch press foreman	Personnel vice-president
Vice-president and controller	Maintenance foreman
Storekeeper	Sales vice-president
Drill press foreman	Production control chief
Production superintendent	Production planning chief
Chairman of the board	Assembly foreman
Engineering vice-president	Purchasing agent
Manufacturing vice-president	Secretary and treasurer
President	

1–23. Costs and benefits. Marks & Spencer, a giant retailer in the United Kingdom, has used a cost-benefit approach to the paper bureaucracy. Looked at in isolation, each form seemed reasonable:

☐ . . . but in terms of the total procedure, the substantial effort required in each department to confirm the accuracy of the information or verify completion of the task seemed to be out of proportion to any value achieved. By challenging the need for detail and highlighting the fact that sensible approximation costs less, the committee succeeded in simplifying many documents and eliminating others.[9]

Describe the rationale that should underlie systems design.

1–24. Focus on financial data. *Business Week* (January 10, 1977, p. 58) reported:

☐ Rockwell's Anderson, a veteran of the company's automotive operations, recalls that when he sat in on meetings at Rockwell's North American Aircraft Operations in the late 1960s, "there'd be 60 or 70 guys talking technical problems, with never a word on profits." Such inattention to financial management helped Rockwell lose the F-15 fighter to McDonnell Douglas, Pentagon sources say. Anderson brought in profit-oriented executives, and he has now transformed North American's staff meetings to the point that "you seldom hear talk of technical problems any more," he says. "It's all financial."

What is your reaction to Anderson's comments? Are his comments related to management accounting?

1–25. Nonprofit systems. The following comments were made by a certified public accountant who has had extensive experience in consulting in service industries and nonprofit organizations: "Valid accounting principles are so basic that, once accepted, it seems incredible that there was ever any question. Accounting doesn't advance on theory, only when somebody's money is at stake."

REQUIRED: During the 1970s and early 1980s hospitals hired consultants in droves to install cost-accounting systems. Why hadn't hospitals used much cost accounting before?

1–26. Measuring costs and benefits. The *Wall Street Journal* (January 31, 1980, p. 1) reported:

☐ A score of U.S. cities—from Decatur, Ill., and Birmingham, Ala., to San Francisco and New York City—have either just completed or plan to build soon downtown convention centers to help them compete for the tourist and business dollar. "There has been a sharp growth in trade shows and the work-shop and educational type of convention," says a spokesman for Grand Rapids, Mich., which just opened a $26.3 million center.

☐ A spokesman for the Trade Show Bureau, an industry group, says more companies are using shows and conventions to build sales leads. Sources estimate it costs a firm $140 for a salesman in the field to contact a new potential customer, while the same contact at a show costs $50 or less.

(1) Explain briefly how management accountants may have arrived at the two estimated costs mentioned in the second paragraph of this extract. (2) How would you classify these accounting activities: scorekeeping, attention directing, or problem solving?

[9] Derek G. Rayner, "A Battle Won in the War on the Paper Bureaucracy," *Harvard Business Review*, January–February 1975, p. 14.

2

INTRODUCTION TO COST-VOLUME RELATIONSHIPS

Learning Objectives

When you have finished studying this chapter, you should be able to

1. Define **variable costs** and **fixed costs** and compute the effects of changes in volume on each of these costs
2. Construct a cost-volume-profit graph from appropriate data
3. From given data, calculate activity volume in both total dollars and total units to (a) break even and (b) achieve a specified target profit
4. Describe the roles of cost-volume analysis and contribution margins in management planning and control
5. Specify the limiting assumptions that underlie cost-volume analysis
6. Distinguish between contribution margin and gross margin
7. Construct and interpret a P/V chart (Appendix 2A)
8. Compute cost-volume-profit relationships on an after-tax basis (Appendix 2B)

How do the costs and revenues of a hospital change as one more patient is admitted for a four-day stay? How are the costs and revenue of an airline affected when one more passenger is boarded at the last moment, or when one more flight is added to the schedule? How should the budget request by the California Department of Motor Vehicles be affected by the predicted increase in the state's population? These questions have a common theme: What will happen to financial results if a specified level of activity or volume fluctuates? Their answers are not easy to obtain, and managers usually resort to some simplifying assumptions, especially concerning cost behavior (that is, how total costs are affected as volume changes). Nevertheless, implicitly or explicitly, managers must frequently answer these questions in order to reach intelligent decisions.

The managers of profit-seeking organizations usually study the relationships of revenue (sales), expenses (costs), and net income (net profit). This study is commonly called cost-volume-profit analysis. The managers of nonprofit organizations also will benefit from the study of cost-volume-profit relationships, primarily because knowledge of how costs fluctuate in response to changes in volume is valuable regardless of whether profit is an objective. After all, no organization has unlimited resources.

The subject matter of this chapter is straightforward. No knowledge of the accountant's assumptions underlying financial reporting is required. After all, in its most fundamental sense, an income statement is merely a presentation of the financial results from matching sales and related costs.

Cost-volume relationships are important to both management and outsiders. For example, the U.S. Securities and Exchange Commission requires the management of all publicly held companies to include a "management's discussion and analysis of the results of operations" in corporate quarterly and annual reports. Some of these analyses are quite detailed, and all focus on the effects of changes in prices and physical quantities sold.

VARIABLE COSTS AND FIXED COSTS

Variable costs and **fixed costs** are usually defined in terms of how a total cost changes in relation to fluctuations in the quantity of some selected activity. Activity bases are diverse: They may be the number of orders processed, the number of lines billed in a billing department, the number of admissions to a theater, the number of pounds handled in a warehouse, the hours of labor worked in an assembly department, the number of rides in an amusement park, the seat-miles on an airline, the dollar sales in a grocery store, or some other index of volume.

If Watkins Products pays its door-to-door sales personnel a 40% straight commission, then the total cost of sales commissions should be 40% of the total sales dollars. If a sports shop buys bags of fish bait at $2 each, then the total cost of fish bait should be $2 times the total number of bags. These are variable costs. They are uniform *per unit*, but their *total* fluctuates in direct proportion to the total of the related activity or volume. These relationships are depicted graphically in Exhibit 2-1. The costs of most merchandise, materials, parts, supplies, commissions, and many types of labor are variable.

If a manufacturer of picture tubes for color television rents a factory for $100,000 per year, then the unit cost of rent applicable to each tube will depend on the total number of tubes produced. If 100,000 tubes are produced, the unit cost will be $1; if 50,000 tubes are produced, $2. This is an example of a fixed cost, a cost that does not change in *total* but becomes progressively smaller on a *per-unit* basis as volume increases. Real estate taxes, real estate insurance, many executive salaries, and straight-line depreciation charges are fixed costs.

COMPARISON OF VARIABLE AND FIXED COSTS

Note carefully from the foregoing examples that the "variable" or "fixed" characteristic of a cost relates to its *total dollar amount* and not to its per-unit amount. A variable cost (the 40% sales commission) is constant per unit, and its *total* dollar amount *changes* proportionally with changes in activity or volume. A fixed cost (the factory rent) varies inversely with activity or volume changes on a per-unit basis but is *constant* in *total* dollar amount. The following table summarizes these relationships:

TYPE OF COST	IF ACTIVITY VOLUME INCREASES (OR DECREASES):	
	Total Cost	Cost Per Unit*
Fixed costs	No change†	Decrease (or increase)
Variable costs	Increase (or decrease)	No change†

*Per unit of activity volume, for example, product units, passenger miles, sales dollars.
†When using data for making predictions, it is usually less confusing to think of fixed costs as a *total* and variable costs as an amount *per unit* of activity.

❏ Relevant Range

A fixed cost is fixed only in relationship to a given period of time—the budget period—and a given, though wide, range of activity called the **relevant range.** Fixed costs may change from budget year to budget year solely because of changes in insurance and property tax rates, executive salary levels, or rent levels. But these items are highly unlikely to change within a given year. In addition, the total budgeted fixed costs may be formulated on the basis of an expected activity level (i.e., volume), say, within a relevant planning range of 40,000 to 85,000 units of production per month. However, operations on either side of the range will result in major salary adjustments or in the layoff or hiring of personnel. For example, assume the total monthly fixed cost within the relevant range is $100,000. If operations fall below 40,000 units, changes in personnel and salaries will slash fixed costs to $60,000. If operations rise above 85,000 units, increases in personnel and salaries will raise fixed costs to $115,000.

EXHIBIT 2-1   Variable-Cost Behavior

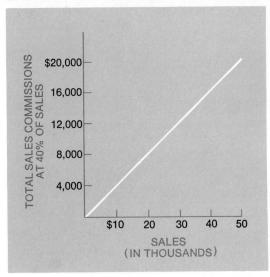

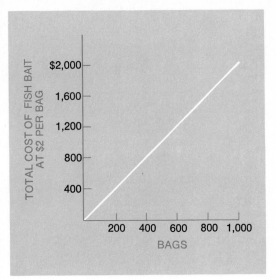

These assumptions—a given time period and a given range—are shown graphically at the top of Exhibit 2-2. The possibility that operations will be outside the relevant range is usually remote. Therefore the three-level refinement at the top of Exhibit 2-2 is usually not graphed. A single horizontal line is typically extended through the plotted activity levels, as at the bottom of the exhibit.

☐ Some Simplifying Assumptions

Nearly every organization has some variable costs and some fixed costs. As you may suspect, it is often difficult to classify a cost as exactly variable or exactly fixed. Many complications arise, including the possibility of costs behaving in some nonlinear way (not behaving as a straight line). For example, as workers learn to process incoming tax forms, productivity rises. This means that total costs may behave like this:

but not like this:

Moreover, costs may simultaneously be affected by more than one activity base. For example, the costs of shipping labor may be affected by *both* the weight and the number of units handled. We shall investigate various facets of this problem in succeeding chapters; for now, we shall assume that any cost may be classified as either variable or fixed. We assume also that a given variable cost is associated with *only one* measure of volume, and that relationship is *linear*.

EXHIBIT
2-2
Fixed Costs
and the
Relevant
Range

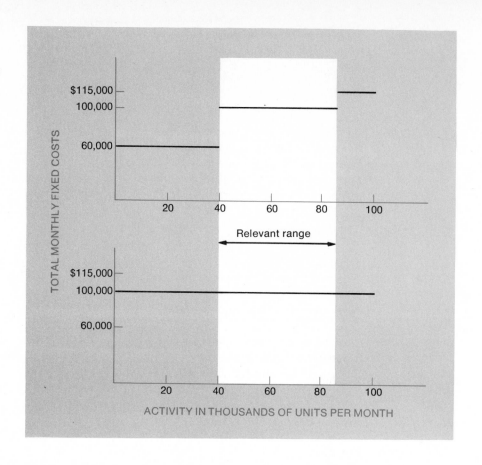

ILLUSTRATION OF COST-VOLUME-PROFIT ANALYSIS

The following situation will be used to demonstrate the techniques and the analytical power of cost-volume-profit analysis. Amy Winston, the manager of food services for the state of California, is trying to decide whether to rent a line of food vending machines for the state's Sacramento buildings. Although the unit prices and acquisition costs differ among individual food items, Winston feels that an average unit selling price of 50¢ and an average unit acquisition cost of 40¢ will suffice for purposes of this analysis. The following revenue and expense relationships are predicted:

	PER UNIT	PERCENT OF SALES
Selling price	$.50	100%
Cost of each item	.40	80
Contribution margin	$.10	20%
Monthly fixed expenses:		
Rent	$1,000	
Wages for replenishing and servicing	4,500	
Other fixed expenses	500	
Total fixed expenses per month	$6,000	

The following six sections will explore various aspects of the above data. A new question or requirement will be stated at the start of each section.

❏ 1. Break-Even Point—Two Analytical Techniques

Express the monthly break-even point in number of units and in dollar sales.

The study of cost-volume-profit relationships is often called *break-even analysis*. The latter is a misnomer because the break-even point—the point of zero net income—is often only incidental to the planning decision at hand. Still, knowledge of the break-even point provides insights into the possible riskiness of certain courses of action.

Consider two basic techniques for computing a break-even point: equation and contribution margin.

a. **Equation technique.** This is the most general form of analysis, the one that may be adapted to any conceivable cost-volume-profit situation. You are familiar with a typical income statement. Any income statement can be expressed in equation form, as follows:

$$sales - variable\ expenses - fixed\ expenses = net\ income\ (1)$$

or

$$sales = variable\ expenses + fixed\ expenses + net\ income\ (1)$$

Let X = number of units to be sold to break even. Then

$$\$.50X = \$.40X + \$6,000 + 0$$
$$\$.10X = \$6,000 + 0$$
$$X = \frac{\$6,000 + 0}{\$.10}$$
$$X = 60,000\ units$$

Total sales in the equation is a price-times-quantity relationship. In the above equation, this was expressed as $.50X. Of course, the *dollar* sales answer in this case could now be obtained by multiplying 60,000 *units* by 50¢, which would yield the break-even dollar sales of $30,000. Another approach is to solve the equation method for total sales *dollars* directly. This method becomes important in those situations where *unit* price and *unit* variable costs are not given. Rather, you must work with variable cost as a *percentage* of each sales *dollar*. Moreover, most companies sell more than one product, and the overall break-even point is often expressed in sales dollars because of the variety of product lines. For example, although radios and television sets cannot be meaningfully added, their sales prices provide an automatic common denominator.

The same equation, this time using the relationship of variable costs and profits as a *percentage* of sales, may be used to obtain the sales in dollars:

Let X = sales in dollars needed to break even. Then

$$X = .80X + \$6,000 + 0$$
$$.20X = \$6,000 + 0$$
$$X = \frac{\$6,000 + 0}{.20}$$
$$X = \$30,000$$

b. **Contribution-margin technique.** If algebra is not one of your strong points, you may prefer to approach cost-volume-profit relationships in the following common-sense arithmetic manner. Every unit sold generates a **contribution margin** or **marginal income,** which is the excess of the sales price over the variable expenses pertaining to the units in question:

Unit sales price	$.50
Unit variable expenses	.40
Unit contribution margin to fixed expenses and net income	$.10

The $.10 unit contribution is divided into total fixed expenses plus a target net income to obtain the number of *units* that must be sold to break even: ($6,000 + 0) ÷ $.10 = 60,000 units.

The computation in terms of *dollar* sales is:

Sales price	100%
Variable expenses as a percentage of dollar sales	80
Contribution-margin percentage	20%

Therefore 20% of each sales dollar is the amount available for the recovery of fixed expenses and the making of net income: ($6,000 + 0) ÷ .20 = $30,000 sales needed to break even. The contribution-margin percentage is based on dollar sales. This percentage is often expressed as a ratio (for example, 20% expressed as .20).

The terms *net income* and *net profit* are used interchangeably. Similarly, *expenses* and *costs* are used interchangeably. In this context, costs refer to the costs (whether variable or fixed) expiring during the period in question.

c. **Relationship of the two techniques.** Reflect on the relationship between the two techniques. The contribution-margin technique is merely a shortcut version of the equation technique. Look at the last three lines in the two solutions given on p. 29 for Equation 1. They read:

TARGET VOLUME	
In Units	**In Dollars**
$.10X = $6,000 + 0	.20X = $6,000 + 0
$X = \dfrac{\$6,000 + 0}{\$.10}$	$X = \dfrac{\$6,000 + 0}{.20}$
X = 60,000 units	X = $30,000

This gives us the shortcut general formulas:

$$\text{target volume in units} = \frac{\text{fixed expenses} + \text{net income}}{\text{contribution margin per unit}} \qquad (2)$$

$$\text{target volume in dollars} = \frac{\text{fixed expenses} + \text{net income}}{\text{contribution-margin ratio}} \qquad (3)$$

Which should you use, the equation or the contribution-margin technique? Use either; the choice is a matter of personal preference or convenience within a particular case.

☐ 2. Graphical Technique

Graph the cost-volume-profit relationships in Requirement 1.

The break-even point is represented by the intersection of the sales line and the total expenses line in Exhibit 2-3. Exhibit 2-3 was constructed by using a sales line and a total expenses line that combined variable and fixed expenses. The procedure (see Exhibit 2-3) is as follows:

Step 1. Select a convenient sales volume, say 100,000 units, and plot the point for total sales dollars at that volume: 100,000 × 50¢ = $50,000. Draw the revenue (i.e., sales) line from the origin to the $50,000 point.

Step 2. Draw the line showing the $6,000 fixed portion of expenses. It should be a horizontal line intersecting the vertical axis at $6,000.

Step 3. Determine the variable portion of expenses at a convenient level of activity: 100,000 units × $.40 = $40,000. Add this to the fixed expenses: $40,000 + $6,000 = $46,000. Plot the point for 100,000 units and $46,000. Then draw a line between this point and the $6,000 fixed cost intercept of the vertical axis. This is the total expenses line. The break-even point is where this line crosses the sales line, 60,000 units or $30,000, namely where total sales revenues exactly equal total costs.

Exhibit 2-3 is the completed break-even graph. The break-even point is only one facet of this cost-volume-profit graph. More generally, the

EXHIBIT 2-3

Cost-
Volume-
Profit Graph

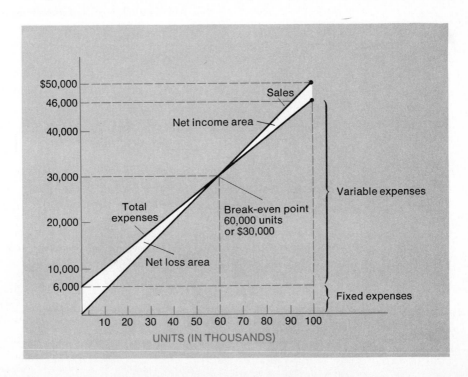

graph shows the profit or loss at *any* rate of activity. Namely, at any given volume, the vertical distance between the sales line and the total expenses line measures the net income or net loss.

The graph portrays only one of a number of methods for picturing cost-volume-profit relationships. The graph often has educational advantages because it shows potential profits over a wide range of volume more easily than numerical exhibits. Whether graphs or other types of exhibits are used depends largely on management's preference.

The business press frequently refers to break-even points. For example, in 1982 a news story stated that "the Big Three auto makers have slashed their sales break-even point in North America from 12.2 million cars and trucks to only 9.1 million this year." Another news story described the efforts of International Harvester Company to "lower the sales break-even point 18%."

☐ 3. Changes in Fixed Expenses

If the $1,000 monthly rent of the vending machines were doubled, find the monthly break-even point: (a) in number of units, (b) in dollar sales.

The fixed expenses would increase from $6,000 to $7,000. Then:

$$\frac{\text{target volume}}{\text{in units}} = \frac{\text{fixed expenses} + \text{net income}}{\text{contribution margin per unit}} = \frac{\$7,000}{\$.10} = 70,000 \text{ units} \quad (2)$$

$$\frac{\text{target volume}}{\text{in dollars}} = \frac{\text{fixed expenses} + \text{net income}}{\text{contribution-margin ratio}} = \frac{\$7,000}{.20} = \$35,000 \quad (3)$$

Note that a one-sixth increase in fixed expenses altered the break-even point by one-sixth: from 60,000 to 70,000 units and from $30,000 to $35,000. This type of relationship always exists, everything else held constant.

☐ 4. Changes in Contribution Margin Per Unit

Assume that the fixed rent is unchanged. (a) If the owner is paid 1¢ per unit as additional rent, find the monthly break-even point in number of units; in dollar sales. (b) If the selling price falls from 50¢ to 45¢ per unit, and the original variable expenses per unit are unchanged, find the monthly break-even point, in number of units; in dollar sales.

a. The variable expenses would be increased from 40¢ to 41¢, the unit contribution margin would be reduced from 10¢ to 9¢, and the contribution-margin ratio would become .18 (9¢ ÷ 50¢).

The original fixed expenses of $6,000 would be unaffected, but the denominators are changed as compared with the denominators used in the solutions to Requirements 1 and 3. Thus:

$$\text{break-even point in units} = \frac{\$6,000}{\$.09} = 66,667 \text{ units} \quad (2)$$

$$\text{break-even point in dollars} = \frac{\$6,000}{.18} = \$33,333 \quad (3)$$

b. A change in unit contribution margin can also be caused by a change in selling price. If the selling price fell from 50¢ to 45¢, and the original variable expenses were unchanged, the unit contribution would be reduced from 10¢ to 5¢ (i.e., 45¢ − 40¢) and the break-even point would soar to 120,000 units (6,000 ÷ 5¢). The break-even point in dollars would also change because the selling price and contribution-margin ratio change: the contribution-margin ratio would be .1111 (5¢ ÷ 45¢). The break-even point, in dollars, would be $54,000 (120,000 units × 45¢), or, using the formula:

$$\text{break-even point in dollars} = \frac{\$6,000}{.1111} = \$54,000 \qquad (3)$$

❑ 5. Target Net Profit and an Incremental Approach

Refer to the original data. If Winston considers $480 per month the minimum acceptable net income, how many units will have to be sold to warrant the adoption of the vending machine plan? Convert your answer into dollar sales.

$$\text{target sales volume in units} = \frac{\text{fixed expenses} + \text{net income}}{\text{contribution margin per unit}} \qquad (2)$$

$$= \frac{\$6,000 + \$480}{\$.10} = 64,800 \text{ units}$$

Another way of getting the same answer is to use your knowledge of the break-even point and adopt an incremental approach. The term **incremental** is widely used in accounting. It refers to the *change* in total results (such as revenue, expenses, or income) under a new condition in comparison with some given or known condition.

In this instance, the given condition is assumed to be the 60,000-unit break-even point. All expenses would be recovered at that volume. Therefore the *change* or *increment* in net income for every unit *beyond* 60,000 would be equal to the contribution margin of $.50 − $.40 = $.10. If $480 were the target net profit, $480 ÷ 10¢ would show that the target volume must exceed the break-even volume by 4,800 units; it would therefore be 60,000 + 4,800 = 64,800 units.

The answer, in terms of *dollar* sales, can then be computed by multiplying 64,800 units by 50¢, or by using the formula:

$$\text{target sales volume in dollars} = \frac{\text{fixed expenses} + \text{net income}}{\text{contribution-margin ratio}} \qquad (3)$$

$$= \frac{\$6,000 + \$480}{.20} = \$32,400$$

To solve directly for sales dollars with the alternative incremental approach, the break-even point, in dollar sales of $30,000, becomes the frame of reference. Every sales dollar beyond that point contributes 20¢ to net profit. Divide $480 by .20. The dollar sales must therefore exceed the break-even volume by $2,400 to produce a net profit of $480; thus the total dollar sales would be $30,000 + $2,400 = $32,400.

These relationships are recapitulated below:

	BREAK-EVEN POINT	INCREMENT	NEW CONDITION
Volume in units	60,000	4,800	64,800
Sales	$30,000	$2,400	$32,400
Variable expenses	24,000	1,920	25,920
Contribution margin	6,000	480	6,480
Fixed expenses	6,000	—	6,000
Net income	$ 0	$ 480	$ 480

☐ 6. Multiple Changes in the Key Factors

Suppose that after the vending machines have been in place awhile, Winston is considering locking them from 6:00 P.M. to 6:00 A.M., which she estimates will save $820 in wages monthly. The cutback from 24-hour service would hurt volume substantially because many nighttime employees use the machines. However, employees could find food elsewhere, so not too many complaints are expected.[1] Should the machines remain available 24 hours per day? Assume that monthly sales would decline by 10,000 units from current sales of (a) 62,000 units and (b) 90,000 units.

First, whether 62,000 or 90,000 units are being sold is irrelevant to the decision at hand. The analysis of this situation consists of constructing and solving equations for conditions that prevail under either alternative and selecting the volume level that yields the highest net profit. However, the incremental approach is much quicker. What is the essence of this decision? We are asking whether the prospective savings in cost exceed the prospective loss in *total* contribution margin in dollars:

Lost total contribution margin, 10,000 units @ $.10	$1,000
Savings in fixed expenses	820
Prospective decline in net income	$ 180

Regardless of the current volume level, whether it be 62,000 or 90,000 units, if we accept the prediction that sales will decline by 10,000 units as accurate, the closing from 6:00 P.M. to 6:00 A.M. will decrease the income by $180:

	DECLINE FROM 62,000 TO 52,000 UNITS		DECLINE FROM 90,000 TO 80,000 UNITS	
Units	62,000	52,000	90,000	80,000
Sales	$31,000	$26,000	$45,000	$40,000
Variable expenses	24,800	20,800	36,000	32,000
Contribution margin	$ 6,200	$ 5,200	$ 9,000	$ 8,000
Fixed expenses	6,000	5,180	6,000	5,180
Net income	$ 200	$ 20	$ 3,000	$ 2,820
Change in net income	($180)		($180)	

[1] The quality of overall working conditions might affect these decisions, even though such factors are difficult to quantify. In particular, if costs or profits do not differ very much between alternatives, the nonquantifiable, subjective aspects may be the deciding factors.

☐ Optimum Combination of Factors

The analysis of cost-volume-profit relationships is one of management's paramount responsibilities. The knowledge of patterns of cost behavior offers insights valuable in planning and controlling short- and long-run operations. This is a major lesson of this book, so we should regard the current material as introductory. Our purpose in this chapter is to provide perspective, rather than to impart an intimate knowledge of the niceties of cost behavior.

The example of the vending machines demonstrated some valuable applications of cost-volume-profit analysis. One of management's principal duties is to discover the most profitable combination of the variable- and fixed-cost factors. For example, automated machinery may be purchased, causing more fixed costs but reducing labor cost per unit. On the other hand, it may be wise to reduce fixed costs in order to obtain a more favorable combination. Thus, direct selling by a salaried sales force may be supplanted by the use of manufacturer's agents who are compensated via sales commissions (variable costs).

Generally, companies that spend heavily for advertising are willing to do so because they have high contribution-margin percentages (airlines, cigarette, and cosmetic companies). Conversely, companies with low contribution-margin percentages usually spend less for advertising and promotion (manufacturers of industrial equipment). Obviously, two companies with the same unit sales volumes at the same unit prices will have different attitudes toward risking an advertising outlay. Assume:

	PERFUME COMPANY	JANITORIAL SERVICE COMPANY
Unit Sales Volume	100,000 Bottles	100,000 Square Feet
Dollar sales at $20 per unit	$2,000,000	$2,000,000
Variable costs	200,000	1,700,000
Contribution margin	$1,800,000	$ 300,000
Contribution-margin percentage	90%	15%

Suppose each company wants to increase sales volume by 10%:

	PERFUME COMPANY	JANITORIAL SERVICE COMPANY
Increase in sales volume, 10,000 × $20	$200,000	$200,000
Increase in contribution margin, 90%, 15%	180,000	30,000

The perfume company would be inclined to increase advertising considerably to boost contribution margin by $180,000. In contrast, the janitorial service company would be foolhardy to spend large amounts to increase contribution margin by $30,000.

Therefore, when the contribution margin is low, great increases in volume are necessary before significant increases in net profits can occur. As sales exceed the break-even point, a high contribution-margin percentage increases profits faster than a small contribution-margin percentage.

☐ Limiting Assumptions

The notion of relevant range, which was introduced when fixed expenses were discussed, is applicable to the entire break-even graph. Almost all break-even graphs show revenue and cost lines extending back to the vertical axis. This is misleading because the relationships depicted in such graphs are valid only within the relevant range that underlies the construction of the graph. Exhibit 2-4 (B), a modification of the conventional break-even graph, partially demonstrates the multitude of assumptions that must be made in constructing the typical break-even graph. Some of these assumptions follow.

1. The behavior of revenues and expenses is accurately portrayed and is linear over the relevant range. The principal differences between the accountant's break-even chart and the economist's are that (a) the accountant's sales line is drawn on the assumption that selling prices do not change with production or sales, and the economist assumes that reduced selling prices are normally associated with increased sales volume; (b) the accountant usually assumes a constant variable expense per unit, and the economist assumes that variable expense per unit does change with production.

2. Expenses may be classified into variable and fixed categories. Total variable

EXHIBIT 2-4
Conventional and Modified Break-Even Graphs

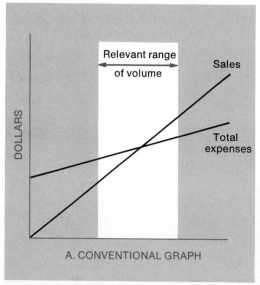

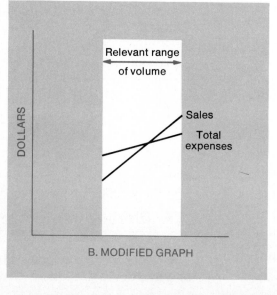

expenses vary directly with volume. Total fixed expenses do not change with volume.

3. Efficiency and productivity will be unchanged.
4. Sales mix will be constant. The **sales mix** is the relative combination of quantities of a variety of company products that compose total sales.
5. The difference in inventory level at the beginning and at the end of a period is insignificant. (The impact of inventory changes on cost-volume-profit analysis is discussed in Chapter 15).

☐ Contribution Margin and Gross Margin

Recall that *contribution margin* was defined as the excess of sales over *all* variable expenses. It may be expressed as a *total* absolute amount, a *unit* absolute amount, a *ratio,* and a *percentage.* Sometimes a **variable expense ratio** or **variable cost ratio** or **variable cost percentage** may be encountered; it is defined as the variable expenses divided by sales. Thus a contribution margin ratio of 20% means that the variable cost ratio is 80%.

The most confusion about terms seems to be the mix-up between *contribution margin* and **gross margin** (which is also called **gross profit**). *Gross margin* is a widely used concept, particularly in the retailing industry. It is defined as the excess of sales over the **cost of goods sold** (that is, the cost of the merchandise that is acquired and resold). The following comparisons from our chapter illustration show the similarities and differences between the contribution margin and the gross margin:

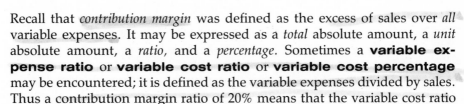

Sales	$.50
Variable costs: Acquisition cost of unit sold	.40
Contribution margin and gross margin are equal	$.10

Thus the basic data for Requirement 1 resulted in no difference between the measure of contribution margin and gross margin. However, recall that Requirement 4a introduced a variable portion of rent. There would now be a difference:

	4a	1
Sales	$.50	$.50
Acquisition cost of unit sold	$.40	.40
Variable rent	.01	
Total variable expense	.41	
Contribution margin	$.09	
Gross margin		$.10

As the preceding tabulation indicates, and as the next chapter will explain more fully, contribution margin and gross margin are not the same concepts. Contribution margin focuses on sales in relation to *all* variable cost behavior, whereas gross margin focuses on sales in relation to a lone item, the acquisition cost of the *merchandise* that has been sold.

Summary

An understanding of cost behavior patterns and cost-volume-profit relationships can help guide a manager's decisions.

Variable costs (and expenses) and fixed costs (and expenses) have contrasting behavior patterns. Their relationship to sales, volume, and net profit is probably best seen on a cost-volume-profit graph. However, the graph should be used with great care. The portrayal of all profit-influencing factors on such a graph entails many assumptions that may hold over only a relatively narrow range of volume. As a tool, the graph may be compared to a meat-ax rather than to a surgeon's scalpel. Cost-volume-profit analysis, as depicted on a graph, is a framework for analysis, a vehicle for appraising overall performance, and a planning device.

Summary Problem For Your Review

❑ Problem

The income statement of Wiley Company is summarized as follows:

Net revenue	$800,000
Less: Expenses, including $400,000 of fixed expenses	880,000
Net loss	$ (80,000)

The manager believes that an increase of $200,000 in advertising outlays will increase sales substantially. Her plan was approved by the chairman of the board.

REQUIRED:
1. At what sales volume will the company break even?
2. What sales volume will result in a net profit of $40,000?

❑ Solution

1. Note that all data are expressed in dollars. No unit data are given. Most companies have many products, so the overall break-even analysis deals with dollar sales, not units. The variable expenses are $880,000 − $400,000, or $480,000. The variable expense ratio is $480,000 ÷ $800,000, or .60. Therefore the contribution-margin ratio is .40.

Let

38

S = break-even sales, in dollars. Then

S = variable expenses + fixed expenses + net profit   (1)

$$S = .60S + (\$400{,}000 + \$200{,}000) + 0$$

$$.40S = \$600{,}000 + 0$$

$$S = \frac{\$600{,}000 + 0}{.40} = \frac{\text{fixed expenses} + \text{target net profit}}{\text{contribution-margin ratio}} \qquad (3)$$

$$S = \$1{,}500{,}000$$

2. $$\text{required sales} = \frac{\text{fixed expenses} + \text{target net profit}}{\text{contribution-margin ratio}} \qquad (3)$$

$$\text{required sales} = \frac{\$600{,}000 + \$40{,}000}{.40} = \frac{\$640{,}000}{.40}$$

$$\text{required sales} = \$1{,}600{,}000$$

Alternatively, we can use an incremental approach and reason that all dollar sales beyond the $1.5 million break-even point will result in a 40% contribution to net profit. Divide $40,000 by .40. Sales must therefore be $100,000 beyond the $1.5 million break-even point in order to produce a net profit of $40,000.

Highlights to Remember

1. Check your understanding of basic terms. As the final section in the chapter emphasized, gross margin and contribution margin have different meanings.

2. Contribution margin may be expressed as a total amount, as an amount per unit, as a ratio, or as a percentage.

3. The assumptions that underlie typical cost-volume-profit analysis are static. A change in one assumption (e.g., total fixed cost or the unit price of merchandise) will affect all the cost-volume-profit relationships on a given graph. The static nature of these assumptions should always be remembered by the managers who use this valuable analytical technique.

Accounting Vocabulary

Contribution margin; cost of goods sold; fixed cost; gross margin; gross profit; incremental; marginal income; relevant range; sales mix; variable cost; variable cost percentage; variable cost ratio; variable expense ratio.

Appendix 2A: The P/V Chart and Sales-Mix Analysis

THE P/V CHART

Exhibit 2-3 can be recast in another form as a so-called P/V chart (a profit-volume graph). This form is preferred by many managers who are interested mainly in the impact of changes in volume on net income. The first graph in Exhibit 2-5 illustrates the chart, using the data in our example. The chart is constructed as follows:

1. The vertical axis is net income in dollars. The horizontal axis is volume in units (or in sales dollars, in many cases).
2. At zero volume, the net loss would be approximated by the total fixed costs: $6,000 in this example.
3. A net income line will slope upward from the $-$6,000 intercept at the rate of the unit contribution margin of 10¢. This line will intersect the volume axis at the break-even point of 60,000 units. Each unit sold beyond the break-even point will add 10¢ to net income. For example, at a volume of 80,000 units, the net income would be $(80,000 - 60,000) \times 10¢ = \$2,000$.

The P/V chart provides a quick, condensed comparison of how alternatives on pricing, variable costs, or fixed costs may affect net income as volume changes. For example, the second graph in Exhibit 2–5 shows how net income and the break-even point would be affected by an increase in selling price from 50¢ to 55¢ and a $1,500 increase in rent. The unit contribution would become 15¢, and the break-even point would fall from 60,000 to 50,000 units:

$$\text{new break-even point} = \$7,500 \div \$.15$$
$$= 50,000 \text{ units}$$

Note also that the net income will increase at a much faster rate as volume increases. At a volume of 80,000 units, the net income would be $(80,000 - 50,000) \times 15¢ = \$4,500$.

EFFECTS OF SALES MIX

The cost-volume-profit analysis in this chapter has focused on a single line of products. In multiproduct firms, sales mix is an important factor in calculating an overall company break-even point. If the proportions of the mix change, the cost-volume-

EXHIBIT 2-5
P/V Chart

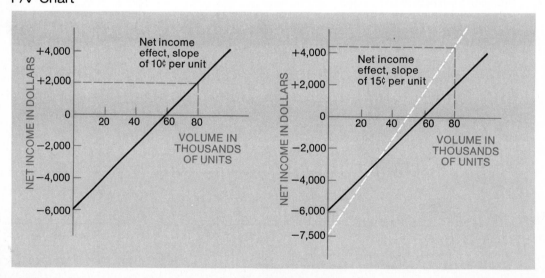

profit relationships also change. When managers choose a sales mix, it can be depicted on a break-even chart or P/V chart by assuming average revenues and costs for a given mix.

For example, suppose that a two-product company has a unit contribution margin of $1 for Product A and $2 for Product B, and that fixed costs are $100,000. The break-even point would be 100,000 units if only A were sold and 50,000 units if only B were sold. Suppose the planned mix is three units of A for each unit of B. The contribution margin for each "package" of products would be (3 × $1) plus (1 × $2), or $5. The average contribution margin per unit of product would be $5 ÷ 4 units in each package = $1.25.[2] The break-even point, assuming that the mix is maintained, would be:

$100,000 ÷ $1.25 = 80,000 units (consisting of 60,000 units of A
and 20,000 of B)

These relationships are shown in Exhibit 2-6. The slopes of the solid lines depict the unit contribution margins of each product. The slope of the broken line depicts the average contribution per unit. Suppose the total planned sales are 160,000 units, consisting of 120,000 units of A and 40,000 of B. Exhibit 2-6 shows that if overall unit sales and mix targets are achieved, net income would be $100,000. However, if the mix changes, net income may be much greater because the proportion of sales of B might be higher than anticipated. The opposite effect

[2] An alternate computation would use a weighted-average approach:

	PLANNED SALES	WEIGHTS	UNIT CONTRIBUTION MARGIN	WEIGHTED AVERAGE
A	3	3/4	$1.00	$ .75
B	1	1/4	2.00	.50
	4			$1.25

EXHIBIT 2-6
P/V Chart and Sales Mix

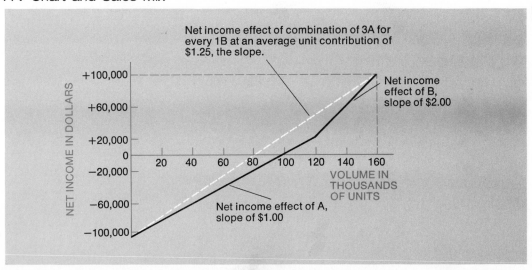

would occur if A sold in a higher proportion than expected. When the sales mix changes, the break-even point and the expected net income at various sales levels are altered.

Management's discussion and analysis of income statements often refers to the effects of changes in sales mix. For example, consider a recent annual report of Deere and Company, a manufacturer of farm equipment: "The increase in the ratio of cost of goods sold to net sales resulted from the higher production costs, a less favorable mix of products sold, and sales incentive programs."

Appendix
2B: Impact of Income Taxes

Private enterprises are subject to income taxes. Reconsider Requirement 5 of the basic illustration in the chapter, where the target income before income taxes was $480. If an income tax were levied at 40%, relationships would be:

Income before income tax	$480	100%
Income tax	192	40
Net income	$288	60%

Note that

$$\text{net income} = \text{income before income taxes} - .40 \,(\text{income before income taxes})$$

$$\text{net income} = .60 \,(\text{income before income taxes})$$

$$\text{income before income taxes} = \frac{\text{net income}}{.60}$$

or

$$\text{income before income taxes} = \frac{\text{target after-tax net income}}{1 - \text{tax rate}}$$

$$\text{income before income taxes} = \frac{\$288}{1 - .40} = \frac{\$288}{.60} = \$480$$

Suppose the target net income after taxes were $288. The only change in the general equation approach would be:

$$\text{target sales} = \text{variable expenses} + \text{fixed expenses} + \frac{\text{target after-tax net income}}{1 - \text{tax rate}}$$

Thus, letting X be the number of units to be sold at 50¢ each with a variable cost of 40¢ each and total fixed costs of $6,000:

$$\$.50X = \$.40X + \$6,000 + \frac{\$288}{1 - .4}$$

$$\$.10X = \$6,000 + \frac{\$288}{.6}$$

$$\$.06X = \$3,600 + \$288 = \$3,888$$

$$X = \$3,888 \div \$.06 = 64,800 \text{ units}$$

Suppose the target net income after taxes were $480. The needed volume would rise to 68,000 units, as follows:

$$\$.50X = \$.40X + \$6,000 + \frac{\$480}{1 - .4}$$

$$\$.10X = \$6,000 + \frac{\$480}{.6}$$

$$\$.06X = \$3,600 + \$480 = \$4,080$$

$$X = \$4,080 \div \$.06 = 68,000 \text{ units}$$

Fundamental Assignment Material

2–1. Cost-volume-profits and vending machines. The Putnam Company operates and services snack vending machines located in restaurants, gas stations, factories, etc. The machines are rented from the manufacturer. In addition, Putnam must rent the space occupied by its machines. The following expense and revenue relationships pertain to a contemplated expansion program of 20 machines.

Fixed monthly expenses:

Machine rental: 20 machines @ $26.75	$ 535
Space rental: 20 locations @ $14.40	288
Wages to service the additional 20 machines	726
Other fixed costs	41
Total monthly fixed costs	$1,590

Other data:

	PER UNIT	PER $100 OF SALES
Selling price	$.50	100%
Cost of snack	.40	80
Contribution margin	$.10	20%

REQUIRED:

These questions relate to the above data unless otherwise noted. **Consider each question independently.**

1. What is the monthly break-even point in dollar sales? In number of units?
2. If 20,000 units were sold, what would be the company's net income?
3. If the space rental were doubled, what would be the monthly break-even point in dollar sales? In number of units?
4. If, in addition to the fixed rent, the vending machine manufacturer was also paid 1¢ per unit sold, what would be the monthly break-even point in dollar sales? In number of units? Refer to the original data.
5. If, in addition to the fixed rent, the machine manufacturer was paid 1¢ for each unit sold in excess of the break-even point, what would the new net income be if 20,000 units were sold? Refer to the original data.

2–2. Exercises in cost-volume-profit relationships. (Alternate is 2–11.) The Avanti Transportation Company specializes in hauling heavy goods over long distances. Avanti's revenue depends on both weights and mileage. Summarized budget data for next year are based on total intercity-vehicle revenue miles of 800,000:

	PER MILE
Average selling price (revenue)	$1.20
Average variable expenses	1.00
Fixed expenses, $120,000	

1. Compute the budgeted net income. Ignore income taxes.
2. Management is trying to decide how various possible conditions or decisions might affect net income. Compute the new net income for each of the following changes. Consider each case independently.
   a. A 10% increase in revenue miles.
   b. A 10% increase in sales price.
   c. A 10% increase in variable expenses.
   d. A 10% increase in fixed expenses.
   e. A 10% increase in fixed expenses in the form of more advertising and a 5% increase in revenue miles.
   f. An average decrease in selling price of 3¢ per mile and a 5% increase in revenue miles. Refer to the original data.
   g. An average increase in selling price of 5% and a 10% decrease in revenue miles.

Additional Assignment Material

2–3. Why is "break-even analysis" a misnomer?

2–4. Distinguish between the equation technique and the unit contribution technique.

2–5. What are the principal differences between the accountant's and the economist's break-even graphs?

2–6. What is the sales mix?

2–7. Explain the *incremental approach* as used in cost-volume-profit analysis.

2–8. **Nature of variable and fixed costs.** "As I understand it, costs such as the salary of the vice-president of transportation operations are variable because the more traffic you handle, the less your unit cost. In contrast, costs such as fuel are fixed because each ton-mile should entail consumption of the same amount of fuel and hence bear the same unit cost." Do you agree? Explain.

2–9. **Basic review exercises.** Fill in the blanks for each of the following independent cases (ignore income taxes):

	SALES	VARIABLE EXPENSES	CONTRIBUTION MARGIN	FIXED EXPENSES	NET INCOME
1.	$900,000	$500,000	$ —	$400,000	$ —
2.	800,000	—	360,000	—	70,000
3.	—	600,000	340,000	300,000	—

2–10. **Basic review exercises.** Fill in the blanks for each of the following independent cases:

	(a) SELLING PRICE PER UNIT	(b) VARIABLE COST PER UNIT	(c) TOTAL UNITS SOLD	(d) TOTAL CONTRIBUTION MARGIN	(e) TOTAL FIXED COSTS	(f) NET INCOME
1.	$10	$ 6	100,000	$ —	$300,000	$ —
2.	20	15	—	100,000	—	11,000
3.	30	20	70,000	—	—	12,000
4.	—	8	80,000	160,000	110,000	—
5.	25	——	120,000	720,000	650,000	—

2–11. Basic review exercises. (Alternate is 2–2.) Each problem is unrelated to the others.

1. Given: Selling price per unit, $20; total fixed expenses, $8,000; variable expenses per unit, $15. Find break-even sales in units.
2. Given: Sales, $40,000; variable expenses, $30,000; fixed expenses, $7,500; net income, $2,500. Find break-even sales.
3. Given: Selling price per unit, $30; total fixed expenses, $32,000; variable expenses per unit, $14. Find total sales in units to achieve a profit of $8,000, assuming no change in selling price.
4. Given: Sales, $50,000; variable expenses, $20,000; fixed expenses, $25,000; net income, $5,000. Assume no change in selling price; find net income if activity volume increases 10%.
5. Given: Selling price per unit, $40; total fixed expenses, $80,000; variable expenses per unit, $30. Assume that if variable expenses are reduced by 20% per unit, the total fixed expenses will be increased by 10%. Find the sales in units to achieve a profit of $16,000, assuming no change in selling price.

2–12. Extensions of chapter illustration. Refer to the basic facts in the chapter illustration. Suppose the selling price was changed to 60¢ in response to a rise in unit variable cost from 40¢ to 45¢. The original data are on page 28.

REQUIRED:

1. Compute the monthly break-even point in number of units and in dollar sales.
2. Refer to the original data. If the rent were halved, what would be the monthly break-even point in number of units and in dollar sales?

2–13. Hospital costs and pricing. A hospital has overall variable costs of 30% of total revenue and fixed costs of $28 million per year.

REQUIRED:

1. Compute the break-even point expressed in total revenue.
2. A patient-day is often used to measure the volume of a hospital. Suppose there are going to be 50,000 patient-days next year. Compute the average daily revenue per patient necessary to break even.

2–14. Motel rentals. The Vanguard Motel has annual fixed costs applicable to its rooms of $1.5 million for its 400-room motel, average daily room rents of $30, and average variable costs of $5 for each room rented. It operates 365 days per year.

REQUIRED:

1. How much net income on rooms will be generated (a) if the motel is completely full throughout the entire year? and (b) if the motel is half-full?
2. Compute the break-even point in number of rooms rented. What percentage occupancy for the year is needed to break even?

2–15. Basic relationships, restaurant. (W. Crum, adapted.) Juan Castillo owns and operates La Cantina Restaurant. His fixed costs are $10,500 per month. Luncheons and dinners are served. The average total bill (excluding tax and tip) is $7 per customer. Juan's present variable costs average $2.80 per meal.

REQUIRED:

1. How many meals must be served to attain a profit before taxes of $4,200 per month?
2. What is Juan's break-even point in number of meals served per month?
3. Juan's rent and his other fixed costs rise to a total of $14,700 per month. Assume that variable costs also rise to $3.75 per meal. If Juan increases his average price to $9, how many meals must he now serve to make $4,200 profit per month?
4. Juan's accountant tells him he may lose 10% of his customers if he increases his prices. If this should happen, what would be Juan's profit per month? Assume that Juan had been serving 3,500 customers per month.
5. Refer to the data in Requirement 4. To help offset the anticipated 10% loss of customers, Juan hires a guitarist to perform for four hours each night for $800 per month. Assume that this would increase the total monthly meals to 3,450. Would Juan's total profit change? By how much?

2–16. **Basic relationships, hotel.** (W. Crum, adapted.) Palm Oasis Hotel has 400 rooms, with a fixed cost of $400,000 per month during the busy season. Room rates average $60 per day with variable costs of $12 per rented room per day. Assume a thirty-day month.

REQUIRED:

1. How many rooms must be occupied per day to break even?
2. How many rooms must be occupied per month to make a profit of $100,000?
3. Assume that Palm Oasis Hotel had these average contribution margins per month from use of space in its hotel:

Leased shops in hotel	$60,000
Meals served, conventions	30,000
Dining room and coffee shop	30,000
Bar and cocktail lounge	20,000

Fixed costs for the total hotel are $400,000 per month. Variable costs are $12 per day per rented room. The hotel has 400 rooms and average 80% occupancy per day. What average rate per day must the hotel charge to make a profit of $100,000 per month?

2–17. **Cost-volume-profit analysis and barbering.** Sidney's Barber Shop in Singapore has five barbers. (Sidney is not one of them.) Each barber is paid $6 per hour and works a 40-hour week and a 50-week year. Depreciation on store fixtures is $500 annually and depreciation on equipment is $1,000 annually. Rent is $500 per month. Assume that the only service performed is the giving of haircuts, the unit price of which is $5.

REQUIRED:

1. Contribution margin per haircut.
2. Annual break-even point, in number of haircuts.
3. What will be operating income if 20,000 haircuts are sold?
4. Suppose the landlord decides to revise the monthly rent to $100 + 10% of revenue per haircut. What is the new contribution margin per haircut? What is the annual break-even point (in number of haircuts)?
5. Ignore Requirements 3 and 4, and assume that the barbers cease to be paid by the hour but receive a 50% commission for each haircut. What is the new contribution margin per haircut? The annual break-even point (in number of haircuts)?
6. Refer to Requirement 5. What would be the operating income if 20,000 haircuts are sold? Compare your answer with the answer in Requirement 3.

7. Refer to Requirement 5. What would be the operating income if the barbers received an 80% commission for each haircut and 20,000 haircuts are sold?

8. Refer to Requirement 5. If 20,000 haircuts are sold, at what rate of commission would Sidney earn the same operating income as he earned in Requirement 3?

2–18. **Fixed costs and relevant range.**   Horizon Computer Consultants has a substantial year-to-year fluctuation in billings to clients. Top management has the following policy regarding the employment of key professional personnel:

IF GROSS ANNUAL BILLINGS ARE	NUMBER OF PERSONS TO BE EMPLOYED	KEY PROFESSIONAL ANNUAL SALARIES AND RELATED EXPENSES
$2,000,000 or less	8	$ 800,000
$2,000,001–$2,400,000	9	900,000
$2,400,001–$2,800,000	10	1,000,000

Top management believes that a minimum of eight individuals should be retained for a year or more even if billings drop drastically below $2 million.

For the past five years, gross annual billings have fluctuated between $2,020,000 and $2,380,000. Expectations for next year are that gross billings will be between $2,100,000 and $2,300,000. What amount should be budgeted for key professional personnel? Graph the relationships on an annual basis, using the two approaches illustrated in Exhibit 2-2. Indicate the relevant range on each graph. You need not use graph paper; simply approximate the graphical relationships.

2–19. **Estimating cost behavior patterns.**   The Mideastern Railroad showed the following results (in millions of dollars):

	19X3	19X2
Operating revenues	$218	$196
Operating expenses:		
Transportation	$ 87	$ 84
Maintenance of way and structures	34	32
Maintenance of equipment	37	34
Traffic	7	6
General	12	11
Payroll taxes	9	9
Property taxes	7	7
Equipment and other rentals	13	12
Total operating expenses	$206	$195
Net railway operating income	$ 12	$ 1

REQUIRED:

Examine the figures in their entirety, not item by item. How do total expenses change in relation to total revenues? That is, if total revenues increase by $1,000, by how much will total expenses increase? What is the apparent contribution-margin percentage? Explain any assumptions that underlie your answer.

2–20. **Movie manager.**   Joan Baker is the manager of Stanford's traditional Sunday Flicks. Each Sunday a film has two showings. The admission price is deliberately set at a very low 50¢. A maximum of 1,650 tickets are sold for each showing. The rental of the auditorium is $100 and labor is $280, including $30 for Baker. Baker must pay the film distributor a guarantee, ranging from $200 to $600 or 50% of gross admission receipts, whichever is higher.

Before and during the show, refreshments are sold; these sales average 12% of gross admission receipts and yield a contribution margin of 40%.

1. On June 3, Baker played *The Graduate*. The film grossed $1,400. The guarantee to the distributor was $500, or 50% of gross admission receipts, whichever is higher. What operating income was produced for the Students Association, which sponsors the showings?
2. Recompute the results if the film grossed $900.
3. The "four-wall" concept is increasingly being adopted by movie producers. This means that the producer pays a fixed rental for the theater for, say, a week's showing of a movie. As a theater owner, how would you evaluate a "four-wall" offer?

2–21. Promotion of championship fight. Newspaper accounts of a Joe Frazier–Muhammad Ali boxing match stated that each fighter would receive a flat fee of $2.5 million in cash. The fight would be shown on closed-circuit television. The central promoter would collect 100% of the receipts and would return 30% to the individual local promoters. He expected to sell 1.1 million seats at a net average price of $10 each. He also was to receive $250,000 from Madison Square Garden (which had sold out its 19,500 seats, ranging from $150 for ringside down to $20, for a gross revenue of $1.25 million); he would not share the $250,000 with the local promoters.

REQUIRED:

1. The central promoter is trying to decide what amount to spend for advertising. What is the most he could spend and still break even on his overall operations, assuming that he would sell 1.1 million tickets?
2. If the central promoter desired an operating income of $500,000, how many seats would have to be sold? Assume that the average price was $10 and the total fixed costs were $8 million.

2–22. Cost-volume-profit relationships and a dog track. The Multnomah Kennel Club is a dog-racing track. Its revenue is derived mainly from attendance and a fixed percentage of the parimutuel betting. Its expenses for a 90-day season are:

Wages of cashiers and ticket takers	$150,000
Commissioner's salary	20,000
Maintenance (repairs, etc.)	20,000
Utilities	30,000
Other expenses (depreciation, insurance, advertising, etc.)	100,000
Purses: Total prizes paid to winning racers	810,000

The track made a contract with the Auto Parking Association to park the cars. Auto Parking charged the track $1.80 per car. A survey revealed that on the average three persons arrived in each car and that there were no other means of transportation except by private automobiles.

The track's sources of revenue are:

Rights for concession and vending	$50,000
Admission charge (deliberately low)	$.80 per person
Percentage of bets placed	10%

1. Assuming that each person bets $25 a night:
   a. How many persons have to be admitted for the track to break even for the season?
   b. What is the total contribution margin at the break-even point?
   c. If the desired profit for the year is $540,000, how many people would have to attend?
2. If a policy of free admission brought a 10% increase in attendance, what would be the new level of profit? Assume that the previous level of attendance was 600,000 people.
3. If the purses were doubled in an attempt to attract better dogs and thus increase attendance, what would be the new break-even point? Refer to the original data and assume that each person bets $25 a night.

2–23. Hospital cost-volume-profit relationships. Dr. Green and Dr. Jones, the two radiologists of the Hong Kong Hospital, have submitted the following costs for operating the Department of Radiology:

Radiologists' salaries	30% of gross receipts
Technicians' and	
clerical salaries	$70,000
Supplies (fixed)	80,000
Depreciation	60,000

This year the department processed 65,000 films with three 200-milliampere X-ray machines. (Their original cost was $200,000 each; their original life expectancy, ten years.) For these processed films the average charge was $6. The 65,000 films represent maximum volume possible with the present equipment.

The physicians have submitted a request for two new 300-milliampere X-ray machines. (Their cost will be $250,000 each; their life expectancy ten years.) They will increase the capacity of the department by 35,000 films per year. Because of their special attachments (i.e., fluoroscopes), it will be possible to take more intricate films, for which a higher charge will be made. The average charge to the patient for each of these additional 35,000 films is estimated at $10. In order to operate the new machines, one highly trained technician must be hired at an annual salary of $15,000. The added capacity will increase the cost of supplies by $20,000.

1. Determine the break-even point in films for the three 200-milliampere X-ray machines. How much do they contribute to the hospital's overall profits?
2. Determine the break-even point if the two new 300-milliampere X-ray machines are added to the department, assuming a sales mix based on maximum capacity. How much will be contributed to the hospital's overall profit, assuming they are operated at maximum volume?

2–24. Church enterprise. A California law permits a game of chance called BINGO when it is offered by specified not-for-profit institutions, including churches. Reverend John O'Toole, the pastor of a new parish in suburban Los Angeles, is investigating the desirability of conducting weekly BINGO nights. The parish has no hall, but a local hotel would be willing to commit its hall for a lump-sum rental of $300 per night. The rent would include cleaning, setting up and taking down tables and chairs, and so on.

1. BINGO cards would be provided by a local printer in return for free advertising thereon. Door prizes would be donated by local merchants. The services of clerks, callers, security force, and others would be donated by volunteers.

Admission would be $2.50 per person, entitling the player to one card; extra cards would be $1.50 each. Father O'Toole also learns that many persons buy extra cards, so there would be an average of four cards played per person. What is the maximum in total cash prizes that the church may award and still break even if 100 persons attend each weekly session?

2. Suppose the total cash prizes are $400. What will be the church's operating income if 50 persons attend? If 100 persons attend? If 150 persons attend? Briefly explain effects of the cost behavior on income.

3. After operating for ten months, Father O'Toole is thinking of negotiating a different rental arrangement but keeping the prize money unchanged. Suppose the rent is $200 weekly plus $1 per person. Compute the operating income for attendance of 50, 100, and 150 persons, respectively. Explain why the results differ from those in Requirement 2.

2–25. **Effects of changes in costs.** (CMA.) All-Day Candy Company is a wholesale distributor of candy. The company services grocery, convenience, and drugstores in a large metropolitan area.

Small but steady growth in sales has been achieved by the All-Day Candy Company over the past few years while candy prices have been increasing. The company is formulating its plans for the coming fiscal year. Presented below are the data used to project the current year's after-tax net income of $110,400.

Average selling price per box	$4.00
Average variable costs per box:	
Cost of candy	$2.00
Selling expenses	.40
Total	$2.40
Annual fixed costs	
Selling	$160,000
Administrative	280,000
Total	$440,000
Expected annual sales volume	
(390,000 boxes)	$1,560,000
Tax rate	40%

Manufacturers of candy have announced that they will increase prices of their products an average of 15% in the coming year, owing to increases in raw material (sugar, cocoa, peanuts, etc.) and labor costs. All-Day Candy Company expects that all other costs will remain at the same rates or levels as the current year.

REQUIRED:

1. What is All-Day Candy Company's break-even point in boxes of candy for the current year?

2. What selling price per box must All-Day Candy Company charge to cover the 15% increase in the cost of candy and still maintain the current contribution-margin ratio? Read Appendix 2B. (Also see Problem 2–36.)

2–26. **Traveling expenses.** (A. Roberts.) Harold Nuget is a traveling inspector for the Environmental Protection Agency. He uses his own car and the agency reimburses him at 18¢ per mile. Harold claims he needs 21¢ per mile just to break even.

George Barr, the district manager, decides to look into the matter. He is able to compile the following information about Harold's expenses:

Oil change every 3,000 miles	$ 12
Maintenance (other than oil) every 6,000 miles	180
Yearly insurance	400
Auto cost $10,800 with an average cash trade-in value of $6,000; has a useful life of three years.	
Gasoline is approximately $2 per gallon and Harold averages 20 miles per gallon.	

When Harold is on the road, he averages 120 miles a day. The manager knows that Harold does not work Saturdays or Sundays, has ten working days vacation and six holidays, and spends approximately fifteen working days in the office.

REQUIRED:

1. How many miles per year would the inspector have to travel to break even at the current rate of reimbursement?
2. What would be an equitable mileage rate?

2–27. **Adding a product.** Jiminy's Greenlawn Tap, a pub located in a college community, serves as a gathering place for the university's more social scholars. Jiminy sells beer on draft and all brands of bottled beer at a contribution margin of 40¢ a beer.

Jiminy is considering also selling hamburgers. His reasons are twofold. First, sandwiches would attract daytime customers. A hamburger and a beer are a quick lunch. Second, he has to meet competition from other local bars, some of which provide more extensive menus.

Jiminy analyzed the costs as follows:

Monthly fixed expenses:	
Wages of cook	$1,000
Other	200
Total	$1,200

	PER HAMBURGER
Variable expenses:	
Rolls	$ .05
Meat @ $1.40 per pound (7 hamburgers per pound)	.20
Other	.05
Total	$ .30

Jiminy planned a selling price of 55¢ per hamburger to lure many customers.

REQUIRED:

For all questions, assume a 30-day month.

1. What are the monthly and daily break-even points, in number of hamburgers?
2. What are the monthly and daily break-even points, in dollar sales?
3. At the end of two months, Jiminy finds he has sold 3,600 hamburgers. What is the net profit per month on hamburgers?
4. Jiminy thinks that at least 60 extra beers are sold per day because he has these hamburgers available. This means that 60 extra people come to the bar or that 60 buy an extra beer because they are attracted by the hamburgers. How does this affect Jiminy's monthly income?

Introduction to
Cost-Volume
Relationships

51

5. Refer to Requirement 3. How many extra beers would have to be sold per day so that the overall effects of the hamburger sales on monthly operating income would be zero?

2–28. Hospital costs. (Heavily adapted from CPA.) The Lincoln Hospital operates several special departments. Each department pays space and bed charges on a fixed yearly basis, and services such as meals and laundry are charged as used. During 19X5 the pediatrics department billed each patient an average of $65 per day, had a capacity of 60 beds, and collected a gross revenue of $1,138,800. Expenses charged by the hospital to the pediatrics department for 19X5 are detailed below.

	BASIS OF ALLOCATION	
	Patient-Days	Bed Capacity
Meals	$ 42,952	
Janitorial		$ 12,800
Laundry	28,000	
Laboratory	94,800	
Maintenance	5,200	7,140
General administrative services		131,760
Rent		275,320
Pharmacy	73,800	
Other	18,048	25,980
	$262,800	$453,000

A separate contract is negotiated each year regarding nursing staff. Each nurse receives an annual salary of $15,000 from the hospital, and at the end of the year each department is charged according to the following schedule.

	NURSES SUPPLIED
ANNUAL PATIENT-DAYS	(assumed)
10,000–14,000	20
Over 14,000	25

You have been asked to assist the head of the Pediatrics Clinic in determining the 19X6 operating budget and renegotiating the nursing contract for 19X6. The cost system for space and services will be unchanged in 19X6.

REQUIRED:

1. Considering only the space and service fees charged by the hospital (before nursing fees), how many patient-days will be required in 19X6 for the pediatrics department to break even?
2. Now *including* the nursing charges, how many patient-days will be required for the pediatrics department to break even in 19X6?
3. The head of the pediatrics department is considering offering the nursing center a flat nursing rate of $22.50 per patient-day, rather than the two-level system employed in 19X5. What will be the break-even point (in patient-days) under this plan (including the proposed nursing fee)?

2–29. Analysis of airline results. Texas Air Corporation owns Texas International Airlines and Continental Airlines. Its actual operating statistics for the three months ended June 30 in a recent quarterly report follow:

	CURRENT YEAR	PRECEDING YEAR
Revenue passengers carried	946,603	1,044,697
Revenue passenger miles (000's)*	549,179	577,071
Scheduled aircraft miles flown	9,472,766	8,595,308
Available seat miles (000's)	971,028	839,720
Passenger load factor	56.6%	?
Yield per revenue passenger mile†	$?	$ .0884

*A revenue passenger mile is one passenger carried one mile. For example, two passengers carried 800 miles would be 1,600 revenue passenger miles.

†Total revenue divided by revenue passenger miles.

The president of Texas Air commented:

☐ In the second quarter, airline revenues were nearly $64 million, a 25.6% increase compared to the preceding year. Revenue passenger miles, however, declined 5%, the first quarterly decline since 1976, primarily as a result of weakened economic conditions. Meanwhile, the yield per passenger mile increased 32% as a result of several fare increases made to counter spiralling costs.

REQUIRED:

1. (a) Compute the total passenger revenue in the second quarter of the preceding year. (b) Also compute the passenger load factor.
2. Compute the yield per passenger mile in the current year.
3. Assume that variable costs during the current quarter were 5¢ per available seat mile. Also assume that the yield per revenue passenger mile was unaffected by the increase in the load factor. Suppose the passenger load factor had increased from 56.6% to 57.6%; compute the increase in operating income that would have been attained.

Assignment Materials For Appendixes _____

2–30. **P/V chart.** Consider the example on page 28. Suppose the rent were cut from $1,000 to $504, the cost per item raised from 40¢ to 47¢, and the selling price raised to 55¢.

REQUIRED:

1. Compute the new break-even point in units.
2. Draw a new P/V chart similar to the second one in Exhibit 2-5, page 40.
3. Compute and plot the new net income at a volume of 80,000 units.

2–31. **P/V chart and sales mix.** The Grimm Company has three products—X, Y, and Z—having contribution margins of $2, $3, and $6, respectively. The president is planning to sell 200,000 units in the forthcoming period, consisting of 80,000 X, 100,000 Y, and 20,000 Z. The company's fixed costs for the period are $406,000.

REQUIRED:

1. What is the company's break-even point in units, assuming that the given sales mix is maintained?
2. Prepare a P/V chart for a volume of 200,000 units. Have a broken line represent the average contribution margin per unit and have solid lines represent the net income effects of each product by showing their unit contributions as the slopes of each line. What is the total contribution margin at a volume of 200,000 units? Net income?

3. What would net income become if 80,000 units of X, 80,000 units of Y, and 40,000 units of Z were sold? What would be the new break-even point if these relationships persisted in the next period?

2–32. **Product mix and break-even analysis.** The Frozen Entree Company specializes in preparing two delicious food items that are frozen and shipped to many of the finer restaurants in the New York area. As a diner orders the item, the restaurant heats and serves it. The budget data for 19X4 are:

	PRODUCT	
	veal oscar	chicken kiev
Selling price	$5	$4
Variable expenses	2	2
Contribution margin	$3	$2
Number of units expected to be sold	20,000	30,000

Fixed expenses have been assigned, $33,000 to veal and $16,000 to chicken.

REQUIRED:

1. Compute the break-even point in units for each product.
2. Suppose the entrees were made in the same facilities, delivered on the same trucks, and so on. Suppose a local chicken processor began a competitive operation on the chicken item, cutting the price so severely that Frozen Entree instantly dropped the chicken item for all of 19X4. Suppose also that the company's fixed costs were unaffected.
   a. What would be the break-even point for the company as a whole, assuming no chicken were produced?
   b. Suppose instead that only chicken and no veal were produced. What would be the break-even point for the company as a whole?
3. Draw a break-even graph for the company as a whole, using an average selling price and an average variable expense per unit. What is the break-even point under this aggregate approach? What is the break-even point if you add together the individual break-even points that you computed in Requirement 1? Why is the aggregate break-even point different from the sum of the individual break-even points?

2–33. **Patient mix.** (Adapted from J. Suver and B. Neumann, "Patient Mix and Break-even Analysis," *Management Accounting*, LVIII, No. 7 [January 1977], 38–40.) A hospital has the following cost structure and patient mix: fixed costs, $1 million; daily revenue rate, $120; variable costs, $40 per patient-day.

TYPE OF PATIENT		REIMBURSEMENT BASIS PER PATIENT-DAY	
Self-pay	20%	Revenue rate	$120
Private insurance	25	Revenue rate	120
Medicare	30	Specified costs or revenue rate, whichever is lower	110
Medicaid	25	Specified costs only	100

REQUIRED:

1. What level of total revenue must be achieved to break even?
2. How many patient-days must be achieved to break even? If the mix is unchanged, how many patient-days for each type of patient are necessary to break even?

3. The application of cost-volume-profit analysis in a hospital will depend on many objectives of top management. For instance, the hospital may be committed to take all types of patients as a matter of its community responsibilities. Suppose the hospital is able to eliminate the Medicare and Medicaid patients; how many patient-days are required to break even?

2–34. **Income taxes.** Review the illustration in Appendix 2B. Suppose the income tax rate were 30% instead of 40%.

REQUIRED: How many units would have to be sold to achieve a target net income of (1) $288 and (2) $480? Show your computations.

2–35. **Income taxes and cost-volume-profit analysis.** Suppose the Litzen Moving Company has a 40% income tax rate, a contribution-margin ratio of 30%, and fixed costs of $120,000. How much sales are necessary to achieve an after-tax income of $66,000?

2–36. **Income taxes.** (CMA.) Refer to Problem 2–25. What volume of sales in dollars must the All-Day Candy Company achieve in the coming year to maintain the same net income after taxes as projected for the current year if the selling price of candy remains at $4 per box and the cost of candy increases 15%?

2–37. **Income taxes on hotels.** The Galvez Hotel has annual fixed costs applicable to rooms of $1.5 million for its 300-room hotel, average daily room rates of $40, and average variable costs of $6 for each room rented. It operates 365 days per year. The hotel is subject to an income tax rate of 30%.

REQUIRED:
1. How many rooms must the hotel rent to earn a net income after taxes of $1 million? Of $500,000?
2. Compute the break-even point in number of rooms rented. What percentage occupancy for the year is needed to break even?

2–38. **Income taxes.** The Quick Snack Company has a chain of fast-food restaurants with the following income pattern:

Average sales check for each customer		$3.00
Costs of food	$1.10	
Other variable costs	.30	1.40
Contribution margin		$1.60

Fixed costs are $200,000 per year. The income tax rate is 35%.

REQUIRED: What total revenue must be achieved to obtain a desired net income after taxes of $100,000?

2–39. **Multiple choice.** (CMA.) Study Appendix 2B. The Able Company has one department that produces three replacement parts for the company. However, only one part can be produced in any month because of the adjustments that must be made to the equipment. The department can produce up to 15,000 units of any one of the three parts in each month. The company expresses the monthly after-tax cost-volume-profit relationships for each part using an equation method. The format of the equations and the equation for each replacement part are given below.

Introduction to
Cost-Volume
Relationships

55

EQUATION FORMAT

$$(ATR) \times [(SP - VC) \times U - FC]$$

ATR = after-tax rate
SP = selling price
VC = variable cost
U = units
FC = fixed costs

PART	PART EQUATIONS
AL45	.6 [($4.00-$1.25) U − $33,400]
BT62	.6 [($4.05-$2.55) U − $15,000]
GM17	.6 [($4.10-$2.00) U − $22,365]

Select the best answer for each of the following items.

1. The contribution margin per unit for Part BT62 is

    a. $4.05
    b. $2.55
    c. $ .50

    d. $1.50
    e. None of these

2. The break-even volume in units for Part GM17 is

    a. 10,650 units
    b. 6,390 units
    c. 17,750 units

    d. 13,419 units
    e. Some other amount

3. If Able Company produces and sells 13,000 units of Part AL45, the amount of Able's after-tax net income attributable to this product would be

    a. $8,090
    b. $2,350
    c. $1,410

    d. $940
    e. Some other amount

4. The number of units of Part BT62 required to be produced and sold to contribute $4,140 to Able's net income after-tax is

    a. 14,600 units
    b. 12,800 units
    c. 5,400 units

    d. 9,000 units
    e. Some other amount

5. The production and unit sales volume level at which Able Company will be indifferent as between Parts BT62 and GM17 is

    a. 7,365 units
    b. 4,092 units
    c. 10,380 units

    d. 12,275 units
    e. Some other amount

6. The maximum effect on Able's after-tax net income that can be realized when production in this department is at capacity is

    a. $4,710
    b. $4,500
    c. $5,481

    d. $9,135
    e. Some other amount

3

INTRODUCTION TO MANUFACTURING COSTS

Learning Objectives

When you have finished studying this chapter, you should be able to

1. Define the following terms and concepts and explain how they are related: **cost, cost objective, cost accumulation,** and **cost allocation**
2. Define and identify examples of each of the three major elements in the cost of a manufactured product
3. Differentiate between product costs and period costs, identifying examples of each
4. Explain how the financial statements of merchandisers and manufacturers differ because of the types of goods they sell
5. Show the effects that the basic transactions of a manufacturing company can have on the balance sheet equation
6. Construct model income statements of a manufacturing company in both the functional form and the contribution form

Some form of cost accounting is applicable to manufacturing companies, retail stores, insurance companies, medical centers, and nearly all types of organizations. Throughout this book we shall consider both nonmanufacturing and manufacturing organizations, but we shall start with the manufacturing company because it is the most general case—embracing production, marketing, and general administration functions. You can then apply this overall framework to any organization.

CLASSIFICATIONS OF COSTS

☐ Cost Accumulation and Cost Objectives

A **cost** may be defined as a sacrifice or giving up of resources for a particular purpose. Costs are frequently measured by the monetary units (for example, dollars or francs) that must be paid for goods and services. Costs are initially recorded in elementary form and then grouped in different ways to facilitate various decisions such as evaluating managers and subunits of the organization, expanding or deleting products or territories, and replacing equipment.

To help make decisions, managers want the *cost of something*. This something is called a **cost objective,** which may be defined as *any activity for which a separate measurement of costs is desired*. Examples of cost objectives include departments, products, territories, miles driven, bricks laid, patients seen, tax bills sent, checks processed, student hours taught, and library books shelved.

The cost-accounting system typically (1) accumulates costs by some "natural" classification such as materials or labor and (2) then allocates (traces) these costs to cost objectives. **Cost accumulation** is the gathering of costs in some organized way via an accounting system. **Cost allocation** is the assignment of and reassignment of a cost or group of costs to one or more cost objectives. Exhibit 3-1 illustrates how a company might use materials in two main departments for manufacturing several different products. Note that the cost of, say, the metal used may be accumulated initially by keeping a tabulation of the amounts withdrawn from the raw-material storage center by each department. In turn, the metal used by each department is allocated to the products worked on in that department.

Cost-accounting systems vary in complexity. They tend to become more detailed as management seeks more accurate data for decision making. A news story about Mark Controls Company, a manufacturer in the valve industry, said: "The key to Mark's success so far has been tough financial controls and methodical emphasis on profit margins." The company had previously relied on broad averages. The story continued: "The company set up a computerized costing system that calculated the precise cost and profit margin for each of the 15,000 products the company sold. Since then, about 15% of those products have been dropped from the company's line because they were insufficiently profitable."

How "precise" can cost allocations be? Probably never as precise as

EXHIBIT 3-1

Cost Accumulation and Allocation

1. Cost accumulation

2. Cost allocation to cost objectives:

a) To departments*

b) To products†

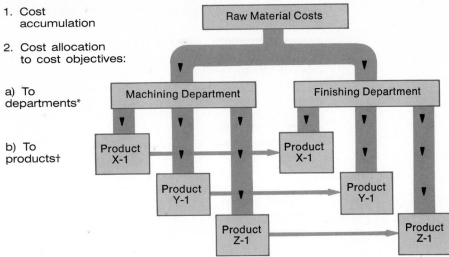

*Purpose: to evaluate performance of manufacturing departments.
†Purpose: to obtain costs of various products for valuing inventory, determining income, and judging product profitability.

might be desired. Nevertheless, managers have increasingly discovered that reliance on broad averages is not enough in today's competitive world.

This introductory chapter concentrates on the big picture of how manufacturing costs are accumulated and classified. A variety of cost-accounting systems allocate these costs to the products worked on. These systems are described in some detail in three separate chapters (13, 14, and 15) in this book. However, such detail may be studied at almost any stage of an introductory course.

❑ Elements of Manufacturing Costs

The same general approach of cost accumulation and cost allocation that was just illustrated for raw materials is also applicable to other manufacturing costs. Manufacturing is the transformation of materials into other goods through the use of labor and factory facilities. There are three major elements in the cost of a manufactured product: (1) **direct materials,** (2) **direct labor,** and (3) **factory overhead.**

1. **Direct materials.** All materials that are physically identified as a part of the finished goods and that may be traced to the finished goods in an economically feasible way. Examples are iron castings, lumber, aluminum sheets, and subassemblies. Direct materials often do *not* include minor items such as nails or glue. Why? Because the costs of tracing insignificant items do not seem worth the possible benefits of having more precise product costs. Such items are usually called *supplies* or *indirect materials* and are classified as a part of the factory overhead described below.

2. **Direct labor.** All labor that is physically traceable to the finished goods in an economically feasible way. Examples are the labor of machine operators and of assemblers. Much labor, such as that of janitors, forklift-truck operators, plant guards, and storeroom clerks, is considered to be *indirect labor* because of the impossibility or economic infeasibility of tracing such activity to specific

Introduction to Manufacturing Costs

59

products via physical observation. Indirect labor is classified as a part of factory overhead.

3. **Factory overhead.** All costs other than direct material or direct labor that are associated with the manufacturing process. Other terms used to describe this category are **factory burden, manufacturing overhead, manufacturing expenses,** and **indirect manufacturing costs.** The last term is a clearer descriptor than factory overhead, but factory overhead will be used most frequently in this book because it is briefer. Two major subclassifications of factory overhead are

   a. **Variable factory overhead.** Examples are power, supplies, and most indirect labor. Whether the cost of a specific category of indirect labor is variable or fixed depends on its behavior in a given company. In this book, unless we specify otherwise, indirect labor will be considered a variable rather than a fixed cost.

   b. **Fixed factory overhead.** Examples are supervisory salaries, property taxes, rent, insurance, and depreciation.

Two of the three major elements are sometimes combined in cost terminology as follows. **Prime cost** consists of (1) + (2), direct materials plus direct labor. **Conversion cost** consists of (2) + (3), direct labor plus factory overhead.

RELATIONSHIPS OF INCOME STATEMENTS AND BALANCE SHEETS

This section assumes a basic familiarity with income statements and balance sheets, as covered by any beginning course in financial accounting or by Chapter 17. However, the reader can easily understand most of the terms explained here without having such familiarity.

❏ Product Costs and Period Costs

Accountants frequently refer to *product costs* and *period costs.* **Product costs** generally are identified with goods produced or purchased for resale. Product costs are initially identified as part of the inventory on hand; in turn, these product costs (inventoriable costs) become expenses (in the form of *cost of goods sold*) only when the inventory is sold. In contrast, **period costs** are costs that are being deducted as expenses during the current period without having been previously classified as product costs.

The distinctions between product costs and period costs are best understood by example. Examine the top half of Exhibit 3-2. A merchandising company (retailer or wholesaler) acquires goods for resale without changing their basic form. The *only* product cost is the purchase cost of the merchandise. Unsold goods are held as merchandise inventory cost and shown as an asset on a balance sheet. As the goods are sold, their costs become expense in the form of "cost of goods sold."

A merchandising company also has a variety of selling and administrative expenses, which are the major examples of period costs (noninventoriable costs). They are referred to as period costs because they are deducted from revenue as expenses without ever having been regarded as a part of inventory.

EXHIBIT 3-2

Relationships of Product Costs and Period Costs

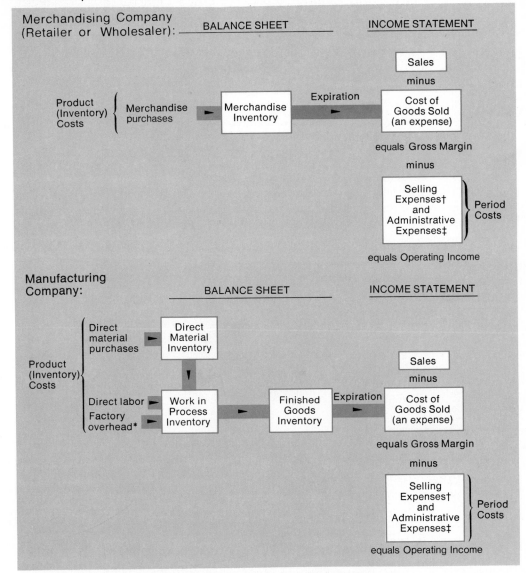

*Examples: indirect labor, factory supplies, insurance and depreciation on plant.

†Examples: insurance on salespersons' cars, depreciation on salespersons' cars, salespersons' salaries.

‡Examples: insurance on corporate headquarters building, depreciation on office equipment, clerical salaries.

Note particularly that where insurance and depreciation relate to the manufacturing function, they are inventoriable; but where they relate to selling and administration, they are not inventoriable.

In manufacturing accounting, as the bottom half of Exhibit 3-2 illustrates, direct materials are transformed into salable form with the help of direct labor and factory overhead. All these costs are product costs because they are allocated to inventory until the goods are sold. As in merchandising accounting, the selling and administrative expenses are not regarded as product costs but are treated as period costs.

❑ Balance Sheet Presentation

As Exhibit 3-2 shows, balance sheets of manufacturers and merchandisers differ with respect to inventories. The merchandise inventory account is supplanted in a manufacturing concern by three inventory classes. The purpose of these various classifications is to trace all product costs through the production process to the time of sale. The classes are

Direct-material inventory: materials on hand but not yet issued to the production line

Work-in-process inventory: cost of uncompleted goods still on the production line containing appropriate amounts of the three major manufacturing costs (direct material, direct labor, and factory overhead)

Finished-goods inventory: fully completed goods not yet sold

The only essential difference between the structure of the balance sheet of a manufacturer and that of the balance sheet of a retailer or wholesaler would appear in their respective current-asset sections (numbers are assumed):

Current-Asset Sections of Balance Sheets

MANUFACTURER			RETAILER OR WHOLESALER	
Cash		$ 4,000	Cash	$ 4,000
Receivables		25,000	Receivables	25,000
Finished goods	$32,000			
Work in process	22,000			
Direct material	23,000		Merchandise	
Total inventories		77,000	inventories	77,000
Other current assets		1,000	Other current assets	1,000
Total current assets		$107,000	Total current assets	$107,000

❑ Unit Costs for Product Costing

Most often, product costing is accomplished by heavy use of unit costs. Assume the following:

Total cost of goods manufactured (10,000,000 units)	$40,000,000
Total units manufactured	10,000,000
Unit cost of product for inventory purposes ($40,000,000 ÷ 10,000,000)	$4

The unit cost facilitates the accounting for inventory valuation and income measurement. If some of the 10 million units manufactured are still unsold at the end of the period, a part of the $40 million cost of goods manufactured will be "held back" as a cost of the ending inventory of finished goods (and shown as an asset on a balance sheet.) The remainder becomes "cost of goods sold" for the current period (that is, shown as an expense on the income statement).

In the income statements, the detailed reporting of selling and administrative expenses is typically the same for manufacturing and merchandising organizations, but the cost of goods sold is different:

MANUFACTURER	RETAILER OR WHOLESALER
Manufacturing cost of goods produced and then sold, usually composed of the three major elements of cost: direct materials, direct labor, and factory overhead	Merchandise cost of goods sold, usually composed of the purchase cost of items, including freight in, that are acquired and then resold

Consider the *additional assumed* details as they are presented in the model income statement of Exhibit 3-3. The $40 million cost of goods manufactured is subdivided into the major components of direct materials, direct labor, and factory overhead.

The terms "costs" and "expenses" are often used loosely by accountants and managers. "Expenses" denote all costs being deducted from (matched against) revenue in a given period. On the other hand, "costs" is a much broader term; for example, "cost" is used to describe an asset (the cost of inventory) and an expense (the cost of goods sold). Thus manufacturing costs are funneled into an income statement as an expense (in the form of cost of goods sold) via the multistep inventory procedure, as indi-

EXHIBIT 3-3

Model Income Statement, Manufacturing Company

Sales (8,000,000 units @ $10)			$80,000,000
Cost of goods manufactured and sold:			
Beginning finished-goods inventory		$ –0–	
Cost of goods manufactured:			
Direct materials used	$20,000,000		
Direct labor	12,000,000		
Factory overhead:			
Variable factory overhead	2,000,000		
Fixed factory overhead	6,000,000	40,000,000	
Cost of goods available for sale		$40,000,000	
Ending finished-goods inventory, 2,000,000 units @ $4		8,000,000	
Cost of goods sold (an expense)			32,000,000
Gross margin or gross profit			$48,000,000
Less other expenses:			
Selling costs (an expense)		$30,000,000	
General and administrative costs (an expense)		8,000,000	38,000,000
Operating income (also net income in this example)			$10,000,000

cated earlier in Exhibit 3-2. In contrast, selling and general administrative costs are commonly deemed expenses immediately as they are incurred.

Common Mistakes

Before proceeding, please take a moment to review some key distinctions made in Exhibits 3-2 and 3-3. Otherwise these new terms and classifications become blurred.

Distinguish sharply between the merchandising accounting and the manufacturing accounting for such costs as insurance, depreciation, and wages. In merchandising accounting, all such items are period costs (expenses of the current period). In manufacturing accounting, many of such items are related to production activities and thus, as factory overhead, are product costs (become expenses as the inventory is sold).

In both merchandising and manufacturing accounting, selling and general administrative costs are period costs. Thus the inventory cost of a manufactured product *excludes* sales salaries, sales commissions, advertising, legal, public relations, and the president's salary. *Manufacturing* overhead is traditionally regarded as a part of finished-goods inventory cost, whereas *selling* expenses and *general administrative* expenses are not.[1]

Relation to Balance Sheet Equation

Exhibit 3-4 relates the theory of product costing to the analysis of the balance sheet equation. For simplicity, all acquisitions and dispositions of resources are assumed to be for cash. The same dollar amounts are used in Exhibits 3-3 and 3-4 except that Exhibit 3-4 introduces the idea of an inventory of materials. That is, $30 million of direct materials were acquired, $20 million were used, and $10 million were left in inventory at the end of the period.

Trace the effects of each summary transaction, step by step, in Exhibit 3-4. As the bottom of Exhibit 3-4 indicates, the ending balance sheet accounts would be:

Cash	$ 92,000,000	Paid-in capital	$100,000,000
Direct-materials inventory	10,000,000	Retained income	10,000,000*
Work-in-process inventory	—		
Finished-goods inventory	8,000,000		
Total assets	$110,000,000	Total equities	$110,000,000

* Retained income arose because of profitable operations, which produced income of $10 million. For the detailed income statement, see Exhibit 3-3.

[1] Some accountants maintain that product costs become period costs as the goods are sold. In their minds, there is no difference between the terms "period costs" and "expenses" because both represent all costs that are being deducted from revenue during the current period. However, the distinction in this book consists of two steps: (1) Is the cost a product cost or a period cost? and (2) When do the product costs and the period costs become expenses? The product costs become expenses as the goods are sold, whereas the period costs become expenses as incurred.

EXHIBIT 3-4

Analysis of Balance Sheet Equation for Manufacturing Costs
(In millions of dollars)

| | | ASSETS | | | | | EQUITIES | |
| | | | | | | | | Stockholders' equity | |
Transactions	Cash +	Direct-Materials Inventory +	Work-in-Process Inventory +	Finished-Goods Inventory	= Liabilities +	Paid-in Capital +	Retained Income
Beginning balances	100				=	100	
1. Purchase of direct materials	−30	+30			=		
2. Direct materials used		−20	+20		=		
3. Acquire direct labor	−12		+12		=		
4. Acquire factory overhead	−8		+8		=		
5. Complete the goods			−40	+40	=		
6a. Revenue	+80				=		+80 (Revenue)
6b. Cost of goods sold				−32	=		−32 (Expense)
7. Selling costs	−30				=		−30 (Expense)
8. General and administrative costs	−8				=		−8 (Expense)
Ending balances	92 +	10 +	0 +	8	=	100 +	10

❑ Direct and Indirect Costs

Admittedly, the area of manufacturing costs contains a thicket of new terms. One of your main tasks in studying this chapter is to understand these terms. For example, a distinction was made earlier in this chapter between costs that are "direct" and "indirect" with respect to a *particular* cost objective—the manufactured product. In other settings, the direct-indirect distinction may pertain to a different cost objective, for example, a department. Thus the wages of a janitor who works solely in the assembly department may be regarded as a direct cost of the department but as an indirect cost of the products worked on within that department. However, unless otherwise stated, throughout this book the direct-indirect distinction will pertain only to the *product* as the cost objective.

TWO TYPES OF INCOME STATEMENTS

❑ Detailed Costs of a Manufacturing Company

A fresh example may clarify many of the cost terms and distinctions explored thus far. Assume that the Samson Company for 19X2 has direct-material costs of $7 million and direct-labor costs of $4 million. Assume also that the company incurred the indirect manufacturing costs (factory overhead) illustrated in Exhibit 3-5 and the selling and administrative expenses illustrated in Exhibit 3-6. Total sales were $20 million.

Finally, assume that the units produced are equal to the units sold. That is, there is no change in inventory levels. In this way, we avoid some complications that are unnecessary and unimportant at this stage.[2]

Note that Exhibits 3-5 and 3-6 contain subdivisions of costs between variable and fixed classifications. Many companies do not make such subdivisions. Furthermore, when such subdivisions are made, sometimes arbitrary decisions are necessary as to whether a given cost is variable or fixed, or partially variable and partially fixed (for example, repairs). Nevertheless, to aid decision making, an increasing number of companies are attempting to report the extent to which their costs are approximately variable or fixed.

❑ Functional Approach

Exhibit 3-7 presents the income statement in the form used by most companies. The theory followed is called the **functional approach** or **absorption costing** or **traditional costing** or **full costing.** It is the theory also illustrated in Exhibit 3-3, page 63, whereby all indirect manufacturing costs (both variable plus fixed factory overhead) are considered as inventoriable or product costs that become an expense in the form of manufacturing cost of goods sold as sales occur.

[2] These complexities are discussed in Chapters 13, 14, and 15. (If preferred, Chapters 13 or 14 may be studied immediately after Chapter 3 without loss of continuity.)

EXHIBIT
3-5

SAMSON COMPANY
Schedules of Indirect Manufacturing Costs
(which are product costs)
For the Year Ended December 31, 19X2
(In thousands of dollars)

Schedule 1: Variable Costs

Supplies (lubricants, expendable tools, coolants, sandpaper)	$ 150	
Indirect labor (janitors, forklift operators)	700	
Repairs	100	
Power	50	$1,000

Schedule 2: Fixed Costs

Foremen's salaries	$ 200	
Employee training	90	
Factory picnic and holiday party	10	
Supervisory salaries, except foremen's salaries	700	
Depreciation, plant and equipment	1,800	
Property taxes	150	
Insurance	50	3,000
Total indirect manufacturing costs		$4,000

Take a moment to compare Exhibits 3-3 and 3-7. Note that gross profit or gross margin is the difference between sales and the *manufacturing* cost of goods sold. Note too that the *primary classifications* of costs on the income statement are by three major management *functions:* manufacturing, selling, and administrative.

EXHIBIT
3-6

SAMSON COMPANY
Schedules of Selling and Administrative
Expenses (which are period costs)
For the Year Ended December 31, 19X2
(In thousands of dollars)

Schedule 3: Selling Expenses

Variable:		
Sales commissions	$ 700	
Shipping expenses for products sold	300	$1,000
Fixed:		
Advertising	$ 700	
Sales salaries	1,000	
Other	300	2,000
Total selling expenses		$3,000

Schedule 4: Administrative Expenses

Variable:		
Some clerical wages	$ 80	
Computer time rented	20	$ 100
Fixed:		
Office salaries	$ 100	
Other salaries	200	
Depreciation on office facilities	100	
Public-accounting fees	40	
Legal fees	100	
Other	360	900
Total administrative expenses		$1,000

EXHIBIT 3-7

SAMSON COMPANY
Functional Income Statement
For the Year Ended
December 31, 19X2
(In thousands of dollars)

Sales		$20,000
Less **manufacturing** costs of goods sold:		
Direct material	$7,000	
Direct labor	4,000	
Indirect **manufacturing costs** (Schedules 1 plus 2)	4,000	15,000
Gross margin or gross profit		$ 5,000
Selling expenses (Schedule 3)	$3,000	
Administrative expenses (Schedule 4)	1,000	
Total **selling** and **administrative** expenses		4,000
Operating income		$ 1,000

EXHIBIT 3-8

SAMSON COMPANY
Contribution Income Statement
For the Year Ended
December 31, 19X2
(In thousands of dollars)

Sales		$20,000
Less **variable** expenses:		
Direct material	$ 7,000	
Direct labor	4,000	
Variable indirect manufacturing (Schedule 1)	1,000	
Total **variable** manufacturing cost of goods sold	$12,000	
Variable selling expenses (Schedule 3)	1,000	
Variable administrative expenses (Schedule 4)	100	
Total **variable** expenses		13,100
Contribution margin		$ 6,900
Less **fixed** expenses:		
Manufacturing (Schedule 2)	$ 3,000	
Selling (Schedule 3)	2,000	
Administrative (Schedule 4)	900	5,900
Operating income		$ 1,000

Note: Schedules 1 and 2 are in Exhibit 3-5. Schedules 3 and 4 are in Exhibit 3-6.

❏ Contribution Approach

Exhibit 3-8 presents the income statement in the "contribution" form used by an increasing number of companies for internal (management accounting) purposes. Even though a standard format is used for external purposes, a company can and often does adopt a different format for internal purposes if the expected benefits of making decisions exceed the extra costs of using different reporting systems simultaneously.

The theory followed by Exhibit 3-8 has been called the **contribution approach, variable costing, direct costing,** or **marginal costing.** For decision purposes, the most important difference between the contribution approach and the functional approach is the emphasis of the former on the distinction between variable and fixed costs. The *primary classifications* of costs are by *variable and fixed cost behavior patterns,* not by *business functions.*

The contribution income statement provides a contribution margin, which is computed after deducting *all* variable costs, *including* variable selling and administrative costs. This approach facilitates the computation of the impact on net income of changes in sales, and it dovetails neatly with the cost-volume-profit analysis illustrated in the preceding chapter.

The contribution approach stresses the lump-sum amount of fixed costs to be recouped before net income emerges. This highlighting of total fixed costs helps to attract management attention to fixed-cost behavior and control when both short-run and long-run plans are being made. Keep in mind that advocates of this contribution approach do not maintain that fixed costs are unimportant or irrelevant; but they do stress that the distinctions between behaviors of variable and fixed costs are crucial for certain decisions.

The implications of the *functional approach* and the *contribution approach* for decision making are discussed in the next chapter, using Exhibits 3-7 and 3-8.

Summary

The most important aspect of intelligent cost planning and control is an understanding of cost behavior patterns and influences. The most basic behavior pattern of costs may be described as either variable or fixed. The contribution approach to preparing an income statement emphasizes this distinction and is a natural extension of the cost-volume-profit analysis used in decisions. In contrast, the functional approach emphasizes the distinction among three major management functions: manufacturing, selling, and administration.

READERS WHO NOW DESIRE A MORE DETAILED TREATMENT OF PRODUCT COSTING MAY JUMP TO THE STUDY OF CHAPTER 13 OR 14 WITHOUT LOSING CONTINUITY. IN TURN, CHAPTER 15 MAY BE STUDIED IMMEDIATELY AFTER CHAPTER 7 IF DESIRED. INSTRUCTORS DIFFER REGARDING THE APPROPRIATE SEQUENCE OF CHAPTERS AND TOPICS. MANY INSTRUCTORS PREFER TO ASSIGN CHAPTER 13 OR 14 NEXT.

Summary Problem For Your Review

❑ Problem

1. Review the illustrations in Exhibits 3-5 through 3-8. Suppose that all variable costs fluctuate in direct proportion to units produced and sold, and that all fixed costs are unaffected over a wide range of production and sales. What would operating income have been if sales (at normal selling prices) had been $20.9 million instead of $20.0 million? Which statement, the functional income statement or the contribution income statement, did you use as a framework for your answer? Why?

2. Suppose employee training (Exhibit 3-5) was regarded as a variable rather than a fixed cost at a rate of $90,000 ÷ 1,000,000 units, or 9¢ per unit. How would your answer in part 1 change?

1. Operating income would increase from $1,000,000 to $1,310,500, computed as follows:

Increase in revenue	$ 900,000
Increase in total contribution margin:	
Contribution-margin ratio in contribution income	
statement (Exhibit 3-8) is $6,900,000 ÷ $20,000,000 = .345	
Ratio times revenue increase is .345 × $900,000	$ 310,500
Increase in fixed expenses	-0-
Operating income before increase	1,000,000
New operating income	$1,310,500

Computations are easily made by using data from the contribution income statement. In contrast, the costs in the traditional functional income statement must be analyzed and divided into variable and fixed categories before the effect on operating income can be estimated.

2. The contribution-margin ratio would be lower because the variable costs would be higher by 9¢ per unit: ($6,900,000 − $90,000) ÷ $20,000,000 = .3405.

	GIVEN LEVEL	HIGHER LEVEL	DIFFERENCE
Revenue	$20,000,000	$20,900,000	$900,000
Variable expenses ($13,100,000 + $90,000)	13,190,000	13,783,550	593,550
Contribution margin at .3405	6,810,000	7,116,450	306,450
Fixed expenses ($5,900,000 − $90,000)	5,810,000	5,810,000	—
Operating income	$ 1,000,000	$ 306,450	$306,450

Highlights to Remember

1. Many new terms were introduced in this chapter. Review them to make sure you know their exact meaning.
2. Manufacturing costs (direct material, direct labor, and factory overhead) are traditionally regarded as product costs (inventoriable costs).
3. In contrast, selling and administrative costs are accounted for as period costs; hence they are typically deducted from revenue as expenses in the period incurred.

Accounting Vocabulary

Absorption costing; contribution approach; conversion cost; cost; cost accumulation; cost allocation; cost objective; direct costing; direct labor; direct material; factory burden; factory overhead; full costing; functional approach; idle time; indirect labor; indirect manufacturing costs; manufacturing expenses; manufacturing overhead; marginal costing; overtime premium; period costs; prime cost; product costs; traditional costing; variable costing.

Appendix

3: Classification of Labor Costs⎯⎯⎯⎯⎯

The terminology for labor costs is usually the most confusing. Each organization seems to develop its own interpretation of various labor-cost classifications. We begin by considering some commonly encountered labor-cost terminology.

For our purposes, we categorize the terminology as follows:

Direct labor (already defined)
Indirect labor:
    Forklift-truck operators (internal handling of materials)
    Janitors
    Plant guards
    Rework labor (time spent by direct laborers redoing defective work)
    Overtime premium paid to *all* factory workers
    Idle time
Payroll fringe costs

All factory labor costs, other than those for direct labor, are usually classified as **indirect labor costs,** a major component of indirect manufacturing costs. The term *indirect labor* is usually divided into many subsidiary classifications. The wages of forklift-truck operators are generally not commingled with janitors' salaries, for example, although both are regarded as indirect labor.

Costs are classified in a detailed fashion primarily in an attempt to associate a specific cost with its specific cause, or reason for incurrence. Two classes of indirect labor need special mention: overtime premium and idle time.

Overtime premium paid to all factory workers is usually considered a part of overhead. If a lathe operator earns $8 per hour for straight time, and time and one-half for overtime, the premium is $4 per overtime hour. If the operator works 44 hours, including four overtime hours, in one week, the gross earnings are classified as follows:

Direct labor: 44 hours × $8	$352
Overtime premium (factory overhead): 4 hours × $4	16
Total earnings	$368

Why is overtime premium considered an indirect cost rather than direct? After all, it can usually be traced to specific batches of work. It is usually not considered a direct charge because the scheduling of production jobs is generally random. For example, assume that Jobs No. 1 through 5 are scheduled for a specific workday of ten hours, including two overtime hours. Each job requires two hours. Should the job scheduled during hours 9 and 10 be assigned the overtime premium? For example, suppose you brought your automobile to a shop for repair by 8:00 A.M. Through random scheduling, your auto was repaired during hours 9 and 10 as Job No. 5. When you came to get your car, you learned that all the overtime premium had been added to your bill. You probably would not be overjoyed.

Thus, in most companies, the overtime premium is not allocated to any specific job. Instead, it is prorated to all jobs. The latter approach does not penalize a particular batch of work solely because it happened to be worked on during the overtime hours. Instead, the overtime premium is considered to be attributable to the heavy overall volume of work, and its cost is thus regarded as indirect manufacturing costs (factory overhead).

Another subsidiary classification of indirect-labor costs is **idle time.** This cost typically represents wages paid for unproductive time caused by machine breakdowns, material shortages, sloppy production scheduling, and the like. For example, if the same lathe operator's machine broke down for three hours during the week, the operator's earnings would be classified as follows:

Direct labor: 41 hours × $8	$328
Overtime premium (factory overhead): 4 hours × $4	16
Idle time (factory overhead): 3 hours × $8	24
Total earnings	$368

The classification of factory *payroll fringe costs* (e.g., employer contributions to social security, life insurance, health insurance, pensions, and miscellaneous other employee benefits) differs from company to company. In most companies these are classified as indirect manufacturing costs. In some companies, however, the fringe benefits related to direct labor are charged as an additional direct-labor cost. For instance, a direct laborer, such as a lathe operator whose gross wages are computed on the basis of $8 an hour, may enjoy fringe benefits totaling, say, $1 per hour. Most companies tend to classify the $8 as direct-labor cost and the $1 as factory overhead. Other companies classify the entire $9 as direct-labor cost. The latter approach is conceptually or theoretically preferable, because most of these costs are also a fundamental part of acquiring labor services.

Fundamental Assignment Material

3–1. Contribution and functional income statements. (Alternate is 3-32.) The following information is taken from the records of the Kingsville Company for the year ending December 31, 19X2. There were no beginning or ending inventories.

Sales	$10,000,000	Long-term rent, factory	$ 100,000
Sales commissions	500,000	Factory superintendent's	
Advertising	200,000	salary	30,000
Shipping expenses	300,000	Foremen's salaries	100,000
Administrative executive		Direct material used	4,000,000
salaries	100,000	Direct labor	2,000,000
Administrative clerical		Cutting bits used	60,000
salaries (variable)	400,000	Factory methods research	40,000
Fire insurance on		Abrasives for machining	100,000
factory equipment	2,000	Indirect labor	800,000
Property taxes on		Depreciation on	
factory equipment	10,000	equipment	300,000

REQUIRED:

1. Prepare a contribution income statement and a functional income statement. If you are in doubt about any cost behavior pattern, decide on the basis of whether the total cost in question will fluctuate substantially over a wide range of volume. Prepare a separate supporting schedule of indirect manufacturing costs subdivided between variable and fixed costs.
2. Suppose that all variable costs fluctuate directly in proportion to sales, and that fixed costs are unaffected over a wide range of sales. What would operating income have been if sales had been $10.5 million instead of $10.0 million? Which income statement did you use to help get your answer? Why?

3–2. Frequently encountered terms. Refer to the functional income statement of your solution to the preceding problem. Give the amounts for the following: (1) prime costs, (2) manufacturing expenses, (3) conversion costs, and (4) factory burden.

Additional
Assignment Material _____

3–3. "Advertising is noninventoriable." Explain.

3–4. "Departments are not cost objects or objects of costing." Do you agree? Explain.

3–5. "Manufacturing cost of goods sold is a special category of expense." Do you agree? Explain.

3–6. "Unexpired costs are always inventory costs." Do you agree? Explain.

3–7. "Miscellaneous supplies are always indirect costs." Do you agree? Explain.

3–8. Distinguish between the two prime costs.

3–9. "Glue or nails become an integral part of the finished product, so they would be direct material." Do you agree? Explain.

3–10. What is the advantage of the contribution approach as compared with the traditional approach?

3–11. Distinguish between manufacturing and merchandising.

3–12. Cost accumulation and allocation. The S Company incurred raw-material costs of $400,000. The machining department used $300,000, and the finishing department, $100,000. Product A flowed through both departments, incurring 10% of the machining department's raw-material costs and 5% of the finishing department's raw-material costs. What was the raw-material cost of Product A?

3–13. Cost accumulation and allocation. A company has two departments, machining and finishing. For a given period, suppose the following costs were incurred by the company as a whole: direct material, $120,000; direct labor, $60,000; and manufacturing overhead, $78,000. The grand total costs were $258,000.

The machining department incurred 80% of the direct-material costs, but only 30% of the direct-labor costs. As is commonplace, manufacturing overhead incurred by each department was allocated to products in proportion to the direct-labor costs of products within the departments.

Three products were produced:

PRODUCT	DIRECT MATERIAL	DIRECT LABOR
X–1	50%	33⅓%
Y–1	25	33⅓
Z–1	25	33⅓
Total for the machining department	100%	100%
X–1	33⅓%	40%
Y–1	33⅓	40
Z–1	33⅓	20
Total added by finishing department	100%	100%

The manufacturing overhead incurred by the machining department and allocated to all products therein amounted to: machining, $36,000; finishing, $42,000.

1. Compute the total costs incurred by the machining department and added by the finishing department.
2. Compute the total costs of each product that would be shown as finished-goods inventory if all the products were transferred to finished stock upon completion.

3–14. Relating costs to cost objectives.   A company uses a functional cost system. Prepare headings for two columns: (1) assembly department costs and (2) products assembled. Fill in the two columns for each of the costs below. If a specific cost is direct to the department but indirect to the product, place a *D* in column 1 and an *I* in column 2. The costs are: materials used, supplies used, assembly labor, material-handling labor (transporting materials between and within departments), depreciation—building, assembly foreman's salary, and the building and grounds supervisor's salary.

3–15. Classification of manufacturing costs.   Classify each of the following as direct or indirect (*D* or *I*) with respect to product, and as variable or fixed (*V* or *F*) with respect to whether the cost fluctuates in total as activity or volume changes over wide ranges of activity. You will have two answers, *D* or *I* and *V* or *F*, for *each* of the ten items:

1. Foreman training program
2. Abrasives (sandpaper, etc.)
3. Cutting bits in a machinery department
4. Food for a factory cafeteria
5. Factory rent
6. Salary of a factory storeroom clerk
7. Workmen's compensation insurance in a factory
8. Cement for a roadbuilder
9. Steel scrap for a blast furnace
10. Paper towels for a factory washroom

3–16. Variable costs and fixed costs; manufacturing and other costs.   For each of the numbered items, choose the appropriate classifications for a job-order manufacturing company (e.g., custom furniture, job printing). If in doubt about whether the cost behavior is basically variable or fixed, decide on the basis of whether the total cost will fluctuate substantially over a wide range of volume. Most items have two answers among the following possibilities with respect to the cost of a particular job:

a. Variable cost
b. Fixed cost
c. General and administrative cost
d. Selling cost
e. Manufacturing costs, direct
f. Manufacturing costs, indirect
g. Other (specify)

Sample answers:

Direct material	a, e
President's salary	b, c
Bond interest expense	b, g (financial expense)

Items for your consideration:

1. Sandpaper
2. Supervisory salaries, production control
3. Supervisory salaries, assembly department
4. Supervisory salaries, factory storeroom
5. Company picnic costs
6. Overtime premium, punch press
7. Idle time, assembly
8. Freight out
9. Property taxes

10. Factory power for machines
11. Salespersons' commissions
12. Salespersons' salaries
13. Welding supplies
14. Fire loss
15. Paint for finished products

16. Heat and air-conditioning, factory
17. Material-handling labor, punch press
18. Straight-line depreciation, salespersons' automobiles

3–17. **Meaning of technical terms.** Refer to Exhibit 3-3, page 63. Give the amounts of the following with respect to the cost of goods available for sale: (1) prime costs, (2) conversion costs, (3) factory burden, and (4) manufacturing expenses.

3–18. **Product and period costs.** Refer to Exhibit 3-3, page 63. Suppose that $30 million of direct material had been purchased.

REQUIRED:

Using Exhibit 3-2 as a guide, sketch how the costs in Exhibit 3-3 are related to balance sheets and income statements. In other words, prepare an exhibit like 3-2, inserting the numbers from Exhibit 3-3 to the extent you can.

3–19. **Presence of ending work in process.** Refer to Exhibits 3-3 and 3-4. Suppose that manufacturing costs were the same, but there was an ending work-in-process inventory of $5 million. The cost of the completed goods would therefore be $35 million instead of $40 million. Suppose also that sales and the cost of goods sold are unchanged.

REQUIRED:

1. Recast the income statement of Exhibit 3-3, p. 63.
2. What lines and ending balances would change in Exhibit 3-4 and by how much?

3–20. **Balance sheet equation.** Review Exhibit 3-4. Assume that the G Company had a beginning balance of $800,000 cash and paid-in capital. The following transactions occurred in 19X2 (in thousands):

1. Purchase of direct materials for cash	$350
2. Direct materials used	300
3. Acquire direct labor for cash	160
4. Acquire factory overhead for cash	200
5. Complete all goods that were started	?
6a. Revenue (all sales are for cash)	600
6b. Cost of goods sold (half of the goods completed were sold)	?
7. Selling costs for cash	100
8. General and administrative costs for cash	40

REQUIRED:

Prepare an analysis similar to Exhibit 3-4. What are the ending balances of cash, direct materials, finished goods, paid-in capital, and retained income?

3–21. **Balance sheet equation.** Refer to the preceding problem. Suppose that some goods were still in process that cost $100,000. Half the goods completed were sold. However, the same revenue was generated even though fewer goods were sold. What are the balances of all the accounts in the ending balance sheet?

3–22. **Straightforward functional statement.** Consider the following data (in thousands) for a given period:

Sales	$700
Direct materials	200
Direct labor	150
Indirect manufacturing costs	170
Selling and administrative expenses	160

There were no beginning or ending inventories. Compute the (1) manufacturing cost of goods sold, (2) gross profit, (3) operating income, (4) conversion cost, and (5) prime cost.

3–23. Straightforward contribution income statement. Consider the following data (in thousands) for a given period:

Sales	$770
Direct materials	300
Direct labor	140
Variable factory overhead	60
Variable selling and administrative expenses	100
Fixed factory overhead	110
Fixed selling and administrative expenses	45

There were no beginning or ending inventories. Compute the (1) variable manufacturing cost of goods sold, (2) contribution margin, and (3) operating income.

3–24. Straightforward functional and contribution statement. Consider the following data (in millions) and fill in the blanks. There were no beginning or ending inventories.

a.	Sales	$960
b.	Direct materials used	400
c.	Direct labor	200
	Factory overhead:	
d.	Variable	100
e.	Fixed	50
f.	Variable manufacturing cost of goods sold	____
g.	Manufacturing cost of goods sold	____
	Selling and administrative expenses:	
h.	Variable	90
i.	Fixed	80
j.	Gross profit	____
k.	Contribution margin	____
l.	Prime costs	____
m.	Conversion costs	____
n.	Operating income	____

3–25. Functional statement. Consider the following data (in thousands) for a given period. Assume there are no inventories. Fill in the blanks.

Sales	$____
Direct materials	370
Direct labor	____
Factory overhead	____
Manufacturing cost of goods sold	780
Gross margin	120
Selling and administrative expenses	____
Operating income	20
Conversion cost	____
Prime cost	600

3–26. Contribution income statement. Consider the following data (in thousands) for a given period. Assume there are no inventories.

Direct labor	$200
Direct materials	210
Variable factory overhead	80
Contribution margin	200
Fixed selling and administrative expenses	100
Operating income	10
Sales	970

REQUIRED:

Compute the (1) variable manufacturing cost of goods sold, (2) variable selling and administrative expenses, and (3) fixed factory overhead.

3–27. **Overtime premium.** Study the chapter appendix. An automobile dealer has a service department. You have brought your car for repair at 8:00 A.M. When you come to get your car after 6:00 P.M., you notice that your bill contains a charge under "labor" for "overtime premium." When you inquire about the reason for the charge, you are told, "We worked on your car from 5:00 P.M. to 6:00 P.M. Our union contract calls for wages to be paid at time-and-a-half after eight hours. Therefore our ordinary labor charge of $25 per hour was billed to you at $37.50."

REQUIRED:

1. Should the overtime premium be allocated only to cars worked on during overtime hours? Explain.
2. Would your preceding answer differ if the dealer arranged to service your car at 8:00 P.M. as a special convenience to you? Explain.

3–28. **Payroll fringe costs.** Study the chapter appendix. Direct labor is often accounted for at the gross wage rate, and the related "fringe costs" such as employer payroll taxes and employer contributions to health-care plans are accounted for as part of overhead. Therefore the $9 gross pay per hour being paid to Mary Locke, a direct laborer, might cause related fringe costs of $3 per hour.

REQUIRED:

1. Suppose Locke works 40 hours during a particular week as an auditor for a public accounting firm, 30 hours for Client A and 10 for Client B. What would be the cost of direct labor? Of general overhead?
2. The firm allocates costs to each client. What would be the cost of "direct labor" on the Client A job? The Client B job?
3. How would you allocate general overhead to the Client A job? The Client B job?
4. Suppose Locke works a total of 50 hours (30 for A and 20 for B), 10 of which are paid on the basis of time-and-one-half. What would be the cost of direct labor? Of general overhead?
5. Given the facts in Requirement 4, what would be the cost of "direct labor" on the Client A job? The Client B job?

3–29. **Review of Chapters 2 and 3.** The Dischinger Company provides you with the following miscellaneous data regarding operations in 19X2:

Sales	$100,000
Direct material used	40,000
Direct labor	15,000
Fixed manufacturing overhead	20,000
Fixed selling and administrative expenses	10,000
Gross profit	20,000
Net loss	5,000

There are no beginning or ending inventories.

Compute the (1) variable selling and administrative expenses, (2) contribution margin in dollars, (3) variable manufacturing overhead, (4) break-even point in sales dollars, and (5) manufacturing cost of goods sold.

3–30. **Review of Chapters 2 and 3.** The Dietz Corporation provides you with the following miscellaneous data regarding operations for 19X4:

Break-even point (in sales dollars)	$ 66,667
Direct material used	22,000
Gross profit	25,000
Contribution margin	30,000
Direct labor	30,000
Sales	100,000
Variable manufacturing overhead	5,000

There are no beginning or ending inventories.

Compute the (1) fixed manufacturing overhead, (2) variable selling and administrative expenses, and (3) fixed selling and administrative expenses.

3–31. **Review of Chapters 2 and 3.** (D. Kleespie.) A. Lee Company manufactured and sold 1,000 "Sams" during November. Selected data for this month follow:

Sales	$100,000
Direct materials used	21,000
Direct labor	16,000
Variable manufacturing overhead	13,000
Fixed manufacturing overhead	14,000
Variable selling and administrative expenses	?
Fixed selling and administrative expenses	?
Contribution margin	40,000
Operating income	22,000

There were no beginning or ending inventories.

1. What were the variable selling and administrative expenses for November?
2. What were the fixed selling and administrative expenses for November?
3. What was the cost of goods sold during November?
4. Without prejudice to your earlier answers, assume that the fixed selling and administrative expenses for November amounted to $14,000.
   (a) What was the break-even point in units for November?
   (b) How many units must be sold to earn a target operating income of $12,000?
   (c) What would the selling price per unit have to be if the company wanted to earn an operating income of $17,000 on the sale of 900 units?

3–32. **Straightforward income statements.** (Alternate is 3–1.) The Millbrae Company had the following manufacturing data for the year 19X6 (in thousands of dollars):

Beginning inventories	$None
Direct material purchased	400
Direct material used	360
Direct labor	370
Supplies	20
Utilities—variable portion	40
Utilities—fixed portion	12
Indirect labor—variable portion	90
Indirect labor—fixed portion	40
Depreciation	100
Property taxes	20
Supervisory salaries	60

Selling expenses were $300,000 (including $50,000 that were variable) and general administrative expenses were $150,000 (including $30,000 that were variable). Sales were $1.8 million.

Direct labor and supplies are regarded as variable costs.

REQUIRED:

1. Prepare two income statements, one using the contribution approach and one the functional approach.
2. Suppose that all variable costs fluctuate directly in proportion to sales, and that fixed costs are unaffected over a very wide range of sales. What would operating income have been if sales had been $2.0 million instead of $1.8 million? Which income statement did you use to help obtain your answer? Why?

3–33. **Meaning of technical terms.**   Refer to the functional income statement of your solution to the preceding problem. Give the amounts of the following: (1) prime cost, (2) conversion cost, (3) factory burden, (4) manufacturing expenses, and (5) ending inventory of direct materials.

4

RELEVANT COSTS AND SPECIAL DECISIONS— PART ONE

Learning Objectives

When you have finished studying this chapter, you should be able to

1. Identify the relationships among the main elements of the decision process: information, predictions, decisions, implementation, and feedback

2. Discriminate between relevant and irrelevant information for making decisions

3. Analyze data by the contribution approach to support a decision for accepting or rejecting a special sales order

4. Compute a target sales price by various approaches and identify their advantages and disadvantages in determining sales prices

5. Analyze data by the relevant-cost approach to support a decision for adding or deleting a product line

6. Analyze data to determine how to maximize profits within the constraints of a given productive capacity

Managers' special decisions pervade a variety of areas and spans of time. By definition, special decisions occur with less regularity than the typical daily or weekly operating decisions of a hotel, hospital, or manufacturer. The pricing of an unusual sales order is an example of a special decision. Other examples are adding programs, services, or products; selecting equipment; selling products at a certain stage of manufacturing or processing them further; and repairing municipal automobiles internally or buying the repair service from outside suppliers. Unique factors bear on all these special decisions. However, there is a general approach that will help the executive make wise decisions in *any* problem-solving situation. The term "relevant" has been overworked in recent years; nevertheless the general approach herein will be labeled as the *relevant-cost approach*. Coupled with the contribution approach, the ability to distinguish relevant from irrelevant items is the key to making special decisions.

Throughout this and the next chapter, in order to concentrate on a few major points, we shall ignore the time value of money (which is discussed in Chapter 11) and income taxes (which are discussed in Chapter 12).

THE ACCOUNTANT'S ROLE IN SPECIAL DECISIONS

❏ Accuracy and Relevance

Accountants have an important role in the problem-solving process, not as the decision makers but as collectors and reporters of **relevant information.** Their reports must provide valid data—numbers that measure the quantities pertinent to the decision at hand. Many managers want the accountant to offer recommendations about the proper decision, even though the final choice always rests with the operating executive.

The distinction between precision and relevance should be kept in mind. Ideally, the data should be *precise* (accurate) and *relevant* (pertinent). However, as we shall see, figures can be precise but irrelevant, or imprecise but relevant. For example, the university president's salary may be $100,000 per year, to the penny, but may have no bearing on the question of whether to buy or rent data-processing equipment. As has often been said, it is better to be roughly right than precisely wrong.

❏ Qualitative and Quantitative Factors

The aspects of each alternative may be divided into two broad categories, *qualitative* and *quantitative*. Qualitative factors are those for which measurement in dollars and cents is difficult and imprecise; yet a qualitative factor may easily be given more weight than a measurable saving in cost. For example, the opposition of a militant union to new labor-saving machinery may cause an executive to defer or even reject completely the contemplated installation. Or, the chance to manufacture a component oneself for less than the supplier's selling price may be rejected because acceptance might lead to the company's long-run dependency on the supplier for other sub-assemblies. Quantitative factors are those that may more easily be reduced to dollars and cents—for example, projected costs of alternative materials, of direct labor, and of overhead. The accountant, statistician, and mathematician try to express as many decision factors as feasible in quantitative terms. This approach reduces the number of qualitative factors to be judged.

MEANING OF RELEVANCE: THE MAJOR CONCEPTUAL LESSON

Decision making is essentially choosing among several courses of action. The available courses of action are the result of an often time-consuming formal or informal search and screening process, perhaps carried on by a company team that includes engineers, accountants, and operating executives.

The accountant's role in problem solving is primarily that of a technical expert on cost analysis. The accountant's responsibility is to be certain that the manager is guided by relevant data, information that will lead the manager to the best decision.

❏ Definition of Relevance

Consider the final stages of the decision-making process. Two (or more) courses of action are aligned, and a comparison is made. The decision is based on the difference in the effect of the two on future performance. The key question is, What difference does it make? The relevant information is the *expected future data* that will *differ* among alternatives.

The ideas in the preceding paragraph deserve elaboration because they have such wide application. Historical, or past, data have no *direct* bearing on the decision. Historical data may be helpful in the formulation of *predictions*, but past figures, in themselves, are irrelevant to the decision itself simply because they are not the expected future data that managers must use in intelligent decison making. Decisions affect the future. Nothing can alter what has already happened; all past costs are down the drain as far as current or future decisions are concerned.

Of the expected future data, only those that will differ among alternatives are relevant to the decision. Any item is irrelevant if it will remain the same regardless of the alternative selected. For instance, if the department manager's salary will be the same regardless of the products stocked, his or her salary is irrelevant to the selection of products.[1]

[1] The time value of money is ignored here; it is discussed in Chapter 11. Strictly interpreted, differences in future data are affected by both magnitude and timing. Therefore, expected future data with the same magnitude but different timing can be relevant.

The following examples will help us summarize the sharp distinctions needed for proper cost analysis for special decisions.

You habitually buy gasoline from either of two nearby gasoline stations. Yesterday you noticed that one station is selling gasoline at $2.00 per gallon; the other, at $1.90. Your automobile needs gasoline, and, in making your choice of stations, you *assume* that these prices are unchanged. The relevant costs are $2.00 and $1.90, the expected future costs that will differ between the alternatives. You use your past experience (i.e., what you observed yesterday) for predicting today's price. Note that the relevant cost is not what you paid in the past, or what you observed yesterday, but what you *expect to pay* when you drive in to get gasoline. This cost meets our two criteria: (a) it is the expected future cost, and (b) it differs between the alternatives.

You may also plan to have your car lubricated. The recent price at each station was $8.50, and this is what you anticipate paying. This expected future cost is irrelevant because it will be the same under either alternative. It does not meet our second criterion.

Exhibit 4-1 sketches the decision process and uses the following decision as an illustration. A manufacturer is thinking of using aluminum instead of copper in a line of desk lamps. The cost of direct material will decrease from 30¢ to 20¢. The elaborate mechanism in Exhibit 4-1 seems unnecessary for this decision. After all, the analysis in a nutshell is:

	ALUMINUM	COPPER	DIFFERENCE
Direct material	$.20	$.30	$.10

The cost of copper used for this comparison undoubtedly came from historical-cost records, but note that the relevant costs in the above analysis are both expected future costs.

The direct-labor cost will continue to be 70¢ per unit regardless of the material used. It is irrelevant because our second criterion—an element of difference between the alternatives—is not met:

	ALUMINUM	COPPER	DIFFERENCE
Direct material	$.20	$.30	$.10
Direct labor	.70	.70	—

Therefore, we can safely exclude direct labor. There is no harm in including irrelevant items in a formal analysis, provided that they are included properly. However, clarity is usually enhanced by confining the reports to the relevant items only.

EXHIBIT 4-1 *(Place a clip on this page for easy reference.)*
Decision process and role of information

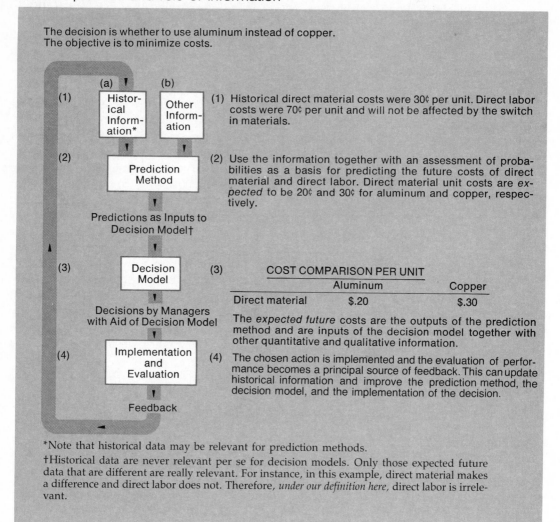

The decision is whether to use aluminum instead of copper.
The objective is to minimize costs.

(1) **Historical direct material costs were 30¢ per unit. Direct labor costs were 70¢ per unit and will not be affected by the switch in materials.**

(2) Use the information together with an assessment of probabilities as a basis for predicting the future costs of direct material and direct labor. Direct material unit costs are *expected* to be 20¢ and 30¢ for aluminum and copper, respectively.

(3)

COST COMPARISON PER UNIT

	Aluminum	Copper
Direct material	$.20	$.30

The *expected future* costs are the outputs of the prediction method and are inputs of the decision model together with other quantitative and qualitative information.

(4) The chosen action is implemented and the evaluation of performance becomes a principal source of feedback. This can update historical information and improve the prediction method, the decision model, and the implementation of the decision.

*Note that historical data may be relevant for prediction methods.

†Historical data are never relevant per se for decision models. Only those expected future data that are different are really relevant. For instance, in this example, direct material makes a difference and direct labor does not. Therefore, *under our definition here,* direct labor is irrelevant.

❑ Role of Predictions

Reflect on Exhibit 4-1. It provides a helpful overview. Box 1(a) represents historical accounting data that are usually supplied by the accounting system, whereas box 1(b) represents other data, such as price indices or industry statistics, that are usually gathered from outside the accounting system. Regardless of their source, the historical data in step 2 help the formulation of *predictions.* Although historical data are often used as a guide to predicting, they are irrelevant per se to the decision itself.

In turn, in step 3 these predictions become inputs to the **decision model,** the method for making the choice. In this case our decision model has a simple form: compare the predicted unit costs and select the alternative bearing the lesser cost.

Exhibit 4-1 will be referred to frequently. It displays the major conceptual lesson in this chapter. This and the next chapter will show how the notion of relevant costs combined with the contribution approach may be applied to various particular decisions. Note that the analytical approach is consistent, regardless of the particular decision encountered. The contribution approach to cost analysis, which was introduced in the preceding chapter, facilitates analysis for a variety of decisions. In this chapter we shall examine the following decisions: (1) special sales orders, (2) pricing policies, (3) deleting or adding product lines or departments, and (4) using available capacity.

THE SPECIAL SALES ORDER

❏ Illustrative Example

Consider the special sales order decision by selecting data from Exhibits 3-7 and 3-8, page 68. We are deliberately returning to these exhibits to underscore their general importance. The main data are summarized again in Exhibit 4-2.

The differences in the emphasis and format of the two income statements in Exhibit 4-2 may be unimportant as long as the accompanying cost analysis leads to the same set of decisions. But these two approaches sometimes lead to different unit costs that must be interpreted warily.

EXHIBIT 4-2

Functional and contribution forms of the income statement

SAMSON COMPANY
Income Statement
For the Year Ended December 31, 19X2
(In thousands of dollars)

FUNCTIONAL FORM		CONTRIBUTION FORM		
Sales	$20,000	Sales		$20,000
Less manufacturing cost of		Less variable ex-		
goods sold	15,000	penses:		
Gross margin or gross profit	$ 5,000	Manufacturing	$12,000	
Less selling and administra-		Selling and ad-		
tive expenses	4,000	ministrative	1,100	13,100
Operating income	$ 1,000	Contribution margin		$ 6,900
		Less fixed expenses:		
		Manufacturing	$ 3,000	
		Selling and ad-		
		ministrative	2,900	5,900
		Operating income		$ 1,000

In our illustration, suppose that 1 million units of product, such as some automobile replacement part, were made and sold. Under the functional costing approach, the unit manufacturing cost of the product would be $15,000,000 ÷ 1,000,000, or $15 per unit. Suppose a mail-order house near year-end offered Samson $13 per unit for a 100,000-unit special order that would not affect regular business in any way, would not raise any antitrust issues concerning price discrimination, would not affect total fixed costs, would not entail any additional variable selling and administrative expenses, and would use some otherwise idle manufacturing capacity. Should Samson accept the order? Perhaps the question should be stated more sharply: What is the difference in the short-run financial results between not accepting and accepting? Again, the key question is, What difference does it make?

❑ Correct Analysis

The correct analysis employs the contribution approach and concentrates on the final overall results. As Exhibit 4-3 shows, only the variable manufacturing costs are affected by the particular order, at a rate of $12 per unit. All other variable costs and all fixed costs are unaffected and may therefore be safely ignored in making this special-order pricing decision. Note how the necessary cost analysis is facilitated by the contribution approach's distinction between variable- and fixed-cost behavior patterns. The total short-run income will increase by $100,000 if the order is accepted—de-

EXHIBIT 4-3

Comparative predicted income statements, contribution approach

SAMSON COMPANY
For the Year Ended December 31, 19X2
(In thousands of dollars)

	WITHOUT SPECIAL ORDER, 1,000,000 UNITS	WITH SPECIAL ORDER, 1,100,000 UNITS	SPECIAL-ORDER DIFFERENCE, 100,000 UNITS Total	Per Unit
Sales	$20,000	$21,300	$1,300	$13
Less variable expenses:				
Manufacturing	$12,000	$13,200	$1,200	$12
Selling and administrative	1,100	1,100	—	—
Total variable expenses	$13,100	$14,300	$1,200	$12
Contribution margin	$ 6,900	$ 7,000	$ 100	$ 1
Less fixed expenses:				
Manufacturing	$ 3,000	$ 3,000	—	—
Selling and administrative	2,900	2,900	—	—
Total fixed expenses	$ 5,900	$ 5,900	—	—
Operating income	$ 1,000	$ 1,100	$ 100	$ 1

spite the fact that the unit selling price of $13 is less than the functional (full) manufacturing cost of $15 computed below:

Total manufacturing costs from Exhibit 4-2	$15,000,000
Divided by units produced	1,000,000
Unit cost of product	$15

Incorrect Analysis

Faulty cost analysis sometimes occurs because of misinterpretation of unit fixed costs. Some managers may erroneously use the $15 full manufacturing cost per unit to make the following prediction for the year (in thousands of dollars):

	WITHOUT SPECIAL ORDER 1,000,000 units	WITH SPECIAL ORDER 1,100,000 units	SPECIAL-ORDER DIFFERENCE 100,000 units
Sales	20,000	21,300	1,300
Less manufacturing cost of goods sold @ $15	15,000	16,500	1,500
Gross margin	5,000	4,800	(200)
Selling and administrative expenses	4,000	4,000	—
Operating income	1,000	800	(200)

The $1.5 million increase in costs is computed by multiplying $15 times 100,000 units. Of course, the fallacy in this approach is the regarding of a fixed cost (fixed manufacturing cost) as though it behaved in a variable manner. Avoid the assumption that unit costs may be used indiscriminately as a basis for predicting how total costs will behave. Instead, follow what was called Robert McNamara's First Law of Analysis when he was U.S. secretary of defense: "Always start by looking at the grand total. Whatever problem you are studying, back off and look at it in the large." In this context, that law means, "Beware of unit costs. When in doubt, convert all costs into totals to get the big picture."

Confusion of Variable and Fixed Costs

To underscore the above law's message, focus on the relationship between total fixed manufacturing costs and a fixed manufacturing cost per unit of product:

fixed cost per unit of product
$$= \frac{\text{total fixed manufacturing costs}}{\text{some selected volume level used as the denominator}}$$

$$= \frac{\$3,000,000}{1,000,000} = \$3$$

The typical cost-accounting system attempts to serve two purposes simultaneously: *planning and control* and *product costing*. The total fixed cost for *budgetary planning and control purposes* can be graphed as a lump sum:

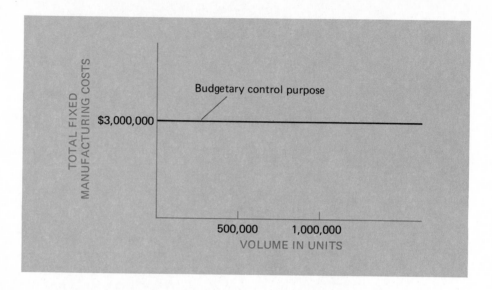

For *product-costing purposes*, however, the functional (full) costing approach implies that these *fixed* costs have a *variable* cost behavior pattern:

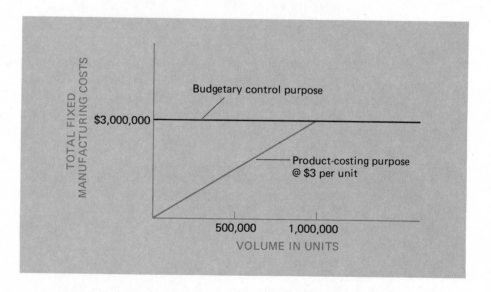

The addition of 100,000 units will *not* add any *total* fixed costs. However, the analytical pitfall is to include 100,000 × $3 = $300,000 in the predictions of increases in total costs.

In short, the increase in manufacturing costs should be computed by multiplying 1,000,000 units by $12, not by $15. The $15 includes a $3 component that will not affect the total manufacturing costs as volume changes.

Spreading Fixed Costs

As we just saw, the unit cost–total cost distinction can become particularly troublesome when analyzing fixed-cost behavior. Assume the same facts concerning the special order as before except that the order was for 250,000 units at a selling price of $11.50. The analytical pitfalls of unit-cost analysis can be avoided by using the contribution approach and concentrating on totals (in thousands of dollars):

	WITHOUT SPECIAL ORDER 1,000,000 units	WITH SPECIAL ORDER 1,250,000 units	SPECIAL-ORDER DIFFERENCE 250,000 units
Sales	20,000	22,875	2,875*
Variable manufacturing costs	12,000	15,000	3,000†
Other variable costs	1,100	1,100	—
Total variable costs	13,100	16,100	3,000
Contribution margin	6,900	6,775	(125)‡

*250,000 × $11.50 selling price of special order.
†250,000 × $12.00 variable manufacturing cost per unit of special order.
‡250,000 × $.50 negative contribution margin per unit of special order.

Short-run income will fall by $125,000 (that is, 250,000 units × $.50) if the special order is accepted. No matter how the fixed manufacturing costs are "unitized" and "spread" over the units produced, their total of $3 million will be *unchanged* by the special order (in thousands of dollars):

	WITHOUT SPECIAL ORDER 1,000,000 units	WITH SPECIAL ORDER 1,250,000 units	SPECIAL-ORDER DIFFERENCE 250,000 units
Contribution margin (as above)	6,900	6,775	(125)
Total fixed costs:			
At an average rate of $3,000,000 ÷ 1,000,000 = $3.00	3,000		—
At an average rate of $3,000,000 ÷ 1,250,000 = $2.40		3,000	—
Contribution to other fixed costs and operating income	3,900	3,775	(125)

No matter how fixed costs are spread for *unit* product-costing purposes, the *total* fixed costs will be unchanged. This is true even though fixed costs *per unit* have fallen from $3.00 to $2.40. The moral is: Beware of unit costs when analyzing fixed costs. Think in terms of totals instead.

❏ Factors That Influence Prices

Many managers say that they use cost-plus pricing—that is, they compute an average unit cost and add a "reasonable" markup that will generate an adequate return on investment. This entails circular reasoning because price, which influences sales volume, is based upon average **full cost** per unit, which in turn is partly determined by the underlying volume of sales. Also, the "plus" in cost-plus is rarely an unalterable markup. Its magnitude depends on the behavior of competitors and customers. Three major factors influence pricing decisions: customers, competitors, and costs.

Customers always have an alternative source of supply, can substitute one material for another, and may make a part rather than buy it if the vendor's prices are too high.

Competitors will usually react to price changes made by their rivals. Tinkering with prices is usually most heavily influenced by the price setter's expectations of competitors' reactions.

The maximum price that may be charged is the one that does not drive the customer away. The minimum price is zero; companies may give out free samples to gain entry into a market. A more practical guide is that, in the short run, the *minimum* price to be quoted, *subject to consideration of long-run effects,* should be the costs that may be avoided by not landing the order—often all variable costs.

❏ Target Pricing

When a company has little influence over price, it usually sells at the market price and tries, by controlling costs, to achieve profitable operations. When a company can set its own prices, its procedures are often a combination of shrewd guessing and mysterious folklore. Often the first step is to accumulate costs and add a markup. This is the target price. Subsequent adjustments may be made "in light of market conditions."

Target prices might be based on a host of different markups based on a host of different definitions of cost. Thus there are many ways to arrive at the *same target price.* They simply reflect different arrangements of the components of the same income statement.

Exhibit 4-4 displays the relationships of costs to target selling prices. The percentages there represent four popular markup formulas for pricing: (1) as a percentage of variable manufacturing costs, (2) as a percentage of total variable costs, (3) as a percentage of all costs, and (4) as a percentage of functional (full) manufacturing costs. Of course, the percentages differ. For instance, the markup on variable manufacturing costs is 66.67% and on functional (full) manufacturing costs is 33.33%. Regardless of the formula used, the pricing decision maker will be led toward the *same* target price. For a volume of 1 million units, assume that the target selling price is $20 per unit. If the decision maker is unable to obtain such a price consistently, the company will not achieve its $1 million operating-income objective or its desired operating-income percentage of sales.

EXHIBIT 4-4 *(Put a clip on this page for easy reference.)*

Relationships of Costs to Target Selling Prices
(In thousands of dollars, except for percentages)

			ALTERNATE MARKUP PERCENTAGES TO ACHIEVE TARGET SALES
	Target sales	$20,000	
	Variable costs:		
(1)	Manufacturing	$12,000*	($20,000 − $12,000) ÷ $12,000 = 66.67%
	Selling and administrative	1,100	
(2)	Total variable costs	$13,100	($20,000 − $13,100) ÷ $13,100 = 52.67%
	Fixed costs		
	Manufacturing	$ 3,000*	
	Selling and administrative	2,900	
	Total fixed costs	$ 5,900	
(3)	Total of all costs	$19,000	($20,000 − $19,000) ÷ $19,000 = 5.26%
	Operating income	$ 1,000	

*A frequently used formula is based on functional (full) *manufacturing* costs:
[$20,000 − ($12,000 + $3,000)] ÷ $15,000 = 33.33%.

☐ Advantages of Contribution Approach

When it is used intelligently, the contribution approach has some advantages over the functional (full) costing approach. Most often, the latter fails to highlight different cost behavior patterns.

First, the contribution approach offers more-detailed information because variable- and fixed-cost behavior patterns are explicitly delineated. Since the contribution approach is sensitive to cost-volume-profit relationships, it is a helpful basis for developing pricing formulas.

Second, a normal or target-pricing formula can be as easily developed by the contribution approach as by full-costing approaches, as was shown in Exhibit 4-4.

Third, the contribution approach offers insight into the short-run versus long-run effects of cutting prices on special orders. For example, assume the same cost behavior patterns as in Exhibit 4-3, page 86. The 100,000-unit order added $100,000 to operating income at a selling price of $13, which was $7 below the target selling price of $20 and $2 below the full manufacturing cost of $15. The implication there, given all the stated assumptions, was in favor of accepting the order. No general answer can be given, but the relevant information was more easily generated by the contribution approach. Recall the possible analyses:

	CONTRIBUTION APPROACH	FUNCTIONAL (FULL) COSTING APPROACH
Sales, 100,000 units @ $13	$1,300,000	$1,300,000
Variable manufacturing costs @ $12	1,200,000	
Full manufacturing costs @ $15		1,500,000
Apparent change in operating income	$ 100,000	$−200,000

Should the offer be accepted? Compare the two approaches. Under the functional approach, the decision maker has no direct knowledge of cost-volume-profit relationships. The decision maker makes the decision by hunch. On the surface the offer is definitely unattractive because the price of $13 is $2 below full manufacturing costs.

Under the contribution approach, the decision maker sees a short-run advantage of $100,000 from accepting the offer. Fixed costs will be unaffected by whatever decision is made and operating income will increase by $100,000. Still, there often are long-run effects to consider. Will acceptance of the offer undermine the long-run price structure? In other words, is the short-run advantage of $100,000 more than offset by high probable long-run financial disadvantages? The decision maker may think so and may reject the offer. But—and this is important—by doing so the decision maker is, in effect, saying that he or she is willing to forgo $100,000 now in order to protect his or her long-run market advantages. Generally, the decision maker can assess problems of this sort by asking whether the probability of long-run benefits is worth an "investment" equal to the forgone contribution margin ($100,000 in this case). Under functional approaches, the decision maker must ordinarily conduct a special study to find the immediate effects. Under the contribution approach, the manager has a system that will routinely and more surely provide such information.

❑ Advantages of Functional (Full) Costing Approach

Our general theme of focusing on relevant costs also extends into the area of pricing. To say that either a contribution approach or a full-cost approach provides the better guide to pricing decisions is a dangerous oversimplification of one of the most perplexing problems in business. Lack of understanding and judgment can lead to unprofitable pricing regardless of the kind of cost data available or cost-accounting system used.

Frequently, managers are reluctant to employ a contribution approach because of fears that variable costs will be substituted indiscriminately for full costs and will therefore lead to suicidal price cutting. This should *not* occur if the data are used wisely. However, if the top managers perceive a pronounced danger of underpricing when variable-cost data are revealed, they may justifiably prefer a full-cost approach for guiding pricing decisions.

Various versions of full-cost pricing are still far more widely used in practice than the contribution approach. Why? In addition to the reasons already mentioned, the following have been offered:

1. Simplicity. Full-cost formula pricing meets the cost-benefit test. It is too costly to conduct individual cost-volume tests for the many (sometimes thousands) products that a company offers.

2. There is much uncertainty about the shape of the demand curves and the correct price-output decisions. Full-cost pricing copes with this uncertainty by not encouraging managers to take too many risks.

3. Full-cost pricing tends to promote price stability. Managers prefer price stability because it eases their professional lives, primarily because planning is more dependable.

4. Full-cost pricing provides the most defensible basis for justifying prices to all interested parties, including government antitrust investigators.

In brief, full-cost pricing provides convenient reference points to simplify hundreds or thousands of pricing decisions. A complete discussion of pricing is beyond the scope of this book.[2] However, a contribution approach should clarify the major classes of information that bear on the pricing decision.

DELETION OR ADDITION OF PRODUCTS OR DEPARTMENTS

Consider a discount department store that has three major departments: groceries, general merchandise, and drugs. Management is considering dropping groceries, which have consistently shown a net loss. The present annual net income is reported in the following table (in thousands of dollars):

| | | DEPARTMENTS | | |
	Total	Groceries	General Merchandise	Drugs
Sales	$1,900	$1,000	$800	$100
Variable cost of goods sold and expenses	1,420	800	560	60
Contribution margin	$ 480 (25%)	$ 200 (20%)	$240 (30%)	$ 40 (40%)
Fixed expenses (salaries, depreciation, insurance, property taxes, etc.):				
Avoidable	$ 265	$ 150	$100	$ 15
Unavoidable	180	60	100	20
Total fixed expenses	$ 445	$ 210	$200	$ 35
Operating income	$ 35	$ (10)	$ 40	$ 5

Sometimes the terms *avoidable* and *unavoidable* costs are used in conjunction with special decison making. **Avoidable costs** are those costs that will not continue if an ongoing operation is changed or deleted; in contrast, **unavoidable costs** are those costs that will continue. Avoidable costs include department salaries and other costs that could be avoided by not operating the specific department. Unavoidable costs include many **common costs,** which are defined as those costs of facilities and services that are shared by user departments. Examples are store depreciation, heating, air conditioning, and general management expenses.

Assume first that the only alternatives to be considered are to drop or continue the grocery department. Assume further that the total assets invested would not be affected by the decision. The vacated space would be

[2] For example, many laws prohibit price discrimination—that is, quoting different selling prices for identical goods or services. Obviously there are also many other complications, which are explored in books on economics and marketing.

idle, and the unavoidable costs would not be changed. Which alternative would you recommend? An analysis follows (in thousands of dollars):

| INCOME STATEMENTS | STORE AS A WHOLE | | |
	a Keep Groceries	b Drop Groceries	a − b Difference
Sales	$1,900	$900	$1,000
Variable expenses	1,420	620	800
Contribution margin	$ 480	$280	$ 200
Avoidable fixed expenses	265	115	150

Profit contribution to
  common space and other
  unavoidable costs
	$ 215	$165	$ 50

Common space and other unavoidable costs	180	180	—
Operating income	$ 35	$ (15)	$ 50

The preceding analysis shows that matters would be worse, rather than better, if groceries were dropped and the vacated facilities left idle. In short, as the income statement shows, groceries bring in a contribution margin of $200,000, which is $50,000 more than the $150,000 fixed expenses that would be saved by closing the grocery department.

Assume now that the space made available by the dropping of groceries would be used by an expanded general merchandise department. The space would be occupied by merchandise that would increase sales by $500,000, generate a 30% contribution-margin percentage, and have avoidable fixed costs of $70,000. The picture would then be improved by an increase in operating income of $65,000 − $35,000 = $30,000:

| | TOTAL | GENERAL
MERCHANDISE | DRUGS |
	(In Thousands of Dollars)		
Sales	$1,400	$800 + $500	$100
Variable expenses	970	560 + 350	60
Contribution margin	$ 430	$240 + $150	$ 40
Avoidable fixed expenses	185	100 + 70	15
Contribution to common space and other unavoidable costs	$ 245	$140 + $ 80	$ 25
Common space and other unavoidable costs*	180		
Operating income	$ 65		

*Includes former grocery fixed costs, which were allocations of common costs that will continue regardless of how the space is occupied.

As the following summary analysis demonstrates, the objective is to obtain, from a given amount of space or capacity, the maximum contribution to the payment of those costs that remain unaffected by the nature of the product sold (in thousands of dollars):

	PROFIT CONTRIBUTION OF GIVEN SPACE		
	Groceries	Expansion of General Merchandise	Difference
Sales	$1,000	$500	$500 U
Variable expenses	800	350	450 F
Contribution margin	$ 200	$150	$ 50 U
Avoidable fixed expense	150	70	80 F
Contribution to common space and other unavoidable costs	$ 50	$ 80	$ 30 F

F = Favorable difference resulting from replacing groceries with general merchandise.
U = Unfavorable difference.

In this case, the general merchandise will not achieve the dollar sales volume that groceries will, but the higher markups and the lower wage costs (mostly because of the diminished need for stocking and checkout clerks) will bring more favorable net results.

An extremely large U.S. grocery chain, A&P, ran into profit difficulties during the 1970s. It began retrenching by closing many stores. Management's lack of adequate information about individual store operations made the closing program a hit-or-miss affair. *Fortune* (November 6, 1978) reported:

☐ . . . Because of the absence of detailed profit-and-loss statements, and a cost-allocation system that did not reflect true costs, A&P's strategists could not be sure whether an individual store was really unprofitable. For example, distribution costs were shared equally among all the stores in a marketing area without regard to such factors as a store's distance from the warehouse. Says one close observer of the company: "When they wanted to close a store, they had to wing it. They could not make rational decisions, because they did not have a fact basis."

CONTRIBUTION TO PROFIT PER UNIT OF LIMITING FACTOR

When a multiple-product plant is being operated at capacity, decisions as to which orders to accept must often be made. The contribution approach is also applicable here, because the product to be pushed or the order to be accepted is the one that makes the biggest *total* profit contribution per unit of the **limiting factor.**

The contribution approach must be used wisely, however. Sometimes a major pitfall is the erroneous tendency to favor those products with the biggest contribution-margin ratios per sales dollar.

Assume that a company has two products:

PER UNIT	PRODUCT A	PRODUCT B
Selling price	$20	$30
Variable costs	16	21
Contribution margin	$ 4	$ 9
Contribution-margin ratio	20%	30%

Which product is more profitable? Product B apparently is more profitable than A: However, one important fact has been purposely withheld—the time that it takes to produce each product. If 10,000 hours of capacity are available, and three units of A can be produced per hour in contrast to one unit of B, your choice would be A because it contributes the most profit per hour, the *limiting, critical,* or *scarce factor* in this example:

	A	B
1. Units per hour	3	1
2. Contribution margin per unit	$4	$9
Contribution margin per hour (1) × (2)	$12	$9
Total contribution for 10,000 hours	$120,000	$90,000

The limiting, critical, or scarce factor is the item that restricts or constrains the production or sale of a given product. Thus the criterion for maximizing profits, for a given capacity, is to obtain the greatest possible contribution to profit per unit of the limiting or critical factor. The limiting factor in the above example may be machine-hours or labor-hours. In the discount store example it was square feet of floor space. It may be cubic feet of display space. In such cases, a ratio such as the conventional gross-profit percentage (gross profit ÷ selling price) is an insufficient clue to profitability because profits also depend on the stock turnover (number of times the average inventory is sold per year).

EXHIBIT
4-5

	REGULAR DEPARTMENT STORE	DISCOUNT DEPARTMENT STORE
Retail price	$4.00	$3.50
Cost of merchandise	3.00	3.00
Contribution to profit per unit	$1.00 (25%)	$ .50 (14+%)
Units sold per year	10,000	22,000
Total contribution to profit, assuming the same space allotment in both stores	$10,000	$11,000

The success of the suburban discount department stores illustrates the concept of the contribution to profit per unit of limiting factor. These stores have been satisfied with subnormal markups because they have been able to increase turnover and thus increase the contribution to profit per unit of space, as Exhibit 4-5 illustrates, using hypothetical numbers.

Summary

The accountant's role in problem solving is primarily that of a technical expert on cost analysis. The accountant's responsibility is to be certain that the manager uses **relevant data** in guiding his or her decisions. Accountants and managers must have a penetrating understanding of relevant costs.

To be relevant to a particular decision, a cost must meet two criteria: (1) it must be an expected **future** cost; and (2) it must be an element of **difference** among the alternatives. All **past (historical or sunk)** costs are in themselves irrelevant to any **decision** about the future, although they often provide the best available basis for the **prediction** of expected future data.

The combination of the relevant-costing and contribution approaches is a fundamental framework, based on economic analysis, that may be applied to a vast range of problems.

Summary
Problems For Your Review

❏ Problem One

1. Return to the basic illustration in Exhibit 4-3, page 86. Suppose a special order like that described in conjunction with Exhibit 4-3 had the following terms: selling price would be $13.50 instead of $13.00, but a manufacturer's agent who had acquired the potential order would have to be paid a flat fee of $40,000 if the order was accepted. What would be the new operating income if the order was accepted?

2. Assume the same facts concerning the special order as before, except that the order was for 250,000 units at a selling price of $11.50. Some managers have been known to argue for acceptance of such an order as follows: Of course, we will lose 50¢ each on the variable manufacturing costs, but we will gain 60¢ per unit by spreading our fixed manufacturing costs over 1.25 million units instead of 1 million units. Consequently, we should take the offer because it represents an advantage of 10¢ per unit:

Old fixed manufacturing cost per unit, $3,000,000 ÷ 1,000,000	$3.00
New fixed manufacturing cost per unit, $3,000,000 ÷ 1,250,000	2.40
"Saving" in fixed manufacturing costs per unit	$ .60
Loss on variable manufacturing costs per unit, $11.50 − $12.00	.50
Net saving per unit in manufacturing costs	$ .10

Explain why this is faulty thinking.

Relevant Costs
and Special
Decisions—
Part One

97

☐ Problem Two

Consider the following news story:

☐ SALT LAKE CITY (UPI)—Mayor Ted Wilson says Sen. William Proxmire, D-Wis., had better stop taking his daily $12 federally funded showers before he criticizes Salt Lake City's $145,000 wave-making machine.

☐ Wilson awarded Proxmire a "Golden Hypocrisy" award Tuesday in exchange for the "Golden Fleece" award the senator gave the U.S. Interior Department for spending taxpayers' money to make waves in a Salt Lake swimming pool so that desert dwellers could have an aquatic experience known only to coastal swimmers.

☐ Proxmire gives out a Golden Fleece award monthly to people, projects, and organizations he believes are ripping off the taxpayers through wasteful spending.

☐ But Wilson predicted that 180,000 people—the city's entire population—would use the pool annually. He also criticized Proxmire for taking advantage of luxuries provided for senators.

☐ The mayor said it cost taxpayers $12.35 a day for Proxmire to shower in the Senate gymnasium after he jogs to work.

☐ "If he showers every day the Senate is in session, it costs the taxpayer $2,470 a year for a publicly paid shower," said Wilson.

☐ "I am giving him my Golden Hypocrisy Award in recognition of the senator's ability to find fault in others and myopically overlook his own waste."

☐ Wilson, who was a congressional aide before his election as mayor, said he calculated the cost of a Senate shower through his own observations. He said only about 15 of the 100 senators use the gym, which costs about $200,000 a year to operate.

☐ "This means Sen. Proxmire costs the taxpayers $12.35 every time he takes a shower."

☐ Proxmire attacked the wave-making machine as the "biggest, most ridiculous" example of wasteful government spending during November.

☐ He said if the government follows the rationale used to justify the wave-making machine, "hard-pressed taxpayers will next be asked to fund ski slopes in Florida, mountain scenery in Indiana, igloos in Death Valley and tropical rain forests in Wisconsin."

REQUIRED:

1. Compute the total cost and the unit cost per swim per year for making waves. Assume that the equivalent of (a) 180,000 and (b) 90,000 swimmers use the pool once during the year. Also assume that the machine will last five years and will have annual fixed operating costs of $11,000 for power and maintenance.

2. Analyze Mayor Wilson's response to Senator Proxmire. Using the mayor's data, compute the number of days the Senate is usually in session per year.

3. Compute the total cost and the unit cost per visit to the gymnasium if (a) 15, (b) 30, and (c) 90 of the senators use the gym and shower each day the Senate is in session.

4. (a) How does your computation of unit cost in Requirement 3a compare with the $12.35 calculated by Wilson? (b) Give a possible explanation for the difference between Wilson's and your computations.

☐ Solution to Problem One

1. The easiest way to solve this part is to work from the $100,000 increase in income already shown in the final column of Exhibit 4-3:

Operating income based on $13 price	$100,000
Increase in selling price per unit is $13.50 minus $13, or $.50. Increase in revenue, $.50 × 100,000 units	50,000
Increase in fixed expenses, special fee	(40,000)
New operating income	$110,000

2. Regardless of how the fixed manufacturing costs are "unitized" or "spread" over the units produced, their *total* of $3 million will be *unchanged* by the special order. As the tabulation on page 97 indicates, short-run income will fall by 250,000 units × ($12.00 − $11.50) = $125,000 if the special order is accepted.

❑ Solution to Problem Two

This problem is worthwhile because it (a) underscores the roles of total costs and unit costs in evaluating frequently encountered discussions and (b) is amusing.

1. Annual costs in total:

Depreciation, $145,000 ÷ 5	$29,000
Fixed operating costs	11,000
Total	$40,000

a. Unit costs, $40,000 ÷ 180,000 = $.2222

b. Unit costs, $40,000 ÷ 90,000 = $.4444

2. Number of days in session = $2,470 ÷ $12.35 = 200. The total cost is probably entirely fixed except for soap, water, towels, and slight fluctuations in energy bills because of variations in hot-water usage. Wilson's analysis seems unjustified. He implies that each visit by Proxmire increases the *total* expenses of operating the gym by $12.35. In fact, each visit has virtually no effect on *total* expenses.

Students should also ponder how Wilson might have accused Proxmire of incurring a higher unit cost per shower if the senator took only one or ten showers per year instead of two hundred. When a fixed cost is divided by some unit measure of activity, the lower the activity, the higher the unit cost. See the next part for examples.

3. a.

Total operating costs per year	$200,000
Visits per year, 15 senators × 200 days	3,000
Unit cost per visit and shower	$66.67

b. If 30 senators visit, the unit cost would drop to $200,000 ÷ (30 × 200) = $200,000 ÷ 6,000 = $33.33.

c. If 90 senators visit: $200,000 ÷ (90 × 200) = $11.11.

4. a. The $66.67 is obviously much higher than the $12.35 quoted by Wilson.

b. Two possible explanations are:

Wilson erred in his computations. Wilson's criticisms of Proxmire would have been even more dramatic if they had been based on the analysis in 3a.

Another possible explanation is that Wilson conducted a sophisticated analysis and somehow decided that $12.35 represented the true variable portion of the operating costs.

Highlights to Remember

The following are among the more important generalizations regarding various decisions:

1. Wherever feasible, think in terms of total costs rather than unit costs. Too often, unit costs are regarded as an adequate basis for predicting changes in total costs. This assumption is satisfactory when analyzing variable costs, but it is frequently misleading when analyzing fixed costs.

2. A common error is to regard all unit costs indiscriminately, as if all costs were variable costs. Changes in volume will affect *total* variable costs but not *total* fixed costs. The

danger then is to predict total costs assuming that all unit costs are variable. The correct relationships are:

| | BEHAVIOR AS VOLUME FLUCTUATES | |
	Variable Cost	Fixed Cost
Cost per unit	No change	Change
Total cost	Change	No change

3. The contribution approach to pricing special sales orders offers helpful information because the forgone contribution can be quantified as the investment currently being made to protect long-run benefits.

4. The key to obtaining the maximum profit from a given capacity is to obtain the greatest possible contribution to profit per unit of the limiting or scarce factor.

Accounting Vocabulary

Avoidable cost: common cost; decision model; full cost; limiting factor; relevant information; unavoidable cost.

Fundamental Assignment Material

4–1. **Special order.** Consider the following details of the income statement of the Monarch Pen Company for the year ended December 31, 19X3:

Sales	$10,000,000
Less manufacturing cost of goods sold	6,000,000
Gross margin or gross profit	$ 4,000,000
Less selling and administrative expenses	3,100,000
Operating income	$ 900,000

Monarch's fixed manufacturing costs were $2.4 million and its fixed selling and administrative costs were $2.3 million. Sales commissions of 3% of sales are included in selling and administrative expenses.

The company had sold 2 million pens. Near the end of the year, McDonald's Corporation, the well-known purveyor of hamburgers, had offered to buy 150,000 pens on a special order. To fill the order, a special clip bearing the McDonald's emblem would have had to be made for each pen. McDonald's intended to use the pens in special promotions during early 19X4.

Even though Monarch had some idle plant capacity, the president rejected the McDonald's offer of $660,000 for the 150,000 pens. He said:

☐ The McDonald's offer is too low. We'd avoid paying sales commissions, but we'd have to incur an extra cost of 20¢ per clip for the emblem and its assembly with the pens. If Monarch sells below its regular selling prices, it will begin a chain reaction of competitors' price cutting and of customers wanting special deals. I believe in pricing at no lower than 8% above our full costs of $9,100,000 ÷ 2,000,000 units = $4.55 per unit plus the extra 20¢ per clip less the savings in commissions.

REQUIRED:

1. Using the contribution approach, prepare an analysis similar to that in Exhibit 4-3. Use four columns: without the special order, with the special order, and the special-order difference shown in total and per unit. Exhibit 4-3 is on page 86.
2. By what percentage would operating income increase or decrease if the order had been accepted? Do you agree with the president's decision? Why?

4-2. **Analysis of unit costs.** The Porterfield Company manufactures small appliances, such as electric can openers, toasters, food mixers, and irons. The peak season is at hand, and the president is trying to decide whether to produce more of the company's standard line of can openers or its premium line that includes a built-in knife sharpener, a better finish, and a higher-quality motor. The unit data follow:

	PRODUCT	
	Standard	Premium
Selling price	$25	$31
Direct material	$ 7	$ 9
Direct labor	2	1
Variable factory overhead	2	3
Fixed factory overhead	6	9
Total cost of goods sold	$17	$22
Gross profit per unit	$ 8	$ 9

The sales outlook is very encouraging. The plant could operate at full capacity by producing either product or both products. Both the standard and the premium products are processed through the same departments. Selling and administrative costs will not be affected by this decision, so they may be ignored.

Many of the parts are produced on automatic machinery. The factory overhead is allocated to products by developing separate rates per machine-hour for variable and fixed overhead. For example, the total fixed overhead is divided by the total machine-hours to get a rate per hour. Thus the amount of overhead allocated to products is dependent on the number of machine-hours allocated to the product. It takes one hour of machine time to produce one unit of the standard product.

Direct labor may not be proportionate with overhead because many workers operate two or more machines simultaneously.

REQUIRED:

Which product should be produced? If more than one should be produced, indicate the proportions of each. Show computations. Explain your answer briefly.

Additional Assignment Material

4-3. "A ratio such as the conventional gross-profit percentage is an insufficient clue to profitability." Do you agree? Explain.

4-4. What three major factors influence pricing decisions?

4-5. Why are customers one of the three factors influencing prices?

4–6. "I don't believe in assigning only variable costs to a job for guiding pricing. This results in suicidal underpricing." Do you agree? Why?

4–7. "The distinction between precision and relevancy should be kept in mind." Explain.

4–8. Distinguish between the quantitative and qualitative aspects of decisions.

4–9. "Any future cost is relevant." Do you agree? Explain.

4–10. Why are historical or past data irrelevant to special decisions?

4–11. Give four examples of limiting or scarce factors.

4–12. **Review of key exhibit.** Exhibit 4-1, page 84, is important because it displays the key steps in management activities and the related role of information. Note how historical information is an input to the prediction method, but historical information is not an input to the decision model. Review the exhibit to be sure you understand these relationships.

4–13. **Pinpointing relevant costs.** You are planning to see a motion picture and you can attend either of two theaters. You have only a small budget for entertainment, so prices are important. You have attended both theaters recently. One charged $4 for admission; the other charged $5. You habitually buy popcorn in the theater—each theater charged $1. The motion pictures now being shown are equally attractive to you, but you are virtually certain that you will never see the picture forgone now.

REQUIRED: | Identify the relevant costs. Explain your answer.

4–14. **Information and decisions.** Suppose a company's historical costs for the manufacture of a calculator were as follows: direct materials, $2.20 per unit; direct labor, $3.00 per unit. Management is trying to decide whether to replace some materials with different materials. The replacement should cut material costs by 10% per unit. However, direct-labor time will increase by 5% per unit. Moreover, direct-labor rates will be affected by a recent 10% wage increase.

Prepare an exhibit like Exhibit 4-1, showing where and how the data about direct material and direct labor fit in the decision process.

4–15. **Unit costs and total costs.** You are a college professor who belongs to a faculty club. Annual dues are $120. You use the club solely for lunches, which cost $3 each. You have not used the club much in recent years and are wondering whether to continue your membership.

REQUIRED:

1. You are confronted with a variable-cost plus a fixed-cost behavior pattern. Plot each on a graph, where the vertical axis is total cost and the horizontal axis is volume in number of lunches. Also plot a third graph that combines the previous two graphs.
2. What is the cost per lunch if you pay for your own lunch once a year? Twelve times a year? Two hundred times a year?
3. Suppose the average price of lunches elsewhere is $4. (a) How many lunches must you have at the faculty club so that the total costs of the lunches would be the same regardless of where you ate for that number of lunches? (b) Suppose you ate 250 lunches a year at the faculty club. How much would you save in relation to the total costs of eating elsewhere?

4–16. **A&P's closing of stores.** Page 95 refers to the A&P's closing of stores.

1. The company's labor costs as a percentage of sales increased in some markets, such as the Long Island and Pittsburgh divisions, even after allowing for normal increases in wage rates. How could this effect occur?

2. The company manufactured many of its own products. In the mid-1970s the company operated forty-six plants. Twenty-one were bakeries. The others manufactured a variety of goods, from frozen potatoes to mouthwash. What impact would the store closings probably have on the manufacturing plants and on the total operating income?

4–17. **Profit per unit of space.**

1. Several successful chains of discount department stores have merchandising policies that differ considerably from those of the traditional downtown department stores. Name some characteristics of these discount stores that have contributed to their success.
2. Food chains have typically regarded, perhaps, 20% of selling price as an average target gross profit on canned goods and similar grocery items. What are the limitations of such an approach? Be specific.

4–18. **Accepting a low bid.**   The Vittetaw Company, a maker of a variety of metal and plastic products, is in the midst of a business downturn and is saddled with many idle facilities. The National Hospital Supply Company has approached Vittetaw to produce 300,000 nonslide serving trays. National will pay $1.20 each.

Vittetaw predicts that its variable costs will be $1.30 each. However, its fixed costs, which had been averaging $1 per unit on a variety of other products, will now be spread over twice as much volume. The president commented, "Sure we'll lose 10¢ each on the variable costs, but we'll gain 50¢ per unit by spreading our fixed costs. Therefore, we should take the offer, because it represents an advantage of 40¢ per unit."

REQUIRED: Do you agree with the president? Why? Suppose the regular business had a current volume of 300,000 units, sales of $600,000, variable costs of $390,000, and fixed costs of $300,000.

4–19. **Variable costs and prices.**   A supplier to an automobile manufacturer has the following conversation with the manufacturer's purchasing manager:

☐ SUPPLIER: You did not predict the heavy demands. To keep up with your unforeseen demands over the coming quarter, we will have to work six days per week instead of five. Therefore, I want a price increase in the amount of the overtime premium that I must pay.

☐ MANUFACTURER: You have already recouped your fixed costs, so you are enjoying a hefty contribution margin on the sixth day. So quit complaining!

REQUIRED: | Should the supplier get an increase in price? Explain.

4–20. **Target selling prices.**   Consider the following data from a budgeted income statement (in thousands of dollars):

Target sales	$30,000
Variable costs:	
Manufacturing	15,000
Selling and administrative	3,000
Total variable costs	18,000
Fixed costs:	
Manufacturing	5,000
Selling and administrative	2,000
Total fixed costs	7,000
Total of all costs	25,000
Operating income	$ 5,000

Compute the following markup formulas that would be used for obtaining the same target selling prices as a percentage of (1) total variable costs, (2) all costs, (3) variable manufacturing costs, and (4) functional (full) manufacturing costs.

4–21. Cost analysis and pricing. The budget for the Bright Printing Company for 19X2 follows:

Sales		$1,000,000
Direct material	$180,000	
Direct labor	320,000	
Overhead	400,000	900,000
Net income		$ 100,000

The company typically uses a so-called cost-plus pricing system. Direct material and direct labor are computed, overhead is added at a rate of 125% of direct labor, and one-ninth of the total cost is added to obtain the selling price.

Mr. Bright has placed a $10,000 bid on a particularly large order with a cost of $1,800 direct material and $3,200 direct labor. The customer informs him that he can have the business for $8,900, take it or leave it. If Mr. Bright accepts the order, total sales for 19X2 will be $1,008,900.

Mr. Bright refuses the order, saying: "I sell on a cost-plus basis. It is bad policy to accept orders at below cost. I would lose $100 on the job."

The company's annual fixed overhead is $160,000.

REQUIRED:

1. What would net income have been with the order? Without the order? Show your computations.
2. Give a short description of a contribution approach to pricing that Bright might follow. Include a stipulation of the pricing formula that Bright should routinely use if he hopes to obtain a target net income of $100,000.

4–22. Formulas for pricing. Adrian Corporation, a building contractor, constructs houses in tracts, often building as many as twenty homes simultaneously. The president of the corporation, Ms. Adrian, has budgeted costs for an expected number of houses in 19X7 as follows:

Direct materials	$2,000,000
Direct labor	1,000,000
Job construction overhead	1,000,000
Cost of jobs	$4,000,000
Selling and administrative costs	1,000,000
Total costs	$5,000,000

The job construction overhead includes approximately $400,000 of fixed costs, such as the salaries of supervisors and depreciation on equipment. The selling and administrative costs include $200,000 of variable costs, such as sales commissions and bonuses that depend fundamentally on overall profitability.

Ms. Adrian wants an operating income of $1 million for 19X7.

REQUIRED:

Compute the average target profit percentage for setting prices as a percentage of

1. Prime costs (direct materials plus direct labor)
2. The full "cost of jobs"
3. The variable "cost of jobs"

4. The full "cost of jobs" plus selling and administrative costs
5. The variable "cost of jobs" plus variable selling and administrative costs

4–23. **Pricing a special order.** The Metroproducts Corporation has an annual plant capacity of 2,400 product units. Its predicted operations for the year are:

Production and sales of 2,000 units, total sales	$90,000
Manufacturing costs:	
Fixed (total)	$30,000
Variable (per unit)	$13
Selling and administrative expenses:	
Fixed (total)	$15,000
Variable (per unit)	$4

REQUIRED:

Compute, ignoring income taxes:

1. If the company accepts a special order for 200 units at a selling price of $19 each, how would the *total* predicted net income for the year be affected, assuming no effect on regular sales at regular prices?
2. Without decreasing its total net income, what is the lowest *unit price* for which the Metroproducts Corporation could sell an additional 100 units not subject to any variable selling and administrative expenses, assuming no effect on regular sales at regular prices?
3. In solving Requirement 2 above, list the numbers given in the problem that are irrelevant (not relevant).
4. Compute the expected annual net income (with no special orders) if plant capacity can be doubled by adding additional facilities at a cost of $250,000. Assume that these facilities have an estimated life of five years with no residual scrap value, and that the current unit selling price can be maintained for all sales. Total sales are expected to equal the new plant capacity each year. No changes are expected in variable costs per unit or in total fixed costs except for depreciation.

4–24. **Pricing and contribution approach.** The Big Western Transportation Company has the following operating results to date for 19X3:

Operating revenues	$50,000,000
Operating costs	40,000,000
Operating income	$10,000,000

A large Los Angeles manufacturer has inquired about whether Western would be interested in trucking a large order of its parts to San Francisco. Steve Minkler, operations manager, investigated the situation and estimated that the "fully distributed" costs of servicing the order would be $40,000. Using his general pricing formula, he quoted a price of $50,000. The manufacturer replied: "We'll give you $35,000, take it or leave it. If you do not want our business, we'll truck it ourselves or go elsewhere."

A cost analyst had recently been conducting studies of how Big Western's operating costs tended to behave. She found that $32 million of the $40 million could be characterized as variable costs. Minkler discussed the matter with her and decided that this order would probably generate cost behavior little different from Big Western's general operations.

REQUIRED:

1. Using a contribution format, prepare an analysis for Minkler.
2. Should Big Western accept the order? Explain.

4–25. Pricing by auto dealers. Many automobile dealers have an operating pattern similar to that of Lance Motors, a dealer in Ohio. Each month, Lance initially aims at a unit volume quota that approximates a break-even point. Until the break-even point is reached, Lance has a policy of relatively lofty pricing, whereby the "minimum deal" must contain a sufficiently high markup to ensure a contribution to profit of no less than $250. After the break-even point is attained, Lance tends to quote lower prices for the remainder of the month.

REQUIRED: What is your opinion of this policy? As a prospective customer, how would you react to this policy?

4–26. Pricing of education. You are the director of continuing education programs for a well-known university. Courses for executives are especially popular, and you have developed an extensive menu of one-day and two-day courses that are presented in various locations throughout the nation. The performance of these courses for the current fiscal year, which is almost ended, is:

Tuition revenue	$2,000,000
Costs of courses	800,000
Contribution margin	1,200,000
General administrative expenses	300,000
Operating income	$ 900,000

The costs of the courses include fees for instructors, rentals of classrooms, advertising, and any other items, such as travel, that can be easily and exclusively identified as being caused by a particular course.

The general administrative expenses include your salary, your secretary's compensation, and related expenses, such as a lump-sum payment to the university's central offices as a share of university overhead.

The enrollment for your final course of the year is forty students, who have paid $150 each. Two days before the course is to begin, a city manager phones your office. "Do you offer discounts to nonprofit institutions?" he asks. "If so, we'll send ten managers. But our budget will not justify our spending more than $75 per person." The extra cost of including these ten managers would entail lunches at $10 each and course materials at $20 each.

REQUIRED:
1. Prepare a tabulation of the performance for the full year, including the final course. Assume that the costs of the final course for the forty enrollees' instruction, travel, advertising, rental of hotel classroom, lunches, and course materials would be $2,500. Show a tabulation in four columns: before final course, final course with forty registrants, effect of ten more registrants, and grand totals.
2. What major considerations would probably influence the pricing policies for these courses? For setting regular university tuition in private universities?

4–27. Demand analysis. (SMA, adapted.) The Aurora Manufacturing Limited produces and sells one product. During 19X4 the company manufactured and sold 50,000 units at $25 each. Existing production capacity is 60,000 units per year.

In formulating the 19X5 budget, management is faced with a number of decisions concerning product pricing and output. The following information is available:

1. A market survey shows that the sales volume is very much dependent on the selling price. For each $1 drop in selling price, sales volume would increase by 10,000 units.
2. The company's expected cost structure for 19X5 is as follows:
   a. Fixed cost (regardless of production or sales activities), $360,000

b. Variable costs per unit (including production, selling, and administrative expenses), $16

3. To increase annual capacity from the present 60,000 to 90,000 units, additional investment for plant, building, equipment, etc., of $200,000 would be necessary. The estimated average life of the additional investment would be ten years, so the fixed costs would increase by an average of $20,000 per year. (Expansion of less than 30,000 additional units of capacity would cost only slightly less than $200,000.)

REQUIRED:

Indicate, with reasons, what the level of production and the selling price should be for the coming year. Also indicate whether the company should approve the plant expansion. Show your calculations. Ignore income tax considerations and the time value of money.

4–28. **Pricing strategy.** The Germane Company has the following cost behavior pattern for the unique ashtrays that it manufactures and sells:

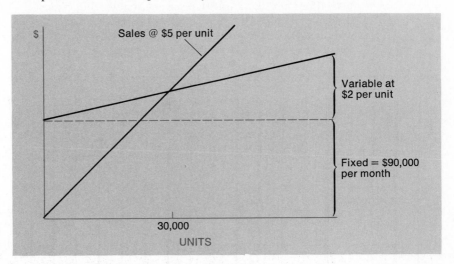

REQUIRED:

1. What is the break-even point in units?
2. If sales were at 40,000 units, would you then be inclined to cut the selling price? Why?
3. If sales were at 20,000 units, would you then be inclined to cut the selling price? Why?

4–29. **Avoiding confusion of variable and fixed costs.** A manufacturer had a fixed factory overhead budget for 19X2 of $10 million. The company planned to make and sell 2 million units of the product, a communications device. All variable manufacturing costs per unit were $11. The budgeted income statement contained the following:

Sales	$40,000,000
Manufacturing cost of goods sold	32,000,000
Gross margin	8,000,000
Deduct selling and administrative expenses	6,000,000
Operating income	$ 2,000,000

For simplicity, assume that the actual variable costs per unit and the total fixed costs were exactly as budgeted.

1. Compute the budgeted fixed factory overhead per unit.
2. Near the end of 19X2 a large computer manufacturer offered to buy 100,000 units for $1.2 million on a one-time special order. The president of the manufacturing firm stated: "The offer is a bad deal. It's foolish to sell below full manufacturing costs per unit. I realize that this order will have only a modest effect on selling and administrative costs. They will increase by a $5,000 fee paid to our sales agent."

   Compute the effect on operating income if the offer is accepted.
3. What factors should the president consider before finally deciding whether to accept the offer?
4. Suppose the original budget for fixed manufacturing costs was $10 million, but budgeted units of product were 1 million. How would your answers to Requirements 1 and 2 change? Be specific.

4–30. Dropping a product line. A local Woolworth's store sells many products. It has a restaurant with a counter that extends almost the length of the store. Management is considering dropping the restaurant, which has consistently shown an operating loss. The predicted income statements, in thousands of dollars, follow (for ease of analysis, only three product lines are shown):

	TOTAL	GENERAL MERCHANDISE	GARDEN PRODUCTS	RESTAURANT
Sales	5,000	4,000	400	600
Variable expenses	3,390	2,800	200	390
Contribution margin	1,610 (32%)	1,200 (30%)	200 (50%)	210 (35%)
Fixed expenses (compensation, depreciation, property taxes, insurance, etc.)	1,110	750	50	310
Operating income	500	450	150	(100)

The $310,000 of fixed expenses include the compensation of restaurant employees of $100,000. These employees will be released if the restaurant is abandoned. All counters and equipment are fully depreciated, so none of the $310,000 pertains to such items. Furthermore, their disposal values will be exactly offset by the costs of removal and remodeling.

If the restaurant is dropped, the manager will use the vacated space for either (a) more general merchandise, or (b) more garden products. The expansion of general merchandise would not entail hiring any additional salaried help, but more garden products would require an additional person at an annual cost of $25,000. The manager thinks that sales of general merchandise would increase by $300,000; garden products, by $200,000. The manager's modest predictions are partially based on the fact that she thinks the restaurant has helped lure customers to the store and thus improved overall sales. If the restaurant is closed, that lure would be gone.

Should the restaurant be closed? Explain, showing computations.

4–31. Utilization of passenger jets. In 19X2 Continental Air Lines, Inc., filled 50% of the available seats on its Boeing 707 jet flights, a record about 15% below the national average.

Continental could have eliminated about 4% of it runs and raised its average load considerably. But the improved load factor would have reduced profits. Give reasons for or against this elimination. What factors should influence an airline's scheduling policies?

When you answer this question, suppose that Continental had a basic package of 3,000 flights per month that had an average of 100 seats available per flight. Also suppose that 52% of the seats were filled at an average ticket price of $50 per flight. Variable costs are about 70% of revenue.

Continental also had a marginal package of 120 flights per month that had an average of 100 seats available per flight. Suppose that only 20% of the seats were filled at an average ticket price of $40 per flight. Variable costs are about 50% of this revenue. Prepare a tabulation of the basic package, marginal package, and total package, showing percentage of seats filled, revenue, variable expenses, and contribution margin.

4–32. **Airline costs.** An executive of Trans World Airlines (TWA) stated:

☐ Under the Civil Aeronautics Board load factor standard, any shortfall below 55 percent is treated as presumptive managerial guilt of overscheduling. Thus, if the industry expects 116 billion *passenger miles* of traffic [a *passenger mile* is one person moved one mile], all we have to do is limit *seat miles* to 211 billion [a *seat mile* is one seat moved one mile]. . . . For us the smallest meaningful unit in capacity planning is not the seat mile, but the schedule. And each schedule generates a large, inflexible, indivisible batch of seat miles. . . . We cannot slice 5 percent off the airplane.

TWA analyzed its New York–Phoenix schedule for the year ended October 1977. This round trip produced revenues of $4.9 million. Fully allocated costs were $5.2 million, consisting of (a) $3.5 million "out-of-pocket costs" specifically created by this schedule (examples are fuel, crew pay, landing fees, and passenger-handling costs), and (b) $1.7 million of allocated fixed costs (examples are the rental of the terminal at Kennedy Airport, the depreciation on the central overhaul base in Kansas City).

REQUIRED: I   Should TWA give up its New York–Phoenix round-trip schedule? Explain.

4–33. **Nonprofit fund-raising.** (CMA, adapted.) Janice Watson recently was appointed executive director of a charitable foundation. The foundation raises the money for its activities in a variety of ways, but the most important source of funds is an annual mail campaign.

The annual mail campaign and accompanying public relations efforts are designed to raise the major share of the foundation's annual budget. Although large amounts of money are raised each year from the mail campaign, the year-to-year growth in the amount derived from the mail solicitation has been lower than expected by the foundation's board. In addition, the board wants the mail campaign to project the image of a well-run and fiscally responsible organization in order to build a base for future contributions. Consequently, the major focus of Watson's efforts in her first year will be devoted to the mail campaign.

The campaign takes place in the spring of each year. The foundation staff makes every effort to secure newspaper, radio, and television coverage of the foundation's activities for several weeks before the mail campaign. In prior years, the foundation has mailed brochures that describe its charitable activities to a large number of people and requested contributions from them. The addresses for the mailing are generated from the foundation's own file of past contributors and from mailing lists purchased from brokers.

The foundation staff is considering three alternative brochures for use in the upcoming campaign. All three will be 8½" × 11" in size. The simplest and the one sure to be ready and available on a timely basis for bulk mailing is a sheet of white paper with a printed explanation of the foundation's program and a request for funds. A more expensive brochure on colored stock will contain pictures as well as printed copy. However, this brochure may not be ready in time to take advantage of bulk postal rates, but there is no doubt that it can be ready in time for mailing at first-class postal rates. The third alternative would be an elegant, multicolored brochure printed on glossy paper with photographs as well as printed copy. The printer assures the staff that it will be ready on time to meet the first-class mailing schedule but asks for a delivery date one week later just in case there are production problems.

The foundation staff has assembled the following cost and revenue information (see accompanying schedule) for mailing the three alternative brochures to 2 million potential contributors. The postal rates are 2¢ per item for bulk mail and 13¢ per item for presorted first-class mail. First-class mail is more likely to be delivered on a timely basis than bulk mail. The charge by outside companies who will be hired to handle the mailing is 1¢ per unit for the plain and colored paper brochures and 2¢ per unit for the glossy paper one.

REQUIRED:

1. Calculate the net revenue contribution for each brochure for each viable mailing alternative.
2. The foundation must choose one of the three brochures for this year's campaign. The criteria established by the board—net revenue raised, image as a well-run organization, and image as a fiscally responsible organization—must be considered when making the choice. Evaluate the three alternative brochures in terms of the three criteria.

| TYPE OF BROCHURE | BROCHURE COSTS | | | | REVENUE POTENTIAL ($000 OMITTED) | | |
	Design	Type Setting	Unit Paper Cost	Unit Printing Cost	Bulk Mail	First Class	Late First Class
Plain paper	$ 300	$ 100	$.005	$.003	$1,200	—	—
Colored paper	$1,000	$ 800	$.008	$.010	$2,000	$2,200	—
Glossy paper	$3,000	$2,000	$.018	$.040	—	$2,500	$2,200

4–34. **Terminology and straightforward interpretations of unit costs.** Following is the income statement of a manufacturer of slacks:

BULOW COMPANY
Income Statement
For the Year Ended December 31, 19X4

	TOTAL	PER UNIT
Sales	$36,000,000	$36
Less manufacturing cost of goods sold	20,000,000	20
Gross margin	$16,000,000	$16
Less selling and administrative expenses	15,000,000	15
Operating income	$ 1,000,000	$ 1

Bulow had manufactured 1 million units, which had been sold to various clothing wholesalers and department stores. At the start of 19X5, the president, Rosalie Bulow, dropped dead of a stroke. Her son, Samuel, became the new president. Sam had worked for fifteen years in the marketing phases of the business. He knew very little about accounting and manufacturing, which were his mother's strengths.

Sam had several questions for you, including inquiries regarding the pricing of special orders.

1. To prepare better answers, you decide to recast the income statement in contribution form. Variable manufacturing cost was $15 million. Variable selling and administrative expenses, which were mostly sales commissions, shipping expenses, and advertising allowances paid to customers based on units sold, were $9 million.

2. Sam asks, "I can't understand financial statements until I know the meaning of various terms. In scanning my mother's assorted notes, I found the following pertaining to both total and unit costs: *functional manufacturing cost, full manufacturing cost, variable cost, full cost, fully allocated cost, fully distributed cost, gross margin, contribution margin.* Using our data for 19X4, please give me a list of these costs, their total amounts, and their per unit amounts."

3. "Near the end of 19X4 I brought in a special order from Macy's for 50,000 slacks at $30 each. I said I'd accept a flat $8,000 sales commission instead of the usual 6% of selling price, but my mother refused the order. She usually upheld a relatively rigid pricing policy, saying that it was bad business to accept orders that did not at least generate full manufacturing cost plus 80% of full manufacturing cost.

   "That policy bothered me. We had idle capacity. The way I figured, our manufacturing costs would go up by 50,000 × $20 = $1,000,000, but our selling and administrative expenses would only go up by $8,000. That would mean additional operating income of 50,000 × ($30 − $20) minus $8,000, or $500,000 minus $8,000, or $492,000. That's too much money to give up just to maintain a general pricing policy. Was my analysis of the impact on operating income correct? If not, please show me the correct additional operating income."

4. After receiving the explanations offered in Requirements 2 and 3, Sam said: "Forget that I had the Macy's order. I had an even bigger order from J. C. Penney. It was for 250,000 units and would have filled the plant completely. I told my mother I'd settle for no commission. There would have been no selling and administrative costs whatsoever because J. C. Penney would pay for the shipping and would not get any advertising allowances.

   "J. C. Penney offered $14.40 per unit. Our fixed manufacturing costs would have been spread over 1.25 million instead of 1 million units. Wouldn't it have been advantageous to accept the offer? Our old fixed manufacturing costs were $5 per unit. The added volume would reduce that cost more than our loss on our variable costs per unit.

   "Am I correct? What would have been the impact on total operating income if we had accepted the order?"

4–35. **Using available facilities.** The Lowe Company manufactures electronic subcomponents that can be sold at the end of Process A or can be processed further in Process B and sold as special parts for a variety of intricate electronic equipment. The entire output of Process A can be sold at a market price of $2 per unit. The output of Process B has been generating a sales price of $5.50 for three years, but the price has recently fallen to $5.10 on assorted orders.

Helen Tobin, the vice-president of marketing, has analyzed the markets and the costs. She thinks that the B output should be dropped whenever its price falls below $4.50 per unit. The total available capacity of A and B is interchangeable, so all facilities should currently be devoted to producing B. She has cited the following data:

Total OH is same whether you produce A or B

<table>
<tr><td colspan="3" align="center">**OUTPUT OF A**</td></tr>
<tr><td>Selling price, after deducting
  relevant selling costs</td><td></td><td>$2.00</td></tr>
<tr><td>Direct materials</td><td>$1.00</td><td></td></tr>
<tr><td>Direct labor</td><td>.20</td><td></td></tr>
<tr><td>SAME ↑ Manufacturing overhead</td><td>.60</td><td></td></tr>
<tr><td>Cost per unit</td><td></td><td>1.80</td></tr>
<tr><td>Operating profit</td><td></td><td>$ .20</td></tr>
<tr><td colspan="3" align="center">**OUTPUT OF B**</td></tr>
<tr><td>Selling price, after deducting
  relevant selling costs</td><td></td><td>$5.10</td></tr>
<tr><td>Transferred-in variable cost
  from A</td><td>$1.20</td><td></td></tr>
<tr><td>Additional direct materials</td><td>1.50</td><td></td></tr>
<tr><td>Direct labor</td><td>.40</td><td></td></tr>
<tr><td>Same Manufacturing overhead</td><td>1.20*</td><td></td></tr>
<tr><td>Cost per unit</td><td></td><td>4.30</td></tr>
<tr><td>Operating profit</td><td></td><td>$ .80</td></tr>
</table>

*For additional processing to make B.

Direct-materials and direct-labor costs are variable. The total overhead is fixed; it is allocated to units produced by predicting the total overhead for the coming year and dividing this total by the total hours of capacity available.

The total hours of capacity available are 600,000. It takes one hour to make 60 units of A and two hours of additional processing to make 60 units of B.

REQUIRED:

1. If the price of B for the coming year is going to be $5.10, should A be dropped and all facilities devoted to the production of B? Show computations.
2. Prepare a report for the vice-president of marketing to show the lowest possible price for B that would be acceptable.
3. Suppose that 50% of the manufacturing overhead were variable. Repeat Requirements 1 and 2. Do your answers change? If so, how?

4–36. **Review of Chapters 2, 3, 4.** The Smart Co. has the following cost behavior patterns:

Production range in units	0–5,000	5,001–10,000	10,001–15,000	15,001–20,000
Nonvariable costs	$150,000	$220,000	$250,000	$270,000

Maximum production capacity is 20,000 units per year. Variable costs per unit are $30 at all production levels.

REQUIRED:

Each situation described below is to be considered independently.

1. Production and sales are expected to be 11,000 units for the year. The sales price is $50 per unit. How many additional units need to be sold, in an unrelated market, at $40 per unit to show a total overall net income of $8,000 for the year?
2. The company has orders for 23,000 units at $50. If it desired to make a minimum overall net income of $148,000 on these 23,000 units, what unit purchase price would it be willing to pay a subcontractor for 3,000 units? Assume

that the subcontractor would act as Smart's agent, deliver the units to customers directly, and bear all related costs of manufacture, delivery, etc. The customers, however, would pay Smart directly as goods were delivered.

3. Production is currently expected to be 7,000 units for the year at a selling price of $50. By how much may advertising or special promotion costs be increased to bring production up to 14,500 units and still earn a total net income of 4% of dollar sales?

4. Net income is currently $125,000. Nonvariable costs are $250,000. However, competitive pressures are mounting. A 5% decrease in price will not affect sales volume but will decrease net income by $37,500. What is the present volume, in units? Refer to the original data.

4–37. **Review of Chapters 2, 3, 4.** The Hansen Company is a processor of a Bacardi-mix concentrate. Sales are made principally to liquor distributors throughout the country.

The company's income statements for the past year and the coming year are being analyzed by top management.

HANSEN COMPANY Income Statements		FOR THE YEAR 19X1 JUST ENDED		FOR THE YEAR 19X2 TENTATIVE BUDGET
Sales 1,500,000 gallons in 19X1		$900,000		$1,000,000
Cost of goods sold:				
Direct material	$450,000		$495,000	
Direct labor	90,000		99,000	
Factory overhead:				
Variable	18,000		19,800	
Fixed	50,000	608,000	50,000	663,800
Gross margin		$292,000		$ 336,200
Selling expenses:				
Variable				
Sales commissions (based				
on dollar sales)	$ 45,000		$ 50,000	
Shipping and other	90,000		99,000	
Fixed:				
Salaries, advertising, etc.	110,000		138,000	
Administrative expenses:				
Variable	12,000		13,200	
Fixed	40,000	297,000	40,000	340,200
Operating income		$ −5,000		$ −4,000

REQUIRED:

Consider each requirement independently.

Unless otherwise stated, assume that all unit costs of inputs such as material and labor are unchanged. Also, assume that efficiency is unchanged—that is, the labor and quantity of material consumed per unit of output are unchanged. Unless otherwise stated, assume that there are no changes in fixed costs.

1. The president has just returned from a management conference at a local university, where he heard an accounting professor criticize conventional income statements. The professor had asserted that knowledge of cost behavior patterns was of key importance in determining managerial strategies. The president now feels that the income statement should be recast to harmonize with cost-volume-profit analysis—that is, the statement should have three major sections: sales, variable costs, and fixed costs. Using the 19X1 data,

Relevant Costs
and Special
Decisions—
Part One

113

prepare such a statement, showing the contribution margin as well as operating income.

2. Comment on the changes in each item in the income statement. What are the most likely causes for each increase? For example, have selling prices been changed for 19X2? How do sales commissions fluctuate in relation to units sold or in relation to dollar sales?

3. The president is unimpressed with the 19X2 budget: "We need to take a fresh look in order to begin moving toward profitable operations. Let's tear up the 19X2 budget, concentrate on 19X1 results, and prepare a new comparative 19X2 budget under each of the following assumptions:

   a. A 5% average price cut will increase unit sales by 20%.
   b. A 5% average price increase will decrease unit sales by 10%.
   c. A sales commission rate of 10% and a 3⅓% price increase will boost unit sales by 10%.

   Prepare the budgets for 19X2, using a contribution-margin format and three columns. Assume that there are no changes in fixed costs.

4. The advertising manager maintains that the advertising budget should be increased by $100,000 and that prices should be increased by 10%. Resulting unit sales will soar by 25%. What would be the expected operating income under such circumstances?

5. A nearby distillery has offered to buy 300,000 gallons in 19X2 if the unit price is low enough. The Hansen Company would not have to incur sales commissions or shipping costs on this special order, and regular business would be undisturbed. Assuming that 19X2's regular operations will be exactly like 19X1's, what unit price should be quoted in order for the Hansen Company to earn an operating income of $5,000 in 19X2?

6. The company chemist wants to add a special ingredient, an exotic flavoring that will add 2¢ per gallon to the Bacardi-mix costs. He also wants to replace the ordinary grenadine now used, which costs 3¢ per gallon of mix, with a more exquisite type costing 4¢ per gallon. Assuming no other changes in cost behavior, how many units must be sold to earn an operating income of $5,000 in 19X2?

RELEVANT COSTS AND SPECIAL DECISIONS— PART TWO

Learning Objectives

When you have finished studying this chapter, you should be able to

1. Analyze given data to support a decision to make or buy certain parts or products
2. Identify the opportunity-cost concept and apply it to an analysis for choosing the best use of available facilities
3. Identify the uses and limitations of allocating joint costs
4. Use either an incremental analysis or an opportunity-cost analysis to determine whether individual joint products should be processed beyond the split-off point
5. Distinguish between relevant and irrelevant items in arriving at decisions concerning disposal of obsolete inventory and replacement of equipment
6. Identify the nature, causes, and remedies of a serious motivational problem that might block a desirable decision to dispose of old equipment and replace it with new equipment

The key question in relevant-cost analysis was introduced and explained in the preceding chapter: What difference does it make? This chapter extends the application of such analysis. The contribution approach is illustrated for make-or-buy decisions and sell-or-process-further decisions. Particular attention is given to the relationships between past and future data, using the decision to replace equipment as an illustration.

MAKE OR BUY

❏ Make or Buy and Idle Facilities

Manufacturers are often confronted with the question of whether to make or buy a product. For example, should we manufacture our own parts and subassemblies or buy them from vendors? The qualitative factors may be of paramount importance. Sometimes the manufacture of parts requires special know-how, unusually skilled labor, rare materials, and the like. The desire to control the quality of parts is often the determining factor in the decision to make them. Then, too, companies hesitate to destroy mutually advantageous long-run relationships by erratic order giving, which results from making parts during slack times and buying them during prosperous times. They may have difficulty in obtaining any parts during boom times when there are shortages of material and workers and no shortage of sales orders.

What are the quantitative factors relevant to the decision of whether to make or buy? The answer, again, depends on the context. A key factor is whether there are idle facilities. Many companies make parts only when their facilities cannot be used to better advantage.

Assume that the following costs are reported:

B COMPANY
Cost of Making Part No. 900

	TOTAL COST FOR 20,000 UNITS	COST PER UNIT
Direct material	$ 20,000	$ 1
Direct labor	80,000	4
Variable factory overhead	40,000	2
Fixed factory overhead	80,000	4
Total costs	$220,000	$11

Another manufacturer offers to sell B Company the same part for $10. Should B Company make or buy the part?

Although the $11 unit cost shown above seemingly indicates that the company should buy, the answer is rarely obvious. The key question is the difference in expected future costs as between the alternatives. If the $4 fixed overhead per unit represents those costs (e.g., depreciation, property taxes, insurance, allocated executive salaries) that will continue regardless of the decision, the entire $4 becomes irrelevant.

Again, it is risky to say categorically that only the variable costs are relevant. Perhaps $1 of the fixed costs will be saved if the parts are bought instead of made. For instance, suppose $20,000 is the salary of a foreman who will be released or transferred to another productive assignment. In other words, fixed costs that may be avoided in the future are relevant.

For the moment, let us assume that the capacity now used to make parts will become idle if the parts are purchased. The relevant computations follow:

	PER UNIT		TOTALS	
	Make	Buy	Make	Buy
Direct material	$1		$ 20,000	
Direct labor	4		80,000	
Variable factory overhead	2		40,000	
Fixed factory overhead that can be avoided by not making (foreman's salary)	1		20,000	
Total relevant costs	$8	$10	$160,000	$200,000
Difference in favor of making		$2		$40,000

☐ Essence of Make or Buy: Utilization of Facilities

The choice in our example is not really whether to make or buy; it is how best to utilize available facilities. Although the data above indicate that making the part is the better choice, the figures are not conclusive—primarily because we have no idea of what can be done with the manufacturing facilities if the component is bought. Only if the released facilities are to remain idle are the figures above valid.

If the released facilities can be used advantageously in some other manufacturing activity (to produce a contribution to profits of, say, $55,000) or can be rented out (say, for $35,000), these alternatives also may merit consideration. The two courses of action have become four (figures are in thousands):

	MAKE	BUY AND LEAVE FACILITIES IDLE	BUY AND RENT	BUY AND USE FACILITIES FOR OTHER PRODUCTS
Rent revenue	$ —	$ —	$ 35	$ —
Contribution from other products	—	—	—	55
Obtaining of parts	(160)	(200)	(200)	(200)
Net relevant costs	$(160)	$(200)	$(165)	$(145)

The analysis indicates that buying the parts and using the vacated facilities for the production of other products is the alternative that should yield best results in this case.

In sum, the make-or-buy decision should focus on relevant costs in a particular decision context. In all cases, companies should relate make-or-buy decisions to the long-run policies for the use of capacity:

☐ One company stated that it solicits subcontract work for *other* manufacturers during periods when sales of its own products do not fully utilize the plant, but that such work cannot be carried on regularly without expansion of its plant. The profit margin on subcontracts is not sufficiently large to cover these additional costs and hence work is accepted only when other business is lacking. The same company sometimes meets a period of high volume by *purchasing* parts or having them made by subcontractors. While the cost of such parts is usually higher than the cost to make them in the company's own plant, the additional cost is less than it would be if they were made on equipment which could be used only part of the time.[1]

OPPORTUNITY COSTS

An **opportunity cost** is the *maximum* available contribution forgone by using limited resources for a particular purpose. It represents a forsaken alternative, so the "cost" differs from the usual kind in the sense that it is not the *outlay cost* that accountants and managers typically encounter and discuss. An **outlay cost** entails a cash disbursement sooner or later; that is, the outlay-cost idea provides the basis for the typical historical-cost valuations of assets.

Consider a hospital administrator who is trying to decide how to use some space vacated by the pediatrics clinic. The administrator has tabulated three choices in a straightforward way. The numbers favor laboratory testing, which will generate a contribution to income that is $30,000 greater than that of the eye clinic:

	(1) EXPAND LABORATORY TESTING	(2) EXPAND EYE CLINIC	(3) RENT TO GIFT SHOP MANAGER*
Expected future revenue	$70,000	$50,000	$4,000
Expected future costs	30,000	40,000	—
Contribution to income	$40,000	$10,000	$4,000

*The gift shop is run by an independent retailer who pays the hospital a yearly rental. He wants to expand his present space.

In fact the manager may have a dozen possible uses for that space. Instead of listing all of them, she may pick the *best* (the rental) from among the ten alternatives that she does not want to consider in any detail and incorporate the forgone contribution as a cost of her final two alternatives. Therefore, the above data could be tabulated as follows, using the notion of opportunity cost:

[1] *The Analysis of Cost-Profit Relationships*, National Association of Accountants, Research Series No. 17, p. 552.

	(1) EXPAND LABORATORY TESTING		(2) EXPAND EYE CLINIC	
Expected future revenue		$70,000		$50,000
Expected future costs:				
Outlay costs	$30,000		$40,000	
Opportunity cost— rent forgone	4,000	34,000	4,000	44,000
Contribution to income		$36,000		$ 6,000

The numbers have been analyzed correctly under both tabulations. They show a $30,000 difference in favor of the laboratory and thus answer the key query: What difference does it make? A comparison of the two tabulations shows how the concept of opportunity cost is a practical means of narrowing the number of alternatives under consideration.

Sometimes an individual may want to focus on only two alternatives from the start. For instance, Joan Bickerton, a certified public accountant, may be employed by a large accounting firm at a salary of $35,000 per year. She may want to begin her own independent practice. Her analysis of alternatives follows:

	INDEPENDENT PRACTICE	EMPLOYEE
Revenue	$90,000	$35,000
Costs	43,000	—
Net income	$47,000	$35,000

Like many individuals, Bickerton may prefer to tabulate the numerical effects as follows:

		INDEPENDENT PRACTICE
Revenue		$90,000
Costs:		
Outlay costs	$43,000	
Opportunity cost— forgone salary	35,000	78,000
Net income		$12,000

The correct key difference, $12,000, will be generated by either tabulation. Some accountants and managers regard the opportunity-cost format of the second tabulation as being more confusing than the straightforward presentation of the first tabulation. Choose either approach. The choice is a matter of taste. Obviously, if the choice is framed as in the second tabulation (entering practice versus not entering), the failure to recognize an opportunity cost will misstate the difference between alternatives.

Note that opportunity costs are seldom incorporated into formal accounting systems, particularly for external reporting. Such costs represent incomes forgone by rejecting alternatives; therefore opportunity costs do not involve cash receipts or outlays. Accountants usually confine their recording to those events that ultimately involve exchanges of assets. Accountants confine their history to alternatives selected rather than those rejected, primarily because of the impracticality or impossibility of accumulating meaningful data on what might have been.

JOINT PRODUCT COSTS AND INCREMENTAL COSTS

❏ Nature of Joint Products

The preceding chapter referred to **common costs** as the cost of facilities and services shared by user departments. Sometimes accountants use the term *common cost* as a synonym for *joint cost*. In this book, however, *joint* will be restricted to the narrower meaning of **joint product costs.** The latter term is defined as the costs of manufactured goods of relatively significant sales values that are produced by a process or a series of processes and that are not identifiable as different individual products until after a certain stage of production known as the **split-off point.** Examples include petroleum products, chemicals, lumber, flour milling, leather tanning, copper mining, soap making, and meat packing. A meat-packing company cannot kill a sirloin steak; it has to slaughter a steer, which supplies various cuts of dressed meat, hides, and trimmings.

The split-off point is that juncture of production where the joint products become individually identifiable. Any costs beyond that stage are called *separable costs* because they are not part of the joint process and can be exclusively identified with individual products.

An illustration should clarify the meaning of these new terms. Suppose a company produces two chemical products, X and Y, as a result of a particular joint process. The joint-processing cost is $100,000. Both products are sold to the petroleum industry to be used as ingredients of gasoline. The relationships follow:

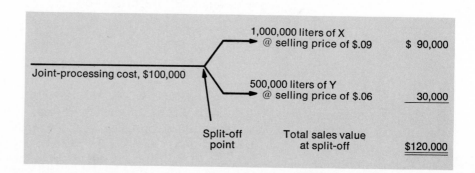

Joint-processing cost, $100,000

1,000,000 liters of X
@ selling price of $.09 $ 90,000

500,000 liters of Y
@ selling price of $.06   30,000

Split-off   Total sales value
point   at split-off $120,000

Management frequently faces decisions of whether to sell joint products at split-off or to process some or all products further. Suppose the 500,000 liters of Y can be processed further and sold to the plastics industry as Product YA, an ingredient for plastic sheeting, at an additional cost of 8¢ per liter for manufacturing and distribution. The net sales price of YA would be 16¢ per liter.

Product X will be sold at the split-off point, but management is undecided about Product Y. Should Y be sold or should it be processed into YA? The joint costs must be incurred to reach the split-off point, so they do not differ between alternatives and are completely irrelevant to the question of whether to sell or process further. The only approach that will yield valid results is to concentrate on the separable costs and revenue *beyond* split-off, as shown in Exhibit 5-1.

EXHIBIT 5-1

	SELL AT SPLIT-OFF AS Y	PROCESS FURTHER AS YA	DIFFERENCE
Revenue	$30,000	$80,000	$50,000
Separable costs beyond split-off, @ $.08	—	40,000	40,000
Income effects	$30,000	$40,000	$10,000

This analysis shows that it would be $10,000 more profitable to process Y beyond split-off than to sell Y at split-off. Briefly, it is profitable to extend processing or to incur additional distribution costs on a joint product if the difference in revenue exceeds the difference in expenses.

For decisions regarding whether to sell or process further, the most straightforward analysis is as shown above. Alternatively, an opportunity-cost format would be:

	PROCESS FURTHER	
Revenue		$80,000
Outlay cost: separable cost beyond split-off, @ $.08	$40,000	
Opportunity cost: sales value of Y at split-off	30,000	70,000
Income effects		$10,000

This format is merely a different way of recognizing another alternative (sell Y at split-off) when considering the decision to process further individually. When they are properly analyzed, decision alternatives may be compared either by excluding the idea of opportunity costs altogether, as Exhibit 5-1 shows, or by encompassing opportunity costs, as is shown here. The key difference, $10,000, is generated either way.

❏ Incremental or Differential Costs

Two important points deserve mentioning here. First, the allocation of joint costs would not affect the decision, as Exhibit 5-2 demonstrates. The joint costs are not allocated in the exhibit, but no matter how they might be allocated, the total income effects would be unchanged.

Second, the title of the last column in Exhibit 5-2 contains terms that are frequently encountered in cost analysis for special decisions. **Incremental costs** (sometimes called **differential costs**) are, in any given situation, the difference between the total costs of each alternative. In this situation, the *incremental revenue* is $50,000, the *incremental cost* is $40,000, and the *incremental income* is $10,000. Each is the difference between the corresponding items under the alternatives being considered. In an analysis that showed only the differences, called an *incremental analysis*, only column 3 would be shown. In a *total analysis* all three sets of columns are shown. The choice of an incremental or a total analysis is a matter of individual preference.

❏ Danger of Allocation

Earlier discussions in this and the preceding chapter have emphasized the desirability of concentrating on totals and of carefully examining unit costs and allocations of fixed costs. For example, the total common costs may only be partially affected by changes in departments or products. Similarly, the allocations of joint product costs to units of product is fraught with analytical perils.

Joint product costs are routinely allocated to products for purposes of inventory valuation and income determination. For example, some of the costs attributable to Product X will ordinarily be allocated to any ending inventory of X. Such allocations are useful for inventory purposes *only*. For decisions of selling a joint product or processing it further, joint cost allocations should be ignored. Not only are they irrelevant, they may be downright misleading.

Two conventional ways of allocating joint costs to products are widely used: *physical units* and *relative sales values*. If physical units were used, the joint costs would be allocated as follows:

	LITERS	WEIGHTING	ALLOCATION OF JOINT COSTS	VALUE AT SPLIT-OFF
X	1,000,000	10/15 × $100,000	$ 66,667	$ 90,000
Y	500,000	5/15 × $100,000	33,333	30,000
	1,500,000		$100,000	$120,000

This approach shows that the $33,333 joint cost of producing Y exceeds its $30,000 value at split-off, seemingly indicating that Y should not be produced. However, such an allocation is not helpful in making production decisions. Neither of the two products could be produced separately. In

EXHIBIT 5-2

Firm as a Whole							
	(1) ALTERNATIVE ONE			(2) ALTERNATIVE TWO			(3) INCREMENTAL OR DIFFERENTIAL EFFECTS
	X	Y	Total	X	YA	Total	
Revenue	$90,000	$30,000	$120,000	$90,000	$80,000	$170,000	$50,000
Joint costs			$100,000		—	$100,000	—
Separable costs			—		40,000	40,000	40,000
Total costs			$100,000			$140,000	$40,000
Income effects			$ 20,000			$ 30,000	$10,000

such a case, as we have already seen, the allocation of joint costs would not be relevant in deciding what to do with each product individually after split-off.

Costing in proportion to *relative sales values* at split-off is another popular way of allocating joint costs:

	RELATIVE SALES VALUE	WEIGHTING	ALLOCATION OF JOINT COSTS
X	$ 90,000	90/120 × $100,000	$ 75,000
Y	30,000	30/120 × $100,000	25,000
	$120,000		$100,000

Now each product would be assigned a joint cost portion that is less than its value at split-off. Note how the allocation of a cost to a particular product such as Y is dependent not only on the sales value of Y but also on the sales value of X. However, here again the joint cost allocation has no bearing on whether Y should be sold as Y or processed further to become YA.

IRRELEVANCE OF PAST COSTS

As defined early in Chapter 4, a relevant cost is (a) an expected future cost (b) that will differ among alternatives. The contribution aspect of relevant-cost analysis has shown that those expected future costs that will not differ are irrelevant to choosing among alternatives. Now we return to the idea that all past costs are also irrelevant to such decisions.

☐ Obsolete Inventory

A company has 100 obsolete missile parts that are carried in inventory at a manufacturing cost of $100,000. The parts can be (1) remachined for $30,000, and then sold for $50,000; or (2) scrapped for $5,000. Which should be done?

This is an unfortunate situation; yet the $100,000 cost is irrelevant to the decision to remachine or scrap. The only relevant factors are the expected future revenue and costs:

Relevant Costs and Special Decisions— Part Two

123

	REMACHINE	SCRAP	DIFFERENCE
Expected future revenue	$ 50,000	$ 5,000	$45,000
Expected future costs	30,000	—	30,000
Relevant excess of revenue over costs	$ 20,000	$ 5,000	$15,000
Accumulated historical inventory costs*	100,000	100,000	—
Net overall loss on project	$ (80,000)	$ (95,000)	$15,000

*Irrelevant because it is not an element of difference as between the alternatives.

We could completely ignore the **historical cost** and still arrive at the $15,000 difference, the key figure in the analysis.

❑ Book Value of Old Equipment

For now, we shall not consider all aspects of equipment-replacement decisions, but we shall turn to one that is widely misunderstood—the role of the book value of the old equipment. **Book value** is defined here as the original (historical) acquisition cost of a fixed asset less its accumulated depreciation. Consider the following data:

	OLD MACHINE	REPLACEMENT MACHINE
Original cost	$10,000	$8,000
Useful life in years	10	4
Current age in years	6	0
Useful life remaining in years	4	4
Accumulated depreciation	$ 6,000	0
Book value	$ 4,000	Not acquired yet
Disposal value (in cash) now	$ 2,500	Not acquired yet
Disposal value in 4 years	0	0
Annual cash operating costs (maintenance, power, repairs, coolants, etc.)	$ 5,000	$3,000

We have been asked to prepare a comparative analysis of the two alternatives. Before proceeding, consider some important concepts. The most widely misunderstood facet of replacement analysis is the role of the book value of the old equipment in the decision. The book value, in this context, is sometimes called a **sunk cost,** which is really just another term for historical or past cost. All historical costs are always irrelevant to choosing among alternative courses of action. Therefore the book value of the old equipment is always irrelevant to replacement decisions. At one time or another, we all like to think that we can soothe our wounded pride arising from having made a bad purchase decision by using the item instead of replacing it. The fallacy here is in erroneously thinking that a current or future action can influence the long-run impact of a past outlay. All past costs are down the drain. *Nothing* can change what has already happened.

We can apply our definition of decision relevance to four commonly encountered items:

1. *Book value of old equipment.* Irrelevant, because it is a past (historical) cost. Therefore depreciation on old equipment is irrelevant.

2. *Disposal value of old equipment.* Relevant (ordinarily), because it is an expected future inflow that usually differs among alternatives.

3. *Gain or loss on disposal.* This is the algebraic difference between 1 and 2. It is therefore a meaningless combination of book value, which is always irrelevant, and disposal value, which is usually relevant. The combination form, *loss* (or *gain*) on *disposal*, blurs the distinction between the irrelevant book value and the relevant disposal value. Consequently, it is best to think of each separately.[2]

4. *Cost of new equipment.* Relevant, because it is an expected future outflow that will differ among alternatives. Therefore depreciation on new equipment is relevant.

Exhibit 5-3 should clarify the above assertions. It deserves close study. Book value of old equipment is irrelevant regardless of the decision-making technique used. The "difference" column in Exhibit 5-3 shows that the $4,000 book value of the old equipment is not an element of difference between alternatives and could be completely ignored for decision-making purposes. No matter what the *timing* of the charge against revenue, the *amount* charged is still $4,000, regardless of any available alterna-

[2] For simplicity, we ignore income tax considerations and the effects of the interest value of money in this chapter. But book value is irrelevant even if income taxes are considered, because the relevant item is then the tax cash flow, not the book value. Using the approach in Exhibit 4-1, the book value is essential information for the *prediction method* (step 2), but the expected future income tax cash outflows are the relevant information for the *decision model* (step 3). The prediction method would be: Disposal value, $2,500 − Book value, $4,000 = Loss on disposal, $1,500. If the income tax rate is 50%, the income tax cash saving would be $750. This $750 would be the expected future cash flow that is relevant input to the decision model. For elaboration, see Chapter 12.

EXHIBIT
5-3

Cost Comparison—Replacement of Equipment Including Relevant and Irrelevant Items			
	FOUR YEARS TOGETHER		
	Keep	Replace	Difference
Cash operating costs	$20,000	$12,000	$8,000
Old equipment (book value):			
Periodic write-off as depreciation	4,000	—	—
or			
Lump-sum write-off		4,000*	—
Disposal value	—	−2,500*	2,500
New machine, written off periodically as depreciation	—	8,000	−8,000
Total costs	$24,000	$21,500	$2,500

The advantage of replacement is $2,500 for the four years together.

*In a formal income statement, these two items would be combined as "loss on disposal" of $1,500.

tive. In either event, the undepreciated cost will be written off with the same ultimate effect on profit.[3] The $4,000 creeps into the income statement either as a $4,000 offset against the $2,500 proceeds to obtain a $1,500 *loss on disposal* in one year, or as $1,000 depreciation in each of four years. But how it appears is irrelevant to the replacement decision. In contrast, the $2,000 annual depreciation on the new equipment *is* relevant because the total $8,000 depreciation is a future cost that may be avoided by not replacing.

❑ Examining Alternatives Over the Long Run

The foregoing is the first example that has looked beyond one year. A useful technique is to view the alternatives over their entire lives and then compute annual average results. In this way, peculiar nonrecurring items (such as loss on disposal) will not obstruct the long-run view that must necessarily be taken in almost all special managerial decisions.

Exhibit 5-4 concentrates on relevant items only. Note that the same answer (the $2,500 net difference) will be produced even though the book value is completely omitted from the calculations. The only relevant items are the cash operating costs, the disposal value of the old equipment, and the depreciation on the new equipment. To demonstrate that the amount of the book value will not affect the answer, suppose the book value of the old equipment is $500,000 rather than $4,000. Your final answer will not be changed. The cumulative advantage of replacement will still be $2,500. (If you are in doubt, rework this example, using $500,000 as the book value.)

MOTIVATION AND CONFLICT OF MODELS

❑ Influence of Loss

Reconsider our replacement example in light of the following sequence, which was originally presented in Exhibit 4-1, page 84:

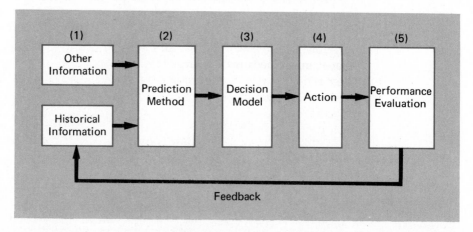

[3] We are deliberately ignoring income tax factors for the time being. If income taxes are considered, the *timing* of the writing off of fixed-asset costs may influence income tax pay-

EXHIBIT
5-4

Cost Comparison—Replacement of Equipment, Relevant Items Only			
	FOUR YEARS TOGETHER		
	Keep	**Replace**	**Difference**
Cash operating costs	$20,000	$12,000	$8,000
Disposal value of old equipment	—	−2,500	2,500
Depreciation—new equipment	—	8,000	−8,000
Total relevant costs	$20,000	$17,500	$2,500

Assume that the decision model (box 3) specifies: choose the alternative that will minimize cumulative total costs over the four years. The analysis in Exhibit 5-4 indicates replace rather than keep. In the "real world," would the manager replace? The answer frequently depends on whether the manager believes that the decision model is consistent with the performance evaluation model (box 5). Conflict arises when managers are told to use one model for decision making, and their performance is then evaluated via a performance evaluation model that is inconsistent with the decision model. In this instance, if the manager's performance were to be evaluated by the typical accrual accounting model, a loss of $1,500 on the disposal of the old equipment would appear for the first year under the "replace" choice, but not under the "keep" choice:

	KEEP	**REPLACE**
Cash operating costs	$5,000	$3,000
Depreciation	1,000	2,000
Loss on disposal ($4,000 − $2,500)	—	1,500
Total charges against revenue	$6,000	$6,500

The performance evaluation model for the first year indicates lower charges against revenue of $6,500 − $6,000 = $500. The manager would be inclined to keep.

Note the motivational factors here. A manager may be reluctant to replace simply because the large loss on disposal would severely harm his or her reported profit performance in the first year. Many managers and accountants would not replace the old machine because it would entail recognizing the $1,500 "loss on disposal," whereas retention would allow spreading the $4,000 book value over four years in the form of "depreciation expense" (a more appealing term than "loss on disposal"). This demonstrates how overemphasis on short-run income may conflict with the objective of maximizing income over the long run, especially if managers are transferred periodically to different responsibilities.

ments. In this example, there will be a small real difference: the present value of $4,000 as a tax deduction now versus the present value of a $1,000 tax deduction each year for four years. But this difference in *future* income tax flows is the *relevant* item—not the book value of the old fixed asset per se. See Chapter 12.

❑ Reconciling the Models

The conflict between decision models and performance evaluation models just described is a pervasive problem in practice. Unfortunately, there are no easy solutions. In theory, the synchronization of these models seems obvious. Merely design a performance evaluation model that harmonizes exactly with the decision model. In our equipment example, this would mean predicting year-by-year income effects over the planning horizon for four years, noting that the first year would be poor, and following up accordingly.

The trouble is that systems rarely accommodate each decision in this fashion, one at a time. Consequently, the results of a single decision are encompassed along with many other decisions in an overall performance report. In such cases, the manager may predict the first-year effects and be inhibited from taking the longer view that may be preferable in the eyes of top management.

This one-year-at-a-time approach is especially prevalent in many not-for-profit organizations where budgets are approved on a year-to-year basis and the use of feedback is not well developed. Occasionally, managers will be tempted to underestimate costs in order to obtain initial approval and then come back year after year for supplementary amounts that were not provided for in the original budget request. Moreover, through the years many colleges and universities have accepted donations for new facilities such as buildings and research equipment without providing sufficiently for lifelong maintenance and repairs. There is a danger that the value of such resources will be exceeded by the costs of operating them.

❑ Distinguishing Between Decisions

Consider the following relationships:

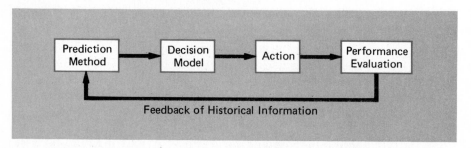

Ponder Decision A, the original choice of the equipment. The feedback regarding Decision A may easily affect the predictions concerning Decision B, the buying of new equipment. For instance, existing equipment was supposed to last ten years. However, if superior equipment is at hand, then the useful life of the old equipment has turned out to be six instead of ten years. Given this feedback, how believable is the new prediction that the proposed equipment will last four years? Thus the evaluation of the performance of Decision A provides vital feedback that should improve Decision B.

The financial impact of Decision A should not be confused with the financial impact of Decision B. Above all, Decision B should not be forced to bear any "loss" already suffered by Decision A. In the equipment example, having the $1,500 loss on disposal (or the $4,000 book value) affect the measurement of Year 1's performance for Decision B (replacing) would be faulty thinking. The relationships should be kept in perspective: Decision A should be separated from Decision B. Mixing them together may lead to the wrong choice when Decision B is made.

IRRELEVANCE OF FUTURE COSTS THAT WILL NOT DIFFER

The past costs in the preceding two examples were not an element of difference among the alternatives. As noted, the $100,000 inventory of obsolete parts and the $4,000 book value of old equipment were included under both alternatives and were irrelevant because they were the same for each alternative under consideration.

There are also expected *future* costs that may be irrelevant because they will be the same under all feasible alternatives. These, too, may be safely ignored for a particular decision. The salaries of many members of top management are illustrations of expected future costs that will not be affected by the decision at hand.

Other examples include many fixed costs that will be unaffected by such considerations as whether Machine X or Machine Y is selected, or whether a special order is accepted. However, it is not merely a case of saying that fixed costs are irrelevant and variable costs are relevant. Variable costs can be irrelevant. For instance, sales commissions might be paid on an order regardless of whether the order was filled from Plant G or Plant H. Variable costs are irrelevant whenever they do not differ among the alternatives at hand. Our preceding example showed that fixed costs (cost of new equipment) can be relevant. Fixed costs are relevant whenever they differ under the alternatives at hand.

BEWARE OF UNIT COSTS

The pricing illustration in the preceding chapter showed that unit costs should be analyzed with care in decision making. There are two major ways to go wrong: (a) the inclusion of irrelevant costs, such as the $3 allocation of unavoidable fixed costs in the make-or-buy example that would result in a unit cost of $11 instead of the relevant unit cost of $8; and (b) comparisons of unit costs not computed on the same volume basis, as the following example demonstrates. Generally, it is advisable to use total costs rather than unit costs. Then, if desired, the totals may be unitized. Machinery sales personnel, for example, often brag about the low unit costs of using the new machines. Sometimes they neglect to point out that the unit costs are based on outputs far in excess of the volume of activity of their prospective customer.

Assume that a new $100,000 machine with a five-year life can produce 100,000 units a year at a variable cost of $1 per unit, as opposed to a variable cost per unit of $1.50 with an old machine. Is the new machine a worthwhile acquisition?

It is attractive at first glance. If the customer's expected volume is 100,000 units, unit-cost comparisons are valid, provided that new depreciation is also considered. Assume that the disposal value of the old equipment is zero. Because depreciation is an allocation of historical cost, the depreciation on the old machine is irrelevant. In contrast, the depreciation on the new machine is relevant because the new machine entails a future cost that can be avoided by not acquiring it:

	OLD MACHINE	NEW MACHINE
Units	100,000	100,000
Variable costs	$150,000	$100,000
Straight-line depreciation	—	20,000
Total relevant costs	$150,000	$120,000
Unit relevant costs	$ 1.50	$ 1.20

However, if the customer's expected volume is only 30,000 units per year, the unit costs change in favor of the old machine:

	OLD MACHINE	NEW MACHINE
Units	30,000	30,000
Variable costs	$45,000	$30,000
Straight-line depreciation	—	20,000
Total relevant costs	$45,000	$50,000
Unit relevant costs	$ 1.50	$1.6667

DECISION MODELS AND UNCERTAINTY

The decision models illustrated in this and the preceding chapter employed accrual accounting models, whereby the effects on net income under various alternatives were compared and the alternative with the best income effect was chosen. Other decision models are discussed in later chapters. (For example, Chapters 11 and 12 cover discounted-cash-flow models for equipment-replacement decisions. Many readers may prefer to jump directly to Chapters 11 and 12 immediately after completing their study of this chapter. This can be done without breaking continuity.)

It is vitally important to recognize that throughout this and other chapters, dollar amounts of future sales and operating costs are assumed to be known with certainty in order to highlight and to simplify various important points. In practice, the forecasting of these key figures is generally the most difficult aspect of decision analysis. For elaboration, see Chapter 16, which explores the implications of uncertainty in decision contexts.

Summary

Relevant-cost analysis, which makes heavy use of the contribution approach, concentrates on expected future data that will differ among alternatives. As Exhibit 4-1 (page 84) shows, clear distinctions should be made between past data, which may be helpful in formulating predictions, and the predicted data that are the inputs to decision models. Numerous illustrations in Chapters 4 and 5 underscore these fundamental ideas.

Summary Problem for Your Review

❏ Problem

Exhibit 5-5 contains data for the Block Company for the year just ended. The company makes parts that are used in the final assembly of its finished product.

REQUIRED:

1. During the year, a prospective customer in an unrelated market offered $82,000 for 1,000 finished units. The latter would be in addition to the 100,000 units sold. The regular sales commission rate would have been paid. The president rejected the order because "it was below our costs of $97 per unit." What would operating income have been if the order had been accepted?

2. A supplier offered to manufacture the year's supply of 100,000 parts for $13.50 each. What would be the effect on operating income if the Block Company purchased rather than made the parts? Assume that $350,000 of the separable fixed costs assigned to parts would have been avoided if the parts were purchased.

3. The company could have purchased the parts for $13.50 each and used the vacated space for the manufacture of a deluxe version of its major product.

EXHIBIT 5-5

	A + B COMPANY AS A WHOLE	A FINISHED PRODUCT*	B PARTS
Sales: 100,000 units, @ $100	$10,000,000		
Variable costs:			
Direct material	$ 4,900,000	$4,400,000	$ 500,000
Direct labor	700,000	400,000	300,000
Variable factory overhead	300,000	100,000	200,000
Other variable costs	100,000	100,000	—
Sales commissions, @ 10% of sales	1,000,000	1,000,000	—
Total variable costs	$ 7,000,000	$6,000,000	$1,000,000
Contribution margin	$ 3,000,000		
Separable fixed costs	$ 2,300,000	$1,900,000	$ 400,000
Common fixed costs	400,000	320,000	80,000
Total fixed costs	$ 2,700,000	$2,220,000	$ 480,000
Operating income	$ 300,000		

*Not including the cost of parts (column B).

Assume that 20,000 deluxe units could have been made (and sold in addition to the 100,000 regular units) at a unit variable cost of $70, exclusive of parts and exclusive of the 10% sales commission. The sales price would have been $110. All of the fixed costs pertaining to the parts would have continued, because these costs related primarily to the manufacturing facilities utilized. What would operating income have been if Block had bought the necessary parts and made and sold the deluxe units?

❏ Solution

1. Costs of filling special order:

Direct material	$49,000
Direct labor	7,000
Variable factory overhead	3,000
Other variable costs	1,000
Sales commission, @ 10% of $82,000	8,200
Total variable costs	$68,200
Selling price	82,000
Contribution margin	$13,800

Operating income would have been $300,000 + $13,800, or $313,800, if the order had been accepted. In a sense, the decision to reject the offer implies that the Block Company is willing to invest $13,800 in immediate gains forgone (an opportunity cost) in order to preserve the long-run selling-price structure.

2. Assuming that $350,000 of the fixed costs could have been avoided by not making the parts and that the other fixed costs would have been continued, the alternatives can be summarized as follows:

	MAKE	BUY
Purchase cost		$1,350,000
Variable costs	$1,000,000	
Avoidable fixed costs	350,000	
Total relevant costs	$1,350,000	$1,350,000

If the facilities used for parts were to become idle, the Block Company would be indifferent as to whether to make or buy. Operating income would be unaffected.

3.

Sales would increase by 20,000 units, @ $110		$2,200,000
Variable costs exclusive of parts would increase by 20,000 units, @ $70	$1,400,000	
Plus the sales commission, 10% of $2,200,000	220,000	1,620,000
Contribution margin on 20,000 units		$ 580,000
Parts: 120,000 rather than 100,000 would be needed		
Buy 120,000, @ $13.50	$1,620,000	
Make 100,000, @ $10 (only the variable costs are relevant)	1,000,000	
Excess cost of outside purchase		620,000
Fixed costs, unchanged		—
Disadvantage of making deluxe units		$ (40,000)

Operating income would decline to $260,000 ($300,000 − $40,000, the disadvantage of selling the deluxe units). The deluxe units bring in a contribution margin of $580,000, but the additional costs of buying rather than making parts is $620,000, leading to a net disadvantage of $40,000.

Highlights to Remember

The following are among the more important generalizations regarding various decisions:

1. Make-or-buy decisions are, fundamentally, examples of obtaining the most profitable utilization of given facilities.
2. Sometimes the notion of an opportunity cost is helpful in cost analysis. An opportunity cost is the maximum sacrifice in rejecting an alternative; it is the maximum earning that might have been obtained if the productive good, service, or capacity had been applied to some alternative use. The opportunity-cost approach does not affect the important final differences between the courses of action, but the format of the analysis differs.
3. Joint product costs are irrelevant in decisions about whether to sell at split-off or process further.
4. Incremental costs or differential costs are the differences in the total costs under each alternative.
5. The book value of old equipment is always irrelevant in replacement decisions. This cost is often called a **sunk cost.** Disposal value, however, is generally relevant.
6. Generally, it is advisable to use total costs, rather than unit costs, in cost analysis.
7. Managers are often motivated to reject desirable economic decisions because of a conflict between the measures used in the decision model and the performance evaluation model.

Accounting Vocabulary

Book value;   common cost;   differential cost;   historical cost;   incremental cost; joint product costs;   opportunity cost;   outlay cost;   split-off point;   sunk cost.

Fundamental Assignment Material

5–1. **Replacing old equipment.**   (Alternates are 5–29 and 5–33.) Suppose a university's old photocopying machine has three years of useful life remaining. It originally cost $15,000, has accumulated depreciation of $6,000, and thus has a book value of $9,000. It can be sold for $5,700 cash now, but it will have no disposal value at the end of three years.

A new machine will have a useful life of three years. It is available for $12,000. It will have no disposal value at the end of three years. The new machine will reduce cash operating costs for power, maintenance, toner, and supplies from $8,000 to $5,000 annually. Income taxes and the time value of money are to be ignored.

Relevant Costs and Special Decisions— Part Two

133

1. Prepare a cost comparison similar to Exhibit 5-3. Which alternative seems preferable? (Exhibit 5-3 is on p. 125.)
2. Prepare a cost comparison similar to Exhibit 5-4. Which tabulation is clearer, this one or the one in Requirement 1? (Exhibit 5-4 is on p. 127.)
3. Prepare a simple "shortcut" or direct analysis to support your choice of alternatives.

5–2. Decision and performance models. (Alternate is 5–34.) Refer to the preceding problem.

1. Suppose the "decision model" favored by top management consisted of a comparison of a three-year accumulation of cash under each alternative. As the manager of office operations, which alternative would you choose? Why?
2. Suppose the "performance evaluation model" emphasized the minimization of overall costs of photocopying operations for the first year. Which alternative would you choose?

Additional
Assignment Material

5–3. "I had a chance to rent my summer home for two weeks for $150. But I chose to have it idle. I didn't want strangers living in my summer house." What term in this chapter describes the $150? Why?

5–4. There are two major reasons why unit costs should be analyzed with care in decision making. What are they?

5–5. "Accountants do not formally record opportunity costs in the accounting records." Why?

5–6. Distinguish between an opportunity cost and an outlay cost.

5–7. Distinguish between an incremental cost and a differential cost.

5–8. "Past costs are indeed relevant in most instances because they provide the point of departure for the entire decision process." Do you agree? Why?

5–9. Which of the following items are relevant in replacement decisions? Explain.
   a. Book value of old equipment
   b. Disposal value of old equipment
   c. Cost of new equipment

5–10. "No technique applicable to the problem of joint product costing should be used for management decisions regarding whether a product should be sold at the split-off point or processed further." Do you agree? Explain.

5–11. "Incremental cost is the addition to costs from the manufacture of one unit." Do you agree? Explain.

5–12. Relevant investment. Tim O'Rourke had obtained a new truck with a list price, including options, of $10,000. The dealer had given him a "generous trade-in allowance" of $3,000 on his old truck that had a wholesale price of $2,000. Sales tax was $600.

The annual cash operating costs of the old truck were $3,000. The new truck was expected to reduce these costs by one-third.

Compute the original investment in the new truck. Explain your reasoning.

5–13. Weak division. (S. Goodman.) The Goodman Company paid $5 million in cash four years ago to acquire a company manufacturing magnetic tape drives. This company has been operated as a division of Goodman and has lost $500,000 each year since its acquisition.

The outlook for this division is: (a) it should break even this year and the next; and (b) two years from now, when a new product is fully developed, it should return a net profit of $500,000 per year for the foreseeable future.

Recently the Apex Corporation offered to purchase the division from Goodman for $3 million. The president of Goodman commented, "I've got an investment of $7 million to recoup ($5 million plus losses of $500,000 for each of four years). I have finally got this situation turned around, so I oppose selling the division now."

Prepare a response to the president's remarks. Indicate how to make this decision. Be as specific as possible.

5–14. **Opportunity cost.** Francine Abrams, M.D., is a psychiatrist who is in heavy demand. Even though she has raised her fees considerably during the past five years, Dr. Abrams still cannot accommodate all the patients who wish to see her.

Abrams has conducted six hours of appointments a day, six days a week, for 48 weeks a year. Her fee averages $130 per hour.

Her variable costs are negligible and may be ignored for decision purposes. Ignore income taxes.

REQUIRED:

1. Abrams is weary of working a six-day week. She is considering taking every other Saturday off. What would be her annual income (a) if she worked every Saturday and (b) if she worked every other Saturday?
2. What would be her opportunity cost for the year of not working every other Saturday?
3. Assume that Dr. Abrams has definitely decided to take every other Saturday off. She loves to repair her sports car by doing the work herself. If she works on her car during half a Saturday when she otherwise would not see patients, what is her opportunity cost?

5–15. **Hospital opportunity cost.** The University Hospital has some extra space that has been idle for some time because of the declining birthrates in the area. Alice Zaloff, the chief administrator, has been considering several alternatives:

a. Use the space for a new diagnostic laboratory for conducting tests that have been sent to outside laboratories until now.
b. Rent the space to an outside contractor who wants to expand the gift shop space already being leased from the hospital.
c. Do nothing because other demands for space are bound to arise later.

The outside laboratory tests in question amount to 3,000 per year at an average cost to the hospital of $60 each. The administrator predicts that the same tests could be conducted internally for $110,000 per year, including the cost of technicians and depreciation on new equipment, which would have a useful life of three years with zero residual value.

The gift shop operator has offered a three-year agreement that would provide the hospital with $60,000 in yearly rent.

REQUIRED:

Prepare a tabulation of the total relevant costs of the decision alternatives, omitting the concept of opportunity costs in one tabulation and using it in the second tabulation. As the administrator, which tabulation would you prefer to get if you could only receive one?

5–16. **Hotel rooms and opportunity costs.** The Sheraton Corporation operates many hotels throughout the world. One of its New York hotels is facing difficult times because of the opening of several new competing hotels.

To accommodate its flight personnel, American Airlines has offered Sheraton a contract for the coming year that provides a rate of $50 per night per room for a minimum of fifty rooms for 365 nights. This contract would assure Sheraton of selling fifty rooms of space nightly, even if some of the rooms are vacant on some nights.

The Sheraton manager has mixed feelings about the contract. On several peak nights during the year, the hotel could sell the same space for $95 per room.

REQUIRED:

1. Suppose the contract is signed. What is the opportunity cost of the fifty rooms on October 20, the night of a big convention of retailers when every midtown hotel room is occupied? What is the opportunity cost on December 28, when only ten of these rooms would be expected to be rented at an average rate of $75?
2. If the year-round rate per room averaged $90, what percentage of occupancy of the fifty rooms in question would have to be rented to make Sheraton indifferent about accepting the offer?

5–17. **Extension of preceding problem.** (A. Wheelock.) Assume the same facts as in the preceding problem. However, also assume that the variable costs per room per day are $10.

REQUIRED:

1. Suppose the best estimate is a 54% general occupancy rate at an average $90 room rate for the next year. Should Sheraton accept the contract?
2. What percentage of occupancy of the fifty rooms in question would have to make Sheraton indifferent about accepting the offer?

5–18. **Hotel pricing and discounts.** (A. Wheelock.) A growing corporation in a large city has offered a 200-room Holiday Inn a one-year contract to rent 40 rooms at reduced rates of $60 per room instead of the regular rate of $80 per room. The corporation will sign the contract for 365-day occupancy because its visiting manufacturing and marketing personnel are virtually certain to use all the space each night.

Each room occupied has a variable cost of $5 per night (for cleaning, laundry, lost linens, and extra electricity).

The hotel manager expects an 85% occupancy rate for the year, so she is reluctant to sign the contract.

REQUIRED:

1. Compute the total contribution margin for the year with and without the contract.
2. Compute the lowest room rate that the hotel should accept on the contract so that the total contribution margin would be the same with or without the contract.

5–19. **Special air fares.** The manager of operations of United Airlines is trying to decide whether to adopt a new discount fare. Focus on one 134-seat 727-200 airplane now operating at a 55.2% load factor. That is, on the average the airplane has $.552 \times 134 = 74$ passengers. The regular fares produce an average revenue of 12¢ per passenger mile.

Suppose an average 40% fare discount (which is subject to restrictions regarding time of departure and length of stay) will produce three new additional passengers. Also suppose that three of the previously committed passengers accept the restrictions and switch to the discount fare from the regular fare.

REQUIRED:

1. Compute the total revenue per airplane mile with and without the discount fares.
2. Suppose the maximum allowed allocation to new discount fares is 46 seats. These will be filled. As before, some previously committed passengers will

accept the restrictions and switch to the discount fare from the regular fare. How many will have to switch so that the total revenue per mile will be the same either with or without the discount plan?

5–20. Relevant cost and special order. Confirmation Quality Company's *unit* costs of manufacturing and selling a given item at an activity level of 10,000 units per *month* are:

Manufacturing costs:	
Direct materials	$2.00
Direct labor	2.50
Variable overhead	0.80
Fixed overhead	1.20
Selling expenses:	
Variable	3.00
Fixed	0.80

The unit selling price is $11.

REQUIRED:

Ignore income taxes in all requirements. These four parts have no connection with each other.

1. Compute the *annual* net income at a selling price of $11 per unit.
2. Compute the expected *annual* net income if the volume can be increased by 20% when the selling price is reduced by $1. Assume the implied cost behavior patterns are correct.
3. The company desires to seek an order for 5,000 units from a foreign customer. The variable selling expenses will be reduced by 40%, but the fixed costs for obtaining the order will be $3,500. Domestic sales will not be affected. Compute the minimum break-even price per unit to be considered.
4. The company has an inventory of 2,000 units of this item left over from last year's model. These must be sold through *regular channels* at reduced prices. The inventory will be valueless unless sold this way. What unit cost is relevant for establishing the minimum selling price of these 2,000 units?

5–21. Make or buy. McCain Company manufactures automobile parts. It frequently subcontracts work to other manufacturers, depending on whether McCain's facilities are fully occupied. McCain is about to make some final decisions regarding the use of its manufacturing facilities for the coming year.

The following are the costs of making Part K426, a key component of an emission control system:

	TOTAL COST FOR 60,000 UNITS	COST PER UNIT
Direct material	$ 300,000	$ 5
Direct labor	480,000	8
Variable factory overhead	360,000	6
Fixed factory overhead	300,000	5
Total manufacturing costs	$1,440,000	$24

Another manufacturer has offered to sell the same part to McCain for $22 each. The fixed overhead consists of depreciation, property taxes, insurance, and supervisory salaries. All of the fixed overhead would continue if McCain bought the component except that the costs of $120,000 pertaining to some supervisory and custodial personnel could be avoided.

1. Assume that the capacity now used to make parts will become idle if the parts are purchased. Should the parts be made or bought? Show computations.
2. Assume that the capacity now used to make parts will either (a) be rented to a nearby manufacturer for $50,000 for the year or (b) be used to make carburetors that will yield a profit contribution of $80,000. Should Part K426 be made or bought? Show computations.

5–22. **Conceptual approach.** A large automobile-parts plant was constructed four years ago in an Ohio city served by two railroads. The PC Railroad purchased forty specialized 60-foot freight cars as a direct result of the additional traffic generated by the new plant. The investment was based on an estimated useful life of twenty years.

Now the competing railroad has offered to service the plant with new 86-foot freight cars, which would enable more efficient shipping operations at the plant. The automobile company has threatened to switch carriers unless PC Railroad buys ten new 86-foot freight cars.

The PC marketing management wants to buy the new cars, but PC operating management says: "The new investment is undesirable. It really consists of the new outlay plus the loss on the old freight cars. The old cars must be written down to a low salvage value if they cannot be used as originally intended."

Evaluate the comments. What is the correct conceptual approach to the quantitative analysis in this decision?

5–23. **Meaning of allocation of joint costs.**

1. Examine the illustration on joint costs that appears on pp. 120–123. Suppose the joint costs were allocated on the basis of liters. Prepare an income statement by product line on the assumption that Product Y was (a) sold at split-off or (b) processed further.
2. Repeat Requirement 1, assuming that the joint costs were allocated on the basis of net realizable values (relative sales values) at split-off.
3. Which set of income statements is more meaningful, those in Requirement 1 or in 2? Why?

5–24. **Joint products.** (CPA.) From a particular joint process, Watkins Company produces three products, X, Y, and Z. Each product may be sold at the point of split-off or processed further. Additional processing requires no special facilities, and production costs of further processing are entirely variable and traceable to the products involved. In 19X3 all three products were processed beyond split-off. Joint production costs for the year were $60,000. Sales values and costs needed to evaluate Watkin's 19X3 production policy follow:

| PRODUCT | UNITS PRODUCED | NET REALIZABLE VALUES (SALES VALUES) AT SPLIT-OFF | ADDITIONAL COSTS AND SALES VALUES IF PROCESSED FURTHER | |
			Sales Values	Added Costs
X	6,000	$25,000	$42,000	$9,000
Y	4,000	41,000	45,000	7,000
Z	2,000	24,000	32,000	8,000

Joint costs are allocated to the products in proportion to the relative physical volume of output. Answer the following multiple-choice questions:

1. For units of Z, the unit production cost most relevant to a sell-or-process-further decision is (a) $5, (b) $12, (c) $4, (d) $9.
2. To maximize profits, Watkins should subject the following products to additional processing: (a) X only, (b) X, Y, and Z, (c) Y and Z only, (d) Z only.

5–25. Joint costs. Two products, A and B, had been allocated $30,000 of joint costs each, using the net-realizable-value method. Net realizable value is the ultimate selling price less separable costs of completion and marketing. The products' ultimate sales values were $70,000 and $90,000, respectively. The separable costs for A were $20,000. What were the separable costs for B?

5–26. Joint products: sell or process further. The Burns Company produced three joint products at a joint cost of $100,000. These products were processed further and sold as follows:

PRODUCT	SALES	ADDITIONAL PROCESSING COSTS
A	$245,000	$200,000
B	330,000	300,000
C	175,000	100,000

The company has had an opportunity to sell at split-off directly to other processors. If that alternative had been selected, sales would have been: A, $56,000; B, $28,000; and C, $56,000.

The company expects to operate at the same level of production and sales in the forthcoming year.

REQUIRED:

Consider all the available information, and assume that all costs incurred after split-off are variable.

1. Could the company increase operating income by altering its processing decisions? If so, what would be the expected overall operating income?
2. Which products should be processed further and which should be sold at split-off?

5–27. Joint costs and decisions. A petrochemical company has a batch process whereby 1,000 gallons of a raw material are transformed into 100 pounds of X-1 and 400 pounds of X-2. Although the joint costs of their production are $900, both products are worthless at their split-off point. Additional separable costs of $250 are necessary to give X-1 a sales value of $750 as Product A. Similarly, additional separable costs of $100 are necessary to give X-2 a sales value of $750.

REQUIRED:

You are in charge of the batch process and the marketing of both products. (Show your computations for each answer.)

1. a. Assuming that you believe in assigning joint costs on a physical basis, allocate the total profit of $250 per batch to Products A and B.
   b. Would you stop processing one of the products? Why?
2. a. Assuming that you believe in assigning joint costs on a net-realizable-value (relative-sales-value) basis, allocate the total operating profit of $250 per batch to Products A and B. If there is no market for X-1 and X-2 at their split-off point, a net realizable value is usually imputed by taking the ultimate sales values at the point of sale and working backward to obtain approximated "synthetic" relative sales values at the split-off point. These synthetic values are then used as weights for allocating the joint costs to the products.
   b. You have internal product-profitability reports in which joint costs are assigned on a net-realizable-value basis. Your chief engineer says that, after seeing these reports, he has developed a method of obtaining more of Product B and correspondingly less of Product A from each batch, without changing the per-pound cost factors. Would you approve this new

method? Why? What would the overall operating profit be if 50 more pounds of B were produced and 50 less pounds of A?

5-28. Joint costs and incremental analysis. (CMA.) Helene's, a high-fashion women's dress manufacturer, is planning to market a new cocktail dress for the coming season. Helene's supplies retailers in the east and mid-Atlantic states.

Four yards of material are required to lay out the dress pattern. Some material remains after cutting, which can be sold as remnants.

The leftover material could also be used to manufacture a matching cape and handbag. However, if the leftover material is to be used for the cape and handbag, more care will be required in the cutting, which will increase the cutting costs.

The company expected to sell 1,250 dresses if no matching cape or handbag were available. Helene's market research reveals that dress sales will be 20% higher if a matching cape and handbag are available. The market research indicates that the cape and/or handbag will not be sold individually but only as accessories with the dress. The various combinations of dresses, capes, and handbags which are expected to be sold by retailers are as follows:

	PERCENT OF TOTAL
Complete sets of dress, cape, and handbag	70%
Dress and cape	6
Dress and handbag	15
Dress only	9
Total	100%

The material used in the dress costs $12.50 a yard, or $50.00 for each dress. The cost of cutting the dress if the cape and handbag are not manufactured is estimated at $20.00 a dress, and the resulting remnants can be sold for $5.00 for each dress cut out. If the cape and handbag are to be manufactured, the cutting costs will be increased by $9.00 per dress. There will be no salable remnants if the capes and handbags are manufactured in the quantities estimated.

The selling prices and the costs to complete the three items once they are cut are:

	SELLING PRICE PER UNIT	UNIT COST TO COMPLETE (EXCLUDES COST OF MATERIAL AND CUTTING OPERATION)
Dress	$200.00	$80.00
Cape	27.50	19.50
Handbag	9.50	6.50

REQUIRED:

1. Calculate Helene's incremental profit or loss from manufacturing the capes and handbags in conjunction with the dresses.
2. Identify any nonquantitative factors which could influence Helene's management in its decision to manufacture the capes and handbags which match the dress.

5-29. Book value of old equipment. (Alternates are 5-1 and 5-33.) Consider the following data:

	OLD EQUIPMENT	PROPOSED NEW EQUIPMENT
Original cost	$20,000	$13,500
Useful life in years	8	3
Current age in years	5	0
Useful life remaining in years	3	3
Accumulated depreciation	$12,500	0
Book value	7,500	*
Disposal value (in cash) now	4,000	*
Annual cash operating costs	0	0
(maintenance, power, repairs, lubricants, etc.)	$ 7,000	$ 3,000

*Not acquired yet.

REQUIRED:

1. Prepare a cost comparison of all relevant items for the next three years together.
2. Prepare a cost comparison that includes both relevant and irrelevant items.
3. Prepare a comparative statement of the total charges against revenue for the first year. Would the manager be inclined to buy the new equipment? Explain.

5–30. **New machine.** A new $200,000 machine is expected to have a four-year life and a terminal value of zero. It can produce 80,000 units a year at a variable cost of $2 per unit. The variable cost is $3 per unit with an old machine, which has a book value of $80,000. It is being depreciated on a straight-line basis at $20,000 per year. It too is expected to have a terminal value of zero. Its current disposal value is also zero because it is highly specialized equipment.

The salesman of the new machine prepared the following comparison:

	NEW MACHINE	OLD MACHINE
Units	80,000	80,000
Variable costs	$160,000	$240,000
Straight-line depreciation	50,000	20,000
Total cost	$210,000	$260,000
Unit cost	$ 2.625	$ 3.25

He said, "The new machine is obviously a worthwhile acquisition. You will save 62½¢ for every unit you produce."

REQUIRED:

1. Do you agree with the salesman's analysis? If not, how would you change it? Be specific.
2. Prepare an analysis of total and unit costs if the annual volume is 40,000 units.
3. At what annual volume would both the old and new machines have the same total relevant costs?

Relevant Costs and Special Decisions— Part Two

141

5–31. **Make or buy.** The Rohr Company's old equipment for making subassemblies is worn out. The company is considering two courses of action: (a) completely replacing the old equipment with new equipment, or (b) buying subassemblies from a reliable outside supplier, who has quoted a unit price of $1 on a seven-year contract for a minimum of 50,000 units per year.

Production was 60,000 units in each of the past two years. Future needs for the next seven years are not expected to fluctuate beyond 50,000 to 70,000 units per year. Cost records for the past two years reveal the following unit costs of manufacturing the subassembly:

Direct material	$ .25
Direct labor	.40
Variable overhead	.10
Fixed overhead (including $.10 depreciation and $.10 for direct departmental fixed overhead)	.25
	$1.00

The new equipment will cost $188,000 cash, will last seven years, and will have a disposal value of $20,000. The current disposal value of the old equipment is $10,000.

The salesman for the new equipment has summarized his position as follows: The increase in machine speeds will reduce direct labor and variable overhead by 35¢ per unit. Consider last year's experience of one of your major competitors with identical equipment. They produced 100,000 units under operating conditions very comparable to yours and showed the following unit costs:

Direct material	$.25
Direct labor	.10
Variable overhead	.05
Fixed overhead, including depreciation of $.24	.40
	$.80

REQUIRED:

For purposes of this case, assume that any idle facilities cannot be put to alternative use. Also assume that 5¢ of the old Rohr unit cost is allocated fixed overhead that will be unaffected by the decision.

1. The president asks you to compare the alternatives on a total-annual-cost basis and on a per-unit basis for annual needs of 60,000 units. Which alternative seems more attractive?
2. Would your answer to Requirement 1 change if the needs were 50,000 units? 70,000 units? At what volume level would Rohr be indifferent between make and buy? Show your computations.
3. What factors, other than the above, should the accountant bring to the attention of management to assist them in making their decision? Include the considerations that might be applied to the outside supplier.

For additional analysis, see Problem 11–46.

5–32. **Relevant costs of auto ownership.** Joan Robbins, a dairy inspector for the state of Wisconsin, used her private automobile for work purposes and was reimbursed by the state at a rate of 22¢ per mile. Robbins was unhappy about the rate, so she was particularly interested in a publication of the Federal Highway Administration, "The Cost of Owning and Operating an Automobile." The publication contained a "work sheet for first-year auto costs":

```
   1. Amount paid for your car .......................  $ .........
   2. First-year mileage .............................    .........
   3. First-year depreciation .........................  $ .........
   4. Insurance ....................................  $ .........
   5. License, other fees or taxes ....................  $ .........
   6. Interest on auto loan ...........................  $ .........
   7. Maintenance, repairs, tires .....................  $ .........
   8. Fuel and oil ..................................  $ .........
   9. Parking, garaging, tolls .......................  $ .........
  10. Total of Lines 3 through 9 ......................  $ .........
  11. Line 10 divided by Line 2 .......................  $ .........
      Line 11 is your first-year per-mile cost.
```

Robbins paid $9,000 for her new car. She expected to drive it 20,000 miles per year. The highway administration work sheet calls for depreciation at 33% of original cost for the first year, 25% the second year, and 20% the third year.

Insurance is $400. License and other fees amount to $200. Interest on her $6,000 auto loan is $720 for the first year, $480 for the second year, and $240 for the third year. The highway booklet said that the following charges might be expected for maintenance for every 10,000 miles: $120 for the first year, $240 for the second year, and $480 for the third year. Parking and tolls would cost an average of 1¢ per mile, and fuel and oil 6¢ per mile.

REQUIRED:

1. Compute the total first-year cost of automobile ownership. Compute the cost per mile if the following miles were driven: 10,000, 20,000, and 30,000.
2. Is the reimbursement rate of 22¢ a "fair" rate?
3. Joan and a friend use her car for a 400-mile journey. They agree in advance "to split the costs of using the car, fifty-fifty." How much should Joan's friend pay?
4. What if Joan had paid cash for her car rather than borrowed $6,000? Would the costs change? By how much? Explain.
5. Suppose Joan was thinking of buying a second car exactly like the first and on the same financial terms, but she would confine the second car to personal use of 5,000 miles per year. The total mileage of the two cars taken together would still be 20,000 miles. What would be the first-year cost of operating a second car? The average unit cost? What costs are relevant? Why?
6. Robbins has owned the car one year. She has switched to a local job that does not require a car. What costs are relevant to the question of selling the car and using other means of transportation?

5–33. **Role of old equipment in replacement.** (Alternates are 5–1 and 5–29.) On January 2, 19X1, the Buxton Company installed a brand-new $81,000 special molding machine for producing a new product. The product and the machine have an expected life of three years. The machine's expected disposal value at the end of three years is zero.

On January 3, 19X1, Jim Swain, a star salesman for a machine tool manufacturer, tells Mr. Buxton: "I wish I had known earlier of your purchase plans. I can supply you with a technically superior machine for $100,000. The old machine can be sold for $16,000. I guarantee that our machine will save $35,000 per year in cash operating costs, although it too will have no disposal value at the end of three years."

Mr. Buxton examines some technical data. Although he had confidence in Swain's claims, Buxton contends: "I'm locked in now. My alternatives are clear: (a) disposal will result in a loss; (b) keeping and using the 'old' equipment avoids such a loss. I have brains enough to avoid a loss when my other alternative is recognizing a loss. We've got to use that equipment till we get our money out of it."

The annual operating costs of the old machine are expected to be $60,000, exclusive of depreciation. Sales, all in cash, will be $900,000 per year. Other annual cash expenses will be $800,000 regardless of this decision. Assume that the equipment in question is the company's only fixed asset. Note that the facts in this problem are probed more deeply in Problems 11–33 and 12–36.

REQUIRED:

Ignore income taxes and the time value of money.

1. Prepare statements of cash receipts and disbursements as they would appear in each of the next three years under both alternatives. What is the total net difference in cash flow for the three years?
2. Prepare income statements as they would appear in each of the next three years under both alternatives. Assume straight-line depreciation. What is the total difference in net income for the three years?
3. Assume that the cost of the "old" equipment was $1 million rather than $81,000. Would the net difference computed in Requirements 1 and 2 change? Explain.
4. As Jim Swain, reply to Buxton's contentions.
5. What are the irrelevant items in each of your presentations for Requirements 1 and 2? Why are they irrelevant?

5–34. Decision and performance models. (Alternate is 5–2.) Refer to the preceding problem.

1. Suppose the "decision model" favored by top management consisted of a comparison of a three-year accumulation of wealth under each alternative. Which alternative would you choose? Why? (Accumulation of wealth means cumulative increase in cash.)
2. Suppose the "performance evaluation model" emphasized the net income of a subunit (such as a division) each year rather than considering each project, one by one. Which alternative would you choose? Why?
3. Suppose the same quantitative data existed, but the "enterprise" was a post office of the U.S. Postal Service. Would your answers to the first two parts change? Why?

5–35. Relevant-cost analysis. Following are the unit costs of making and selling a single product at a normal level of 5,000 units per month and a current unit selling price of $75:

Manufacturing costs:	
Direct material	$20
Direct labor	12
Variable overhead	8
Fixed overhead	
(total for the year, $300,000)	5
Selling and administrative expenses:	
Variable	15
Fixed (total for the year, $540,000)	9

REQUIRED:

Consider each requirement separately. Label all computations, and present your solutions in a form that will be comprehensible to the company president.

1. This product is usually sold at a rate of 60,000 units per year. It is predicted that a rise in price to $80 will decrease volume by 5%. How much may advertising be increased under this plan without having annual net profit fall below the current level?
2. The company has received a proposal from an outside supplier to make and ship this item directly to the company's customers as sales orders are forwarded. Variable selling and administrative costs would fall 40%. If the supplier's proposal is accepted, the company will use its own plant to produce a

CHAPTER 5
144

new product. The new product would be sold through manufacturer's agents at a 10% commission based on a selling price of $20 each. The cost characteristics of this product, based on predicted yearly normal volume, are as follows:

	PER UNIT
Direct material	$ 3
Direct labor	6
Variable overhead	4
Fixed overhead	3
Manufacturing costs	$16
Selling and administrative expenses:	
Variable	10% of selling price
Fixed	$ 1

What is the maximum price per unit that the company can afford to pay to the supplier for subcontracting the entire old product? Assume the following:

a. Total fixed factory overhead and total fixed selling expenses will not change if the new product line is added.

b. The supplier's proposal will not be considered unless the present annual net income can be maintained.

c. Selling price of the old product will remain unchanged.

THE MASTER BUDGET: THE OVERALL PLAN

Learning Objectives

When you have finished studying this chapter, you should be able to

1. Define **budget** and identify its major advantages to an organization

2. Distinguish between master budgets and capital budgets

3. Distinguish between operating budgets and financial budgets

4. List the principal steps in preparing a master budget

5. Construct the supporting schedules and main statements for a master budget

6. Identify the two primary uses of a financial-planning model

Management—and many investors and bank loan officers—have become increasingly aware of the merits of formal business plans. This chapter provides a condensed view of the overall business plan for the forthcoming year (or less)—the master budget. The major technical work of the budgetary accountant involves expected future data rather than historical data. There is also a major philosophical difference: The advocates of budgeting maintain that the process of preparing the budget forces executives to become better administrators. Budgeting puts planning where it belongs—in the forefront of the manager's mind.

This chapter provides a bird's-eye view of planning for the organization as a whole. We will see that planning requires all the functions of a business to blend together. We will see the importance of an accurate sales forecast. Most of all, we should begin to appreciate why budgeting is helpful. Budgeting is primarily attention directing because it helps managers to focus on operating or financial problems early enough for effective planning or action.

This book stresses how accounting helps the *operating* performance of management (how effectively assets are acquired and utilized). But the *financing* function (how funds for investment in assets are obtained) is also important. That is why this chapter examines cash budgets as well as operating budgets. Successful organizations are usually characterized by both superior operating management *and* superior financial management. Business failures are frequently traceable to management's shirking of the financial aspects of its responsibilities.

CHARACTERISTICS OF BUDGETS

☐ Definition of Budget

A budget is a formal quantitative expression of management plans. The master budget summarizes the goals of all subunits of an organization—sales, production, distribution, and finance. It quantifies targets for sales, production, net income, and cash position, and for any other objective that management specifies. The master budget usually consists of a statement of expected future income, a balance sheet, a statement of cash receipts and disbursements, a statement of changes in financial position, and supporting schedules. These statements are the culmination of a series of planning decisions arising from a detailed, rigorous look at the organization's future.

Of course, budgets can also be used on an individual level. For instance, a student may budget in a detailed or general way regarding food for the coming week or month, hours of study before examinations, and so forth.

☐ Advantages of Budgets

Many skeptics who have never used budgets are quick to state, "I suppose budgeting is okay for the other fellow's business, but *my* business is different. There are too many uncertainties and complications to make budgeting worthwhile for me." But the same managers, when prodded for details, usually reveal that they are planning incessantly, but in an informal way. Perhaps the best way to combat such a short-sighted attitude is to name others in the same industry who are zealous about budgeting and who, inevitably, are among the industry's leaders. An organization that adopts formal budgeting usually becomes rapidly convinced of its helpfulness and would not consider regressing to its old-fashioned, nonbudgeting days. The benefits of budgeting almost always clearly outweigh the cost and the effort.

Some kind of budget program is bound to be useful to any organization, regardless of its size or its uncertainties. The major benefits are:

1. Budgeting, by formalizing the managers' responsibilities for planning, compels them to think ahead.
2. Budgeting provides definite expectations that are the best framework for judging subsequent performance.
3. Budgeting aids managers in coordinating their efforts, so that the objectives of the organization as a whole harmonize with the objectives of its parts.

❏ Formalization of Planning

The principal advantage of budgeting is probably that it forces managers to think ahead—to anticipate and prepare for changing conditions. The budgeting process makes planning an explicit management responsibility. Too often, managers operate from day to day, extinguishing one business brush fire after another. They simply have no time for any tough-minded thinking beyond the next day's problems. Planning takes a back seat or is actually obliterated by workaday pressures.

The trouble with the day-to-day approach to managing an organization is that objectives are never crystallized. Without goals, company operations lack direction, problems are not foreseen, and results are hard to interpret. Advocates of budgeting correctly maintain that most business emergencies can be avoided by careful planning.

In an interview published in the *San Francisco Chronicle*, May 27, 1983, Carl E. Reichardt, chief executive officer of Wells Fargo, commented:

❏ I say our budget is the most important thing we do. I like to have all the debates over with when it is adopted. I'm not too sympathetic about hearing a lot of excuses after the fact. If budget planning is done well, there is no room for infighting and personality conflicts.

❏ Expectations as a Framework for Judging Performance

As a basis for judging actual results, budgeted goals and performance are generally regarded as being more appropriate than past performance. The news that a company had sales of $10 million this year, as compared with $8 million the previous year, may or may not indicate that the company has been effective and has achieved maximum success. Perhaps sales should have been $11 million this year. The major drawback of using historical data for judging performance is that inefficiencies may be concealed in the past performance. Moreover, the usefulness of comparisons with the past is also limited by intervening changes in economic conditions, technology, competitive maneuvers, personnel, and so forth.

Another benefit of budgeting is that key personnel are informed of what is expected of them. Nobody likes to drift along, not knowing what his or her boss expects or hopes to achieve.

Coordination and Communication

Coordination is the meshing and balancing of an organization's resources so that its overall objectives are attained—so that the goals of the individual manager harmonize with goals of the organization as a whole. The budget is the means for communicating overall objectives and for blending the objectives of all departments.

Coordination requires, for example, that purchasing officers integrate their plans with production requirements, and that production officers use the sales budget to help them anticipate and plan for the employees and plant facilities they will require. The budgetary process obliges executives to visualize the relationship of their department to other departments, and to the company as a whole.

A budget is not a cure-all for existing organizational ills. It will not solve the problems created by a bumbling management or a faulty information system. The budget is a device whose value depends on its being administered astutely in conjunction with an information system that is attuned to a coordinated organization.

HUMAN RELATIONS

Middle management's attitude toward budgets will be heavily influenced by the attitude of top management. The chief executives must offer whole-hearted support if a budgetary program is to achieve maximum benefits.

The ability to adhere to a budget is often an important factor in judging a manager's performance, and naturally, budgets are usually not the most popular aspect of a manager's professional life. Budgets pinpoint a manager's performance and direct his or her superior's attention to trouble spots. Few individuals are ecstatic about any techniques used by the boss to check their performance. Budgets are therefore sometimes regarded by middle management as embodiments of nickel-nursing, restrictive, negative top-management attitudes.

These misconceptions can be overcome by persuasive education and salesmanship. The budget should not be an unpleasant instrument for harassing the employee. Properly used, it will be a positive aid in setting standards of performance, in motivating toward goals, in metering results, and in directing attention to the areas that need investigation. *The budget is inanimate*; however, its administration is a delicate task because everyone it affects must understand and accept the notion that the budget is primarily designed to help, not hinder.

The supreme importance of the human relations aspects of budgeting cannot be overemphasized. Too often, top management and its accountants are overly concerned with the mechanics of budgets, whereas the effectiveness of any budgeting system depends directly on whether the managers it affects understand it and accept it. Ideally, managers should be cooperative and cost-conscious. Budgets that are imposed upon managers tend to be less effective than budgets that are formulated with the active participation of managers. This subject is explored more fully in Chapters 9 and 10.

TYPES OF BUDGETS

❑ Time Span

The planning horizon for budgeting can vary from a year (or less) to many years, depending on budget objectives and on the uncertainties involved. Long-range budgets, called *capital budgets,* are often prepared for particular projects such as equipment purchases, locations of plant, and additions of product lines. **Master budgets,** which consolidate an organization's overall plans for a shorter span of time, are usually prepared on an annual basis. The annual budget may be subdivided on a month-to-month basis, or perhaps on a monthly basis for the first quarter and on a quarterly basis for the three remaining quarters.

※ **Continuous budgets** are increasingly being used. These are master budgets that perpetually add a month in the future as the month just ended is dropped. Continuous budgets are desirable because they compel managers to think specifically about the forthcoming twelve months and thus maintain a stable planning horizon.

❑ Classification of Budgets

The terms used to describe assorted budget schedules vary from company to company. Sometimes budgets are called **pro-forma statements** because they are forecasted financial statements, in contrast to statements of actual results.

The master budget, accompanied by subsidiary schedules, can be classified as follows:

A. Operating budget
   1. Sales budget
   2. Production budget (for manufacturing companies)
      a. Materials used and material purchases
      b. Direct labor
      c. Indirect manufacturing costs (factory overhead)
      d. Changes in inventory levels
   3. Cost-of-goods-sold budget (for merchandising and manufacturing companies)
   4. Selling-expense budget
   5. Administrative-expense budget
   6. Budgeted income statement

B. Financial budget
  1. Capital budgets (long-range expectations for specific projects)
  2. Cash budget: cash receipts and disbursements
  3. Budgeted balance sheet
  4. Budgeted statement of changes in financial position or budgeted statement of sources and applications of funds

Exhibit 6-1 presents a condensed diagram of the various parts of the master budget for a nonmanufacturing company. The two major parts of the master budget are the operating budget and the financial budget. The **operating budget** focuses on the income statement and its supporting schedules. The **financial budget** focuses on the effect that the operating budget and other plans (such as capital expenditures and repayments of debt) will have on cash.

In addition to the master budget there are countless forms of special budgets and related reports. For example, a report might be prepared containing various cost-volume-profit forecasts that might be encountered, depending on assorted management decisions and economic conditions.

EXHIBIT
6-1

Master
Budget for
Nonmanu-
facturing
Company

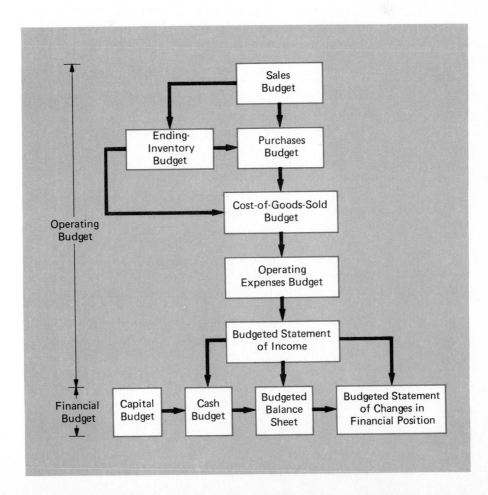

❏ Description of Problem

Try to prepare the budget schedules required for the solution of this illustrative problem. Use the basic steps described after the problem. Do not rush. This is a comprehensive illustration that will require some step-by-step thinking and some reflection before a full understanding can be achieved. Although this illustration may seem largely mechanical, remember that the master-budgeting process generates key decisions regarding pricing, product lines, capital expenditures, research and development, personnel assignments, and so forth. Therefore the first draft of a budget leads to decisions that prompt subsequent drafts before a final budget is chosen. Suppose R Company is a retailer of a wide variety of household items. The company rents a number of retail stores and also has a local door-to-door sales force.

The R Company's newly hired accountant has persuaded management to prepare a budget to aid financial and operating decisions. Because this is the company's first attempt at formal budgeting, the planning horizon is only four months, April through July. In the past, sales have increased during the spring season. Collections lag behind and cash is needed for purchases, wages, and other operating outlays. In the past, the company has met this cash squeeze with the help of six-month loans from banks.

Exhibit 6-2 is the closing balance sheet for the fiscal year just ended. Sales in March were $40,000. Monthly sales are forecasted as follows:

April	$50,000	July	$50,000
May	$80,000	August	$40,000
June	$60,000		

Sales consist of 60% cash and 40% credit. All credit accounts are collected in the month following the sales. The $16,000 of accounts receivable on March 31 represents credit sales made in March (40% of $40,000). Uncollectible accounts are negligible and are to be ignored.

At the end of any month, the R Company wishes to maintain a basic inventory of $20,000 plus 80% of the cost of goods to be sold in the following month. The cost of merchandise sold averages 70% of sales. Therefore the inventory, on March 31, is $20,000 + .8 (.7 × April sales of $50,000) = $20,000 + $28,000 = $48,000. The purchase terms available to the R Company are net, 30 days. A given month's purchases are paid as follows: 50% during that month and 50% during the next month.

Wages and commissions are paid semimonthly, half a month after they are earned. They are divided into two portions: monthly fixed wages of $2,500 and commissions, equal to 15% of sales, which are uniform throughout each month. Therefore the March 31 balance of Accrued Wages and Commissions Payable consists of (.5 × $2,500) + .5 (.15 × $40,000) = $1,250 + $3,000 = $4,250. This $4,250 will be paid on April 15. A used delivery truck will be purchased for $3,000 cash in April.

EXHIBIT
6-2

R COMPANY
Balance Sheet
March 31, 19X1

ASSETS

Current assets:		
Cash	$10,000	
Accounts receivable,		
net (.4 × March sales of $40,000)	16,000	
Merchandise inventory,		
$20,000 + .8 (.7 × April sales of $50,000)	48,000	
Unexpired insurance	1,800	$ 75,800
Plant assets:		
Equipment, fixtures, and other	$37,000	
Accumulated depreciation	12,800	24,200
Total assets		$100,000

EQUITIES

Current liabilities:		
Accounts payable		
(.5 × March purchases of $33,600)	$16,800	
Accrued wages and commissions payable		
($1,250 + $3,000)	4,250	$ 21,050
Owners' equity		78,950
Total equities		$100,000

Other monthly expenses are:

Miscellaneous expenses	5% of sales, paid as incurred
Rent	$2,000, paid as incurred
Insurance	$200 expiration per month
Depreciation, including truck	$500

The company desires to maintain a minimum cash balance of $10,000 at the end of each month. Money can be borrowed or repaid in multiples of $1,000, at an interest rate of 18% per annum. Management does not want to borrow any more cash than necessary and wants to repay as promptly as possible. At the time the principal is repaid, interest is computed and paid only on the portion of principal that is repaid. Assume that borrowing takes place at the beginning, and repayment at the end, of the months in question.

Special note: By now it may be obvious that a basic knowledge of financial accounting (see Chapter 17) is necessary to cope with this illustrative problem.

1. Using the data given, prepare the following detailed schedules:
   a. Sales budget
   b. Cash collections from customers
   c. Purchases budget
   d. Disbursements for purchases
   e. Operating expense budget
   f. Disbursements for operating expenses

2. Using the data given and the schedules you have compiled, prepare the following major statements:
   a. Budgeted income statement for four months ending July 31, 19X1
   b. Budgeted statement of cash receipts and disbursements by months, including details of borrowings, repayments, and interest
   c. Budgeted balance sheet as of July 31, 19X1

For consistency with the numbering scheme used in this book, label your responses to Requirement 2 as Exhibits 6-3, 6-4, and 6-5, respectively. Note that Schedules *a*, *c*, and *e* will be needed to prepare Exhibit 6-3, and Schedules *b*, *d*, and *f* will be needed to prepare Exhibit 6-4.

❏ Basic Steps in Preparing Operating Budget

The basic steps in preparing budgeted income statements follow. Use the steps to prepare your own schedules. Then examine the schedules in the Solution.

Step 1. The sales budget (Schedule *a*) is the starting point for budgeting, because inventory levels, purchases, and operating expenses are generally geared to the rate of sales activity. Trace the final column in Schedule *a* to Exhibit 6-3. In nonprofit organizations, forecasts of revenue or some level of services are also the focal point for budgeting. Examples are patient revenues expected by hospitals and donations to be received by churches. If no revenues are generated, as in the instances of municipal fire protection, a desired level of service is predetermined.

	MARCH	APRIL	MAY	JUNE	JULY	APRIL–JULY TOTAL
Schedule a: Sales Budget						
Credit sales, 40%	$16,000	$20,000	$32,000	$24,000	$20,000	
Cash sales, 60%	24,000	30,000	48,000	36,000	30,000	
Total sales, 100%	$40,000	$50,000	$80,000	$60,000	$50,000	$240,000
Schedule b: Cash Collections						
Cash sales this month		$30,000	$48,000	$36,000	$30,000	
100% of last month's credit sales		16,000	20,000	32,000	24,000	
Total collections		$46,000	$68,000	$68,000	$54,000	

Step 2. After sales are budgeted, the purchases budget (Schedule *c*) can be prepared. The total merchandise needed will be the sum of the desired ending inventory plus the amount needed to fulfill budgeted sales demand. The total need will be partially met by the beginning inventory; the remainder must come from planned purchases. Therefore these purchases are computed as follows: Purchases = Desired ending inventory + Cost of goods sold − Beginning inventory. Trace the final column of Schedule *c* to Exhibit 6-3, p. 156.

	MARCH	APRIL	MAY	JUNE	JULY	APRIL–JULY TOTAL
Schedule c: Purchases Budget						
Ending inventory	$48,000	$64,800	$ 53,600	$48,000	$42,400	
Cost of goods sold	28,000*	35,000	56,000	42,000	35,000	$168,000
Total needed	$76,000	$99,800	$109,600	$90,000	$77,400	
Beginning inventory	42,400†	48,000	64,800	53,600	48,000	
Purchases	$33,600	$51,800	$ 44,800	$36,400	$29,400	
Schedule d: Disbursements for Purchases						
50% of last month's purchases		$16,800	$ 25,900	$22,400	$18,200	
50% of this month's purchases		25,900	22,400	18,200	14,700	
Disbursements for merchandise		$42,700	$ 48,300	$40,600	$32,900	

*.7 × March sales of $40,000 = $28,000.
†$20,000 + .8(.7 × March sales of $40,000) = $20,000 + $22,400 = $42,400.

Step 3. The budgeting of operating expenses is dependent on various factors. Many operating expenses are directly influenced by month-to-month fluctuations in sales volume. Examples are sales commissions and delivery expenses. Other expenses are not directly influenced (e.g., rent, insurance, depreciation, certain types of payroll). In this solution, Schedule *e* summarizes these expenses. Trace the final column of Schedule *e* to Exhibit 6-3, the budgeted income statement.

	MARCH	APRIL	MAY	JUNE	JULY	APRIL–JULY TOTAL
Schedule e: Operating Expense Budget						
Wages, all fixed*	$ 2,500	$ 2,500	$ 2,500	$ 2,500	$ 2,500	
Commission (15% of current month's sales)	6,000	7,500	12,000	9,000	7,500	
Total wages and commissions	$ 8,500	$10,000	$14,500	$11,500	$10,000	$46,000
Miscellaneous expenses (5% of current month's sales)		2,500	4,000	3,000	2,500	12,000
Rent*		2,000	2,000	2,000	2,000	8,000
Insurance*		200	200	200	200	800
Depreciation*		500	500	500	500	2,000
Subtotal		$ 5,200	$ 6,700	$ 5,700	$ 5,200	$22,800
Total operating expenses		$15,200	$21,200	$17,200	$15,200	$68,800

*Monthly amounts are given in the statement of the problem.

	APRIL	MAY	JUNE	JULY
Schedule f: Disbursements for Operating Expenses:				
Wages and commissions:				
50% of last month's expenses	$ 4,250	$ 5,000	$ 7,250	$ 5,750
50% of this month's expenses	5,000	7,250	5,750	5,000
Total wages and commissions	$ 9,250	$12,250	$13,000	$10,750
Miscellaneous expenses	2,500	4,000	3,000	2,500
Rent	2,000	2,000	2,000	2,000
Total disbursements	$13,750	$18,250	$18,000	$15,250

Step 4. Steps 1 through 3 will provide enough information for a budgeted statement of income from operations (Exhibit 6-3). The income statement is complete except for interest expense, which cannot be computed until the cash budget is prepared.

☐ The Financial Budget

The second major part of the master budget is the financial budget, which consists of the capital budget, cash budget, ending balance sheet, and statement of changes in financial position. This chapter focuses on the cash budget and the ending balance sheet. Chapters 11 and 12 focus on the capital budget. In our illustration, the $3,000 purchase of the used truck

EXHIBIT
6-3

R COMPANY Budgeted Income Statement For the Four Months Ended July 31, 19X1			
		DATA	**SOURCE OF DATA**
Sales		$240,000	Schedule a
Cost of goods sold		168,000	Schedule c
Gross margin		$ 72,000	
Operating expenses:			
Wages and commissions	$46,000		Schedule e
Rent	8,000		Schedule e
Miscellaneous expenses	12,000		Schedule e
Insurance	800		Schedule e
Depreciation	2,000	68,800	Schedule e
Income from operations		$ 3,200	
Interest expense		675	Exhibit 6-4*
Net income		$ 2,525	

*For May, June, and July: $30 + $405 + $240 = $675.

would be included in the capital budget. The statement of changes in financial position (Chapter 18) is beyond the scope of this illustration.

❑ Basic Steps in Preparing Cash Budget

The **cash budget** is a statement of planned cash receipts and disbursements. It is heavily affected by the month-to-month effects that the level of operations summarized in the budgeted income statement will have on cash. The cash budget has the following major sections:

w. The beginning cash balance plus cash receipts yield the total cash available for needs, before financing. Cash receipts depend on collections from customers' accounts receivable and cash sales (Schedule b) and on other operating sources such as miscellaneous rental income. Trace Schedule b to Exhibit 6-4. Studies of the collectibility of accounts receivable are a prerequisite to accurate forecasting. Key factors include collection experience and average time lag between sales and collections.

x. Cash disbursements:
   (1) Purchases depend on the credit terms extended by suppliers and the bill-paying habits of the buyer (Schedule d, which should be traced to Exhibit 6-4).
   (2) Payroll depends on wage, salary, or commission terms and on payroll dates (Schedule f, which should be traced to Exhibit 6-4).
   (3) Other costs and expenses (Schedule f) depend on timing and credit terms. Note that depreciation and the expiration of insurance do not entail a cash outlay.
   (4) Other disbursements include outlays for fixed assets, long-term investments, installment payments on purchases, and the like. In this problem, the only "other disbursement" is $3,000 for the truck.

y. Financing requirements depend on how the total cash available w (in Exhibit 6-4) compares with the total cash needed. Needs include the disbursements x plus the ending cash balance z desired. The financing plans will depend on the relationship of cash available to cash sought. If there is an excess, loans may be repaid or temporary investments made. The pertinent outlays for

EXHIBIT 6-4

R COMPANY
Budgeted Statement of Cash Receipts and Disbursements
For the Four Months Ended July 31, 19X1

	APRIL	MAY	JUNE	JULY
Cash balance, beginning	$10,000	$10,550	$10,970	$10,965
Cash receipts:				
Collections from customers (Schedule **b**)	46,000	68,000	68,000	54,000
w.* Total cash available for needs, before financing	56,000	78,550	78,970	64,965
Cash disbursements:				
Merchandise (Schedule **d**)	42,700	48,300	40,600	32,900
Operating expenses (Schedule **f**)	13,750	18,250	18,000	15,250
Truck purchase (given)	3,000	—	—	—
x. Total disbursements	59,450	66,550	58,600	48,150
Minimum cash balance desired	10,000	10,000	10,000	10,000
Total cash needed	69,450	76,550	68,600	58,150
Excess (deficiency) of total cash available over total cash needed before current financing	(13,450)	2,000	10,370	6,815
Financing:				
Borrowings (at beginning)	14,000†			
Repayments (at end)	—	(1,000)	(9,000)	(4,000)
Interest (at 18% per annum)‡	—	(30)	(405)	(240)
y. Total effects of financing	14,000	(1,030)	(9,405)	(4,240)
z. Cash balance, ending (w + y − x)	$10,550	$10,970	$10,965	$12,575

Note: Expired insurance and depreciation do not entail cash outlays.

*Letters are keyed to the explanation in the text.

†Borrowings and repayments of principal are made in multiples of $1,000, at an interest rate of 18% per annum.

‡Interest computations: .18 × $1,000 × 2/12 = $30; .18 × $9,000 × 3/12 = $405; .18 × $4,000 × 4/12 = $240.

interest expenses are usually contained in this section of the cash budget. Trace the calculated interest expense to Exhibit 6-3, which will then be complete (ignoring income taxes).

z. The ending cash balance is $w + y - x$. Financing y may have a positive (borrowing) or a negative (repayment) effect on the cash balance. The illustrative cash budget shows the pattern of short-term, self-liquidating financing. Seasonal peaks often result in heavy drains on cash, for merchandise purchases and operating expenses, before the sales are made and cash is collected from customers. The resulting loan is self-liquidating—that is, the borrowed money is used to acquire merchandise for sale, and the proceeds from the sale are used to repay the loan. This "working-capital cycle" moves from cash to inventory to receivables and back to cash.

Cash budgets help management to avoid having unnecessary idle cash, on the one hand, and unnecessary nerve-racking cash deficiencies, on the other. An astutely mapped financing program keeps cash balances in reasonable relation to needs.

☐ Budgeted Balance Sheet

The final step is the preparation of the budgeted balance sheet (Exhibit 6-5). Each item is projected in accordance with the business plan as ex-

EXHIBIT 6-5

R COMPANY
Budgeted Balance Sheet
July 31, 19X1

ASSETS

Current assets:

Cash (Exhibit 6-4)	$12,575	
Accounts receivable (.40 × July sales of $50,000) (Schedule **a**)	20,000	
Merchandise inventory (Schedule **c**)	42,400	
Unexpired insurance ($1,800 old balance − $800 expired)	1,000	$ 75,975

Plant:

Equipment, fixtures, and other ($37,000 + truck, $3,000)	$40,000	
Accumulated depreciation ($12,800 + $2,000 depreciation)	14,800	25,200
Total assets		$101,175

EQUITIES

Current liabilities:

Accounts payable (.5 × July purchases of $29,400) (Schedule **d**)	$14,700	
Accrued wages and commissions payable (.5 × $10,000) (Schedule **e**)	5,000	$ 19,700
Owners' equity ($78,950 + $2,525 net income)		81,475
Total equities		$101,175

Note: Beginning balances were used as a start for the computations of unexpired insurance, plant, and owners' equity.

pressed in the previous schedules. Specifically, the beginning balances at March 31 would be increased or decreased in light of the expected cash receipts and disbursements in Exhibit 6-4 and in light of the effects of noncash items appearing on the income statement in Exhibit 6-3. For example, unexpired insurance of $1,800 (the balance on March 31) minus the $800 expiring over four months would affect the balance sheet, even though it is a noncash item.

When the complete master budget is formulated, management can consider all the major financial statements as a basis for changing the course of events. For example, the initial formulation may prompt management to try new sales strategies to generate more demand. Or management may explore the effects of various ways of adjusting the timing of receipts and disbursements. In any event, the first draft of the master budget is rarely the final draft. In this way, the budgeting process becomes an integral part of the management process itself in the sense that *planning* and *budgeting* are indistinguishable.

THE DIFFICULTIES OF SALES FORECASTING

As you have seen in the foregoing illustration, the sales forecast is the foundation of the entire master budget. The accuracy of estimated production schedules and of cost to be incurred depends on the detail and accuracy, in dollars and in units, of the forecasted sales.

The sales forecast is usually prepared under the direction of the top sales executive. All of the following factors are important: (1) past patterns of sales; (2) the estimates made by the sales force; (3) general economic and competitive conditions; (4) specific interrelationships of sales and economic indicators, such as gross national product or industrial production indexes; (5) changes in prices; (6) market research studies; and (7) advertising and sales promotion plans.

Sales forecasting usually combines various techniques. Opinions of the sales staff are sought. Statistical methods are often used. Correlations between sales and economic indicators help make sales forecasts more reliable. In most cases, the quantitative analysis provided by economists and members of the market research staff provide valuable help but not outright answers. The opinions of line management heavily influence the final setting of sales forecasts.

Pricing policies can have pronounced effects on sales. Management's assessment of price elasticities (the effect of price changes on the physical volume sold) will influence the sales forecast. A company may not offer the same unit price to all customers (because of differences in costs of serving different markets). In such cases, a detailed analysis of both units to be sold as well as dollar sales is needed for each price category before a final sales forecast can be aggregated.

Sales forecasting is still somewhat mystical, but its procedures are becoming more formal and are being viewed more seriously because of the intensity of competitive pressures. Although this book does not encompass a detailed discussion of the preparation of the sales budget, the importance of an accurate sales forecast cannot be overstressed.

In recent years, the formal use of statistical probabilities has been applied to the problem of sales forecasting. (See Chapter 16 for an elaboration.) Moreover, financial-planning models and simulation have enabled managers to get a quantitative grasp on the ramifications of various sales strategies.[1]

Governments and other nonprofit organizations also face a problem similar to sales forecasting. For example, the budget for city revenues may depend on a variety of items such as predicted property taxes, traffic fines, parking fees, and city income taxes. In turn, property taxes depend on the extent of new construction and general increases in real estate values. Thus the budget is based on a variety of assumptions and past results.

Financial-Planning Models and Simulation

In most cases, the master budget is the best practical approximation to a formal model of the total organization: its objectives, its inputs, and its outputs. If the master budget serves as a "total decision model" for top

[1] For a survey of forecasting techniques, see S. Makridakis and S. Wheelwright, "Forecasting: Issues & Challenges for Marketing Management," *Journal of Marketing*, October 1977, pp. 24–38. Also see Wheelwright and Makridakis, eds., *The Handbook of Forecasting—A Manager's Guide* (New York: John Wiley, 1982); and Makridakis, Wheelwright, and McGee, *Forecasting Methods and Applications*, 2nd ed. (New York: John Wiley, 1983).

management, then decisions about strategies for the forthcoming period may be formulated and altered during the budgetary process. Traditionally, this has been a step-by-step process whereby tentative plans are gradually revised as executives exchange views on various aspects of expected activities.

In the future, much of the interaction and interdependence of the decisions will probably be formalized in mathematical simulation models—"total models" that are sometimes called financial-planning models.[2] These models are mathematical statements of the relationships in the organization among all the operating and financial activities, and of other major internal and external factors that may affect decisions.

Financial models include all the ingredients for preparing a master budget. However, they can also be used for long-range planning decisions. For example, if managers want to predict the impact of adding a new product line, they can obtain budgeted financial statements for many future years. For instance, at Dow Chemical Company, 140 separate cost inputs, constantly revised, are fed into the model. Such factors as major raw-material costs and prices by country and region are monitored weekly. Multiple contingency plans rather than a single master plan are used more widely than before.[3]

Many models are constructed and working. They are used for budgeting, for revising budgets with little incremental effort, and for comparing a variety of decision alternatives as they affect the entire firm. The models speed the budgetary process because the sensitivity of income and cash flows to various decisions can be tested promptly via a simulation. Management can react quickly to events and to revisions in predictions of various aspects of operations. Moreover, mathematical probabilities can be incorporated into these models, so that uncertainty can be dealt with explicitly rather than informally.

The computer has enabled managers to shorten their reaction time. For example, at a New Jersey utility, Public Service Electric and Gas Company, the total corporate plan is run once a day, on average. Measures are generated of the financial impact on costs and equipment utilization of such business decisions as a cutback in fuel purchases during an unexpectedly warm winter week. Equally important is the speed of the computer. The executive vice-president said, "If an oil embargo were announced tomorrow, within 24 hours we would know the major impact of it and could begin reacting."[4]

Summary

The master budget expresses management's overall operating and financing plan. It outlines company objectives and steps for achieving them. The budgetary process compels managers to think ahead and to prepare for changing conditions. Budgets are aids in setting

[2] Vincent R. LoCascio, "Financial Planning Models," *Financial Executive*, Vol. 40, No. 3.
[3] "What-if Help for Management," *Business Week*, January 21, 1980, p. 73.
[4] "Computer Games That Planners Play," *Business Week*, December 18, 1978, p. 66.

standards of performance, motivating personnel toward goals, measuring results, and directing attention to the areas that most need investigation.

Summary Problem for Your Review

❏ Problem

Before attempting to solve the homework problems, review the R Company illustration in this chapter.

Highlights to Remember

1. Budgets deserve more respect than they usually receive. Some companies use different words to emphasize the positive nature of budgeting. They will refer to *profit planning* or *targeting* instead of plain old *budgeting.* Nevertheless, the nature of the process is the same regardless of the label.

2. For most organizations, budgets meet the cost-benefit test. That is, they are installed voluntarily because top management believes they can help managers throughout the organization.

3. The cornerstone of the budget is the sales forecast. All current operating and financial planning is generally tied to the expected volume of sales.

4. The human factors in budgeting are more important than the mechanics. Top management must support a budgetary program wholeheartedly. The job of educating personnel and selling them on the budget is everlasting, but essential, if those who are affected by the budget are to understand it and accept it. The master budget should be a powerful aid to the most crucial decisions of top management. Often it falls far short of that role because its potential is misunderstood. Instead of being regarded as a management tool, in many cases the budget is unfortunately looked upon as a necessary evil.

Accounting Vocabulary

Cash budget; continuous budget; financial budget; master budget; operating budget; pro-forma statements.

Fundamental Assignment Material

Special note: Problem 6-1 provides a single-problem review of the entire chapter. Those readers who prefer to concentrate on the fundamentals in smaller chunks should consider Problems 6-15, 6-16, 6-17, and 6-20 or 6-23.

6–1. Master budget.   (Alternates are 6-32 and 6-33.) A retailing subsidiary of a widely diversified company has a strong belief in using highly decentralized management. You are the new manager of one of its small "Apex" stores (Store No. 82). You know much about how to buy, how to display, how to sell, and how to reduce shoplifting. However, you know little about accounting and finance.

Top management is convinced that training for higher management should include the active participation of store managers in the budgeting process. You have been asked to prepare a complete master budget for your store for April, May, and June. You are responsible for its actual full preparation. All accounting is done centrally, so you have no expert help on the premises. In addition, tomorrow the branch manager and the assistant controller will be here to examine your work; at that time they will assist you in formulating the final budget document. The idea is to have you prepare the budget a few times so that you gain more confidence about accounting matters. You want to make a favorable impression on your superiors, so you gather the following data as of March 31, 19X1:

		RECENT AND PROJECTED SALES:	
Cash	$ 11,000		
Inventory	300,000		
Accounts receivable	261,000	February	$200,000
Net furniture and fixtures	150,000	March	250,000
Total assets	$722,000	April	500,000
		May	300,000
Accounts payable	$340,000	June	300,000
Owner's equity	382,000	July	200,000
Total equities	$722,000		

Credit sales are 90% of total sales. Credit accounts are collected 80% in the month following the sale and 20% in the next following month. Assume that bad debts are negligible and can be ignored. The accounts receivable on March 31 are the result of the credit sales for February and March: $(.20 \times .90 \times \$200,000 = \$36,000) + (1.00 \times .90 \times \$250,000 = \$225,000) = \$261,000$. The average gross profit on sales is 40%.

The policy is to acquire enough inventory each month to equal the following month's projected sales. All purchases are paid for in the month following purchase.

Salaries, wages, and commissions average 20% of sales; miscellaneous variable expenses, 4% of sales. Fixed expenses for rent, property taxes, and miscellaneous payroll and other items are $40,000 monthly. Assume that these expenses require cash disbursements each month. Depreciation is $2,000 monthly.

In April, $40,000 is going to be disbursed for fixtures acquired in March. The March 31 balance of accounts payable includes this amount.

Assume that a minimum cash balance of $10,000 is to be maintained. Also assume that all borrowings are effective at the beginning of the month and all repayments are made at the end of the month of repayment. Interest is paid only at the time of repaying principal. Interest rate is 8% per annum; round out interest computations to the nearest ten dollars. All loans and repayments of principal must be made in multiples of a thousand dollars.

REQUIRED:

1. Prepare a budgeted income statement for the coming quarter, a budgeted statement of monthly cash receipts and disbursements (for the next three months), and a budgeted balance sheet for June 30, 19X1. All operations are evaluated on a before-income-tax basis. Also, because income taxes are disbursed from corporate headquarters, they may be ignored here.
2. Explain why there is a need for a bank loan and what operating sources supply cash for repaying the bank loan.

Additional
Assignment Material_____

6–2. What factors influence the sales forecast?

6–3. "There are too many uncertainties and complications to make budgeting worthwhile in my business." Do you agree? Explain.

6–4. What is the major technical difference between historical and budgeted financial statements?

6–5. What are the major benefits of budgeting?

6–6. Why is budgeted performance better than past performance, as a basis for judging actual results?

6–7. What is *coordination?*

6–8. "Education and salesmanship are key features of budgeting." Explain.

6–9. "Capital budgets are plans for managing long-term debt and common stock." Do you agree? Explain.

6–10. "*Pro-forma* statements are those statements prepared in conjunction with continuous budgets." Do you agree? Explain.

6–11. What is the difference between an operating budget and a financial budget?

6–12. Why is the sales forecast the starting point for budgeting?

6–13. What is a self-liquidating loan?

6–14. What is the principal objective of a cash budget?

6–15. **Sales budget.** A retail store has the following data:

Accounts receivable, May 31: (.6 × May sales of $300,000) = $180,000.

Monthly forecasted sales: June, $250,000; July, $220,000; August, $280,000; September, $310,000.

Sales consist of 40% cash and 60% credit. All credit accounts are collected in the month following the sales. Uncollectible accounts are negligible and may be ignored.

REQUIRED: Prepare a sales budget schedule and a cash collections budget schedule for June, July, and August.

6–16. **Purchase budget.** A retail store plans the following inventory levels (at cost) at the end of

May, $170,000; June, $150,000; July, $190,000; August, $160,000

Sales are expected to be: June, $350,000; July, $250,000; August, $330,000. Cost of goods sold is 60% of sales.

Purchases in April had been $190,000; in May, $160,000. A given month's purchases are paid as follows: 10% during that month; 80% the next month; and the final 10% the next month.

REQUIRED: Prepare budget schedules for June, July, and August for purchases and for disbursements for purchases.

6–17. **Operating expenses budget.** A retail store has the following budgeted sales, which are uniform throughout the month:

May, $300,000; June, $250,000; July, $220,000; August, $280,000

Employees earn fixed salaries of $12,000 monthly and commissions of 10% of the current month's sales. Disbursements are made semimonthly, half a month after salaries and commissions are earned.

Other expenses are rent, $3,000, paid on the first of each month for that month's occupancy; miscellaneous expenses, 6% of sales, paid as incurred; insurance, $300 per month, related to a one-year policy that was paid for on January 2; and depreciation, $1,900 per month.

REQUIRED: Prepare budget schedules for June, July, and August for operating expenses and for disbursements for operating expenses.

6–18. Purchase budget. The inventory of a retail store was $160,000 on May 31. The manager was upset because the inventory was too high. She has adopted the following policies regarding merchandise purchases and inventory. At the end of any month, the inventory should be $10,000 plus 90% of the cost of goods to be sold during the following month. The cost of merchandise sold averages 60% of sales. Purchase terms are generally net, 30 days. A given month's purchases are paid as follows: 20% during that month and 80% during the following month.

Purchases in May had been $150,000. Sales are expected to be: June, $250,000; July, $220,000; August, $280,000; and September, $310,000.

REQUIRED:
1. Compute the amount by which the inventory on May 31 exceeded the manager's policies.
2. Prepare budget schedules for June, July, and August for purchases and for disbursements for purchases.

6–19. Inventory planning. Ramirez Company manufactures many furniture items, including four-legged tables for playing games. Each table is assembled from one square top, four legs, and eight supporting crosspieces (two between each pair of legs). The following data pertain to the budgeted production of tables for the fourth quarter of a given year. The budgeted sales are 18,000 tables.

| | ITEM TO BE PRODUCED | |
	Tables	Legs
Budgeted inventory, September 30	2,400	4,000
Budgeted inventory, December 31	2,800	3,500

REQUIRED: Prepare a schedule of budgeted production of tables and legs.

6–20. Cash budget. Consider the following:

FAVARO COMPANY
Budgeted Income Statement
For the Month Ended June 30, 19X9
(in thousands)

Sales		$240
Inventory, May 31	$ 40	
Purchases	160	
Available for sale	$200	
Inventory, June 30	30	
Cost of goods sold		170
Gross margin		$ 70
Operating expenses:		
Wages	$ 30	
Utilities	2	
Advertising	9	
Depreciation	1	
Office expenses	3	
Insurance and property taxes	2	47
Operating income		$ 23

The cash balance, May 31, 19X9, is $38,000. Sales proceeds are collected as follows: 40% month of sale, 40% second month, 20% third month.

Accounts receivable are $120,000 on May 31, 19X9, consisting of $30,000 from April sales and $90,000 from May sales.

Accounts payable on May 31, 19X9, are $120,000. Favaro Company pays 25% of purchases during the month of purchase and the remainder during the following month. All operating expenses requiring cash are paid during the month of recognition. However, insurance and property taxes are paid annually in December.

REQUIRED: Prepare a cash budget for June. Confine your analysis to the given data. Ignore income taxes and other possible items that might affect cash.

6–21. Cash collection budget. Volyum Company's experience indicates that cash collections from customers tend to occur in the following pattern:

Collected within cash discount period in month of sale	50%
Collected within cash discount period in first month after month of sale	10
Collected after cash discount period in first month after month of sale	25
Collected after cash discount period in second month after month of sale	13
Never collected	2
Total sales in any month (before cash discounts)	100%
Cash discount allowable as a percentage of invoice price	1%

Compute the total cash budgeted to be collected in March if sales are predicted as $200,000 for January, $300,000 for February, and $400,000 for March.

6–22. Budget computations for purchases and borrowing. Nuts & Bolts, Inc., needs your help in computing two of the estimates for its budget for a certain period.

a. The company plans to produce during the period 15,000 units of Product X and 20,000 units of Product Y. It uses 5 units of material K for each X and 3 units of K for each Y. The beginning inventory of K is 12,000 units, and the desired ending inventory is 18,000 units. How many K units must your company purchase during the period?
b. The company forecasts cash receipts of $330,000 and cash disbursements of $365,000. If the beginning cash balance is $26,000 and the desired ending cash balance is $20,000, how much cash must be borrowed during the period?

6–23. Cash budget. Consider the following cash budget. Compute amounts for the lettered spaces.

	MAY	JUNE
Cash balance, beginning	A	E
Cash receipts from customers	80,000	140,000
Total cash available before financing	100,000	F
Cash disbursements:		
Merchandise	70,000	60,000
Operating expenses	20,000	25,000
Acquisition of equipment	30,000	—
Total disbursements	120,000	85,000
Minimum cash balance desired	B	B
Total cash needed	130,000	G

Excess (deficiency) of total cash available over total cash needed before current financing	C	H
Financing:		
Borrowings (at beginning)*	D	
Repayments (at end)	—	I
Interest (at 18% per annum)	—	J
Total effects of financing	D	K
Cash balance, ending	E	L

*Borrowings and repayments of principal are made in multiples of $1,000. Interest is to be paid when loans are paid.

6–24. **Multiple choice.** (CPA.) The Zel Co., a wholesaler, budgeted the following sales for the indicated months:

	June 19X1	July 19X1	August 19X1
Sales on account	$1,500,000	$1,600,000	$1,700,000
Cash sales	200,000	210,000	220,000
Total sales	$1,700,000	$1,810,000	$1,920,000

All merchandise is marked up to sell at its invoice cost plus 25%. Merchandise inventories at the beginning of each month are at 30% of that month's projected cost of goods sold.

Select the best answer for each of the following items:

1. The cost of goods sold for the month of June 19X1 is anticipated to be (a) $1,530,000, (b) $1,402,500, (c) $1,275,000, (d) $1,190,000, (e) none of these.
2. Merchandise purchases for July 19X1 are anticipated to be (a) $1,605,500, (b) $1,474,400, (c) $1,448,000, (d) $1,382,250, (e) none of these.

6–25. **Miscellaneous computations.** (H. Schaefer.) These questions relate to the preparation of budgets for *the year 19X6*. Each question is independent of the others.

a. Sales are predicted to be 30,000 units per month for the first six months and 40,000 units per month for the last six months. The January 1 balance in accounts receivable is $50,000. The accounts receivable are predicted to experience a one-month turnover cycle. The predicted sales price is $2. All sales are on a credit basis. Compute (1) predicted sales revenue, (2) predicted December 31 balance in Accounts Receivable, (3) predicted cash collections from accounts receivable.

b. The January 1 balance in prepaid rent is $400. Rent is paid on the last day of the month prior to the month for which it applies; e.g., the April rent is paid on March 31. The present rent contract is for $400 per month, and the last payment is scheduled for May 31. A new contract is expected to be signed for $500 per month, the first payment being on June 30. The new contract is expected to be in effect for twelve months. Compute (1) predicted rent expense, (2) predicted December 31 balance in Prepaid Rent, (3) predicted cash payments for rent.

6–26. **Cash budget.** Kay Sharon is the manager of an extremely successful gift shop, Gifts for Charities, which is operated for the benefit of local charities. From the data below, she wants a cash budget showing expected cash receipts and disbursements for the month of April, and the cash balance expected as of April 30, 19X1:

Bank note due April 10: $100,000 plus $5,000 interest
Depreciation for April: $3,000
Two-year insurance policy due April 14 for renewal: $3,000, to be paid in cash
Planned cash balance, March 31, 19X1: $100,000
Merchandise purchases for April: $700,000, 40% paid in month of purchase, 60% paid in next month
Customer receivables as of March 31: $100,000 from February sales, $600,000 from March sales
Payrolls due in April: $120,000
Other expenses for April, payable in April: $60,000
Accrued taxes for April, payable in June: $9,000
Sales for April: $1,400,000, half collected in month of sale, 40% in next month, 10% in third month
Accounts payable, March 31, 19X1: $600,000

REQUIRED: I   Prepare the cash budget.

6–27. Cash collections and disbursements.   (CPA.) The following information was available from Montero Corporation's books:

19X2	PURCHASES	SALES
January	$42,000	$72,000
February	48,000	66,000
March	36,000	60,000
April	54,000	78,000

Collections from customers are normally 70% in the month of sale, 20% in the month following the sale, and 9% in the second month following the sale. The balance is expected to be uncollectible. Montero takes full advantage of the 2% discount allowed on purchases paid for by the tenth of the following month. Purchases for May are budgeted at $60,000, while sales for May are forecasted at $66,000. Cash disbursements for expenses are expected to be $14,400 for the month of May. Montero's cash balance at May 1 was $22,000.

REQUIRED: Prepare the following schedules:

1. Expected cash collections during May
2. Expected cash disbursements during May
3. Expected cash balance at May 31

6–28. Purchases and sales budgets.   (CMA, adapted.) The Russon Corporation is a retailer whose sales are all made on credit. Sales are billed twice monthly, on the tenth of the month for the last half of the prior month's sales and on the twentieth of the month for the first half of the current month's sales. The terms of all sales are 2/10, net 30. Based upon past experience, the collection experience of accounts receivable is as follows:

Within the discount period	80%
On the 30th day	18%
Uncollectible	2%

The sales value of shipments for May 19X0 and the forecast for the next four months are:

May (actual)	$500,000
June	600,000
July	700,000
August	700,000
September	400,000

Russon's average markup on its products is 20% of the sales price.

Russon purchases merchandise for resale to meet the current month's sales demand and to maintain a desired monthly ending inventory of 25% of the next month's sales. All purchases are on credit with terms of net 30. Russon pays for one-half of a month's purchases in the month of purchase and the other half in the month following the purchase.

All sales and purchases occur uniformly throughout the month.

REQUIRED:

1. How much cash can Russon Corporation plan to collect from accounts receivable collections during July 19X0?

   a. $574,000
   b. $662,600
   c. $619,000

   d. $608,600
   e. None of these

2. How much cash can Russon plan to collect in September from sales made in August 19X0?

   a. $337,400
   b. $343,000
   c. $400,400

   d. $280,000
   e. None of these

3. The budgeted dollar value of Russon's inventory on August 31, 19X0 will be

   a. $110,000
   b. $80,000
   c. $112,000

   d. $100,000
   e. Some amount other than those given

4. How much merchandise should Russon plan to purchase during June 19X0?

   a. $520,000
   b. $460,000
   c. $500,000

   d. $580,000
   e. None of these

5. The amount Russon should budget in August 19X0 for the payment of merchandise is

   a. $560,000
   b. $500,000
   c. $667,000

   d. $600,000
   e. None of these

6–29. **Importance of sales forecast.** A retail department of a local chain of department stores sells a plain and a fancy box of hard candy. The candy is purchased in individual plastic-wrapped packages from a local candy manufacturer, and two types of boxes are purchased from a local container manufacturer. The store clerks use a back room for boxing the candy, as the need arises. Purchasing and selling prices have been stable, and no price changes are anticipated.

It is near the end of October. Orders must be placed today for delivery by November 1. These orders are to provide sufficient stock to last through the Christmas season.

Federal Reserve statistics for the local area show retail department store sales to be 2% over last year, for the period January 1–September 30. The store's top management anticipates an increase of 1% in dollar sales of ordinary items and of 10% in dollar sales of luxury items this year, as compared with last year.

Other data are:

| | LAST YEAR | | THIS YEAR | |
	November	December	Inventory October 31	Target Inventory December 31
Selling price per box, $1.50 fancy and $1.00 plain Boxes sold:				
Plain	4,000	7,000		
Fancy	4,000	12,000		
Plastic-wrapped packages			1,000	600
Number of boxes:				
Plain			200	100
Fancy			500	100
Purchase costs: Candy, per package $.40 Box, plain $.05 Box, fancy $.20				

REQUIRED:

Prepare the following:

1. Budgeted sales of plain candy, in boxes and in total dollars, for November and December
2. Budgeted sales of fancy candy, in boxes and in total dollars, for November and December
3. Packages and total cost of needed candy purchases
4. Number and total cost of needed plain boxes
5. Number and total cost of needed fancy boxes

6–30. **Sales forecasting.** In each of the accompanying diagrams A through E, the dollar value of a sales order is contrasted with the quantity of product or service sold. Assume a single product in each case.

REQUIRED:

1. What pricing policy is reflected by these order patterns (assuming that all customers are rational)?
2. Why are these patterns relevant to a sales forecast?

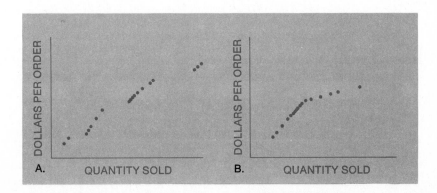

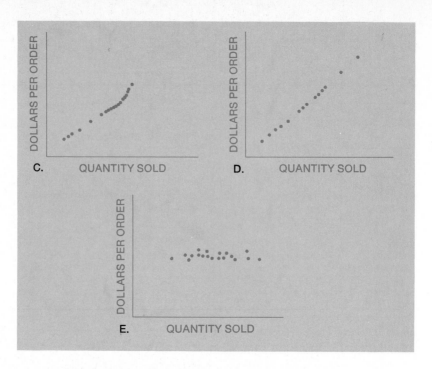

6–31. Cash budget. Prepare a statement of estimated cash receipts and disbursements for October 19X2, for the Rourk Company, which sells one product. On October 1, 19X2, part of the trial balance showed:

Cash	$ 6,000	
Accounts receivable	19,500	
Allowance for bad debts		$2,400
Merchandise inventory	12,000	
Accounts payable, merchandise		9,000

The company's purchases are payable within ten days. Assume that one-third of the purchases of any month are due and paid for in the following month.

The unit invoice cost of the merchandise purchased is $10. At the end of each month it is desired to have an inventory equal in units to 50% of the following month's sales in units.

Sales terms include a 1% discount if payment is made by the end of the calendar month. Past experience indicates that 60% of the billings will be collected during the month of the sale, 30% in the following calendar month, 6% in the next following calendar month. Four percent will be uncollectible. The company's fiscal year begins August 1.

Unit selling price	$	15
August actual sales		15,000
September actual sales		45,000
October estimated sales		36,000
November estimated sales		27,000
Total sales expected in the fiscal year		450,000

Exclusive of bad debts, total budgeted selling and general administrative expenses for the fiscal year are estimated at $68,500, of which $21,000 is fixed expense (inclusive of a $9,000 annual depreciation charge). These fixed expenses are incurred uniformly throughout the year. The balance of the selling and general administrative expenses vary with sales. Expenses are paid as incurred.

6–32. **Prepare master budget.** (Alternates are 6-1 and 6-33.) The Loebl Company wants a master budget for the next three months, beginning January 1, 19X2. It desires an ending minimum cash balance of $4,000 each month. Sales are forecasted at an average selling price of $4 per unit. Inventories are supposed to equal 125% of the next month's sales in units except for the end of March. The March 31 inventory in units should be 75% of the next month's sales. Merchandise costs are $2 per unit. Purchases during any given month are paid in full during the following month. All sales are on credit, payable within thirty days, but experience has shown that 40% of current sales is collected in the current month, 40% in the next month, and 20% in the month thereafter. Bad debts are negligible.

Monthly operating expenses are as follows:

Wages and salaries	$12,000
Insurance expired	100
Depreciation	200
Miscellaneous	2,000
Rent	100 + 10% of sales

Cash dividends of $1,000 are to be paid quarterly, beginning January 15, and are declared on the fifteenth of the previous month. All operating expenses are paid as incurred, except insurance, depreciation, and rent. Rent of $100 is paid at the beginning of each month, and the additional 10% of sales is paid quarterly on the tenth of the month following the quarter. The next settlement is due January 10.

The company plans to buy some new fixtures, for $2,000 cash, in March.

Money can be borrowed and repaid in multiples of $500, at an interest rate of 18% per annum. Management wants to minimize borrowing and repay rapidly. Interest is computed and paid when the principal is repaid. Assume that borrowing takes place at the beginning, and repayments at the end, of the months in question. Money is never borrowed at the beginning and repaid at the end of the *same* month. Compute interest to the nearest dollar.

ASSETS AS OF DECEMBER 31:		LIABILITIES AS OF DECEMBER 31:	
Cash	$ 4,000	Accounts payable	
Accounts receivable	16,000	(merchandise)	$28,750
Inventory	31,250	Dividends payable	1,000
Unexpired insurance	1,200	Rent payable	7,000
Fixed assets, net	10,000		$36,750
	$62,450		

Recent and forecasted sales:

October	$30,000	December	$20,000	February	$60,000	April	$36,000
November	20,000	January	50,000	March	30,000		

1. Prepare a master budget, including a budgeted income statement, balance sheet, statement of cash receipts and disbursements, and supporting schedules.
2. Explain why there is a need for a bank loan and what operating sources provide the cash for the repayment of the bank loan.

6–33. **Deviations from master budget.** (Alternates are 6-1 and 6-32.) Review the major illustration in the chapter. It is the end of July. Operations have been exactly in accordance with the budget except that July sales were $40,000 instead of $50,000. Purchases for July were not affected by the drop in sales, but commissions, cash, accounts receivable, and notes payable were among the accounts affected.

Prepare a summary analysis of the effects. That is, how would Schedules *a, b, e,* and *f* be affected, as well as Exhibits 6-3, 6-4, and 6-5? Include a list of all new balances in Exhibit 6-5.

6–34. **Budgeting, pricing, and service industries.** Most law firms have two broad ranks of attorneys: associates, who work for salaries, and partners, who share any income generated before taxes. You are an experienced associate of James Milne and Company, a small but prestigious law firm. James Milne, the senior partner, has asked you to analyze the following budget data with the aim of setting a fee structure for 19X4:

	DEPARTMENT		
	Probate	Tax	TOTAL
Number of partners	2	3	5
Budgeted partner-hours billable			
to clients	3,200	4,500	7,700
Number of associates	2	6	8
Budgeted associate-hours billable			
to clients	3,000	8,400	11,400
Total hours	6,200	12,900	19,100
Budgeted expenses for the firm:			
Secretarial staff and receptionist			$110,000
Library services			40,000
Rent			52,000
Janitorial services			14,000
Supplies and photocopying			30,000
Telephone			11,000
General expenses			15,000
			$272,000

Associates receive salaries and benefits of $40,000 per person per year.

James Milne kept abreast of the general pricing practices of other law firms. The billing rate for associates was $40 per hour, and he said it would be unthinkable for his firm to do otherwise. However, because of the general high quality of the work performed by his firm, the senior partner was confident that a partner could be billed out at $80 to $125 per hour. Milne also told you that, on an average, the partners expected an income after all expenses, but before income taxes, of $100,000 each.

REQUIRED:

1. Compute the average billing rate per partner-hour for 19X4.
2. All expenses for 19X4 were exactly the same as budgeted. You have been asked to repeat for 19X5 what you did in Requirement 1. All expenses are expected to be the same as the actual expenses for 19X4. However, because of their superior work in 19X4, the associates will be provided greater responsibility and greater breadth of experience. What that entailed, you learned, was that the associates would work more hours and the partners would work fewer. The budgeted billable hours for 19X5 were:

| | DEPARTMENT | | |
	Probate	Tax	TOTAL
Partners	2,400	3,300	5,700
Associates	3,800	9,600	13,400
Total hours	6,200	12,900	19,100

You also learned that the partners still expected to receive $100,000 each on the average. The market remained such that an associate could still only be billed out at $40 per hour.

7

FLEXIBLE BUDGETS AND STANDARDS FOR CONTROL

Learning Objectives

When you have finished studying this chapter, you should be able to

1. Distinguish between static budgets and flexible budgets
2. Compute and use a budget formula in the construction of a flexible budget
3. Use the flexible-budget approach to compute (a) sales volume variances and (b) flexible budget variances
4. List the four usual stages in the evolution of a control system for an organization
5. Distinguish between budget amounts and standard amounts
6. Distinguish between perfection standards and currently attainable standards
7. Compute the price and efficiency variances for direct material and direct labor
8. Identify the typical responsibilities for controlling variances in material and labor costs

The essence of control is feedback—the comparison of actual performance with planned performance. Flexible budgets and standard costs are major attention-directing techniques for planning and for providing feedback regarding individual costs. Throughout this chapter, to stress some basic ideas, we shall continue to assume that each cost is either variable or fixed; in the next chapter we shall consider various cost behavior patterns in more detail.

This chapter has two major sections. Part One provides a general overview of flexible budgets without getting into details of the analysis of variances. Part Two introduces price and efficiency variances.

❏ PART ONE Flexible Budgets

STATIC-BUDGET COMPARISONS

As Chapter 6 shows, budgets may be developed on a companywide basis to cover all activities, from sales to direct materials to sweeping compounds, and from spending on a new plant to expected drains on petty cash. A budget may be expressed on an accrual basis or on a cash-flow basis; it may be highly condensed or exceedingly detailed. All the budgets discussed in Chapter 6 are *static* (inflexible). A **static budget** is defined as a budget prepared for only one level of activity (e.g., volume of sales). To illustrate: A typical master-planning budget is a plan tailored to a single target volume level of, say, 100,000 units. All results would be compared with the original plan, regardless of changes in ensuing conditions—even though, for example, volume turned out to be only 90,000 units instead of the original 100,000.

Consider a simplified illustration. Suppose the Dominion Company, a one-department firm in Singapore, manufactured and sold a special kind of carry-on flight luggage that required several hand operations. The product had some variations, but it was viewed essentially as a single product bearing one selling price.

The master budget for the forthcoming month included the condensed income statement shown in Exhibit 7-1, column 2. The actual results are in column 1. The master budget called for the production and sales of 9,000 units, but only 7,000 units were actually produced and sold. There were no beginning or ending inventories.

The master budget was based on detailed expectations for the given month, including a careful forecast of sales. The performance report in Exhibit 7-1 compares the actual results with the master budget. **Performance report** is a general term that usually means a comparison of actual results with some budget. In particular, note that the volume of activity, as measured by sales, was substantially below the budget. The budget in Exhibit 7-1 is an example of a static budget.

Exhibit 7-1 is difficult to analyze. Recall that Chapter 1 defined *variance* as a deviation of an actual result from the expected or budgeted result. Clearly, sales are below expectations, but the favorable variances regarding the variable costs are deceptive. Considering the lower-than-projected

EXHIBIT
7-1

DOMINION COMPANY
Performance Report Using Static Budget
For the Month Ended June 30, 19X1

	ACTUAL	MASTER (STATIC) BUDGET	VARIANCE
Units	7,000	9,000	2,000
Sales	$168,000	$216,000	$48,000 U
Variable costs:			
Direct material	$ 21,350	$ 27,000	$ 5,650 F
Direct labor	61,500	72,000	10,500 F
Labor to transport materials internally and provide general support	11,100	14,400	3,300 F
Idle time	3,550	3,600	50 F
Cleanup time	2,500	2,700	200 F
Other indirect labor	800	900	100 F
Miscellaneous supplies	4,700	5,400	700 F
Variable manufacturing costs	$105,500	$126,000	$20,500 F
Shipping expenses (selling)	5,000	5,400	400 F
Duplication, telephone, etc. (administrative)	2,000	1,800	200 U
Total variable costs	$112,500	$133,200	$20,700 F
Contribution margin	$ 55,500	$ 82,800	$27,300 U
Fixed costs:			
Factory supervision	$ 14,700	$ 14,400	$ 300 U
Rent of factory	5,000	5,000	—
Depreciation of factory equipment	15,000	15,000	—
Other fixed factory costs	2,600	2,600	—
Fixed manufacturing costs	$ 37,300	$ 37,000	$ 300 U
Fixed selling and administrative costs	33,000	33,000	—
Total fixed costs	$ 70,300	$ 70,000	$ 300 U
Operating income (loss)	$ (14,800)	$ 12,800	$27,600 U

F = Favorable cost variances occur when actual costs are less than budgeted costs.
U = Unfavorable cost variances occur when actual costs are greater than budgeted costs.

level of activity, was cost control really satisfactory? The comparison of actual results with a static budget does not give much help in answering that question.

FLEXIBLE-BUDGET COMPARISONS

As president of the Dominion Company, you would probably want a performance report that better pinpoints some major variances between the master budget and the actual results. To get a better basis for analysis, a flexible budget is introduced. The **flexible budget** (also called **variable budget**) is based on knowledge of cost behavior patterns. It is prepared for a range, rather than a single level, of activity; it is essentially a set of budgets that can be tailored to any level of activity. Ideally, the flexible budget is compiled after obtaining a detailed analysis of how each cost is affected by changes in activity. Exhibit 7-2 shows how a flexible budget might appear.

The costs in Exhibit 7-2 can be graphed as in Exhibit 7-3. As these exhibits show, a mathematical function or formula can summarize the cost behavior as $70,000 per month plus $14.80 per unit. Although we have assumed that the graph is valid for the range of 7,000 to 9,000 units, costs are unlikely to behave in accordance with such a pat formula beyond either side of this range. Inasmuch as the activity was 7,000 units, the pertinent flexible budget is in the 7,000-unit column of Exhibit 7-2.

Flexible budgets have the following distinguishing features: (a) they are prepared for a range of activity instead of a single level; (b) they supply a dynamic basis for comparison because they are automatically geared to changes in volume.

EXHIBIT 7-2 (Place a clip on this page for easy reference.)

DOMINION COMPANY
Flexible Budget
For the Month Ended June 30, 19X1

	BUDGET FORMULA PER UNIT	VARIOUS LEVELS OF ACTIVITY		
Units	—	7,000	8,000	9,000
Sales	$24.00	$168,000	$192,000	$216,000
Variable costs:				
Direct material	$ 3.00	$ 21,000	$ 24,000	$ 27,000
Direct labor	8.00	56,000	64,000	72,000
Labor to transport materials internally and provide general support	1.60	11,200	12,800	14,400
Idle time	.40	2,800	3,200	3,600
Cleanup time	.30	2,100	2,400	2,700
Other indirect labor	.10	700	800	900
Miscellaneous supplies	.60	4,200	4,800	5,400
Variable manufacturing costs	$14.00	$ 98,000	$112,000	$126,000
Shipping expenses (selling)	.60	4,200	4,800	5,400
Duplication, telephone, etc.	.20	1,400	1,600	1,800
Total variable costs	$14.80	$103,600	$118,400	$133,200
Contribution margin	$ 9.20	$ 64,400	$ 73,600	$ 82,800
Fixed costs:				
Factory supervision		$ 14,400	$ 14,400	$ 14,400
Rent of factory		5,000	5,000	5,000
Depreciation of factory equipment		15,000	15,000	15,000
Other fixed factory costs		2,600	2,600	2,600
Fixed manufacturing costs		$ 37,000	$ 37,000	$ 37,000
Fixed selling and administrative costs		33,000	33,000	33,000
Total fixed costs*		$ 70,000	$ 70,000	$ 70,000
Operating income (loss)		$ (5,600)	$ 3,600	$ 12,800

*Note that the budget formula for fixed costs is $70,000 per month. Therefore the budget formula for total costs is $14.80 per unit plus $70,000 per month. The graph in Exhibit 7-3 portrays these relationships.

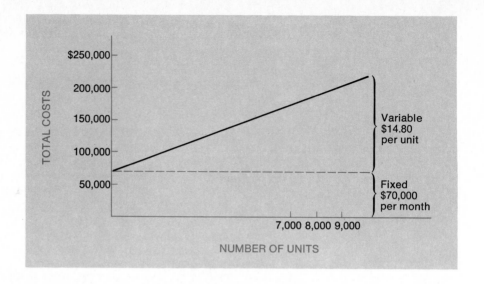

EXHIBIT 7-3

Dominion Company graph of flexible budget of costs

TOTAL COSTS

$250,000

200,000

150,000

100,000

50,000

Variable $14.80 per unit

Fixed $70,000 per month

7,000 8,000 9,000

NUMBER OF UNITS

The flexible-budget approach says, "Give me any activity level you choose, and I'll provide a budget tailored to that particular volume." Flexible budgets may be useful both before and after the period in question. They may be helpful when managers are trying to choose among various ranges of activity for planning purposes. They may also be helpful at the end of the period when managers are trying to analyze actual results.

ISOLATING THE VARIANCES

Pause a moment to reflect on the analytical problem. The company had an original plan, and the president may seek an explanation of why the plan was not achieved; in other words, a manager may desire a more penetrating analysis of the variances in Exhibit 7-1. The analysis can become quite detailed. However, as a start, consider how the variances can be divided into two major categories:

1. Variances from a revenue target (sometimes called a volume target or, in the case of a production manager, a scheduled production target).[1] In this book, this variance will be called a **sales volume variance,** although its label will vary from company to company. It emphasizes the idea that the marketing function usually has the primary responsibility for reaching the sales level called for in the master budget.

[1] Sometimes this is generically called an *effectiveness* variance, as distinguished from all other measures, which are loosely called *efficiency* variances. Effectiveness is the accomplishment of a predetermined objective. Efficiency is an optimum relationship between input and output. Given any level of output, did the manager control his inputs as he should have? Performance may be both effective and efficient, but either condition can occur without the other. For example, a company may set 200,000 units as a production objective. Subsequently, because of material shortages, only 150,000 units may be produced with 100% efficiency— performance would be ineffective but efficient. In contrast, 200,000 units may be produced on schedule but with a considerable waste of labor and materials—performance would be effective but inefficient.

2. Variances arising from changes in unit prices (or unit costs), here called **price variances,** and from inefficient utilization of inputs, here called **efficiency variances.**

The trouble with the static budget, as Exhibit 7-1 shows, is its failure to distinguish between these various facets of a manager's performance. However, Exhibit 7-4 gives a condensed view of how these variances can be isolated by using a flexible budget as an explanatory bridge between the master (static) budget and the actual results.

Column 4 in Exhibit 7-4 focuses on the sales volume variance. It shows that the underachievement of sales by 2,000 units and $48,000 resulted in an $18,400 decrease in attained contribution margin and hence an $18,400 decrease in operating income. Note that unit prices are held constant in this part of the analysis—that is, the net sales volume variance is computed by using the budgeted contribution margin per unit:

sales volume variance = budgeted unit contribution margin ×
difference between the master budgeted
sales in units and the actual sales in units

= $9.20 × (9,000 − 7,000)
= $18,400, unfavorable

Without the flexible budget in column 3, this sales volume variance cannot be isolated.

Column 2 presents the **flexible-budget variances,** which are the differences between actual amounts and the flexible-budget amounts for the actual output achieved. These variances arise from *price* changes and *inefficient* uses of inputs. The focus is on the difference between actual costs and flexible budgeted costs when *both* are at the 7,000-unit level of

EXHIBIT 7-4 (Place a clip on this page for easy reference.)

DOMINION COMPANY
Summary of Performance
For the Month Ended June 30, 19X1

	(1) ACTUAL RESULTS AT ACTUAL PRICES*	(2) (1)−(3) FLEXIBLE- BUDGET VARIANCES†	(3) FLEXIBLE BUDGET FOR ACTUAL OUTPUT ACHIEVED‡	(4) (3)−(5) SALES VOLUME VARIANCES	(5) MASTER (STATIC) BUDGET*
Physical units	7,000	—	7,000	2,000 U	9,000
Sales	$168,000	$ —	$168,000	$48,000 U	$216,000
Variable costs	112,500	8,900 U	103,600	29,600 F	133,200
Contribution margin	$ 55,500	$8,900 U	$ 64,400	$18,400 U	$ 82,800
Fixed costs	70,300	300 U	70,000	—	70,000
Operating income	$ (14,800)	$9,200 U	$ (5,600)	$18,400 U	$ 12,800

U = Unfavorable.
*Figures are from Exhibit 7-1.
†Figures are shown in more detail in Exhibit 7-5.
‡Figures are from the 7,000-unit column in Exhibit 7-2.

activity. Again, without the flexible budget in column 3, these variances cannot be separated from the effects of changes in sales volume.

If the president wants to pursue this analysis of cost control beyond the summary in Exhibit 7-4, the cost performance report in Exhibit 7-5 may be of help. Even if the president were not interested in probing further, some lower-level managers might be so inclined. Exhibit 7-5 gives a line-by-line sizeup, showing how most of the costs that had seemingly favorable variances when a static budget was used as a basis for comparison have, in reality, unfavorable variances. These flexible-budget variances may be analyzed in even more depth by being subdivided further, at least for the more important material and labor costs, as shown later in the section "Standards for Material and Labor."

EXHIBIT 7-5 (Place a clip on this page for easy reference.)

DOMINION COMPANY
Cost Control Performance Report
For the Month Ended June 30, 19X1

	ACTUAL COSTS INCURRED	FLEXIBLE BUDGET*	FLEXIBLE-BUDGET VARIANCES†	EXPLANATION
Units	7,000	7,000	—	
Variable costs:				
Direct material	$ 21,350	$ 21,000	$ 350 U	Lower prices, but higher usage
Direct labor	61,500	56,000	5,500 U	Higher wage rates and higher usage
Labor to transport materials internally and provide general support	11,100	11,200	100 F	
Idle time	3,550	2,800	750 U	Excessive machine breakdowns
Cleanup time	2,500	2,100	400 U	Needs more investigation
Other indirect labor	800	700	100 U	
Miscellaneous supplies	4,700	4,200	500 U	Higher prices and higher usage
Variable manufacturing costs	$105,500	$ 98,000	$7,500 U	
Shipping expenses (selling)	5,000	4,200	800 U	Use of air freight
Duplication, telephone, etc.	2,000	1,400	600 U	Needs more investigation
Total variable costs	$112,500	$103,600	$8,900 U	
Fixed costs:				
Factory supervision	$ 14,700	$ 14,400	$ 300 U	Unanticipated salary increase
Rent of factory	5,000	5,000	—	
Depreciation of factory equipment	15,000	15,000	—	
Other fixed factory costs	2,600	2,600	—	
Fixed manufacturing costs	$ 37,300	$37,000	$ 300 U	
Fixed selling and administrative costs	33,000	33,000	—	
Total fixed costs	$ 70,300	$ 70,000	$ 300 U	
Total variable and fixed costs	$182,800	$173,600	$9,200 U	

F = Favorable. U = Unfavorable.
*From 7,000-unit column in Exhibit 7-2, p. 177.
†This represents a line-by-line breakdown of the variances in column 2 of Exhibit 7-4.

In most organizations, systems for accumulating and analyzing data evolve gradually. For example, when small businesses are founded, planning and control decisions are based at first almost wholly on the manager's *personal observations* of operations. It does not take long for the manager to realize that keeping some *historical records* would be a net benefit. That is, the additional bookkeeping costs are clearly outweighed by the greater likelihood of a series of better decisions regarding extensions of trade credit to customers, negotiating with suppliers and bankers, and so on. Furthermore, comparing the current period's sales, costs, or income with the preceding period's helps in the evaluation of performance and the preparation of new plans.

Personal observation and historical records, however, are often not enough. Managers desire to reduce emergency decision making by planning more carefully, and the *master (static) budget* is helpful in this regard. Furthermore, the master budget provides a better benchmark for evaluating performance. That is, managers want to know more than how they have done currently in relation to last period's performance; they also want to know how they have done *currently* in relation to their *current* targeted performance.

This chapter has shown that some managers are willing to pay for more help in the form of *flexible budgets*, which are key aids in mapping an explanatory trail from the master budget to the actual results.

Thus the evolution of control systems is often from personal observation, to historical records, to master (static) budgets, to flexible budgets (and standard costs, which are described in the next section). Note that one control tool does not *replace* another; instead, each control tool is *added* to the others. The systems become more costly, but they are perceived by the managers who buy them as leading to net benefits in the form of a better set of collective operating decisions.

This concludes the presentation of an overall view of flexible budgets and standards. Subsequent sections probe the subject more deeply.

Summary
Problem for Your Review

❏ Problem One

Refer to the data contained in the illustration just concluded.

Suppose actual production and sales were 8,500 units instead of 7,000 units. (a) Compute the sales volume variance. Is the performance of the marketing function the sole explanation for this variance? Why? (b) Using a flexible budget, compute the budgeted contribution margin, budgeted operating income, budgeted direct material, and budgeted direct labor.

❑ Solution to Problem One

(a) sales volume variance = budgeted unit contribution margin
× difference between the master-
budgeted sales in units and the actual
sales in units
= \$9.20 × (9,000 − 8,500) = \$4,600 U

This variance is labeled as a sales volume variance because it quantifies the impact on net income of the deviation from an original sales target—while holding price and efficiency factors constant. Of course, the failure to reach target sales may be traceable to a number of causes beyond the control of the marketing force, including strikes, material shortages, and storms.

(b) The budget formulas in Exhibit 7-2 are the basis for the following answers:

Budgeted contribution margin = \$9.20 × 8,500 = \$78,200
Budgeted operating income   = \$78,200 − \$70,000 fixed costs = \$8,200
Budgeted direct material   = \$3.00 × 8,500 = \$25,500
Budgeted direct labor   = \$8.00 × 8,500 = \$68,000

❑ PART TWO: Price and Efficiency Variances

This part of the chapter shows how flexible-budget variances may be analyzed further by being subdivided into price and efficiency variances.

STANDARDS FOR MATERIAL AND LABOR

Standard costs are the building blocks of a budgeting and feedback system. A **standard cost** is a carefully predetermined cost that should be attained, usually expressed per unit.

❑ Difference Between Standards and Budgets

How does a standard amount differ from a budget amount? If standards are currently attainable, as they are assumed to be in this book, there is no conceptual difference. However, as it is most widely used, the term *standard cost* refers to a *single* unit. In contrast, the term *budgeted cost* refers to a *total*. For example, the standard cost of direct material in Exhibit 7-2 shows:

	BUDGET FORMULA PER UNIT	FLEXIBLE BUDGET FOR VARIOUS LEVELS OF ACTIVITY		
Units	1	7,000	8,000	9,000
Direct material	\$3.00	\$21,000	\$24,000	\$27,000

The standard cost is \$3 per unit. The budgeted cost is \$21,000 if 7,000 units are to be produced. It may help to think of a standard as a budget for the production of a single unit. In many companies, the terms *budgeted performance* and *standard performance* are used interchangeably.

In practice, direct material and direct labor are often said to be controlled with the help of *standard costs*, whereas all other costs are usually said to be controlled with the help of *departmental overhead budgets*. This distinction probably arose because of different timing and control techniques for various costs. Direct material and direct labor are generally relatively costly and are easily identifiable for control purposes. Therefore techniques for planning and controlling these costs are relatively refined. Overhead costs are combinations of many individual items, none of which by itself justifies an elaborate control system. In consequence, use of direct material may be closely watched on an hourly basis; direct labor, on a daily basis; and factory overhead, on a weekly or monthly basis.

All of this leads to the following straightforward approach (using assumed figures for a factory in Singapore), which we will pursue throughout the remainder of this book. The *standard* is a *unit* idea; the *budget* is a *total* idea. Using the data in Exhibit 7-2, p. 177:

	STANDARDS		
	(1) Standard Inputs Allowed for Each Unit of Output Achieved	(2) Standard Price per Unit of Input	BUDGET FOR 7,000 UNITS OF OUTPUT*
Direct material	5 pounds	$ .60	$21,000
Direct labor	2 hours	4.00	56,000
Other costs (detailed)	Various	Various	96,600

*Col. (1) × (2) × 7,000.

❏ Role of Past Experience

The study of past behavior patterns is typically a fundamental step in formulating a standard or a budgeted cost. Although the study of past cost behavior is a useful starting point, a budgeted cost should not merely be an extension of past experience. Inefficiencies may be reflected in prior costs. Changes in technology, equipment, and methods also limit the usefulness of comparisons with the past. Also, performance should be judged in relation to some currently attainable goal, one that may be reached by skilled, diligent, superior effort. Concern with the past is justified only insofar as it helps prediction. Management wishes to plan what costs *should be*, not what costs *have been*.

❏ Current Attainability: The Most Widely Used Standard

What standard of expected performance should be used? Should it be so severe that it is rarely, if ever, attained? Should it be attainable 50% of the time? Eighty percent? Twenty percent? Individuals who have worked a lifetime in setting standards for performance disagree, so there are no universal answers to these questions.

Two types of standards deserve mention here, perfection standards and currently attainable standards. *Perfection standards* (often also called *ideal standards*) are expressions of the absolute minimum costs possible under the best conceivable conditions, using existing specifications and equipment. No provision is made for shrinkage, spoilage, machine break-downs, and the like. Those who favor this approach maintain that the resulting unfavorable variances will constantly remind managers of the perpetual need for improvement in all phases of operations. These stand-ards are not widely used, however, because they have an adverse effect on employee motivation. Employees tend to ignore unreasonable goals.

Currently attainable standards are those that can be achieved by *very efficient* operations. Expectations are set high enough so that em-ployees regard their fulfillment as possible, though perhaps not probable. Allowances are made for normal shrinkage, waste, and machine break-downs. Variances tend to be unfavorable, but managers accept the stand-ards as being reasonable goals.

The major reasons for using currently attainable standards are:

1. The resulting standard costs serve multiple purposes. For example, the same cost may be used for cash budgeting, inventory valuation, and budgeting departmental performance. In contrast, perfection standards cannot be used per se for cash budgeting because financial planning will be inaccurate.[2]

2. They have a desirable motivational impact on employees. The standard rep-resents reasonable future performance, not fanciful ideal goals or antiquated goals geared to past performance.

❑ Focus on Both Inputs and Outputs

To see how the analysis of variances can be pursued more fully, reconsider the direct material and direct labor in Exhibit 7-5 (p. 180). We continue our illustration and assume that the following actually occurred:

Direct material: 36,810 pounds of inputs were used at an actual unit price of 58¢ for a total actual cost of $21,350.

Direct labor: 15,000 hours of inputs were used at an actual hourly price (rate) of $4.10, for a total actual cost of $61,500.

These additional data enable us to subdivide the flexible-budget vari-ances into separate price and efficiency variances:

	ACTUAL COSTS INCURRED	FLEXIBLE BUDGET	FLEXIBLE-BUDGET VARIANCE	PRICE VARIANCE*	EFFICIENCY VARIANCE*
Direct material	$21,350	$21,000	$ 350 U	$ 736 F	$1,086 U
Direct labor	61,500	56,000	5,500 U	1,500 U	4,000 U

*Computations to be explained shortly.

[2] If standards are not currently attainable because they are perfection or outdated, the amount budgeted for financial (cash) planning purposes has to differ from the standard. Otherwise, projected income and cash disbursements will be forecasted incorrectly. In such cases, perfection or outdated standards may be used for compiling performance reports, but "expected variances" are stipulated in the master budget for financial planning. For example, if unusually strict labor standards are used, the standard cost per finished unit may be $8 despite the fact that top management anticipates an unfavorable performance variance of 40¢ per unit. In the master budget, the total labor costs would be $8.40 per unit: $8 plus an expected variance of 40¢.

The flexible-budget totals for direct material and direct labor are also sometimes expressed as total *standard costs allowed,* computed as follows:

$$\begin{pmatrix} \text{units of} \\ \text{good} \\ \text{output} \end{pmatrix} \times \begin{pmatrix} \text{input allowed} \\ \text{per unit of} \\ \text{output} \end{pmatrix} \times \begin{pmatrix} \text{standard} \\ \text{unit price} \\ \text{of input} \end{pmatrix} = \begin{pmatrix} \text{total standard} \\ \text{cost allowed} \end{pmatrix}$$

Direct material: 7,000 units × 5 pounds × $.60 per pound = $21,000
Direct labor: 7,000 units × 2 hours   × $4.00 per hour = $56,000

Before reading on, note particularly that the flexible-budget amounts (that is, the standard costs allowed) are tied to an initial question, What was the *output* achieved? Always first ask yourself, What was the good output? Then proceed with your computations of the total standard cost allowed for the good output achieved.

☐ Price and Efficiency Variances

Two commonly encountered variances are

Price variance—the difference between actual unit prices and budgeted unit prices multiplied by the actual quantity of goods or services in question
Efficiency variance—the difference between the quantity of actual inputs (such as pounds of materials or number of direct-labor hours) and the quantity of inputs that should have been allowed for any *actual output achieved* (such as finished goods) multiplied by some budgeted price

The assessment of performance is facilitated by separating the items that are subject to the manager's direct influence from those that are not. The general approach is to separate *price* factors from *efficiency* factors. Price factors are less subject to immediate control than are efficiency factors, principally because of external forces, such as general economic conditions and unforeseeable price changes. Even when price factors are regarded as outside of company control, it is still desirable to isolate them to obtain a sharper focus on the efficient usage of the goods or services in question.

"Efficiency" is a relative measure that is often expressed as the ratio of inputs to outputs. That is, the concept of efficiency requires our knowing both *inputs* and *outputs* and their interrelationships. "Perfect" efficiency would be some approximation of an optimal relationship between inputs and outputs.[3]

☐ Price and Efficiency Variance Computations

Consider the detailed computations of price and efficiency variances:
Price variance: The difference between actual unit prices of inputs and standard unit prices *multiplied by the actual inputs:*

[3] *Price* and *efficiency* will be used throughout this book to describe these two classes of variances. In practice, the price variance is often called a **rate** variance when it is used in conjunction with labor. Similarly, the efficiency variance is often called a **usage** or **quantity** variance when it is used in conjunction with materials.

$$\text{price variance} = \begin{pmatrix} \text{difference in} \\ \text{unit price} \\ \text{of inputs} \end{pmatrix} \times \begin{pmatrix} \text{actual} \\ \text{inputs} \\ \text{used} \end{pmatrix}$$

For direct material:

$$= (\$.58 - \$.60) \times 36{,}810 \text{ pounds}$$
$$= \$736 \text{ F}$$

For direct labor:

$$= (\$4.10 - \$4.00) \times 15{,}000 \text{ hours}$$
$$= \$1{,}500 \text{ U}$$

Efficiency variance: For any given level of output (e.g., units produced), the efficiency variance is the difference between the inputs that should have been used and the inputs that were actually used—holding unit prices of inputs constant at the standard unit price:[4]

$$\text{efficiency variance} = \begin{pmatrix} \text{inputs} & \text{inputs that} \\ \text{actually} - \text{should have} \\ \text{used} & \text{been used} \end{pmatrix} \times \begin{pmatrix} \text{standard} \\ \text{unit price} \\ \text{of inputs} \end{pmatrix}$$

$$= \begin{pmatrix} \text{actual} & \text{standard} \\ \text{pounds or} - \text{allowed pounds} \\ \text{hours used} & \text{or hours for} \\ & \text{good output} \end{pmatrix} \times \begin{pmatrix} \text{standard} \\ \text{unit price} \\ \text{of inputs} \end{pmatrix}$$

For direct materials:

$$= [36{,}810 - (7{,}000 \text{ units} \times 5 \text{ pounds})] \times \$.60$$
$$= (36{,}810 - 35{,}000) \times \$.60$$
$$= 1{,}810 \times \$.60$$
$$= \$1{,}086 \text{ U}$$

For direct labor:

$$= [15{,}000 - (7{,}000 \text{ units} \times 2 \text{ hours})] \times \$4.00$$
$$= (15{,}000 - 14{,}000) \times \$4.00$$
$$= 1{,}000 \times \$4.00$$
$$= \$4{,}000 \text{ U}$$

Evidently, the direct-labor efficiency variance warrants further investigation because it is easily the largest variance of all.

Variance analysis does *not* provide any answers. But it raises questions, provides clues, and directs attention. For instance, one possible explanation, among many, for this set of variances is that a manager might have made a trade-off and lost—that is, the manager might have purchased, at a favorable price, some materials that were slightly substandard, resulting in excessive waste as indicated by the unfavorable efficiency variance.

❏ A General Approach

Exhibit 7-6 presents the foregoing analysis in a format that deserves close study. The general approach is at the top of the exhibit; the specific applica-

---

[4] Expressed algebraically, these variances are $V_p = (AP - SP) \times AQ$ and $V_e = (AQ - SQ) \times SP$, where V_p = price variance, V_e = efficiency variance, AP = actual unit price of inputs, SP = standard unit price of inputs, AQ = actual quantity of inputs, and SQ = standard quantity of inputs allowed for good output.

EXHIBIT 7-6   *(Place a clip on this page for easy reference.)*

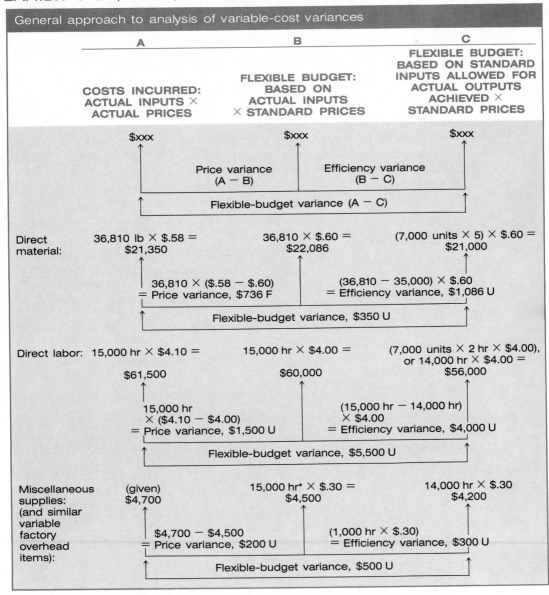

General approach to analysis of variable-cost variances

	A	B	C
	COSTS INCURRED: ACTUAL INPUTS × ACTUAL PRICES	**FLEXIBLE BUDGET: BASED ON ACTUAL INPUTS × STANDARD PRICES**	**FLEXIBLE BUDGET: BASED ON STANDARD INPUTS ALLOWED FOR ACTUAL OUTPUTS ACHIEVED × STANDARD PRICES**
	$xxx	$xxx	$xxx

Price variance (A − B) Efficiency variance (B − C)

Flexible-budget variance (A − C)

Direct material:
36,810 lb × $.58 = $21,350   36,810 × $.60 = $22,086   (7,000 units × 5) × $.60 = $21,000

36,810 × ($.58 − $.60) = Price variance, $736 F   (36,810 − 35,000) × $.60 = Efficiency variance, $1,086 U

Flexible-budget variance, $350 U

Direct labor:
15,000 hr × $4.10 = $61,500   15,000 hr × $4.00 = $60,000   (7,000 units × 2 hr × $4.00), or 14,000 hr × $4.00 = $56,000

15,000 hr × ($4.10 − $4.00) = Price variance, $1,500 U   (15,000 hr − 14,000 hr) × $4.00 = Efficiency variance, $4,000 U

Flexible-budget variance, $5,500 U

Miscellaneous supplies: (and similar variable factory overhead items):
(given) $4,700   15,000 hr* × $.30 = $4,500   14,000 hr × $.30 = $4,200

$4,700 − $4,500 = Price variance, $200 U   (1,000 hr × $.30) = Efficiency variance, $300 U

Flexible-budget variance, $500 U

U = Unfavorable. F = Favorable.
*For comments, see the section "Limitations of Price and Efficiency Variances" in text.

tions then follow. Even though the exhibit may seem unnecessarily complex at first, its repeated use will solidify your understanding of variance analysis. Of course, the other budget variances in Exhibit 7-5 could be further analyzed in the same manner in which direct material and direct labor are analyzed in Exhibit 7-6. The pursuit of such a detailed investigation depends on the manager's perception as to whether the extra benefits will exceed the extra cost of such detective work.

Flexible Budgets and Standards for Control

187

A graphical approach sometimes clarifies the relationships. For example, the direct-labor analysis in the middle of Exhibit 7-6 is also portrayed in Exhibit 7-7. The cost function is linear, sloping upward at a standard rate (price) of $4 per hour.

Note that volume is expressed in hours instead of in physical units of product. This is a common practice. Most departments have a variety of products; when the variety of units is added together, the result is frequently a nonsensical sum. Therefore all units of output are expressed in terms of the standard inputs of hours allowed for their production. Hours thus become the common denominator for measuring total volume. Production, instead of being expressed as, say, 12,000 chairs and 3,000 tables, is frequently expressed as 14,000 *standard hours allowed* (or *standard hours worked*, or *standard hours earned*, or most accurately as *standard hours of input allowed for outputs achieved*).

Another key idea illustrated in Exhibits 7-6 and 7-7 is the versatility of the flexible budget. A flexible budget is geared to volume, and Exhibit 7-7 shows that volume can be measured in terms of *actual inputs* alone, *actual outputs achieved* alone, or both. Both measures are shown in the graph; they

**EXHIBIT
7-7**

Graphical
analysis of
direct labor

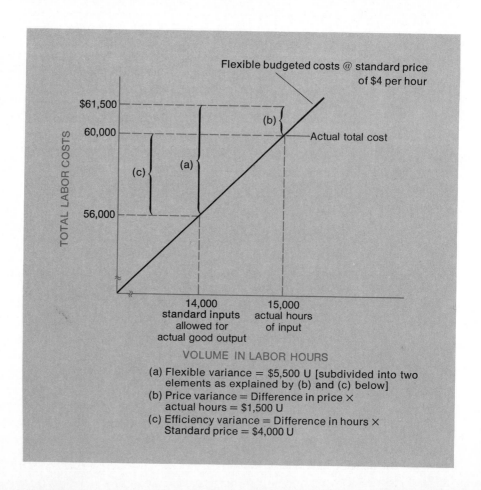

(a) Flexible variance = $5,500 U [subdivided into two elements as explained by (b) and (c) below]
(b) Price variance = Difference in price × actual hours = $1,500 U
(c) Efficiency variance = Difference in hours × Standard price = $4,000 U

are necessary to obtain separate identification of price and efficiency variances.

When used in this book, unless stated otherwise, the term *flexible-budget variance* will mean the difference between columns A and C in Exhibit 7-6, the difference between actual costs and the flexible budget based on the standard inputs allowed for actual outputs achieved.

Please reread the preceding four paragraphs before going on. They contain key ideas and terms that warrant scrutiny.

❑ Limitations of Price and Efficiency Variances

The division of variances into two neat categories of "price" and "efficiency" is a good first step. However, it is a crude split, and its limitations should be kept in mind. In particular, the individual overhead items may be hard to subdivide in this way. For instance, the flexible budget for supplies is budgeted in Exhibit 7-5 at $4,200, based on a formula of 60¢ per unit.

In practice, a simple but fragile assumption underlies the usual efficiency-variance computation for variable-overhead items: Variable-overhead costs fluctuate in direct proportion to direct-labor hours. Therefore the efficiency variance for a variable-overhead item such as supplies is a measure of the extra overhead (or savings) incurred *solely* because the actual *direct-labor hours* used differed from the standard hours allowed:

$$\text{overhead efficiency variance} = \text{standard overhead rate per hour} \times (\text{actual direct-labor hours of inputs} - \text{standard direct-labor hours allowed})$$
$$= \$.30 \times (15{,}000 - 14{,}000)$$
$$= \$300 \text{ unfavorable}$$

Because direct labor was inefficiently used by 1,000 hours under this approach, we would expect the related usage of supplies to be proportionately excessive wholly because of labor inefficiency. However, whether in fact this direct relationship exists depends on specific circumstances.

To recapitulate, ponder why there was a $500 supplies variance in Exhibit 7-5. The implications of the analysis in Exhibit 7-6 follow:

Actual costs	$4,700
Efficiency variance—The amount that would be expected to be incurred **because of the inefficient use of direct labor,** 1,000 hr × $.30 =	$300
Price variance—The amount unexplained by the efficiency variance. It could arise from unit price changes for various supplies—but it could also arise simply from the general waste and sloppy use of these supplies. In short, this, too, could be partially or completely traceable to **more efficiency,** even though it is labeled as a price variance. (Incidentally, for this reason, many practitioners call this type of overhead variance a **spending** variance rather than a price variance.)	200
Budget variance	500
Budgeted amount in flexible budget	$4,200

Above all, the limitations of these analyses of variances should be underscored. The *only* way to discover why overhead performance did not agree with a budget is to investigate possible causes, line item by line item. However, the price-efficiency distinctions provide a handy springboard for a more rigorous analysis.

CONTROLLABILITY AND VARIANCES

❏ Responsibility for Material Variances

In most companies, the *acquisition* of materials or merchandise entails different control decisions than their *use*. The purchasing executive of a manufacturing company worries about getting raw materials at favorable prices, whereas the production executive concentrates on using them efficiently. The merchandise manager of a large grocery company will be responsible for skillful buying of foodstuffs, but the store manager will be responsible for their sale and for minimizing losses from shrinkage, shoplifting, and the like. Thus the responsibility for price variances usually rests with the purchasing officer, and the responsibility for efficiency variances usually rests with the production manager or sales manager.

Price variances are often regarded as measures of forecasting ability rather than of failure to buy at specified prices. Some control over the price variance is obtainable by getting many quotations, buying in economical lots, taking advantage of cash discounts, and selecting the most economical means of delivery. Price variances may lead to decisions to change suppliers or freight carriers.

However, failure to meet price standards may result from a sudden rush of sales orders or from unanticipated changes in production schedules, which in turn may require the purchasing officer to buy at uneconomical prices or to request delivery by air freight. In such cases, the responsibility may rest with the sales manager or the head of production scheduling, rather than with the purchasing officer.

❏ Responsibility for Labor Variances

In most companies, because of union contracts or other predictable factors, labor prices can be foreseen with much greater accuracy than can prices of materials. Therefore labor price variances tend to be relatively insignificant.

Labor, unlike material and supplies, cannot ordinarily be stored for later use. The acquisition and use of labor occur simultaneously. For these reasons, labor rate variances are usually charged to the same manager who is responsible for labor usage.

Labor price variances may be traceable to faulty predictions of the labor rates. However, the more likely causes include (1) the use of a single average standard labor price for a given operation that is, in fact, performed by individuals earning slightly different rates because of seniority; (2) the assignment of a worker earning, perhaps, $9 per hour to a given operation that should be appointed to a less-skilled worker earning, say, $7 per hour; and (3) the payment of hourly rates, instead of prescribed piece rates, because of low productivity.

☐ Causes of Efficiency Variances

The general approach to analyzing efficiency variances is probably best exemplified by the control of direct materials in standard cost systems. The budget of the production department manager is usually based on a *standard formula* or a *Standard Bill of Materials*. This is a specification of the physical quantities allowed for producing a specified number of acceptable finished units. These quantities are then compared with the quantities actually used.

What does the manager do with the variances? The manager seeks explanations for their existence. Common causes of efficiency variances include improper handling, inferior quality of material, poor workmanship, changes in methods, new workers, slow machines, broken cutting tools, and faulty blueprints.

☐ Trade-Offs Among Variances

Variance analysis can be useful for focusing on how various aspects of operations are meeting expectations. However, a standard cost system should not be a straitjacket that prevents the manager from aiming at the overall organization objectives. Too often, each unfavorable variance is regarded as, ipso facto, bad; and each favorable variance is regarded as, ipso facto, good.

Managers sometimes deliberately acquire off-standard material at unusually low prices. They hope that the favorable price variances will exceed any resulting unfavorable efficiency variances caused by heavy spoilage or unusual labor-hours. Thus, if the manager guesses correctly, the decision was favorable despite the unfavorable label pinned on the efficiency variances. Because there are so many interdependencies among activities, an "unfavorable" or a "favorable" label should not lead the manager to jump to conclusions. By themselves, such labels merely raise questions and provide clues. They are attention directors, not answer givers. The chapter appendix discusses these interdependencies in more depth.

☐ When to Investigate Variances

When should variances be investigated? Frequently the answer is based on subjective judgments, hunches, guesses, and rules of thumb. The most troublesome aspect of feedback is in deciding when a variance is significant enough to warrant management's attention. For some items, a small deviation may prompt follow-up. For other items, a minimum dollar amount or 5%, 10%, or 25% deviations from budget may be necessary before investigations commence. Of course, a 4% variance in a $1 million material cost may deserve more attention than a 20% variance in a $10,000 repair cost. Therefore, rules such as "Investigate all variances exceeding $5,000 or 25% of standard cost, whichever is lower," are common.

Variance analysis is subject to the same cost-benefit test as other phases of an information system. The trouble with the foregoing rules of thumb is that they are too frequently based on subjective assessments, guesses, or hunches. The field of statistics offers tools to help reduce these subjective features. These tools help answer the cost-benefit question, and they help separate variances caused by random events from variances that are controllable.

Accounting systems have traditionally implied that a standard is a single acceptable measure. Practically, the accountant (and everybody else) realizes that the standard is a *band* or *range* of possible acceptable outcomes. Consequently, the accountant expects variances to fluctuate randomly within some normal limits. A random variance, by definition, calls for no corrective action to an existing process. In short, random variances are attributable to chance rather than to management's implementation decisions.

Summary

Management is best aided by carefully prepared standards and budgets representing what should be accomplished. These standards should be based on material specifications and on work measurement rather than on past performance, because the latter too often conceals past inefficiencies.

Currently attainable standards are the most widely used because they usually have the most desirable motivational impact and because they may be used for a variety of accounting purposes, including financial planning, as well as for monitoring departmental performance.

When standards are currently attainable, there is no logical difference between standards and budgets. A standard is a unit concept, whereas a budget is a total concept. In a sense, the standard is the budget for one unit.

Flexible budgets are geared to changing levels of activity rather than to a single static level. They may be tailored to a particular level of sales or production volume—before or after the fact. They tell how much cost should be or should have been incurred for any level of output, which is usually expressed either in product units of output or in standard direct-labor hours allowed for that output.

The evaluation of performance is aided by a feedback comparison of actual results with budgeted expectations, as summarized in Exhibit 7-4. The flexible-budget idea helps managers to get an explanation of why the master budget was not achieved. Variances are often divided into sales volume, price, and efficiency variances. In practice, the efficiency factors are more important because they are subject to more direct management influence than are prices of materials or labor.

CHAPTER 15, WHICH MAY BE STUDIED NOW IF DESIRED, PROBES THE ANALYSIS OF VARIANCES IN MORE DEPTH, PARTICULARLY WITH RESPECT TO FIXED OVERHEAD AND INVENTORIES.

Summary
Problem for Your Review _____

(Problem One appeared earlier in this chapter.)

❑ Problem Two

The following questions are based on the data contained in the illustration used in the chapter, p. 184:

1. Suppose the following were the actual results for the production of 8,500 units: Direct material: 46,000 pounds of inputs were used at an actual unit price of 55¢, for a total actual cost of $25,300.

    Direct labor: 16,500 hours of inputs were used at an actual hourly price (rate) of $4.20, for a total actual cost of $69,300.

    Compute the flexible-budget variance and the price and efficiency variances for direct material and direct labor. Present your answers in the form shown in Exhibit 7-6, p. 187.

2. Suppose the company is organized so that the purchasing manager bears the primary responsibility for the acquisition prices of materials, and the production manager bears the primary responsibility for efficiency but no responsibility for unit prices. Assume the same facts as in Requirement 1 except that the purchasing manager acquired 60,000 pounds of materials. This means that there is an ending inventory of 14,000 pounds. Would your variance analysis of materials in Requirement 1 change? Why? Show computations to support your answer.

❑ Solution To Problem Two

1.

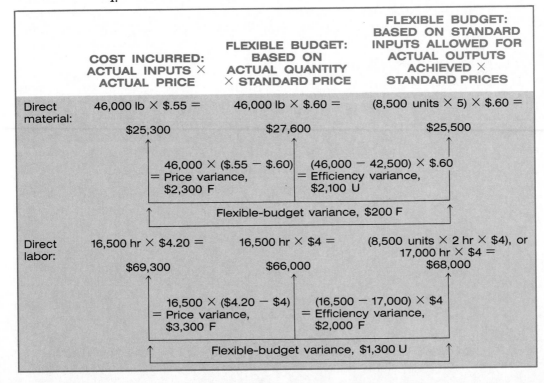

2. Whether the variance analysis in Requirement 1 would change depends on how the information system is designed. In many organizations, price variances for materials are isolated at the most logical control point—time of purchase rather than time of use. In turn, the production or operating departments that later use the materials are always charged at some predetermined so-called budget or standard unit price, never at actual unit prices. Under this procedure the price-variance analysis would be conducted in the purchasing department and the efficiency-variance analysis in the production department. This represents a slight modification of the approach in Requirement 1 as follows:

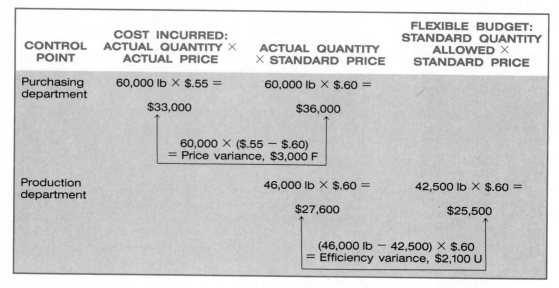

CONTROL POINT	COST INCURRED: ACTUAL QUANTITY × ACTUAL PRICE	ACTUAL QUANTITY × STANDARD PRICE	FLEXIBLE BUDGET: STANDARD QUANTITY ALLOWED × STANDARD PRICE
Purchasing department	60,000 lb × $.55 = $33,000	60,000 lb × $.60 = $36,000	
		60,000 × ($.55 − $.60) = Price variance, $3,000 F	
Production department		46,000 lb × $.60 = $27,600	42,500 lb × $.60 = $25,500
		(46,000 lb − 42,500) × $.60 = Efficiency variance, $2,100 U	

Note that the efficiency variance is the same in Requirements 1 and 2. However, the flexible-budget variance would not now be the algebraic sum of the price and efficiency variances because here the price variance is computed by using the actual quantity *purchased* instead of the actual quantity *used*.

Highlights to Remember

1. There is a similarity in approach to the control of all costs that are regarded as variable. The price variance is the difference in price multiplied by actual quantity. The efficiency variance is the difference in quantity multiplied by standard price.

2. Some important relationships deserve attention:

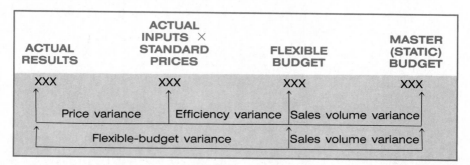

ACTUAL RESULTS	ACTUAL INPUTS × STANDARD PRICES	FLEXIBLE BUDGET	MASTER (STATIC) BUDGET
XXX	XXX	XXX	XXX
	Price variance	Efficiency variance	Sales volume variance
	Flexible-budget variance		Sales volume variance

3. Price variances help managers gauge the impact of price fluctuations on actual results. Moreover, price variances permit the exclusion of price effects from all *other* variances.

4. The first question to ask in solving standard-cost problems is, What was the good output achieved? The second question often asked is, What were the standard direct-labor hours allowed for the good output achieved?

Accounting Vocabulary

Budget variance; currently attainable standards; efficiency variance; flexible budget; flexible-budget variances; performance report; price variance; quantity variance; rate variance; sales volume variances; spending variance; standard cost; static budget; usage variance; variable budget.

Appendix 7: Mutual Price and Efficiency Effects

The usual breakdown of variances into price and efficiency is not theoretically perfect because there may be a small mutual price-efficiency effect. A production foreman and a purchasing agent might argue over the following situation. The direct material is 1,000 pounds @ $1 and is intended to produce 1,000 good finished units. The performance report shows the use of 1,150 pounds @ $1.20 to produce 1,000 good finished units.

The ordinary analysis of variances would appear as follows:

Actual quantity × Actual price, or 1,150 × $1.20 =		$1,380
Price variance = Difference in price ×		
Actual pounds = ($1.20 − $1) × 1,150 =	$230 U	
Efficiency variance = Difference in quantity ×		
Standard price = (1,150 − 1,000) × $1 =	150 U	
Total variance explained		380 U
Standard quantity of inputs allowed for units		
produced × Standard price = 1,000 × $1 =		$1,000

The small area in the upper right-hand corner of the graphic analysis (Exhibit 7-8) may be the area of controversy. The purchasing officer might readily accept responsibility for the price variance on the 1,000 pounds in the standard allowance but might also claim that the extra $30 buried in the $230 total variance is more properly attributable to the production foreman. After all, if the foreman had produced in accordance with the standard, the extra 150 pounds would not have been needed. But this distinction is not often made, simply because it usually involves a small sum. However, we should be aware that the conventional variance analysis, which includes the joint price-efficiency variance ($30 in this case) as a part of an overall price variance, has logical deficiencies.

In practice, the efficiency variance is considered much more important than the price variance because the manager can exert more direct influence over the efficiency variance. Consequently, the performance report on efficiency should minimize the possibility of the production manager's criticisms of any accounting or measurement methods. Joint price-efficiency variance is less likely to cause arguments if it is buried in the total price variance than if it is buried in the efficiency variance.

EXHIBIT 7-8 Graphical analysis of variances

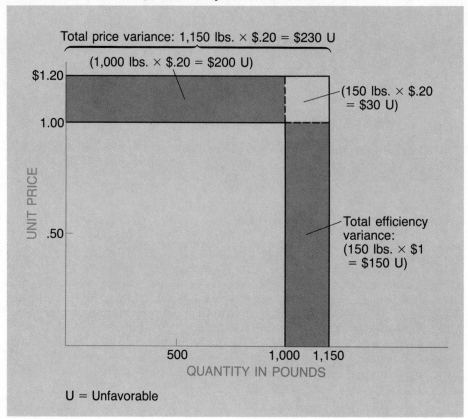

U = Unfavorable

Assignment Material

Special note: Problem 7–1 covers Part One of the chapter; 7–2 covers Part Two. Similarly, Problems 7–21 through 7–30 cover Part One; 7–31 through 7–44 cover Part Two. Problem 7–44 is a review and is accompanied by answers. Problem 7–46 covers all the major points in the chapter.

Fundamental Assignment Material

7–1. **Flexible and static budgets.** (Alternates are 7–26, 7–27, and 7–28.) Azure Transportation Company executives have had trouble interpreting operating performance for a number of years. The company has used a budget based on detailed expectations for the forthcoming quarter. For example, the condensed performance report for a recent quarter for a midwestern branch was (in dollars):

	BUDGET	ACTUAL	VARIANCE
Net revenue	10,000,000	9,500,000	500,000 U
Fuel	200,000	196,000	4,000 F
Repairs and maintenance	100,000	98,000	2,000 F
Supplies and miscellaneous	1,000,000	985,000	15,000 F
Variable payroll	6,700,000	6,500,000	200,000 F
Total variable costs*	8,000,000	7,779,000	221,000 F
Supervision	200,000	200,000	—
Rent	200,000	200,000	—
Depreciation	600,000	600,000	—
Other fixed costs	200,000	200,000	—
Total fixed costs	1,200,000	1,200,000	—
Total costs charged against revenue	9,200,000	8,979,000	221,000 F
Operating income	800,000	521,000	279,000 U

U = Unfavorable.   F = Favorable.

*For purposes of this analysis, assume that all these costs are totally variable. In practice, many are mixed and have to be subdivided into variable and fixed components before a meaningful analysis can be made. Also assume that the prices and mix of services sold remain unchanged.

Although the branch manager was upset about not obtaining enough revenue, he was happy that his control performance was favorable; otherwise his net operating income would be even worse.

His immediate superior, the vice-president for operations, was totally unhappy and remarked: "I can see some merit in comparing actual performance with budgeted performance because we can see whether actual revenue coincided with our best guess for budget purposes. But I can't see how this performance report helps me evaluate the cost control performance of the department head."

REQUIRED:

1. Prepare a columnar flexible budget for expected costs at $9, $10, and $11 million levels of revenue. Include both variable and fixed costs in your budget.
2. Express Requirement 1 in formula form.
3. Prepare a condensed summary similar to Exhibit 7-4 that might better trace the effects on operating income of the deviations of actual results from the original plans. (Exhibit 7-4 is on p. 179.)

7–2. **Direct-material and direct-labor variances.** The Kenneth Company manufactures metal giftware that is hand-shaped and hand-painted. The following standards were developed for a luxury line of vases:

	STANDARD INPUTS ALLOWED FOR EACH UNIT OF OUTPUT ACHIEVED	STANDARD PRICE PER UNIT OF INPUT
Direct materials	12 ounces	$ 4.00 per pound
Direct labor	.5 hour	20.00 per hour

During April, 50,000 vases were scheduled for production. However, only 48,000 were actually produced.

Direct materials used amounted to 40,000 pounds at a unit price of $3.50 per pound. Direct labor actually was paid $21.00 per hour, and 26,000 hours were used.

REQUIRED:

1. Compute the standard cost per vase for direct materials and direct labor. (There are sixteen ounces in one pound.)

2. Compute the price variances and efficiency variances for direct materials and direct labor.
3. Based on these sketchy data, what clues for investigation are provided by the variances?

Additional Assignment Material

7-3. "Price variances should be computed even if prices are regarded as being outside of company control." Do you agree? Explain.

7-4. "Failure to meet price standards is the responsibility of the purchasing officer." Do you agree? Explain.

7-5. Why do labor price variances tend to be insignificant?

7-6. What are the key questions in the analysis and follow-up of variances?

7-7. What are some common causes of quantity variances?

7-8. Why is the joint price-quantity variance buried in the price variance rather than in the quantity variance?

7-9. What two basic questions must be asked in approaching the control of all costs?

7-10. Why do the techniques for controlling overhead differ from those for controlling direct material and direct labor?

7-11. "The flex in the flexible budget relates solely to variable costs." Do you agree? Explain.

7-12. How does the variable-overhead price variance differ from the labor price variance?

7-13. Why are standard hours superior to actual hours as an index of activity?

7-14. "A standard is a band or range of acceptable outcomes." Criticize.

7-15. What are standard costs? Why is their use preferable to comparisons of actual data with past data?

7-16. "Direct material and direct labor may be included in a flexible budget." Do you agree? Explain.

7-17. Why should a budgeted cost not be merely an extension of past experience?

7-18. Distinguish between perfection and currently attainable standards.

7-19. What is the difference between a standard amount and a budget amount?

7-20. What are expected variances?

7-21. **National Park Service.** The National Park Service prepared the following budget for one of its national parks for 19X4:

Revenue from fees	$4,000,000
Variable costs (miscellaneous)	400,000
Contribution margin	$3,600,000
Fixed costs (miscellaneous)	3,600,000
Operating income	$ 0

The fees were based on an average of 50,000 vehicle-admission days (vehicles multiplied by number of days in parks) per week for the twenty-week season, multiplied by average entry and other fees of $4 per vehicle-admission day.

The season was booming for the first four weeks. However, there was a wave of thievery and violence during the fifth week. Grizzly bears killed four campers during the sixth week and two during the seventh week. As a result, the number of visitors to the park dropped sharply during the remainder of the season.

Total revenue fell by $1 million. Moreover, extra rangers and police had to be hired at a cost of $200,000. The latter was regarded as a fixed cost.

REQUIRED:

Prepare a columnar summary of performance, showing the original budget, sales volume variances, flexible budget, flexible-budget variances, and actual results.

7–22. Flexible budget. Escriva Company made 150,000 units of product in a given year. The total manufacturing costs of $170,000 included $50,000 of fixed costs. Assume that no price changes will occur in the following year and that no changes in production methods are applicable. Compute the budgeted cost for producing 200,000 units in the following year.

7–23. Basic flexible budget. The superintendent of police of the city of Santa Clara is attempting to predict the costs of operating a fleet of police cars. Among the items of concern are fuel, 15¢ per mile; and depreciation per car per year, $4,000.

REQUIRED:

The manager is preparing a flexible budget for the coming year. Prepare the flexible-budget amounts for fuel and depreciation for ten cars at a level of 30,000, 40,000, and 50,000 miles.

7–24. Flexible budget. Consider the following data for a given month:

	BUDGET FORMULA PER UNIT	VARIOUS LEVELS OF VOLUME		
Units	—	4,000	5,000	6,000
Sales	$20	$?	$?	$?
Variable costs:				
Direct material	?	48,000	?	?
Fuel	1	?	?	?
Fixed costs:				
Depreciation		?	12,000	?
Executive salaries		?	?	50,000

REQUIRED:

1. Fill in the unknowns.
2. Draw a freehand graph of the flexible budget for the cost items shown here.

7–25. Basic flexible budget. The budgeted prices for materials and direct labor per unit of finished product are $12 and $5, respectively. The production manager is delighted about the following data:

	MASTER BUDGET	ACTUAL COSTS	VARIANCE
Direct materials	$120,000	$110,000	$10,000 F
Direct labor	50,000	47,000	3,000 F

Is the manager's happiness justified? Prepare a report that might provide a more-detailed explanation of why the master budget was not achieved. Good output was 8,500 units.

7–26. Summary performance report. (Alternates are 7–1, 7–27, and 7–28.) Consider the following data:

Master budget data: sales, 20,000 units at $30 per unit; variable costs, $20 per unit; fixed costs, $150,000

Actual results at actual prices: sales, 24,000 units at $31 per unit; variable costs, $525,000; fixed costs, $155,000

REQUIRED:

1. Prepare a summary performance report similar to Exhibit 7–4, p. 179.
2. Fill in the blanks:

Master-budget operating income		$ —
Variances:		
Sales volume variances	$ —	
Flexible-budget variances	—	—
Actual operating income		$ —

7–27. Summary explanation. (Alternates are 7–1, 7–26, and 7–28.) Consider the following data. Except for physical units, all quantities are in dollars:

	ACTUAL RESULTS AT ACTUAL PRICES	FLEXIBLE-BUDGET VARIANCES	FLEXIBLE BUDGET	SALES VOLUME VARIANCES	MASTER (STATIC) BUDGET
Physical units	100,000	—	?	?	90,000
Sales	?	8,000 F	?	?	900,000
Variable costs	620,000	?	600,000	?	?
Contribution margin	?	?	?	?	?
Fixed costs	?	10,000 U	?	?	260,000
Operating income	?	?	?	?	?

REQUIRED:

1. Fill in the unknowns.
2. Give a brief summary explanation of why the original target operating income was not attained.

7–28. Explanation of variance in income. (Alternates are 7–1, 7–26, and 7–27.) The H & R Income Tax Service processes income tax returns that result in standard contribution margins averaging 60% of dollar sales and average selling prices of $30 per return. Average productivity is four returns per hour. Some preparers work for sales commissions and others for an hourly rate. The master budget for 19X2 had predicted sales of 900,000 returns, but only 800,000 returns were processed.

Fixed costs of rent, supervision, advertising, and other items were budgeted at $11 million, but they were exceeded by $1 million because of extra advertising in an attempt to boost revenue.

There were no variances from the average selling prices, but the actual commissions paid to preparers and the actual productivity per hour resulted in flexible-budget variances (that is, total price and efficiency variances) for variable costs of $1.1 million unfavorable.

The president was unhappy because the budgeted operating income of $5.2 million was not achieved. He said, "Sure, we had unfavorable variable-cost variances, but our operating income was down far more than that. Please explain why."

REQUIRED: Explain why the budgeted operating income was not attained. Use a presentation similar to Exhibit 7-4. Enough data have been given to permit you to construct the complete exhibit by filling in the known items and then computing the unknown. Complete your explanation by summarizing what happened, using no more than three sentences. (Exhibit 7-4 is on p. 179.)

7–29. Summary of airline performance. Consider the following performance of an airline for a given year (in thousands of dollars):

	ACTUAL RESULTS AT ACTUAL PRICES	MASTER BUDGET	VARIANCE
Revenue	?	150,000	?
Variable expenses	100,000	97,500*	2,500 U
Contribution margin	?	52,500	?
Fixed expenses	38,500	37,500	1,000 U
Operating income	?	15,000	?

*Includes jet fuel of $45,000.

The master budget had been based on budgeted revenue passenger mile of 15¢. A revenue passenger mile is one paying passenger flown one mile. An average airfare decrease of 8% had helped generate an increase in passenger miles flown that was 10% in excess of the master budget for the year.

The price per gallon of jet fuel fell below the price used to formulate the master budget. The average price decline for the year was 12%.

REQUIRED: 1. As an explanation for the president, prepare a summary performance report that is similar to Exhibit 7-4, p. 179.
2. Assume that the use of fuel was at the same level of efficiency as predicted in the master budget. What portion of the flexible-budget variance for variable expenses is attributable to jet fuel expenses? Explain.

7–30. University flexible budgeting. (CMA, adapted.) The University of Boyne offers an extensive continuing education program in many cities throughout the state. For the convenience of its faculty and administrative staff and also to save costs, the university operates a motor pool. The motor pool operated with twenty vehicles until February of this year, when an additional automobile was acquired. The motor pool furnishes gasoline, oil, and other supplies for the cars and hires one mechanic who does routine maintenance and minor repairs. Major repairs are done at a nearby commercial garage. A supervisor manages the operations.

Each year the supervisor prepares an operating budget, informing university management of the funds needed to operate the pool. Depreciation on the automobiles is recorded in the budget in order to determine the costs per mile.

The schedule below presents the annual budget approved by the university. The actual costs for March are compared with one-twelfth of the annual budget.

UNIVERSITY MOTOR POOL
Budget Report
For March 19X6

	ANNUAL BUDGET	ONE-MONTH BUDGET	MARCH ACTUAL	OVER* UNDER
Gasoline	$ 72,000	$ 6,000	$ 9,100	$3,100*
Oil, minor repairs, parts, and supplies	3,600	300	380	80*
Outside repairs	2,700	225	50	175
Insurance	6,000	500	525	25*
Salaries and benefits	30,000	2,500	2,500	—
Depreciation	26,400	2,200	2,310	110*
	$140,700	$11,725	$14,865	$3,140*
Total miles	600,000	50,000	63,000	
Cost per mile	$ .2345	$ .2345	$ .2360	
Number of automobiles	20	20	21	

The annual budget was constructed upon the following assumptions:

    a. 20 automobiles in the pool
    b. 30,000 miles per year per automobile
    c. 15 miles per gallon per automobile
    d. $1.80 per gallon of gas
    e. $.006 per mile for oil, minor repairs, parts, and supplies
    f. $135 per automobile in outside repairs

The supervisor is unhappy with the monthly report comparing budget and actual costs for March; he claims it presents his performance unfairly. His previous employer used flexible budgeting to compare actual costs with budgeted amounts.

REQUIRED:

1. Employing flexible-budgeting techniques, prepare a report that shows budgeted amounts, actual costs, and monthly variation for March.
2. Explain briefly the basis of your budget figure for outside repairs.

7–31. Material and labor variances. Consider the following data:

	DIRECT MATERIAL	DIRECT LABOR
Costs incurred: actual inputs × actual prices incurred	$100,000	$70,000
Actual inputs × standard prices	110,000	65,000
Standard inputs allowed for actual outputs achieved × standard prices	115,000	61,000

REQUIRED:

Compute the price, efficiency, and flexible-budget variances for direct material and direct labor. Use *U* or *F* to indicate whether the variances are unfavorable or favorable.

7–32. Material and labor variances. Consider the following data:

	DIRECT MATERIAL	DIRECT LABOR
Actual price per unit of input (pounds and hours)	$14	$ 9
Standard price per unit of input	$12	$10
Standard inputs allowed per unit of output	5	2
Actual units of input	48,000	23,000
Actual units of output (product)	10,000	10,000

1. Compute the price, efficiency, and flexible-budget variances for direct material and direct labor. Use *U* or *F* to indicate whether the variances are unfavorable or favorable.
2. Prepare a plausible explanation for the performance.

7–33. Efficiency variances. Assume that 10,000 units of a particular item were produced. Suppose the standard direct-material allowance is two pounds per unit, at a cost per pound of $2. Actually, 21,000 pounds of materials (input) were used to produce the 10,000 units (output).

Similarly, assume that it is supposed to take four direct-labor hours to produce one unit, and that the standard hourly labor cost is $3. But 41,000 hours (input) were used to produce the 10,000 units in this Hong Kong factory.

Compute the efficiency variances for direct material and direct labor.

7–34. Hospital costs. A hospital cafeteria used a flexible budget. The expectation for January volume was 20,000 meals. Hourly paid extra dishwashers were budgeted at $4,000, computed on the basis of an average wage rate of $4 per hour. The following data were compiled for January, when 20,000 meals were actually served and the dishwashers actually worked 1,200 hours:

	ACTUAL	BUDGET	VARIANCE
Dietary department: Wages—dishwashers	$4,560	$4,000	$560 U

U = Unfavorable.

1. Compute the price and efficiency variances. What might be some possible reasons for the variances?
2. Suppose 24,000 meals had been served. Compute the price and efficiency variances.

7–35. Straightforward variance analysis. The Macao Company uses a standard cost system. The month's data regarding its single product follow:

Material purchased and used, 6,700 pounds
Direct-labor costs incurred, 11,000 hours, $41,800
Variable overhead costs incurred, $9,500
Finished units produced, 2,000
Actual material cost, $.90 per pound
Variable overhead rate, $.90 per hour
Standard direct-labor cost, $4 per hour
Standard material cost, $1 per pound
Standard pounds of material in a finished unit, 3
Standard direct-labor hours per finished unit, 5

Prepare schedules of all variances, using the format of Exhibit 7-6, p. 187.

7–36. Standard material allowances. (CMA.) Danson Company is a chemical manufacturer that supplies industrial users. The company plans to introduce a new chemical solution and needs to develop a standard product cost for this new solution.

The new chemical solution is made by combining a chemical compound (nyclyn) and a solution (salex), boiling the mixture, adding a second compound (protet), and bottling the resulting solution in 10-liter containers. The initial mix, which is 10 liters in volume, consists of 12 kilograms of nyclyn and 9.6 liters of salex. A 20% reduction in volume occurs during the boiling process. The solution is then cooled slightly before 5 kilograms of protet are added; the addition of protet does not affect the total liquid volume.

The purchase prices of the raw materials used in the manufacture of this new chemical solution are as follows:

Nyclyn	$1.30 per kilogram
Salex	1.80 per liter
Protet	2.40 per kilogram

REQUIRED: Determine the standard quantity for each of the raw materials needed to produce a 10-liter container of Danson Company's new chemical solution and the standard materials cost of a 10-liter container of the new product.

7–37. **Similarity of direct-labor and variable-overhead variances.** The Acme Company has had great difficulty controlling costs in Singapore during the past three years. Last month a standard cost and flexible-budget system was installed. A condensation of results for a department follows:

	EXPECTED BEHAVIOR PER STANDARD DIRECT-LABOR HOUR	TOTAL BUDGET VARIANCE
Lubricants	$ .30	$200 F
Other supplies	.20	150 U
Rework	.40	300 U
Other indirect labor	.50	300 U
Total variable overhead	$1.40	$550 U

F = Favorable. U = Unfavorable.

The department had initially planned to manufacture 6,000 units in 4,000 standard direct-labor hours allowed. However, material shortage and a heat wave resulted in the production of 5,400 units in 3,900 actual direct-labor hours. The standard wage rate is $3.50 per hour, which was 20¢ higher than the actual average hourly rate.

REQUIRED:
1. Prepare a detailed performance report with two major sections: direct labor and variable overhead.
2. Prepare a summary analysis of price and efficiency variances for direct labor and for variable overhead, using the format of Exhibit 7-6, p. 187.
3. Explain the similarities and differences between the direct-labor and variable-overhead variances. What are some of the likely causes of the overhead variances?

7–38. **Graphical analysis of direct labor.**   An air-conditioning service company uses "mechanics" to rebuild and maintain equipment. It has developed flexible budgets and standards for much of its work. The following partially completed graph displays a recent month's performance of direct labor regarding the jobs subject to these standards:

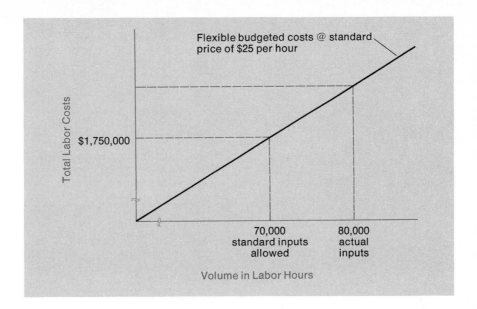

Flexible budgeted costs @ standard price of $25 per hour

Total Labor Costs

$1,750,000

70,000
standard inputs
allowed

80,000
actual
inputs

Volume in Labor Hours

The standard inputs allowed for the actual output achieved were 70,000 hours. The mechanics have a strong union. They earn $30 per hour. Apprentices earn less, and they do some of the same work as the mechanics; thus the average standard price per hour is $25. Because a higher-than-usual proportion of apprentices worked last month, the actual amounts paid were $23 per hour for a total of 80,000 hours of input, or $1,840,000.

REQUIRED:

1. Compute the price and efficiency variances for direct labor.
2. Complete and fully label the graph. Enter and identify the flexible-budget variance, the price variance, and the efficiency variance.

7–39. **Variance analysis.** The Hong Kong Company uses standard costs and a flexible budget. The purchasing agent is responsible for material price variances, and the production manager is responsible for all other variances. Operating data for the past week are summarized as follows:

Finished units produced: 5,000.
Direct material: Purchases, 10,000 lb. @ $1.50. Standard price, $1.60 per lb. Used, 5,400 lb. Standard allowed per unit produced, 1 lb.
Direct labor: Actual costs, 8,000 hours @ $3.05, or $24,400. Standard allowed per good unit produced, 1½ hours. Standard price per direct-labor hour, $3.
Variable manufacturing overhead: Actual costs, $8,800. Budget formula is $1 per standard direct-labor hour.

REQUIRED:

1. *a.* Material purchase-price variance
   b. Material efficiency variance
   c. Direct-labor price variance
   d. Direct-labor efficiency variance
   e. Variable manufacturing-overhead price variance
   f. Variable manufacturing-overhead efficiency variance
   (*Hint:* For a format, see Requirement 2 of the solution to the second Summary Problem for Your Review, p. 194.)
2. *a.* What is the budget allowance for direct labor?
   b. Would it be any different if production were 6,000 good units?

Flexible
Budgets and
Standards for
Control

Multiple choice.   (CPA.)

1. Information on Westcott Company's direct-labor costs is as follows:

Standard direct-labor rate	$3.75
Actual direct-labor rate	$3.50
Standard direct-labor hours	10,000
Direct-labor usage (efficiency)	
variance—unfavorable	$4,200

What were the actual hours worked, rounded to the nearest hour? (a) 10,714, (b) 11,120, (c) 11,200, (d) 11,914.

2. Information on Kennedy Company's direct-material costs is as follows:

Standard unit price	$3.60
Actual quantity purchased	1,600
Standard quantity allowed	
for actual production	1,450
Materials purchase price	
variance—favorable	$ 240

What was the actual purchase price per unit, rounded to the nearest penny? (a) $3.06, (b) $3.11, (c) $3.45, (d) $3.75.

7–41. Labor variances.   The city of Houston has a sign shop where street signs of all kinds are manufactured and repaired. The manager of the shop uses standards to judge performance. However, because a clerk mistakenly discarded some labor records, the manager has only partial data for October. He knows that the total direct-labor variance was $880, favorable, and that the standard labor price was $6 per hour. Moreover, a recent pay raise produced an unfavorable labor price variance for October of $320. The actual hours of input were 1,600.

REQUIRED:

1. Find the actual labor price per hour.
2. Determine the standard hours allowed for the output achieved.

7–42. Variable-overhead variances.   You have been asked to prepare an analysis of the overhead costs in the billing department of a hospital. As an initial step, you prepare a summary of some events that bear on overhead for the most recent period. The variable-overhead budget variance was $4,000, unfavorable. The standard variable-overhead price per billing was 5¢. Ten bills per hour is regarded as standard productivity per clerk. The total overhead incurred was $168,500, of which $110,000 was fixed. There were no variances for fixed overhead. The variable-overhead price variance was $2,000, favorable.

REQUIRED:

Find the following:

1. Variable-overhead efficiency variance
2. Actual hours of input
3. Standard hours allowed for output achieved

7–43. Material and labor variances.   Consider the following data:

	DIRECT MATERIAL	DIRECT LABOR
a. Actual price per unit of input (pounds and hours)	$ 9	?
b. Standard price per unit of input	$10	$12
c. Standard inputs per unit of output	4	?

d. Actual units of input		?	?
e. Actual units of output (product)		?	?
f. Actual inputs × actual prices		?	?
g. Actual inputs × standard prices		?	$114,000
h. Standard inputs allowed for actual output achieved × standard prices		$200,000	?
i. Price variance		$ 23,000 F	?
j. Efficiency variance		?	$ 6,000 F
k. Flexible-budget variance		$ 7,000 U	$ 1,250 F

REQUIRED:

1. Solve for the unknowns. (You may be helped by following the format in Exhibit 7-6, page 187.)
2. Prepare a plausible explanation for the performance.

7–44. **Review problem on standards and flexible budgets; answers provided.** The Singapore Company makes a variety of leather goods. It uses standard costs and a flexible budget to aid planning and control. Budgeted variable overhead at a 60,000-direct-labor-hour level is $36,000.

During April the company had an unfavorable variable-overhead efficiency variance of $1,200. Material purchases were $322,500. Actual direct-labor costs incurred were $187,600. The direct-labor efficiency variance was $6,000, unfavorable. The actual average wage price was 20¢ lower than the average standard wage price.

The company uses a variable-overhead rate of 20% of standard direct-labor *cost* for flexible-budgeting purposes. Actual variable overhead for the month was $41,000.

REQUIRED:

Compute the following amounts; then use *U* or *F* to indicate whether requested variances are unfavorable or favorable.

1. Standard direct-labor cost per hour
2. Actual direct-labor hours worked
3. Total direct-labor price variance
4. Total flexible budget for direct-labor costs
5. Total direct-labor variance
6. Variable-overhead price variance in total

Answers to Problem 7–44:

1. $3. The variable-overhead price is $.60, obtained by dividing $36,000 by 60,000 hours. Therefore the direct-labor price must be $.60 ÷ .20 = $3.
2. 67,000 hours. Actual costs, $187,600 ÷ ($3 − $.20) = 67,000 hours.
3. $13,400 F. 67,000 actual hours × $.20 = $13,400.
4. $195,000. Efficiency variance was $6,000, unfavorable. Therefore, excess hours must have been $6,000 ÷ $3 = 2,000. Consequently, standard hours allowed must be 67,000 − 2,000 = 65,000. Flexible budget = 65,000 × $3 = $195,000.
5. $7,400 F. $195,000 − $187,600 = $7,400 F; or $13,400 F − $6,000 U = $7,400 F.
6. $800 U. Flexible budget = 65,000 × $.60 = $39,000. Total variance = $41,000 − $39,000 = $2,000 U. Price variance = $2,000 − $1,200 efficiency variance = $800 U.

7–45. **Combined or joint price-quantity variance and incentives.** Study the chapter appendix. The Howell Company had an incentive system that rewarded managers each Christmas for cost savings on materials. The manager of purchasing received 10% of any favorable price variance accumulated for the fiscal year ending November 30. Similarly, the production manager received 10% of the favorable efficiency (quantity) variances. In addition, each manager received 10% of the favorable net material variances. Note, however, that all variances were included in the computations—that is, an unfavorable variance in one month would offset a favorable variance in another month.

In the opinion of the company president, this system had worked reasonably well in past years. Of course, because of the sensitivity of the incentive system, the standards were carefully specified and adjusted each quarter. Only minimal inventories were kept at any time. Bonuses had varied from zero to 20% of the managers' base salaries. The purchasing manager's base salary for a recent fiscal year ending November 30 was $24,000; the production manager's was $30,000.

The operating results on Material A for a recent month were:

Purchase-price variance	$ 72,000 U
Efficiency variance	36,000 U
Net material variance	$108,000 U

Two pounds of Material A was the standard quantity allowed for every unit of a particular finished product, a chemical used in petroleum refining. One hundred thousand units of the chemical had been manufactured. The average price actually paid for Material A was 30¢ per pound in excess of the standard price.

REQUIRED:

1. What number of pounds of Material A was purchased?
2. Find the standard price per pound of Material A.
3. What is the total standard cost allowed for material components of the finished product?
4. As the purchasing manager, what is your opinion of the bonus system? Would your answer be the same if the actual raw-material price paid had been 70¢ per pound? Explain fully.
5. As the production manager, what is your opinion of the bonus system? Why?
6. Why is part of the bonus dependent on the net material variance?
7. Assume that some bonus system tied to variance analysis is maintained. What changes would you recommend?

7–46. **Review of major points in chapter.** The following questions are based on the data contained in the illustration used in the chapter, p. 184:

1. Suppose actual production and sales were 8,000 units instead of 7,000 units. (a) Compute the sales volume variance. Is the performance of the marketing function the sole explanation for this variance? Why? (b) Using a flexible budget, compute the budgeted contribution margin, the budgeted operating income, budgeted direct material, and budgeted direct labor.
2. Suppose the following were the actual results for the production of 8,000 units:

    Direct material: 42,000 pounds were used at an actual unit price of 56¢, for a total actual cost of $23,520.

    Direct labor: 16,500 hours were used at an actual hourly rate of $4.10, for a total actual cost of $67,650.

    Compute the flexible-budget variance and the price and efficiency variances for direct materials and direct labor. Present your answers in the form shown in Exhibit 7–6, p. 187.
3. Suppose the company is organized so that the purchasing manager bears the primary responsibility for the acquisition prices of materials, and the production manager bears the primary responsibility for efficiency but no responsibility for unit prices. Assume the same facts as in Requirement 2 except that the purchasing manager acquired 60,000 pounds of materials. This means that there is an ending inventory of 18,000 pounds. Would your variance analysis of materials in Requirement 2 change? Why? Show computations.

VARIATIONS OF COST BEHAVIOR PATTERNS

When we refer to **cost behavior patterns,** we generally mean the relationship of total costs to changes in the volume of activity. Until this chapter, we have concentrated on two basic linear-cost behavior patterns: variable and fixed. Now we shall examine some variations of these patterns that have proved helpful for planning and control. Then we shall explore the problem of how to determine cost behavior patterns so that useful predictions and evaluations can be made.

ENGINEERED, DISCRETIONARY, AND COMMITTED COSTS

During the 1960s, a classification of costs evolved as follows:

FIXED COSTS:	VARIABLE COSTS:
Committed	Engineered
Discretionary	Discretionary*

*Only a few variable costs belong in the discretionary classification, as explained below.

We shall describe these types of costs, beginning with **committed fixed costs.**

❏ Fixed Costs and Capacity

Fixed costs, also called *capacity costs*, measure the cost of providing the capability to operate at a particular capacity for such activities as manufacturing, sales, administration, and research. They reflect the capability for sustaining a planned volume of activity.

The size of fixed costs is influenced by long-run marketing conditions, technology, and the methods and strategies of management. Examples of the methods and strategies of management include sales salaries versus sales commissions and one-shift versus two-shift operations. Fixed costs are often the result of a trade-off decision whereby lower variable costs are attained in exchange for higher fixed costs. For example, automatic equipment may be acquired by banks, post offices, or hospitals to reduce labor costs.

Generally, a heavier proportion of fixed to variable costs lessens management's ability to respond to short-run changes in economic conditions and opportunities. Still, unwillingness to incur fixed costs reveals an aversion to risk that may exclude a company from profitable ventures. For instance, the launching of new products often requires very large fixed costs for research, advertising, equipment, and working capital.

❏ Committed Fixed Costs

For planning and control, fixed costs may be usefully subdivided into committed and discretionary categories. **Committed fixed costs** consist largely of those fixed costs that arise from the possession of plant, of equipment, and of a basic organization. Examples are depreciation, property taxes, rent, insurance, and the salaries of key personnel. These costs are affected primarily by long-run sales forecasts that, in turn, indicate the long-run capacity needs.

The behavior of committed fixed costs can best be viewed by assuming a zero volume of activity in an enterprise that fully expects to resume normal activity (for example, during a strike or a shortage of materials that forces a complete shutdown of activity). The committed fixed costs are all those organization and plant costs that continue to be incurred and that cannot be reduced without injuring the organization's competence to meet long-range goals. Committed fixed costs are the least responsive of the fixed costs because they tend to be less affected by month-to-month and year-to-year decisions.

In planning, the focus is on the impact of these costs over a number of years. Such planning usually requires tailoring the capacity to future demand for the organization's products in the most economical manner. For example, should the store size be 50,000 square feet, or 80,000, or 100,000? Should the gasoline station have one, or two, or more stalls for servicing automobiles? Such decisions usually involve selecting the point of optimal trade-off between present and future operating costs. That is, constructing excess capacity now may save costs in the long run because construction costs per square foot may be much higher later. On the other hand, if the forecast demand never develops, the organization may have to bear the costs of owning facilities that are idle.

These decisions regarding capital expenditures are generally shown in an annual budget called the *capital budget* or *capital-spending budget*. As you will recall, the *master budget* is based primarily on the annual sales forecast, the cornerstone of budgeting. Similarly, all capital-spending decisions are ultimately based on long-range sales forecasts. Capital budgeting is discussed in Chapters 11 and 12.

Once buildings are constructed and equipment is installed, little can be done in day-to-day operations to affect the *total level* of committed costs. From a control standpoint, the objective is usually to increase current utilization of facilities because this will ordinarily increase net income.

There is another aspect to the control problem, however. A follow-up, or audit, is needed to find out how well the ensuing utilization harmonizes with the decision that authorized the facilities in the first place. The latter approach helps management to evaluate the wisdom of its past long-range decisions and, in turn, should improve the quality of future decisions.

❏ Discretionary Fixed Costs

Discretionary fixed costs (sometimes called **managed** or **programmed costs**) are fixed costs (a) that arise from periodic (usually yearly) **budget appropriation** decisions that directly reflect top-management policies regarding the maximum permissible amounts to be incurred, and (b) that do not have a demonstrable optimum relationship between inputs (as measured by the costs) and outputs (as measured by sales, services, or production). Discretionary costs may have no particular relation to volume of activity. Examples vary among organizations and include child day-care services, staging an opera, research and development, advertising, sales promotion, charitable donations, management consulting services, and many employee-training programs. Conceivably, such costs could be reduced almost entirely for a given year in dire times, whereas the committed costs would be much more difficult to reduce.

Discretionary fixed costs are decided upon by management at the start of the budget period. Goals are selected, the means for their attainment are chosen, the maximum expense to be incurred is specified, and the total amount to be spent is appropriated. For example, a state government may appropriate $5 million for an advertising campaign to encourage tourism. In the give-and-take process of preparing the master budget, the discretionary costs are the most likely to be revised.

Discretionary fixed costs represent an assortment of manufacturing, selling, administrative, and research items. For example, a large portion of discretionary fixed costs may consist of salaries for sales personnel, accountants, clerks, and engineers, and often appear in the income statement lumped under the heading "General Selling and Administrative Expense." As in the case of committed costs, the resources acquired should be carefully planned and fully utilized if net income is to be maximized. Unlike committed costs, discretionary costs can be influenced more easily from period to period. It is also harder to measure the utilization of resources acquired via discretionary costs, principally because the results of services such as creative personnel, advertising, research, and training programs are much more difficult to isolate and quantify than the results of utilizing plants and equipment to make products.

The behavior of some discretionary fixed costs is easy to delineate. Advertising, research, donations, and training programs, for example, are usually formulated with certain objectives in mind. The execution of such projects is measured by comparing total expenditures with the appropriation. Because the tendency is to spend the entire budget appropriation, the resulting dollar variances are generally trivial. But planning is far more important than this kind of day-to-day control. The perfect execution of an advertising program—in the sense that the full amount authorized was spent in specified media at predetermined times—will be fruitless if the advertisements are unimaginative and lifeless and if they reach the wrong audience.

The most noteworthy aspect of discretionary fixed costs is that, unlike most other costs, they are not subject to ordinary engineering input-output analysis. For example, an optimum relationship between inputs and outputs can be specified for direct materials because it takes three pounds or five liters or two square feet to make a finished product. In contrast, we are usually unsure of the "correct" amount of advertising, research, management training, donations, management consulting costs, police protection, and programs for health care, education, or consumer protection.

The prominent Philadelphia retailer, John Wanamaker, supposedly said (*Wharton Magazine*, Summer 1982): "Fifty percent of my advertising budget is wasted. I know that. My problem is I don't know which half is being wasted."

The U.S. Department of Education can quantify the inputs (for example, the amount spent on planning, research, and evaluation and on writing regulations), but the outputs and the relation between inputs and outputs are harder to quantify. Systems can be designed to ensure that the research and the regulations are concerned with the subjects deemed most important by the decision makers, but there is no convincing way of knowing how much is enough in any absolute sense.

Engineered and Discretionary Variable Costs

An **engineered cost** is any cost that has an explicit, specified physical relationship with a selected measure of activity. Most variable costs fit this classification. An "engineered" variable cost exists when an optimum relationship between inputs and outputs has been carefully determined by work-measurement techniques, which are described below. In fact, **efficiency** has been defined as the relationship between inputs and outputs. For example, an automobile may have exact specifications: one battery, one radiator, two fan belts, and so forth. Direct material and direct labor are prime examples of engineered costs.

Many managers and accountants tend to use "variable cost" and "engineered cost" interchangeably, as if they were synonymous. Usually, this error is harmless. However, as noted at the start of the chapter, although most variable costs are engineered, some fit a discretionary classification; depending on management policy, other costs may go up and down with sales (or production) merely because management has predetermined that the organization can afford to spend a certain percentage of the sales dollar for such items as research, donations, and advertising. Such discretionary costs would have a graphical pattern of variability, but not for the same reasons as direct materials or direct labor. An increase in these costs may be due to management's authorization to spend "because we can afford it" rather than to an engineered cause-and-effect relationship between such costs and sales.

ENGINEERED VERSUS DISCRETIONARY COSTS

Work Measurement for Control

Work measurement is the careful analysis of a task, its size, the methods used in its performance, and its efficiency. Its objective is to determine the workload in an operation and the number of employees necessary to perform that work efficiently.

The work-measurement approach is based on a fundamental premise: Permanent improvement in any performance is impossible unless the work is measured. The premise is a natural accompaniment for the idea of desired efficiency, which is an optimal relationship between inputs and outputs. Therefore, to know whether efficiency exists, we must have some quantification of both inputs and outputs.

Variations of
Cost Behavior
Patterns

213

During the 1980s, many financial services organizations, such as banks and insurance companies, have turned to work measurement. For example, American Express (Am Ex) has conducted extensive work-measurement programs that have increased productivity in replacing lost credit cards, issuing new cards, responding to inquiries, and performing other functions. For example, Am Ex now takes two weeks instead of four weeks to issue new credit cards.

❏ Origins of Work Measurement

Work-measurement techniques were initially developed for planning and control of manufacturing rather than of nonmanufacturing activities. This occurred because inputs and outputs in the manufacturing areas are easier to identify and measure. The measurement of direct material consumed and finished units produced is straightforward. It is much more difficult to obtain a measurement for relating the inputs of advertising and sales promotion activity to the outputs of sales or contribution margins.

As the input-output relationships become less defined, management tends to abandon any formal work-measurement techniques and, instead, relies almost wholly on the individual and his or her supervisor for successful control. Consequently, the role of personal observation is paramount and formal cost control is approached from a discretionary-cost rather than from an engineered-cost (work-measurement) viewpoint, especially in many areas of nonmanufacturing. However, despite the difficulties of implementation, work measurement is getting more attention from nonmanufacturing organizations as they seek to improve their efficiency.

In recent years, work measurement has been extended into nonprofit organizations as well as into the selling and administrative clerical areas of profit-seeking organizations. In fact, federal government agencies are heavy users of work measurement in such diverse areas as the auditing of income tax returns, the processing of social security checks, and the sorting of mail.

❏ Control-Factor Units

The specific techniques used to measure the work include time and motion study, observation of a random sample of the work (work sampling), and the estimation, by a work-measurement analyst and a line supervisor, of the amount of time required for the work (time analysis).

The workload is often expressed in **control-factor units,** which are used in formulating the budget. For example, the control-factor units in a payroll department might include operations performed on time cards, on notices of change in the labor rate, on notices of employee promotion, on new employment and termination reports, and on routine weekly and monthly reports. All of these would be timed. The estimated workload would then be used for determining the required labor force and budgetary allowance.

Examples of other operations and appropriate control-factor units include:

OPERATION	UNIT OF MEASURE (CONTROL-FACTOR UNIT)
Billing	Lines per hour
Warehouse labor	Pounds or cases handled per day
Packing	Pieces packed per hour
Posting accounts receivable	Postings per hour
Mailing	Pieces mailed per hour

Based on work measurement, standards are set for activities. For example, Pan American World Airways has the following standards:

1. Answering reservations: pick up 85% of all calls within twenty seconds
2. Checking passengers in: process 85% of the passengers within five minutes
3. Handling baggage: deliver the last bag stowed in the belly of a large airplane within thirty-five minutes

☐ The Engineered-Cost Approach

There is much disagreement about how clerical costs should be controlled. Advocates of work measurement favor a more rigorous approach, which essentially regards these costs as engineered. In practice, a discretionary-fixed-cost approach is more often found.

Assume that ten payroll clerks are employed by a government agency, and that each clerk's operating efficiency *should be* the processing of the payroll records of 500 employees per month. This might be called the *perfection standard* for the work. In the month of June, the payroll records of 4,700 individuals were processed by these ten clerks. Each clerk earns $1,800 per month.

The engineered-cost approach to this situation is to base the budget formula on the unit cost of the individual pay record processed: $1,800 ÷ 500 records, or $3.60. Therefore the budget allowance for payroll-clerk labor would be $3.60 × 4,700, or $16,920. Assume that the ten employees worked throughout the month. The following performance report would be prepared (*U* means unfavorable):

	ACTUAL COST (10 × $1,800)	FLEXIBLE BUDGET: TOTAL STANDARD INPUTS ALLOWED FOR ACTUAL OUTPUT PRODUCED (4,700 × $3.60)	BUDGET VARIANCE
Payroll-clerk labor	$18,000	$16,920	$1,080 U

Essentially, two decisions must be made in this operation. The first is a policy decision involving such questions as How many clerks do we need? How flexible should we be? How divisible is the task? Should we use part-time help? Should we hire and fire as the volume of work fluctuates? The implication of these questions is that once the hiring decision is made, the total costs incurred can be predicted easily—$18,000 in our example.

The second decision concentrates on day-to-day control, on how efficiently the given resources are being utilized. Thus the work-measurement approach to ongoing control is an explicit and formal attempt to measure the utilization of resources by

1. Assuming a proportionately variable budget and the complete divisibility of the workload into small units.
2. Generating a budget variance that assumes a comparison of actual costs with the perfection standard—the cost that would be incurred if payroll-clerk labor could be turned on and off like a faucet. In this case, the variance of $1,080 informs management that there was overstaffing. The workload capability was 5,000 pay records, not the 4,700 actually processed. The extra cost of $1,080 resulted from operating in a way that does not attain the lowest possible cost. The $1,080 might also be considered as the amount that management is currently investing to provide stability in the work force.

Critics of work measurement will often assert that such a formal approach is not worth its cost because strong labor unions and other forces prevent managers from fine-tuning the size of the work force. Defenders of work measurement will respond that managers must know the costs of various labor policies. For instance, if the cost of overstaffing becomes exorbitant, the pertinent provisions in a labor contract may become key bargaining issues when the contract is about to be renewed. In recent years, airlines have provided numerous illustrations of this bargaining.

❑ The Discretionary-Fixed-Cost Approach

Work-measurement techniques are not used in the vast majority of organizations. Consequently, the tendency is to rely on the experience of the department head and his or her superior for judging the size of the work force needed to carry out the department's functions. There is a genuine reluctance to overhire because there is a corresponding slowness in discharging or laying off people when volume slackens. As a result, temporary peak loads are often met by hiring temporary workers or by having the regular employees work overtime.

In most cases, the relevant range of activity during the budget period can be predicted with assurance, and the work force needed for the marketing and administrative functions can readily be determined. If management refuses, consciously or unconsciously, to control costs in rigid accordance with short-run fluctuations in activity, these costs, in effect, become discretionary—that is, their total amount is relatively fixed and unresponsive to short-run variations in volume.

The practical effects of the discretionary-fixed-cost approach are that the budgeted costs and the actual costs tend to be very close, so that resulting budget variances are small. Follow-ups to see that the available resources are being fully and efficiently utilized are regarded as the managers' responsibility, a duty that can be carried through by face-to-face control and by records of physical quantities (for example, pounds handled per day in a warehouse, pieces mailed per hour in a mailing room) that do not have to be formally integrated into the accounting records in dollar terms.

Hence there is a conflict between common practice and the objective of work measurement, which is to treat most costs as engineered and to therefore subject them to short-range management control. The moral is that management's attitudes and its planning and controlling decisions often determine whether a cost is discretionary fixed or engineered variable. A change in policy can transform a budgeted fixed cost into a budgeted variable cost, and vice versa.

Banks have applied work measurement to the clearing of checks. For example, the fluctuations in the volume of checks to be processed and cleared can be predicted. Accordingly, banks have scheduled portions of their work force to coincide with the budgeted volumes. Therefore, some wages expenses that would otherwise be fixed can become variable.

In sum, the discretionary and engineered approaches may be compared as in Exhibit 8-1. The graphs there provide an overview of how differing philosophies of budgeting and control may be adopted for a cost that has *the same underlying behavior pattern.*

EXHIBIT
8-1

	BUDGET AS AN ENGINEERED VARIABLE COST	BUDGET AS A DISCRETIONARY FIXED COST
Actual cost incurred	$18,000	$18,000
Budget allowance	16,920*	18,000
Variance	1,080 U	0

*Rate = $18,000 ÷ 5,000 records, or $3.60 per record; total = 4,700 records @ $3.60 = $16,920.

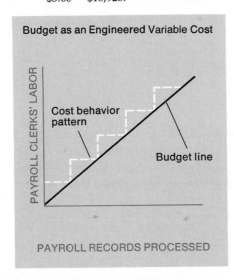

Budget as an Engineered Variable Cost

PAYROLL CLERKS' LABOR

Cost behavior pattern

Budget line

PAYROLL RECORDS PROCESSED

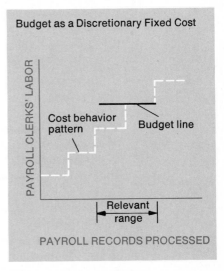

Budget as a Discretionary Fixed Cost

PAYROLL CLERKS' LABOR

Cost behavior pattern

Budget line

Relevant range

PAYROLL RECORDS PROCESSED

❑ Negotiated Static Budgets

The most popular ways of controlling discretionary fixed costs are personal observation and negotiated static budgets. Salaries tend to constitute the bulk of departmental discretionary costs. Because of the difficulties of identifying a convincing relationship between inputs and outputs, most organizations rely heavily on appropriate hiring and supervision as a way of controlling a department's discretionary costs. That is, personal observation by supervisors is a key to ensuring that human resources are used appropriately.

Managers and their superiors tend to negotiate an appropriate lump sum that forms the static budget for discretionary costs. By definition, the "appropriate" amounts of discretionary costs are difficult to establish. Hence tradition, rules of thumb, industry custom, and formulas often affect the final budget figures. For example, a lump sum of 2% of last year's sales may be appropriated for the forthcoming year's research budget.

Negotiated static budgets can be subclassified as incremental and zero-base. Each will be discussed in sequence.

❑ Incremental Budgets

Ordinary incremental budgets are easily the most popular. The budget is based on the previous period's budget and actual results as givens. The budget amount is then changed in accordance with expectations for the next period. For example, a budget for a research department might be increased because of increases in salaries or additions of new personnel for a new project, or both.

Priority incremental budgets are similar to ordinary incremental budgets; however, they require managers to specify the activities that would be added or deleted if the budgetary appropriation were increased or decreased by, say, 10%. This procedure is an inexpensive way of forcing managers to indicate some key priorities. Superior managers can then evaluate the stated priorities before approving the final budget.

❑ Zero-Base Budgeting

Zero-base budgeting (ZBB) is an elaborate, time-consuming practice of having managers justify their activities and costs as if they were being undertaken for the first time. Zero-base budgeting gets at fundamental questions by requiring managers to document the following steps:

1. Determine goals, operations, and costs of all activities under the manager's jurisdiction.
2. Explore alternative means of conducting each activity. (This is a desirable attribute of any budgeting system for discretionary costs.)
3. Evaluate alternative budget levels for various levels of effort for each activity.

4. Establish measures of workload and performance.
5. Rank all activities in order of their importance to the organization.

Zero-base budgeting has been receiving increased attention in non-profit organizations:

☐ Zero-base budgeting is especially adaptable to discretionary cost areas in which service and support are the primary outputs. It is this characteristic that has attracted the interest of governmental officials, as most expenditures of government can be classified as discretionary in nature.[1]

Zero-base budgeting became highly fashionable after Jimmy Carter installed the practice for all federal government agencies. Although ZBB yields benefits, it requires much time and effort. It has lost some popularity as a yearly endeavor, but its basic ideas are probably worth applying sequentially through various departments every five years or so.[2] Meanwhile, priority incremental budgeting warrants annual use.

Summary Problem for Your Review

☐ Problem One

Reconsider the first illustration in the chapter, page 215. Suppose eleven employees worked throughout the month, but only 5,000 pay records were processed.

REQUIRED:

1. Prepare a performance report that presents actual, budgeted, and budget variance columns for the month. Use (a) a discretionary-cost approach and (b) an engineered-cost approach.
2. Suppose the workers have been reasonably efficient. What do the budget variances in 1a and 1b tell the manager?
3. Assume that an engineered-cost approach to control is used, even though management has deliberately overstaffed. This means that management must provide for an "expected variance" or "budgeted variance" for cash-planning purposes. For preparing a budgeted statement of cash receipts and disbursements, what amount would be budgeted for payroll-clerk labor?

☐ Solution to Problem One

1. a. Discretionary-fixed-cost approach:

	ACTUAL COST	BUDGET	BUDGET VARIANCE
Payroll-clerk labor (11 × $1,800)	$19,800	$19,800	—

[1] See G. Minmier and R. Hermanson, "A Look at Zero Base Budgeting—The Georgia Experience," *Atlanta Economic Review*, 26, No. 4 (July–August 1976), 6.
[2] See *Streamlining Zero-Base Budgeting Will Benefit Decision-Making*, Report to the Congress, Comptroller-General, PAD-79-45, 1979.

b. Engineered-variable-cost approach:

	ACTUAL COST	FLEXIBLE BUDGET: TOTAL STANDARD INPUTS ALLOWED FOR ACTUAL OUTPUTS ACHIEVED (5,000 × $3.60)	BUDGET VARIANCE In Dollars	In Equivalent Persons
Payroll-clerk labor	$19,800	$18,000	$1,800 U	1.0 U

Note the addition of an equivalent-persons column that was not required here, nor was it illustrated earlier. Many managers want this information because it provides a gauge of the physical extent of overstaffing.

2. Managers control operations in many ways. A basic way is personal observation, which is always used regardless of what accounting approach is favored. The budget variance in 1a tells the manager nothing. A discretionary-cost approach essentially determines a flat amount to be spent for a given planning period and relies on personal observation or other informal ways to judge if the "right" amount of cost is being incurred.

The budget variance in 1b measures the extra amount the manager is paying to keep a stable work force. Proponents of this approach maintain that the variance of $1,800 or one equivalent person keeps management abreast of the extra cost of maintaining the current number of personnel. This work-measurement approach maintains that clerical workloads must be formally measured before control can really succeed.

The chapter emphasizes that management attitudes and policies are often of determining importance in characterizing a cost as fixed or variable. If managers think that the incremental benefits from a formal engineered-variable-cost approach do not justify its incremental costs, they will continue to rely on a discretionary-cost approach. Thus there is no single "best" way to control costs. The preferable way depends on the type of organization and type of operations subject to control.

3. This question was included here to call attention to the fact that management may use one budget figure for motivation and control and a different budget figure for cash planning. The master budget would include $19,800 as a part of the budgeted statement of cash receipts and disbursements. A detailed presentation would show:

Payroll-clerk labor:	
Flexible control-budget allowance	$18,000
Expected flexible control-budget variance	1,800
Total budget allowance for cash disbursements	$19,800

DETERMINING HOW COSTS BEHAVE

❏ Major Assumptions

Before costs can be classified and appropriately controlled, managers must be familiar with how the costs in question behave. As we know, costs often do not fit snugly into strictly variable and strictly fixed categories. Instead, there are a variety of *cost behavior patterns*, more technically described as *cost functions*. A **cost function** is a relationship between a cost and one or more variables. The dependent variable is frequently denoted as y (for example, some measure of total cost of repairs); the independent variable, as x (for example, some measure of related activity or volume of inputs or outputs). The problem facing the accountant or manager is frequently called **cost estimation** or **cost approximation,** which is the attempt to specify some underlying relation between x and y over a stipulated *relevant range* of x that may be of interest. That is, given any quantification of the independent variable x (e.g., total miles driven), how much will the dependent variable y be (e.g., total repair costs)?

In practice, such cost approximations are typically based on two major simplifying and often heroic assumptions:

1. The cost function is linear over the relevant range. This straight-line approximation is often regarded as sufficiently precise for most decision uses.

2. The "true" cost behavior can be sufficiently explained by one independent variable (miles driven) instead of more than one (miles driven, weather, weight carried, model year of the vehicle, and so forth).

❑ Focus on Costs and Benefits

As this book has stressed, whether these simplifying assumptions are justified is a cost-benefit question to be answered on a situation-by-situation basis. Managers tend to rely on exceedingly rough approximations until the buying of finer cost estimation models promises net collective benefits from more desirable operating decisions.

To summarize, given assumptions of linearity and of one independent variable, each item of cost has some underlying "true" behavior pattern, whose expected value, $E(y)$, has the following form:

$$E(y) = A + Bx$$

where A and B are the true (but unknown) parameters. (A **parameter** is a constant, such as A, or a coefficient, such as B, in a model or system of equations.)

Working with historical data, the cost analyst usually develops a formula approximation of the underlying relationship:

$$y' = a + bx$$

where y' is the calculated value as distinguished from the observed value y, and a and b are the approximations of the true A and B.

❑ Variety of Cost Functions

To illustrate the major types of cost functions, we now examine the corresponding graphic solutions to the basic formula: $y' = a + bx$.

A *proportionately variable cost* is the classical variable cost that was introduced in Chapter 2. Its total fluctuates in direct proportion to changes in x:

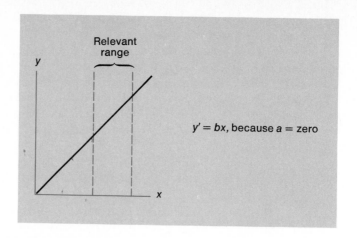

A *fixed cost* does not fluctuate in total as x changes within the relevant range:

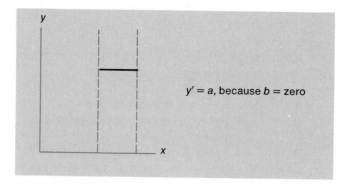

A *mixed* or *semivariable cost* is a combination of variable and fixed elements. That is, its total fluctuates as x changes within the relevant range, but not in direct proportion. Instead, its behavior accords with the basic formula:

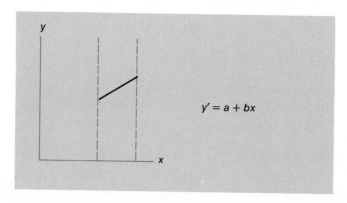

A *step-function cost* is nonlinear because of the breaks in its behavior pattern:

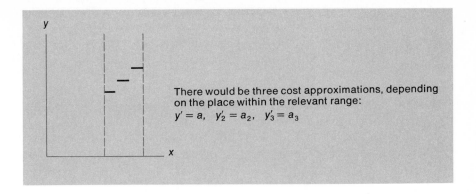

There would be three cost approximations, depending on the place within the relevant range:
$$y' = a, \quad y'_2 = a_2, \quad y'_3 = a_3$$

☐ Criteria for Choosing Functions

The critical tasks in choosing among possible cost functions are to approximate the appropriate slope coefficient (defined as the amount of increase in y for each unit increase in x) and the constant or intercept (defined as the value of y when x is zero). The cost function is determined on the basis of some plausible theory that supports the relationships between the dependent and the independent variable—not on the basis of sample observations alone. There are many variables that move together and are therefore referred to as being highly *correlated.* But no conclusions about causes and effects are warranted. For instance, studies have shown a high positive correlation between teachers' salaries and liquor consumption. There are also many teacher members of Alcoholics Anonymous, but no cause-and-effect relationships have been demonstrated.

The following criteria should help in obtaining accurate approximations of cost functions:

1. *Economic plausibility.* The relationship must be credible. Personal observation, when it is possible, probably provides the best evidence of a relationship. The engineered-cost approach described earlier is an example of heavy reliance on observed technical relationships between inputs and outputs.

2. *Goodness of fit.* The cost analyst uses tests of closeness of fit for personal reassurance about the choice of a plausible cost function. Such tests, which are briefly described later, may be limited to scatter diagrams or may entail full-fledged formal statistical **regression analysis.**[3]

Note especially that both of these criteria are used together in choosing a cost function; each is a check on the other. Knowledge of both cost accounting and operations is helpful. For example, repairs are often made when output is low because the machines can be taken out of service at these times. Therefore, if repair costs were recorded as each repair was made, scatter diagrams and regression analysis would show repair costs declining as output increased, whereas engineers know that the *timing* of

[3] In the latter case, so-called specification analysis is also conducted to be sure that certain assumptions are satisfied. Then the sample values a and b are the best available estimates of the population values A and B. For an expanded discussion, see C. Horngren, *Cost Accounting: A Managerial Emphasis,* 5th ed. (Englewood Cliffs, N.J.: Prentice-Hall, 1982), Chap. 24.

the repair is often discretionary—the true cause-and-effect relationship is a tendency for many repair costs to increase (perhaps in steplike fashion) as activity increases. Consequently, these costs should be analyzed separately; otherwise the true extent of variability of costs with output will be masked.[4]

Note too how criteria 1 and 2 interrelate. For example, a clerical overhead cost may show a high correlation with the number of records processed and an even higher correlation with the number of factory machine-hours worked. Our knowledge of operations confirms the first relationship; in contrast, there is a less convincing theoretical basis for the second.

❑ Methods of Linear Approximation

There are many methods of approximating cost functions, including (a) *the industrial engineering method*, (b) *account analysis*, (c) *high-low points*, (d) *visual fit*, (e) *simple regression*, and (f) *multiple regression*. These methods are not mutually exclusive; frequently, two or more are used to prevent major blunders. In many organizations, each of these six methods is used in succession over the years as the need for more accurate approximations becomes evident.

The *industrial engineering method*, sometimes called the *analytic method*, searches for the most efficient means of obtaining wanted output. It entails a systematic review of materials, supplies, labor, support services, and facilities. Time and motion studies are sometimes used. Any input-output relationship that is observable is an obvious candidate for the engineering method. For example, in the manufacturing of bicycles, one handlebar and two wheels are needed per bicycle. But the engineering method is of little help when relationships are infeasible or impossible to observe on an individual cost basis. Examples are relationships between various overhead costs and output. Then other methods come to the fore.

In *account analysis*, the analyst proceeds through the detailed ledger accounts, one by one, and classifies each into one of two categories, variable or fixed. In so doing, analysts may use their past experience intuitively and nothing else. More likely, they will at least study how total costs behave over a few periods before making judgments.

An examination of the accounts is obviously a necessary first step, no matter whether cost functions are approximated by means of simple inspection of the accounts or by multiple regression. Familiarity with the data is needed to avoid the analytical pitfalls that abound in regression analysis.

A major disadvantage of the account analysis method is its inherent subjectivity. The *high-low* method is slightly less subjective because at least it employs a series of samples and relies on two of their results, the highest cost and the lowest cost. It will be illustrated in a subsequent section.

The *visual-fit, simple-regression*, and *multiple-regression* methods have a distinct advantage because *all sample points* (not just two), are used in deter-

[4] George J. Benston, "Multiple Regression Analysis of Cost Behavior," *Accounting Review*, 41, No. 4, 663.

EXHIBIT
8-2

Mixed cost

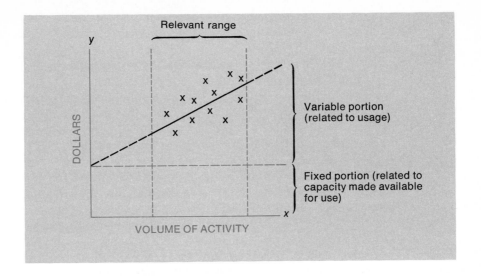

mining the cost function. A visual fit is applied by drawing a straight line through the cost points on a scatter diagram, which consists of a plotting on a graph of individual dots that represent various experienced costs at various activity levels. The line in Exhibit 8-2 could have been fitted visually.

There are no objective tests to ensure that the line fitted visually is the most accurate representation of the underlying data. Consequently, regression analysis is a more systematic approach.[5] Under certain assumptions, it has measures of probable error. **Regression analysis** refers to the measurement of the average amount of change in one variable (e.g., shipping cost) that is associated with unit increases in the amounts of one or more other variables. When only two variables are studied (e.g., shipping costs in relation to units shipped), the analysis is called *simple regression;* when more than two variables are studied (e.g., shipping costs in relation to units shipped and to the weight of those units shipped), it is called *multiple regression.*[6]

APPROXIMATING A COST FUNCTION

❏ Mixed Costs

We have previously discussed the nature of the proportionately variable cost, the fixed cost, and the step-function cost, so this section will concentrate on the *mixed cost* (often called *semivariable cost*). Exhibit 8-2 gives a closer look at a mixed cost. The fixed portion is usually the result of *providing* the capability to operate at a particular capacity, whereas the variable portion is the result of *using* the available capacity. For example, a copy-making machine often has a fixed monthly rental plus a variable cost based

[5] For elaboration, see Horngren, *Cost Accounting,* Chap. 24.
[6] For elaboration, see Benston, "Multiple Regression Analysis of Cost Behavior," pp. 657–72.

on the copies produced. Other examples include costs of rented trucks, power, telephone, repairs and maintenance, clerks, accountants, and janitors.

Ideally, there should be no accounts for mixed costs. All such costs should be subdivided into two accounts, one for the variable portion and one for the fixed portion. In practice, these distinctions are rarely made in the recording process because of the difficulty of analyzing day-to-day cost data into variable and fixed sections. Costs such as power, indirect labor, repairs, and maintenance are generally accounted for in total. It is typically very difficult to decide, as such costs are incurred, whether a particular invoice or work ticket represents a variable or fixed item. Moreover, even if it were possible to make such distinctions, the advantages might not be worth the additional clerical effort and costs. Whenever cost classifications are too refined, the perpetual problem of getting accurate source documents is intensified.

In sum, mixed costs are merely a blend of two unlike cost behavior patterns; they do not entail new conceptual approaches. Anybody who obtains a working knowledge of the planning and controlling of variable and fixed costs, separately, can adapt to a mixed-cost situation when necessary.

In practice, where a report is divided into two main cost classifications, variable and fixed, mixed costs tend to be included in the variable category even though they may not have purely variable behavior. At first glance, such arbitrary classification may seem undesirable and misleading. However, within a particular organization, the users of the reports usually have an intimate knowledge of the fundamental characteristics of the cost in question. Therefore they can temper their interpretation accordingly.

❏ Budgeting Mixed Costs

How should mixed costs be budgeted? Sometimes it is relatively easy to separate the cost into its fixed and variable elements. For example, the rental for a leased computer or photographic reproduction machine may be subdivided:

Photocopying costs—variable @ 3¢ per copy	XXXX
Photocopying costs — fixed @ $200 per month	XXXX

Alternatively, a flexible budget may be prepared that contains a single-line item:

	TOTALS AT VARIOUS VOLUMES		
Photocopying costs ($200 per month plus 3¢ per copy)	XXXX	XXXX	XXXX

Other mixed costs are harder to analyze: For example, how do repairs and maintenance, indirect factory labor, clerical labor, and miscellaneous overhead relate to decisions concerning changes in general volume of work in the form of more sales, more inquiries, more telephone calls, more letters, and so forth? The relationships are often hazy and difficult to pinpoint in any systematic way. Still, the decision makers want to know how these costs are affected by volume so that they can weigh their operating alternatives more intelligently.

❏ Data for Illustration

The city of Northvale operates several municipal golf courses that require varying maintenance attention, depending on the season of the year. The assistant city manager has begun to collect data on the cost of repairing the various types of power equipment used (for example, golf carts and power lawn mowers). She is concerned because repairs have been billed individually by an outside firm as each piece of equipment fails to perform. She is considering various alternatives, including buying a service contract for a flat fee or creating her own equipment repair department.

To date she has compiled the following data:

	GROUNDSKEEPER LABOR-HOURS (x)	REPAIR EXPENSE (y)
August	2,200	$2,300
September	2,300	2,500
October	1,900	2,000
November	1,200	2,000
December	1,200	2,000
January	900	1,500
February	700	1,400
March	1,100	1,400
April	1,400	1,600

She realizes that many more data should be gathered before jumping to conclusions about how costs behave. She also wishes that more-detailed classifications were available (for example, by acreage in specific golf courses, by types and age of equipment, and perhaps by number of rounds played at each course). But she has decided to use the above data as a start.

❏ Analysis of Graphs

The first graph in Exhibit 8-3 is a scatter diagram of the preceding data. The analyst should scrutinize the data to see whether a strong relationship exists between the costs of repair and groundskeeper labor-hours. Also, the analyst uses the scatter diagram as a key to deciding whether the relationship can be followed sufficiently closely by a *linear* approximation— that is, a straight line fitted through the dots.

The second graph in Exhibit 8-3 shows the straight line that has been fitted by the *statistical method of least squares*, which is described in more

Variations of
Cost Behavior
Patterns
227

EXHIBIT
8-3

Fitting A
Line (graph
not drawn
completely
to scale.
For the
latter, see
Exhibit 8-4.)

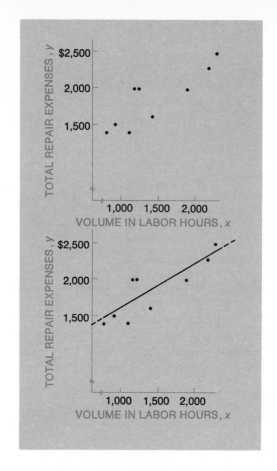

detail in the appendix to this chapter. The formula for the straight line is:

$$y' = a + bx$$
$$y' = \$983 + \$.609x$$

That is, repair costs fluctuate over the relevant range of 700 to 2,300 hours at a rate of $983 per month plus $.609 per labor-hour.

❑ Focus on Relevant Range

The line in Exhibit 8-3 is extended backward from the relevant range to intersect the y-axis at $983. The extension is deliberately shown as a dashed line to emphasize the focus on the relevant range. The manager is concerned with how costs behave within the relevant range, not with how they behave at zero volume. Therefore the $983 intercept must be kept in perspective. It is often called a fixed cost, but it is really a fixed or constant component of the formula that provides the best available linear approximation of how a mixed cost behaves within the relevant range. The manager is ordinarily not concerned about cost behavior at extremely low or high volumes.

❑ Use of High-Low Method

The high-low method uses two observations rather than all the observations for constructing the line. A high representative point (rather than an "outlier" that seems nonrepresentative) and a low representative point are chosen. The resultant line is extended back to intersect the vertical axis. The intercept becomes the "fixed" portion and the slope becomes the "variable" portion of the formula for the mixed cost.

The same results can be achieved via algebra:

	LABOR-HOURS (x)	REPAIR EXPENSES (y)
High (h)	2,300	$2,500
Low (L)	700	1,400
Difference	1,600	$1,100

$$\text{variable rate} = \frac{y_h - y_l}{x_h - x_l} = \frac{\$1,100}{1,600} = \$.6875 \text{ per labor-hour}$$

fixed component = total mixed cost less variable component

$$\text{at } x_h = \$2,500 - \$.6875(2,300)$$
$$= \$2,500 - \$1,581 = \$919$$

or

$$\text{at } x_l = \$1,400 - \$.6875(700)$$
$$= \$1,400 - \$481 = \$919$$

Therefore,

mixed-cost formula = $919 per month plus $.6875 per labor-hour

Compare this high-low formula with the least-squares formula, which was $983 per month plus $.609 per labor-hour. At a 1,000-hour level of volume, cost predictions would be:

high-low formula: $919 + $.6875(1,000) = $1,606.50

least-squares formula: $983 + $.609(1,000) = $1,592.00

In this illustration, the differences seem too small to have any influence on decisions. However, the high-low method is statistically inefficient. For example, if 40 data points were available, the high-low would use only 2 and disregard the other 38. Because of the danger of relying on extreme points, which may not be representative of normal situations, the high-low method is not recommended.

❑ Unreliability of High-Low Method

The graph in Exhibit 8-4 shows the unreliability of the high-low method. The graph is merely the second one of Exhibit 8-3, which showed a least-squares line fitted to the data, plus two high-low lines, marked as (1) and (2). High-low line (1) is the one we just computed algebraically. High-low line (2) is based on the choice of the alternative low point in the data:

	LABOR-HOURS (x)	REPAIR EXPENSES (y)
High (h)	2,300	$2,500
Low (L)	1,100	1,400
Difference	1,200	$1,100

$$\text{variable rate} = \frac{y_h - y_l}{x_h - x_l} = \frac{\$1,100}{1,200} = \$.9167 \text{ per labor-hour}$$

fixed component = total mixed cost less variable component

$$\text{at } x_h = \$2,500 - \$.9167(2,300)$$
$$= \$2,500 - \$2,108 = \$392$$

or

$$\text{at } x_l = \$1,400 - \$.9167(1,100)$$
$$= \$1,400 - \$1,008 = \$392$$

Therefore,

mixed-cost formula = $392 per month plus $.9167 per labor-hour

Thus we have two strikingly different mixed-cost formulas provided by the same high-low method. The watchword is beware. Use all, or nearly all, the data points, not just two, as a basis for cost estimation.

EXHIBIT
8-4

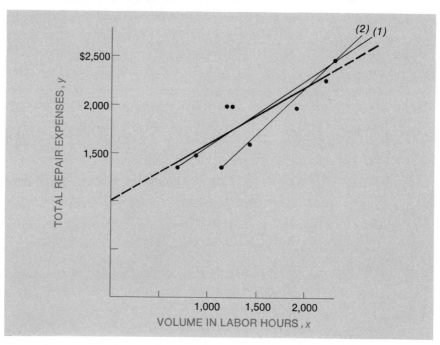

Summary

Managers who know cost behavior patterns are better equipped to make intelligent planning and control decisions. The division of costs into engineered, discretionary, and committed categories highlights the major factors that influence cost incurrence. Management policies often determine whether a cost will be planned and controlled as an engineered cost or as a discretionary cost.

Predictions of how costs will behave in response to various actions usually have an important bearing on a wide number of decisions. The cost function used to make these predictions is usually a simplification of underlying relationships. Whether this simplification is justified depends on how sensitive the manager's decisions are to the errors that the simplifications may generate. In some cases, additional accuracy may not make any difference; in other cases, it may be significant. The choice of a cost function is a decision concerning the costs and benefits of information.

Summary Problem for Your Review_____

(Problem One appeared earlier in this chapter.)

☐ Problem Two

The Delite Company has its own power plant. All costs related to the production of power have been charged to a single account, Power. We know that the total cost for power was $24,000 in one month and $28,000 in another month. Total machine-hours in those months were 120,000 and 160,000, respectively. Express the cost behavior pattern of the Power account in formula form.

☐ Solution to Problem Two

$$\text{variable rate} = \frac{\text{change in mixed cost}}{\text{change in volume}} = \frac{\$28,000 - \$24,000}{160,000 - 120,000}$$

$$= \frac{\$4,000}{40,000} = \$.10 \text{ per machine-hour}$$

fixed component = total mixed cost less variable component
at 160,000-hour level = $28,000 − $.10(160,000) = $12,000
or, at 120,000-hour level = $24,000 − $.10(120,000) = $12,000
cost formula = $12,000 per month + $.10 per machine-hour

Highlights to Remember

1. Costs may be divided for planning and control purposes as follows:

TYPE OF COST	MAJOR CONTROL TECHNIQUES	TIME SPAN AND FEEDBACK
Engineered	Flexible budgets and standards	Short
Discretionary	Personal observation and negotiation of static budgets	Longer
Committed	Capital budgeting*	Longest

*Discussed in Chapters 11 and 12.

2. From time to time, you will undoubtedly find that these distinctions among engineered, discretionary, and committed costs are useful. However, these are subjective decisions, so expect some ambiguity as to whether a given cost is, say, committed or discretionary. For example, the salaries of supervisory or other highly prized personnel who would be kept on the payroll at zero activity levels are often regarded as committed costs; but some organizations may classify them as discretionary costs. Arguments about whether such types of costs should be classified as committed or discretionary are a waste of time—these matters must be settled on a case-by-case basis. In a given organization, quick agreement regarding an appropriate classification is usually achieved.

3. The section on work measurement illustrates the overall theme of this book regarding control systems. Two alternative systems have been *described*, but note that one is not *advocated* here as being superior to the other. Such judgments can safely be made only in the specific circumstances facing a given organization.

4. Although a particular *system* has not been advocated here, a *method for choosing* among the systems is favored. Essentially, it is the cost-benefit method. That is, the manager or systems designer should assess (1) the expected benefits from, say, a proposed clerical work-measurement system in the form of a better collective set of operating behaviors or decisions against (2) the expected costs of a more formal system, including behavioral costs and the costs of educating employees.

Accounting Vocabulary

Budget appropriation; committed fixed costs; control-factor unit; cost approximation; cost behavior pattern; cost estimation; cost function; discretionary costs; efficiency; managed (or programmed) costs; ordinary incremental budget; parameter; priority incremental budget; regression analysis; work measurement; zero-base budgeting.

Appendix
8: Method of Least Squares

The method of least squares is the most accurate device for formulating the *past behavior* of a mixed cost.

The line itself is not plotted visually, however; it is located by means of two simultaneous linear equations:

$$\Sigma xy = a\Sigma x + b\Sigma x^2 \tag{1}$$

$$\Sigma y = na + b\Sigma x \tag{2}$$

where a is the fixed component, b is the variable cost rate, x is the activity measure, y is the mixed cost, n is the number of observations, and the Greek letter Σ (sigma) means summation.

For example, assume that nine monthly observations of repair costs are to be used as a basis for developing a budget formula. A scatter diagram indicates a mixed-cost behavior in the form $y = a + bx$. Computation of the budget formula by the method of least squares is shown in Exhibit 8-5. Substitute the values from Exhibit 8-5 into Equations 1 and 2:

$$\$25,520,000 = 12,900a + 21,090,000b \quad (1)$$

$$\$16,700 = 9a + 12,900b \quad (2)$$

repeat equation 1:

$$\$25,520,000 = 12,900a + 21,090,000b$$

multiply equation 2
by 1,433.3333
(which is 12,900 ÷ 9):

subtract.

$$\frac{\$23,936,667}{\$1,583,333} = \frac{12,900a + 18,490,000b}{2,600,000b}$$

$$b = \$.6089742$$

substitute $.6089742
for b in equation 2:

$$\$16,700 = 9a + 12,900(\$.6089742)$$

$$\$16,700 = 9a + \$7,855.7671$$

$$9a = \$8,844.233$$

$$a = \$982.69255$$

Therefore the formula for the total repair expenses is $983 per month plus $.609 per labor-hour.

A scatter diagram should also be prepared to see whether the derived line seems to fit the existing cost data to a satisfactory degree. If not, then factors other than volume or activity have also significantly affected total cost behavior. In such instances, multiple regression techniques may have to be used.

EXHIBIT 8-5

Least Squares Computation of Budget Formula for Mixed Cost

MONTH	LABOR-HOURS x	TOTAL MIXED COST y	xy	x^2
August	2,200	$ 2,300	$ 5,060,000	4,840,000
September	2,300	2,500	5,750,000	5,290,000
October	1,900	2,000	3,800,000	3,610,000
November	1,200	2,000	2,400,000	1,440,000
December	1,200	2,000	2,400,000	1,440,000
January	900	1,500	1,350,000	810,000
February	700	1,400	980,000	490,000
March	1,100	1,400	1,540,000	1,210,000
April	1,400	1,600	2,240,000	1,960,000
	12,900	$16,700	$25,520,000	21,090,000

SOURCE: *Adapted from "Separating and Using Costs as Fixed and Variable," N.A.A. Bulletin, Accounting Practice Report No. 10 (New York, June 1960), p. 13. For a more thorough explanation, see any basic text in statistics or Horngren, Cost Accounting, Chap. 24.*

Fundamental Assignment Material

8–1. **Clerical work measurement.** (Alternate is 8–23.) San Marino Pest Control Company has many small accounts receivable. Work measurement of billing labor has shown that one billing clerk can process 2,000 customers' accounts per month. The company employs thirty billing clerks at an annual salary of $19,200 each. The outlook for next year indicates a decline in the number of customers, from 59,900 to 56,300 per month.

REQUIRED:

1. Assume that management has decided to continue to employ the thirty clerks despite the expected drop in billings. Show two approaches, the engineered-cost approach and the discretionary-fixed-cost approach, to the budgeting of billing labor. Show how the *performance report* for the year would appear under each approach.
2. Assume that the workers are reasonably efficient. (a) Interpret the budget variances under the engineered-cost approach and the discretionary-fixed-cost approach. (b) What should management do to exert better control over clerical costs?
3. Some managers favor using tight budgets as motivating devices for controlling operations. In these cases, the managers really expect an unfavorable variance and must allow, in financial planning, for such a variance so that adequate cash will be available as needed. What would be the budgeted variance, also sometimes called expected variance, in this instance if an engineered-cost approach were used?

8–2. **Types of cost behavior.** Identify the following as (a) proportionately variable costs, (b) discretionary fixed costs, (c) committed fixed costs, (d) mixed or semivariable costs, (e) step-function costs, (f) discretionary variable costs, and (g) engineered variable costs.

1. Straight-line depreciation on desks in the office of a certified public accountant.
2. Rental payment by the Federal Bureau of Investigation on a five-year lease for office space in a private office building.
3. Sales commissions based on revenue dollars. Payments made to advertising salespersons employed by radio station KCBS, San Francisco.
4. Advertising costs, a lump sum budgeted and paid by Coca-Cola.
5. Crew supervisor in a Sears mail-order house. A new supervisor is added for every seven workers employed.
6. Public relations employee compensation paid by Mobil Oil Company.
7. Jet fuel costs of United Airlines.
8. Compensation of lawyers employed internally for Ford Motor Company.
9. Total costs of renting trucks by the city of Palo Alto. Charge is a lump sum of $300 per month plus 20¢ per mile.
10. Advertising allowances granted to wholesalers by Stroh Brewing Company on a per-case basis.
11. Total repairs and maintenance of a school building.

8–3. **Division of mixed costs into variable and fixed components.** The president and the controller of the Warner Transformer Company have agreed that refinement of the company cost classifications will aid planning and control decisions. They have asked you to approximate the formula for variable and fixed-cost behavior of repairs and maintenance from the following sparse data:

MONTHLY ACTIVITY IN DIRECT-LABOR HOURS	MONTHLY REPAIR AND MAINTENANCE COSTS INCURRED
3,000	$1,700
5,000	2,300

8–4. Why are fixed costs also called capacity costs?

8–5. How do committed costs differ from discretionary costs?

8–6. How do the methods and philosophies of management affect cost behavior?

8–7. "Ideally, there should be no accounts for mixed costs." Explain.

8–8. Describe how mixed costs are budgeted.

8–9. "Variable costs are those that should fluctuate directly in proportion to sales." Do you agree? Explain.

8–10. How does the basic behavior of the cost of raw materials differ from that of clerical services?

8–11. "For practical budgeting purposes, costs do not have to be proportionately variable in order to be regarded as variable." Explain.

8–12. "The objective in controlling step costs is to attain activity at the highest volume for any given step." Explain.

8–13. What is the primary determinant of the level of committed costs?

8–14. What is the primary determinant of the level of discretionary costs?

8–15. "Planning is far more important than day-to-day control of discretionary costs." Do you agree? Explain.

8–16. What is *work measurement?*

8–17. Why are committed costs the stickiest of the fixed costs?

8–18. "An unfavorable variance for discretionary costs would measure the failure to spend the entire appropriation." Do you agree? Explain.

8–19. **Attitudes toward work measurement.** At a management conference, a proponent of work measurement stated, "Before you can control, you must measure." Another executive complained, "Why bother to measure when work rules and guaranteed employment provisions in labor union contracts prevent discharging workers, using part-time employment, and using overtime!"

REQUIRED:

Evaluate these comments. Summarize your personal attitudes toward the use of work measurement.

8–20. **Government work measurement.** The auditor general of the state of California conducted a study of the Department of Motor Vehicles. The auditor's report said that the department's work standards, which were set in 1939, allow ten minutes for typing and processing a driver's license application. But a 1977 study of 40 of its 147 field offices showed that it takes only six minutes. The report said: "The continued use of the ten-minute standard results in the overstaffing of 158 positions at an unnecessary annual cost of $1.9 million."

REQUIRED:

Name four governmental activities that are likely candidates for using work measurement as a means for control.

8–21. **Government work measurement.** The Internal Revenue Service has an auditing system where an auditor scrutinizes income tax returns after they have been prescreened with the help of computer tests for normal ranges of deductions claimed by taxpayers. A standard cost of $4 per tax return has been used, based on work-measurement studies that allow twenty minutes per return. Each agent has a workweek of five days at eight hours per day.

The audit supervisor has the following data regarding performance for the most recent four-week period, when 8,000 returns were processed.

	ACTUAL COSTS	FLEXIBLE BUDGET	VARIANCE
Salaries	$38,400*	?	?

* 20 auditors × $480 salary per week × 4 weeks.

1. Compute the flexible-budget allowance and the variance.
2. The supervisor believes that audit work should be conducted more productively and that superfluous personnel should be transferred to field audits. If the above data are representative, how many auditors should be transferred?
3. Enumerate some possible reasons for the variance.

8–22. Zero-base budgeting. (CMA.) There has been much recent publicity about a budgeting system called "zero-base" budgeting. The system can be applied in governmental, not-for-profit, and profit-making organizations. Its proponents believe it represents a significant change in the budgeting process for most types of organizations and that it therefore leads to more effective use of limited resources.

REQUIRED:

1. Describe the zero-base budgeting system.
2. Explain how the proponents of zero-base budgeting say it differs from the traditional budgeting process.
3. Identify the advantages and disadvantages of the zero-base budgeting system.

8–23. Clerical work measurement. (Alternate is 8–1.) The Northeastern Transportation Company has many small customers. Billing labor used to be controlled by careful personal observation, but a year ago a formal system of work measurement was added to aid control.

A management consultant developed work standards that allowed 150 bills per day per billing clerk. The company employs ten clerks at a salary of $300 per five-day week.

To avoid confusion regarding comparisons from month to month, interim performance focuses on reporting periods of four weeks each. A recent four-week period showed that 27,000 bills had been processed by the ten clerks.

1. How would a performance report show the budget variance for the four-week period under (a) a discretionary-fixed-cost approach and (b) an engineered-cost approach?
2. What factors might influence management regarding the size of the clerical force for the billing operation?
3. Sometimes top management uses one budget for cash-planning purposes and a second budget for cost-control purposes. If an engineered-cost approach is used, top management might have an "expected variance" embedded in the cash-planning budget. What would be the "expected" or "budgeted" variance in this case?

8–24. Nonlinear behavior. The following graph contains a linear function, which is the linear approximation of the nonlinear "true" cost function also shown.

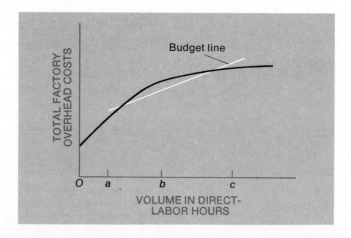

1. Will the flexible budget be higher or lower than what the budgeted "true" costs would be at *Oa*, *Ob*, and *Oc*?
2. Would you prefer to use the "true" cost curve for budgeting and for decision purposes? Why?

8–25. Separation of hospital X-ray mixed costs into variable and fixed components. A staff meeting has been called at St. Joseph's Hospital by the new administrator. She has examined the income statement and is particularly interested in the X-ray department. The chief radiologist, Dr. Ruiz, has demanded an increase in prices to cover the increased repair costs because of the opening of an outpatient clinic. She claims it is costing more per X-ray for this expense.

The administrator has asked you to approximate the fundamental variable- and fixed-cost behavior of repairs and maintenance for the X-ray department and to prepare a graphic report she can present to Dr. Ruiz. Data for the relevant range follow:

	X-RAYS PER MONTH	MONTHLY REPAIR AND MAINTENANCE COST INCURRED
Low volume	6,000	$3,400
High volume	10,000	5,400

Prepare the requested information. Also prepare a freehand graph to show the administrator.

8–26. University budgeting. Saratoga Business College, a private institution, is preparing a budgeted income statement for the coming academic year ending August 31, 19X4. Tuition revenue for the past two years ending August 31 were 19X3, $500,000; and 19X2, $550,000. Total expenses in 19X3 were $510,000 and in 19X2 were $530,000. No tuition rate changes occurred in 19X2 or 19X3, nor are any expected to occur in 19X4. Tuition revenue is expected to be $520,000 for the year ending August 31, 19X4. What net income should be budgeted for next year, assuming that the implied cost behavior patterns remain unchanged?

8–27. College income. Many private universities try to recover about one-third of their total costs from tuition revenue. The remainder is recovered via endowment income and charitable donations. Stanford University is preparing a budgeted income statement for the coming fiscal year, which will end on August 31, 19X6. Tuition revenue for the past two fiscal years was: 19X5, $54 million; and 19X4, $48 million. Total expenses were: 19X5, $165.6 million; and 19X4, $153.6 million. No tuition rate changes occurred in 19X4 or 19X5. If the tuition rate is not changed in 19X6, tuition revenue is expected to be $60 million.

1. What is the implied cost behavior pattern faced by the university? That is, what is the university's fixed- and variable-cost equation in relation to tuition revenue?
2. If historical patterns persist, what total expenses are expected by the university in 19X6?
3. What are the analytical defects in using the volume of tuition revenue as a basis for predicting costs? As financial vice-president of the university, what basis would you prefer?

8–28. Work measurement in a hospital. The billing procedures in a hospital require ponderous detail. A large hospital introduced a work-measurement program and established a standard rate of four bills per hour. Extensive studies had concluded that the typical bill contains 40 lines. Each billing clerk received an hourly labor rate of $8 and worked five days per week, eight hours per day.

REQUIRED:

1. The billing supervisor has asked you to prepare a performance report for billing labor for a recent eight-week period when ten clerks were employed and 10,000 bills were processed. Show the actual cost, flexible budget, and the variance.
2. The hospital administrator has followed the work-measurement application with intense interest. A consultant had suggested that all variances should be expressed in terms of "equivalent persons" in addition to dollar amounts. The administrator has asked you to compute the variance in terms of "equivalent persons."
3. The administrator told the supervisor: "As you know, the trustees, the government agencies, and the patients are really criticizing us for soaring hospitalization costs. This work-measurement system leads me to think we are overstaffed with billing labor. As a start, we ought to reduce the work force by the number of equivalent persons shown by the variance analysis."

   The supervisor was upset. She then took a careful random sample of 500 of the bills that were processed. Her count showed a total of 25,000 lines in the sample. As the supervisor, prepare a reply to the administrator.

8–29. Identifying cost behavior patterns.   At a seminar, a cost accountant spoke on the classification of different kinds of cost behavior.

Ann Falk, a hospital administrator who heard the lecture, identified several hospital costs and classified them. After her classification, Falk presented you with the following list of costs and asked you to classify their behavior as one of the following: variable; step; mixed; discretionary fixed; or committed fixed:

1. Straight-line depreciation of operating room equipment
2. Costs incurred by Dr. Raun in cancer research
3. Costs of services of ABC Hospital Consultant Firm
4. Repairs made on hospital furniture
5. Nursing supervisors' salaries (a supervisor is added for each 45 nursing personnel)
6. Leasing costs of X-ray equipment ($9,500 a year plus 30¢ per film)
7. Training costs of an administrative resident
8. Blue Cross insurance for all full-time employees

8–30. Various cost behavior patterns.   In practice, there is often a tendency to simplify approximations of cost behavior patterns, even though the "true" underlying behavior is not simple. Choose from the accompanying graphs A through H the one that matches the numbered items. Indicate by letter which graph best fits each of the situations described.

The vertical axes of the graphs represent total dollars of factory costs incurred, and the horizontal axes represent total production. The graphs may be used more than once.

1. Cost of sheet steel for a manufacturer of refrigerators
2. Guaranteed annual wage plan, whereby workers get paid for 40 hours of work per week at zero or low levels of production that require working only a few hours weekly
3. Cost of machining labor that tends to decrease per unit as workers gain experience
4. Depreciation on a straight-line basis
5. Water bill under drought conditions, which entails a flat fee for the first 100,000 gallons and then an increasing unit cost for every additional batch of 10,000 gallons used

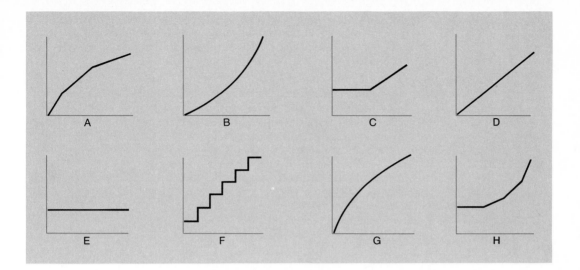

6. Salaries of assistant foremen, where one assistant foreman is added for every ten assembly workers added
7. Natural gas bill consisting of a fixed component, plus a constant variable cost per thousand cubic feet after a specified number of cubic feet are used
8. Availability of quantity discounts, where the cost per unit falls as each price break is reached
9. Price rise of an increasingly scarce raw material as the volume used increases

8–31. **Least squares.** Assume that total operating overhead of a trucking company is a function of the gross ton-miles of work to be performed. The past records show (in thousands):

	DATE			
	10/1	10/2	10/3	10/4
Gross ton miles	800	1,200	400	1,600
Total operating costs	$350	$350	$150	$550

REQUIRED:

1. Draw a scatter diagram.
2. Use simple regression to fit a line to the data. What is the equation of the line? Plot the line. This example is used only to illustrate the least-squares method. When the number of observations is small, as in this example, additional analysis should be performed to determine whether the results are reliable.

8–32. **Method of least squares and sales forecasts.** (SMA, adapted.) The Progressive Company Ltd. has recorded the following sales since its inception in 19M2:

19M2	$10,000	19M8	$125,000
19M3	20,000	19M9	150,000
19M4	30,000	19N0	180,000
19M5	45,000	19N1	220,000
19M6	70,000	19N2	270,000
19M7	90,000		

Variations of
Cost Behavior
Patterns

239

1. Calculate 19N3 sales, using the least-squares method.
2. If the directors have determined from an outside consultant that the cyclical factor in 19N4 will cause sales to be 10% above the forecast trend, what will they amount to?

8–33. **Least-squares analysis.** Suppose a manufacturer is troubled by fluctuations in labor productivity and wants to compute how direct-labor costs are related to the various sizes of batches of output. The workers in question set up their own jobs on complex machinery. The following data show the results of a random sample of ten batches of a given kind:

BATCH SIZE	DIRECT-LABOR COSTS	BATCH SIZE	DIRECT-LABOR COSTS
x	y	x	y
15	$180	25	$300
12	140	22	270
20	230	9	110
17	190	18	240
12	160	30	320

REQUIRED:

1. Prepare a scatter diagram.
2. Using least-squares analysis, compute the equation of the line relating labor costs and size of batch.
3. Predict the labor costs for a lot size of 20.
4. Using a high-low method, repeat Requirements 2 and 3. Should the manager use the high-low method or the least-squares method? Explain.

8–34. **Nonlinear costs.** The U.S. Government Printing Office has used a flexible budget for the overhead of one of its press departments. At a level of 15,000 direct-labor hours, its total overhead is budgeted at $80,000; at a level of 23,000 hours, at $96,000.

In March, the department took 21,000 hours of input for work that should have taken 19,000 standard allowed hours. Actual overhead costs incurred were $98,000.

REQUIRED:

1. Compute the flexible-budget variance for March. Subdivide the variance into a price variance and an efficiency variance.
2. Special cost studies were conducted later in the year that developed the following approximation for relating overhead to direct-labor hours (DL):

$$\text{Total overhead} = \$53,000 + \$1DL + \$100\sqrt{DL}$$

If this cost function had been used in March as the flexible-budget formula (instead of the linear budget used previously), what would have been the flexible-budget variance for March? The price variance? The efficiency variance? Round your square roots to the nearest hour.

8–35. **Nonlinear behavior and banking.** Managers are often troubled by not really knowing how overhead is affected by their operating decisions. As a result, they are uncomfortable when they use the simple "linear approximations" that are commonly encountered. Suppose a bank is contemplating the introduction of a new "one-price" banking service, whereby a flat monthly fee will provide a combination of "free" checking, safety deposit, and other services.

Suppose the underlying (but unidentified) overhead-cost behavior would be:

VOLUME LEVEL IN NUMBER OF ACCOUNTS	TOTAL OVERHEAD COSTS PER YEAR
1,000	$34,000
2,000	40,000
3,000	45,000
4,000	49,000
5,000	64,000
6,000	85,000

REQUIRED:

1. A committee is trying to predict what costs are relevant. After much heated discussion, predictions were made for two "representative" volumes: 2,000 accounts and 5,000 accounts. A flexible budget was to be constructed based on a "high-low" analysis of these two volumes. Compute the formula for the flexible-budget line.
2. What predictions would be produced by the flexible budget developed in Requirement 1 for each of the tabulated levels of activity? Use a table to compare these predictions with the "true" cost behavior, showing the difference between the "true" cost behavior and the linear approximation.
3. Plot the two sets of predictions on a graph.
4. Assume that the new service has been introduced. The manager in charge is convinced that a special television campaign can increase volume from the current level of 2,000 accounts to a level of 4,000 accounts. These additional accounts would bring an additional contribution to income of $64,000 before considering the predicted increase in total overhead cost and before considering the cost of $50,000 for the television campaign. If the manager were guided by the linear flexible-budget formula, would she launch the campaign? Show computations. If she did launch the campaign, by how much would income change if 2,000 more accounts were achieved?
5. As an operating manager responsible for budgetary control of overhead, would you regard the linear budget allowances for 4,000 and 6,000 accounts as too tight or too loose? Why?
6. A top executive of the bank commented: "I think we should have a more accurate budgetary system." Do you agree? Explain.

8–36. **Two independent variables in hospital.** The underlying cost behavior pattern of overhead in South Chicago Hospital is linear but is affected by two independent variables: number of patients and the number of days each patient stays. The latter, called *patient-days*, is computed by multiplying the number of patients by the days each stayed. The number of patients influences costs because the first day of the stay tends to require more overhead costs than subsequent days. In sum, the actual cost behavior pattern is:

$$\text{total overhead} = a + bx_1 + cx_2$$

where a = intercept, b = rate per patient-day, and c = rate per patient.

For simplicity, the flexible budget for overall overhead behavior is based on patient-days:

$$\text{total overhead} = a + bx_1$$

At the end of a period, the hospital administrator was disturbed that the overhead variance was highly unfavorable. She commented: "A large part of that variance is attributable to Medicare and similar reimbursement plans. Some people place aged parents in the hospital for a couple of days and go away for a short holiday."

REQUIRED:

Given these facts and the underlying cost behavior, was the flexible-budget variance overstated or understated? Suppose the more costly and more accurate flexible-budget formula had been developed. Would the variance be higher or lower than the variance produced by the simple formula? Why?

RESPONSIBILITY ACCOUNTING AND COST ALLOCATION

Learning Objectives

When you have finished studying this chapter, you should be able to

1. Define and contrast cost centers, profit centers, and investment centers, and explain how a responsibility accounting structure can promote desirable management behavior

2. Recognize the major purposes for allocating costs

3. Prepare a segmented income statement, using the contribution approach to cost allocation

4. Distinguish between the economic performance of an organization segment and the performance of the segment manager

5. Use recommended guidelines to allocate the variable and fixed costs of service departments to other organization segments

6. Identify the principal approaches to solving the allocation problem for the central costs of an organization

7. Use the direct and step-down methods to allocate service department costs to user departments

This chapter is the first of a two-chapter overview of how management accounting systems are designed. It describes some typical approaches and focuses on the factors that should influence management's choice of systems. We learn that no single system is inherently superior to another. The "best" system is the one that consistently leads to a collective set of subordinate managers' decisions that are desired by higher-level managers. The relative costs of each system must also be considered.

GENERAL IDEAS OF RESPONSIBILITY ACCOUNTING

❑ Responsibility Accounting and Motivation

Ideally, organizations are structured by top managers who subdivide activities and stipulate a hierarchy of managers who oversee predetermined spheres of activities and who have some latitude to make decisions in those spheres. Some type of responsibility accounting usually accompanies this delegation of decision making. **Responsibility accounting** is a system of accounting that recognizes various responsibility centers throughout the organization and reflects the plans and actions of each of these centers by assigning particular revenues and costs to the one having the pertinent responsibility. It is also called **profitability accounting** and **activity accounting.**

Responsibility accounting emphasizes a major lesson for both managers and accountants—that is, the behavior of managers is often heavily influenced by how their performance is measured. Thus accounting is usually far from being a sterile, secondary part of a manager's professional life. Instead, the accounting system often plays a key role in motivating managers toward or away from the desires of top management. The motivational impact of the responsibility approach is described in the following:

❑ The sales department requests a rush production. The plant scheduler argues that it will disrupt his production and cost a substantial though not clearly determined amount of money. The answer coming from sales is: "Do you want to take the responsibility of losing the X Company as a customer?" Of course the production scheduler does not want to take such a responsibility, and he gives up, but not before a heavy exchange of arguments and the accumulation of a substantial backlog of ill feeling. Analysis of the payroll in the assembly department, determining the costs involved in getting out rush orders, eliminated the cause for argument. Henceforth, any rush order was accepted with a smile by the production scheduler, who made sure that the extra cost would be duly recorded and charged to the sales department—"no questions asked." As a result, the tension created by rush orders disappeared completely; and, somehow, the number of rush orders requested by the sales department was progressively reduced to an insignificant level.[1]

A 1983 news story regarding quality control in the automobile industry also illustrates the motivational impact of responsibility accounting. A former Ford engineer said that he often watched suspect vehicles being

[1] Raymond Villers, "Control and Freedom in a Decentralized Company," *Harvard Business Review*, XXXII, No. 2, 95.

manufactured: "Bonuses were figured on how many cars we produced, not how well we made them. When the customer discovered the defect, it was charged to warranties, not to our plant."

☐ Cost Centers and Profit Centers

Areas of responsibility take many forms, including

1. **Cost centers**—formal reporting of costs only
2. **Profit centers**—formal reporting of revenues and expenses
3. **Investment centers**—formal reporting of revenues, expenses, and related investment

A **cost center** is the smallest segment of activity or area of responsibility for which costs are accumulated. Typically, cost centers are departments, but in some instances a department may contain several cost centers. For example, although an assembly department may be supervised by one foreman, it may contain several assembly lines. Sometimes each assembly line is regarded as a separate cost center with its own assistant foreman.

A **profit center** is a segment of a business, often called a division, that is responsible for both revenue and expenses.[2] An **investment center** goes a step further; its success is measured not only by its income but also by relating that income to its invested capital. In practice, the term *investment center* is not widely used. Instead, *profit center* is used indiscriminately to describe segments that are always assigned responsibility for revenue and expenses but may or may not be assigned responsibility for the related invested capital.

☐ Illustration of Responsibility Accounting

The simplified organization chart in Exhibit 9-1 will be the basis for our illustration of how responsibility accounting is used in the motel industry. The manager at the motel level has freedom to make many operating decisions, including some repairs and building improvements.

Exhibit 9-2 provides an overall view of responsibility reporting. Start with the lowest level and work toward the top. See how the reports are integrated through three levels of responsibility. All the variances may be subdivided for further analysis, either in these reports or in more-detailed reports.

Trace the $38,000 total from the Los Banos manager's report to the Western vice-president's report. The vice-president's report merely summarizes the final results of the motels under his jurisdiction. He may also want copies of the detailed statements for each motel manager responsible to him.

Also trace the $297,000 total from the Western vice-president's report to the president's report. The president's report includes data for her own

[2] In some settings, particularly in nonprofit organizations, the term *revenue center* is used instead of *profit center* because profit (as ordinarily conceived) is not the primary mission of the subunit. For example, an army motor pool might be called a revenue center if it charged users for its vehicles instead of not charging.

EXHIBIT 9-1 Siesta Motels, Inc. Simplified Organization Chart

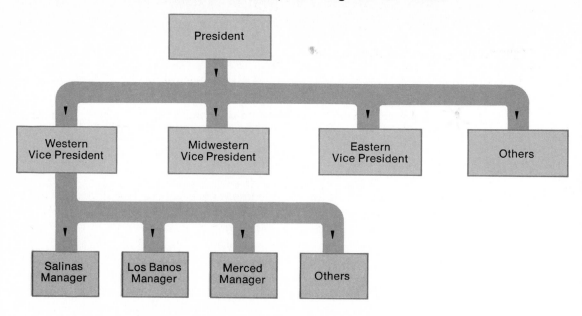

corporate office plus a summarization of the entire company's operating income performance.

☐ Format of Feedback Reports

This set of illustrative reports shows only the budgeted amount and the variance, which is defined as the difference between the budgeted and the actual amounts. This places the focus on the variances and illustrates *management by exception*, which means that the executive's attention is concentrated on the important deviations from budgeted items. In this way, managers do not waste time on those parts of the reports that reflect smoothly running phases of operations.

Of course, this illustration represents only one possible means of presenting a report of performance. Another common reporting method shows three sets of dollar figures instead of two sets. Moreover, the variances could also be expressed in terms of percentages of budgeted amounts. For example, revenue in Los Banos could appear as follows:

	BUDGET		ACTUAL RESULTS		VARIANCE: FAVORABLE (UNFAVORABLE)		VARIANCE: PERCENT OF BUDGETED AMOUNT	
	This Month	Year to Date	This Month	Year to Date	This Month	Year to Date	This Month	Year to Date
Revenue	$80	$250	$85	$265	$5	$15	6.3%	6.0%

The full performance report would contain a similar line-by-line analysis of all items.

EXHIBIT
9-2

SIESTA MOTELS, INC.
Responsibility Accounting at Various Levels
(In thousands of dollars)

PRESIDENT'S MONTHLY RESPONSIBILITY REPORT

	Budget		Variance: Favorable (Unfavorable)	
	This Month	Year to Date	This Month	Year to Date
President's office	(90)	(300)	(9)	(30)
Western vice-president	297	850	(8)	50
Midwestern vice-president	400	1,300	20	(100)
Eastern vice-president	350	1,050	46	130
Others	300	1,000	50	100
Operating income	1,257	3,900	99	150

WESTERN VICE-PRESIDENT'S MONTHLY RESPONSIBILITY REPORT

	Budget		Variance: Favorable (Unfavorable)	
	This Month	Year to Date	This Month	Year to Date
Vice-president's office	(20)	(40)	(2)	4
Salinas	29	(20)	(1)	(5)
Los Banos	38	133	3	16
Merced	30	90	2	10
Others	220	687	(10)	25
Operating income	297	850	(8)	50

LOS BANOS MANAGER'S MONTHLY RESPONSIBILITY REPORT

	Budget		Variance: Favorable (Unfavorable)	
	This Month	Year to Date	This Month	Year to Date
Revenue	80	250	5	15
Housekeeping and supplies	12	30	1	4
Heat, light, power	3	10	(1)	(2)
Advertising and promotion	2	7	–	(2)
Repairs and maintenance	4	10	(2)	(1)
General	11	30	–	2
Depreciation	10	30	–	–
Total expenses	42	117	(2)	1
Operating income	38	133	3	16

Other data are often included in performance evaluation reports. For example, the motel industry characteristically includes the percentage of occupany of rooms and the average rate per room. Restaurants will show the number of meals served and the average selling price per meal.

The exact format adopted in a particular organization depends heavily on user preferences. For instance, some companies focus on the budgeted income statement for the year. As each month unfolds, the managers receive the original plan *for the year* compared with the revised plan *for the year*. The revised plan provides management with the best available prediction of how the year's results will eventually turn out.

Even though formats and intent of responsibility reports may be geared to satisfy the preferences of the managers in a particular organization, the following fundamentals are typically followed:

1. Show total costs, unit costs, and physical amounts of inputs and outputs. Most managers prefer simple reports. Consequently, some of these data may be omitted or condensed; when in doubt, more data rather than less data are furnished.

2. Keep the terminology, time spans, and various internal reports consistent. In this way, budgeted figures can easily be compared with actual results and with budgets and actual results of previous and future periods.

❏ Responsibility and Incentive

Responsibility accounting has innate attraction for most top managers because it facilitates the delegation of decision making. That is, each middle manager is given command of a subunit together with some authority. In return, responsibility accounting supplies the basic means of evaluating each manager's performance. Consequently, in addition to keeping top management informed, a responsibility accounting system helps give individual managers incentive via performance reports.

A **controllable cost** has been defined as any cost that is subject to the influence of a given *manager* of a given *responsibility center* for a given *time span*. The degree of controllability is often hard to establish. To try to focus on the manager's performance as an individual administrator, responsibility reporting often excludes or segregates items that are judged as not subject to the manager's control. For example, a foreman's performance report may be confined to usage of direct material, direct labor, and supplies, and exclude depreciation, rent, and property taxes. In a prison or hospital, or in many hotels, the costs on a laundry department performance report might be confined to soap and labor; depreciation on the building and equipment would be excluded.

❏ Who Gets Blamed?

Responsibility accounting, budgets, variances, and the entire library of accounting techniques are basically neutral devices. However, they are frequently misused as negative weapons, as being a means of placing blame or finding fault. Viewed positively, they are a means of assisting managers so that future improvements in decisions are more easily attained. Moreover, they facilitate the delegation of decision making to lower levels, providing the autonomy that is almost always treasured by managers.

The "blame-placing" attitude reveals a misunderstanding of the rationale of responsibility accounting, which basically asks, "Which individual in the organization is in the best position to *explain why* a specific outcome occurred? Let's trace costs down to that level so that the feedback coming from performance evaluation is as well informed as feasible."

In many circumstances, the degree of the manager's control or influence over the outcome may be minimal—but responsibility accounting still is favored. For example, the price of gold to a jewelry manufacturer may be beyond the influence of anybody within the organization. Still, somebody usually is in the best position to explain the *price* of gold, and another is in the best position to explain the *quantity* of gold consumed. The latter individual typically has a budget based on a standard (budgeted) unit price of gold rather than on its actual unit price.

The purchasing manager may have little influence over the price of the commodities acquired. Nevertheless, responsibility accounting is still applicable. He or she has *the most information* about prices. Managers are expected to bear risks even though they may have limited control over many outcomes.

In sum, responsibility accounting presses accountability down to the person who has the most information and the greatest potential day-to-day influence over the revenue or cost in question. This person must bear the responsibility, and so must his or her superiors. And this person's fundamental reporting responsibility is to explain the outcome regardless of the personal influence over the result.

COST ALLOCATION IN GENERAL

To be credible, responsibility accounting depends on appropriate cost allocations. The term **cost allocation** is used here as general label for all tracing of various costs to cost objectives such as departments or products. Like air and water, problems of cost allocation are everywhere. University presidents, city managers, hospital administrators, and corporate executives inevitably face these difficult problems. This section describes some general approaches to the solutions, but there are no easy answers.

❑ Cost Allocation as a Term

As Chapter 3 pointed out, cost allocation is fundamentally a problem of linking (1) some cost or groups of costs with (2) one or more cost objectives (examples are products, departments, and divisions). In short, cost allocation tries to identify (1) with (2) via some cost function.

The linking of (1) with (2) is accomplished by a **cost-allocation base.** Such a base is the common denominator used to trace the cost or costs in question to the cost objectives. For example, the total direct-labor cost and many indirect costs are frequently expressed as costs *per hour.* Direct-labor hours are an illustration of a cost-allocation base.

Major costs, such as newsprint for a newspaper and direct professional labor for a law firm, may be allocated to departments, jobs, and projects on an item-by-item basis, using cost-allocation bases such as tonnage consumed or direct-labor hours used. Other costs, taken one at a time, are not important enough to justify being allocated individually.

These costs are *pooled* and then allocated as pools. A **cost pool** is a group of individual costs that is allocated to *cost objectives* in some plausible way. An example would be a university's allocating the operating costs of a registrar's office to its colleges on the basis of the number of students in each college.

The literature is not consistent in the use of terms in this area, so be sure to pinpoint the meaning of terms in specific situations. You may encounter terms such as *allocate, reallocate, trace, assign, distribute, redistribute, load, apportion,* and *reapportion* being used interchangeably to describe the same cost-accounting practice. The terms *apply* or *absorb* tend to have the narrower meaning of costs traced to *products* rather than to *departments.*

❏ Four Purposes of Allocation

What logic should be used for allocating costs from one segment to other segments of an organization? This question bothers many internal users and suppliers of services in all organizations, including nonprofit organizations. The answer should begin with a determination of the principal purpose or purposes of the cost allocation.

Costs are allocated for four major purposes:

1. *To predict the economic effects of planning and control decisions.* Examples are the addition of a new course in a university, the addition of a new flight or an additional passenger on an airline, and the addition of a new specialty in a medical clinic. Some costs are obviously associated with particular decisions. Other costs are admittedly associated, but the nature of the association is hard to establish in any convincing way.

2. *To obtain desired motivation.* Cost allocations are sometimes made to promote goal coordination and managerial effort. Examples are decisions to allocate or not to allocate a given cost, depending on top management's predictions regarding collective management behavior. Consequently, in some organizations there is no cost allocation for legal or internal auditing services or internal management consulting services because top management wants to encourage their use. In other organizations there is a cost allocation for such items to spur managers to take an interest in a particular activity or to compare the costs and benefits of the use of specified services. Examples are allocations of research costs and of "carrying" costs, such as an "opportunity" or "imputed" interest cost on receivables or inventories.

3. *To compute income and asset valuations.* Costs are allocated to products and projects to measure their inventory costs and their profit contributions.

4. *To obtain a mutually agreeable price.* The best examples are in regulated industries and in government contracts based on a negotiated price that provides for costs plus some profit based on costs.[3] These contracts are used when ordinary market prices do not seem applicable. In these instances, cost allocations become substitutes for the usual working of the marketplace. That is, cost allocations are a way of using a "cost-accounting pricing system" as a substitute for the "free-market pricing system."

[3] Regarding government contracts, see the statements on cost allocation issued by the Cost Accounting Standards Board. Also see H. Wright and J. Bedingfield, *Government Contract Accounting* (Washington, D.C.: Federal Publications, 1983).

Ideally, all four purposes would be served simultaneously by a single cost allocation. The allocation of raw-material usage to departments, products, managers, and contracts might reach this ideal occasionally. But thousands of managers and accountants will testify that for most costs the ideal is rarely achieved. Instead, cost allocations are often a major source of discontent and confusion to the affected parties. When all four purposes are unattainable simultaneously, the manager and the accountant should start attacking a cost-allocation problem by trying to identify which of the purposes should dominate in the particular situation at hand.

THE CONTRIBUTION APPROACH TO ALLOCATION

Many organizations combine the contribution approach and responsibility accounting; they report by cost behavior pattern as well as by degrees of controllability. To do so, they must contend with problems of cost allocation. Consider an illustration of a retail grocery company. It might have the basic organizational design shown in Exhibit 9-3.

Exhibit 9-4 displays the contribution approach to reporting and cost allocation. Study this important exhibit carefully. It provides perspective on how a reporting system can be designed to stress cost behavior pat-

EXHIBIT 9-3

Organization Chart of Retail Grocery Company

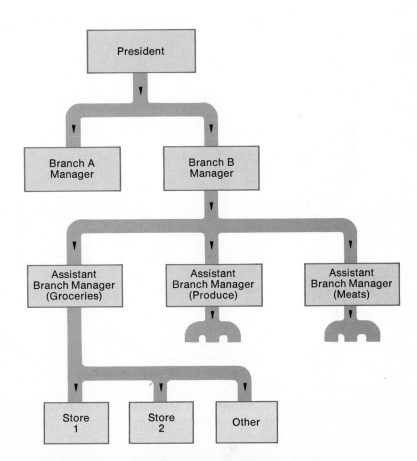

terns, controllability, manager performance, and subunit performance simultaneously.

Contribution Margin

As demonstrated in previous chapters, the contribution margin, which is revenues minus all variable expenses (line (a) in Exhibit 9-4), is especially helpful for predicting the impact on income of short-run changes in volume. Incidentally, in this case, if management prefers, a gross margin or gross profit (revenue minus the cost of the merchandise sold) could be inserted just after cost of merchandise sold. This is a good example of how gross margin and contribution margin differ. The principal example of variable operating expenses are the wages and payroll-related costs for most store personnel.

Any expected changes in income may be quickly calculated by multiplying increases in dollar sales by the contribution-margin ratio. Suppose the contribution-margin ratio for meats is 20%. Then a $1,000 increase in sales of meats should produce a $200 increase in income (.20 × $1,000 = $200). (This assumes, of course, no changes in selling prices or operating conditions.)

Segment and Manager Performance

A **segment** is defined as any part of an organization or line of activity for which separate determination of revenue and costs is obtained. When they analyze performance, many proponents of responsibility accounting distinguish sharply between the *segment* (department, division, store, motel) as an economic investment and the *manager* as a professional decision maker. Managers frequently have little influence over many factors that affect economic performance. For instance, the manager of a motel may be relatively helpless if an energy crisis reduces automobile traffic or if unseasonable weather ruins the ski season.

Similarly, the manager of a retail store may have influence over some local advertising but not other advertising, some fixed salaries but not other salaries, and so forth. Moreover, the meat manager at both the branch and store levels for the retail grocery company may have zero influence over store depreciation and the president's salary.

Contribution Controllable by Segment Managers

The controllable contribution (item (b) in Exhibit 9-4) and the segment contribution (item (c) in Exhibit 9-4) are attempts to underscore the distinction between subunit (segment) performance and manager performance.

The term "segment managers" is used in the exhibit to represent a general description of the manager of any subunit of any organization. Examples are nursing supervisors, shipping room foremen, police captains, and fire station chiefs.

Note that fixed costs controllable by the segment manager are deducted from the contribution margin to obtain the contribution controllable by segment managers. These are usually discretionary fixed costs. Exam-

EXHIBIT 9-4

The Contribution Approach:
Model Income Statement, by Segments*
(In thousands of dollars)

	RETAIL FOOD COMPANY AS A WHOLE	COMPANY BREAKDOWN INTO TWO DIVISIONS		POSSIBLE BREAKDOWN OF BRANCH B ONLY				POSSIBLE BREAKDOWN OF BRANCH B, MEATS ONLY		
		Branch A	Branch B	Not Allocated†	Groceries	Produce	Meats	Not Allocated†	Store 1	Store 2
Net sales	$4,000	$1,500	$2,500	—	$1,300	$300	$900	—	$600	$300
Variable costs:										
Cost of merchandise sold	$3,000	$1,100	$1,900	—	$1,000	$230	$670	—	$450	$220
Variable operating expenses	260	100	160	—	100	10	50	—	35	15
Total variable costs	$3,260	$1,200	$2,060	—	$1,100	$240	$720	—	$485	$235
(a) Contribution margin	$ 740	$ 300	$ 440	—	$ 200	$ 60	$180	—	$115	$ 65
Less: Fixed costs controllable by segment managers‡	260	100	160	$ 20	40	10	90	$ 30	35	25
(b) Contribution controllable by segment managers	$ 480	$ 200	$ 280	$(20)	$ 160	$ 50	$ 90	$(30)	$ 80	$ 40
Less: Fixed costs controllable by others§	200	90	110	20	40	10	40	10	22	8
(c) Contribution by segments	$ 280	$ 110	$ 170	$(40)	$ 120	$ 40	$ 50	$(40)	$ 58	$ 32
Less: Unallocated costs¶	100									
(d) Income before income taxes	$ 180									

*Three different types of segments are illustrated here: branches, product lines, and stores. As you read across, note that the focus becomes narrower: from Branch A and B, to Branch B only, to Meats in Branch B only.

†Only those costs clearly identifiable to a product line should be allocated.

‡Examples are certain advertising, sales promotion, salespersons' salaries, management consulting, training and supervision costs.

§Examples are depreciation, property taxes, insurance, and perhaps the segment manager's salary.

¶These costs are not clearly or practically allocable to any segment except by some highly questionable allocation base.

ples of these discretionary costs are some local advertising but not all advertising and some fixed salaries but not the manager's own salary.

In many organizations, managers have some latitude to trade off some variable costs for fixed costs. To save variable material and labor costs, managers might make heavier outlays for machinery, labor-saving devices, quality control inspectors, maintenance, management consulting fees, employee training programs, and so on. Moreover, decisions on advertising, research, and sales promotion have effects on sales volumes and hence on contribution margins. That is why the contribution margin alone is not a satisfactory measure of manager performance. However, the controllable contribution attempts to capture the results of these trade-offs.

The distinctions in Exhibit 9-4 among which items belong in what cost classification are inevitably not clear-cut. For example, determining controllability is always a problem when service department costs are allocated to other departments. Should the store manager bear a part of the branch headquarters costs? If so, how much and on what basis? How much, if any, store depreciation or lease rentals should be deducted in computing the controllable contribution? There are no pat answers to these questions. They are worked out in various ways from organization to organization. Again, for management control purposes there are no constraints of external accounting principles[4] on designing acceptable management accounting systems. The answers depend fundamentally on what reporting system will bring the most net benefits in terms of motivation and collective decisions.

Consider the fixed costs that are deducted between items (a) and (b) in Exhibit 9-4. The "not allocated" columns show amounts of $20,000 and $30,000, respectively. This approach recognizes that perhaps some clusters of costs should not be allocated below specified levels in the organization's hierarchy. For instance, the $20,000 may include secretarial salaries of the Branch B general manager that may not be allocated; similarly, the $30,000 in that same line may include costs of general meat advertisements that may not be allocated to individual stores.

❑ Contribution by Segments

The contribution by segments, line (c) in Exhibit 9-4, is an attempt to approximate the economic *performance of the segment*, as distinguished from the *performance of its manager*. The "fixed costs controllable by others" typically include committed costs (such as depreciation and property taxes) and discretionary costs (such as the subunit manager's salary). These costs are examples of items that are minimally influenced by the segment manager within a reporting period of a year or less.

Exhibit 9-4 shows an "unallocated costs" line immediately before line (d). They might include central corporate costs such as the costs of the

---

[4] FASB *Statement No. 14*, "Financial Reporting for Segments of a Business Enterprise," requires that companies' external financial statements include information about operations in different industries, foreign operations and export sales, and major customers. Disclosure of profit contribution (revenue less only those operating expenses that are directly traceable to a segment) is encouraged but not required.

president's office and many costs of the legal and accounting activities. When a persuasive "cause-and-effect" or "benefits-received" justification for allocating such costs cannot be found, many organizations favor not allocating them to segments.

The contribution approach highlights the relative objectivity of various measures of performance evaluation. The contribution margin tends to be the most objective. As you read downward, the allocations become more difficult, and the resulting measures of contributions or income become more subject to dispute. In contrast, the traditional functional approach to income statements rarely hesitates to use full-cost allocations. Therefore, it tends to offer less-sharp distinctions between variable and fixed costs and between controllable and uncontrollable costs.

HOW TO ALLOCATE FOR PLANNING AND CONTROL

❏ General Guides

What causes costs to occur? The *causes* of costs are the very same activities that are usually chosen to be cost objectives. Examples are products produced, letters typed, and patients seen. The *effects* of these activities are various costs. Therefore the manager and the accountant should search for some cost-allocation base that establishes a convincing relationship between the cause and the effect and that permits reliable predictions of how costs will be affected by decisions regarding the activities.

The preferred guides for allocating service department costs are:

1. Use responsibility accounting and flexible budgets for each service (staff) department, just as they are used for each production or operating (line) department. When feasible, maintain distinctions between variable-cost pools and fixed-cost pools.

2. Allocate variable- and fixed-cost pools separately. This is sometimes called the dual method of allocation. Note that one service department (such as a computer department) can contain a variable-cost pool and a fixed-cost pool. That is, costs may be pooled within and among departments if desired.

3. Establish part or all of the details regarding cost allocation in advance of rendering the service rather than after the fact.

❏ Using the Guides

To illustrate these guides, consider a simplified example of a computer department of a university that serves two major users, the School of Earth Sciences and the School of Engineering. The computer mainframe was acquired on a five-year lease that is not cancelable unless prohibitive cost penalties are paid.

How should costs be allocated to the user departments? Suppose there are two major purposes for the allocation: (1) predicting economic effects of the use of the computer and (2) motivating toward optimal usage.

Apply the guides enumerated earlier:

1. Analyze the costs of the computer department in detail. Divide the costs into two pools, one for variable costs and one for fixed costs. Suppose the flexible-budget formula for the forthcoming fiscal year is $100,000 monthly fixed costs plus $200 variable cost per hour of computer time used.
2. *Allocate separately* the variable-cost pool and the fixed-cost pool.
3. *Establish in advance* the details regarding the cost allocation.

Guides (2) and (3) will be considered together in the following sections on variable-cost pools and fixed-cost pools.

❏ Variable-Cost Pool

Ideally, the variable-cost pool should be allocated as follows:

(budgeted unit rate) × (actual quantities of service units used)

The cause-and-effect relationship is clear: the heavier the usage, the higher the total costs. In this example, the rate used would be the budgeted rate of $200 per hour.

The use of *budgeted* cost rates rather than *actual* cost rates for allocating variable costs of service departments protects the using departments from intervening price fluctuations and also often protects them from inefficiencies.

The most desirable procedure for allocating variable-cost pools is to know the complete cost of various services in advance. For example, the cost of a repair job would be predetermined based on budgeted cost rates multiplied by the budgeted or standard hours of input allowed for accomplishing specified repairs. User department managers sometimes complain more vigorously about the poor management of a service department than about the choice of a cost-allocation base (such as direct-labor dollars or number of employees). Such complaints are less likely if the service department managers have budget responsibility and the user departments are protected from short-run price fluctuations and inefficiencies.

❏ Fixed-Cost Pool

Ideally, the fixed-cost pool should be allocated as follows:

(budgeted fraction of capacity available for use)
× (total budgeted fixed costs)

Before exploring the implications of this approach, consider our example. Suppose the deans had originally predicted the following long-run average monthly usage: earth sciences, 210 hours, and engineering, 490 hours, a total of 700 hours. The fixed-cost pool would be allocated as follows:

	EARTH SCIENCES	ENGINEERING
Fixed costs per month:		
210/700, or 30% of $100,000	$30,000	
490/700, or 70% of $100,000		$70,000

This predetermined lump-sum approach is based on the long-run capacity *available* to the user, regardless of actual usage from month to month. The reasoning is that the level of fixed costs is affected by long-range planning regarding the overall level of service and the *relative* expected usage, not by *short-run* fluctuations in service levels and relative usage.

A major strength of the use of capacity *available* rather than capacity *used* for allocating *budgeted* fixed costs is that short-run allocations to user departments are not affected by the *actual* usage of *other* user departments. Such a budgeted lump-sum approach is more likely to have the desired motivational effects with respect to the ordering of service in both the short run and the long run.

❏ Fixed Pool and Actual Usage

In practice, the use of capacity available as a base for allocating fixed-cost pools is seldom followed. Instead, actual usage is the base employed. Suppose the computer department allocated the total actual costs after the fact, a weakness followed by many service departments. At the end of the month, total *actual* costs would be allocated in proportion to the *actual* hours used by the consuming departments. Compare the costs borne by the two schools:

If 600 hours are used:

Total costs incurred, $100,000 + 600($200) = $220,000	
Earth Sciences: 200/600 × $220,000 =	$ 73,333
Engineering: 400/600 × $220,000 =	146,667
Total cost allocated	$220,000

What happens if Earth Sciences uses only 100 hours during the following month while Engineering still uses 400 hours?

If 500 hours are used:

Total costs incurred, $100,000 + 500($200) = $200,000	
Earth Sciences: 100/500 × $200,000 =	$ 40,000
Engineering: 400/500 × $200,000 =	160,000
Total cost allocated	$200,000

Engineering has done nothing differently, but it must bear higher costs of $13,333, an increase of 9%. Its short-run costs are dependent on what *other* consumers have used, not on its own actions. This phenomenon is caused by a faulty allocation method for the *fixed* portion of total costs, a method whereby the allocations are highly sensitive to fluctuations in the actual volumes used by the various consuming departments. This weakness is avoided by the dual approach that provides for a predetermined lump-sum allocation of fixed costs.

To consider further the use of *budgeted* rates for allocating *variable* costs, return to our data for 600 hours. Suppose inefficiencies in the computer department caused the variable costs to be $140,000 instead of the 600 hours × $200, or $120,000 budgeted. A common weakness of cost allocation is to allocate the costs of inefficiencies to the consumer departments. To remedy this weakness, many cost-allocation schemes would allocate only the $120,000 to the consuming departments and would let the $20,000 remain as an unallocated unfavorable budget variance of the computer department. This is responsibility accounting in action, and it reduces the resentment of user managers. The allocation of costs of inefficiency seems unjustified because the "consuming departments" have to bear another department's cost of waste.

Most consumers prefer to know the total price in advance. They become nervous when an automobile mechanic or a contractor undertakes a job without specifying prices. As a minimum, they like to know the hourly rates that they must bear.

Cost-allocation systems should motivate the service department manager to control operating costs. Therefore, predetermined unit prices (at least) should be used. Where feasible, predetermined total prices should be used for various kinds of work based on flexible budgets and standards.

To illustrate, when we have our automobiles repaired, we are routinely given firm total prices for various types of services. Furthermore, in the short run these prices are not affected by the volume of work handled on a particular day. Imagine your feelings if you came to an automobile service department to get your car and were told: "Our daily fixed overhead is $1,000. Yours was the only car in our shop today,[5] so we are charging you the full $1,000. If we had processed 100 cars today, your charge would have been only $10."

❑ Troubles with Using Lump Sums

If fixed costs are allocated on the basis of long-range plans, there is a natural tendency on the part of consumers to underestimate their planned usage and thus obtain a smaller fraction of the cost allocation. Top management can counteract these tendencies by monitoring predictions and by following up and utilizing feedback to keep future predictions more honest.

In some organizations there are even definite rewards in the form of salary increases for managers who are skillful as accurate predictors. Moreover, some cost-allocation methods provide for penalties for underpredictions. For example, if a manager predicts usage of 210 hours and then demands 300 hours, either he doesn't get the hours or he pays a dear price for every hour beyond 210.

---

[5] Similarly, consider a news reporter's comment on medical costs: "When they thought I had a heart attack, I was glad to know they were giving me the Rolls Royce treatment. For 30 hours of observation in a coronary ward the bill topped $700. The cost was higher than needed because I was the only one in it."

❏ Allocating Central Costs

Many central costs, such as the president's salary and related expenses, public relations, legal, income tax planning, companywide advertising, and basic research, are difficult to allocate in any feasible, convincing way. Therefore many companies do not allocate them at all. Other companies use allocation bases such as the revenue of each division, the cost of goods sold of each division, the total assets of each division, or the total costs of each division (before allocation of the central costs).

The desperate search for such allocation bases is a manifestation of a widespread, deep-seated belief that all costs must somehow be fully allocated to all parts of the organization. The flimsy assumptions that might underlie such allocations are widely recognized, but most managers accept them as a fact of a manager's life—as long as all managers seem to be treated alike and thus "fairly."

The use of the above bases may provide a rough indication of cause-and-effect relationships. Basically, however, they represent a "soak-the-rich" or "ability-to-bear" philosophy of cost allocation. For example, the costs of companywide advertising, such as the goodwill sponsorship of a program on a noncommercial television station, might be allocated to all products and divisions on the basis of the dollar sales in each. But such costs precede sales. They are discretionary costs as determined by management policies, not by sales results.

❏ Choice of Allocation Bases

A persuasive allocation base for central services is usage, either actual or estimated. Many organizations, however, regard such measurements as infeasible. For example, 60% of the companies in a large survey use sales revenue as an allocation base.[6]

Not all central services are allocated in the same manner. The costs of such services as public relations, top-corporate-management overhead, real estate department, and corporate-planning department are the least likely to be allocated on the basis of usage; the most likely are data processing, advertising, and operations research.[7]

Companies that allocate central costs by usage tend to generate less resentment. Consider the experience of J. C. Penney Co. (*Business Week*, April 12, 1982, p. 107):

❏ The controller's office wanted subsidiaries such as Thrift Drug Co. and the insurance operations to base their share of corporate personnel, legal, and auditing costs on their revenues. The subsidiaries contended that they maintained their own personnel and legal departments, and should be assessed far less.

   . . . The subcommittee addressed the issue by asking the corporate departments to approximate the time costs involved in servicing the sub-

[6] R. Vancil, *Decentralization: Managerial Ambiguity by Design* (New York: Financial Executives Research Foundation, 1979), p. 235.

[7] *Ibid.*, p. 250. Also see J. Fremgen and S. Liao, *The Allocation of Corporate Indirect Costs* (New York: National Association of Accountants, 1981).

sidiaries. The final allocation plan, based on these studies, cost the divisions less than they were initially assessed but more than they had wanted to pay. Nonetheless, the plan was implemented easily.

❑ Using Budgeted Allocation Bases

Again, if the costs of central services are to be allocated, the use of *budgeted* sales or some other *budgeted* allocation base is preferred to the use of *actual* sales. At least this method means that the short-run costs of a given consuming department will not be affected by the fortunes of other consuming departments.

For example, suppose central advertising were allocated on the basis of potential sales in two territories:

| | TERRITORY | | | |
	A	B	TOTAL	PERCENT
Budgeted sales	$500	$500	$1,000	100%
Central advertising allocated	$ 50	$ 50	$ 100	10%

Consider the possible differences in allocations when actual sales become known:

| | TERRITORIES | |
	A	B
Actual sales	$300	$600
Central advertising:		
1. Allocated on basis of budgeted sales	$50	$50
or		
2. Allocated on basis of actual sales	$33	$67

Compare allocation 1 with 2. Allocation 1 is preferable. It indicates a low ratio of sales to advertising in Territory A. It directs attention to where it is deserved. In contrast, allocation 2 soaks Territory B with more advertising cost because of the *achieved* results and relieves Territory A because it had lesser success. This is another example of the analytical confusion that can arise when cost allocations to one consuming department are dependent on the activity of other consuming departments.

THE PRODUCT-COSTING PURPOSE

❑ Relating Costs to Outputs

Until this point, we have concentrated on cost allocation to divisions, departments, and similar segments of an entity. Cost allocation is often carried one step further—to the outputs of these departments, however defined. Examples are *products* such as automobiles, furniture, and newspapers. Other examples are personal *services* such as hospitalization and education.

Costs are allocated to products for inventory valuation purposes and for decision purposes such as pricing, adding products, and promoting products. Cost allocation is also performed for cost reimbursement purposes. For example, many public and private health programs reimburse hospitals for the "costs" of rendering services to patients.

The general approach to allocating costs to final products or services is:

1. Prepare budgets for all departments, including the *operating (line)* or *production* or *revenue-producing* departments that work directly on the final product or service and the *service (staff* or *support)* departments that help the operating departments.
2. Choose the most logical cost-allocation bases that seem economically feasible.
3. Allocate the costs of the service departments to the operating departments. The operating departments have now been allocated all the costs: their direct department costs and the service department costs.
4. Allocate (apply) the total costs accumulated in item 3 to the products or services that are the outputs of the operating departments.

☐ Allocation of Service Department Costs

The foregoing steps can be illustrated in a hospital setting. The output of a hospital is not as easy to define as the output of a factory. The objective is the improved health of patients, but that is hard to quantify. Consequently, the output of revenue-producing departments might be the following:

DEPARTMENT	MEASURES OF OUTPUT*
Radiology	X-ray films processed
Laboratory	Tests administered
Daily patient services†	Patient-days of care (that is, the number of patients multiplied by the number of days of each patient's stay)

*These become the product cost objectives, the various revenue-producing activities of a hospital.

†There would be many of these departments, such as obstetrics, pediatrics, and orthopedics. Moreover, there may be both in-patient and out-patient care.

As you undoubtedly suspect, the allocation of hospital costs to cost objectives is marked by trade-offs between costs and the possible benefits to be derived from more elaborate cost allocations. Because hospitals are often reimbursed by "third-party" payors based on allocated costs, hospital administrators have become increasingly interested in how the costs of various departments might be allocated to the measures of revenue-producing output.

To keep the data manageable, suppose there are only three service departments in addition to the revenue-producing departments just mentioned:
Administrative and Fiscal Services, Plant Operations and Maintenance,
and Laundry.

1. *Prepare departmental budgets.* All six departments would prepare responsibil-
   ity-center budgets for operating their own areas as efficiently and effectively
   as possible. These budgets would be confined to their "direct departmental
   costs" that are the primary responsibility of the particular department manager. Examples of such costs are salaries and supplies.

2. *Choose allocation bases.* Common allocation bases for various hospital service
   departments are shown in Exhibit 9-5. Exhibit 9-6 shows the allocation bases
   and relationships of our sample hospital.

3. *Allocate service department costs.* There are two popular ways to allocate:

   Method One, **Direct Method.** As the name implies, this method ignores other service departments when any given service department's costs
   are allocated to the revenue-producing (operating) departments. For example, as Exhibit 9-7 shows, the service rendered by Plant Operations and Maintenance to Laundry is not considered. The direct method is popular. Its outstanding virtue is simplicity.

   Method Two, **Step-down Method.** Hospitals are increasingly being
   required to use this method, which has been used by many manufacturing
   companies for years. As Exhibit 9-7 shows, the step-down method recognizes
   that service departments render their benefits to other service departments as
   well as to revenue-producing departments. A sequence of allocations is chosen, usually by starting with the service department that renders the greatest
   service (as measured by costs) to the greatest number of other departments.
   The last service department in the sequence is the one that renders the least
   service to the least number of other departments. Therefore, once a depart-

**EXHIBIT
9-5**

Hospital Cost-Allocation Bases*

Purchasing—Costs of supplies used by each center; "other" direct expenses.

Nursing service, administrative office—Hours of nursing service supervised;
estimated supervision time.

Pharmacy—Amount of requisitions priced at retail; number of requisitions;
special studies.

Medical records—Estimated time spent on records; number of patient-days;
number of admissions.

Admitting—Number of admissions.

Plant operations and maintenance—Square feet of area occupied; work orders.

Laundry and linens—Pounds of soiled laundry processed; pounds weighted
by degree of care (nurses' uniforms would be double- or triple-weighted to
allow for starching or pressing).

Administrative and Fiscal Services—Accumulated costs in each department
before these costs are allocated; number of personnel. This is a general
cost center that should be subdivided into several cost centers and be
allocated on different bases.

*For a thorough discussion, see *Cost Finding and Rate Setting for Hospitals* (Chicago: American
Hospital Association).

EXHIBIT 9-6

Cost-Allocation Bases by Department

	SERVICE DEPARTMENTS			REVENUE DEPARTMENTS		
	Administrative and Fiscal Services	Plant Operations and Maintenance	Laundry	Radiology	Laboratory	Daily Patient Services
Direct departmental costs	$ —	$800,000	$200,000	$1,000,000	$400,000	$1,600,000
Square feet occupied	—	—	5,000	12,000	3,000	80,000
Pounds	—	—	—	80,000	20,000	300,000

ment's costs are allocated to other departments, no subsequent service department costs are allocated back to it.

Administrative and Fiscal Services will be allocated on the basis of the relative costs of other departments and will be allocated first. Because it would be awkward to allocate a department's own costs to itself, its costs are not included in the allocation base.

Plant Operations and Maintenance will be allocated second on the basis of square feet occupied, and none will be allocated back to Administrative and Fiscal Services. Therefore no square footage is presented for these two departments in this exhibit.

Laundry will be allocated third; none will be allocated back to the first two departments, *even though the first two departments may have used laundry services.* Sometimes special studies of relative usage of services are made to establish what percentage should go to various consuming departments. For example, the hospital administrator's salary might be allocated separately in proportion to the time she spends on each department. This allocation might be unchanged for a year or two. Similarly, laundry might be weighed periodically on a sampling basis and the results used as a predetermined means of allocation for a year regardless of interim usage.

4. *Allocate (apply) the total costs to products.* The final step is sometimes called *cost application,* whereby total departmental costs are applied to a revenue-producing product. Our illustration in Exhibit 9-7 is a hospital, but the same fundamental approach is used for manufactured products, for research projects in universities, and for client cases in social welfare departments.

Compare Methods One and Two in Exhibit 9-7. In many instances, the final product costs may not differ enough to warrant investing in a cost-allocation method that is any fancier than the direct method.[8] But sometimes even small differences may be significant to a government agency or anybody paying for a large volume of services based on costs. For example, in Exhibit 9-7 the "cost" of an "average" laboratory test is either $11.37 or $10.90. This may be significant for the fiscal committee of the hospital's board of trustees, who must decide on hospital prices. Thus cost allocation often is a technique that helps answer the vital question, "Who should pay for what, and how much?"

[8] The most defensible theoretical accuracy is generated by the *reciprocal method,* which is rarely used in practice because of its complexity. Simultaneous equations and linear algebra are used to solve for the impact of mutually interacting services, such as between Administrative and Fiscal Services and Plant Operations. See C. Horngren, *Cost Accounting: A Managerial Emphasis,* 5th ed. (Englewood Cliffs, N.J.: Prentice-Hall, 1982), Chap. 14.

EXHIBIT 9-7

Allocation of Service Department Costs: Two Methods

ALLOCATION BASE— FROM EXHIBIT 9–6	ADMINISTRATIVE AND FISCAL SERVICES (ACCUMULATED COSTS)	PLANT OPERATIONS AND MAINTENANCE (SQ. FOOTAGE)	LAUNDRY (LB)	RADIOLOGY	LABORATORY	DAILY PATIENT SERVICES
Method One, Direct Method						
Direct departmental costs before allocation	$1,000,000	$800,000	$200,000	$1,000,000	$400,000	$1,600,000
Administrative and fiscal services	(1,000,000)	–	–	333,333*	133,333	533,334
Plant operations and maintenance		(800,000)	–	101,052†	25,263	673,685
Laundry			(200,000)	40,000‡	10,000	150,000
Total budgeted costs				$1,474,385	$568,596	$2,957,019
Product output in films, tests, and patient-days, respectively				60,000	50,000	30,000
Cost per unit of output				$ 24.573	$ 11.372	$ 98.567
Method Two, Step-down Method						
Direct department costs before allocation	$1,000,000	$800,000	$200,000	$1,000,000	$400,000	$1,600,000
Administrative and fiscal services	(1,000,000)	200,000§	50,000	250,000	100,000	400,000
Plant operations and maintenance		(1,000,000)	50,000¶	120,000	30,000	800,000
Laundry			(300,000)	60,000#	15,000	225,000
Total budgeted costs				$1,430,000	$545,000	$3,025,000
Product output in films, tests, and patient-days, respectively				60,000	50,000	30,000
Cost per unit of output				$ 23.833	$ 10.900	$ 100.833

Notes: The cost-allocation bases are from Exhibit 9–6:

*$1,000,000 ÷ ($1,000,000 + $400,000 + $1,600,000) = 33⅓%; 33⅓% × $1,000,000 = $333,333; etc.

†$800,000 ÷ (12,000 + 3,000 + 80,000) = $8.4210526 × 12,000 sq. ft. = $101,052; etc.

‡$200,000 ÷ (80,000 + 20,000 + 300,000) = $.50; $.50 × 80,000 = $40,000; etc.

§$1,000,000 ÷ ($800,000 + $200,000 + $1,000,000 + $400,000 + $1,600,000) = 25%; 25% × $800,000 = $200,000; etc.

¶$1,000,000 ÷ (5,000 + 12,000 + 3,000 + 80,000) = $10.00; $10.00 × 5,000 sq. ft. = $50,000; etc.

$300,000 ÷ (80,000 + 20,000 + 300,000) = $.75; $.75 × 80,000 = $60,000; etc.

Summary

Responsibility accounting assigns particular revenues and costs to the individual in the organization who has the greatest potential day-to-day influence over them.

Costs are allocated for four major purposes: (1) prediction of economic effects of decisions, (2) motivation, (3) income and asset measurement, and (4) pricing.

The contribution approach to the income statement and to the problems of cost allocation is accounting's most effective method of helping management to evaluate performance and make decisions. Allocations are made with thoughtful regard for the purpose of the information being compiled. Various subdivisions of net income are drawn for different purposes. The contribution approach distinguishes sharply between various degrees of objectivity in cost allocations.

Where feasible, fixed costs of service departments should be reallocated by using predetermined monthly lump sums for providing a basic capacity to serve. Variable costs should be reallocated by using a predetermined standard unit rate for the services actually utilized.

Summary Problem for Your Review

❏ Problem

Review the section "How to Allocate for Planning and Control" and the example of the use of the computer by the university. Recall that the flexible-budget formula was $100,000 monthly plus $200 per hour of computer time used. Based on long-run predicted usage, the fixed costs were allocated on a lump-sum basis, 30% to Earth Sciences and 70% to Engineering.

1. Show the total allocation if Earth Sciences used 210 hours and Engineering used 420 hours in a given month. Assume that the actual costs coincided exactly with the flexible-budgeted amount.

2. Assume the same facts as in part 1 except that the fixed costs were allocated on the basis of actual hours of usage. Show the total allocation of costs to each school. As the dean of Earth Sciences, would you prefer this method or the method in part 1? Explain.

❏ Solution

1.

	EARTH SCIENCES	ENGINEERING
Fixed costs per month:		
210/700, or 30% of $100,000	$30,000	
490/700, or 70% of $100,000		$70,000
Variable costs @ $200 per hour:		
210 hours	42,000	
420 hours		84,000
Total costs	$72,000	$154,000

2.

	EARTH SCIENCES	ENGINEERING
Fixed costs per month:		
210/630 × $100,000	$33,333	
420/630 × $100,000		$ 66,667
Variable costs, as before	42,000	84,000
Total costs	$75,333	$150,667

The dean of Earth Sciences would probably be unhappy. His school has operated exactly in accordance with the long-range plan. Nevertheless, Earth Sciences is bearing an extra $3,333 of fixed costs because of what *another* consumer is using. He would prefer the method in part 1 because it insulates Earth Sciences from short-run fluctuations in costs caused by the actions of other users.

Highlights to Remember

1. The aim of responsibility accounting is *not* to place blame. Instead, it is to evaluate performance and provide feedback so that future operations can be improved. The central question is, Who has the most information? not Who bears the blame?

2. The selection of a cost-allocation method should be influenced by how the results of the alternative allocation methods affect decisions. Full-cost allocations are widespread, apparently because accountants and managers feel that these methods generally induce better decisions than partial-cost allocations.

Accounting Vocabulary

Allocation; controllable cost; cost-allocation base; cost application; cost centers; cost pool; direct method; investment centers; profit centers; responsibility accounting; segment; step-down method.

Fundamental Assignment Material

9–1. Responsibility of purchasing agent. (Alternate is 9–19.) Stribling Electronics Company, a privately held enterprise, has a subcontract from a large aerospace company on the West Coast. Although Stribling was low bidder, the aerospace company was reluctant to award the business to Stribling, a newcomer to this kind of activity. Consequently, Stribling assured the aerospace company of its financial strength by submitting its audited financial statements. Moreover, Stribling agreed to a penalty clause of $2,000 per day to be paid by Stribling for each day of late delivery for whatever cause.

Linda Yu, the Stribling purchasing agent, is responsible for acquiring materials and parts in time to meet production schedules. She placed an order with a Stribling supplier for a critical manufactured component. The supplier, who had a reliable record for meeting schedules, gave Yu an acceptable delivery date. Yu checked up several times and was assured that the component would arrive at Stribling on schedule.

On the date specified by the supplier for shipment to Stribling, Yu was informed that the component had been damaged during final inspection. It was delivered ten days late. Yu had allowed four extra days for possible delays, but Stribling was six days late in delivering to the aerospace company. Hence a penalty of $12,000 was paid.

REQUIRED: | What department should bear the penalty? Why?

9–2. Hospital equipment. (Alternate is 9–24.) A regional health-planning agency must approve the acquisition of specified medical equipment before the hospitals in the region can qualify for cost-based reimbursement related to that equipment. That is, hospitals cannot bill government agencies for the later use of the equipment unless the agencies originally authorized the acquisition.

Two hospitals in the region proposed the acquisition and sharing of some expensive X-ray equipment to be used for unusual cases. The depreciation and related fixed costs of operating the equipment were predicted at $10,000 per month. The variable costs were predicted at $20 per patient procedure.

The planning agency asked each hospital to predict how much each hospital would use the equipment over its expected useful life of five years. Hospital A predicted an average usage of 60 procedures per month; B, of 40 procedures. The agency regarded this information as critical to the size and degree of sophistication that would be justified. That is, if the number of procedures exceeded a certain quantity per month, a different configuration of space, equipment, and personnel would be acquired that would mean higher fixed costs per month.

REQUIRED:

1. Suppose fixed costs are allocated on the basis of the hospitals' predicted average utilization per month. Variable costs are allocated on the basis of $20 per procedure, the budgeted variable-cost rate for the current fiscal year. In October, A had 40 procedures and B had 40 procedures. Compute the total costs allocated to A and to B.
2. Suppose the manager of the equipment had various operating inefficiencies so that the total October costs were $12,400. Would you change your answers in Requirement 1? Why?
3. A traditional method of cost allocation does not use the method in Requirement 1. Instead, an allocation rate depends on the actual costs and actual volume encountered. The actual costs are totaled for the month and divided by the actual number of procedures conducted during the month. Suppose the actual costs agreed exactly with the flexible budget for a total of 80 actual procedures. Compute the total costs allocated to A and to B. Compare the results with those in Requirement 1. What is the major weakness in this traditional method? What are some of its possible behavioral effects?
4. Describe any undesirable behavioral effects of the method described in Requirement 1. How would you counteract any tendencies toward deliberate false predictions of long-run usage?

9–3. Allocating central costs. The Western Railroad allocates all central corporate overhead costs to its divisions. Some costs, such as specified internal auditing and legal costs, are identified on the basis of time spent. However, other costs are harder to allocate, so the revenue achieved by each division is used as an allocation base. Examples of such costs were executive salaries, travel, secretarial, utilities, rent, depreciation, donations, corporate planning, and general marketing costs.

Allocations on the basis of revenue for 19X4 were (in millions):

DIVISION	REVENUE	ALLOCATED COSTS
Shasta	$ 60	$ 3
Southern	120	6
Valley	120	6
Total	$300	$15

In 19X5, Shasta's revenue remained unchanged. However, Valley's revenue soared to $140 million because of unusually bountiful crops. The latter are troublesome to forecast because unpredictable weather has a pronounced influence on volume. Southern had expected a sharp rise in revenue, but severe competitive conditions resulted in a decline to $100 million. The total cost allocated on the basis of revenue was again $15 million, despite rises in other costs. The president was pleased that central costs did not rise for the year.

REQUIRED:

1. Compute the allocations of costs to each division for 19X5.
2. How would each division manager probably feel about the cost allocation in 19X5 as compared with 19X4? What are the weaknesses of using revenue as a basis for cost allocation?
3. Suppose the budgeted revenues for 19X5 were $60, $120, and $140, respectively, and the budgeted revenues were used as a cost-allocation base. Compute the allocations of costs to each division for 19X5. Do you prefer this method to the one used in Requirement 1? Why?
4. Many accountants and managers oppose allocating any central costs. Why?

Additional Assignment Material

9–4.   "Variable costs are controllable and fixed costs are uncontrollable." Do you agree? Explain.

9–5.   "Managers may trade off variable costs for fixed costs." Give three examples.

9–6.   What two major factors influence controllability?

9–7.   "Material costs are controllable by a production department foreman." Do you agree? Explain.

9–8.   "The contribution margin is the best measure of short-run performance." Do you agree? Why?

9–9.   What is the most controversial aspect of the contribution approach to cost allocation?

9–10.   Give three guides for the allocation of service department costs.

9–11.   "A commonly misused basis for allocation is dollar sales." Explain.

9–12.   How should national advertising costs be allocated to territories?

9–13.   Give five terms that are sometimes used as substitutes for the term *allocate*.

9–14.   How do the terms *apply* or *absorb* differ from *allocate*?

9–15.   What is *dual allocation*?

9–16.   "Always try to distinguish between the performance of a segment and its manager." Why?

9–17.   Give four examples of segments.

9–18. Hospital depreciation allocation. Many hospital accounting systems are designed so that depreciation on buildings and fixed equipment is collected in a separate cost pool and then allocated to departments, usually on the basis of square feet of space occupied. In contrast, depreciation of major movable equipment is allocated directly to the departments that use such equipment.

Is square feet a logical allocation base? Explain.

9–19. Responsibility accounting. (CMA, adapted.) (Alternate is 9–1.) The Fillep Company operates a standard cost system. The variances for each department are calculated and reported to the department manager. It is expected that the manager will use the information to improve his operations and recognize that it is used by his superiors when they are evaluating his performance.

John Smith was recently appointed manager of the assembly department of the company. He has complained that the system as designed is disadvantageous to his department. Included among the variances charged to the departments is one for rejected units. The inspection occurs at the end of the assembly department. The inspectors attempt to identify the cause of the rejection so that the departments where the error occurred can be charged with it. But not all errors can easily be identified with a department. The nonidentified units are totaled and apportioned to the departments according to the number of identified errors. The variance for rejected units in each department is a combination of the errors caused by the department plus a portion of the unidentified causes of rejects.

REQUIRED:

1. Is John Smith's complaint valid? Explain the reason(s) for your answer.
2. What would you recommend that the company do to solve its problem with John Smith and his complaint?

9–20. Responsibility for a stable employment policy. The Fast-Weld Metal Fabricating Company has been manufacturing machine tools for a number of years and has an industrywide reputation for doing high-quality work. The company has been faced with irregularity of output over the years. It has been company policy to lay off welders as soon as there was insufficient work to keep them busy, and to rehire them when demand warranted. The company, however, now has poor labor relations and finds it very difficult to hire good welders because of its layoff policy. Consequently, the quality of the work has continually been declining.

The plant manager has proposed that the welders, who earn $6 per hour, be retained during slow periods to do menial plant maintenance work that is normally performed by workers earning $3.85 per hour in the plant maintenance department.

You, as controller, must decide the most meaningful accounting procedure to handle the wages of the welders doing plant maintenance work. What department or departments should be charged with this work, and at what rate? Discuss the implications of your plan.

9–21. Cost of passenger traffic. Southern Pacific Railroad (SP) has a commuter operation that services passengers along a route between San Jose and San Francisco. Problems of cost allocation were highlighted in a 1983 news story about SP's application to the Public Utilities Commission (PUC) for a rate increase. The PUC staff claimed that the "avoidable annual cost" of running the operation was $700,000, in contrast to SP officials' claim of a loss of $9 million. PUC's estimate was based on what SP would be able to save if it shut down the commuter operation.

The SP loss estimate was based on a "full-allocation-of-costs" method, which allocates a share of common maintenance and overhead costs to the passenger service.

If the PUC accepted its own estimate, a 25% fare increase would have been justified, whereas SP sought a 96% fare increase.

The PUC stressed that commuter costs represent less than 1% of the system-wide costs of SP, and that 57% of the commuter costs are derived from some type of allocation method—sharing the costs of other operations.

SP's representative stated that "avoidable cost" is not an appropriate way to allocate costs. He said that "it is not fair to include just so-called above-the-rail costs" because there are other real costs associated with commuter service. Examples are maintaining smoother connections and making more frequent track inspections.

REQUIRED:

1. As Public Utilities commissioner, what approach toward cost allocation would you favor for making decisions regarding fares? Explain.
2. How would fluctuations in freight traffic affect commuter costs under the SP method?

9–22. Responsibility accounting, profit centers, and the contribution approach. Consider the following data for the year's operations of an automobile dealer:

General dealership overhead	$ 100,000
Advertising of vehicles	100,000
Sales commissions, vehicles	40,000
Sales salaries, vehicles	50,000
Sales of vehicles	2,000,000
Sales of parts and service	500,000
Cost of vehicle sales	1,600,000
Parts and service materials	150,000
Parts and service labor	200,000
Parts and service overhead	50,000

The president of the dealership has long regarded the markup on material and labor for the parts and service activity as the amount that is supposed to cover all parts and service overhead plus all general overhead of the dealership. In other words, the parts and service department is viewed as a cost-recovery operation, and the sales of vehicles as the income-producing activity.

REQUIRED:

1. Prepare a departmentalized operating statement that harmonizes with the views of the president.
2. Prepare an alternative operating statement that would reflect a different view of the dealership operations. Assume that $10,000 and $50,000 of the $100,000 general overhead can be allocated with confidence to the parts and service department and to sales of vehicles, respectively. The remaining $40,000 cannot be allocated except in some highly arbitrary manner.
3. Comment on the relative merits of Requirements 1 and 2.

9–23. Divisional contribution, performance, and segment margins. The president of the Midwestern Railroad wants to obtain an overview of his operations, particularly with respect to comparing freight and passenger business. He has heard about some new "contribution" approaches to cost allocations that emphasize cost behavior patterns and so-called *contribution margins, contributions controllable by segment managers,* and *contributions by segments.* Pertinent data for the year ended December 31, 19X2, follow.

Total revenue was $100 million, of which $90 million was freight traffic and $10 million was passenger traffic. Fifty percent of the latter was generated by Division 1; 40% by Division 2; and 10% by Division 3.

Total variable costs were $56 million, of which $44 million was freight traffic. Of the $12 million allocable to passenger traffic, $4.4, $3.7, and $3.9 million could be allocated to Divisions 1, 2, and 3, respectively.

Total separable discretionary fixed costs were $10 million, of which $9.5 million applied to freight traffic. Of the remainder, $100,000 could not be allocated to specific divisions, although it was clearly traceable to passenger traffic in general. Divisions 1, 2, and 3 should be allocated $300,000, $70,000, and $30,000, respectively.

Total separable committed costs, which were not regarded as being controllable by segment managers, were $30 million, of which 90% was allocable to freight traffic. Of the 10% traceable to passenger traffic, Divisions 1, 2, and 3 should be allocated $1.8 million, $420,000, and $180,000, respectively; the balance was unallocable to a specific division.

The common fixed costs not clearly allocable to any part of the company amounted to $1 million.

REQUIRED:

1. The president asks you to prepare statements, dividing the data for the company as a whole between the freight and passenger traffic and then subdividing the passenger traffic into three divisions.
2. Some competing railroads actively promote a series of one-day sightseeing tours on summer weekends. Most often, these tours are timed so that the cars with the tourists are hitched on with regularly scheduled passenger trains. What costs are relevant for making decisions to run such tours? Other railroads, facing the same general cost picture, refuse to conduct such sightseeing tours. Why?
3. For purposes of this analysis, even though the numbers may be unrealistic, suppose that Division 2's figures represented a specific run for a train instead of a division. Suppose further that the railroad has petitioned government authorities for permission to drop Division 2. What would be the effect on overall company net income for 19X3, assuming that the figures are accurate and that 19X3 operations are in all other respects a duplication of 19X2 operations?

9–24. **Allocation of costs.** (Alternate is 9–2.) The Galvez Transportation Company has one service department and two operating departments. A flexible budget is used. The budgeted cost behavior pattern of the service department is $500,000 monthly plus 80¢ per 1,000 ton-miles operated in Departments P and Q. (Ton-miles are the number of tons carried times the number of miles traveled.) The actual monthly costs of the service department are allocated on the basis of the ton-miles operated.

REQUIRED:

1. Galvez processed 400 million ton-miles of traffic in April, half in each operating department. The actual costs of the service department were exactly equal to those predicted by the flexible budget. Compute the costs that would be allocated to each operating department.
2. Suppose Department P's region was plagued by strikes, so that the freight handled was much lower than originally anticipated. P moved only 100 million ton-miles of traffic. Department Q handled 200 million ton-miles. The actual costs were exactly as budgeted for this lower level of activity. Compute the costs that would be allocated to P and Q. Note that the total costs will be lower.
3. Refer to the facts in Requirement 1. Various inefficiencies caused the service department to incur costs of $900,000. Compute the costs to be allocated to P and Q. Are the allocations justified? If not, what improvement do you suggest?
4. Refer to the facts in Requirement 2. Assume that assorted investment outlays for equipment and space in the service department were made to provide a basic maximum capacity to serve Department P at a level of 390,000 ton-miles

and Department Q at a level of 210,000 ton-miles. Suppose fixed costs are allocated on the basis of this capacity to serve. Variable costs are allocated by using a predetermined standard rate per 1,000 ton-miles. Compute the costs to be allocated to each department. What are the advantages of this method over other methods?

9–25. Hospital cost allocation. The laboratory of a hospital has developed the following relative value weightings based on the amount of time necessary to complete specific types of tests:

	WEIGHTING	NUMBER OF TESTS PERFORMED
Sugar, quantitative	1.0	1,375
Bleeding time	0.8	2,340
White cell count	0.6	4,675
Chlorides	1.9	584
Sedimentation rate	0.7	3,280
Tissues, surgical, frozen section	10.0	603

The total costs of these tests were $139,392. You are to allocate the costs to the tests as a basis for reimbursements from health-care agencies. Compute the cost rate per individual test.

9–26. Hospital allocation base. Myra Keller, the administrator of Mount Sinai Hospital, has become interested in obtaining more accurate cost allocations on the basis of cause and effect. The $80,000 of laundry costs had been allocated on the basis of 400,000 pounds processed for all departments, or 20¢ per pound.

Keller is concerned that government health-care officials will require weighted statistics to be used for cost allocation. She asks you, "Please develop a revised base for allocating laundry costs. It should be better than our present base, but not be overly complex either."

You study the situation and find that the laundry processed a large volume of uniforms for student nurses and physicians, and for dietary, housekeeping, and other personnel. In particular, the coats or jackets worn by personnel in the radiology department took unusual care.

A special study of laundry for radiology revealed that 5,000 of the 10,000 pounds were jackets and coats that were five times as expensive to process as regular laundry items. A number of reasons explained the difference, but it was principally because of unusual handwork.

Ignore the special requirements of the departments other than radiology. Revise the cost-allocation base and compute the new cost-allocation rate. Compute the total cost charged to radiology using pounds and using the new base.

9–27. Direct and step-down methods of allocation. A factory has three service departments:

	BUDGETED DEPARTMENT COSTS
Cafeteria, revenue $100,000 less expenses of $220,000	$ 120,000
Engineering	2,400,000
General factory administration	970,000

Cost-allocation bases are budgeted as follows:

PRODUCTION DEPARTMENTS	EMPLOYEES	ENGINEERING HOURS WORKED FOR PRODUCTION DEPARTMENTS	TOTAL LABOR-HOURS
Machining	100	40,000	250,000
Assembly	450	15,000	600,000
Finishing and painting	50	5,000	120,000

REQUIRED:

1. All service department costs are allocated directly to the production departments without allocation to other service departments. Show how much of the budgeted costs of each service department are allocated to each production department. To plan your work, examine Requirement 2 before undertaking Requirement 1.

2. The company has decided to use the step-down method of cost allocation. General factory administration would be allocated first, then cafeteria, then engineering. Cafeteria employees had 30,000 labor-hours per year. There were 50 engineering employees with 100,000 total labor-hours. Recompute the results in Requirement 1, using the step-down method. Show your computations. Compare the results in Requirements 1 and 2. Which method of allocation do you favor? Why?

9–28. **Direct and step-down methods of allocation.** The X Company has prepared departmental overhead budgets for normal activity levels before reapportionments, as follows:

Building and grounds	$ 10,000
Personnel	1,000
General factory administration*	26,090
Cafeteria—operating loss	1,640
Storeroom	2,670
Machining	34,700
Assembly	48,900
	$125,000

*To be reapportioned before cafeteria.

Management has decided that the most sensible product costs are achieved by using departmental overhead rates. These rates are developed after appropriate service department costs are reapportioned to production departments.

Bases for reapportionment are to be selected from the data on the following page:

DEPARTMENT	DIRECT-LABOR HOURS	NUMBER OF EMPLOYEES	SQUARE FEET OF FLOOR SPACE OCCUPIED	TOTAL LABOR-HOURS	NUMBER OF REQUISITIONS
Building and grounds		—	—	—	
Personnel*		—	2,000	—	
General factory administration		35	7,000	—	
Cafeteria— operating loss		10	4,000	1,000	
Storeroom		5	7,000	1,000	
Machining	5,000	50	30,000	8,000	2,000
Assembly	15,000	100	50,000	17,000	1,000
	20,000	200	100,000	27,000	3,000

*Basis used is number of employees.

1. Allocate service department costs by the step-down method. Develop over-head rates per direct-labor hour for machining and assembly.
2. Same as in Requirement 1, using the direct method.
3. What would be the blanket plantwide factory-overhead application rate, as-suming that direct-labor hours are used as a cost-allocation base?
4. Using the following information about two jobs, prepare three different total-overhead costs for each job, using rates developed in Requirements 1, 2, and 3.

| | DIRECT-LABOR HOURS | |
	MACHINING	ASSEMBLY
Job 88	18	2
Job 89	3	17

9–29. **Review of Chapters 1–9.** (H. Schaefer.) As you are about to depart on a business trip, your accountant hands you the following information about your Singapore division:

a. Master budget for the fiscal year just ended on October 31, 19X1:

Sales	$700,000
Manufacturing cost of goods sold	560,000
Manufacturing margin	$140,000
Selling and administrative expenses	100,000
Operating income	$ 40,000

b. Budgeted sales and production mix:

Product A	40,000 units
Product B	60,000 units

c. Standard variable manufacturing cost per unit:

Product A
Direct material	10 pieces	@ $0.25	$2.50
Direct labor	1 hour	@ $3.00	3.00
Variable overhead	1 hour	@ $2.00	2.00
			$7.50

Product B
Direct material	5 pounds	@ $0.10	$0.50
Direct labor	.3 hours	@ $2.50	0.75
Variable overhead	.3 hours	@ $2.50	0.75
			$2.00

d. All budgeted selling and administrative expenses are common, fixed expenses; 60% are discretionary expenses.
e. Actual income statement for the fiscal year ended October 31, 19X1:

Sales	$700,000
Manufacturing cost of goods sold	571,400
Manufacturing margin	$128,600
Selling and administrative expenses	97,000
Operating income	$ 31,600

f. Actual sales and production mix:

Product A	42,000 units
Product B	56,000 units

g. Budgeted and actual sales prices:

Product A	$10
Product B	5

h. Schedule of the actual *variable* manufacturing cost of goods sold by product; actual quantities in parentheses:

Product A:	Material	$106,800 (427,200 pieces)
	Labor	123,900 (42,000 hours)
	Overhead	86,100 (42,000 hours)
Product B:	Material	33,600 (280,000 pounds)
	Labor	42,500 (17,000 hours)
	Overhead	42,500 (17,000 hours)
		$435,400

i. Products A and B are manufactured in separate facilities. Of the *budgeted* fixed manufacturing cost, $120,000 is separable as follows: $40,000 to product A and $80,000 to product B. Ten percent of these separate costs is discretionary. All other budgeted fixed manufacturing expenses, separable and common, are committed.

    The purpose of your business trip is a board of directors meeting. During the meeting it is quite likely that some of the information from your accountant will be discussed. In anticipation you set out to prepare answers to possible questions. (There are no beginning or ending inventories.)

1. Determine the firm's *budgeted* break-even point, overall contribution-margin ratio, and contribution margins per unit by product.
2. Considering products A and B as *segments* of the firm, find the *budgeted* "contribution by segments" for each.
3. It is decided to allocate the *budgeted* selling and administrative expenses to the segments (in part 2 above) as follows: committed costs on the basis of budgeted unit sales mix and discretionary costs on the basis of actual unit sales mix. What are the final expense allocations? Briefly appraise the allocation method.
4. How would you respond to a proposal to base commissions to salespersons on the sales (revenue) value of orders received? Assume all salespersons have the opportunity to sell both products.
5. Determine the firm's *actual* "contribution margin" and "contribution controllable by segment managers" for the fiscal year ended October 31, 19X1. Assume *no* variances in committed fixed costs.
6. Determine the "sales volume variance" for each product for the fiscal year ended October 31, 19X1.
7. Determine and identify all variances in *variable* manufacturing costs by product for the fiscal year ended October 31, 19X1.

Suggested Readings

ANTHONY, R., and R. HERZLINGER, *Management Control in Nonprofit Organizations*, rev. ed. Homewood, Ill.: Richard D. Irwin, 1980.

CAPLAN, EDWIN H., *Management Accounting and Behavioral Science*. Reading, Mass.: Addison-Wesley, 1971.

CAPLAN, EDWIN H., and J. CHAMPOUX, *Cases in Management Accounting: Context and Behavior*. New York: National Association of Accountants, 1978.

CHENALL, R., G. HARRISON, and D. WATSON, eds., *Organizational Context of Management Accounting*. Boston: Pitman, 1981.

FREMGEN, J., and S. LIAO, *The Allocation of Corporate Indirect Costs*. New York: National Association of Accountants, 1981.

HOPWOOD, A., *Accounting and Human Behavior*. Englewood Cliffs, N.J.: Prentice-Hall, 1976.

KAPLAN, R., *Advanced Management Accounting*. Englewood Cliffs, N.J.: Prentice-Hall, 1982.

LAWLER, E., and J. RHODE, *Information and Control in Organizations*. Pacific Palisades, Calif.: Goodyear, 1976.

LIBBY, R., *Accounting and Human Information Processing*. Englewood Cliffs, N.J.: Prentice-Hall, 1981.

LIKERT, RENSIS, *The Human Organization, Its Management and Value*. New York: McGraw-Hill, 1967.

LIVINGSTONE, J. L., ed., *Managerial Accounting: The Behavioral Foundations*. Columbus, Ohio: Grid, 1975.

SCHIFF, JONATHAN B., *Readings in Managerial Accounting*. Princeton, N.J.: Dow Jones/Arno Press Books, 1980.

10

PROFIT CENTERS AND TRANSFER PRICING

Learning Objectives

When you have finished studying this chapter, you should be able to

1. Describe the role of management accounting systems in relation to top-management goals and subgoals and in relation to organization structure

2. Explain the implications of goal congruence and managerial effort in the design of systems

3. Define **decentralization** and identify its expected benefits and costs

4. Define **transfer prices** and identify their purpose

5. Identify the relative advantages and disadvantages of basing transfer prices on total costs, variable costs, and market prices

6. Compute ROI and residual income and contrast them as criteria for judging the performance of organization segments

7. Identify the relative advantages and disadvantages of using various bases for measuring the invested capital used by organization segments

This chapter continues the overview of management control systems that was introduced in the preceding chapter. Special attention is given to how to judge one system versus another and to two widely used aids in measuring performance: (1) transfer prices and (2) rate of return on investment (hereafter often called ROI).

JUDGING A MANAGEMENT CONTROL SYSTEM

How should managers and accountants judge a management accounting system, often called a management control system? Too often, judgments focus on physical or data-processing aspects, emphasizing the detection of fraud and compliance with various legal requirements. However, a broader focus is preferable. Systems exist primarily to improve the collective decisions within an organization.

❏ Top-Management Goals and Subgoals

The starting point for judging a system is the specification of a top-management goal (or set of goals). Some managements will delineate a single goal, such as the maximization of profit over the long run. Such a lofty overall goal is too vague for most subordinates. Consequently, many organizations specify multiple goals and accompany them with some form of measurement for evaluating performance.[1]

Top management's subgoals are frequently called by other names, such as *key-result areas, critical success factors, key variables,* or *critical variables.* Some critics maintain that they should not be called goals at all; instead they should be labeled as key *means* of obtaining a single, dominant overall goal such as long-run profitability.

To illustrate the use of multiple goals, consider the General Electric Company, which has stated that organizational performance will be measured in the following eight areas:

1. Profitability
2. Market position
3. Productivity
4. Product leadership
5. Personnel development

6. Employee attitudes
7. Public responsibility
8. Balance between short-range and long-range goals

Note that the first goal, profitability, usually is measured in terms of a single year's results. The thrust of the other goals is to offset the inclination of managers to maximize short-run profits to the detriment of long-run profits.

Regarding the emphasis on short-run profits, consider the following 1983 news story about Campbell, the company that makes soups and other

[1] Some organizations express goals in unique ways. For example, consider the Gavilan Bank of Gilroy, California, Report to Shareholders, 1976: "Greed is our vital force. It is the major influence in our program of expansion. . . . As Samuel Butler said, 'Money is always on the brain so long as there is a brain in reasonable order.'"

food items: "Management was resorting increasingly to short-term methods to improve the bottom line. In weak quarters, the advertising budget was pared—sometimes eliminated. Marketing employees recall that expensive new products were often discouraged."

Overstress on any single goal, whether it be short-run profits or some other goal, usually does not promote long-run profitability. Instead, coordination of goals is blocked; one goal may be achieved while others are neglected:

> *Example.* The Moscow Cable Company decided to reduce copper wastage and actually slashed it by 60% in a given year. The value of the scrap recovered was only $40,000 instead of the $100,000 originally budgeted. However, when top management in the central government perceived this to be an undesirable shortfall of value, the plant was fined $45,000 for not meeting its scrap budget.

As the Moscow Cable example illustrates, the design of a system includes choosing accounting reports that evaluate performance and affect rewards or penalties. Managers often face trade-off decisions. That is, which goals should be emphasized or de-emphasized? For example, one way to increase market share, at least in the short run, is to cut selling prices. In turn, however, profitability may be hurt. These trade-offs, this juggling of goals, are major keys to the successes or failures of the managers and the segments they oversee.

❑ Working Within Constraints

Systems should be distinguished from *goals* and from **organization structures.** The latter are defined here as the way top management has arranged the lines of responsibility within an entity. For example, one company may be organized primarily by *functions,* such as manufacturing and sales; another company by *divisions* bearing profit responsibility, such as the eastern and western divisions; and other companies by some hybrid arrangement.

Occasionally the systems designer may be in a position to persuade top management that goals or organization structures deserve revamping before the system is redesigned. But most of the time, changes in control systems are piecemeal improvements rather than grandiose replacements. Thus, typically the designer must work within the constraints of given goals and organization structures.

To recapitulate, the judge or designer of systems should ordinarily consider the following:

1. Top-management goals
2. Subgoals or key-result areas
3. Trade-offs among the goals in items 1 and 2
4. Organization structure
5. Systems design in light of the above

An illustration may clarify these distinctions. Suppose top managers specify their goal: Earnings for the coming year should be $50 million. They may use the accounting system to communicate and enforce this goal. Near the end of the year, if the earnings prospects are gloomy, top managers may exert immense pressure to reach the budgeted target. To reach the earnings goal, subordinates may be inclined to reduce current expenses by postponing outlays for maintenance, sales promotion, or research, even though such decisions could cripple future earning power.

We may deplore these decisions, but our criticism should be aimed at top management's choice of goals rather than at the system. Given the goal, the accounting system performed admirably as the helpmate of top management. The system should be judged in light of the goals, whatever they may be. In this example, the top-management goal was actually achieved; the trouble was that the goals may not have been appropriate.

Similarly, top management may be heavily committed to a favored organization structure, such as a university's heavy or light use of formal departments organized by subject area (for example, a department of marketing, a department of statistics). Most often, the design of the system must be made within the given structure.

❏ Cost, Congruence, Managerial Effort

The final selection of a management accounting system should be affected by three major criteria: cost-benefit, goal congruence, and managerial effort.

1. The primary criterion in judging System A versus System B is **cost-benefit.** The choice of a system should be governed by weighing the collective costs and benefits, given the particular circumstances of the specific organization. The benefits are often difficult to measure. The overall cost-benefit theme basically says that all systems are imperfect and that System A is superior to System B if A is likely to generate a more desirable set of collective operating decisions after due consideration is given to the costs of A and B.

2. Two additional criteria help make the primary criterion more concrete: congruence and effort. **Goal congruence** exists when individuals and groups aim at the goals desired by top management. Goal congruence is achieved as managers, when working in their own perceived best interests, make decisions that harmonize with the overall objectives of top management. The challenge is to specify goals (or behaviors) to induce (or at least not discourage) decisions that will blend with top-management goals.

3. **Managerial effort** is defined here as exertion toward a goal. Effort is not confined to its common meaning of a worker producing faster; it includes all conscientious actions (such as watching or thinking) that result in more efficiency and effectiveness. Managerial effort is a matter of degree; it is maximized when individuals and groups *strive* (run rather than walk) toward their goals. Goal congruence can exist with little accompanying effort, and vice versa. For example, students can enroll for a university course because their goal is to learn about, say, managing a government

agency. The dean of the school, the professors, and the students may share the same goal. But goal congruence is not enough. Educators also introduce incentives in the form of a grading system to spur student effort.

Grading is a formal tool of *performance evaluation,* as are accounting performance reports in various organizations. Performance evaluation is a widely used means of improving congruence and effort because most individuals tend to perform better when they expect such feedback.[2]

During the course some students may be irresistibly tempted to skip class sessions and play tennis instead. This would be an example of having plenty of effort aimed at a different and less-important goal. Similarly, managers may eagerly pursue sales in the aggregate without paying sufficient attention to the specified and most important goal of profits, which may be affected differently by different products.

❏ Behavioral Focus

Motivation has been defined as the need to achieve some *selected goal* (the goal congruence) together with the *resulting drive* (the managerial effort) that influences action toward that goal. So the systems designer's problems of congruence and effort may be wrapped together as subparts of the problem of motivation—a problem that often is fruitfully divided into its congruence and effort aspects. Hereafter in this book, the terms "motivational" or "motivation" will refer to both the goal-congruence effects and the managerial effort effects.

Obtaining goal congruence and effort is essentially a behavioral problem. The incessant focus is on the motivational impact of a particular accounting system or method versus another system or method. It may seem strange to view accounting systems in terms of their behavioral effects, but the accountant's task is more complex, more ill-structured, and more affected by the human aspects than many people believe at first glance. A simple awareness of the importance of goal congruence and the effort impacts of systems is at least a first step toward getting a perspective on the design of accounting systems and the selection of accounting techniques.

EVOLUTION OF ACCOUNTING TECHNIQUES

Reconsider the ideas introduced in Chapter 7 in the section on page 181, "Development of Control Systems." As organizations grow, managers cope with their responsibilities by delegating their decision-making powers to subordinates and by coordinating activities through informal and formal control systems, most notably the accounting system. The initial stages of organizations are usually marked by heavy reliance on personal observation and light reliance on formal accounting techniques. But the founders

---

[2] Congruence and effort are also encouraged by compensation. Sometimes a large fraction of executive compensation is based on accounting measurements. For example, a prospectus issued by Golden Nugget, Inc., a Nevada casino operator, said: ". . . the Company entered into a five-year employment contract with an executive and director providing for a salary of $25 per day for each day worked during the term thereof and additional compensation equivalent to $16\frac{2}{3}$ percent of the operating income from the game of poker."

soon learn that accounting techniques can improve decisions. The evolution occurs as follows:

1. *Personal observation.* Managers rely on their eyes and ears to obtain their objectives.
2. *Historical records.* The manager quickly finds that records help operations. Moreover, assorted records must be kept to satisfy legal requirements such as income tax laws. The cost-benefit tests of system design are easily met; without such records, the manager faces lawsuits, fines, or worse.
3. *Static budgets.* The manager finds that historical records are often insufficient because they do not draw attention to the right questions. For example, the manager may be depressed if she discovers that her hospital's actual revenue in 19X1 was only $50 million instead of the $55 million of the previous year. But she may be even more depressed if the budgeted 19X1 revenue was $62 million. The key question, then, is not How did we do in comparison with last year? but How did we do in comparison with our targets for the current year?
4. *Flexible budgets and standards.* Many organizations introduce these techniques to obtain a sharper focus on explaining the separate impact on operations of price, efficiency, and volume factors.
5. *Profit centers.* Organizations use these devices to evaluate the performance of subunits that are assigned responsibility for revenue as well as costs and to provide better motivation.

Reflect on this evolution. Steps 1 and 3 through 5 are usually taken voluntarily rather than being imposed by outside forces. Thus the cost-benefit tests induce managers to invest in more-sophisticated accounting systems as their organizations become harder to control. Furthermore, these new features are *additions* to the old features instead of *replacements* for them.

The conceptual overview here is that systems are typically changed on an incremental basis when top management predicts that the benefits from better collective decisions (improved goal congruence and managerial effort) will exceed the additional costs.

DECENTRALIZATION

❑ Costs and Benefits

Decentralization is the delegation of the freedom to make decisions. The lower in the organization that this freedom exists, the greater the decentralization. Decentralization is a matter of degree along a continuum:

Centralization   Decentralization

Maximum constraints   Minimum constraints
Minimum freedom   Maximum freedom

The benefits of decentralization include: (1) the lower-level managers have the best information concerning local conditions and therefore are able to make better decisions than their superiors; (2) managers acquire the ability to make decisions and other management skills that assist their movement upward in the organization; and (3) managers enjoy higher status from being independent and thus are better motivated.

The costs of decentralization include: (1) managers may make dysfunctional decisions (a) by focusing on and acting to improve their own subunit's performance at the expense of the organization, or (b) by not being aware of all relevant facts; (2) managers tend to duplicate central services that might be less expensive when centralized (accounting, advertising, and personnel are examples); and (3) costs of accumulating and processing information frequently rise. The last is exemplified by responsibility accounting reports that represent a necessary counterbalance to the extension of freedom to make decisions. It is also exemplified by the time that subunit managers often spend with one another in negotiating prices for goods or services that are transferred internally.

Decentralization is more popular in profit-seeking organizations (where outputs and inputs can be measured) than in nonprofit organizations:

> ☐ . . . considerable latitude can safely be given to the operating manager. . . . If poor decisions are made, these are soon revealed through the signal of inadequate profits. Without such a signal, such latitude is dangerous. . . . The budgeting process is extremely important in a nonprofit organization. When resource allocation decisions cannot safely be decentralized, the budget is an essential device for communicating how operating managers are expected to act.[3]

❏ Middle Ground

Philosophies of decentralization differ considerably. Cost-benefit considerations usually result in some management decisions being highly decentralized and vice versa. To illustrate, much of the controller's problem-solving and attention-directing functions may be found at the lower levels, whereas income tax planning and mass scorekeeping such as payroll may be highly centralized.

Decentralization tends to be most successful when the segments or subunits are relatively independent of one another—that is, the decisions of one manager will not affect the fortunes of another manager. If subunits do much internal buying or selling, much buying from the same outside suppliers, or much selling to the same outside markets, they are candidates for heavier centralization.

An earlier part of this chapter stressed cost-benefit tests, goal congruence, and managerial effort as three major criteria that must be considered when designing a control system. A fourth criterion, **subunit autonomy,** must be added if management has pondered the pros and cons and

[3] R. Anthony and R. Herzlinger, *Management Control in Nonprofit Organizations*, rev. ed. (Homewood, Ill.: Richard D. Irwin, 1980), p. 77.

has decided in favor of heavy decentralization. *Subunit autonomy* is defined here as the possession of decision-making power by managers of subunits of an organization. The control system should be designed to respect subunit autonomy to the extent specified by top management. In other words, when top managers openly commit themselves to heavy decentralization, they must refrain from interfering in decisions by subunit managers (except in rare instances).

Meaning of Profit Centers

Do not confuse **profit centers** (accountability for revenue and expenses) with **decentralization** (freedom to make decisions). They are entirely separate concepts, although profit centers clearly are accounting devices that aim to facilitate decentralization. However, one can exist without the other. Some profit-center managers possess vast freedom to make decisions concerning labor contracts, supplier choices, equipment purchases, personnel decisions, and so on. In contrast, other profit-center managers may have to obtain top-management permission for almost all the decisions just mentioned. Indeed, some cost centers may be more heavily decentralized than profit centers if the cost-center managers have more freedom to make decisions.

TRANSFER PRICING

Nature of Transfer Pricing

Transfer prices are the amounts charged by one subunit of an organization for a product or service that it supplies to another subunit of the same organization. Most often, the term is associated with materials, parts, or finished goods. In a most fundamental sense, all cost allocation is a form of transfer pricing, although how to charge the costs of a personnel department to the subunits of a hospital, for example, is referred to as a cost-allocation problem, not a transfer-pricing problem.

Why do transfer-pricing systems exist? The principal reason is to communicate data that help solve the problems of cost-benefit trade-offs, goal congruence, managerial effort, and autonomy. Transfer-pricing systems are judged as all facets of control systems should be judged—by determining whether top-management objectives are being obtained as efficiently and effectively as feasible.

Organizations solve their problems by using market prices for some transfers, standard costs for other transfers, negotiated prices for other transfers, and so forth. Therefore, do not expect to obtain a lone, universally applicable answer in the area of transfer pricing. It is a subject of continuous concern to top management. Whenever there is a lull in a conversation with a manager, try asking, "Do you have any transfer-pricing problems?" The response is usually, "Let me tell you about the peculiar transfer-pricing difficulties in my organization."

❏ Transfers at Cost

When the "transfer price" is some version of cost, such transfer pricing is indistinguishable from the "cost allocation" of interdepartmental services that was discussed in Chapter 9, pages 261–264. Therefore, if you want to study the options and pitfalls of "transfer pricing at cost," merely substitute those words for "cost allocation" as you review those pages.

As an example of a pitfall, transferring at *actual* cost is generally not recommended because it fails to provide the buying subunit with a reliable basis for planning. More important, it fails to provide the supplying division with the incentive to control its costs. Inefficiencies are merely passed along to the buying division. Thus the general recommendation of using budgeted or standard costs instead of actual costs applies to all forms of cost allocation, whether the allocation is called transfer pricing, cost reallocation, or by some other name.

❏ Market Price

When an organization has profit centers, market price should be the prime candidate for setting transfer prices. In this way, the buyers and sellers systematically keep abreast of their internal and external opportunities, and problems of congruence, effort, and autonomy are minimized.

Frequently, internal transfers are made at market-price-minus. That is, the supplier division may avoid some shipping or marketing costs by transferring goods to another division instead of marketing them to outside customers. These savings are often deducted when the transfer price is agreed upon.

Sometimes market prices are not used because they are nonexistent, inapplicable, or impossible to determine. For example, no intermediate markets may exist for specialized parts, or markets may be too thin or scattered to permit the determination of a credible price. In these instances, versions of "cost-plus-a-profit" are used that are supposed to provide a "fair" or "equitable" substitute for regular market prices.

❏ Variable Cost

Although market prices have innate appeal in a profit-center context, they are not cure-all answers to transfer-pricing problems. To illustrate, consider the analysis in Exhibit 10-1. Division A produces a part that may be sold either to outside customers or to Division B, which incorporates the part into a finished product that is then sold to outside customers. The selling prices and "variable" costs per unit are shown in the exhibit. Whether the part should be manufactured by Division A and transferred to Division B depends on the existence of idle capacity in Division A (insufficient demand from outside customers).

As Exhibit 10-1 shows, if there were no idle capacity in Division A, the optimum action would be for A to sell outside at $15, because Division B would incur $8 of variable costs but add only $2 to the selling price of the product ($17 − $15). Using market price would provide the correct motivation for such a decision because, if the part were transferred,

EXHIBIT 10-1

Analysis of Market Prices

DIVISION A		DIVISION B			
Market price of finished part to outsiders	$15	Sales price of finished product			$17
Variable costs per unit	6	Variable costs:			
Contribution margin	$ 9	Division A		$6	
Total contribution for 10,000 units	$90,000	Division B			
		Processing	$4		
		Selling	4	8	14
		Contribution margin			$ 3
		Total contribution for 10,000 units			$30,000

Division B's cost would rise to $15 + $8 = $23, which would be $6 higher than B's prospective revenue of $17 per unit. So B would choose not to buy from A at the $15 market price.

As Exhibit 10-1 also shows, if there were idle capacity in Division A, the optimum action would be to produce the part and transfer it to Division B. If there were no production and transfer, Division B and the company as a whole would forgo a total contribution of $30,000. In this situation, variable cost[4] would be the better basis for transfer pricing and would lead to the optimum decision for the firm as a whole.

☐ Dysfunctional Behavior

Reconsider the situation depicted in Exhibit 10-1. If there were idle capacity in Division A, the optimum transfer price would be the $6 variable cost. Nevertheless, in a decentralized company the Division A manager, working in his own best interests, may argue that the transfer price should be based on the $15 market price rather than $6. If his subunit is a profit center, his incentive is to obtain as high a price as possible above the $6 variable cost because such a price maximizes the contribution to the subunit profit. (Of course, the latter statement assumes that the number of units transferred will be unaffected by the transfer price—an assumption that is often shaky.)

So the solutions to the problems of goal congruence and managerial effort may conflict. From the companywide viewpoint, the desired transfers may not occur because each subunit manager, pursuing his own best interests, could decide against a transfer. This is an example of **dysfunctional behavior,** which is defined as actions taken in conflict with top-management goals. These conflicts are sometimes overcome by having a superior manager impose a "fair" transfer price and insist that a

---

[4] "Variable" is used here (but with misgivings) because the term is so widely used in the literature and in practice. "Variable" should be interpreted broadly here as including all pertinent "outlay" costs (those additional costs that will be incurred by the production of the units in question.) For example, if a special lump-sum outlay such as a setup cost were engendered by the order for 10,000 units, it would be added to the "variable" costs in Exhibit 10–1 for purposes of this analysis.

transfer be made. But the managers of subunits within an organization that has an announced policy of decentralization often regard such orders as undermining their autonomy. So the imposition of a price may satisfy the congruence and managerial effort criteria but not satisfy the autonomy criterion. Transfer pricing thus becomes a delicate balancing act in systems design.

The general difficulties are exemplified by the following:

☐ Levels of the subunits tried to make their results look good at each other's expense. One widespread result: Inflated transfer payments among the Gulf subunits as each one vied to boost its own bottom line. A top manager commented, "Gulf doesn't ring the cash register until we've made an outside sale."[5]

❏ Use of Incentives

What should top management of a decentralized organization do if it sees dysfunctional decisions being made at the subunit level? As usual, the answer is "It depends." If top management steps in and forces transfers, it undermines autonomy. This may have to be done occasionally, but if top management imposes its will too often, the organization is in substance being recentralized. Of course, if the decision were indeed not to give autonomy, the organization could be redesigned by combining the two subunits.

Top managers who are proponents of decentralization will be more reluctant to impose their desires. Instead, they will make sure that both A and B managers understand all the facts, are good company citizens, and will make sacrifices for the company as a whole. If they think a dysfunctional decision is going to be made anyway, some top managers swallow hard and accept the subunit manager's judgments.

Keep in mind that a decentralized setup is usually initiated primarily because top managers think that the subunit managers have more information at the local level that permits these subordinates to make better collective decisions about all sorts of options. Therefore, second-guessing the local managers really means that the top manager is saying, "I know more than you do about the condition of the local markets."

Being a good corporate citizen may be one way to appeal to subunit managers to make goal-congruent decisions, but building in some formal incentives typically is far more persuasive. As a result, some companies would try various incentives in reaction to our illustration in Exhibit 10-1. For example, the contribution to the company as a whole, $30,000 in the idle-capacity case, would be split between A and B, perhaps equally, perhaps in proportion to the variable costs of each, or perhaps via negotiation.[6]

---

[5] "Gulf Oil Goes Back to What It Knows Best," *Business Week,* January 31, 1977, p. 80. Richard Vancil, *Decentralization: Managerial Ambiguity by Design* (New York: Financial Executives Research Foundation, 1979), covers problems of decentralization and transfer pricing in more depth.

[6] Other examples include using the dual allocation described in the preceding chapter—that is, transfer at standard variable cost. In addition, a predetermined lump-sum charge is made for fixed costs, based on a long-run commitment of the buyer to support the supplier. In this way the buyer's month-to-month decisions are not influenced by the supplier's fixed costs.

Exhibit 10-2 shows the criteria and choices faced by top management when designing a management control system. Using the criterion of cost-benefit and the motivational criteria of congruence and effort, top management chooses responsibility centers (e.g., cost center versus profit center), performance measures, and rewards. The term *incentives* was used in the preceding paragraph. As used in this context, **incentives** are defined as those informal and formal performance measures and rewards that enhance goal congruence and managerial effort. For example, how the $30,000 in Exhibit 10-1 is split between A and B affects the measures of their performance. In turn, the performance measures may affect the managers' rewards.

Numerous performance measurement choices have been described in this book. Examples include whether to use tight or loose standards, whether to measure divisional performance by contribution margins or operating incomes, and whether to allocate central corporate costs to divisions.

Research about rewards has generated a basic principle that is simple and important: Individuals are motivated to perform in a way that leads to rewards. Managers tend to focus their efforts in areas where performance is measured and where their performance affects rewards. Rewards are both monetary and nonmonetary. Examples include pay raises, bonuses, promotion, praise, self-satisfaction, elaborate offices, and private dining rooms. For our purposes, punishments are negative rewards.

Research also shows that the more objective the measures of performance, the more likely the manager will provide effort. That is why accounting measures are important. They provide relatively objective evaluations of performance. Moreover, if individuals believe that their behavior fails to affect their measure of performance, they will not see the connection between performance and rewards.[7]

The choice of rewards clearly belongs within an overall system of management control. However, the design of a reward system is mainly

EXHIBIT 10-2

Criteria and Choices

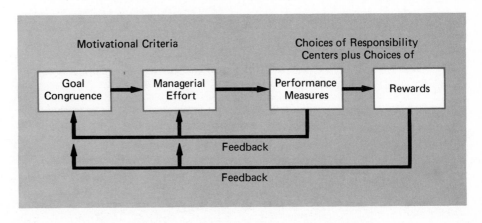

[7] For a summary of this research, see E. Lawler and J. Rhode, *Information and Control in Organizations* (Pacific Palisades, Calif.: Goodyear, 1976), especially Chaps. 4 and 5.

the concern of top managers, who frequently get advice from many sources besides accountants.

THE NEED FOR MANY TRANSFER PRICES

Previous sections have pointed out that there is seldom a single transfer price that will ensure the desired decisions. The "correct" transfer price depends on the economic and legal circumstances and the decision at hand. We may want one transfer price for congruence and a second for incentive. Furthermore, the optimal price for either may differ from that employed for tax reporting or for other external needs.

Income taxes, property taxes, and tariffs often influence the setting of transfer prices so that the firm as a whole will benefit, even though the performance of a subunit may suffer. To minimize tariffs and domestic income taxes, a company may want to set an unusually low selling price for a domestic division that ships goods to foreign subsidiaries in countries where the prevailing tax rates are lower. To maximize tax deductions for percentage depletion allowances, which are based on revenue, a petroleum company may want to transfer crude oil to other subunits at as high a price as legally possible.

Transfer pricing is also influenced in some situations because of state fair-trade laws and national antitrust acts. Because of the differences in national tax structures around the world or because of the differences in the incomes of various divisions and subsidiaries, the firm may wish to shift profits and "dump" goods, if legally possible. These considerations are additional illustrations of the limits of decentralization where heavy interdependencies exist and of why the same company may use different transfer prices for different purposes.

Summary Problem for Your Review

❏ Problem One

Examine Exhibit 10-1, page 287. In addition to the data there, suppose Division A has fixed manufacturing costs of $400,000 and expected annual production of 100,000 units. The "fully allocated cost" per unit was computed as follows:

Variable costs per unit	$ 6
Fixed costs, $400,000 ÷ 100,000 units	4
Fully allocated cost per unit	$10

REQUIRED:

Assume that Division A has idle capacity. Division B is considering whether to buy 10,000 units to be processed further and sold for $17. The additional costs shown in Exhibit 10-1 for Division B would prevail. If transfers were based on fully allocated cost, would the B manager buy? Why? Would the company as a whole benefit if the B manager decided to buy? Why?

❑ Solution to Problem One

B would not buy. Fully allocated costing may occasionally lead to dysfunctional decisions. The resulting transfer price of $10 would make the acquisition of parts unattractive to B:

Division B:		
Sales price of final product		$ 17
Deduct costs:		
Transfer price per unit paid to A		
(fully allocated cost)	$10	
Additional costs (from Exhibit 10-1):		
Processing	$4	
Selling	4	8
Total costs to B		18
Contribution to profit of B		$ −1
Contribution to company as a whole		
(from Exhibit 10-1)		$ 3

As Exhibit 10-1 shows, the company as a whole would benefit by $30,000 ($10,000 units × $3) if the units were transferred.

The major lesson here is that, when idle capacity exists in the supplier division, transfer prices based on fully allocated costs may induce the wrong decisions. Working in his or her own best interests, the B manager has no incentive to buy from A.

MEASURES OF PROFITABILITY

❑ Return on Investment

A favorite objective of top management is to maximize profitability. The trouble is that profitability does not mean the same thing to all people. Is it net income? Income before taxes? Net income percentage based on revenue? Is it an absolute amount? A percentage?

Too often, managers stress net income or income percentages without tying the measure into the investment associated with the generating of the income. A better test of profitability is the rate of **return on investment (ROI),** defined in general as a measure of income or profit divided by the investment required to help obtain the income or profit. That is, given the same risks, for any given amount of resources required, the investor wants the maximum income. To say that Project A has an income of $200,000 and Project B has an income of $150,000 is an insufficient statement about profitability. The required investment in A may be $500,000, and the required investment in B may be only $150,000. Based on rate of return, all other things being equal, A's return would be much less than B's.

The ROI measure is a useful common denominator. It can be compared with rates inside and outside the organization and with opportunities in other projects and industries. It is affected by two major ingredients:

$$\text{rate of return on invested capital} = \frac{\text{income}}{\text{invested capital}}$$

$$= \frac{\text{income}}{\text{revenue}} \times \frac{\text{revenue}}{\text{invested capital}}$$

$$= \text{income percentage of revenue} \times \text{capital turnover}$$

The terms of this equation are deliberately vague at this point because various versions of income, revenue, and invested capital are possible. Ponder the components of the equation. The rate of return is the result of the combination of two items, **income percentage of revenue** and **capital turnover.** An improvement in either without changing the other will improve the rate of return on invested capital.

Consider an example of these relationships:

	RATE OF RETURN ON INVESTED CAPITAL	=	INCOME REVENUE	×	REVENUE INVESTED CAPITAL
Present outlook	20%	=	$\frac{16}{100}$	×	$\frac{100}{80}$
Alternatives:					
1. Increase income percentage by reducing expenses	25%	=	$\frac{20}{100}$	×	$\frac{100}{80}$
2. Increase turnover by decreasing investment in inventories	25%	=	$\frac{16}{100}$	×	$\frac{100}{64}$

Alternative 1 is a popular way to improve performance. An alert management tries to decrease expenses without reducing sales in proportion or to boost sales without increasing related expenses in proportion.

Alternative 2 is less popular, but it may be a quicker way to improve performance. Increasing this turnover of invested capital means generating higher revenue for each dollar invested in such assets as cash, receivables, or inventories. There is an optimal level of investment in these assets. Having too much is wasteful, but having too little may hurt credit standing and the ability to compete for sales.

❏ ROI or Residual Income?

Most managers agree that the rate of return on investment is the ultimate test of profitability. Intelligently used, ROI can help guide decision making. However, some companies favor emphasizing an *absolute amount* of income rather than a *rate* of return. This approach is called **residual income (RI).** For example, residual income may be defined as follows:

	FIGURES ASSUMED
Divisional net income after taxes	$900,000
Minus imputed interest on average invested capital	800,000
Equals residual income	$100,000

Suppose the average invested capital in the division for the year was $10 million. The corporate headquarters assesses an "imputed" interest charge of 8%: (.08 × $10,000,000 = $800,000). The word "imputed" in this context means that the charge is made regardless of whether the corporation as a whole has actually incurred an interest cost in the ordinary sense of a cash disbursement. The rate represents the minimum acceptable rate for investments in that division.

Why do some companies (such as General Electric) prefer RI to ROI? The ROI approach shows:

Divisional net income after taxes	$900,000
Average invested capital	$10,000,000
Return on investment	9%

Residual income is favored for reasons of goal congruence and managerial effort. Under ROI, the basic message is, "Go forth and maximize your rate of return, a percentage." Thus managers of highly profitable divisions may be reluctant to invest in projects at, say, 15% if their division is currently earning, say, 18%, because their average ROI would be reduced.

From the viewpoint of the company as a whole, top management may want this division manager to accept any projects that earn 15% or more. Under RI, the manager would be inclined to invest in projects earning more than 15% even if his or her division were currently earning 18%. The basic message is, "Go forth and maximize residual income, an absolute amount."

DISTINCTION BETWEEN MANAGERS AND INVESTMENTS

As Chapter 9 explained (see Exhibit 9-4, p. 252), a distinction should be made between the performance of the division manager and the performance of the division as an investment by the corporation. Managers should be evaluated on the basis of their controllable performance (in many cases some controllable contribution in relation to controllable investment). For other decisions, "such as new investment or a withdrawal of funds from the division, the important thing is the success or failure of the divisional venture, not of the men who run it."[8]

---

[8] David Solomons, *Divisional Performance: Measurement and Control* (Homewood, Ill.: Richard D. Irwin, 1968), p. 84. Solomons also discusses residual income.

This distinction helps clarify some vexing difficulties. For example, top management may want to use an investment base to gauge the economic performance of a retail store, but the *manager* may best be judged by focusing on income and forgetting about any investment allocations. If investment is assigned to the manager, the aim should be to assign controllable investment only. Controllability depends on what *decisions* managers can make regarding the size of the investment base. In a highly decentralized company, for instance, the manager can influence the size of all his or her assets and can exercise judgment regarding the appropriate amount of short-term credit and perhaps some long-term credit.

KEY ROLE OF BUDGET

❏ Management by Objectives

Management by objectives (MBO) is a term that describes the joint formulation by a manager and his or her superior of a set of goals and of plans for achieving the goals for a forthcoming period. For our purposes here, the terms *goals* and *objectives* are synonyms. The plans often take the form of a responsibility accounting budget (together with supplementary goals such as levels of management training and safety that may not be incorporated into the accounting budget). The manager's performance is then evaluated in relation to these agreed-upon budgeted objectives.

Regardless of whether it is so labeled, a management-by-objectives approach lessens the complaints about lack of controllability because of its stress on *budgeted results.* That is, a budget is negotiated between a particular manager and his or her superior for a *particular* time period and a *particular* set of expected outside and inside influences. In this way, a manager may more readily accept an assignment to a less successful subunit. This is preferable to a system that emphasizes absolute profitability for its own sake. Unless focus is placed on currently attainable results, able managers will be reluctant to accept responsibility for subunits that are in economic trouble.

Thus, skillful budgeting and intelligent performance evaluation will go a long way toward overcoming the common lament: "I'm being held responsible for items beyond my control."

❏ Tailoring Budgets for Managers

Many of the troublesome motivational effects of performance evaluation systems can be minimized by the astute use of budgets. The desirability of tailoring a budget to particular managers cannot be overemphasized. For example, either an ROI or an RI system can promote goal congruence and managerial effort if top management gets everybody to focus on what is currently attainable in the forthcoming budget period. Typically, divisional managers do not have complete freedom to make major investment decisions without checking with senior management.

In sum, our cost-benefit approach provides no universal answers with respect to such controversial issues as historical values versus current values or return on investment versus residual income. Instead, using a cost-benefit test, each organization must judge for itself whether an alternative control system or accounting technique will improve collective decision making. The latter is the primary criterion.

Too often, the literature engages in pro-and-con discussion about which alternative is more perfect or truer than another in some logical sense. The cost-benefit approach is not concerned with "truth" or "perfection" by itself. Instead, it asks, "Do you think your perceived 'truer' or 'more logical' system is worth its added cost? Or will our existing imperfect system provide about the same set of decisions if it is skillfully administered?"[9]

DEFINITIONS OF INVESTED CAPITAL AND INCOME

☐ Many Investment Bases

Consider the following balance sheet classifications:

Current assets	$ 400,000	Current liabilities	$ 200,000
Property, plant, and		Long-term liabilities	400,000
equipment	800,000		
Construction in progress	100,000	Stockholders' equity	700,000
Total assets	$1,300,000	Total equities	$1,300,000

Possible definitions of invested capital include

1. *Total assets.* All assets are included, $1,300,000.
2. *Total assets employed.* All assets except agreed-upon exclusions of vacant land or construction in progress, $1,300,000 − $100,000 = $1,200,000.
3. *Total assets less current liabilities.* All assets except that portion supplied by short-term creditors, $1,300,000 − $200,000 = $1,100,000. This is sometimes expressed as *long-term invested capital;* note that it can also be computed by adding the long-term liabilities and the stockholders' equity, $400,000 + $700,000 = $1,000,000.
4. *Stockholders' equity.* Focuses on the investment of the owners of the business, $700,000.

All of the above are computed as averages for the period under review. These averages may be based simply on the beginning and ending balances or on more complicated averages that weigh changes in investments through the months.

For measuring the performance of division managers, any of the three asset bases is recommended rather than stockholders' equity. If the division manager's mission is to utilize all assets as best he or she can

Profit Centers
and Transfer
Pricing

295

without regard to their financing, then base 1 is best. If top management directs the manager to carry extra assets that are not currently productive, then base 2 is best. If the manager has direct control over obtaining short-term credit and bank loans, then base 3 is best.[10] In practice, base 1 is used most often, although base 3 is not far behind.

A few companies allocate long-term debt to their divisions and thus have an approximation of the stockholders' equity in each division. However, this practice has doubtful merit. Division managers typically have little responsibility for the long-term *financial* management of their divisions, as distinguished from *operating* management. You might compare how the investment base of a division manager of Company A might differ radically from the investment base of a comparable division manager of Company B if A bore heavy long-term debt and B were debt-free.

❏ Allocation to Divisions

Various definitions of income for the segments of an organization were discussed in Chapter 9, page 253, so they will not be repeated here. Just as cost allocations affect income, asset allocations affect the invested capital of particular divisions. The aim is to allocate in a manner that will be goal-congruent, will spur managerial effort, and will recognize subunit autonomy insofar as possible. Incidentally, as long as the managers feel that they are being treated uniformly, they tend to be more tolerant of the imperfections of the allocation.

A frequent criterion for asset allocation is avoidability. That is, the amount allocable to any given segment for the purpose of evaluating the division's performance is the amount that the corporation as a whole could avoid by not having that segment. Commonly used bases for allocation, when assets are not directly identifiable with a specific division, include:

ASSET CLASS	POSSIBLE ALLOCATION BASE
Corporate cash	Budgeted cash needs, as discussed below
Receivables	Sales weighted by payment terms
Inventories	Budgeted sales or usage
Plant and equipment	Usage of services in terms of long-run forecasts of demand or area occupied

The allocation of central corporate assets often parallels the allocation of central corporate costs. Where the allocation of an asset would indeed be arbitrary, many managers feel that it is better not to allocate.

Should cash be included under controllable investment if the balances are strictly controlled by corporate headquarters? Arguments can be made for both sides, but the manager is usually regarded as being responsible for

[10] Reece and Cool, "Measuring Investment Center Performance," surveyed the practices of 620 companies. Of these, 459 used investment centers; 51% deducted external current payables in calculating an investment center's asset base.

the volume of business generated by the division. In turn, this volume is likely to have a direct effect on the overall cash needs of the corporation.

Central control of cash is usually undertaken to reduce the holdings from what would be used if each division had a separate account. Fluctuations in cash needs of each division will be somewhat offsetting, and backup borrowing power is increased. These factors make allocation of cash to the subunits difficult.

The allocation of cash on the basis of sales dollars seldom gets at the economic rationale of cash holdings. As Chapter 6 explains, cash needs are influenced by a host of factors, including payment terms of customers and creditors.

If the criterion of avoidability is used, the cash assignments should be done in recognition of offsetting "portfolio" effects. For example, Division A might have a cash deficiency of $1 million in February, but Division B might have an offsetting cash excess of $1 million. Taken together for the year, Divisions A, B, C, D, and others might require a combined investment in cash of, say, $16 million if each were independent entities but only $8 million if cash were controlled centrally. Hence, if Division C would ordinarily require a $4 million investment in cash as a separate entity, it would be allocated an investment of only $2 million as a subunit of a company where cash was controlled centrally.

MEASUREMENT ALTERNATIVES

❏ Valuation of Assets

There is a widespread tendency to have one asset measure serve many masters. Should the assets contained in the investment base be valued at net book value (original cost less accumulated depreciation), some version of current value, or some other way? Practice is overwhelmingly in favor of using net book value:[11]

	NUMBER	PERCENTAGE
Gross book value	63	14%
Net book value	389	85
Replacement cost	10	2
Other	2	0
No answer	8	2
Total	472*	103%

*Number of responding companies was 459. Includes multiple responses. Note that only 2% used replacement cost, a remarkably low percentage in light of the inflation of the 1970s.

Historical cost has been widely criticized for many years as providing a faulty basis for decision making and performance evaluation. As Chapters 4 and 5 point out, historical costs are irrelevant per se for making economic

[11] Reece and Cool, "Measuring Investment Center Performance," p. 42.

decisions. Despite these criticisms, and despite the increasing external requirements for using current values such as replacement costs for asset valuation,[12] managers have been slow to depart from historical cost.

Why is historical cost so widely used? Some critics would say that sheer ignorance is the explanation. But a more persuasive answer comes from cost-benefit analysis. Accounting systems are costly. Historical records must be kept for many legal purposes; therefore they are already in place. No additional money must be spent to obtain an evaluation of performance based on the historical-cost system. Furthermore, many managements believe that such a system provides the desired goal congruence and managerial effort. That is, a more sophisticated system will not radically improve the collective operating decisions that are desired. In short, the historical-cost system is good enough for the *routine* evaluation of performance. In nonroutine instances, such as replacing equipment or deleting a product line, managers will conduct special studies to gather any current valuations that seem relevant.

Sooner or later the required disclosures of "current costs" in American external reporting will probably also cause their wider use internally. Such current-value information must be gathered in a routine manner to satisfy external requirements. When current values are already available, the incremental costs (including the high costs of educating personnel) of using such values for internal performance measurement purposes are much less imposing than when current values must be installed from scratch.

❏ Budgets and Inflation

There is probably a major reason for the reluctance to rush toward adopting current values in internal accounting: Managers do not believe that collective decisions will be significantly affected by the routine collection of current-value data. Why? Because managers are already predicting the effects of inflation when they prepare their budgets.

Put another way, most well-managed organizations do not use a historical-cost system by itself. The alternatives available to managers are not:

Historical Cost System	versus	Current- Value System

More accurately stated, the alternatives are:

Budgeting System (comparing budgeted and historical data)	versus	Budgeting System (comparing budgeted and current-value data)

[12] See Chapter 20 for a discussion of the use of current values and general-price-level indexes as a basis of asset valuation and income measurement.

If the latter is an accurate depiction of choices, most managers seem to prefer to concentrate on improving their existing budgeting systems. The existing systems already cause managers to worry about the effects of inflation.

❑ Plant and Equipment: Gross or Net?

Net book value is the carrying amount of an asset, net of any related accounts (such as *accumulated depreciation*). **Gross book value** is the carrying amount of an asset before deducting any related amounts.

Although net book value is extensively used, gross book value was used by 14% of the companies surveyed. The proponents of gross book value maintain that it facilitates comparisons between years and between plants or divisions.

Consider an example of a $600,000 piece of equipment with a three-year life and no residual value:

YEAR	OPERATING INCOME BEFORE DEPRECIATION	DEPRECIATION	OPERATING INCOME	AVERAGE INVESTMENT			
				Net Book Value	Rate of Return	Gross Book Value	Rate of Return
1	$260,000	$200,000	$60,000	$500,000	12%	$600,000	10%
2	260,000	200,000	60,000	300,000	20%	600,000	10%
3	260,000	200,000	60,000	100,000	60%	600,000	10%

The rate of return on net book value goes up as the equipment ages; note that it could increase even if operating income gradually declined through the years. In contrast, the rate of return on gross book value is unchanged if operating income does not change; moreover, the rate would decrease if operating income gradually declined through the years.

The advocates of using net book value maintain:

1. It is less confusing because it is consistent with the assets shown on the conventional balance sheet and with the net income computations.
2. The major criticism of net book value is not peculiar to its use for ROI purposes. It is really a criticism of using historical cost as a basis for evaluation.

This author is not enchanted with the gross book value method because of its inherent inconsistency. To show depreciation on an income statement and not deduct it on the balance sheet seems like an awkward means of remedying some peculiarities of historical-cost accounting. Instead, if net book value is yielding unsatisfactory measures of performance, serious consideration should be given to revising the straight-line patterns of depreciation[13] or to using current values.

[13] Solomons, *Divisional Performance*, p. 135. He discusses these issues at length on pages 134–42.

Whatever their merits, neither the ROI nor the residual-income method can be used without considering the cost of capital. Critical questions include (a) what minimum rates to specify; (b) when and by how much minimum rates should be altered; and (c) whether the same minimum rates should be used in each segment of the organization. If a uniform rate is used and many divisions are currently earning different rates, the use of a very low rate will surely drive ROI down toward such a rate. Moreover, frequent changes in the rate may be demoralizing as well as nonoptimal. For example, it might lead to acceptance of an 11% prospective return when the minimum rate is 11%, and rejection of a 15% prospective rate when the minimum rate is 16%.

Modern financial theory supports the use of different rates for different divisions. Portfolio theory provides the analytical framework for the investment decision under uncertainty. The firm would be viewed as a collection of different classes of assets whose income streams bear different risks. The minimum desired rates of return are functions of risk. Various divisions face different risks. Therefore a different minimum desired rate should be used for each division, based on the relative investment risk of each.[14]

The Reece and Cool survey revealed the following practices:

Survey question: If you use ROI (alone or with residual income), how do you set an investment center's target or budgeted ROI percentage?
Survey responses:

	NUMBER	PERCENTAGE
All investment centers are expected to earn the same ROI	30	7%
Each investment center is assigned its own target ROI based on its profit potential	294	64
Investment centers are not given target ROIs	105	23
No answer or not applicable	30	7
Total	459	101%*

*Because of rounding.

The majority practice is roughly consistent with modern financial theory. Note also how a budgeted ROI can be adjusted to allow for special circumstances facing a division. In developing target rates within a division, top management would be consistent with modern financial theory by using different rates for different divisional assets. For example, one rate may be used for investments in current assets and another rate for plant assets.

[14] James Van Horne, *Financial Management and Policy*, 6th ed. (Englewood Cliffs, N.J.: Prentice-Hall, 1983), Chap. 8, gives a detailed discussion of the finance issues summarized here.

Accounting textbooks, including this one, do not discuss at length the problem of timing. However, timing is an important factor to consider when an information system is designed. For instance, the costs of gathering and processing information and the need for frequent feedback for controlling current operations may lead to using historical-cost measures rather than replacement costs. The need for replacement costs, realizable values, and economic values tends to be less frequent, so the systems are not designed for providing such information routinely.

Admittedly, this point was made earlier in the chapter. Nevertheless, it is repeated here because it is a likely explanation of why actual practice seems to differ so markedly from what theory may prefer. The essence of the matter is that management seems unwilling to pay for more elegant information because its extra costs exceed its prospective benefits.

Another aspect of timing underscores why management accounting systems are seldom static. A system that works well in 1984 may not suffice in 1987. Why? Because top management's desires and the attitudes of various managers may change. For example, top management may not allocate the costs of the internal auditing department in 1984 in order to encourage all managers to use auditing services. In 1987 top management may begin allocating auditing services in order to discourage use.

WHY PROFIT CENTERS?

The literature contains many criticisms of profit centers on the grounds that managers are given profit responsibility without commensurate authority. Therefore, the criticism continues, the profit center is "artificial" because the manager is not free to make a sufficient number of the decisions that affect his or her profit.

Such criticisms confuse profit centers and decentralization; early in this chapter, we stressed that one can exist without the other. The fundamental question in deciding between using a cost center or a profit center for a given subunit is not whether heavy decentralization exists. Instead, the fundamental question is, "Will a profit center better solve the problems of goal congruence and management effort than a cost center? In other words, do I predict that a profit center will induce the managers to make a better collective set of decisions from the viewpoint of the organization as a whole?"

All control systems are imperfect. Judgments about their merits should concentrate on which alternative system will bring the actions top management seeks. For example, a plant may be a "natural" cost center because the plant manager has no influence over decisions concerning the marketing of its products. Still, some companies impose profit responsibility on the plant manager by either creating some transfer price above cost or by including the marketing costs on the plant manager's income statement. Why? Because it has changed the plant manager's behavior. How?

Profit Centers
and Transfer
Pricing

301

Instead of being concerned solely with running an efficient cost center, the plant manager now "naturally" considers quality control more carefully and reacts to customers' special requests more sympathetically. The profit center obtained the desired plant-manager behavior that the cost center failed to achieve.

From the viewpoint of top management, plant managers often have more influence on sales than is apparent at first glance. This is an example of how systems may evolve from cost centers to profit centers and an example of the first-line importance of predicting behavior effects when an accounting control system is designed.

CONTROL SYSTEMS IN NONPROFIT ORGANIZATIONS

Most nonprofit organizations have more difficulty in identifying objectives or goals than do profit-seeking organizations. There is no profit, no "bottom line" that so often serves as a powerful incentive in private industry. Furthermore, monetary incentives are generally less effective in nonprofit organizations. For example, many managers seek positions in nonprofit organizations primarily for nonmonetary rewards.

Control systems in nonprofit organizations will never be as highly developed as in profit-seeking organizations for several reasons, including:

1. Organizational goals or objectives are less clear. Moreover, they are often multiple, requiring trade-offs.
2. Professionals (for example, teachers, attorneys, physicians, scientists, economists) tend to dominate nonprofit organizations. They are usually less receptive to the installation or improvement of formal control systems.[15]
3. Measurements are more difficult:
   a. There is no profit measure.
   b. There are heavy amounts of discretionary fixed costs.
   c. The relationships of inputs to outputs are hard to specify and measure. Attempts to relate inputs to outputs via work measurement are often resisted.

Additional difficulties arise because of the lesser role of the marketplace, the greater role of politics, and the vague sense of responsibility because "ownership" of nonprofit organizations is often ill-defined.

Budgeting was originally developed in the public sector as a way of providing accountability. However, the management uses of budgets have been unimpressive. Too often, the budget is regarded as a means of obtaining money, not as a means of planning and control. Thus the process of budgeting in the public sector is often a matter of playing bargaining games with higher authorities to get the largest possible authorization of discretionary fixed costs.

[15] Anthony and Herzlinger, *Nonprofit Organizations*, pp. 34–58, discuss differences between nonprofit and other organizations. Also see R. Anthony and J. Dearden, *Management Control Systems*, 5th ed. (Homewood, Ill.: Richard D. Irwin, 1984).

Summary

The starting point for judging a management accounting or management control system is the specification of top-management goals and subgoals. Systems typically are designed within the constraints of a given set of goals and a given organization structure. The final selection of a system depends on criteria of cost-benefit, goal congruence, and managerial effort. Above all, top management should predict which alternative system is more likely to produce the best collective set of operating decisions in light of the costs of the systems.

As organizations grow, decentralization of some management functions becomes desirable. Decentralization immediately raises problems of obtaining decisions that are coordinated with the objectives of the organization as a whole. Ideally, planning and control systems should provide information that (a) aims managers toward decisions that are goal-congruent, (b) provides feedback (evaluation of performance) that improves managerial effort, and (c) preserves subunit autonomy. Note that the common thread of these problems is motivation.

Transfer-pricing systems are often used as a means of communicating information among subunits and of measuring their performance. Problems of transfer pricing and cost allocations are similar. Proper choices vary from situation to situation.

Choices of performance measures (such as return on investment and residual income) and rewards (such as bonuses and increases in salaries) can heavily affect goal congruence and managerial effort. To affect managerial behavior, strong links must exist between effort, performance, and rewards.

Summary
Problem for Your Review

(Problem One appeared earlier in this chapter.)

☐ Problem Two

A division has assets of $200,000 and operating income of $60,000.

1. What is the division's ROI?
2. If interest is imputed at 14%, what is the residual income?
3. What effects on management behavior can be expected if ROI is used to gauge performance?
4. What effects on management behavior can be expected if residual income is used to gauge performance?

☐ Solution to Problem Two

1. $60,000 ÷ $200,000 = 30\%$
2. $60,000 - .14($200,000) = $60,000 - $28,000 = $32,000$
3. If ROI is used, the manager is prone to reject projects that do not earn an ROI of at least 30%. From the viewpoint of the organization as a whole, this may be undesirable be-

cause its best investment opportunities may lie in that division at a rate of, say, 22%. If a division is enjoying a high ROI, it is less likely to expand if it is judged via ROI than if it is judged via residual income.

If residual income is used, the manager is inclined to accept all projects whose expected ROI exceeds the minimum desired rate. The manager's division is more likely to expand because his or her goal is to maximize a dollar amount rather than a rate.

Highlights to Remember

1. Choices must usually be made between two or more imperfect systems. Incremental rather than radical improvements are typically achieved. That is, there is no immaculate substitution whereby a perfect System A replaces an imperfect System B.

2. When arguments arise regarding whether current values should be a routine part of performance measurement, the role of budgets should not be overlooked. Budgets deserve more respect because they do induce managers to consider the effects of future price changes.

3. Profit centers are usually associated with heavily decentralized organizations, whereas cost centers are usually associated with heavily centralized organizations. However, profit centers and decentralization are separate ideas; one can exist without the other.

4. Although this point was not mentioned in the chapter, any control system requires enthusiastic support from senior management if it is to be taken seriously by subordinates. Indeed, top-management support is so important that it deserves nearly as much prominence as goal congruence as a major criterion in designing systems.

Accounting Vocabulary

Capital turnover;   decentralization, dysfunctional behavior;   goal congruence;   gross book value;   incentive;   income percentage of revenue;   management by objectives (MBO);   managerial effort;   net book value,   organization structure;   profit center; residual income;   return on investment (ROI);   subunit autonomy;   transfer price.

Fundamental Assignment Material

10–1. Rate of return and transfer pricing.   Consider the following data regarding budgeted operations of a company division:

Average available assets:	
Receivables	$100,000
Inventories	300,000
Plant and equipment, net	200,000
Total	$600,000
Fixed overhead	$200,000
Variable costs	$1 per unit
Desired rate of return on average available assets	25%
Expected volume	100,000 units

REQUIRED:

1. a. What average unit sales price is needed to obtain the desired rate of return on average available assets?

b. What would be the expected asset turnover?

c. What would be the operating income percentage on dollar sales?

2. a. If the selling price is as computed above, what rate of return will be earned on available assets if sales volume is 120,000 units?

b. If sales volume is 80,000 units?

3. Assume that 30,000 units are to be sold to another division of the same company and that only 70,000 units can be sold to outside customers. The other division manager has balked at a tentative selling price of $4. She has offered $2.25, claiming that she can manufacture the units herself for that price. The manager of the selling division has examined his own data. He has decided that he could eliminate $40,000 of inventories, $60,000 of plant and equipment, and $20,000 of fixed overhead if he did *not* sell to the other division and sold only 70,000 units to outside customers. Should he sell for $2.25? Show computations to support your answer.

10–2. Transfer-pricing dispute. A transportation-equipment manufacturer, Chalmers Corporation, is heavily decentralized. Each division head has full authority on all decisions regarding sales to internal or external customers. Division P has always acquired a certain equipment component from Division S. However, when informed that Division S was increasing its unit price to $220, Division P's management decided to purchase the component from outside suppliers at a price of $200.

Division S had recently acquired some specialized equipment that was used primarily to make this component. The manager cited the resulting high depreciation charges as the justification for the price boost. He asked the president of the company to instruct Division P to buy from S at the $220 price. He supplied the following:

P's annual purchases of component	2,000 units
S's variable costs per unit	$190
S's fixed costs per unit	$ 20

REQUIRED:

1. Suppose there are no alternative uses of the S facilities. Will the company as a whole benefit if P buys from the outside suppliers for $200 per unit? Show computations to support your answer.

2. Suppose internal facilities of S would not otherwise be idle. The equipment and other facilities would be assigned to other production operations that would otherwise require an additional annual outlay of $29,000. Should P purchase from outsiders at $200 per unit?

3. Suppose that there are no alternative uses for S's internal facilities and that the selling price of outsiders drops $15. Should P purchase from outsiders?

4. As the president, how would you respond to the request of the manager of S? Would your response differ, depending on the specific situations described in Requirements 1 through 3 above? Why?

Additional Assignment Material

10–3. "There are corporate objectives other than profit." Name four.

10–4. What is the most important question in judging the effectiveness of a measure of performance?

10–5. What eight areas has General Electric Company used to avoid over-emphasis of one performance measure?

10–6. Give three examples of how managers may improve short-run performance to the detriment of long-run results.

10–7. "The essence of decentralization is the use of profit centers." Do you agree? Explain.

10–8. Why are cost-based transfer prices in common use?

10–9. Why are transfer-pricing systems needed?

10–10. Why are interest expense and income taxes ordinarily excluded in computing incomes that are related to asset bases?

10–11. What is the major benefit of the ROI technique for measuring performance?

10–12. "There is an optimum level of investment in any asset." Explain.

10–13. "Just as there may be different costs for different purposes, there may be different rates of return for different purposes." Explain.

10–14. Simple calculations. You are given the following data:

G| Sales | $100,000,000 |
| Invested capital | $ 20,000,000 |
| Return on investment | 10% |

REQUIRED:

1. Turnover of capital   5
2. Net income   2,000,000
3. Net income as a percentage of sales   ← 2%

10–15. Simple calculations. Fill in the blanks:

	DIVISION		
	A	**B**	**C**
Income percentage of revenue	8%	2%	6%
Capital turnover	2	10	4
Rate of return on invested capital	16 %	20%	24%

10–16. Simple calculations. Consider the following data:

	DIVISION		
	A	**B**	**C**
Invested capital	$1,200,000	$ 800,000	$ 1,000,000
Revenue	4,800,000	2,400,000	10,000,000
Income	144,000	144,000	100,000

REQUIRED:

1. For each division, compute the income percentage of revenue, the capital turnover, and the rate of return on invested capital.
2. Which division is the best performer? Explain.
3. Suppose each division is assessed an imputed interest rate of 10% on invested capital. Compute the residual income for each division.

10–17. Simple calculations. Consider the data shown on the next page.

REQUIRED:

1. Prepare a similar tabular presentation, filling in all blanks.
2. Which division is the best performer? Explain.
3. Suppose each division is assessed an imputed interest rate of 10% on invested capital. Compute the residual income for each division.

	DIVISION		
	X	Y	Z
Invested capital	$1,000,000	$2,000,000	$1,500,000
Income	$150,000	$ 240,000	$ 150,000
Revenue	$5,000,000	$6,000,000	$3,000,000
Income percentage of revenue	3%	4 %	5 %
Capital turnover	5	3	2
Rate of return on invested capital	15 %	12%	10 %

10–18. Margins and turnover. Return on investment is often expressed as the product of two components—capital turnover and margin on sales. You are considering investing in one of three companies, all in the same industry, and are given the following information:

	COMPANY		
	X	Y	Z
Sales	$5,000,000	$ 2,500,000	$50,000,000
Income	500,000	250,000	250,000
Capital	2,000,000	20,000,000	20,000,000

REQUIRED:

1. Why would you desire the breakdown of return on investment into margin on sales and turnover on capital?
2. Compute the margin on sales, turnover on capital, and return on investment for the three companies, and comment on the relative perfomance of the companies as thoroughly as the data permit.

10–19. Comparison of asset and equity bases. Company A has assets of $1 million and a long-term, 6% debt of $500,000. Company B has assets of $1 million and no long-term debt. The annual operating income (before interest) of both companies is $200,000.

REQUIRED:

Compute the rate of return on

1. Assets available
2. Stockholders' equity

Evaluate the relative merits of each base for appraising operating management.

10–20. Finding unknowns. Consider the following data:

	DIVISION		
	J	K	L
Income	$210,000	$1,000,000	$2,520,000
Revenue	$2,100,000	$20,000,000	$42,000,000
Invested capital	$700,000	$5,000,000	$21,000,000
Income percentage of revenue	10%	5%	6 %
Capital turnover	3	4	2
Rate of return on invested capital	30 %	20%	12%
Imputed interest rate on invested capital	25%	15%	10 %
Residual income	$35,000	$ 250,000	$ 420,000

1. Prepare a similar tabular presentation, filling in all blanks.
2. Which division is the best performer? Explain.

10–21. ROI or residual income. W. R. Grace Co. is a large integrated conglomerate with shipping, metals, and mining operations throughout the world. The general manager of the ferrous metals division has been directed to submit his proposed capital budget for 19X1 for inclusion in the companywide budget.

The division manager has for consideration the following projects, all of which require an outlay of capital. All projects have equal risk.

PROJECT	INVESTMENT REQUIRED	RETURN
1	$6,000,000	$1,380,000
2	2,400,000	768,000
3	1,750,000	245,000
4	1,200,000	216,000
5	800,000	160,000
6	350,000	98,000

The division manager must decide which of the projects to take. The company has a cost of capital of 15%. An amount of $15 million is available to the division for investment purposes.

REQUIRED:

1. What will be the total investment, total return, return on capital invested, and residual income of the rational division manager if
   a. The company has a rule that all projects promising at least 20% or more should be taken
   b. The division manager is evaluated on his ability to maximize his return on capital invested (assume that this is a new division with no invested capital)
   c. The division manager is expected to maximize residual income as computed by using the 15% cost of capital
2. Which of the three approaches will induce the most effective investment policy for the company as a whole?

10–22. Evaluating divisional performance. As the chief executive officer of Acme Company, you examined the following measures of the performance of three divisions (in thousands of dollars):

DIVISION	NET ASSETS BASED ON Historical Cost	NET ASSETS BASED ON Replacement Cost	OPERATING INCOME BASED ON* Historical Cost	OPERATING INCOME BASED ON* Replacement Cost
X	$10,000	$10,000	$1,800	$1,800
Y	30,000	37,500	4,500	4,100
Z	20,000	32,000	3,200	2,600

*The differences in operating income between historical and replacement cost are attributable to the differences in depreciation expenses.

REQUIRED:

1. Calculate for each division the rate of return on net assets and the residual income based on historical cost and on replacement cost. For purposes of calculating residual income, use 10% as the minimum desired rate of return.
2. Rank the performance of each division under each of the four different measures computed in Requirement 1.

3. What do these measures indicate about the performance of the divisions? Of the division managers? Which measure do you prefer? Why?

10–23. Using gross or net book value of fixed assets. Assume that a particular plant acquires $400,000 of fixed assets with a useful life of four years and no residual value. Straight-line depreciation will be used. The plant manager is judged on income in relation to these fixed assets. Annual net income, after deducting depreciation, is $40,000.

Assume that sales, and all expenses except depreciation, are on a cash basis. Dividends equal net income. Thus, cash in the amount of the depreciation charge will accumulate each year. The plant manager's performance is judged in relation to fixed assets because all current assets, including cash, are considered under central-company control.

REQUIRED:

1. Prepare a comparative tabulation of the plant's rate of return and the company's overall rate of return based on
   a. Gross (i.e., original cost) assets.
   b. Net book value of assets. Assume (unrealistically) that any cash accumulated remains idle.
2. Evaluate the relative merits of gross assets and net book value of assets as investment bases.

10–24. Management by objectives. (CMA.) John Press is the chief executive officer of Manfield Company. Press has a financial management background and is known throughout the organization as a "no-nonsense" executive. When Press became chief executive officer, he emphasized cost reduction and savings and introduced a comprehensive cost control and budget system. The company goals and budget plans were established by Press and given to his subordinates for implementation. Some of the company's key executives were dismissed or demoted for failing to meet projected budget plans. Under the leadership of John Press, Manfield has once again become financially stable and profitable after several years of poor performance.

Recently Press has become concerned with the human side of the organization and has become interested in the management technique referred to as "management by objectives" (MBO). If there are enough positive benefits of MBO, he plans to implement the system throughout the company. However, he realizes that he does not fully understand MBO because he does not understand how it differs from the current system of establishing firm objectives and budget plans.

REQUIRED:

1. Briefly explain what "management by objectives" entails and identify its advantages and disadvantages.
2. Does the management style of John Press incorporate the human value premises and goals of MBO? Explain your answer.

10–25. Multiple goals and profitability.[16] The following are multiple goals of the General Electric Company:

1. Profitability
2. Market position
3. Productivity
4. Product leadership
5. Personnel development
6. Employee attitudes
7. Public responsibility
8. Balance between short-range and long-range goals

General Electric is a Goliath corporation with sales of about $25 billion and assets of $19 billion in 1983. It had approximately 170 responsibility centers called

[16] Adapted from a problem originally appearing in R. H. Hassler and Neil E. Harlan, *Cases in Controllership* (Englewood Cliffs, N.J.: Prentice-Hall).

"departments," but that is a deceiving term. In most other companies, these departments would be called divisions. For example, some GE departments have sales of over $300 million.

Each department manager's performance is evaluated annually in relation to the specified multiple goals. A special measurements group was set up in 1952 to devise ways of quantifying accomplishments in each of the areas. In this way, the evaluation of performance would become more objective as the various measures were developed and improved.

1. How would you measure performance in each of these areas? Be specific.
2. Can the other goals be encompassed as ingredients of a formal measure of profitability? In other words, can profitability *per se* be defined to include the other goals?

10–26. Salesmen's compensation plan. You are sales manager of a manufacturing firm whose sales are subject to month-to month variations, depending upon the individual salesman's efforts. A new salary-plus-bonus plan has been in effect for four months and you are reviewing a sales performance report. The plan provides for a base salary of $400 per month, a $500 bonus each month if the salesman's monthly quota is met, and an additional commission of 5% on all sales over the monthly quota.

		SALESMAN A	SALESMAN B	SALESMAN C
January	Quota	$30,000	$10,000	$50,000
	Actual	10,000	10,000	60,000
February	Quota	$10,300	$10,300	$61,800
	Actual	20,000	10,300	40,000
March	Quota	$20,600	$10,600	$41,200
	Actual	35,000	5,000	60,000
April	Quota	$36,050	$ 5,150	$61,800
	Actual	15,000	5,200	37,000

Evaluate the compensation plan. Be specific. What changes would you recommend?

10–27. Profit centers and transfer pricing in an automobile dealership. A large automobile dealership is installing a responsibility accounting system and three profit centers: parts and service; new vehicles; and used vehicles. Each department manager has been told to run his shop as if he were in business for himself. However, there are interdepartmental dealings. For example:

a. The parts and service department prepares new cars for final delivery and repairs used cars prior to resale.
b. The used-car department's major source of inventory has been cars traded in as part payment for new cars.

The owner of the dealership has asked you to draft a company policy statement on transfer pricing, together with specific rules to be applied to the examples cited. He has told you that clarity is of paramount importance because your statement will be relied upon for settling transfer-pricing disputes.

10–28. Role of economic value and replacement value. "To me, economic value is the only justifiable basis for measuring plant assets for purposes of evaluating performance. By economic value, I mean the present value of expected future services. Still, we do not even do this upon acquisition of new assets—that is, we may compute a positive net present value, using discounted cash flow; but we record the asset at no more than its cost. In this way, the excess present value is not shown in the initial balance sheet. Moreover, the use of replacement costs in subsequent years is also unlikely to result in showing economic values; the replacement cost will probably be less than the economic value at any given instant of an asset's life.

"Market values are totally unappealing to me because they represent a second-best alternative value—that is, they ordinarily represent the maximum amount obtainable from an alternative that has been rejected. Obviously, if the market value exceeds the economic value of the assets in use, they should be sold. However, in most instances, the opposite is true; market values of individual assets are far below their economic value in use.

"The obtaining and recording of total present values of individual assets based on discounted-cash-flow techniques is an infeasible alternative. I, therefore, conclude that replacement cost (less accumulated depreciation) of similar assets producing similar services is the best practical approximation of the economic value of the assets in use. Of course, it will facilitate the evaluation of the division's performance more easily than the division manager's performance."

REQUIRED: Critically evaluate the above comments. Please do not wander; concentrate on the issues described by the quotation.

10-29. **Variable cost as a transfer price.** A product's variable cost is $2 and its market value is $3 at a transfer point from Division S to Division P. Division P's variable cost of processing the product further is $2.25, and the selling price of the final product is $4.75.

REQUIRED:
1. Prepare a tabulation of the contribution margin per unit for Division P performance and overall performance under the two alternatives of (a) processing further and (b) selling to outsiders as the transfer point.
2. As Division P manager, which alternative would you choose? Explain.

10–30. **Transfer pricing.** Refer to Problem 10–2, Requirement 1 only. Suppose Division S could modify the component at an additional variable cost of $10 per unit and sell the 2,000 units to other customers for $225. Then would the entire company benefit if P purchased the 2,000 components from outsiders at $200 per unit?

10–31. **Transfer pricing.** The Never Die Division of Durable Motors Company produces water pumps for automobiles. It has been the sole supplier of pumps to the Automotive Division and charges $10 per unit, the current market price for very large wholesale lots. The pump division also sells to outside retail outlets, at $12.50 per unit. Normally, outside sales amount to 25% of a total sales volume of 2 million pumps per year. Typical combined annual data for the division follow:

Sales	$21,250,000
Variable costs, @ $8 per pump	$16,000,000
Fixed costs	2,000,000
Total costs	$18,000,000
Gross margin	$ 3,250,000

The Sure Life Pump Company, an entirely separate entity, has offered the Automotive Division comparable pumps at a firm price of $9 per unit. The Never Die Division claims that it can't possibly match this price because it could not earn any margin at $9.

1. Assume you are the manager of the Automotive Division. Comment on the Never Die Division's claim. Assume that normal outside volume cannot be increased.
2. The Never Die Division feels that it can increase outside sales by 1.5 million pumps per year by increasing fixed costs by $2 million and variable costs by $1 per unit while reducing the selling price to $12. Assume that maximum capacity is 2 million pumps per year. Should the division reject intracompany business and concentrate on outside sales?

10–32. Transfer pricing. Newmill Enterprises runs a chain of drive-in hamburger stands on Cape Cod during the ten-week summer season. The manager of each stand is told to act as if he owned the stand and is judged on his profit performance. Newmill Enterprises has rented a soft-ice-cream machine for the summer, to supply its stands with ice cream for their frappés. Rent for the machine is $1,000. Newmill is not allowed to sell ice cream to other dealers because it cannot obtain a dairy license. The manager of the ice-cream machine charges the stands $3 per gallon. Operating figures for the machine for the summer are as follows:

Sales to the stands (10,000 gallons at $3)		$30,000
Variable costs, @ $1.60 per gallon	$16,000	
Fixed costs:		
Rental of machine	1,000	
Other fixed costs	4,000	21,000
Operating margin		$ 9,000

The manager of the Clam Bar, one of the Newmill drive-ins, is seeking permission to make a contract to buy ice cream from an outside supplier at $2.40 a gallon. The Clam Bar uses 2,000 gallons of soft ice cream during the summer. Frank Redmond, controller of Newmill Enterprises, refers this request to you. You determine that the Other Fixed Costs of operating the machine will decrease by $500 if the Clam Bar purchases from an outside supplier. He wants an analysis of the request in terms of overall company objectives and an explanation of your conclusion. What is the appropriate transfer price?

10–33. Transfer-pricing concession. (CMA, adapted.) The Ajax Division of Gunnco Corporation, operating at capacity, has been asked by the Defco Division of Gunnco to supply it with Electrical Fitting No. 1726. Ajax sells this part to its regular customers for $7.50 each. Defco, which is operating at 50% capacity, is willing to pay $5 each for the fitting. Defco will put the fitting into a brake unit that it is manufacturing on essentially a cost-plus basis for a commercial airplane manufacturer.

Ajax has a variable cost of producing fitting No. 1726 of $4.25. The cost of the brake unit as being built by Defco is as follows:

Purchased parts—outside vendors	$22.50
Ajax fitting No. 1726	5.00
Other variable costs	14.00
Fixed overhead and administration	8.00
	$49.50

Defco believes the price concession is necessary to get the job.

The company uses return on investment and dollar profits in the measurement of division and division-manager performance.

1. Consider that you are the division controller of Ajax. Would you recommend that Ajax supply fitting No. 1726 to Defco? Why or why not? (Ignore any income tax issues.)
2. Would it be to the short-run economic advantage of the Gunnco Corporation for the Ajax Division to supply the Defco Division with fitting No. 1726 at $5 each? (Ignore any income tax issues.) Explain your answer.
3. Discuss the organizational and manager-behavior difficulties, if any, inherent in this situation. As the Gunnco controller, what would you advise the Gunnco Corporation president do in this situation?

10–34. Review of major points in chapter. (D. Kleespie.) The C/J Company is a large company that uses the decentralized form of organizational structure and considers each of its divisions as a (profit) investment center. Division L is currently selling 10,000 "widgets" annually, although it has sufficient productive capacity to produce 14,000 units per year. Variable manufacturing costs amount to $20 per unit, while the total fixed costs amount to $80,000. These 10,000 widgets are sold to outside customers at $40 per unit.

Division M, also a part of the C/J Company, has indicated that it would like to buy 1,000 widgets from Division L, but at a price of $39 per unit. This is the price Division M is currently paying an outside supplier.

REQUIRED:

1. Compute the effect on the operating income of the company as a whole if Division M purchases the 1,000 widgets from Division L.
2. What is the minimum price that Division L should be willing to accept for these 1,000 widgets?
3. What is the maximum price that Division M should be willing to pay for these 1,000 widgets?
4. Suppose instead that Division L is currently producing and selling 14,000 widgets annually to outside customers. What is the effect on the overall C/J Company operating income if Division L is required by top management to sell 1,000 widgets to Division M at (a) $20 per unit and (b) $39 per unit?
5. For this question only, assume that Division L is currently earning an annual operating income of $33,000, and the division's average invested capital is $300,000. The division manager has an opportunity to invest in a proposal that will require an additional investment of $20,000 and will increase annual operating income by $2,000. (a) Should the division manager accept this proposal if the C/J Company uses ROI in evaluating the performance of its divisional managers? (b) If the company uses residual income? (Assume an "imputed interest" charge of 9%.)

10–35. Transfer-pricing principles. A consulting firm, INO, is decentralized with twenty-five offices around the country. The headquarters is based in Orange County, California. Another operating division is located in Los Angeles, fifty miles away. A subsidiary printing operation, We Print, is located in the headquarters building. Top management has indicated the desirability of the Los Angeles office's utilizing We Print for printing reports. All charges are eventually billed to the client, but INO was concerned about keeping such charges competitive.

We Print charges Los Angeles the following:

Photographing page for offset printing (a setup cost)	$.30
Printing cost per page	.015

At this rate, We Print sales have a 60% contribution margin to fixed overhead.

Outside bids for 50 copies of a 135-page report needed immediately have been:

EZ Print	$145.00
Quick Service	128.25
Fast Print	132.00

These three printers are located within a five-mile radius of INO Los Angeles and can have the reports ready in two days. A messenger would have to be sent to drop off the original and pick up the copies. The messenger usually goes to headquarters, but in the past, special trips have been required to deliver the original or pick up the copies. It takes three to four days to get the copies from We Print (because of the extra scheduling difficulties in delivery and pickup).

Quality control of We Print is poor. Reports received in the past have had wrinkled pages and have occasionally been miscollated or had pages deleted. (In one circumstance an intracompany memorandum indicating INO's economic straits was inserted in a report. Fortunately, the Los Angeles office detected the error before the report was distributed to the clients.) The degree of quality control in the three outside print shops is unknown.

(Although the differences in costs may seem immaterial in this case, regard the numbers as significant for purposes of focusing on the key issues.)

REQUIRED:

1. If you were the decision maker at INO Los Angeles, to which print shop would you give the business? Is this an optimal economic decision from the entire corporation's point of view?
2. What would be the ideal transfer price in this case, if based only on economic considerations?
3. Time is an important factor in maintaining the goodwill of the client. There is potential return business from this client. Given this perspective, what might be the optimal decision for the company?
4. Comment on the wisdom of top management in indicating that We Print should be utilized.

10-36. Profit centers and central services. Easthall Company, a manufacturer of a variety of small appliances, has an engineering consulting department (ECD). The department's major task has been to help the production departments improve their operating methods and processes.

For several years the consulting services have been charged to the production departments based on a signed agreement between the managers involved. The agreement specifies the scope of the project, the predicted savings, and the number of consulting hours required. The charge to the production department is based on the costs to the engineering department of the services rendered. For example, senior engineer hours cost more per hour than junior engineer hours. An overhead cost is included. The agreement is really a "fixed-price" contract. That is, the production manager knows his total cost of the project in advance. A recent survey revealed that production managers have a high level of confidence in the engineers.

The ECD department manager oversees the work of about forty engineers and ten draftsmen. He reports to the engineering manager, who reports to the vice-president of manufacturing. The ECD manager has the freedom to increase or decrease the number of engineers under his supervision. The ECD manager's performance is based on many factors, including the annual incremental savings to the company in excess of the costs of operating the ECD department.

The production departments are profit centers. Their goods are transferred to subsequent departments, such as a sales department or sales division, at prices that approximate market prices for similar products.

Top management is seriously considering a "no-charge" plan. That is, engineering services would be rendered to the production departments at absolutely no cost. Proponents of the new plan maintain that it would motivate the production managers to take keener advantage of engineering talent. In all other respects, the new system would be unchanged from the present system.

REQUIRED:

1. Compare the present and proposed plans. What are their strong and weak points? In particular, will the ECD manager tend to hire the "optimal" amount of engineering talent?
2. Which plan do you favor? Why?

Suggested Readings

ANTHONY, R. N., and J. DEARDEN, *Management Control Systems: Cases and Readings*, 4th ed. Homewood, Ill.: Richard D. Irwin, 1980.

BENKE, R., and J. EDWARDS, *Transfer Pricing: Techniques and Uses*. New York: National Association of Accountants, 1980.

DERMER, J. *Management Planning and Control Systems*. Homewood, Ill.: Richard D. Irwin, 1977.

GOLDSCHMIDT, YAAQOV, *Information for Management Decisions*. Ithaca, N.Y., and London: Cornell University Press, 1970.

HORNGREN, CHARLES T., *Cost Accounting: A Managerial Emphasis*, 5th ed. Chaps. 5, 19, 20. Englewood Cliffs, N.J.: Prentice-Hall, 1982.

KAPLAN, R., *Advanced Management Accounting*. Englewood Cliffs, N.J.: Prentice-Hall, 1982.

SOLOMONS, DAVID, *Divisional Performance: Measurement and Control*. New York: Financial Executives Research Foundation, 1965. Reprinted in paperback form in 1968 by Richard D. Irwin.

VANCIL, RICHARD, *Decentralization: Managerial Ambiguity by Design*. New York: Financial Executives Research Foundation, 1979.

11

CAPITAL BUDGETING: AN INTRODUCTION

Learning Objectives

When you have finished studying this chapter, you should be able to

1. Identify the assumptions of the discounted-cash-flow (DCF) models
2. Compute a project's net present value (NPV)
3. Compute a project's internal rate of return (IRR)
4. Apply the decision rules for the two DCF models (NPV and IRR)
5. Use sensitivity analysis in evaluating projects
6. Use the incremental approach in determining the NPV difference between two projects
7. Use the payback model and the accounting rate-of-return model and compare them with the DCF models
8. Identify the methods for reconciling the conflict between using a DCF model for making a decision and the accrual accounting model for evaluating the related performance

Should we replace the equipment? Should we add this product to our line? Managers must make these and similar decisions having long-range implications; they are called **capital-budgeting** decisions. Capital-budgeting decisions are faced by managers in all types of organizations, including religious, medical, and governmental subunits. Many different decision models are used for capital budgeting. In this chapter we deal mostly with the accountant's problem-solving function; we compare the uses and limitations of various capital-budgeting models, with particular emphasis on relevant-cost analysis.

FOCUS ON PROGRAMS OR PROJECTS

The planning and controlling of operations typically have a *time-period* focus. For example, the chief administrator of a university will be concerned with all activities for a given academic year. But the administrator will also be concerned with longer-range matters that tend to have an individual *program* or *project* focus. Examples are new programs in educational administration or health-care education, joint law-management programs, new athletic facilities, new trucks, or new parking lots. In fact, the ideas of *portfolio theory* in finance have sometimes been extended so that the operating management of many organizations is perceived as the ongoing overseeing of a collection of individual investments.

This chapter concentrates on the planning and controlling of those programs or projects that affect more than one year's financial results. Such decisions inevitably entail investments of resources that are often called *capital outlays*. Hence the term *capital budgeting* has arisen to describe the long-term planning for making and financing such outlays.

Capital-budgeting problems affect almost all organizations. For example, decisions about hospital location, size, and equipment are usually crucial because of the magnitude of the financial stakes and the murkiness of future developments, particularly in technology. Because the unknowable factors are many, the well-managed organizations tend to gather and quantify as many knowable factors as is feasible before a decision is made. In addition, because organizations have limited resources, they must choose *among* various investments. Thus a basis of comparison must be established. In response to these concerns, many decision models have evolved, including discounted cash flow (DCF), payback, and accrual accounting models. The DCF model is becoming increasingly popular and is conceptually more attractive than the other two models.

DISCOUNTED-CASH-FLOW MODEL

☐ Major Aspects of DCF

The old adage that a bird in the hand is worth two in the bush is applicable to the management of money. A dollar in the hand today is worth more than a dollar to be received (or spent) five years from today, because the use of money has a cost (interest), just as the use of a building or an automobile may have a cost (rent). Because the discounted-cash-flow model explicitly and systematically weighs the time value of money, it is the best method to use for long-range decisions.

Another major aspect of DCF is its focus on *cash* inflows and outflows rather than on *net income* as computed in the accrual accounting sense. As we shall see, students without a strong accounting background have an advantage here. They do not have to unlearn the accrual concepts of accounting, which accounting students often incorrectly try to inject into discounted-cash-flow analysis.

There are two main variations of DCF: (a) net present value (NPV) and (b) internal rate of return (IRR). A brief summary of the tables and formulas used is included in Appendix B at the end of this book. Do not be frightened by the mathematics of compound interest. We shall confine our study to present-value tables, which may seem imposing but which are simple enough to be taught in many grade-school arithmetic courses. Before reading on, be sure you understand Appendix B at the end of this book, pages 675–681.

> *Example.* The following example will be used to illustrate the concepts. A buildings and grounds manager of a campus of the University of California is contemplating the purchase of some lawn maintenance equipment that will increase efficiency and produce cash operating savings of $2,000 per year. The useful life of this project is four years, after which the equipment will have a net disposal value of zero. Assume that the equipment will cost $6,074 now and that the minimum desired rate of return is 10% per year.

REQUIRED:

1. Compute the project's net present value.
2. Compute the expected internal rate of return on the project.

☐ Net Present Value

One type of discounted-cash-flow approach may be called the **net-present-value method.** It assumes some minimum desired rate of return. The minimum rate is often called the **required rate, hurdle rate, cutoff rate, discount rate, target rate,** or **cost of capital.** All expected future cash flows are discounted to the present, using this minimum desired rate. If the result is positive, the project is desirable, and vice versa. When choosing among several investments, the one with the largest net present value is most desirable.

Requirement 1 of our example will be used to demonstrate the net-present-value approach:

1. Prepare a diagram of relevant cash flows, including the outflow at time zero, the date of acquisition. The right-hand side of Exhibit 11-1 shows how these cash flows are sketched. Outflows are in parentheses. Although a sketch is not essential, it clarifies thought.

2. Choose the correct compound interest table. Find the discount factor from the correct row and column. Multiply the discount factors by the cash amounts in the sketch.

3. Sum the individual present values. If the total is zero or positive, the project should be accepted; if negative, rejected.

Exhibit 11-1 shows a net present value of $264, so the investment is desirable. The manager would be able to invest $264 more, or a total of $6,338 (i.e., $6,074 + $264), and still earn 10% on the project.

The higher the minimum desired rate of return, the lower the net present value of the project. At a rate of 16%, the net present value would be $-478 (i.e., $2,000 × 2.798 = $5,596, which is $478 less than the required investment of $6,074). (Present-value factor, 2.798, is taken from Table 2, page 681.) When the desired rate of return is 16%, rather than 10%, the project is undesirable at a price of $6,074.

☐ Assumptions of DCF Model

Before proceeding, consider the assumptions of the DCF model. First, the model assumes a world of certainty: You are absolutely sure that the predicted cash flows will occur at the times specified. Second, the model assumes that the original amount of the investment can be looked upon as being either borrowed or loaned at some specified rate of return.

The assumptions of certainty and the interest effects apply to the net-present-value DCF model as follows. The net present value of $264 (as computed in Exhibit 11-1) implies that if you borrowed $6,074 from a bank at 10% per annum, invested in the project, and repaid the loan in installments with the $2,000 annual cash savings from the project, you would accumulate the same net amount of money as if you had deposited $264 in a savings institution at 10% interest.

Exhibit 11-2 demonstrates these relationships. Suppose that at time zero a friend offered you $264 for the project that you had invested in thirty seconds before and that he would assume the obligation to pay the bank loan. You accept and invest the $264 in a savings account at a compound interest rate of 10% per annum. In our assumed world of certainty, you would be serenely indifferent as between the two alternatives. Pause a moment and study Exhibit 11-2.

Do not proceed until you thoroughly understand Exhibits 11-1 and 11-2. Moreover, compare Approach 1 with Approach 2 in Exhibit 11-1 to see how the two compound interest tables relate to one another. Note how Table 2 is merely a summation of the pertinent present-value factors of Table 1: .909 + .826 + .751 + .683 = 3.169. The 3.169 is shown as 3.170 in Approach 2 because rounding differences occur. That is, if more than three decimal places had been used throughout the calculations, no rounding errors would arise. Note that the fundamental table is Table 1; Table 2 exists as a shortcut to reduce hand calculations when there are a *series* of equal cash flows at equal intervals. In this example, Table 2 accomplishes in one computation what Table 1 accomplishes in four computations.

Investment

> 101%

PV of cash outflows

EXHIBIT 11-1

Net-Present-Value Technique

Original investment, $6,074. Useful life, 4 years. Annual cash inflow from operations, $2,000. Minimum desired rate of return, 10%. Cash outflows are in parentheses; cash inflows are not.

	PRESENT VALUE OF $1, DISCOUNTED @ 10%	TOTAL PRESENT VALUE	SKETCH OF CASH FLOWS AT END OF YEAR				
			0	1	2	3	4

Approach 1: Discounting Each Year's Cash Inflow Separately*

Cash flows:

Annual savings	.909	$1,818		$2,000			
	.826	1,652			$2,000		
	.751	1,502				$2,000	
	.683	1,366					$2,000
Present value of future inflows		$6,338					
Initial outlay	1.000	(6,074)	$(6,074)				
Net present value		$ 264					

Approach 2: Using Annuity Tablet†

Annual savings	3.170	$6,340		$2,000	$2,000	$2,000	$2,000
Initial outlay	1.000	(6,074)	$(6,074)				
Net present value		$ 264‡					

*Present values from Table 1, Appendix B, at the end of this book. (You may wish to put a paper clip on page 680.)
†Present values of annuity from Table 2. (Incidentally, hand-held programmed calculators may give slightly different answers than tables.)
‡Rounded.

EXHIBIT 11-2

Rationale Underlying Net-Present-Value Model (Same Data as in Exhibit 11-1)

alternative one: invest and hold the project.

YEAR	(1) LOAN BALANCE AT BEGINNING OF YEAR	(2) INTEREST AT 10% PER YEAR	(3) (1) + (2) ACCUMULATED AMOUNT AT END OF YEAR	(4) CASH FOR REPAYMENT OF LOAN	(5) (3) − (4) LOAN BALANCE AT END OF YEAR
1	$6,074	$607	$6,681	$2,000	$4,681
2	4,681	468	5,149	2,000	3,149
3	3,149	315	3,464	2,000	1,464
4	1,464	146	1,610	2,000	(390)*

*After repayment of the final $1,610 loan installment, the investor in the project would have $390 left over from the $2,000 cash provided by the project at the end of the fourth year. Therefore the investor would be $390 wealthier at the end of the fourth year.

alternative two: invest, sell the project for $264 an instant later, and deposit the $264 in a savings institution paying 10% interest compounded annually.

YEAR	(1) INVESTMENT BALANCE AT BEGINNING OF YEAR	(2) INTEREST AT 10% PER YEAR	(3) (1) + (2) ACCUMULATED AMOUNT AT END OF YEAR
1	$264	$26	$290
2	290	29	319
3	319	32	351
4	351	35	386*

*The investor would have the same amount of wealth at the end of four years as in Alternative One. The $4 difference between the $386 and the $390 in Alternative One is because of the accumulation of a number of small differences from rounding off amounts. Note especially that stating the net present value at $264 at time zero is equivalent to stating the future amount at $386. The investor is indifferent (given equal riskiness of the two choices) as to whether he has $264 today or $386 four years hence.

☐ Internal Rate of Return

Now consider Requirement 2. The **internal rate of return** has been defined as the discount rate that makes the net present value of a project equal to zero, as Exhibit 11-3 shows. Expressed another way, the internal rate of return can be defined as the discount rate that makes the present value of a project's expected cash inflows equal to the present value of the expected cash outflows, including the investment in the project.

Exhibit 11-3 demonstrates why 12% is the internal rate of return. The 12% rate produces a net present value of zero. The steps in computing the rate of return are:

EXHIBIT 11-3

Two Proofs of Internal Rate of Return

Original investment, $6,074. Useful life, 4 years. Annual cash inflow from operations, $2,000. Internal rate of return (selected by trial-and-error methods), 12%.

	PRESENT VALUE OF $1, DISCOUNTED AT 12%	TOTAL PRESENT VALUE
Approach 1: Discounting Each Year's Cash Inflow Separately*		
Cash flows:		
Annual savings	.893	$ 1,786
	.797	1,594
	.712	1,424
	.636	1,272
Present value of future inflows		$ 6,074†
Initial outlay	1.000	(6,074)
Net present value (the zero difference proves that the rate of return is 12%)		$ 0
Approach 2: Using Annuity Table‡		
Annual savings	3.037	$ 6,074
Initial outlay	1.000	(6,074)
Net present value		$ 0

SKETCH OF CASH FLOWS AT END OF YEAR

	0	1	2	3	4
		$2,000			
			$2,000		
				$2,000	
					$2,000
	$(6,074)				

	0	1	2	3	4
	$(6,074)	$2,000	$2,000	$2,000	$2,000

*Present values from Table 1, Appendix B, page 680.
†Sum is really $6,076 but is rounded.
‡Present values of annuity from Table 2, Appendix B.

1. Construct an equation depicting the relationships, finding the present-value factor in the table that will equate the required investment and the present value of the expected cash inflows:

required investment

$$= \text{annual cash inflow} \times \text{appropriate PV Factor (F)}$$

$$\$6,074 = \$2,000\ F$$

$$F = \frac{\$6,074}{\$2,000} = 3.037$$

Pay back

2. Find the appropriate row in the table that represents the relevant life of the project (four years in this example).
3. Scan the row to find the column that is closest to the present-value factor. In this example, the column closest to 3.037 is 12%.

But suppose the cash inflow were $1,800 instead of $2,000:

$$\$6,074 = \$1,800\ F$$

$$F = \frac{\$6,074}{\$1,800} = 3.374$$

On the Period 4 line of Table 2, the column closest to 3.374 is 8%. This may be close enough for most purposes. To obtain a more accurate rate, interpolation is needed:

	PRESENT-VALUE FACTORS	
6%	3.465	3.465
True rate		3.374
8%	3.312	
Difference	.153	.091

diff. bet 6% - 8%

$$\text{true rate} = 6\% + \frac{.091}{.153}\ (2\%) = 7.2\%$$

diff. bet 6% - 8%

These hand computations become more complex when the cash inflows and outflows are not uniform. Then trial-and-error methods are needed. See the appendix to this chapter for examples. Of course, in practice, canned computer programs are commonly available for such computations.

❑ Meaning of Internal Rate

Exhibit 11-3 shows that $6,074 is the present value, at a rate of return of 12%, of a four-year stream of inflows of $2,000 in cash. Twelve percent is the rate that equates the amount invested ($6,074) with the present value of the cash inflows ($2,000 per year for four years). In other words, if money were borrowed at an effective interest rate of 12%, as Exhibit 11-4 shows, the cash inflow produced by the project would exactly repay the hypothetical loan plus the interest over the four years.

Exhibit 11-4 highlights how the internal rate of return is computed on the basis of the investment tied up in the project from period to period instead of solely the initial investment. The internal rate is 12% of the capital invested during each year. The $2,000 inflow is composed of two parts, as analyzed in columns 3 and 4. Consider Year 1. Column 3 shows the interest on the $6,074 invested capital as .12 × $6,074 = $729. Column 4 shows that $2,000 − $729 = $1,271, the amount of investment recovered at the end of the year. By the end of Year 4, the series of four cash inflows exactly recovers the initial investment plus annual interest at a rate 12% on the as yet unrecovered capital.

Exhibit 11-4 can be interpreted from either the borrower's or the lender's vantage point. Suppose the university borrowed $6,074 from a bank at an interest rate of 12% per annum, invested in the project, and repaid the loan with the project cash flows of $2,000 per year. Each $2,000 payment would represent interest of 12% plus a reduction of the loan balance. At a rate of 12%, the borrower would end up with an accumulated wealth of zero. Obviously, if the borrower could borrow at 12%, and the project could generate cash at more than the 12% rate (that is, in excess of $2,000 annually), the borrower would be able to keep some cash—and the internal rate of return, *by definition*, would exceed 12%. Again the internal rate of return is that which would provide a net present value of zero (no more, no less).

EXHIBIT 11-4

Rationale Underlying Internal Rate-of-Return Model
(Same data as in Exhibit 11–3)

Original investment, $6,074. Useful life, 4 years. Annual cash savings from operations, $2,000. Internal rate of return, 12%.

YEAR	(1) UNRECOVERED INVESTMENT AT BEGINNING OF YEAR	(2) ANNUAL CASH SAVINGS	(3) INTEREST AT 12% PER YEAR (1) × 12%	(4) AMOUNT OF INVESTMENT RECOVERED AT END OF YEAR (2) − (3)	(5) UNRECOVERED INVESTMENT AT END OF YEAR (1) − (4)
1	$6,074	$2,000	$729	$1,271	$4,803
2	4,803	2,000	576	1,424	3,379
3	3,379	2,000	405	1,595	1,784
4	1,784	2,000	216*	1,784	0

*Rounded.

Assumptions: Unrecovered investment at beginning of each year earns interest for whole year. Annual cash inflows are received at the end of each year. For simplicity in the use of tables, all operating cash inflows are assumed to take place at the end of the years in question. This is unrealistic because such cash flows ordinarily occur uniformly throughout the given year, rather than in lump sums at the end of the year. Compound interest tables especially tailored for these more stringent conditions are available, but we shall not consider them here. See R. Vichas, *Handbook of Financial Mathematics, Formulas and Tables* (Englewood Cliffs, N.J.: Prentice-Hall, 1979).

☐ Depreciation and Discounted Cash Flow

Accounting students are sometimes mystified by the apparent exclusion of depreciation from discounted-cash-flow computations. A common homework error is to deduct depreciation. This is a misunderstanding of one of the basic ideas involved in the concept of the discounting. Because the discounted-cash-flow approach is fundamentally based on inflows and outflows of *cash* and not on the *accrual* concepts of revenues and expenses, no adjustments should be made to the cash flows for the periodic allocation of cost called depreciation expense (which is not a cash flow). In the discounted-cash-flow approach, the initial cost of an asset is usually regarded as a *lump-sum* outflow of cash at time zero. Therefore it is wrong to deduct depreciation from operating cash inflows before consulting present-value tables. To deduct periodic depreciation would be a double-counting of a cost that has already been considered as a lump-sum outflow.

☐ Review of Decision Rules

Review the basic ideas of discounted cash flow. The decision maker cannot readily compare an outflow of $6,074 with a series of future inflows of $2,000 each because the outflows and inflows do not occur simultaneously. The net-present-value model expresses all amounts in equivalent terms (in today's dollars at time zero). An interest rate is used to measure the decision maker's time preference for money. At a rate of 12%, the comparison would be:

Outflow in today's dollars	$(6,074)
Inflow equivalent in today's dollars @ 12%	6,074
Net present value	$ 0

Therefore, at a time preference for money of 12%, the decision maker is indifferent about having $6,074 now or a stream of four annual inflows of $2,000 each. If the interest rate were 16%, the decision maker would find the project unattractive because the net present value would be negative:

Outflow	$(6,074)
Inflow equivalent in today's dollars @ 16% = $2,000 × 2.798 (from Table 2) =	5,596
Net present value	$(478)

We can summarize the decision rules offered by these two models as follows:

NET-PRESENT-VALUE MODEL	**INTERNAL RATE-OF-RETURN MODEL**
1. Calculate the net present value, using the minimum desired rate of return as the discount rate.	1. Using present-value tables, compute the internal rate of return by trial-and-error.
2. If the net present value is zero or positive, accept the project; if negative, reject the project.	2. If this rate equals or exceeds the minimum desired rate of return, accept the project; if not, reject the project.

Business Week (December 18, 1978, p. 86) provided an example of using a net-present-value model:

☐ Like many of the amounts being paid in big acquisitions of the last year, the $350 million that Eaton Corp. will have paid this January to acquire Cutler-Hammer Inc. appears to be a stiff price. . . . Eaton is justifying the price in large part by using an old but increasingly popular financial tool: discounted cash flow analysis (DCF). To set the price, Eaton projected the future cash flows it expects from Cutler over the next 5 to 10 years and then discounted them, using a rate that reflects the risks involved in the investment and the time value of the money used. Eaton figures that, based on DCF, Cutler will return at least 12% on its $350 million outlay.

☐ Choosing the Minimum Desired Rate

There are two key aspects of capital budgeting: investment decisions and financing decisions. *Investment decisions* focus on whether to acquire an asset, a project, a company, a product line, and so on. *Financing decisions* focus on whether to raise the required funds via some form of debt or equity or both. This textbook concentrates on the investment decision. Finance textbooks provide ample discussions of financing decisions.

Depending on the risk (that is, the degree of variability in the likely rate of return) and available alternatives, investors usually have some notion of a minimum rate of return that would make various projects desirable investments. The problem of choosing this required rate of return is complex and is really more a problem of finance than of accounting.[1] In general, the higher the risk, the higher the required rate of return. In this book we shall assume that the minimum acceptable rate of return is the opportunity-cost rate. It is given to the accountant by management. It represents the rate that can be earned by the best alternative investments of similar risk.

Note too that the minimum desired rate is not affected by whether the *specific project* is financed by all debt, all ownership capital, or some of both. Thus the cost of capital is not "interest expense" on borrowed money as the accountant ordinarily conceives it. For example, a mortgage-free home

[1] For an excellent discussion, see the chapter on cost of capital in James C. Van Horne, *Financial Management and Policy*, 6th ed. (Englewood Cliffs, N.J.: Prentice-Hall, 1983).

still has a cost of capital—the maximum amount that could be earned with the proceeds if the home were sold.[2]

CAPITAL BUDGETING AND NONPROFIT ORGANIZATIONS

Religious, educational, health-care, governmental, and other nonprofit organizations face a variety of capital-budgeting decisions. Examples include investments in buildings, equipment, weapons systems, and research programs. Thus, even when no revenue is involved, organizations try to choose projects with the least cost for any given set of objectives.

The unsettled question of the appropriate discount rate plagues all types of organizations, profit-seeking and not-for-profit. One thing is certain: As New York City has discovered, capital is not cost-free. A discussion of the appropriate hurdle rate is beyond the scope of this book. Nearly all U.S. departments use 10%. It represents a crude approximation of the opportunity cost to the economy of having investments made by public agencies instead of by private organizations.[3]

Progress in management practices and in the use of sophisticated techniques has generally tended to be faster in profit-seeking organizations. Although DCF is used by federal departments, it is almost unknown at state and local levels of government. Thus there are many opportunities to introduce improved analytical techniques. In general, managers have more opportunities in nonprofit than in profit-seeking organizations to contribute to improved decision making by introducing newer management decision models such as DCF.[4]

UNCERTAINTY AND SENSITIVITY ANALYSIS

❑ No Single Way

In this and other chapters, we almost always work with the expected values (single dollar amounts) of cash flows in order to emphasize and sim-

[2] Avoid a piecemeal approach. It is near-sighted to think that the appropriate hurdle rate is the interest expense on any financing associated with a specific project. Under this faulty approach, a project will be accepted as long as its expected internal rate of return exceeds the interest rate on funds that might be borrowed to finance the project. Thus a project will be desirable if it has an expected internal rate of 11% and a borrowing rate of 9%. The trouble here is that a series of such decisions will lead to a staggering debt that will cause the borrowing rate to skyrocket or will result in an inability to borrow at all. Conceivably, during the next year, some other project might have an expected internal rate of 16% and will have to be rejected, even though it is the most profitable in the series, because the heavy debt permits no further borrowing.

[3] See H. Bierman and S. Smidt, *The Capital Budgeting Decision*, 5th ed. (New York: Macmillan, 1980), Chap. 24; and R. Anthony and R. Herzlinger, *Management Control in Nonprofit Organizations*, rev. ed. (Homewood, Ill.: Richard D. Irwin, 1980), pp. 292–94.

[4] An extensive study by the General Accounting Office cited the U.S. Post Office as being the best of the federal agencies regarding capital budgeting. The Post Office uses discounted cash flow, sensitivity analysis, and postaudits. See *Federal Capital Budgeting: A Collection of Haphazard Practices* (GAO, P.O. Box 6015, Gaithersburg, Md., PAO-81-19, February 26, 1981), p. 6.

plify various important points. These cash flows are subject to varying degrees of risk or uncertainty, defined here as the possibility that the actual cash flow will deviate from the expected cash flow. Nevertheless, as a minimum, a manager must predict the probable outcome of various alternative projects. These expected values really should be analyzed in conjunction with probability distributions, as we see in Chapter 16. However, to stress the fundamental differences among various decision models, in this chapter we deal only with the expected values.

General Electric Company requires planners to use more than just a single number, such as return on investment or assets, to justify programs. "In the last five years we have come to realize that a single-number criterion doesn't work. People can make that number come out whatever way they want."[5]

An alternative to developing probability distributions of anticipated cash flows is to use elaborate screening devices in the early stages of the decision. Consider the Monsanto Company:

☐ Projects are initiated with greater care than in the past. For instance, 47 planning units within Monsanto's six operating companies prepare two-page business-direction papers, which include financial data such as rates of return, information on market shares and competition, as well as an analysis of technology in the field. Top corporate management and operating executives then sift through proposed capital programs and assign priorities. A three-year list of projects is maintained. At present, about 200 are on the drawing boards . . . ; each involves a minimum investment of $2 million and must be cleared by the board of directors.[6]

Other ways to allow for uncertainty include the use of (a) high minimum desired rate of return, (b) short expected useful lives, (c) pessimistic predictions of annual cash flows, (d) simultaneous comparisons of optimistic, pessimistic, and best-guess predictions, and (e) sensitivity analysis.[7] Sensitivity analysis is a "what-if" technique that measures how the expected values in a decision model will be affected by changes in the data. In the context of capital budgeting, sensitivity analysis answers the question, "How will my internal rate of return or net present value be changed if my predictions of useful life or the cash flows are inaccurate?"

☐ Applying Sensitivity Analysis

Although sensitivity analysis may be conducted at any time, it is usually conducted before a decision is made. Suppose that in Exhibit 11-1 the cash inflows were $1,500 annually instead of $2,000. What would be the net present value? The annuity factor of 3.170 would be multiplied by $1,500, producing a gross present value of $4,755 and a negative net present value of $4,755 − $6,074, or $−1,319. Alternatively, management may want to

---

[5] "The Opposites: GE Grows While Westinghouse Shrinks," *Business Week*, January 31, 1977, p. 64.

[6] *Wall Street Journal*, December 30, 1976, pp. 1, 7.

[7] Sensitivity analysis is particularly essential in the risky decisions of acquiring new airplanes. Among the uncertainties are the price of fuel, the prices of used aircraft, and competitor reactions. See *Fortune*, October 18, 1982, p. 120.

know how far cash inflows will have to fall to break even on the investment. In this context, "break even" means the point of indifference, the
point where the net present value is zero. Let X = annual cash inflows and
let net present value = 0; then

$$0 = 3.170(X) - 6,074$$

$$X = \frac{6,074}{3.170} = \$1,916$$

Thus cash inflows can drop only \$84 (\$2,000 − \$1,916) annually to reach
the point of indifference regarding the investment.

Another critical factor is useful life. If useful life were only three
years, the gross present value would be \$2,000 multiplied by 2.487 (from
the Period 3 row in Table 2, Appendix B) or \$4,974, again producing a
negative net present value, \$4,974 − \$6,074, or \$−1,100.

These calculations can also be used in testing the sensitivity of rates of
return. As we saw in the section "Internal Rate of Return," page 321, a fall
in the annual cash inflow from \$2,000 to \$1,800 reduces the rate of return
from 12% to 7.2%.

Of course, sensitivity analysis works both ways. It can measure the
potential increases in net present value or rate of return as well as the
decreases. The major contribution of sensitivity analysis is that it provides
an immediate financial measure of the consequences of possible errors in
forecasting. Therefore it can be very useful because it helps focus on decisions that may be very sensitive indeed, and it eases the manager's mind
about decisions that are not so sensitive.

In addition, sensitivity analysis is applicable to the comparison of
various capital-budgeting decision models. In other words, the results
under the discounted-cash-flow model may be compared with the results,
using the same basic data, generated under simpler models such as payback and accounting rate of return (discussed later in this chapter).

THE NET-PRESENT-VALUE COMPARISON OF TWO PROJECTS

❑ Incremental Versus Total Project Approach

The mechanics of compound interest may appear formidable to those readers who are encountering them for the first time. However, a little practice
with the interest tables should easily clarify the mechanical aspect. More
important, we shall now combine some relevant cost analysis with the
discounted-cash-flow approach. Consider the following example.

A company owns a packaging machine, which was purchased three
years ago for \$56,000. It has a remaining useful life of five years but will
require a major overhaul at the end of two more years at a cost of \$10,000.
Its disposal value now is \$20,000; in five years its disposal value is expected
to be \$8,000, assuming that the \$10,000 major overhaul will be done on
schedule. The cash operating costs of this machine are expected to be
\$40,000 annually.

A salesman has offered a substitute machine for \$51,000, or for

$31,000 plus the old machine. The new machine will reduce annual cash operating costs by $10,000, will not require any overhauls, will have a useful life of five years, and will have a disposal value of $3,000.

REQUIRED: Assume that the minimum desired rate of return is 14%. Using the net-present-value technique, show whether the new machine should be purchased, using (I) a **total project approach;** (II) an **incremental approach.** Try to solve before examining the solution.

The total project approach is straightforward. It compares two or more alternatives by computing the *total* impact on cash flows of *each* alternative and then converting these total cash flows to their present values.

The incremental approach compares two alternatives by computing the *differences* in cash flows between alternatives, and then converting these differences in cash flows to their present values.

A difficult part of long-range decision making is the structuring of the data. We want to see the effects of each alternative on future cash flows. The focus here is on bona fide cash transactions, not on opportunity costs. Using an opportunity-cost approach may yield the same answers, but repeated classroom experimentation with various analytical methods has convinced the author that the following steps are likely to be the clearest:

Step 1. Arrange the relevant cash flows by project, so that a sharp distinction is made between total project flows and incremental flows. The incremental flows are merely algebraic differences between two alternatives. (There are always at least two alternatives. One is the status quo—i.e., doing nothing.) Exhibit 11-5 shows how the cash flows for each alternative are sketched.

Step 2. Discount the expected cash flows and choose the project with the least cost or the greatest benefit. Both the total project approach and the incremental approach are illustrated in Exhibit 11-5; which one you use is a matter of preference. However, to develop confidence in this area, you should work with both at the start. One approach can serve as proof of the accuracy of the other. In this example, the $8,425 net difference in favor of replacement is the ultimate result under either approach.

❑ Analysis of Typical Items Under Discounted Cash Flow

1. FUTURE DISPOSAL VALUES. The disposal value at the date of termination of a project is an increase in the cash inflow in the year of disposal. Errors in forecasting terminal disposal values are usually not crucial because the present value is usually small.

2. CURRENT DISPOSAL VALUES AND REQUIRED INVESTMENT. There are a number of correct ways to analyze this item, all having the same ultimate effect on the decision. Probably the simplest way was illustrated in Exhibit 11-5, where the $20,000 was offset against the $51,000 purchase price, and the actual cash outgo of $31,000 was shown. Generally, the required investment is most easily measured by offsetting the current disposal value of the old assets against the gross cost of the new assets.

3. INVESTMENTS IN RECEIVABLES AND INVENTORIES. Investments in receivables, inventories, and intangible assets are basically no different from investments in plant and equipment. In the discounted-cash-flow model, the initial outlays are entered in the sketch of cash flows at time zero. At the end of the useful life of the project, the original outlays for machines may not be recouped at all or may be partially recouped in the

EXHIBIT 11-5 (Place a clip on this page for easy reference.)

Total Project versus Incremental Approach to Net Present Value

	PRESENT-VALUE DISCOUNT FACTOR, @ 14%	TOTAL PRESENT VALUE	SKETCH OF CASH FLOWS AT END OF YEAR					
			0	1	2	3	4	5
I. TOTAL PROJECT APPROACH								
A. Replace								
Recurring cash operating costs, using an annuity table*	3.433	$(102,990)		($30,000)	($30,000)	($30,000)	($30,000)	($30,000)
Disposal value, end of Year 5	.519	1,557						3,000
Initial required investment	1.000	(31,000)	($31,000)					
Present value of net cash outflows		$(132,433)						
B. Keep								
Recurring cash operating costs, using an annuity table*	3.433	$(137,320)		($40,000)	($40,000)	($40,000)	($40,000)	($40,000)
Overhaul, end of Year 2	.769	(7,690)			(10,000)			
Disposal value, end of Year 5	.519	4,152						8,000
Present value of net cash outflows		$(140,858)						
Difference in favor of replacement		$ 8,425						
II. INCREMENTAL APPROACH								
A – B Analysis Confined to Differences								
Recurring cash operating savings, using an annuity table*	3.433	$ 34,330		$10,000	$10,000	$10,000	$10,000	$10,000
Overhaul avoided, end of Year 2	.769	7,690			$10,000			
Difference in disposal values, end of Year 5	.519	(2,595)						(5,000)
Incremental initial investment	1.000	(31,000)	($31,000)					
Net present value of replacement		$ 8,425						

*Table 2, page 681.

amount of the salvage values. In contrast, the entire original investments in receivables and inventories are usually recouped when the project ends. Therefore, all initial investments are typically regarded as outflows at time zero, and their terminal disposal values are regarded as inflows at the end of the project's useful life.

Thus the expansion of a retail store entails an additional investment in a building and fixtures *plus* inventories. Such investments would be shown in the format of Exhibit 11-5 as follows (numbers assumed):

	SKETCH OF CASH FLOWS					
End of Year	0	1	2		19	20
Investment in building and fixtures	(10)					1
Investment in working capital (inventories)	(6)					6

As the sketch shows, the residual value of the building and fixtures might be small. However, the entire investment in inventories would ordinarily be recouped when the venture was terminated.

The difference between the initial outlay for working capital (mostly receivables and inventories) and the present value of its recovery is the present value of the cost of using working capital in the project. Working capital is constantly revolving in a cycle from cash to receivables to inventories and back to cash throughout the life of the project. But to be sustained, the project requires that money be tied up in the cycle until the project ends.

4. BOOK VALUE AND DEPRECIATION. Depreciation is a phenomenon of accrual accounting that entails an allocation of cost, not a specific cash outlay. Depreciation and book value are ignored in discounted-cash-flow approaches for the reasons mentioned earlier in this chapter, p. 325.

5. INCOME TAXES. In practice, comparison between alternatives is best made after considering tax effects, because the tax impact may alter the picture. (The effects of income taxes are considered in Chapter 12 and may be studied now if desired.)

6. OVERHEAD ANALYSIS. In relevant-cost analysis, only the overhead that will differ among alternatives is pertinent. There is need for careful study of the fixed overhead under the available alternatives. In practice, this is an extremely difficult phase of cost analysis, because it is hard to relate the individual costs to any single project.

7. UNEQUAL LIVES. Where projects have unequal lives, comparisons may be made over the useful life either of the longer-lived project or of the shorter-lived one. For our purposes, we will estimate what the residual values will be at the end of the longer-lived project. We must also assume a reinvestment at the end of the shorter-lived project. This makes sense primarily because the decision makers should extend their time horizon as far as possible. If they are considering a longer-lived project, they should give serious consideration to what would be done in the time interval between the termination dates of the shorter-lived and longer-lived projects.

8. **MUTUALLY EXCLUSIVE PROJECTS.** When the projects are mutually exclusive, so that the acceptance of one automatically entails the rejection of the other (e.g., buying Dodge or Ford trucks), the project that maximizes wealth measured in net present value in dollars should be undertaken.

9. **A WORD OF CAUTION.** The foregoing material has been an *introduction* to the area of capital budgeting, which is, in practice, complicated by a variety of factors: unequal lives; major differences in the size of alternative investments; peculiarities in internal rate-of-return computations; various ways of allowing for uncertainty (see Chapter 16); changes, over time, in desired rates of return; the indivisibility of projects in relation to a fixed overall capital-budget appropriation; inflation (see the next chapter); and more. These niceties are beyond the scope of this introduction to capital budgeting, but the "Suggested Readings" at the end of the chapter will help you pursue the subject in more depth.

OTHER MODELS FOR ANALYZING LONG-RANGE DECISIONS

Although discounted-cash-flow models for business decisions are being increasingly used, they are still relatively new, having been developed and applied for the first time on any wide scale in the 1950s. There are other models with which the manager should at least be somewhat familiar, because they are entrenched in many businesses. These models, which we are about to explain, are conceptually inferior to discounted-cash-flow approaches. Then why do we bother studying them? First, because changes in business practice occur slowly. Second, because where older models such as payback are in use, they should be used properly, even if better models are available. The situation is similar to using a pocket knife instead of a scalpel for removing a person's appendix. If the pocket knife is used by a knowledgeable and skilled surgeon, the chances for success are much better than if it is used by a bumbling layperson.

Of course, as always, the accountant and manager face a cost-and-value-of-information decision when they choose a decision model. Reluctance to use discounted-cash-flow models may be justified if the more familiar payback model or other models lead to the same investment decisions.

One existing technique may be called the emergency-persuasion method. No formal planning is used. Fixed assets are operated until they crumble, product lines are carried until they are obliterated by competition, and requests by a manager for authorization of capital outlays are judged on the basis of past operating performance regardless of its relevance to the decision at hand. These approaches to capital budgeting are examples of the unscientific management that often leads to bankruptcy.

❏ Payback Model

Payback or **payout** or **payoff** is the measure of the time it will take to recoup, in the form of cash inflow from operations, the initial dollars of outlay. Assume that $12,000 is spent for a machine with an estimated useful life of eight years. Annual savings of $4,000 in cash outflow are expected from operations. Depreciation is ignored. The payback calculations follow:

payback time

$$= \frac{\text{initial incremental amount invested}}{\text{uniform annual incremental } \textit{cash} \text{ inflow from operations}}$$

$$P = \frac{I}{O} = \frac{\$12,000}{\$4,000} = 3 \text{ years} \tag{1}$$

The payback model merely measures how quickly investment dollars may be recouped; it does *not* measure profitability. This is its major weakness because a shorter payback time does not necessarily mean that one project is preferable to another.

For instance, assume that an alternative to the $12,000 machine is a $10,000 machine whose operation will also result in a reduction of $4,000 annually in cash outflow. Then

$$P_1 = \frac{\$12,000}{\$4,000} = 3.0 \text{ years}$$

$$P_2 = \frac{\$10,000}{\$4,000} = 2.5 \text{ years}$$

The payback criterion indicates that the $10,000 machine is more desirable. However, one fact about the $10,000 machine has been purposely withheld. Its useful life is only 2.5 years. Ignoring the impact of compound interest for the moment, the $10,000 machine results in zero benefit, while the $12,000 machine (useful life eight years) generates cash inflows for five years beyond its payback period.

The main objective in investing is profit, not the recapturing of the initial outlay. If a company wants to recover its outlay fast, it need not spend in the first place. Then no waiting time is necessary; the payback time is zero. When a wealthy investor was assured by the promoter of a risky oil venture that he would have his money back within two years, the investor replied, "I already have my money."

The payback approach may also be applied to the data in Exhibit 11-5, page 331. What is the payback time?

$$P = \frac{I}{O} = \frac{\$31,000}{\$10,000} = 3.1 \text{ years}$$

However, the formula can be used with assurance only when there are uniform cash inflows from operations. In this instance, $10,000 is saved by avoiding an overhaul at the end of the second year. When cash inflows are not uniform, the payback computation must take a cumulative form— that is, each year's net cash flows are accumulated until the initial investment is recouped:

| | | NET CASH INFLOWS | |
YEAR	INITIAL INVESTMENT	Each Year	Accumulated
0	$31,000	—	—
1	—	$10,000	$10,000
2	—	20,000	30,000
2.1	—	1,000	31,000

[handwritten margin note: Same as Internal Rate of Return]

The payback time is slightly beyond the second year. Straight-line interpolation within the third year reveals that the final $1,000 needed to recoup the investment would be forthcoming in 2.1 years:

$$2 \text{ years} + \left(\frac{\$1,000}{\$10,000} \times 1 \text{ year} \right) = 2.1 \text{ years}$$

☐ Accounting Rate-of-Return Model

how it will be measured

similar to R.O.I.

The label for the **accounting rate-of-return** model or method is not uniform. It is also known as the *accrual accounting rate-of-return model* (a more accurate description), the *unadjusted rate-of-return model*, the *financial-statement model*, the *book-value model*, the *rate-of-return on assets model*, the *accounting model*, and the *approximate rate-of-return model*. Its computations supposedly dovetail most closely with conventional accounting models of calculating income and required investment.

The equations for the accounting rate of return are:

specific

$$\text{accounting rate of return} = \frac{\text{increase in expected average annual operating income}}{\text{initial increase in required investment}} \qquad (2)$$

$$R = \frac{O - D}{I} \qquad (3)$$

where R is the average annual rate of return on initial additional investment, O is the average annual incremental cash inflow from operations, D is the incremental average annual depreciation, and I is the initial incremental amount invested.

Assume the same facts as in our payback illustration: cost of machine, $12,000; useful life, eight years; estimated disposal value, zero; and expected annual savings in annual cash outflow from operations, $4,000. Annual depreciation would be $12,000 ÷ 8 = $1,500. Substitute these values in Equation 3:

$$R = \frac{\$4,000 - \$1,500}{\$12,000} = 20.8\%$$

If the denominator is the "average" investment, which is often assumed for equipment as being the average book value over the useful life, or $12,000 ÷ 2, the rate would be doubled.[8]

☐ Defects of Accounting Rate-of-Return Model

The *accounting rate-of-return* model is based on the familiar financial statements prepared under accrual accounting. Unlike the payback model, the

---

[8] The measure of the investment recovered in the example above is $1,500 per year, the amount of the annual depreciation. Consequently, the average investment committed to the project would decline at a rate of $1,500 per year from $12,000 to zero; hence the average investment would be the beginning balance plus the ending balance ($12,000) divided by 2, or $6,000. Note that when the ending balance is not zero, the average investment will *not* be half the initial investment.

accounting model at least has profitability as an objective. However, it has two major drawbacks.

First, as compared with discounted-cash-flow models, the required investment tends to be understated. The investment base for decision making should include such items as costs of research, sales promotion, and startups, which the accountant usually writes off immediately as expenses.

Second, the accounting model ignores the time value of money. Expected future dollars are unrealistically and erroneously regarded as equal to present dollars. The discounted-cash-flow model explicitly allows for the force of interest and the exact timing of cash flows. In contrast, the accounting model is based on *annual averages*. To illustrate, consider a petroleum company with three potential projects to choose from: an expansion of an existing gasoline station, an investment in an oil well, and the purchase of a new gasoline station. To simplify the calculations, assume a three-year life for each project. Exhibit 11-6 summarizes the comparisons. Note that the accounting rate of return would indicate that all three projects are equally desirable and that the internal rate of return properly discriminates in favor of earlier cash inflows.

Thus the conflict of purposes is highlighted in Exhibit 11-6. The accounting model utilizes concepts of investment and income that were originally designed for the quite different purpose of accounting for periodic income and financial position. The resulting accounting rate of return may be far from the real mark.

However, the accounting model usually facilitates follow-up, because the same approach is used in the forecast as is used in the accounts. Yet

EXHIBIT 11-6

Comparison of Accounting Rates of Return and Internal Rates of Return			
	EXPANSION OF EXISTING GASOLINE STATION	INVESTMENT IN AN OIL WELL	PURCHASE OF NEW GASOLINE STATION
Initial investment	$ 90,000	$ 90,000	$ 90,000
Cash inflows from operations:			
Year 1	$ 40,000	$ 80,000	$ 20,000
Year 2	40,000	30,000	40,000
Year 3	40,000	10,000	60,000
Totals	$120,000	$120,000	$120,000
Average annual cash inflow	$ 40,000	$ 40,000	$ 40,000
Less: Average annual depreciation ($90,000 ÷ 3)	30,000	30,000	30,000
Increase in average annual net income	$ 10,000	$ 10,000	$ 10,000
Accounting rate of return on initial investment	11.1%	11.1%	11.1%
Internal rate of return, using discounted-cash-flow techniques	16.0%*	23.2%*	13.3%*

*Computed by trial-and-error approaches using Tables 1 and 2, pages 680–681. See the appendix to this chapter for a detailed explanation.

exceptions to this ideal situation often occur, commonly arising from the inclusion in the forecast of some initial investment items that are not handled in the same manner in the subsequent accounting records. For example, the accounting for trade-ins and disposal values varies considerably. In practice, spot checks are frequently used on key items.

CONFLICT OF MODELS

❏ Nature of Conflict

Many managers are reluctant to accept DCF models as the best way to make capital-budgeting decisions. Their reluctance stems from the wide usage of the accrual accounting model for evaluating performance. That is, managers become frustrated if they are instructed to use a DCF model for making decisions that are evaluated later by a non-DCF model, such as the typical accrual accounting rate-of-return model.

To illustrate, consider the potential conflict that might arise in the first example of this chapter. Recall that the expected rate of return was 12%, based on an outlay of $6,074 that would generate cash savings of $2,000 for each of four years and no terminal disposal value. Under accrual accounting, using straight-line depreciation, the first-year evaluation of performance would be:

Cash operating savings	$2,000
Straight-line depreciation,	
$6,074 ÷ 4 =	1,519
Effect on net income	$ 481
Accounting rate of return	
on initial book value,	
$481 ÷ $6,074 =	7.9%

Given the above facts, many managers of profit-seeking organizations (where performance is evaluated by accrual accounting models) would be inclined against replacing the equipment despite the internal rate of 12%. Such negative inclinations are especially likely where managers are transferred to new positions every year or two. As Chapter 5 indicated, the reluctance to replace is reinforced (see pp. 128–129) if a heavy book loss on old equipment would appear in Year 1's accrual income statement—even though such a loss would be irrelevant in a properly constructed decision model.

❏ Reconciliation of Conflict

How can the foregoing conflict be reconciled? An obvious solution would be to use the same model for decisions and for evaluating performance. The accrual accounting model is often dominant for evaluating all sorts of performance; that is why many organizations use it for both purposes and do not use a DCF model at all. Critics claim that this nonuse of DCF may lead to many instances of poor capital-budgeting decisions.

Another obvious solution would be to use DCF for both capital-budgeting decisions and the performance evaluation audit. Several organizations use sampling procedures to perform such audits. A major reason for not auditing all capital-budgeting decisions routinely is that most accounting systems are designed to evaluate operating performances of products, departments, divisions, territories, and so on. In contrast, capital-budgeting decisions frequently deal with individual *projects*, not the collection of projects that are usually being managed simultaneously by divisional or department managers.

Some companies have solved the conflict by a dual approach. Managers use both the DCF model and the accrual accounting model at decision-making time. The decision is based on the DCF model, but the performance evaluation is tied back to the accrual accounting model.

The conflicts between the longstanding, pervasive accrual accounting model and various formal decision models represent one of the most serious unsolved problems in the design of management control systems. Top management cannot expect goal congruence if it favors the use of one collection of models for decisions and the use of other models for performance evaluation.[9]

Summary

Capital budgeting is long-term planning for proposed capital outlays and their financing. Projects are accepted if their rate of return exceeds a minimum desired rate of return.

Because the discounted-cash-flow model explicitly and automatically weighs the time value of money, it is the best method to use for long-range decisions. The overriding goal is maximum long-run net cash inflows.

The discounted-cash-flow model has two variations: internal rate of return and net present value. Both models take into account the timing of cash flows and are thus superior to other methods.

The payback model is a popular approach to capital-spending decisions. It is simple and easily understood, but it neglects profitability.

The accounting rate-of-return model is also widely used in capital budgeting, although it is conceptually inferior to discounted-cash-flow models. It fails to recognize explicitly the time value of money. Instead, the accounting model depends on averaging techniques that may yield inaccurate answers, particularly when cash flows are not uniform through the life of a project.

[9] For a fuller discussion, see Charles T. Horngren, *Cost Accounting: A Managerial Emphasis*, 5th ed. (Englewood Cliffs, N.J.: Prentice-Hall, 1982), Chap. 20. Also see Y. Ijiri, "Recovery Rate and Cash Flow Accounting," *Financial Executive*, XLVII (March 1980).

Summary
Problem for Your Review _____

❑ Problem

Review the problem and solution shown in Exhibit 11-5, page 331. Conduct a sensitivity analysis as indicated below. Consider each requirement as independent of other requirements.

1. Compute the net present value if the minimum desired rate of return were 20%.

2. Compute the net present value if predicted cash operating costs were $35,000 instead of $30,000, using the 14% discount rate.

3. By how much may the cash operating savings fall before reaching the point of indifference, the point where the net present value of the project is zero, using the original discount rate of 14%?

❑ Solution

1. Either the total project approach or the incremental approach could be used. The incremental approach would show:

	TOTAL PRESENT VALUE
Recurring cash operating savings, using an annuity table (Table 2):	
2.991 × $10,000 =	$29,910
Overhaul avoided: .694 × $10,000 =	6,940
Difference in disposal values:	
.402 × $5,000 =	(2,010)
Incremental initial investment	(31,000)
Net present value of replacement	$ 3,840

2. Net present value in Exhibit 11-5		$ 8,425
Present value of original $10,000 annual cash operating savings, given in Exhibit 11-5	$34,330	
Present value of reduced savings of $5,000 which is 50% of above	17,165	
Decrease in net present value		17,165
New net present value		$ (8,740)

3. Let X = annual cash operating savings and let net present value = 0. Then

$$0 = 3.433(X) + \$7,690 - \$2,595 - \$31,000$$
$$3.433X = \$25,905$$
$$X = \$ 7,546$$

(Note that the $7,690, $2,595, and $31,000 are at the bottom of Exhibit 11-5.)

If the annual savings fall from $10,000 to $7,546, a decrease of $2,454, the point of indifference will be reached.

An alternative way to obtain the same answer would be to divide the net present value of $8,425 (see bottom of Exhibit 11-5) by 3.433, obtaining $2,454, the amount of the annual difference in savings that will eliminate the $8,425 of net present value.

Highlights to Remember

1. Common errors in DCF analysis include
   a. Deducting depreciation from operating cash inflows
   b. Using the wrong present-value table
   c. Incorrectly analyzing investments in working capital (for example, inventories)
2. A serious practical impediment to the adoption of discounted-cash-flow models is the widespread use of conventional accrual models for evaluating performance. Frequently, the optimal decision under discounted cash flow will not produce a good showing in the early years, when performance is computed under conventional accounting methods. For example, heavy depreciation charges and the expensing rather than capitalizing of initial development costs will hurt reported income for the first year.

Accounting Vocabulary

Accounting method; accounting rate of return; book-value method; capital budgeting; cost of capital; cutoff rate; discount rate; hurdle rate; incremental approach; internal rate of return; net-present-value method; payback; payoff; payout; required rate; target rate; total project approach.

Appendix 11 : Calculations of Internal Rates of Return

EXPANSION OF EXISTING GASOLINE STATION

(Data are from Exhibit 11-6, p. 336.)

$90,000 = Present value of annuity of $40,000 at x percent for three years, or what factor F in the table of the present values of an annuity will satisfy the following equation:

$90,000 = $40,000 F

F = $90,000 ÷ $40,000 = 2.250

Now, on the Year 3 line of Table 2, page 681, find the column that is closest to 2.250. You will find that 2.250 is extremely close to a rate of return of 16%—so close that straight-line interpolation is unnecessary between 14% and 16%. Therefore the internal rate of return is 16%.

INVESTMENT IN AN OIL WELL

Trial-and-error methods must be used to calculate the rate of return that will equate the future cash flows with the $90,000 initial investment. As a start, note that the 16% rate was applicable to a uniform annual cash inflow. But now use Table 1 (p. 680) because the flows are not uniform, and try a higher rate, 22%, because you know that the cash inflows are coming in more quickly than under the uniform inflow:

YEAR	CASH INFLOWS	TRIAL AT 22% Present-Value Factor	TRIAL AT 22% Total Present Value	TRIAL AT 24% Present-Value Factor	TRIAL AT 24% Total Present Value
1	$80,000	.820	$65,600	.806	$64,480
2	30,000	.672	20,160	.650	19,500
3	10,000	.551	5,510	.524	5,240
			$91,270		$89,220

The true rate lies somewhere between 22% and 24% and can be approximated by straight-line interpolation:

INTERPOLATION	TOTAL PRESENT VALUES	
22%	$91,270	$91,270
True rate		90,000
24%	89,220	
Difference	$ 2,050	$ 1,270

Therefore

$$\text{true rate:} = 22\% + \frac{1,270}{2,050} \times 2\%$$

$$= 22\% + 1.2\% = 23.2\%$$

PURCHASE OF A NEW GASOLINE STATION

In contrast to the oil-well project, this venture will have slowly increasing cash inflows. The trial rate should be much lower than the 16% rate applicable to the expansion project. Let us try 12%:

YEAR	CASH INFLOWS	TRIAL AT 12% Present-Value Factor	TRIAL AT 12% Total Present Value	TRIAL AT 14% Present-Value Factor	TRIAL AT 14% Total Present Value
1	$20,000	.893	$17,860	.877	$17,540
2	40,000	.797	31,880	.769	30,760
3	60,000	.712	42,720	.675	40,500
			$92,460		$88,800

INTERPOLATION	TOTAL PRESENT VALUES	
12%	$92,460	$92,460
True rate		90,000
14%	88,800	
	$ 3,660	$ 2,460

$$\text{true rate} = 12\% + \frac{2,460}{3,660} \times 2\%$$

$$= 12\% + 1.3\% = 13.3\%$$

Assignment Material

Special Note: Ignore income taxes. The effects of income taxes are considered in the next chapter.

Fundamental Assignment Material

11–1. Exercises in compound interest: answers supplied.[10] Use the appropriate interest table to compute the following:

a. It is your sixty-fifth birthday. You plan to work five more years before retiring. Then you want to take $5,000 for a round-the-world tour. What lump sum do you have to invest now in order to accumulate the $5,000? Assume that your minimum desired rate of return is

(1) 4%, compounded annually

(2) 10%, compounded annually

(3) 20%, compounded annually

b. You want to spend $500 on a vacation at the end of each of the next five years. What lump sum do you have to invest now in order to take the five vacations? Assume that your minimum desired rate of return is

(1) 4%, compounded annually

(2) 10%, compounded annually

(3) 20%, compounded annually

c. At age sixty, you find that your employer is moving to another location. You receive termination pay of $5,000. You have some savings and wonder whether to retire now.

(1) If you invest the $5,000 now at 4%, compounded annually, how much money can you withdraw from your account each year so that at the end of five years there will be a zero balance?

(2) If you invest it at 10%?

d. At 16%, compounded annually, which of the following plans is more desirable in terms of present values? Show computations to support your answer.

	ANNUAL CASH INFLOWS	
Year	Mining	Farming
1	$10,000	$ 2,000
2	8,000	4,000
3	6,000	6,000
4	4,000	8,000
5	2,000	10,000
	$30,000	$30,000

11–2. Comparison of capital-budgeting techniques. The Putnam Hospital is considering the purchase of a new exercise machine at a cost of $20,000. It should save $4,000 in cash operating costs per year. Its estimated useful life is eight years, and it will have zero disposal value.

[10] The answers appear at the end of the assignment material for this chapter, p. 353.

1. What is the payback time?
2. Compute the net present value if the minimum rate of return desired is 10%. Should the hospital buy? Why?
3. Compute the internal rate of return.
4. Using the accounting rate-of-return model, compute the rate of return on the initial investment.

11–3. **Sensitivity analysis.** The Midwest Railroad is considering the replacement of an old power jack tamper used in the maintenance of track with a new improved version that should save $5,000 per year in net cash operating costs. The old equipment has zero disposal value, but it could be used for the next twelve years. The estimated useful life of the new equipment is twelve years and it will cost $25,000.

REQUIRED:
1. What is the payback time?
2. Compute the internal rate of return.
3. Management is unsure about the useful life. What would be the rate of return if the useful life were (a) six years instead of twelve and (b) twenty years instead of twelve?
4. Suppose the life will be twelve years, but the savings will be $3,000 per year instead of $5,000. What would be the rate of return?
5. Suppose the annual savings will be $4,000 for eight years. What would be the rate of return?

Additional
Assignment Material

11–4. Distinguish between the symbols DCF, NPV, and IRR.

11–5. According to Alexander Pope (1688–1744), "A little learning is a dangerous thing." How might this apply in capital budgeting?

11–6. State a rule that can serve as a general guide to capital-budgeting decisions.

11–7. "If discounted-cash-flow approaches are superior to the payback and the accounting methods, why should we bother to learn the others? All it does is confuse things." Answer this contention.

11–8. What is the basic flaw in the payback model?

11–9. How can the payback model be helpful in capital budgeting?

11–10. Compare the accounting rate-of-return approach and the discounted-cash-flow approach with reference to the time value of money.

11–11. "The higher the interest rate, the less I worry about errors in predicting terminal values." Do you agree? Explain.

11–12. "Double-counting occurs if depreciation is separately considered in discounted-cash-flow analysis." Do you agree? Explain.

11–13. "Problem solving is project-oriented rather than time-period-oriented." Explain.

11–14. Why is capital budgeting likely to receive increasing attention?

11–15. Why is discounted cash flow a superior method for capital budgeting?

11–16. Why should depreciation be excluded from discounted-cash-flow computations?

11–17. Can net present value ever be negative? Why?

11–18. "The higher the minimum rate of return desired, the higher the price that a company will be willing to pay for cost-saving equipment." Do you agree? Explain.

11–19. Why should the incremental approach to alternatives always lead to the same decision as the total project approach?

11–20. "Current disposal values of equipment are always relevant to a replacement decision." Do you agree? Explain.

11–21. "Discounted-cash-flow approaches will not work if the competing projects have unequal lives." Do you agree? Explain.

11–22. Exercise in compound interest. Xerox Corporation plans to enter some new communications business. The company expects to accumulate sufficient cash from its new operations to pay a lump sum of $200 million to Prudential Insurance Company at the end of five years. Prudential will lend money on a promissory note now, will take no payments until the end of five years, and desires 12% interest compounded annually.

REQUIRED:

1. How much money will Prudential lend Xerox?
2. How much will Xerox owe Prudential at the end of Year 1? At the end of Year 2? Show computations.

11–23. Exercise in compound interest. Refer to the preceding problem. Suppose Xerox and Prudential agree on a 12% interest rate compounded annually. However, Xerox will pay a *total* of $40 million annually at the end of *each* of the next five years. How much money will Prudential lend Xerox?

11–24. Exercises in compound interest.

1. A bank offers depositors a lump-sum payment of $10,000 six years hence. If you desire an interest rate of 8% compounded annually, how much would you be willing to deposit? At an interest rate of 16%?
2. Repeat Requirement 1, but assume that the interest rates are compounded semiannually.

11–25. Exercise in compound interest. A building contractor has asked you for a loan. You are pondering various proposals for repayment:

1. Lump sum of $300,000 four years hence. How much will you lend if your desired rate of return is (a) 10% compounded annually, (b) 20% compounded annually?
2. Repeat Requirement 1, but assume that the interest rates are compounded semiannually.
3. Suppose the loan is to be paid in full by equal payments of $75,000 at the end of each of the next four years. How much will you lend if your desired rate of return is (a) 10% compounded annually, (b) 20% compounded annually?

11–26. Basic relationships in interest tables.

1. Suppose you borrow $10,000 now at 16% interest compounded annually. The borrowed amount plus interest will be repaid in a lump sum at the end of eight years. How much must be repaid? Use Table 1 and the basic equation: PV = Future amount × Conversion factor.
2. Assume the same facts as in Requirement 1 except that the loan will be repaid in equal installments at the end of each of eight years. How much must be repaid each year? Use Table 2 and the basic equation: PV_A = Future annual amounts × Conversion factor.

11–27. Deferred annuity exercise. It is your sixtieth birthday. On your sixty-fifth birthday, and on three successive birthdays thereafter, you intend to spend exactly $2,000 for a birthday celebration. What lump sum do you have to invest now in order to have the four celebrations? Assume that the money will earn interest, compounded annually, of 12%.

11–28. Assumptions of DCF model. (R. Jaffee.) A superintendent of a school district has asked you to explain the assumptions underlying the discounted-cash-flow model. He has just learned the *mechanics* of calculating net present value, but he is unclear on its *meaning* and its implications for financial analysis.

Prepare a memorandum of explanation for the superintendent, using an example of an initial investment of $1,000, a project life of three years, and an operating cash savings of $500 at the end of each of the three years. Assume that the minimum desired rate of return is 10%. Use Exhibit 11-2 as a guide for preparing your presentation. The superintendent admires clarity.

11–29. Internal rate of return. Fill in the blanks:

	NUMBER OF YEARS		
	10	20	30
Amount of annual cash inflow*	$ 5,000	$8 433	$20,000
Required initial investment	$19,615	$50,000	$99580
Internal rate of return	22 %	16%	20%

*To be received at the end of each year.

11–30. Internal rate and NPV. Fill in the blanks:

	NUMBER OF YEARS		
	8	18	28
Amount of annual cash inflow*	$ 9,000	$13750.43	$12,000
Required initial investment	$36702	$80,000	$49,884
Internal rate of return	18%	16%	24 %
Minimum desired rate of return	14%	20 %	26%
Net present value	$4175 / 5049	($13,835)	$42816 (7068)

*To be received at the end of each year.

11–31. Illustration of trial-and-error method of computing rate of return. Study Exhibit 11-3. Suppose the annual cash inflow will be $2,500 rather than $2,000. (Exhibit 11-3 is on p. 322.)

REQUIRED: What is the internal rate of return?

11–32. New equipment. The Vail Company has offered to sell some new packaging equipment to the Aspen Company. The list price is $40,000, but Vail has agreed to accept some old equipment in trade. A trade-in allowance of $6,000 was agreed upon. The old equipment was carried at a book value of $7,700 and could be sold outright for $5,000 cash. Cash operating savings are expected to be $5,000 annually for the next twelve years. The minimum desired rate of return is 12%. The old equipment has a remaining useful life of twelve years. Both the old and the new equipment will have zero disposal values twelve years from now.

REQUIRED: Should Aspen buy the new equipment? Show your computations, using the net-present-value method. Ignore income taxes.

11–33. Replacement of equipment. Refer to Problem 5-33. Assume that the new equipment will cost $100,000 in cash, and that the old machine cost $81,000 and can be sold now for $16,000 cash.

REQUIRED:

1. Compute the net present value of the replacement alternative, assuming that the minimum desired rate of return is 10%.
2. What will be the internal rate of return?
3. How long is the payback period on the incremental investment?

11–34. Present values of cash inflows. Pristine Products has just been established. Operating plans indicate the following expected cash flows:

	OUTFLOWS	INFLOWS
Initial investment now	$210,000	$ —
End of year: One	150,000	200,000
Two	200,000	250,000
Three	250,000	300,000
Four	300,000	400,000
Five	300,000	400,000

REQUIRED:

1. Compute the net present value for all of these cash flows. This should be a single amount. Use a discount rate of 14%.
2. Is the internal rate of return more than 14% or less than 14%? Why?

11–35. Fixed and current assets; evaluation of performance. (Alternate is 11–36.) Mercy Hospital has been under pressure to keep costs down. Indeed, the hospital administrator has been managing various revenue-producing centers to maximize contributions to the recovery of the operating costs of the hospital as a whole. The administrator has been considering whether to buy a special-purpose X-ray machine for $190,000. Its unique characteristics would generate additional cash operating income of $50,000 per year for the hospital as a whole.

The machine is expected to have a useful life of six years and a terminal salvage value of $25,000.

The machine is delicate. It requires a constant inventory of various supplies and spare parts. When these items can no longer be used, they are instantly replaced, so an investment of $10,000 must be maintained at all times. However, this investment is fully recoverable at the end of the useful life of the machine.

REQUIRED:

1. Compute the net present value if the required rate of return is 14%.
2. Compute the internal rate of return (to nearest whole percentage).
3. Compute the accounting rate of return on (a) the initial investment and (b) the "average" investment.
4. Why might the administrator be reluctant to base her decision on the DCF model?

11–36. Effects of current assets and residual values. (Alternate is 11–35.) The manager of a department store is considering whether to remodel space that has been devoted to large household appliances. She is thinking of dropping those products and replacing them with expensive high-fashion clothing.

New display fixtures and dressing areas will be needed. They will cost $70,000 and are expected to be useful for five years with a terminal salvage value of $5,000. Additional cash inflows from operations are expected to be $40,000 per year.

To sustain the higher anticipated sales volumes, additional investments in receivables and inventories will be required. An initial investment of $60,000 is needed for these current assets. This level must be maintained steadily. When these activities are terminated, the receivables and inventories will be converted to cash and fully recouped.

The manager has decided to use a five-year planning horizon for this possible use of space. Experience has shown that selling high-fashion clothing is risky, so there is a strong likelihood that the space will be changed at the end of five years.

REQUIRED:

1. Compute (a) net present value, using a required rate of 20%; (b) internal rate of return (to nearest whole percentage); (c) accounting rate of return on the initial investment; and (d) accounting rate of return on the "average" investment.
2. As the store manager, which type of model would you prefer for the purposes of making this decision and of evaluating subsequent performance? Give reasons and compare the principal types of models.

11–37. Capital budgeting with uneven cash flows. The Stanford University Engineering School is considering the purchase of a special-purpose machine for $30,000. It is expected to have a useful life of three years with no terminal salvage value. The university's controller estimates the following savings in cash operating costs:

YEAR	AMOUNT
1	$14,000
2	13,000
3	12,000

REQUIRED:

Compute

1. Payback period
2. Net present value if the required rate of return is 12%
3. Internal rate of return
4. Accounting rate of return (a) on the initial investment and (b) on the "average" investment

11–38. Replacing office equipment. Harvard University is considering replacing its present manual bookkeeping machines (NCR) with faster machines purchased from IBM. The administration is very concerned about the rising costs of operations during the last decade.

In order to convert to IBM, two operators would have to be sent to school. Required training and remodeling would cost $6,000.

Harvard's three NCR machines were purchased for $10,000 each, five years ago. Their expected life was ten years. Their resale value now is $3,000 each and will be zero in five more years. The total cost of the new IBM equipment will be $50,000; it will have zero disposal value in five years.

The three NCR operators are paid $8 an hour each. They usually work a forty-hour week. Machine breakdowns occur monthly on each machine, resulting in repair costs of $50 per month and overtime of four hours, at time-and-one-half, per machine per month, to complete the normal monthly workload. Paper, supplies, etc., cost $100 a month for each NCR.

The IBM system will require only two regular operators, on a regular work-week of forty hours each, to do the same work. Rates are $10 an hour, and no overtime is expected. Paper, supplies, etc., will cost $3,300 annually. Maintenance and repairs are fully serviced by IBM for $1,050 annually. (Assume a 52-week year.)

1. Using discounted-cash-flow techniques, compute the present value of all relevant cash flows, under both alternatives, for the five-year period discounted at 12%.
2. Should Harvard keep the NCR machines or replace them, if the decision is based solely on the given data?
3. What other considerations might affect the decision?

11–39. Replacement decision for railway equipment. The St. Paul Railroad is considering replacement of a Kalamazoo Power Jack Tamper, used for maintenance of track, with a new automatic raising device that can be attached to a production tamper.

The present power jack tamper cost $18,000 five years ago and has an estimated life of twelve years. A year from now the machine will require a major overhaul estimated to cost $5,000. It can be disposed of now via an outright cash sale for $2,500. There will be no value at the end of twelve years.

The automatic raising attachment has a delivered selling price of $74,000 and an estimated life of twelve years. Because of anticipated future developments in combined maintenance machines, it is felt that the machine should be disposed of at the end of the seventh year to take advantage of newly developed machines. Estimated sale value at end of seven years is $5,000.

Tests have shown that the automatic raising machine will produce a more uniform surface on the track than the power jack tamper now in use. The new equipment will eliminate one laborer whose annual compensation, including fringe benefits, is $30,000.

Track maintenance work is seasonal, and the equipment normally works from May 1 to October 31 each year. Machine operators and laborers are transferred to other work after October 31, at the same rate of pay.

The salesman claims that the annual normal maintenance of the new machine will run about $1,000 per year. Because the automatic raising machine is more complicated than the manually operated machine, it is felt that it will require a thorough overhaul at the end of the fourth year at an estimated cost of $7,000.

Records show the annual normal maintenance of the Kalamazoo machine to be $1,200. Fuel consumption of the two machines is equal.

Should the St. Paul keep or replace the Kalamazoo Power Jack Tamper? A 10% rate of return is desired. Compute present values.

The railroad is not currently paying any income tax.

11–40. Discounted cash flow, uneven revenue stream, relevant costs. Mr. Divot, the owner of a nine-hole golf course on the outskirts of a large city, is considering the proposal that this course be illuminated and operated at night. Mr. Divot purchased the course early last year for $75,000. His receipts from operations during the 28-week season were $24,000. Total disbursements for the year, for all purposes, were $15,500.

The required investment in lighting this course is estimated at $20,000. The system will require 150 lamps of 1,000 watts each. Electricity costs 3.2¢ per kilowatt-hour. The expected average hours of operation per night is five. Because of occasional bad weather and the probable curtailment of night operation at the beginning and end of the season, it is estimated that there will be only 130 nights of operation per year. Labor for keeping the course open at night will cost $15 per night. Lamp renewals are estimated at $300 per year; other maintenance and repairs, per year, will amount to 4% of the initial cost of the lighting system. Property taxes on this equipment will be about 2% of its initial cost. It is estimated that the average revenue, per night of operation, will be $90 for the first two years.

Considering the probability of competition from the illumination of other golf courses, Mr. Divot decides that he will not make the investment unless he can make at least 10% per annum on his investment. Because of anticipated competition, revenue is expected to drop to $60 per night for Years 3 through 5. It is estimated that the lighting equipment will have a salvage value of $8,000 at the end of the five-year period.

REQUIRED: Using discounted-cash-flow techniques, determine whether Mr. Divot should install the lighting system.

11–41. Minimizing transportation costs. The Wriston Company produces industrial and residential lighting fixtures at its manufacturing facility located in Los Angeles. Shipment of company products to an eastern warehouse is presently handled by common carriers at a rate of 20¢ per pound of fixtures. The warehouse is located in Cleveland, 2,500 miles from Los Angeles.

The treasurer of Wriston Company is presently considering whether to purchase a truck for transporting products to the eastern warehouse. The following data on the truck are available:

Purchase price	$50,000
Useful life	5 years
Salvage value after 5 years	$5,000
Capacity of truck	10,000 lbs.
Cash costs of operating truck	$.80 per mile

The treasurer feels that an investment in this truck is particularly attractive because of his successful negotiation with X Company to back-haul X's products from Cleveland to Los Angeles on every return trip from the warehouse. X has agreed to pay Wriston $2,400 per load of X's products hauled from Cleveland to Los Angeles up to and including 100 loads per year.

Wriston's marketing manager has estimated that 500,000 pounds of fixtures will have to be shipped to the eastern warehouse each year for the next five years. The truck will be fully loaded on each round trip.

Ignore income taxes. For income tax effects, see Problem 12–39.

REQUIRED:
1. Assume that Wriston requires a minimum rate of return of 20%. Should the truck be purchased? Show computations to support your answer.
2. What is the minimum number of trips that must be guaranteed by the X Company to make the deal acceptable to Wriston, based on the above numbers alone?
3. What qualitative factors might influence your decision? Be specific.

11–42. Investment in machine and working capital. The Schultz Company has an old machine with a net disposal value of $10,000 now and $4,000 five years from now. A new Rapido machine is offered for $60,000 cash or $50,000 with a trade-in. The new machine will result in an annual operating cash outflow of $40,000 as compared with the old machine's annual outflow of $50,000. The disposal value of the new machine five years hence will be $4,000.

Because the new machine will produce output more rapidly, the average investment in inventories will be $160,000 by using the new machine instead of $200,000.

The minimum desired rate of return is 20%. The company uses discounted-cash-flow techniques to guide these decisions.

REQUIRED: Should the Rapido machine be acquired? Show your calculations. Company procedures require the computing of the present value of each alternative. The most desirable alternative is the one with the least cost. Assume PV of $1 at 20% for five years, $.40; PV of annuity of $1 at 20% for five years, $3.

11–43. Uses of warehouse: review of Chapters 5 and 11.

a. The Hiller Company is currently leasing one of its small warehouses to another company for $3,000 per year, on a month-to-month basis.

b. The estimated sales value of the warehouse is $30,000. This price is likely to remain unchanged indefinitely—even if a contemplated public expressway results in the building's condemnation. The building originally cost $20,000 and is being depreciated at $500 annually. Its net book value is $9,000.

c. The Hiller Company is seriously considering converting the warehouse into a retail outlet for selling furniture at ridiculously low discount prices. Such an endeavor would entail remodeling, at a cost of $15,000. The remodeling would be extremely modest because the major attraction would be flimsy furniture at rock-bottom prices. The remodeling can be accomplished over a single weekend.

d. The inventory, cash, and receivables needed to open and sustain the retail outlet would be $50,000. This total is fully recoverable whenever operations terminate.

e. The president, who paid an expressway engineer $1,000 to discover when and where the expressway will be built, is virtually certain that the warehouse will be available for no more than four years. He has asked you to give him an analysis of whether the company should continue to lease the warehouse or convert it to a retail outlet, assuming that the minimum annual rate of return desired is 14% over a four-year planning horizon. Estimated annual operating data, exclusive of depreciation, are:

f.	Sales	$200,000
g.	Operating expenses	177,000
h.	Nonrecurring sales promotion costs at *beginning* of Year 1	20,000
i.	Nonrecurring termination costs at *end* of Year 4	10,000

The president has definitely decided not to sell the warehouse until forced to by condemnation proceedings.

REQUIRED:

1. Show how you would handle the *individual* items on the company's analysis form, which is set up as follows:

		NET PRESENT VALUE	CASH FLOWS IN YEAR				
ITEM	DESCRIPTION		0	1	2	3	4
a.							
b.							
.							
.							
.							
h.							
i.							

Use the following present-value factors: the PV of $1 = $.60 and the PV of an annuity of $1 = $2.90. Ignore income taxes. If you think an item is irrelevant, leave the space blank.

2. After analyzing all the relevant data, compute the net present value. Indicate which course of action, based on the data alone, should be taken.

11–44. Cafeteria facilities. The cafeteria of an office building is open 250 days a year. It offers typical cafeteria-line service. At the noon meal (open to the public), serving-line facilities can accommodate 200 people per hour for the two-hour serving period. The average customer has a thirty-minute lunch hour. Serving facilities are unable to handle the overflow of noon customers with the result that, daily, 200 dissatisfied customers who do not wish to stand in line choose to eat elsewhere. Projected over a year, this results in a considerable loss to the cafeteria.

To tap this excess demand, the cafeteria is considering two alternatives: (a) installing two vending machines, at a cost of $5,000 apiece; or (b) completely revamping present serving-line facilities with new equipment, at a cost of $80,000. The vending machines and serving-line equipment have a useful life of ten years and will be depreciated on a straight-line basis. The minimum desired rate of return for the cafeteria is 10%. The average sale is $1.50, with a contribution margin of 30%. This will remain the same if new serving-line facilities are installed.

Data for alternative *a* (vending machines) are as follows:

Service cost per year is $300; salvage value of each machine at the end of ten years is $500.

Contribution margin is 20%. It is estimated that 60% of the dissatisfied customers will use the vending machines and spend an average of $1.50. The estimated salvage value of the present equipment will net $2,000 at the end of the ten-year period.

Data for alternative *b* (new serving-line facilities) are as follows:

Yearly salary for an extra part-time clerk is $4,000; salvage value of old equipment is $5,000; salvage value of new equipment, at the end of ten years, is $10,000; cost of dismantling old equipment is $1,000. It is estimated that all the previously dissatisfied customers will use the new facilities.

All other costs are the same under both alternatives and need not be considered.

REQUIRED: Using the net-present-value model, which is the better alternative?

11–45. Comparison of investment models. Maria's Pizza Company makes and sells frozen pizzas to local retail outlets. Maria has just inherited $10,000 and has decided to invest it in the business. She is trying to decide between:

Alternative *a:* Buy a $10,000 contract, payable immediately, from a local reputable sales promotion agency. The agency would provide various advertising services, as specified in the contract, over the next ten years. Maria is convinced that the sales promotion would increase cash inflow from operations, through increased volume, by $2,000 per year for the first five years, and by $1,000 per year thereafter. There would be no effect after the ten years had elapsed.

Alternative *b:* Buy new mixing and packaging equipment, at a cost of $10,000, which would reduce operating cash outflows by $1,500 per year for the next ten years. The equipment would have zero salvage value at the end of the ten years. Ignore any tax effect.

REQUIRED:
1. Compute the rates of return on initial investment by the accounting model for both alternatives.
2. Compute the rates of return by the discounted-cash-flow model for both alternatives.
3. Are the rates of return different under the discounted-cash-flow model? Explain.

11–46. Make or buy, discounted cash flow, and accounting rate of return. Refer to Problem 5–31, Requirement 1, page 142.

1. Using a net-present-value analysis, which alternative is more attractive? Assume that the minimum rate of return desired is 8%.
2. Using the accounting rate-of-return method, what is the rate of return on the initial investment?

11–47. New equipment and analysis of operating costs: accounting rate of return. The processing department of Rho Company has incurred the following costs in producing 150,000 units, which is normal volume, during the past year:

Variable	$100,000
Fixed	50,000
	$150,000

The department has been offered some new processing equipment. The salesman says that the new equipment will reduce unit costs by 20¢. The department's old equipment has a remaining useful life of five years, has zero disposal value now, and is being depreciated on a straight-line basis at $5,000 annually. The new equipment's straight-line depreciation would be $30,000 annually. It would last five years and have no disposal value. The salesman pointed out that overall unit costs now are $1, whereas the new equipment is being used by one of Rho's competitors to produce an identical product at a unit cost of 80¢, computed as follows:

Variable costs	$ 80,000
Fixed costs*	80,000
Total costs	$160,000
Divide by units produced	200,000
Cost per unit	$ .80

*Fixed costs include $30,000 depreciation on the new equipment. Rho's supervisory payroll is $10,000 less than this competitor's.

The salesman stated that a saving of 20¢ per unit would add $30,000 to Rho's annual net income.

REQUIRED:

1. Show *specifically* how the salesman computed Rho's costs and prospective savings.
2. As adviser to the Rho Company, evaluate the salesman's contentions and prepare a quantitative summary to support your recommendations for Rho's best course of action. Include the accounting rate-of-return method and the net-present-value method in your evaluation. Assume that Rho's minimum desired rate of return is 10%.

11–48. Replacement decision. Amtrak, a passenger train company subsidized wholly by the U.S. government, has included a dining car on the lone passenger train it operates from Buffalo to Albany, N.Y. Yearly operations of the dining car have shown a consistent loss, which is expected to persist, as follows:

Revenue (in cash)		$200,000
Expenses for food, supplies, etc. (in cash)	$100,000	
Salaries	110,000	210,000
Net loss (ignore depreciation on the dining car itself)		($ 10,000)

The Auto-vend Company has offered to sell automatic vending machines to Amtrak for $22,000, less a $3,000 trade-in allowance on old equipment (which is carried at $3,000 book value, and which can be sold outright for $3,000 cash) now used in the dining car operation. The useful life of the vending equipment is estimated at ten years, with zero scrap value. Experience elsewhere has led executives to predict that the equipment will serve 50% more food than the dining car, but prices will be 50% less, so the new gross receipts will probably be $150,000. The variety and mix of food sold are expected to be the same as for the dining car. A catering company will completely service and supply the machines, paying 10% of gross receipts to the Amtrak company and bearing all costs of food, repairs, etc. All dining car employees will be discharged immediately. Their termination pay will total $30,000. However, an attendant who has some general knowledge of vending machines will be needed for one shift per day. The annual cost to Amtrak for the attendant will be $14,000.

For political and other reasons, the railroad will definitely not abandon its food service. The old equipment will have zero scrap value at the end of ten years.

REQUIRED: Using the above data, compute the following. Label computations. Ignore income taxes.

1. The incremental net present value, in dollars, of the proposed investment. Assume that Congress has specified that a minimum desired rate of return of 10% be used for these types of investments. For this problem, assume that the PV of $1 at 10% to be received at the end of ten years is $.400 and that the PV of an annuity of $1 at 10% for ten years is $6.000.
2. What would be the minimum amount of annual *revenue* that Amtrak would have to receive from the catering company to justify making the investment? Show computations.

☐ Solutions to Exercises in Compound Interest, Problem 11-1

The general approach to these exercises centers on one fundamental question: Which of the two basic tables am I dealing with? No calculations should be made until after this question is answered with assurance. If you made any errors, it is possible that you used the wrong table.

a. From Table 1, page 680:
   (1) $4,110
   (2) $3,105
   (3) $2,010

The $5,000 is an *amount* or *future worth*. You want the present value of that amount:

$$PV = \frac{S}{(1 + i)^n}$$

The conversion factor, $1/(1 + i)^n$, is on line 5 of Table 1. Substituting:

PV = $5,000(.822) = $4,110	(1)
PV = $5,000(.621) = $3,105	(2)
PV = $5,000(.402) = $2,010	(3)

Note that the higher the interest rate, the lower the present value.

b. From Table 2, page 681:
   (1) $2,226.00
   (2) $1,895.50
   (3) $1,495.50

The $500 withdrawal is a uniform annual amount, an annuity. You need to find the present value of an annuity for five years:

PV_A = annual withdrawal (F), where F is the conversion factor.

Substituting:

$$PV_A = \$500(4.452) = \$2,226.00 \tag{1}$$
$$PV_A = \$500(3.791) = \$1,895.50 \tag{2}$$
$$PV_A = \$500(2.991) = \$1,495.50 \tag{3}$$

c. From Table 2:
  (1) $1,123.09
  (2) $1,318.91

You have $5,000, the present value of your contemplated annuity. You must find the annuity that will just exhaust the invested principal in five years:

$$PV_A = \text{annual withdrawal (F)} \tag{1}$$

$$\$5,000 = \text{annual withdrawal (4.452)}$$
$$\text{annual withdrawal} = \$5,000 \div 4.452$$
$$= \$1,123.09$$

$$\$5,000 = \text{annual withdrawal (3.791)} \tag{2}$$
$$\text{annual withdrawal} = \$5,000 \div 3.791$$
$$= \$1,318.91$$

d. From Table 1: Mining is preferable; its present value exceeds farming by $3,852. Note that the nearer dollars are more valuable than the distant dollars.

YEAR	PRESENT-VALUE @ 16% FROM TABLE 1	PRESENT VALUE OF MINING	PRESENT VALUE OF FARMING
1	.862	$8,620	$1,724
2	.743	5,944	2,972
3	.641	3,846	3,846
4	.552	2,208	4,416
5	.476	952	4,760
		$21,570	$17,718

Suggested Readings

BIERMAN, H., and S. SMIDT, *The Capital Budgeting Decision*, 5th ed. New York: Macmillan, 1980.

BOWER, J., *Managing the Resource Allocation Process*. Boston: Harvard Business School, 1970.

CLARK, J., T. HINDELANG, and R. PRITCHARD, *Capital Budgeting*. Englewood Cliffs, N.J.: Prentice-Hall, 1979.

VAN HORNE, JAMES C., *Financial Management and Policy*, 6th ed. Englewood Cliffs, N.J.: Prentice-Hall, 1983.

12

CAPITAL BUDGETING: TAXES AND INFLATION

Learning Objectives

When you have finished studying this chapter, you should be able to

1. Analyze a typical income statement to determine the net after-tax cash inflow from operations

2. Compute the after-tax present values of projects involving straight-line depreciation and accelerated depreciation

3. Explain the effect of an investment tax credit on net present value

4. Explain the after-tax effect on cash of disposing of assets

5. Describe how depreciation is analyzed in various capital-budgeting models

6. Analyze the impact of inflation on capital budgeting

This chapter extends the coverage of the preceding chapter. We are especially concerned with the effect of income taxes on capital-budgeting decisions. However, other topics will also be explored, especially how to analyze the effects of inflation. A chapter appendix covers some conflicts between the net-present-value model and the internal rate of return.

INCOME TAXES AND CAPITAL BUDGETING

❏ General Characteristics

Income taxes are cash disbursements. Income taxes can influence the *amount* and/or the *timing* of cash flows. Their basic role in capital budgeting is no different from that of any other cash disbursement. However, taxes tend to narrow the cash differences between projects. Cash savings in operations will cause an increase in taxable income and thus a partially offsetting increase in tax outlays. For example, a 60% income tax rate would reduce the net attractiveness of $1 million in cash operating savings to $400,000.

U.S. federal income tax rates on ordinary corporate taxable income vary from 16% to 40% of the first $100,000 per year. Taxable income over $100,000 is taxed at 46%. These rates are sometimes subject to additional surcharges that may vary from year to year. State income tax rates vary considerably. In many instances, state plus federal income tax rates are more than 50%. We use a 60% rate in several examples to facilitate computations.

❏ Effects of Depreciation Deductions

Exhibit 12-1 shows the interrelationship of income before taxes, income taxes, and depreciation. Please examine this key exhibit carefully before reading on. Assume that the company has a single fixed asset, equipment purchased for $125,000 cash, which has a five-year life and zero disposal value. The purchase cost, less the estimated disposal value, is tax-deductible in the form of yearly depreciation. Depreciation deductions (and similar deductions that are noncash expenses when deducted) have been called **tax shields** because they protect that amount of income from taxation.

As Exhibit 12-2 shows, the asset represents a valuable future tax deduction of $125,000. The present value of this deduction depends directly on its specific yearly effects on future income tax payments. Therefore the present value is influenced by the depreciation method selected, the tax rates, and the discount rate.

Exhibit 12-2 shows two methods for analyzing the data for capital budgeting, assuming straight-line depreciation.[1] Both lead to the same final answer, a net present value of $15,595. The choice of analytical method is a matter of personal preference. However, Method Two will be used in this chapter. Why? Because it highlights the impact of the alternative depreciation methods on present values.

[1] For simplicity, and to underscore the general approach, the *half-year convention* is ignored here. It is explained later in the chapter.

EXHIBIT
12-1

**Basic Analysis of Income Statement,
Income Taxes, and Cash Flows**

TRADITIONAL INCOME STATEMENT

(S)	Sales	$130,000
(E)	Less: Expenses, excluding depreciation	$ 70,000
(D)	Depreciation (straight line)	25,000
	Total expenses	$ 95,000
	Income before taxes	$ 35,000
(T)	Income taxes @ 60%	21,000
(I)	Net income	$ 14,000

Total after-tax effect on cash is
either S − E − T = $130,000 − $70,000 − $21,000 = $39,000
or I + D = $14,000 + $25,000 = $39,000

ANALYSIS OF THE ABOVE FOR CAPITAL BUDGETING

Cash effects of operations:

(S−E)	Cash inflow from operations: $130,000 − $70,000 =	$ 60,000
	Income tax outflow, @ 60%	36,000
	After-tax inflow from operations (excluding depreciation)	$ 24,000

Effect of depreciation:

(D)	Straight-line depreciation: $125,000 ÷ 5 = $25,000	
	Income tax savings @ 60%	15,000
	Total after-tax effect on cash	$ 39,000

The $125,000 investment really buys two streams of cash: (a) inflows from operations plus (b) savings of income tax outflows (which have the same effect in capital budgeting as additions to cash inflows). The choice of depreciation method will not affect the cash inflows from operations. But different depreciation methods will affect the cash outflows for income taxes. That is, a straight-line method will produce one present value of tax savings, and an accelerated method will produce a different present value. Such differences can be pinpointed more easily if Method Two is used.

❏ Tax Deductions, Cash Effects, and Timing

Before proceeding, review the basic relationships just portrayed (in dollars):

LINE	(A) ITEMS USED IN COMPUTING TAXABLE INCOME	(B) CURRENT PRETAX CASH EFFECT	(C) EFFECT ON INCOME TAX CASH OUTFLOWS @ 60%	(B)-(C) NET CASH EFFECT
1. Sales	130,000	130,000	78,000	52,000
2. Expenses, excluding depreciation	70,000	70,000	42,000	28,000
3. Cash effects of operations	60,000	60,000	36,000	24,000
4. Depreciation	25,000	0	15,000	15,000
5. Net cash effects		60,000	21,000	39,000
6. Income before income taxes	35,000			
7. Income taxes	21,000			
8. Net income	14,000			

EXHIBIT 12-2 *(Place a clip on this page for easy reference.)*

Impact of Income Taxes on Capital-Budgeting Analysis

Assume: Original cost of equipment, $125,000; 5-year life; zero terminal disposal value; pretax annual cash inflow from operations, $60,000; income tax rate, 60%; required after-tax rate of return, 12%. All items are in dollars except discount factors. The after-tax cash flows are from Exhibit 12-1.

	12% DISCOUNT FACTOR, FROM APPROPRIATE TABLES	TOTAL PRESENT VALUE @ 12%		SKETCH OF AFTER-TAX CASH FLOWS AT END OF YEAR					
				0	1	2	3	4	5
Method One (Discount the total annual effects together)									
After-tax effect on cash flow from operations	3.605	140,595			39,000	39,000	39,000	39,000	39,000
Investment	1.000	125,000		(125,000)					
Net present value		15,595							
Method Two (Discount two annual effects separately)									
Cash effects of operations excluding depreciation	3.605	86,520			24,000	24,000	24,000	24,000	24,000
Cash effects of depreciation: Savings of income taxes	3.605	54,075			15,000	15,000	15,000	15,000	15,000
Total after-tax effect on cash		140,595							
Investment	1.000	(125,000)		(125,000)					
Net present value		15,595							

This tabulation highlights why the net cash effects of operations (any of the items on lines 1, 2, and 3) are computed by multiplying the pretax amounts by 1 minus the tax rate, or $1 - .60$, or .40. Thus the after-tax effect of the $70,000 deduction for *cash* expenses (line 2) is $70,000 × .40 = $28,000.

In contrast, the after-tax effects of the *noncash* expenses (depreciation on line 4) are computed by multiplying the tax deduction of $25,000 by the tax rate itself, or $25,000 × .60 = $15,000.

Throughout the illustrations in this chapter, we assume that all income tax flows occur simultaneously with the pretax cash flows. That is, consider line 3. We are ignoring the likelihood that part or all of the $36,000 tax payments related to the $60,000 pretax cash effects of operations of Year 1 may not actually occur until, say, April of Year 2.

This assumption of no lags in income tax effects is also largely in accordance with the facts in the real world. Why? Because both individual and corporate taxpayers generally "pay-as-they-go." That is, tax payments are made throughout the current year, not in one lump sum in the subsequent year.

Another assumption throughout this chapter is that the companies in question are profitable. That is, the companies will have enough taxable income from all sources to utilize all income tax benefits in the situations described.

☐ Accelerated Depreciation

Governments have frequently enacted income tax laws that permit accelerated depreciation instead of straight-line depreciation. **Accelerated depreciation** is defined as any pattern of depreciation that writes off depreciable assets more quickly than does ordinary straight-line depreciation. Inevitably, these laws are aimed at encouraging investments in long-lived assets.

An extreme example clearly demonstrates why accelerated depreciation is attractive to investors. Reconsider the facts in Exhibit 12-2. Suppose, as is the case in England, that the entire initial investment can be written off during Year 1 for income tax reporting. Focus on Method Two to see the rise in net present value from $15,595 to $28,495:

	PRESENT VALUES	
	As In Exhibit 12-2	Complete Write-off During Year 1
Cash effects of operations	$ 86,520	$ 86,520
Cash effects of depreciation	54,075	66,975*
Total after-tax effect on cash	140,595	153,495
Investment	(125,000)	(125,000)
Net present value	$ 15,595	$ 28,495

*Discount factor of .893 for Year 1 × income tax savings of 60% × $125,000.

In summary, the present value of the income tax savings is greater if straight-line depreciation is *not* used. The general decision rule is to select accelerated methods because, as compared with the straight-line method, they maximize the present values of income tax savings. The cumulative *dollar* tax bills may not change when the years are taken together, but the early write-offs defer tax outlays to future periods. The measure of the latter advantage depends on the rate of return that can be gained from funds that would otherwise have been paid as income taxes. The mottoes in income tax planning are: When there is a legal choice, take the deduction sooner rather than later; and recognize taxable income later rather than sooner.

❏ Declining-Balance Depreciation

For years the U.S. income tax laws permitted a popular basic form of accelerated depreciation called **double-declining-balance depreciation** (DDB). This form results in first-year depreciation being twice the amount of straight-line depreciation when zero terminal disposal value is assumed. DDB is computed as follows:

a. Compute the straight-line rate (ignoring the terminal value) by dividing 100% by the useful life. Then double this rate. In our example, 100% ÷ 5 years = 20%. The DDB rate would be 2 × 20% = 40%.

b. To compute the depreciation for any year, multiply the beginning book value by the DDB rate: 40% × $125,000 = $50,000 for the first year; 40% × ($125,000 − $50,000) = $30,000 for the second year, etc.

c. Unmodified, this method would never fully depreciate the book value. Therefore, in the later years of an asset's life, companies have been permitted to switch to the straight-line method. For instance, in our example, the taxpayer could switch to straight-line depreciation for the fourth and fifth years.

❏ Accelerated Cost Recovery System (ACRS)

For most depreciable assets placed in service after December 31, 1980, the U.S. Internal Revenue Service applies the **Accelerated Cost Recovery System** (ACRS). This system requires that depreciation deductions be based on arbitrary "recovery periods" instead of useful lives. Essentially, ACRS has assigned much shorter useful lives to the assets then previously. In brief, ACRS (a) approximates 150% declining-balance depreciation (b) applied *over shorter lives*. In combination, (a) and (b) generally provide greater acceleration of depreciation than ever before.

The key word in all variations of depreciation from the straight-line method based on expected useful service life is *accelerated*. For example, whether declining-balance depreciation is 200%, 175%, or 150% of the straight-line rate, in the early years of an asset's service life there will be higher depreciation than with the straight-line method. Moreover, the use of a straight-line rate over a shorter useful life is also a form of accelerated depreciation. Carried to its extreme, an accelerated depreciation method would call for immediate total write-off in the year of acquisition.

As Exhibit 12-3 shows, property is classified by the number of years over which the acquisition cost is to be recovered through deductions.

EXHIBIT 12-3

Classifications in Accelerated Cost Recovery System (ACRS)	
CLASS	**EXAMPLES OF TYPES OF ASSETS**
3-year	Autos, light trucks, equipment used for research and development
5-year	Most machinery, equipment, furniture and fixtures, heavy trucks
10-year	Public utility property with useful life of eighteen to twenty-five years
15-year	Longer-lived public utility property and real estate in general

Exhibit 12-4 displays the "accelerated depreciation" schedules that must be used, providing that the straight-line method of cost recovery is not elected.[2] Consider the 5-year column. A deduction of 15% is allowed for the year the property was placed in service (its first recovery year), as though it were acquired near the end of the year. Correspondingly, no deduction is allowed in the year of the property's disposition, even if its full cost had not been recovered in prior years. *Salvage values are completely ignored when using these schedules.*

EXHIBIT 12-4

ACRS Recovery Percentages					
			PROPERTY CLASS		
RECOVERY YEAR	**3-Year**	**5-Year**	**10-Year**	**15-Year Public Utility**	**15-Year General Real Estate**
1	25%	15%	8%	5%	12%
2	38	22	14	10	10
3	37	21	12	9	9
4		21	10	8	8
5		21	10	7	7
6			10	7	6
7			9	6	6
8			9	6	6
9			9	6	6
10			9	6	5
11				6	5
12				6	5
13				6	5
14				6	5
15				6	5
	100%	100%	100%	100%	100%

In essence, these ACRS schedules achieve about the same results as would be achieved by declining-balance depreciation methods, given the

---

[2] Under current tax law the taxpayer can always elect to use straight-line cost recovery. When this election is made, several recovery period options are available, as explained later in the chapter.

same expected useful lives. For nearly all ACRS assets, these schedules approximate 150% declining-balance depreciation as applied to the prescribed lives. However, the real estate schedule approximates the 175% declining-balance method.

For example, if an asset in the five-year property class is acquired anytime in 1984 at a cost of $125,000, the cost-recovery deduction will be 15% × $125,000, or $18,750.[3] No matter when the asset is acquired in 1984, the deduction will be 15%. In 1985 the deduction would be 22% × $125,000, or $27,500.

Taxpayers can use 200% declining-balance depreciation for assets acquired before 1981. If so, how can the 150% declining-balance depreciation of ACRS be welcomed? For one major reason: Such assets can now be written off more quickly. For example, much railroad equipment formerly had to be written off over a useful life of forty years. Such equipment can now be written off over only five years. Similarly, many buildings had to be written off over a useful life of twenty-five to forty years. They can now be written off over only fifteen years.

In sum, for many assets, ACRS accelerates depreciation even more than double-declining-balance depreciation. Why? Because the scheduled lives are often much shorter than previously permitted.

❑ ACRS and Straight-Line Depreciation

Accelerated depreciation may not be desirable for some companies. After all, a few companies, especially new ones, expect to suffer taxable losses for a series of years. Such companies may prefer to delay as much in depreciation deductions as is permissible by using a straight-line method of cost recovery.

ACRS does allow straight-line cost recovery to be used over specified lives. For example:

TYPE OF PROPERTY	RECOVERY PERIODS AVAILABLE
3-year	3, 5, or 12 years
5-year	5, 12, or 25 years
10-year	10, 25, or 35 years

If the straight-line method is chosen, the **half-year convention** must be used: Treat all assets placed in service during the year as if they had been placed in service at the year's midpoint. Note how this convention affects our $125,000 asset with a five-year ACRS recovery period:

YEAR	ACCELERATED	STRAIGHT-LINE
1 Half-year convention applied	15%	10%
2	22	20
3	21	20
4	21	20
5	21	20
6	0	10
Total	100%	100%

[3] This deduction represents a half year's depreciation at 150% declining-balance rate: 100% ÷ 5 = 20%, 1.50 × 20% = 30%, 30% ÷ 2 = 15%.

You can readily see that accelerated depreciation generates a higher net present value. If straight-line cost recovery is used, the half-year convention extends the recovery period into the sixth year.

❑ Applying ACRS

Reconsider the data in Exhibit 12-2, page 358. Suppose the useful life of the equipment is ten years instead of five years. However, the ACRS recovery period is five years. Assume that the asset was acquired on January 2, 1984, that is, time zero is at the very start of Year 1; the asset will be disposed of after a full ten years of use. Before ACRS, the taxpayer would probably have used DDB depreciation. If so, ACRS would be welcomed because the net present value of the tax savings would be more than under DDB.

Exhibit 12-5 explains the detailed DDB and ACRS computations. ACRS produces a net present value higher than DDB of $5,138. The latter can be computed by concentrating solely on the effects of the income tax deductions ($53,357 − $48,219 = $5,138) or on the net present values ($14,877 − $9,739 = $5,138).

Focus on the major point: ACRS enhances the net present value of most acquisitions of fixed assets. Why? Because the real useful lives are ignored in favor of specified shorter recovery periods.

❑ Gains or Losses on Disposal

The impact on income taxes of the disposal of equipment for cash can be summarized as follows, using the data from our example under various assumptions. For simplicity, straight-line depreciation is assumed:

		END OF YEAR (IN DOLLARS)		
		5*	3*	3*
(a)	Cash proceeds of sale	10,000	70,000	20,000
	Book value: zero and $125,000 − 3($25,000)	0	50,000	50,000
	Gain (loss)	10,000	20,000	(30,000)
	Effect on income taxes at 60%:			
(b)	Tax saving, an inflow effect			18,000
(c)	Tax paid, an outflow	(6,000)	(12,000)	
	(a) plus (b)			38,000
	(a) minus (c)	4,000	58,000	

*ACRS does not permit a deduction for depreciation in the year of a property's disposition. Therefore, strictly speaking, these disposals would have to occur at the beginning of Years 6 and 4, respectively. For simplicity, the latter complication is not introduced in the examples or the assignment material in this book. That is, ACRS depreciation will be taken in the year of disposal.

Ponder these calculations. Note especially that the total cash inflow effect of disposal at a loss is the selling price plus the income tax savings.

The often-heard expression "What the heck, it's deductible" some-

EXHIBIT 12-5

Effects of Double-Declining-Balance Depreciation and ACRS on Present Values
(Assume same basic data as in Exhibit 12-2, page 358, except useful life is 10 years instead of 5 years.)

YEAR	INCOME TAX DEDUCTION	INCOME TAX SAVINGS AT 60%	12% DISCOUNT FACTOR	PRESENT VALUES
	Double-Declining-Balance:			
	Rate is 100% ÷ 10 years = 10%			
	2 × 10% = 20%			
1	.20 × $125,000 =	$25,000	$15,000	.893	$13,395
2	.20 × ($125,000 − $25,000) =	20,000	12,000	.797	9,564
3	.20 × ($125,000 − $25,000 − $20,000) =	16,000	9,600	.712	6,835
4	.20 × ($125,000 − $25,000 − $20,000 − $16,000) =	12,800	7,680	.636	4,884
5	.20 × ($125,000 − $25,000 − $20,000 − $16,000 − $12,800) =	10,240	6,144	.567	3,484
6	Switch to straight-line is book	8,192	4,915	.507	2,492
7	value of $40,960 ÷ 5 years =	8,192	4,915	.452	2,222
8	$8,192	8,192	4,915	.404	1,986
9		8,192	4,915	.361	1,774
10		8,192	4,915	.322	1,583
	Total present value of DDB				$48,219
	ACRS Rates from Exhibit 12-4:				
1	.15 × $125,000 =	$18,750	$11,250	.893	$10,046
2	.22 × $125,000 =	27,500	16,500	.797	13,150
3	.21 × $125,000 =	26,250	15,750	.712	11,214
4	.21 × $125,000 =	26,250	15,750	.636	10,017
5	.21 × $125,000 =	26,250	15,750	.567	8,930
	Total present value of ACRS				$53,357

Summary Computation of Net Present Values

		PRESENT VALUES	
Cash effects of operations (from Exhibit 12-2)		$ 86,520	$ 86,520
Cash effects of depreciation, income-tax savings:			
Double-declining balance (from above)		48,219	
ACRS (from above)			53,357
Total after-tax effect on cash		134,739	139,877
Investment		(125,000)	(125,000)
Net present value		$ 9,739	$ 14,877

times warps perspective. Even though losses bring income tax savings and gains bring additional income taxes, gains are still more desirable than losses. In the above tabulation, the loss would result in income tax savings of $18,000, but total cash would be increased by $38,000 as compared with the $58,000 generated by selling the asset at a $20,000 gain.[4]

❏ Income Tax Complications

In the foregoing illustrations, believe it or not, we deliberately avoided many possible income tax complications. As all taxpaying citizens know, income taxes are affected by many intricacies, including progressive tax rates, loss carrybacks and carryforwards, a variety of depreciation options, state income taxes, short- and long-term gains, distinctions between capital assets and other assets, offsets of losses against related gains, exchanges of property of like kind, exempt income, and so forth. Moreover, since the early 1970s most depreciable assets have qualified for an **investment tax credit,** which is generally an immediate income tax credit of 10% of the initial cost. This credit is a lump-sum reduction of the income tax cash outflow at time zero or in Year 1. For example, an investment of $125,000 would generate an investment tax credit that would reduce current income tax outflows by .10 × $125,000, or $12,500. Thus, net present value would increase accordingly.

Keep in mind that miscellaneous changes in the tax law occur each year. To illustrate, the investment tax credit has been suspended, reinstated, and changed in many respects through the years. For example, for assets acquired in 1983 and thereafter, the government does not permit the full acquisition cost to be recovered for tax purposes. Instead, the basis for cost recovery must be reduced by one-half of the investment tax credit.

❏ Effects of Investment Tax Credit

To see how the investment tax credit increases net present value, consider the following modification of the original investment in our example. Assume that the cost of the equipment was $131,579 instead of $125,000:

---

[4] In this case, the old equipment was sold outright. Where there is a trade-in of old equipment for new equipment of like kind, special income tax rules result in the gain or loss being added to, or deducted from, the capitalized value of the new equipment. The gain or loss is not recognized in the year of disposal; instead, it is spread over the life of the new asset as an adjustment of the new depreciation charges.

Many gains on the sale of specified assets qualify for taxation at the *capital gains* tax rate, which is currently 28% for corporations. A *capital gain* is the profit on the sale of an asset that is typically not held for resale in the ordinary course of business. Examples of such assets are investments in stocks and bonds, land, and equipment.

Before 1962, gains from disposal of equipment were taxed at the existing capital gains rate. The general rule is that gain on sale of equipment is not a capital gain except in the amount of the sales price in excess of the *original* cost. This complicates the effect on taxes of gains arising on disposal, sometimes resulting in part of the gains being taxed at ordinary income tax rates and part at capital gain rates. For simplicity, this chapter does not introduce these complications but assumes that the ordinary income tax rates apply to the entire gain or loss.

Original cost as in Exhibit 12-5, p. 364		$125,000
Original cost now assumed	$131,579	
10% investment tax credit	13,158	
Original cost less credit		$118,421
Addition to net present value		6,579
Net present value using ACRS depreciation (final number, p. 364)		14,877
Net present value after considering effect of investment tax credit		$ 21,456

The above tabulation summarizes how the investment tax credit increases the net present value by $6,579. The basis for depreciation for ACRS purposes will be $131,579 minus half the investment tax credit, or $131,579 − .5($13,158) = $125,000.[5]

In brief, the original example ignored the existence of any investment tax credit. A straightforward outlay was assumed: investment in equipment, $125,000. The modified example changed the basic facts so that a net outlay was assumed: $131,579 investment in equipment less a $13,158 investment tax credit, a net cash outlay of $118,421. Thus the net present value increases by the $6,579 difference between the $125,000 and the $118,421 net outlay.

Summary Problem for Your Review

❏ Problem One

Reconsider the data in Exhibit 12-5, page 364. Recall that the application of the Accelerated Cost Recovery System provided the following results:

	PRESENT VALUES (PV)
Cash effects of operations	$ 86,520
Cash effects of depreciation on income tax savings using ACRS	53,357
Total after-tax effect on cash	$139,877
Investment	125,000
Net present value (NPV)	$ 14,877

REQUIRED:

Consider each requirement independently.

1. Suppose the equipment was expected to be sold for $20,000 cash immediately after the end of Year 5. Compute the net present value of the investment.

---

[5] Complications abound. In our example, the taxpayer may elect to take an 8% investment tax credit (.08 × $131,579 = $10,526) instead of the 10% credit of ($13,158). By reducing the investment tax credit claimed, the cost-recovery basis of the property would remain at $131,579. For book-length coverage of these and other complications, see *Federal Tax Course* (Englewood Cliffs, N.J.: Prentice-Hall), published annually.

2. Ignore the assumption in Requirement 1. Return to the original data. Suppose the economic life of the equipment was eight years rather than five years. Compute the net present value of the investment, assuming accelerated cost recovery is used.

❏ Solution to Problem One

1. Net present value as given		$14,877
Cash proceeds of sale	$20,000	
Book value	0	
Gain	$20,000	
Income taxes at 60%	12,000	
Total after-tax effect on cash	$ 8,000	
PV of $8,000 to be received in		
5 years at 12%, $8,000 × .567		4,536
NPV of investment		$19,413
2. Net present value as given		$14,877
Add the present value of $24,000 per year for 8 years:		
Discount factor of 4.968 × $24,000 =	$119,232	
Deduct the present value of $24,000 per year for 5 years	86,520	
Increase in present value		32,712
Net present value		$47,589

The investment would be very attractive. Note especially the relationship between ACRS and the economic useful life of the asset. ACRS specifies lives (3, 5, 10, or 15 years) for various types of depreciable assets. The ACRS recovery period is unaffected by the economic useful lives of the assets. Thus the beneficial impact on net present value becomes more pronounced for an asset that before ACRS would have been depreciated over an eight-year life for tax purposes.

CONFUSION ABOUT DEPRECIATION

The meaning of depreciation and book value is widely misunderstood. Pause and consider their role in decisions. Suppose a bank has some printing equipment with a book value of $30,000, an expected terminal disposal value of zero, a current disposal value of $12,000, and a remaining useful life of three years. For simplicity, assume that straight-line depreciation of $10,000 yearly will be taken.

These data should be examined in perspective, as Exhibit 12-6 indicates. In particular, note that the inputs to the decision model are the predicted income tax effects on cash. Book values and depreciation may be necessary for making *predictions*. By themselves, however, they are not inputs to DCF decision models.

The following points summarize the role of depreciation regarding the replacement of equipment:

1. *Accounting rate-of-return model.* As Chapter 5 explained (p. 125), depreciation on old equipment is irrelevant. The total book value ($30,000 in our example) is written off regardless of whether it takes the form of a lump-sum charge

EXHIBIT 12-6   Perspective on Book Value and Depreciation

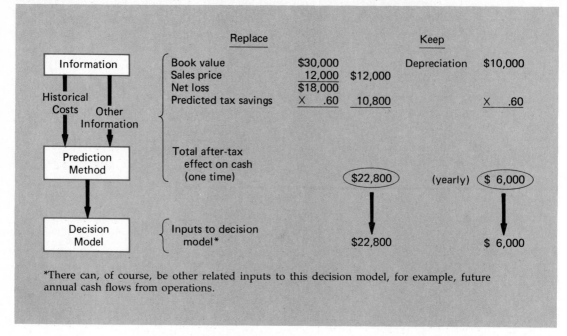

	Replace			Keep	
	Book value	$30,000		Depreciation	$10,000
	Sales price	12,000	$12,000		
	Net loss	$18,000			
	Predicted tax savings	✕ .60	10,800		✕ .60
	Total after-tax effect on cash (one time)		$22,800	(yearly)	$ 6,000
	Inputs to decision model*		$22,800		$ 6,000

*There can, of course, be other related inputs to this decision model, for example, future annual cash flows from operations.

against the $12,000 proceeds of disposal or the form of $10,000 annual depreciation. In contrast, depreciation on new equipment is relevant because it is an expected future cost that will not be incurred if replacement is rejected.

2. *Discounted-cash-flow model.* The investment in equipment is a one-time outlay at zero, so it should not be double-counted as an outlay in the form of depreciation. Depreciation by itself is irrelevant; it is not a cash outlay. However, depreciation must be considered when *predicting income tax cash outflows.*

3. *Relation to income tax cash flows.* Relevant quantities were defined in Chapter 4, page 82, as expected future data that will differ among alternatives. Given this definition, book values and past depreciation are irrelevant in all capital-budgeting decision models. The relevant item is the *income tax cash effect,* not the book value or the depreciation. Using the approach in Exhibit 12-6, the book value and depreciation are essential data for the *prediction method,* but the expected future income tax cash disbursements are the relevant data for the decision model.

CAPITAL BUDGETING AND INFLATION

❏ Watch for Consistency

Inflation may be defined as the decline in the general purchasing power of the monetary unit. Given its importance, especially in recent years, inflation should be specifically and consistently analyzed in a capital-budgeting model.

The minimum desired rate of return (the required rate or hurdle rate) can be subdivided as on page 369, using assumed percentages.

Consider an illustration: purchase cost of equipment, $200,000; useful life, 5 years; zero terminal salvage value; pretax operating cash savings per

(a) Risk-free element—the "pure" rate of interest that is paid on long-term federal bonds	4%
(b) Business-risk element—the "risk" premium that is demanded for taking larger risks	10
(a) + (b) Often called the "real rate"	14%
(c) Inflation element—the premium demanded because of expected deterioration of the general purchasing power of the monetary unit	10
(a) + (b) + (c) Often called the "nominal rate"	24%

year, $83,333 (in 19X0 dollars); income tax rate, 40%; after-tax hurdle rate, 24%, as above. For simplicity, ordinary straight-line depreciation of $200,000 ÷ 5 = $40,000 per year is assumed, and the investment tax credit is ignored.

Exhibit 12-7 displays correct and incorrect ways to analyze the effects of inflation. The key words are *internal consistency*. The correct analysis (a) uses a hurdle rate that includes a 10% element attributable to inflation, and (b) explicitly adjusts the predicted operating cash flows for the effects of inflation. Note that the correct analysis favors the purchase of the equipment, but the incorrect analysis does not.

The incorrect analysis in Exhibit 12-7 is inherently inconsistent. The predicted cash inflows *exclude* adjustments for inflation. Instead, they are stated in 19X0 dollars. However, the discount rate *includes* an element attributable to inflation. Such an analytical flaw may induce an unwise refusal to purchase.

❏ Role of Depreciation

The correct analysis in Exhibit 12-7 shows that the tax effects of depreciation are *not* adjusted for inflation. Why? Because income tax laws permit a depreciation deduction based on the 19X0 dollars invested, nothing more.

Critics of income tax laws emphasize that capital investment is discouraged by not allowing the adjusting of depreciation deductions for inflationary effects. For instance, the net present value in Exhibit 12-7 would be larger if depreciation were not confined to the $40,000 amount per year. The latter generates a $16,000 saving in 19X1 dollars, then $16,000 in 19X2 dollars, and so forth. Defenders of existing U.S. tax laws assert that capital investment is encouraged in many other ways. The most prominent examples are provisions for investment tax credits and for accelerated cost recoveries over lives that are much shorter than the economic lives of the assets.

❏ Improving Predictions and Feedback

The ability to forecast and cope with changing prices is a valuable management skill, especially when inflation is significant. In other words, price variances become more important. Auditing and feedback should help evaluate management's predictive skills.

The adjustment of the operating cash flows in Exhibit 12-7 uses a *general*-price-level index of 10%. However, where feasible use *specific* indexes or tailor-made predictions for price changes in materials, labor, and

EXHIBIT 12-7 (Place a clip on this page for easy reference.)

Inflation and Capital Budgeting

DESCRIPTION	AT 24 PERCENT PV Factor	AT 24 PERCENT Present Value	SKETCH OF RELEVANT CASH FLOWS (IN DOLLARS) 0	1	2	3	4	5
End of Year								
Correct Analysis (Be sure the discount rate includes an element attributable to inflation and adjust the predicted cash flows for inflationary effects.)								
Cash operating inflows:								
Pretax inflow in 19X0 dollars $83,333								
Income-tax effect at 40% 33,333								
After-tax effect on cash $50,000				$55,000*	$60,500	$66,550	$73,205	$80,526
	.806	$ 44,330						
	.650	39,325						
	.524	34,872						
	.423	30,966						
	.341	27,459						
Subtotal		176,952						
Annual depreciation $200,000 ÷ 5 = $40,000 Cash effect of depreciation: savings in income taxes @ 40% = $40,000 × .40 = $16,000	2.745	43,920		$16,000†	$16,000	$16,000	$16,000	$16,000
Investment in equipment	1.000	(200,000)	($200,000)					
Net present value		$ 20,872						
Incorrect Analysis (A common error is to adjust the discount rate as above, but *not* adjust the predicted cash inflows.)								
Cash operating inflows after taxes	2.745	$137,250		$50,000	$50,000	$50,000	$50,000	$50,000
Tax effect of depreciation	2.745	43,920		16,000	16,000	16,000	16,000	16,000
Investment in equipment	1.000	(200,000)	($200,000)					
Net present value		$(18,830)						

*Each year is adjusted for anticipated inflation: $50,000 × 1.10, $50,000 × 1.10², $50,000 × 1.10³, etc.

†The annual savings in income taxes from depreciation will be unaffected by inflation. Why? Because the income-tax deduction must be based on original cost of the asset in 19X0 dollars.

other items. These predictions may have different percentage changes from year to year.

The correct analysis espoused here quantifies predictions in the monetary units of the nominal dollars that will be encountered. That is, predictions for, say, 1988 will be expressed in 1988 dollars. This approach enhances understanding because accounting systems usually produce numbers in then-current dollars. In this manner, subsequent auditing of capital-budgeting decisions is eased. Moreover, the managers are more likely to be more careful about their forecasted inflation rates.[6]

Summary _____

Income taxes can have a significant effect on the desirability of an investment. An outlay for a depreciable asset should result in two streams of cash: (a) inflows from operations plus (b) savings of income tax outflows that may be analyzed as additions to cash inflows.

Accelerated depreciation and investment tax credits increase net present value. They have been heavily used by the U.S. government to encourage investments.

The correct analysis in capital budgeting provides an internally consistent analysis of inflationary aspects. For example, the required rate of return (a) should include an element attributable to anticipated inflation and (b) should specifically adjust predicted operating cash flows for the effects of inflation.

Summary Problems for Your Review _____

(Problem One appeared earlier in this chapter.)

❏ Problem Two

Examine the correct analysis in Exhibit 12-7, page 370. Suppose the cash operating inflows persisted for an extra year. Compute the present value of the inflow for the sixth year. Ignore depreciation.

❏ Problem Three

Examine Exhibit 12-5, page 364. Assume an anticipated inflation rate of 12%. How would you change the present values of depreciation under DDB and ACRS to accommodate the inflation rate?

---

[6] Another correct analysis of inflation uses "real" monetary units (real dollars) exclusively. To be internally consistent, the DCF model would use an inflation-free hurdle rate plus inflation-free operating cash flows. Using the numbers in Exhibit 12–7, the 24% hurdle rate would be lowered to exclude the expected inflation rate, the $50,000 operating cash savings in 19X0 dollars would be used in 19X1, 19X2, 19X3, and so on. Properly used, this type of analysis would lead to the same net present value as the analysis used in Exhibit 12–7. See H. Bierman and S. Smidt, *The Capital Budgeting Decision*, 5th ed. (New York: Macmillan, 1980), pp. 426–33.

❏ Solution to Problem Two

The cash operating inflow would be $50,000 × 1.10^6$, or $80,526 × 1.10$, or $88,579. Its present value would be $88,579 × .275$, the factor from Table 1 (period-6 row, 24% column), or $24,359.

❏ Solution to Problem Three

The DDB and ACRS computations in Exhibit 12-5 would not be changed. The tax effects of depreciation are unaffected by inflation. U.S. income tax laws permit a deduction based on 19X0 dollars, nothing more.

Highlights to Remember

1. Managers have an obligation to avoid income taxes. Avoidance is not evasion. *Avoidance* is the use of legal means to minimize tax payments; *evasion* is the use of illegal means. Income tax problems are often exceedingly complex, so qualified counsel should be sought whenever the slightest doubt exists.

2. When income tax rates and required rates of return are high, the attractiveness of immediate deductions heightens. Consequently, accelerated depreciation is attractive even in the face of tax rate increases in future years.

3. The after-tax impact of operating cash inflows is obtained by multiplying the inflows by 1 minus the tax rate. In contrast, the impact of depreciation on cash flows is obtained by multiplying the depreciation by the tax rate itself.

4. Inflation should be specifically accounted for in a capital-budgeting model. However, expected tax effects of depreciation should not be adjusted because they are unaffected by inflation.

Accounting Vocabulary

Accelerated Cost Recovery System (ACRS); accelerated depreciation; double-declining-balance depreciation (DDB); half-year convention; investment tax credit; tax shield.

Appendix
12: Net Present Value or Internal Rate of Return?

The net-present-value and internal rate-of-return models generally lead to the same decisions. However, sometimes the models conflict when a set of proposals is ranked for rationing a total capital budget. For example, consider the analyses in Exhibit 12-8. For simplicity, ignore income taxes. Use tables to check your understanding of the computations. For instance, the 22% rate is computed as follows:

Discount factor = $5,728 ÷ $2,000 = 2.864
Find the 5-year row in Table 2, p. 681
Scan the row to see that 2.864 is in the 22% column

EXHIBIT 12-8

Ranking of Projects

PROJECT	INVESTMENT	USEFUL LIFE IN YEARS	ANNUAL OPERATING CASH INFLOWS	RANKING		RANKING		
				Internal Rate of Return	Rank	Present Value of Cash Inflows at 10% Hurdle Rate	Net Present Value Amount	Net Present Value Rank
A	$ 5,728	5	$2,000	22%	1	$ 7,582	$1,854	3
B	8,384	10	2,000	20%	2	12,290	3,906	2
C	10,184	15	2,000	18%	3	15,212	5,028	1

Which model is preferable? In principle, the net-present-value model is superior in all instances. Why? Basically because a percentage is inappropriate for discriminating between projects of different sizes.[7] This phenomenon can be clarified by comparing the implicit assumptions made with respect to *rate of return on the reinvestment* of the cash proceeds at the end of the shorter investment's life:

1. The internal rate-of-return model assumes that the reinvestment rate equals the indicated rate of return for the shorter-lived project. Consider how wealth accumulates for Project A:

> Years 1–5, $2,000 per year for 5 years @ 22%
> will accumulate to 2,000 × (1.22)^5 = $15,480
> Years 6–15, $15,480 invested at 22% from 6th
> through 15th year, or $15,480 × (1.22)^{10} = $113,082

2. The net-present-value method assumes that the Project A amount at the end of the fifth year can be reinvested to earn only the *10% required rate of return*:

> Years 1–5, as before, $15,480
> Years 6–15, $15,480 invested at 10% from
> 6th through 15th year, or $15,480 × (1.10)^{10} = $40,156

How can we reconcile these approaches? There is a need for a common terminal date and for explicit assumptions as to the appropriate reinvestment rates for *all* the funds available throughout the lives of the projects. The valid comparisons are fundamentally not between projects but between various courses and combinations of actions.

The rationing of capital is widely followed in practice. But adhering to a fixed ceiling has been widely criticized. For example:

☐ Capital rationing usually results in an investment policy that is less than optimal. In some periods, the firm accepts projects down to its required rate of return; in others, it rejects projects that would provide returns substantially in excess of the required rate. . . . In the final analysis, the firm should accept all proposals yielding more than their required rates of return.[8]

Assignment Material

Special note: Throughout this assignment material, *unless directed otherwise*, assume that

1. All income tax cash flows occur simultaneously with the pretax cash flows
2. Where ACRS is specified, the straight-line option is *not* chosen
3. The companies in question will have enough taxable income from other sources to utilize all income tax benefits from the situations described
4. The investment tax credit can be ignored

[7] S. Keane, "Let's Scrap IRR Once for All," *Accounting*, February 1974, pp. 78–82, uses a series of examples to show that all projects have different sizes unless they have identical initial outlays *and* operating cash flows.

[8] J. Van Horne, *Financial Management and Policy*, 6th ed. (Englewood Cliffs, N.J.: Prentice-Hall, 1983), p. 126. For more discussion of unequal lives, capital rationing, and the merits of net present values versus internal rates of return, see pages 123–26 of Van Horne's book.

Fundamental
Assignment Material _____

12–1. Straight-line depreciation and present values. (Alternate is 12–30.) The president of an electronics company is contemplating acquiring some equipment used for research and development. The equipment will cost $150,000 cash and will have a three-year useful life and zero terminal salvage value. Annual pretax cash savings from operations will be $75,000. The income tax rate is 40%, and the required after-tax rate of return is 16%.

REQUIRED:

1. Compute the net present value, assuming straight-line depreciation of $50,000 yearly. Ignore the investment tax credit.
2. Suppose the asset will be fully depreciated at the end of Year 3, but its disposal value will be $15,000. Compute the net present value. Show computations.
3. Ignore Requirement 2. Suppose the required after-tax rate of return is 12% instead of 16%. Should the equipment be acquired? Show computations.

12–2. ACRS and present values. (Alternate is 12–31.) The president of Chavez Company is considering whether to buy some equipment for the research department. The equipment will cost $150,000 cash and will have a three-year useful life and zero terminal salvage value. Annual pretax cash savings from operations will be $75,000. The income tax rate is 40%, and the required after-tax rate of return is 16%.

REQUIRED:

1. Compute the net present value, assuming ACRS basis of accelerated cost recovery. Should the equipment be acquired? Ignore the investment tax credit.
2. Suppose the economic life of the equipment is four years, which means that there will be $75,000 additional cash savings from operations in the fourth year. Assume ACRS is used. Should the equipment be acquired? Show computations.

12–3. Gains or losses on disposal. (Alternate is 12–32.) An asset with a book value of $40,000 was sold for cash on January 1, 19X6.

REQUIRED:

Assume two selling prices: $50,000 and $25,000. For each selling price, prepare a tabulation of the gain or loss, the effect on income taxes, and the total after-tax effect on cash. The applicable income tax rate is 40%.

12–4. Investment tax credit. (Alternate is 12–33.) Assume that factory equipment is acquired for $200,000 cash. A related 10% investment tax credit is taken.

REQUIRED:

1. Fill in the blanks:

	TOTAL PRESENT VALUE
Acquisition of equipment	$_____
Investment tax credit	$_____

2. What cost of equipment may be used for cost-recovery purposes under ACRS? Explain.

12–5. Inflation and capital budgeting. (Alternate is 12–44.) A manager is contemplating buying equipment: acquisition cost, $90,000; useful life, five years;

zero terminal salvage value; pretax operating cash savings per year, $38,000 in 19X0 dollars; income tax rate, 40%; after-tax hurdle rate, 22%, which includes a 12% element attributable to inflation.

For simplicity, assume ordinary straight-line depreciation of $90,000 ÷ 5 = $18,000 per year. Ignore the investment tax credit.

REQUIRED:

1. Compute the net present value of the equipment by adjusting the $38,000 operating cash flows for inflation, using a 12% rate.
2. Compute the net present value of the equipment by not adjusting the operating cash flows for inflation.
3. Compare your answers in Requirements 1 and 2. What generalizations about capital budgeting and inflation seem warranted?

Additional Assignment Material

12-6. Explain why accelerated depreciation methods are superior to straight-line methods for income tax purposes.

12-7. "Immediate disposal of equipment, rather than its continued use, results in a full tax deduction of the undepreciated cost now—rather than having such a deduction spread over future years in the form of annual depreciation." Do you agree? Explain, using the $30,000 cost of old equipment in Exhibit 12-6, page 368, as a basis for your discussion.

12-8. Name some income tax complications that were ignored in the illustrations in this chapter.

12-9. Distinguish between tax avoidance and tax evasion.

12-10. "Tax planning is unimportant because the total income tax bill will be the same in the long run, regardless of short-run maneuvering." Do you agree? Explain.

12-11. What are the major influences on the present value of a tax deduction?

12-12. Is *tax shield* an apt term for describing depreciation for tax purposes? Why?

12-13. "An investment in equipment really buys two streams of cash." Do you agree? Explain.

12-14. "If income tax rates do not change through the years, my total tax payments will be the same. Therefore I really do not care what depreciation schedule is permitted." Do you agree? Explain.

12-15. Is double-declining-balance depreciation permitted in the United States for tax purposes? Explain.

12-16. "ACRS does not allow straight-line depreciation." Do you agree? Explain.

12-17. Accelerated depreciation can take many forms. Describe two.

12-18. ACRS provides two types of acceleration. Identify them.

12-19. "The ACRS half-year convention causes assets to be depreciated beyond the lives specified in the ACRS recovery schedules." Do you agree? Explain.

12-20. Describe how internal consistency is achieved when considering inflation in a capital-budgeting model.

12-21. Explain how U.S. tax laws fail to adjust for inflation.

12-22. Role of depreciation in decision models. A student of management accounting complained, "I'm confused about how depreciation relates to decisions.

For example, Chapter 5 says that depreciation on old equipment is irrelevant, but depreciation on new equipment is relevant. Chapter 11 said that depreciation was irrelevant in discounted-cash-flow models, but Chapter 12 shows the relevance of depreciation."

REQUIRED: | Prepare a careful explanation that will eliminate the student's confusion.

12–23. **Depreciation, income taxes, cash flows.** Fill in the unknowns (in thousands of dollars):

(S)	Sales	500
(E)	Expenses excluding depreciation	300
(D)	Depreciation	100
	Total expenses	400
	Income before income taxes	?
(T)	Income taxes at 40%	?
(I)	Net income	?
	Cash effects of operations:	
	Cash inflow from operations	?
	Income tax outflow at 40%	?
	After-tax inflow from operations	?
	Effect of depreciation:	
	Depreciation, $100	
	Income tax savings	?
	Total after-tax effect on cash	?

12–24. **Depreciation, income taxes, cash flows.** Fill in the unknowns (in thousands of dollars):

(S)	Sales	?
(E)	Expenses excluding depreciation	?
(D)	Depreciation	200
	Total expenses	900
	Income before income taxes	?
(T)	Income taxes at 40%	?
(I)	Net income	300
	Cash effects of operations:	
	Cash inflow from operations	?
	Income tax outflow at 40%	?
	After-tax inflow from operations	?
	Effect of depreciation:	
	Depreciation, $200	
	Income tax savings	?
	Total after-tax effect on cash	?

12–25. **Nature of investment tax credit.**

1. "An investment tax credit of $100,000 saves income taxes by $100,000 multiplied by the applicable income tax rate." Do you agree? Explain.
2. "New equipment cost $800,000 cash. There was an investment tax credit of $80,000. Consequently, $720,000, less the estimated disposal value, is deductible in the form of yearly depreciation for income tax purposes." Do you agree? Explain.

12–26. ACRS recovery periods. Consider the following business assets: (1) a heavy-duty truck, (2) an office word processor, (3) a commercial building, (4) an industrial packaging machine, and (5) an electron microscope used in industrial research. What is the recovery period for each of these assets under the prescribed ACRS method?

12–27. ACRS depreciation. Federal Express Corporation provides overnight delivery of packages throughout the United States. Consider a light-duty van acquired for $18,000. Using the prescribed ACRS method, compute the depreciation deduction for tax purposes for each of three years. Ignore the investment tax credit.

12–28. ACRS depreciation. Consider the following acquisitions of business assets on October 1, 1984: (1) office furniture, $3,000; (2) light truck, $16,000; and (3) production machinery, $30,000. For each asset, compute the depreciation for tax purposes for 1984 and 1985, as prescribed by ACRS. Ignore the investment tax credit.

12–29. ACRS depreciation. In 1984 the Arnosti Manufacturing Company acquired the following assets and immediately placed them into service:

1. A factory building that cost $30 million
2. A desk-top computer that cost $10,000
3. Special calibration equipment that was used in research and development and cost $5,000
4. An office desk that cost $2,000 but was sold sixteen months later

REQUIRED:

Compute the depreciation for tax purposes, under the prescribed ACRS method in 1984 and 1985. Assume that the building was acquired on January 3, 1984, and that all other assets were acquired on March 1, 1984. Ignore the investment tax credit.

12–30. Straight-line depreciation and present values. (Alternate is 12–1.) Equipment could be acquired for $200,000 cash; five-year life; zero terminal disposal value; annual pretax cash inflow from operations, $80,000; income tax rate, 60%; required after-tax rate of return, 14%.

REQUIRED:

1. Compute the net present value, assuming straight-line depreciation of $40,000 yearly. Should the equipment be acquired? For simplicity, ignore the half-year convention; that is, take a full year's depreciation each year. Ignore the investment tax credit.
2. Suppose the asset will be fully depreciated at the end of Year 5 but its disposal value will be $20,000. Assume that a full year's depreciation is taken in the fifth year. Should the equipment be acquired? Show computations.
3. Ignore Requirement 2. Suppose the required after-tax rate of return is 10% instead of 14%. Should the equipment be acquired? Show computations.

12–31. ACRS and present values. (Alternate is 12–2.) Suppose equipment could be acquired for $200,000 cash on January 2, 19X1 (time zero); five-year life; zero terminal disposal value; annual pretax cash inflow from operations, $80,000; income tax rate, 60%; required after-tax rate of return, 14%.

REQUIRED:

1. Compute the net present value, assuming ACRS basis of accelerated cost recovery. Should the equipment be acquired? Ignore the investment tax credit.
2. Suppose the economic life of the equipment is six years, which means that there will be $80,000 cash inflow from operations in the sixth year. Assume ACRS is used. Should the equipment be acquired? Show computations.

12–32. Income taxes and disposal of assets. (Alternate is 12–3.) Assume that income tax rates are 60%.

1. The book value of an old machine is $20,000. It is to be sold for $8,000 cash. What is the effect of this decision on cash flows, after taxes?
2. The book value of an old machine is $10,000. It is to be sold for $13,000 cash. What is the effect on cash flows, after taxes, of this decision?

12–33. Investment tax credit. (Alternate is 12–4.) A trucking company has acquired a fleet of heavy-duty trucks for $500,000 cash. A related 10% investment tax credit has been taken. The required rate of return is 18% after taxes.

REQUIRED:

1. Describe the effects of the above data on net present value. Be specific.
2. What cost of equipment can be used for cost-recovery purposes under ACRS? Explain.

12–34. Football coaching contract. (H. Schaefer.) Bo Hays, a successful college football coach, has just signed a "million-dollar-plus" contract to coach a new professional team. The contract is a personal services contract for five years with the team's owner, I. M. Rich (if the team is disbanded Bo can still collect from Rich). Under the terms of the contract, Bo will be paid $150,000 cash at the start of the contract plus $150,000 at the end of each of the five years. Rich also agrees to buy a $200,000 house that Bo can use rent-free for all five years.

Rich earns a substantial income from numerous business ventures. His marginal tax rate is about 60%. Bo's cash salary payments are tax deductible to Rich, as are the depreciation expenses on the house. Rich decides to depreciate the house over a twenty-year life with zero salvage value using the straight-line method of depreciation. Rich is certain the house can be sold at the end of five years for a price equal to its remaining book value. For simplicity, assume that ordinary straight-line depreciation (ignoring the half-year convention) is permissible for tax purposes. Ignore the investment tax credit.

REQUIRED:

1. Determine Rich's yearly after-tax cash flows under Bo's contract.
2. Given your answers to Requirement 1, calculate the net present value of the costs of Bo's contract to Rich, assuming Rich employs a 10% minimum desired rate of return. Show your calculations clearly and in an orderly fashion. You may round to the nearest thousand dollars.

12–35. Present value of after-tax cash flows. Rose Optometrics, Inc., is planning to buy new equipment to produce a new product. Estimated data are:

Cash cost of new equipment now	$400,000
Estimated life in years	10
Terminal salvage value	$ 50,000
Incremental revenues per year	$300,000
Incremental expenses per year other than depreciation	$165,000

Use the straight-line method for depreciation and assume a 60% flat rate for income taxes. All revenue and expenses other than depreciation will be received or paid in cash. Use a 14% discount rate. For simplicity, assume that ordinary straight-line depreciation (ignoring the half-year convention) based on a ten-year useful life is permissible for tax purposes. Ignore the investment tax credit. Also assume that the terminal salvage value will affect the depreciation per year. Ignore the investment tax credit.

Compute:

1. Depreciation expense per year
2. Anticipated net income per year
3. Annual net cash inflow
4. Payback period
5. Accounting rate of return on initial investment
6. Net present value

12–36. ACRS and replacement of equipment. Refer to Problem 5–33, page 143. Assume that income tax rates are 60%. The minimum desired rate of return, after taxes, is 6%. Using the net-present-value technique, show whether the proposed equipment should be purchased. Present your solution on both a total project approach and an incremental approach. For illustrative purposes, assume that the old equipment would have been depreciated on a straight-line basis and the proposed equipment on an ACRS basis of accelerated cost recovery. Assume that the equipment is used for research and development.

12–37. ACRS, residual value. The Flan Company estimates that it can save $2,500 per year in annual operating cash costs for the next five years if it buys a special-purpose machine at a cost of $9,000. Residual value is expected to be $900, although no residual value is being provided for in using ACRS (five-year life and accelerated depreciation) for tax purposes. The equipment will be sold at the beginning of the sixth year; for purposes of this analysis assume that the proceeds are received at the end of the fifth year. The minimum desired rate of return, after taxes, is 10%. Assume the income tax rate is 40%.

REQUIRED:

1. Using the net-present-value model, show whether the investment is desirable. Ignore the investment tax credit.
2. Suppose the equipment will produce savings for six years instead of five. Residual value is expected to be the same a year later. Using the net-present-value model, show whether the investment is desirable.

12–38. Purchase of equipment. The O'Hara Company is planning to spend $40,000 for a specialized machine for research on electronic components. The machine is expected to save $13,500 in cash operating costs for each of the next four years. A major overhaul costing $4,000 will occur at the end of the second year and is fully deductible in that year for income tax purposes.

The expected terminal value is $3,000, but no terminal value is being provided for in using ACRS depreciation for tax purposes.

The minimum desired rate of return after taxes is 12%. The applicable income tax rate is 60%. Use an ACRS basis of accelerated cost recovery and a three-year recovery period.

REQUIRED:

1. Using the net-present-value model, show whether the investment is desirable.
2. Suppose an investment tax credit of 6% were available on all new assets acquired having ACRS lives of three years. Would your answer in Requirement 1 change? Explain, assuming that depreciation will not be affected by the tax credit.

12–39. Minimizing transportation costs. The Wriston Company produces industrial and residential lighting fixtures at its manufacturing facility located in Los Angeles. Shipment of company products to an eastern warehouse is presently handled by common carriers at a rate of 20¢ per pound of fixtures. The warehouse is located in Cleveland, 2,500 miles from Los Angeles.

The treasurer of Wriston Company is presently considering whether to purchase a truck for transporting products to the eastern warehouse. The following data on the truck are available:

Purchase price	$50,000
Useful life	5 years
Terminal residual value	zero
Capacity of truck	10,000 lbs.
Cash costs of operating truck	$.80 per mile

The treasurer feels that an investment in this truck is particularly attractive because of his successful negotiation with X Company to back-haul X's products from Cleveland to Los Angeles on every return trip from the warehouse. X has agreed to pay Wriston $2,400 per load of X's products hauled from Cleveland to Los Angeles up to and including 100 loads per year.

Wriston's marketing manager has estimated that 500,000 pounds of fixtures will have to be shipped to the eastern warehouse each year for the next five years. The truck will be fully loaded on each round trip.

Make the following assumptions:

a. Wriston requires a minimum 10% after-tax rate of return.
b. A 40% tax rate.
c. ACRS based on five-year life and accelerated cost recovery.
d. No investment tax credit.

REQUIRED:

1. Should the truck be purchased? Show computations to support your answer.
2. What qualitative factors might influence your decision? Be specific.

12–40. ACRS, disposal value, tax credit. (CMA.) Lamb Company manufactures several lines of machine products. One unique part, a valve stem, requires specialized tools that need to be replaced. Management has decided that the only alternative to replacing these tools is to acquire the valve stem from an outside source. A supplier is willing to provide the valve stem at a unit sales price of $20 provided at least 70,000 units are ordered annually.

Lamb's average usage of valve stems over the past three years has been 80,000 units each year. Expectations are that this volume will remain constant over the next five years. Cost records indicate that unit manufacturing costs for the last several years have been as follows:

Direct material	$ 3.80
Direct labor	3.70
Variable overhead	1.70
Fixed overhead*	4.50
Total unit cost	$13.70

*Depreciation accounts for two-thirds of the fixed overhead. The balance is for other fixed overhead costs of the factory that require cash expenditures.

If the specialized tools are purchased, they will cost $2,500,000 and will have a disposal value of $100,000 after their expected economic life of five years. Straight-line depreciation is used for book purposes, but ACRS is used for tax purposes. The specialized tools are considered three-year property for ACRS purposes; the applicable ACRS rates for the next three years are 25%, 38%, and 37%, respectively. The tools qualify for investment tax credit. Lamb has elected to use the 4% investment tax credit and not reduce the asset basis for ACRS. The company has a 40% marginal tax rate, and management requires a 12% after-tax return on investment.

The sales representative for the manufacture of the new tools stated, "The new tools will allow direct labor and variable overhead to be reduced by $1.60 per unit." Data from another manufacturer using identical tools and experiencing similar operating conditions, except that annual production generally averages 110,000 units, confirms the direct-labor and variable-overhead savings. However, the manufacturer indicates that it experienced an increase in raw material cost due to the higher quality of material that had to be used with the new tools. The manufacturer indicated that its costs have been as follows:

Direct material	$ 4.50
Direct labor	3.00
Variable overhead	.80
Fixed overhead	5.00
Total unit cost	$13.30

REQUIRED:

1. Present a discounted-cash-flow analysis covering the economic life of the new specialized tools to determine whether Lamb Company should replace the old tools or purchase the valve stem from an outside supplier. Give consideration to all typical tax implications. The present value factors for 12% are presented below.

PERIOD	PRESENT VALUE OF $1.00 RECEIVED AT END OF PERIOD	PRESENT VALUE OF ANNUITY OF $1.00 RECEIVED AT END OF EACH PERIOD
1	.89	.89
2	.80	1.69
3	.71	2.40
4	.64	3.04
5	.57	3.61

2. Identify additional factors Lamb Company should consider before a decision is made to replace the tools or purchase the valve stem from an outside supplier.

12–41. **Unequal lives and ranking.** Study Appendix 12. A hospital manager is pondering the following data regarding some diagnostic equipment that is mutually exclusive. That is, the manager will buy only one set of equipment.

PROJECT	INVESTMENT	LIFE	ANNUAL OPERATING CASH INFLOWS
A	$2,864	5	$1,000
B	4,192	10	1,000
C	5,092	15	1,000

REQUIRED:

1. Compute the internal rate of return of each project.
2. Assuming a 10% hurdle rate, compute the net present value of each project.
3. Explain why the rankings of the projects differ depending on which discounted-cash-flow model is used.

12–42. Unequal lives and ranking. Study Appendix 12. The manager of the Good Shepherd Hospital is about to decide which one of two competing research projects to support. The required rate of return is 10%. Other data follow:

PROJECT	INVESTMENT	OPERATING CASH INFLOWS FOR YEAR			
		1	2	3	4
A	$20,000	$24,000	0	0	0
B	20,000	0	0	0	$35,000

REQUIRED:
1. Compute the net present value of each project.
2. Compute the internal rate of return of each project.
3. Compare the results in Requirements 1 and 2. Why do they differ?

12–43. Inflation and nonprofit institution. A hospital is considering the purchase of a photocopying machine for $7,000 on December 31, 19X0, useful life five years, and no residual value. The cash operating savings are expected to be $2,000 annually, measured in 19X0 dollars.

The hurdle rate is 20%, which includes an element attributable to anticipated inflation of 12%.

REQUIRED:
Use the 20% hurdle rate for Requirements 1 and 2:

1. Compute the net present value of the project without adjusting the cash operating savings for inflation.
2. Repeat Requirement 1, adjusting the cash operating savings upward in accordance with the 12% inflation rate.
3. Compare your results in Requirements 1 and 2. What generalizations seem applicable about the analysis of inflation in capital budgeting?

12–44. Sensitivity of capital budgeting to inflation. (Alternate is 12-5.) G. Putnam, the president of a London trucking company, is considering whether to invest £205,000 in new semiautomatic loading equipment that will last five years, have zero scrap value, and generate cash operating savings in labor usage of £80,000 annually, using 19X0 prices and wage rates. It is December 31, 19X0. The minimum desired rate of return is 18% per year after taxes.

REQUIRED:
1. Compute the net present value of the project. Assume a 40% tax rate and ordinary straight-line depreciation of £205,000 ÷ 5 = £41,000 annually.
2. Putnam is wondering if the model in Requirement 1 provides a correct analysis of the effects of inflation. She maintains that the 18% rate embodies an element attributable to anticipated inflation. For purposes of this analysis, she assumes that the existing rate of inflation, 10% annually, will persist over the next five years. Repeat Requirement 1, adjusting the cash operating savings upward in accordance with the 10% inflation rate.
3. What generalizations about the effects of inflation on capital-budgeting models and decisions seem warranted?

12–45. Approaches to inflation. (CMA, adapted.) Catix Corporation is a divisionalized company, and each division has the authority to make capital expenditures up to $200,000 without approval of the corporate headquarters. The corporate controller has determined that the cost of capital for Catix Corporation is 21%. This rate includes an allowance for inflation, which is expected to occur at an average rate of 8% over the next five years. Catix pays income taxes at the rate of 40%.

The Electronics Division of Catix is considering the purchase of an automated assembly and soldering machine for use in the manufacture of its printed circuit boards. The machine would be placed in service in early 1981. The divisional controller estimates that if the machine is purchased, two positions will be eliminated yielding a cost savings for wages and employee benefits. However, the machine would require additional supplies, and more power would be required to operate the machine. The cost savings and additional costs in current 1980 prices are as follows:

Wages and employee benefits of the two positions eliminated ($25,000 each)	$50,000
Cost of additional supplies	$ 3,000
Cost of additional power	$10,000

The new machine would be purchased and installed at the end of 1980 at a net cost of $80,000. If purchased, the machine would be depreciated on a straight-line basis at $20,000 per year for both book and tax purposes. The machine will become technologically obsolete in four years and will have no salvage value at that time.

The Electronics Division compensates for inflation in capital expenditure analyses by adjusting the expected cash flows by an estimated price-level index. The adjusted after-tax cash flows are then discounted using the appropriate discount rate. The estimated year-end index values for each of the next five years are presented below.

YEAR	YEAR-END PRICE INDEX
1980	1.00
1981	1.08
1982	1.17
1983	1.26
1984	1.36
1985	1.47

The Plastics Division of Catix compensates for inflation in capital expenditure analyses by using the inflation-adjusted cost of capital (21%) to discount the project cash flows. The Plastics Division recently rejected a project with cash flows and economic life similar to those associated with the machine under consideration by the Electronics Division. The Plastics Division's analysis of the rejected project was as follows:

Net pretax cost savings	$37,000
Less incremental depreciation expenses	20,000
Increase in taxable income	$17,000
Increase in income taxes (40%)	6,800
Increase in after-tax income	$10,200
Add back noncash expense (depreciation)	20,000
Net after-tax annual cash inflow (unadjusted for inflation)	$30,200
Present value of net cash inflows using a minimum required return of 21%	$76,708
Investment required	(80,000)
Net present value	$ (3,292)

All operating revenues and expenditures occur at the end of the year. Appropriate 21% discount factors follow:

	END OF PERIOD				
	1	2	3	4	5
Single payment	0.83	.68	.56	.47	.39
Annuity	0.83	1.51	2.07	2.54	2.93

REQUIRED:

1. Using the price index provided, prepare a schedule showing the net after-tax annual cash flows adjusted for inflation for the automated assembly and soldering machine under consideration by the Electronics Division.
2. Without prejudice to your answer to Requirement 1, assume that the net after-tax annual cash flows adjusted for inflation for the project being considered by the Electronics Division are as follows:

	1981	1982	1983	1984
Net after-tax annual cash flow adjusted for inflation	$30,000	$35,000	$37,000	$40,000

Calculate the net present value for Electronic Division's project which will be meaningful to management.

3. Evaluate the methods used by the Plastics Division and the Electronics Division to compensate for expected inflation in capital expenditure analyses.

13

PROCESS-COSTING SYSTEMS

Learning Objectives

When you have finished studying this chapter, you should be able to

1. Explain the basic ideas underlying process costing, particularly the expression of output in terms of **equivalent units**
2. Demonstrate how the presence of beginning inventories affects the computations of unit costs under the first-in, first-out and weighted-average methods
3. Compute costs and prepare journal entries for the principal transactions in a process-costing system

Cost-accounting systems have a twofold purpose fulfilled by their day-to-day operations: (1) allocate costs to departments for *planning and control,* and (2) allocate costs to units of product for *product costing.* This is the first of three chapters that emphasize how product costing is accomplished.

THIS CHAPTER MAY BE STUDIED IMMEDIATELY AFTER CHAPTER 3 OR AFTER CHAPTER 14. THE THREE MAJOR PARTS OF THIS CHAPTER MAY BE STUDIED INDEPENDENTLY. INSTRUCTORS WHO PREFER TO FOCUS ON JOB-ORDER COSTING MAY OMIT THIS CHAPTER OR CONFINE THEIR COVERAGE TO THE FIRST MAJOR PART.

❏ PART ONE Introduction to Process Costing

JOB-ORDER AND PROCESS COSTING

The detailed procedures for allocating costs to products vary considerably from industry to industry and company to company. Two contrasting forms of product costing are **job-order costing** and **process costing.** Their principal difference centers on the type of products that are the cost objectives. Job-order costing is found in industries such as printing, construction, and furniture manufacturing, where each unit or batch (job) of product tends to be unique and easily identifiable. Process costing is found where there is mass production of identical units through a sequence of several processes, such as mixing and cooking. Examples include flour, glass, and paint. To see the major difference between job-order costing and process costing, visualize the detail that might support the work-in-process inventory, as diagramed in Exhibit 13-1.

The process-costing approach is less concerned with distinguishing among individual units of product. Instead, accumulated costs for a period, say a month, are divided by quantities produced during that period in order to get broad, average unit costs. Process costing may be adopted in nonmanufacturing activities as well as in manufacturing activities. Examples include dividing the costs of giving state automobile driver's license tests by the number of tests given and dividing the costs of an X-ray department by the number of X-rays processed.

❏ Equivalent Units

Assume that a company produces hand-held calculators in large quantities. Suppose the assembly department produced 1 million units during the year. The manufacturing costs of the assembly department were:

Direct materials added		$ 890,000
Conversion costs:		
Direct labor	$171,000	
Factory overhead	114,000	285,000
Assembly costs to account for		$1,175,000

EXHIBIT
13-1
Comparison
of Job-Order
and Process
Costing

For job-order costing:

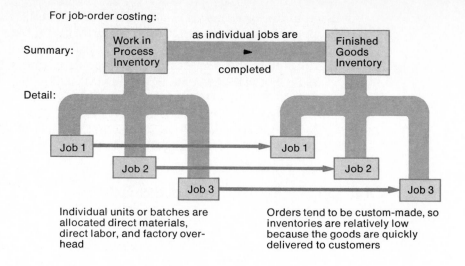

Individual units or batches are allocated direct materials, direct labor, and factory overhead

Orders tend to be custom-made, so inventories are relatively low because the goods are quickly delivered to customers

For process costing:

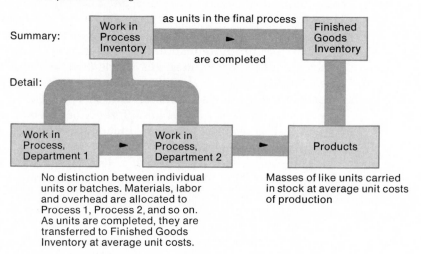

No distinction between individual units or batches. Materials, labor and overhead are allocated to Process 1, Process 2, and so on. As units are completed, they are transferred to Finished Goods Inventory at average unit costs.

Masses of like units carried in stock at average unit costs of production

The unit cost of goods completed would simply be the total cost of $1,175,000 \div 1,000,000$, or $1.175.

The major difficulty in process costing is applying costs to incompleted products—goods still in process at the end of the accounting period. For example, suppose 100,000 calculators were still in process at year-end; only 900,000 were started and completed. All the parts had been made or requisitioned, but only half of the assembly labor had been completed for each of the 100,000 calculators.

What was the output for the year? An obvious answer would be 900,000 completed units plus 100,000 half-completed units. But we should hesitate to express the sum of the output as 1 million units. Why? Because each of the partially completed units is not a perfect substitute for a completed unit. Therefore we express output not as *physical* units, but as *equivalent* units.

Equivalent units is the expression of output in terms of *doses* or *amounts* of resources applied thereto. That is, an equivalent unit is viewed as a collection of work applications necessary to produce one complete physical unit of output. In other words, an equivalent unit is a measure of the factors of production—direct materials, direct labor, and factory overhead.

Recall that direct labor plus factory overhead is called conversion costs. In terms of equivalent units of conversion costs, the ending work in process of 100,000 units half completed is equivalent to 50,000 units of work accomplished. In a like manner, an ending work in process of 750 units two-thirds completed is equivalent to 500 units of work accomplished.

The idea of equivalent units extends to all types of organizations, even though the terminology differs. For example, clinical laboratories often measure volume in terms of weight units. A *weight unit* is an arbitrary unit by which various lab procedures are ranked in terms of the relative combination of labor, supplies, and related costs devoted to each. For instance, a procedure with a weight of two is deemed to use twice the resources as a procedure with a weight of one. An average cost per weight unit is developed, which is then multiplied by the average number of weight units per laboratory procedure to obtain an average unit cost for each laboratory procedure. Radiology departments use a similar "process costing" system. For another example, the beer industry translates its productions into equivalent barrels, even though its output is in the form of various sizes of kegs, cans, and bottles.

❑ Illustration of Process Costing

To illustrate basic process costing, consider how equivalent units are used to compute the product costs of the assembly department.

Example 1

FLOW OF PRODUCTION	PHYSICAL UNITS	EQUIVALENT UNITS DIRECT MATERIALS	EQUIVALENT UNITS CONVERSION COSTS
Started and completed	900,000	900,000	900,000
Work in process, ending inventory	100,000		
Materials added: 100,000 × 1		100,000	
Conversion costs: 100,000 × 1/2			50,000
Units accounted for	1,000,000		
Total work done		1,000,000	950,000
Costs to account for ($1,175,000):			
Direct materials added		$890,000	
Conversion costs ($171,000 + $114,000)			$285,000
Divide by equivalent units		1,000,000	950,000
Unit costs added in assembly		$.89	$.30

The unit costs are used to apply costs to products:

To units completed and transferred to finished goods:		
900,000 × ($.89 + $.30) =		$1,071,000
To units not completed and still in work in process:		
Direct materials, 100,000 × $.89 =	$89,000	
Conversion costs, 50,000 × $.30 =	15,000	104,000
Total costs accounted for		$1,175,000

As indicated in Exhibit 13-1, the general approach to process costing can be diagramed, assuming that there are two sequential departments, fabricating and assembly:

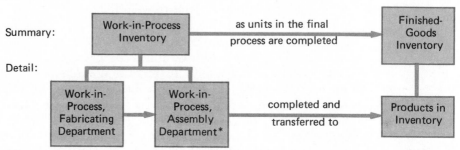

*Assembly department costs of $1,071,000 added to the cost of products completed and transferred to finished-goods inventory. Ending work in process in assembly includes $104,000 of the assembly department's costs.

As you might expect, each manufacturing company develops its own hybrid accounting system to suit its own desires. For example, many companies have so-called **operation costing** systems. In these systems, distinctions are made between batches of product, such as Model A calculators and Model B calculators. Materials are specifically allocated to the batches. Conversion costs are computed for each operation. The final costs of Model A and Model B depend on their particular material components plus what operations were conducted in their manufacture. Obviously, the more materials and the more operations undergone, the more costs are applied to the specific product.[1]

☐ PART TWO Effects of Beginning Inventories

FIVE KEY STEPS

Consider a second example.

[1] For an expanded discussion of operation costing, see Charles T. Horngren, *Cost Accounting: A Managerial Emphasis*, 5th ed. (Englewood Cliffs, N.J.: Prentice-Hall, 1982), pp. 569–74.

Example 2

The Gustavo Company has a fabricating process for cotton textiles. Material is introduced at the beginning of the process in Department A. Conversion costs are applied uniformly throughout the process. As the process is completed, goods are immediately transferred to a finishing process in Department B. Data for the month of April 19X1 follow:

Work in process, beginning inventory	10,000 units, 40% converted,* $64,400 (materials, $51,000; conversion costs, $13,400)
Units started during April	60,000
Units completed during April	30,000
Work in process, ending inventory	40,000 units, 60% converted*
Material cost added during April	$600,000
Conversion costs added during April	$100,000

*Converted means that each unit in process at the inventory date is regarded as being fractionally complete with respect to the conversion costs of the present department only.

Production was inefficient in March. In April severe material price increases occurred. Demand was increasing, so the company began to increase its inventories.

REQUIRED: Compute the cost of goods transferred out of the department during April. Compute the costs of the ending inventory of work in process. Assume (a) first-in, first-out product costing and (b) weighted-average product costing.

Five major steps in accounting for process costs will be described:

Step 1: Summarize physical units
Step 2: Compute output in terms of equivalent units
Step 3: Summarize the total costs to account for, which are the total debits in Work in Process
Step 4: Compute unit costs
Step 5: Compute total costs of work completed and in process

Although shortcuts are sometimes taken, the methodical procession through each of the five steps minimizes error. The first two steps concentrate on what is occurring in physical or engineering terms. The financial impact of the production process is measured in the final three steps.

☐ Step 1: Summarize Physical Units

Step 1 traces the physical units of production. (Where did units come from? Where did they go?) In other words, (a) what are the units to account for? and (b) how are they accounted for? Draw flow charts as a preliminary step, if necessary. Exhibit 13-2 shows these relationships, which may also be expressed as an equation:

beginning inventories + units started = units transferred + ending inventories

The total of the left side of the equation is shown as the units to account for: 10,000 + 60,000 = 70,000 in Exhibit 13-2. The total of the right side is shown as the units accounted for: 10,000 + 20,000 + 40,000 = 70,000 in Exhibit 13-2.

There are 10,000 physical units in process at the start of the period. In addition, 60,000 units were begun during the current period. Of the total of 10,000 + 60,000 = 70,000 units to account for, 40,000 units remained in process at the end of the period. Therefore, 30,000 units were completed during the period, consisting of the 10,000 units from the beginning work in process plus 20,000 units from the 60,000 units started.

EXHIBIT 13-2

Step 1: Summarize Physical Units	
Work in process, beginning inventory	10,000 (40%)*
Started	60,000
To account for	70,000
Completed and transferred out during current period:†	
From beginning inventory	10,000
Started and completed currently	20,000
Work in process, ending inventory	40,000 (60%)*
Accounted for	70,000

*Degrees of completion for conversion costs, at the dates of the work-in-process inventories.
†"Current period" is used as a general term. In this example, the current period is one month, April.

❑ Step 2: Compute Output In Equivalent Units

Express the physical units in terms of work done. Because materials and conversion costs are applied differently, the equivalent output is usually divided into material and conversion-cost categories. For example, instead of thinking of output in terms of physical units, think of output in terms of material doses of work and conversion-cost doses of work. Disregard dollar amounts until **equivalent units** are computed.

Step 2 is illustrated in Exhibit 13-3. Concentrate on the work done in the current period regarding materials. All the materials are introduced as production begins. Consequently, the material component of work in process is "fully completed" as soon as work is started because all doses of material are used at the initial stage of the process. The work done in the current period *includes* the following material in the physical units:

Started and completed currently, 20,000 × 100% =	20,000
Started and still in process at the end, 40,000 × 100% =	40,000
Work done in current period in terms of equivalent units of material	60,000

Note that this total *excludes* the 10,000 units of material added in the *preceding* period to the beginning inventory of the current period.

EXHIBIT 13-3

FLOW OF PRODUCTION	(STEP 1) PHYSICAL UNITS	(STEP 2) EQUIVALENT UNITS	
		Materials	Conversion Costs
Work in process, beginning inventory	10,000 (40%)*		
Started	60,000		
To account for	70,000		
Completed and transferred out during current period:			
From beginning inventory	10,000		6,000
Started and completed currently	20,000	20,000	20,000
Work in process, ending inventory	40,000 (60%)*	40,000	24,000
Accounted for	70,000		
Work done in current period only		60,000	50,000

*Degrees of completion, for conversion costs of this department only, at the dates of the work-in-process inventories.

The equivalent units for conversion costs for the current period are computed as follows. The 30,000 units completed and transferred out consist of the 10,000 units from the beginning inventory plus 20,000 units started and completed in April. The total work done in April on the physical units transferred out plus the ending inventory would be:

To complete the units in beginning inventory, 10,000 × (100% − 40%) =	6,000
To entirely process the units started and completed during current period, 20,000 × 100%	20,000
Equivalent units on goods transferred	26,000
To do the first part of processing on the ending inventory, 40,000 × 60%	24,000
Equivalent units for current period (work done in current period)	50,000

Note that the 50,000 total *excludes* the beginning inventory of 10,000 × 40% = 4,000 equivalent units of conversion costs added in the *preceding* period to the *beginning inventory* of the *current* period.

As shown in Exhibit 13-3, step 2 ends with the "work done in current period only." Such measurements are the keys to judging performance during the current period, April in this illustration.

Step 3: Summarize Total Costs to Account For

Exhibit 13-4 summarizes the total costs to account for, consisting of the beginning balance of work in process ($64,400) plus the current costs ($700,000) added during April. The amounts of materials and conversion costs are also shown because they are frequently necessary for step 4.

Process-Costing Systems

393

EXHIBIT 13-4

Step 3: Summarize Total Costs to Account For	TOTAL COSTS	MATERIALS	CONVERSION COSTS
Work in process, beginning inventory	$ 64,400	$ 51,000	$ 13,400
Current costs	700,000	600,000	100,000
Total costs to account for	$764,400	$651,000	$113,400

FIRST-IN, FIRST-OUT (FIFO) METHOD

The two most-discussed methods of accounting for process-cost inventories are first-in, first-out (FIFO) and weighted-average. We examine each in turn. FIFO will be used to illustrate steps 4 and 5.

❑ Step 4: Compute Unit Costs

The FIFO method rests on a specific assumption regarding the flow of costs. The beginning inventory is regarded as if it were a batch of goods separate and distinct from the goods started *and* completed by a process during the current period. Therefore the unit costs are confined to the work done during the current period. That is, as Exhibit 13-5 demonstrates, the *current* costs (only) are divided by the equivalent units for work done in the current period (only).

Note especially that the beginning inventory costs and equivalent units for work done in the preceding period are *excluded* from the calculations in Exhibit 13-5.

❑ Step 5: Compute Total Costs of Work Completed and in Process

Exhibit 13-6 shows how the costs are finally summarized. The unit costs computed in step 4 are used to determine the total costs of goods completed and work in process. The units completed include 10,000 physical

EXHIBIT 13-5

Step 4: Compute Unit Costs First-in, First-out Method	MATERIALS	CONVERSION COSTS
Current costs only	$600,000	$100,000
Divided by equivalent units for work done in current period only (see step 2)	÷60,000	÷50,000
Unit costs	$ 10	$ 2

EXHIBIT 13-6

Step 5: Total Costs of Work Completed and in Process
First-in, First-out Method

COSTS	TOTALS	Materials	Conversion Costs	Equivalent Whole Unit
				DETAILS
Units completed (30,000)				
From beginning inventory (10,000) (see step 3)	$ 64,400			
Current costs added:				
Materials, none	—			
Conversion costs	12,000		6,000 ($2)	
Total completed from beginning inventory	$ 76,400			
Started and completed this period (20,000)	240,000			20,000 ($12)
Total costs transferred out	$316,400			
Work in process, ending inventory (40,000)				
Materials	$400,000	40,000 ($10)		
Conversion costs	48,000		24,000 ($2)	
Total work in process	$448,000			
Total costs accounted for	$764,400			

units of beginning inventory, which is accounted for as if it were a separate batch. The beginning inventory costs of $64,400 have 6,000 equivalent units × $2 = $12,000 of conversion costs *added* thereto in the current period. Moreover, 20,000 physical units were started and completed during the current period. Therefore they are allocated costs of $10 + $2 = $12 per equivalent whole unit.

The 40,000 physical units of ending work in process have a full 40,000 equivalent units of materials @ $10, but only 60% of 40,000, or 24,000 equivalent units of conversion costs @ $2.

As a final check, the costs are totaled to see if they have been fully accounted for.

Taken together, the five steps provide all the ingredients of a *production cost report*, which is shown in Exhibit 13-7. The format includes many details that some managers may deem unnecessary. For example, the report could be confined to the first column only and omit the data regarding equivalent units and unit costs. Moreover, many accountants favor placing the computations of equivalent units (the top part of Exhibit 13-7) either at the bottom of the report or as a separate schedule.

☐ Journal Entries for Department A

The following transaction-by-transaction summary analysis will explain how product costing is accomplished.

EXHIBIT 13-7   *(Place a clip on this page for easy reference.)*

Department A
Production Cost Report
First-in, First-out Method
For the Month Ended April 30, 19X1

FLOW OF PRODUCTION	(STEP 1) PHYSICAL UNITS	(STEP 2) EQUIVALENT UNITS Materials	Conversion Costs
Work in process, beginning inventory	10,000 (40%)*		
Started	60,000		
To account for	70,000		
Completed and transferred out:			
From beginning inventory	10,000	—	6,000
Started and completed currently	20,000	20,000	20,000
Work in process, ending inventory	40,000 (60%)*	40,000	24,000
Accounted for	70,000	60,000	50,000

COSTS	TOTALS	Materials	Conversion Costs	DETAILS Conversion Costs	Equivalent Whole Unit
Work in process, beginning inventory	$ 64,400	—	—		
Current costs	700,000	$600,000	$100,000		
(Step 3) Total costs to account for	$764,400				
(Step 4) Divide by equivalent units†		÷ 60,000	÷ 50,000		
Cost per equivalent unit		$ 10	$ 2		$ 12
(Step 5) Total costs of work completed and in process:					
Units completed and transferred out (30,000):					
From beginning inventory (10,000)	$ 64,400				
Current costs added:					
Materials, none	—				
Conversion costs	12,000			6,000 ($2)	
Total completed from beginning inventory	$ 76,400				
Started and completed this period (20,000)	240,000				20,000 ($12)
Total costs transferred out	$316,400				
Work in process, ending inventory (40,000):					
Materials	$400,000	40,000 ($10)			
Conversion costs	48,000			24,000 ($2)	
Total work in process	$448,000				
Total costs accounted for	$764,400				

*Degree of completion on conversion costs of this department.
†For work done in current period only.

1. Transaction: Materials added to production, $600,000

Analysis: The asset Work in Process, Department A, an inventory account, is increased. The asset Direct-Materials Inventory is decreased.

Entry: In the journal (explanation omitted):

Work in process, Department A	600,000	
Direct-materials inventory		600,000

Post to the ledger:

Work in Process, Department A		Direct-Materials Inventory	
3/31/X1 Bal. 64,400		1.	600,000
1. 600,000			

2. Transaction: Conversion costs added to production, $100,000

Analysis: The asset Work in Process, Department A, is increased. Various accounts (such as cash and liabilities for payroll and services) are affected.

Entry: In the journal:

Work in process, Department A	100,000	
Various accounts		100,000

Post to the ledger:

Work in Process, Department A		Various Accounts	
3/31/X1 Bal. 64,400		2.	100,000
1. 600,000			
2. 100,000			

3. Transaction: Transfer to Department B

Analysis: The cost of goods completed and transferred is shifted from the inventory account in Department A to a similar inventory account in Department B. The latter has a beginning inventory balance of $221,850, a fact not revealed before in this chapter.

Entry: In the journal:

Work in process, Department B	316,400	
Work in process, Department A		316,400

Post to the ledger:

Work in Process, Department A		Work in Process, Department B	
3/31/X1 Bal. 64,400	3. 316,400	3/31/X1 Bal. 211,850	
1. 600,000		3. 316,400	
2. 100,000			
764,400			
4/30/X1 448,000			

WEIGHTED-AVERAGE METHOD

The weighted-average method is another popular way of obtaining product costs. As in the FIFO method, five steps are recommended.

❑ Steps and 1 and 2

Step 1 is the same for both FIFO and weighted-average. Summarize the physical units as shown in Exhibit 13-2, page 392.

Step 2, the computation of equivalent units, is identical to that shown

EXHIBIT 13-8

Step 2: Compute Output in Equivalent Units, Weighted-Average Method

FLOW OF PRODUCTION	(STEP 1) PHYSICAL UNITS	(STEP 2) EQUIVALENT UNITS	
		Materials	Conversion Costs
Work in process, beginning inventory	10,000 (40%)*		
Started	60,000		
To account for	70,000		
Completed and transferred out during current period:			
From beginning inventory	10,000		6,000
Started and completed currently	20,000	20,000	20,000
Work in process, ending inventory	40,000 (60%)*	40,000	24,000
Accounted for	70,000		
Work done in current period only†		60,000	50,000
Work done in previous period on the beginning inventory		10,000	4,000
Work done to date (that is, done in the current and previous periods)		70,000	54,000

*Degree of completion on conversion costs of this department.

†Note that all computations through this line are identical to those in Exhibit 13–3, page 393.

for FIFO in Exhibit 13-3—except for the necessary addition of the final two line items. As the final lines in Exhibit 13-8 show, the weighted-average method mingles the work done in the current period with the work done in the preceding period on the beginning work in process. The final line represents the *work done to date,* which becomes the basis for computing unit costs in step 3. This contrasts with the *work done in the current period,* which is used in the FIFO method.

Compare the FIFO and weighted-average computations of equivalent units. The key difference is:

FIFO—Equivalent units are the work done in the current period only.

Weighted-average—Equivalent units are the work done to date, which includes all work done in the current period plus work done in the preceding period on the current period's beginning inventory of work in process.

❑ Steps 3, 4, and 5

Step 3, summarizing the total costs to account for, is the same as shown earlier in Exhibit 13-4. The unit costs are calculated in step 4, as shown in Exhibit 13-9.

The weighted-average method has been called a "roll-back" method because the averaging of costs includes the work done in the preceding period on the current period's beginning inventory of work in process. Thus the total costs and the equivalent units mingle the applicable work

EXHIBIT 13-9

Step 4: Compute Unit Costs, Weighted-Average Method

	MATERIALS	CONVERSION COSTS	EQUIVALENT WHOLE UNIT
Total costs to account for (step 3)	$651,000	$113,400	
Divide by equivalent units for work done to date (step 2)	÷70,000	÷54,000	
Unit costs	$ 9.30	$ 2.10	$ 11.40

Step 5: Compile Total Cost of Work Completed and in Process

			DETAILS	
	TOTALS	Materials	Conversion Costs	Equivalent Whole Unit
Units completed and transferred out (30,000)	$342,000			30,000 ($11.40)
Work in process, end (40,000):				
Materials	$372,000	40,000 ($9.30)		
Conversion costs	50,400		24,000 ($2.10)	
Total cost of work in process	$422,400			
Total costs accounted for	$764,400			

begun in the preceding period with the work started during the current period. The total costs include the beginning inventories. The equivalent units include all work done to date on the current month's production, including the beginning inventory of work in process.

Step 5 compiles the total costs of work completed and in process, as shown in the bottom half of Exhibit 13-9.

The computations here are simpler than the comparable FIFO computations in Exhibit 13-6. Why? Because Exhibit 13-6 separately calculated the current costs added to the beginning inventory. No such distinctions are necessary here. Instead, all the units completed are multiplied by a single unit cost, $11.40.

Exhibit 13-10 recapitulates the five steps for the weighted-average method. Compare the recapitulation in the exhibit with the FIFO recapitulation in Exhibit 13-7. The key difference is the choice of equivalent units for computing unit costs:

Weighted average—work done to date
FIFO—work done in current period only

Process-
Costing
Systems

399

Another difference is the mingling of beginning inventory costs with current costs in the weighted-average method and the separate handling of beginning inventory costs in the FIFO method.

EXHIBIT 13-10

Department A
Production Cost Report
Weighted-Average Method
For the Month Ended April 30, 19X1

FLOW OF PRODUCTION	(STEP 1) PHYSICAL UNITS	(STEP 2) EQUIVALENT UNITS	
		Materials	Conversion Costs
Work in process, beginning inventory	10,000 (40%)*		
Started	60,000		
To account for	70,000		
Completed and transferred out	30,000	30,000	30,000
Work in process, ending inventory	40,000 (60%)*	40,000	24,000
Accounted for	70,000	70,000	54,000

COSTS	TOTALS	Materials	Conversion Costs	Equivalent Whole Unit
			DETAILS	
		Materials	Conversion Costs	Equivalent Whole Unit
Work in process, beginning inventory	$ 64,400	$ 51,000	$ 13,400	
Current costs	700,000	600,000	100,000	
(Step 3) Total costs to account for	$764,400	$651,000	$113,400	
Divide by equivalent units†		÷ 70,000	÷ 54,000	
(Step 4) Cost per equivalent unit		$ 9.30	$ 2.10	$ 11.40
(Step 5) Total costs of work completed and in process:				
Units completed and transferred out (30,000)	$342,000			30,000 ($11.40)
Work in process, ending inventory (40,000)				
Materials	$372,000	40,000 ($9.30)		
Conversion costs	50,400		24,000 ($2.10)	
Total work in process	$422,400			
Total costs accounted for	$764,400			

*Degree of completion on conversion costs of this department.
†For work done to date.

Our example produced an ending inventory of work in process as follows:

FIFO	$448,000
Weighted average	422,400

The difference of $448,000 − $422,400 = $25,600, which is 6% of the weighted-average value. The difference was basically caused by a dramatic price increase in materials to $10 per unit and an increase in inventory levels. (The beginning inventory had a material component of $51,000 ÷ 10,000 units = $5.10 per unit.) Ordinarily, the difference in unit costs under the FIFO and weighted-average methods would be far less significant than illustrated here.

❏ PART THREE Transfers in Process Costing

NATURE OF TRANSFERRED-IN UNITS AND COSTS

As goods move from department to department, related costs are also transferred. An example will show how the accounting is accomplished. The same facts as in Example 2 are extended to a second department.

Example 3

The Gustavo Company has a fabricating process for cotton textiles. Material is introduced at the *beginning* of the process in Department A. As the process is completed, goods are immediately transferred to a finishing process in Department B. Additional material is added at the *end* of the process in Department B. Conversion costs are applied uniformly through both processes. Data for B for April follow.

Work in process, beginning inventory	15,000 units 30% converted,* $221,850 (transferred-in costs, $189,000; conversion costs, $32,850)
Units started during April	30,000
Units completed during April	39,000
Work in process, ending inventory	6,000, 50% converted*
Transferred-in costs from Department A during April:	
FIFO method	$316,400
Weighted-average method	$342,000
Material cost added	
during April	$54,600
Conversion costs added	
during April	$168,750

*This means that each unit in process is regarded as being fractionally complete with respect to the conversion costs of the present department only, at the dates of the work-in-process inventories.

REQUIRED:

Compute the cost of goods transferred out of the department during April. Compute the costs of the ending inventory of work in process. Assume (a) first-in, first-out product costing and (b) weighted-average product costing.

The five-step procedure described earlier is still pertinent. Exhibit 13-11 shows for Department B the initial two steps that analyze physical flows and compute equivalent units. Note that material costs pertaining to work in process have no degree of completion regarding the beginning or ending work in process. Why? Because materials are introduced at the *end* of the process in Department B. However, the equivalent units for transferred-in costs are, of course, fully completed at each of the inventory dates because they are introduced at the *beginning* of the process.

Transferred-in costs tend to give students much trouble, so special study is needed here. As far as Department B is concerned, units coming in from Department A may be viewed as if they were the raw materials of Department B introduced at the beginning of the process. However, they are distinguished from materials and are called **transferred-in costs** (or **previous-department costs**), not material costs. That is, we might visualize the situation as if Department B had bought these goods from an outside supplier. Thus Department B's computations must provide for transferred-in costs, as well as for any new material costs added in Department B, and for conversion costs added in Department B.

❑ Transfers and FIFO Method

Exhibit 13-12 displays the FIFO application of costs to products in Department B. The application is similar to the FIFO application in Department A (Exhibit 13-7, p. 396) except that transferred-in costs must now be considered. Before reading on, study Exhibit 13-12 carefully. Concentrate on the bottom half of the exhibit. Note how the divisor equivalent units are based on the steps 1 and 2 shown in Exhibit 13-11. That is, the current costs are divided by equivalent units for the "total work done in current period only." For example, the divisor for conversion costs is 37,500 equivalent units.

In a series of interdepartmental transfers, each department is regarded as a distinct accounting entity. All transferred-in costs during a given period are carried at one unit cost, regardless of whether weighted-average or FIFO methods were used by previous departments.

In summary, although the so-called FIFO method is sometimes used in process-costing situations, only rarely is an application of strict FIFO ever encountered. It should really be called a *modified* or *departmental* FIFO method. Why? Because, although FIFO is applied within a department to compile the cost of goods transferred *out*, the goods transferred *in* during a given period usually bear a single average unit cost as a matter of convenience.[2]

[2] Thus, although the FIFO method as used by Department A may show batches of goods accumulated and transferred at different unit costs, these goods are typically "costed in" by Department B at *one* average unit cost, as Exhibit 13-12 demonstrates ($316,400 ÷ 30,000 = $10.547). In other words, a departmental FIFO method may be used, but in practice the strict FIFO method is modified to the extent that subsequent departments use weighted-average methods for cost transferred in during a given period. If this were not done, the attempt to trace costs on a strict FIFO basis throughout a series of processes would become too burdensome and complicated. For example, a four-department process-cost system could have at least eight or more batches, which would need separate costing by the time costs are transferred to and out of the final department. However, as goods are transferred from the last process to Finished Goods, the records of finished stock could be kept on a strict first-in, first-out method if desired. The clerical burden alone is enough to cause most process-cost industries to reject strict FIFO as a costing method. Therefore the idea of broad averaging is applicable even within the workings of the FIFO method.

EXHIBIT 13-11

Department B
Computation of Output in Equivalent Units
For the Month Ended April 30, 19X1

FLOW OF PRODUCTION	(STEP 1) PHYSICAL UNITS	(STEP 2) EQUIVALENT UNITS		
		Transferred-In Costs	Materials	Conversion Costs
Work in process, beginning inventory	15,000 (30%)*			
Transferred in	30,000			
To account for	45,000			
Completed and transferred out during current period:				
From beginning inventory	15,000	—	15,000	10,500
Started and completed currently	24,000	24,000	24,000	24,000
Work in process, ending inventory:				
Transferred-in costs: 6,000 × 100%	6,000 (50%)*	6,000		
Materials: none			—	
Conversion costs: 6,000 × 50%				3,000
Accounted for	45,000			
Total work done in current period only†		30,000	39,000	37,500
Work done in the preceding period on the beginning inventory		15,000	—	4,500
Work done to date (that is, done in the current and preceding periods)‡		45,000	39,000	42,000

*Degrees of completion on conversion costs in this department only, at the dates of the work-in-process inventories. Note that *material costs* pertaining to work in process have no completion at each of these dates because, in this department, materials are introduced at the end of the process. Note also that transferred-in costs are, of course, fully completed at each of the inventory dates.

†USED FOR FIFO COST METHOD.

‡USED FOR WEIGHTED-AVERAGE COST METHOD.

EXHIBIT 13-12   *(Place a clip on this page for easy reference.)*

Department B
Production Cost Report
First-in, First-out Method
For the Month Ended April 30, 19X1

FLOW OF PRODUCTION	(STEP 1) PHYSICAL UNITS	(STEP 2) EQUIVALENT UNITS		
		Transferred-In Costs	Materials	Conversion Costs
Work in process, beginning inventory	15,000 (30%)*			
Transferred in	30,000			
To account for	45,000			
Completed and transferred out:				
From beginning inventory	15,000	—	15,000	10,500
Started and completed currently	24,000	24,000	24,000	24,000
Work in process, ending inventory	6,000 (50%)*	6,000	—	3,000
Accounted for	45,000	30,000	39,000	37,500

COSTS	TOTALS	DETAILS		
		Transferred-In Costs	Materials	Conversion Costs
Work in process, beginning inventory	$ 221,850			
Current costs	539,750	$ 316,400	$ 54,600	168,750
(Step 3) Total costs to account for	$761,600			
Divide by equivalent units†		÷ 30,000	÷ 39,000	÷ 37,500
(Step 4) Cost per equivalent unit	$16.44666‡	$10.54666	$ 1.40	$ 4.50

404

(Step 5) Total costs of work completed and in process:

Units completed and transferred out (39,000):

From beginning inventory (15,000) $ 221,850

Current costs added:

Materials   15,000 ($1.40)
Conversion costs   10,500 ($4.50)   21,000
                                                                           47,250

Total completed from beginning inventory $ 290,100

Started and completed (24,000) ($16.44666)   394,720

Total costs transferred out $ 684,820

Work in process, ending inventory (6,000):

Transferred-in costs   6,000 (10.54666) $ 63,280

Materials   —   —

Conversion costs   3,000 ($4.50)   13,500

Total work in process $ 76,780

Total costs accounted for $ 761,600

*Degree of completion on conversion costs in this department.

†For work done in current period only.

‡This $16.44666 is the unit cost only for work started and completed this month. However, the unit cost of all units transferred out of this process this month is $684,820 ÷ 39,000 = $17.55949. This average unit cost would be used for the additions to finished goods during April. Unit costs are carried out to five decimal places in this exhibit to prevent rounding errors in the dollar totals. Alternatively, unit costs could be carried out to fewer decimal places, resulting in rounding errors in the totals.

The only essential difference between the weighted-average method as applied to Departments A (Exhibit 13-10, p. 400) and B (Exhibit 13-13) is the accounting for transferred-in costs in Department B. Concentrate on the bottom half of Exhibit 13-13. Pause again, particularly to see the link between the equivalent units in Exhibit 13-11 and the divisor equivalent units in Exhibit 13-13. The total costs to account for are divided by the equivalent units for the "work done to date." For example, the divisor for conversion costs is 42,000 equivalent units.

☐ Journal Entries for Transfers

The analysis of transactions, journal entries, and postings to the ledger are similar in Departments A and B. The journal entries for transfers are summarized as follows:

	FIFO METHOD		WEIGHTED-AVERAGE METHOD	
	Debit	Credit	Debit	Credit
Work in process—Department B	316,400		342,000	
Work in process—Department A		316,400		342,000
To transfer costs from Department A. (For detailed computations, see Exhibits 13-6 and 13-9.)				
Finished goods inventory	684,820		702,000	
Work in process—Department B		684,820		702,000
To transfer costs from Department B. (See Exhibits 13-12 and 13-13.)				

ADDITIONAL FEATURES OF PROCESS COSTING

This chapter's illustrations plus almost all process-cost problems blithely mention various degrees of completion for inventories in process. The accuracy of these estimates depends on the care and skill of the estimator and the nature of the process. Estimating the degree of completion is usually easier for materials than for conversion costs. The conversion sequence usually consists of a number of standard operations or a standard number of hours, days, weeks, or months for mixing, heating, cooling, aging, curing, and so forth. Thus the degree of completion for conversion costs depends on what proportion of the total effort needed to complete one unit or one batch has been devoted to units still in process. In industries where no exact estimate is possible, or, as in textiles, where vast quantities in process prohibit costly physical estimates, all work in process in every department is assumed to be ⅓ or ½ or ⅔ complete. In other cases, continuous processing entails little change of work-in-process levels from month to month.

EXHIBIT 13-13

Department B
Production Cost Report
Weighted-Average Method
For the Month Ended April 30, 19X1

FLOW OF PRODUCTION	(STEP 1) PHYSICAL UNITS	(STEP 2) EQUIVALENT UNITS		
		Transferred-In Costs	Materials	Conversion Costs
Work in process, beginning inventory	15,000 (30%)*			
Transferred in	30,000			
To account for	45,000			
Completed and transferred out	39,000	39,000	39,000	39,000
Work in process, ending inventory	6,000 (50%)*	6,000	—	3,000
Accounted for	45,000	45,000	39,000	42,000

COSTS	TOTALS	DETAILS		
		Transferred-In Costs	Materials	Conversion Costs
Work in process, beginning inventory	$221,850	$189,000	$ —	$ 32,850
Current costs	565,350	342,000	54,600	168,750
(Step 3) Total costs to account for	$787,200	$531,000	$54,600	$201,600
Divide by equivalent units†		÷ 45,000	÷ 39,000	÷ 42,000
(Step 4) Cost per equivalent unit	$ 18.00	$ 11.80	$ 1.40	$ 4.80
Total costs of work completed and in process:				
Units completed and transferred out (39,000)($18)	$702,000			
Work in process, ending inventory (6,000)				
Transferred-in costs	$70,800	6,000 ($11.80)		
Materials	—			
Conversion costs	14,400			3,000 ($4.80)
Total work in process	$ 85,200			
Total costs accounted for	$787,200			

*Degree of completion on conversion costs of this department.
†For work done to date.

Consequently, in such cases, work in process is safely ignored and monthly production costs are assigned solely to goods completed.

For convenience, direct labor and factory overhead have been lumped together in the examples in this chapter. Accounting for factory overhead is discussed more fully in the next chapter.

Process costing is often marked by significant shrinkage, evaporation, spoilage, and waste. As a general rule, the costs of the related units are separately identified. If deemed as being within normal limits, such costs are allocated to the good units produced. If abnormal spoilage occurs, such costs are written off as a separate expense (loss) of the current period instead of being allocated to the good units. A detailed explanation of these topics is beyond the scope of this introduction to process costing.

Summary

Process costing is used for inventory costing when there is continuous, mass production of like units. The key concept in process costing is that of equivalent units, the expression of output during a given period in terms of doses or amounts of work applied thereto.

Five basic steps may be used in solving process-cost problems. Process costing is complicated by varying amounts of cost factors, by the presence of beginning inventories, and by the presence of costs transferred in from prior departments.

Two widely advocated process-costing techniques are known as the *weighted-average* and *first-in, first-out* methods. However, standard costs are the most widely used; they are simpler and more useful than other techniques for both product-costing and control purposes.

Summary Problem for Your Review

Review each example in this chapter and obtain the solutions on your own. Then check your work against the solutions, which appear in the various exhibits.

Highlights to Remember

1. This introduction to process costing has concentrated on general approaches. The FIFO method has been explored primarily to illustrate how the equivalent units for the current period provide the key measures of the work accomplished during a given period (April in our examples). This type of measurement is used widely for planning and controlling materials and labor, especially when linked with the standard-costing systems described in Chapter 7. The weighted-average method has been covered primarily because it is widely used in practice for product-costing purposes, as distinguished from planning and control purposes.

2. The practice of expressing work in terms of equivalent whole units is widespread in both manufacturing and nonmanufacturing situations. For example, universities measure the number of part-time students attending night courses in terms of full-time equivalents.

3. Part Three of this chapter covers the more difficult phases of process costing. Avoid these common pitfalls:

   a. Transferred-in costs from previous departments should be included in your calculations. Such costs should be treated as if they were another kind of material cost, because each department is treated as a separate entity. In other words, when successive departments are involved, transferred goods from one department become all or a part of the raw materials of the next department, although they are called *transferred-in costs,* not raw materials.

   b. In calculating costs to be transferred on a first-in, first-out basis, do not overlook the costs attached at the beginning of the period to goods that were in process but are now included in the goods transferred. For example, do not overlook the $221,850 in Exhibit 13-12.

   c. Unit costs may fluctuate between periods. Therefore, transferred goods may contain batches accumulated at different unit costs (see point b). These goods, when transferred to the next department, are typically valued by that next department at *one* average unit cost.

Accounting Vocabulary

Equivalent units; job-order costing; operation costing; previous-department costs; process; process costing; transferred-in costs.

Fundamental Assignment Material

13–1. Coverage of Part One of chapter. (Alternates are 13–8 and 13–9.) Wong Company produces transistor radios in large quantities. The manufacturing costs during January were:

Direct materials added		$ 48,000
Conversion costs		
Direct labor	$40,000	
Factory overhead	36,000	76,000
Assembly costs to account for		$124,000

There was no beginning inventory of work in process. Suppose work on 10,000 radios was begun during January, but only 9,000 radios were fully completed. All the parts had been made or placed in process, but only half of the labor had been completed for each of the radios.

For simplicity, assume that this is a one-department company.

REQUIRED:

1. Compute the equivalent units and unit costs for January.
2. Compute the costs of units completed and transferred to finished goods. Also compute the cost of the ending work in process.

13–2. Coverage of Part Two of chapter. (Alternate is 13–25.) The Caceras Company manufactures hand-held calculators. Material is introduced at the beginning of the process in Department A. Conversion costs are applied uniformly throughout the process. As the process is completed, goods are immediately transferred to a finishing process in Department B.

Data for the month of June 19X1 follow:

Work in process, May 31, 12,000 units, 25% converted, $168,600: materials, $137,400; conversion costs, $31,200

Units started during June	75,000
Units completed during June	57,000
Work in process, June 30, 30,000 units, 50% converted:	
Material cost added during June	$750,000
Conversion costs added during June	$552,000

REQUIRED:

Compute the total cost of goods transferred out of the department during June. Compute the total costs of the ending work in process. Show computations in an orderly manner. Use the weighted-average method. (For the FIFO method and journal entries, see Problems 13–28 and 13–29.)

13–3. Coverage of Part Three of chapter. (Alternate is 13–38.) A company has two processes. Material is introduced at the *beginning* of the process in Department A, and additional material is added at the *end* of the process in Department B. Conversion costs are applied uniformly throughout both processes. As the process in Department A is completed, goods are immediately transferred to Department B; as goods are completed in Department B, they are transferred to Finished Goods.

Data for the month of March are shown below for Department B:

Work in process, beginning inventory	12,000 units 66⅔% converted,* $26,100 (transferred-in costs, $15,600; conversion costs, $10,500)
Units started during March	?
Units completed during March	44,000
Work in process, ending inventory	16,000, 37½% converted*
Material cost added during March	$13,200
Conversion costs added during March	$63,000
Transferred-in costs from Department A during March	$45,600

*This means that each unit in process is regarded as being fractionally complete with respect to the conversion costs of the present department only, at the dates of the work-in-process inventories.

REQUIRED:

1. Prepare a schedule for Department B showing the computation of output in equivalent units for March.
2. Prepare a schedule of the total costs of units completed and transferred to finished goods and the total costs of the ending work in process. Use the weighted-average method. (For the FIFO method, see Problem 13–37.)

Additional Assignment Material for Part One ____

13–4. Give three examples of industries where process-costing systems are probably used.

13–5. Give three examples of not-for-profit organizations where process-costing systems are probably used.

13–6. Give three examples of equivalent units in various organizations.

13–7. "There are hybrid cost-accounting systems." Explain.

13–8. **Straightforward computations.** (Alternates are 13–1 and 13–9.)
Garcia Company produces hand-held calculators in large quantities. The manufacturing costs of the assembly department were:

Direct materials added		$ 950,000
Conversion costs:		
Direct labor	$200,000	
Factory overhead	160,000	360,000
Assembly costs to account for		$1,310,000

For simplicity, assume that this is a one-department company and that there was no beginning work in process.

Suppose 1 million units were begun. There were 800,000 units completed and transferred to finished goods. The 200,000 units in ending work in process were fully completed regarding direct materials but half-completed regarding conversion costs.

REQUIRED:

1. Compute the equivalent units and unit costs.
2. Compute the costs of units completed and transferred to finished goods. Also compute the cost of the ending work in process.

13–9. **Straightforward computations.** (Alternates are 13–1 and 13–8.)
A department produces textile products. All direct materials are introduced at the start of the process. Conversion costs are incurred uniformly throughout the process.

In May there was no beginning inventory. Units started, completed, and transferred, 400,000. Units in process, May 31, 80,000. Each unit in ending work in process was 75% converted. Costs incurred during May: direct materials, $3,360,000; conversion costs, $920,000.

REQUIRED:

1. Compute the total work done in equivalent units and the unit cost for May.
2. Compute the cost of units completed and transferred. Also compute the cost of units in ending work in process.

13–10. **Nonprofit process costing.** The Internal Revenue Service must process millions of income tax returns yearly. When the taxpayer sends in his return, documents such as withholding statements and checks are matched against the data on page one. Then various other inspections of the data are conducted. Of course, some returns are more complicated than others, so the expected time allowed to process a return is geared to an "average" return.

Some work-measurement experts have been closely monitoring the processing at a particular branch. They are seeking ways to improve productivity.

Suppose 1 million returns were received on April 15. On April 22, the work-measurement teams discovered that all supplies (punched cards, inspection check-sheets, and so on) had been affixed to the returns, but 40% of the returns still had to undergo a final inspection. The other returns were fully completed.

REQUIRED:

1. Suppose the final inspection represents 20% of the overall processing time in this process. Compute the total work done in terms of equivalent units.
2. The materials and supplies consumed were $150,000. For these calculations, materials and supplies are regarded just like direct materials. The conversion costs were $1,380,000. Compute the unit costs of materials and supplies and of conversion.
3. Compute the cost of the tax returns not yet completely processed.

13–11. Uneven flow. A one-department company manufactured basic hand-held calculators. Various materials were added at various stages of the process. The outer front shell and the carrying case, which represented 10% of the total material cost, were added at the final step of the assembly process. All other materials were considered to be "in process" by the time the calculator reached a 50% stage of completion.

Ninety-one thousand calculators were started in production during 19X1. At year-end, 5,000 calculators were in various stages of completion, but all of them were beyond the 50% stage and on the average they were regarded as being 80% completed.

The following costs were incurred during the year: direct materials, $181,000; conversion costs, $450,000.

REQUIRED:

1. Prepare a schedule of physical units, equivalent units, and unit costs.
2. Tabulate the cost of goods completed and the cost of ending work in process.

13–12. Two materials. The following data pertain to the mixing department for April:

Units:	
Work in process, March 31	0
Units started	50,000
Completed and transferred to finishing department	35,000
Costs:	
Material P	$250,000
Material Q	$105,000
Conversion costs	$176,000

Material P is introduced at the start of the process, while material Q is added when the product reaches an 80% stage of completion. Conversion costs are incurred uniformly throughout the process.

The ending work in process is 60% completed.

REQUIRED:

1. Compute the equivalent units and unit costs for April.
2. Compute the total cost of units completed and transferred to finished goods. Also compute the cost of the ending work in process.

Additional Assignment Material for Part Two _____

13–13. Identify the major distinction between the first two and the final three steps of the five major steps in accounting for process costs.

13–14. Present an equation that describes the physical flow in process costing.

13–15. Why is "work done in the current period only" a key measurement of equivalent units?

13–16. "The beginning inventory is regarded as if it were a batch of goods separate and distinct from the goods started *and* completed by a process during the current period." What method of process costing is being described?

13–17. "Equivalent units are the work done to date." What method of process costing is being described?

13–18. "Ordinarily, the differences in unit costs under FIFO and weighted-average methods are insignificant." Do you agree? Explain.

13–19. **Physical units.** Fill in the unknowns in physical units:

FLOW OF PRODUCTION	CASE A	CASE B
Work in process, beginning inventory	1,000	3,000
Started	4,000	?
Completed and transferred	?	8,000
Work in process, ending inventory	3,000	2,000

13–20. **Multiple choice.** The Ace Company had computed the physical flow (of physical units) for Department A, for the month of April, as follows:

Units completed:	
From work in process on April 1	10,000
From April production	30,000
	40,000

Materials are added at the beginning of the process. Units of work in process at April 30 were 8,000. The work in process at April 1 was 80% complete as to conversion costs and the work in process at April 30 was 60% complete as to conversion costs. What are the equivalent units of production for the month of April using the FIFO method? Choose one of the following combinations:

	MATERIALS	CONVERSION COSTS
a.	38,000	36,800
b.	38,000	38,000
c.	48,000	44,800
d.	48,000	48,000

13–21. **Equivalent units.** Fill in the unknowns:

FLOW OF PRODUCTION IN UNITS	(STEP 1) PHYSICAL UNITS	(STEP 2) EQUIVALENT UNITS Direct Materials	(STEP 2) EQUIVALENT UNITS Conversion Costs
Work in process, beginning inventory	20,000*		
Started	70,000		
To account for	90,000		
Completed and transferred:			
From beginning inventory	?	?	?
Started and completed currently	?	?	?
Work in process, ending inventory	5,000†	?	?
Accounted for	90,000		
Work done in current period only		?	?
Work done in previous period on the beginning inventory		?	?
Work done to date		?	?

*Degree of completion: direct materials, 90%; conversion costs, 20%.
†Degree of completion: direct materials, 70%; conversion costs, 80%.

13–22. Compute equivalent units. Consider the following data for June:

	PHYSICAL UNITS
Started in June	50,000
Completed in June	45,000
Ending inventory, work in process	15,000
Beginning inventory, work in process	10,000

The beginning inventory was 70% complete regarding materials and 30% complete regarding conversion costs. The ending inventory was 40% complete regarding materials and 80% complete regarding conversion costs.

REQUIRED: Prepare a schedule of equivalent units for the work done during June only and the work done to date.

13–23. FIFO and unit material costs. The Lee Company uses the FIFO process-cost method. Consider the following for March:

Beginning inventory, 20,000 units, 80% completed regarding materials, which cost $100,000
Units completed, 75,000
Cost of materials placed in process during March, $341,000
Ending inventory, 10,000 units, 30% completed regarding materials

REQUIRED: Compute the material cost per equivalent unit for the work done in March only. No units were lost or spoiled.

13–24. FIFO method, conversion cost. Given the following information, compute the unit conversion cost for the month of June for the Holloway Company, using the FIFO process-cost method. Show details of your calculation.

Units completed, 30,000
Conversion cost in beginning inventory, $7,500
Beginning inventory, 5,000 units with 60% of conversion cost
Ending inventory, 10,000 units with 60% of conversion cost
Conversion costs put into production in June, $99,000

13–25. Weighted-average process-costing method. (Alternate is 13–2.) The Nifty Paint Co. uses a process-cost system. Materials are added at the beginning of a particular process and conversion costs are incurred uniformly. Work in process at the beginning is assumed 50% complete; at the end, 40%. One gallon of material makes one gallon of product. Data follow:

Beginning inventory	900 gallons
Direct materials added	12,100 gallons
Ending inventory	400 gallons
Conversion costs incurred	$18,465
Cost of direct materials added	$52,030
Conversion costs, beginning inventory	$ 1,951
Cost of direct materials, beginning inventory	$ 2,570

REQUIRED: Use the weighted-average method. Prepare a schedule of output in equivalent units and a schedule of application of costs to products. Show the cost of goods completed and of ending work in process. (For the FIFO method and journal entries, see the next two problems.)

13–26. FIFO computations. Refer to the preceding problem. Using FIFO, repeat the requirements.

13–27. Journal entries. Refer to the data in Problem 13–25. Prepare summary journal entries for the use of direct materials and conversion costs. Also prepare a journal entry for the transfer of goods completed, assuming that the goods are transferred from Department A to Department B.

13–28. **FIFO method.** Refer to Problem 13–2. Using FIFO costing, repeat the requirements.

13–29. **Journal entries.** Refer to the data in Problem 13–2. Prepare summary journal entries for the use of direct materials and conversion costs. Also prepare a journal entry for the transfer of the goods completed and transferred from Department A to Department B.

Additional Assignment Material for Part Three___

13–30. "Transferred-in costs are those incurred in the preceding period." Do you agree? Explain.

13–31. Why should the accountant distinguish between *transferred-in costs* and *new material costs* for a particular department?

13–32. "The FIFO method should really be called the modified FIFO or departmental FIFO method." Do you agree? Explain.

13–33. "The total costs to account for are divided by the equivalent units for the work done to date." Does this quotation describe the weighted-average method or does it describe FIFO?

13–34. Under what conditions can significant amounts of work in process be safely ignored in process costing?

13–35. Describe the general approach to process costing followed when significant spoilage occurs.

13–36. "Transferred-in costs may be regarded as if they were another type of material cost." Do you agree? Explain.

13–37. **FIFO method.** Refer to Problem 13–3. Repeat Requirement 2, using FIFO.

13–38. **Weighted-average method.** (Alternate is 13–3.) A company has two processes. Material is introduced at the *beginning* of the process in Department A, but no material is added in Department B, which is the finishing department. Conversion costs are applied uniformly throughout both processes. As the process in Department A is completed, goods are immediately transferred to Department B; as goods are completed in Department B, they are transferred to Finished Goods.

Simplified data for Department B for the month of November are shown below:

Work in process, beginning inventory	300 units ⅓ converted, $5,530 (transferred-in costs, $4,680; conversion costs, $850)
Units started during November	?
Units completed during November	500
Work in process, ending inventory	300, ⅔ converted
Cost transferred in from Department A during November	$7,000
Conversion costs added during November	$3,000

1. Prepare a schedule showing the computation of output in equivalent units for November.
2. Prepare a schedule of the total costs of units completed and transferred to finished goods and the total costs of the ending work in process. Use the weighted-average method. (For the FIFO method, see the next problem.)

13–39. **FIFO method.** Refer to the preceding problem. Repeat Requirement 2, using FIFO.

13–40. **FIFO and weighted-average.** Consider these April data for Department B:

	PHYSICAL UNITS	EQUIVALENT UNITS Transferred In	Materials	Conversion
Work in process, beginning	?			
Started	?			
To account for	20,000			
Completed and transferred out:				
From beginning inventory	?	?	?	?
Started and completed				
currently	9,000	?	?	?
Work in process, ending	5,000	?	?	?
Accounted for	?			
Work done during April only		?	?	?
Work done before April on the				
beginning inventory		?	?	?
Work done to date		?	?	?

Materials are added at the beginning of the process in Department B. Conversion costs are incurred uniformly throughout the process. The beginning inventory was 50% converted; ending inventory was 20% converted.

REQUIRED:

1. Fill in the unknowns.
2. Suppose Department B March conversion costs associated with the April beginning inventory were $7,600 and current conversion costs in April for all production were $26,000. Compute the appropriate unit conversion costs under the (a) FIFO method and (b) weighted-average method.
3. Suppose current transferred-in costs during April were $112,000. The March transferred-in costs associated with the April beginning inventory were $42,000. Compute the appropriate unit transferred-in costs under the (a) FIFO method and (b) weighted-average method.

14

JOB-COSTING SYSTEMS AND OVERHEAD APPLICATION

The purpose of this and the next chapter is to show how data may be accumulated within an accounting system and how various alternative methods of applying costs to products affect inventories and income determination. These are essentially scorekeeping tasks. Management makes policy decisions, at one time or another, regarding methods of product costing. Because such decisions affect the way net income will be determined, managers should know the various approaches to product costing. Moreover, as we have seen previously, a knowledge of product-costing techniques will enhance a manager's understanding of product costs, particularly when the latter are used for pricing and evaluating product lines. Keep in mind that product costing is separable from control. That is, a good planning and control system may be coupled with any of a number of product-costing practices.

This chapter is designed so that it may be studied immediately after Chapter 3 without loss of continuity. Therefore, to begin, please review the first two sections of Chapter 3 ("Classifications of Costs" and "Relationships of Income Statements and Balance Sheets") and the Chapter 3 Appendix ("Classification of Labor Costs"). It is not necessary to review the other parts of Chapter 3.

To permit the utmost flexibility, this chapter is also designed so that it may be studied independently from the immediately preceding chapter on process costing.

Our focus in this and the next chapter is on manufacturing costs, because accountants view selling, administrative, and other nonmanufacturing costs as being expenses immediately and therefore totally excludable from costs of *product*.

DISTINCTION BETWEEN JOB COSTING AND PROCESS COSTING

Recall that Chapter 3 defined *cost objective* as any activity for which a separate measurement of costs is desired. Two principal cost objectives were illustrated: departments and products. Cost-accounting systems have a twofold purpose fulfilled by their day-to-day operations: (1) allocate costs to departments for planning and control, hereafter for brevity's sake often called *control*, and (2) allocate costs to units of product for *product costing*.

Two extremes of product costing are usually termed **job-order costing** and **process costing.** *Job-order* (or *job-cost* or *production-order*) accounting methods are used by companies whose products are readily identified by individual units or batches, each of which receives varying degrees of attention and skill. Industries that commonly use job-order methods include construction, printing, aircraft, furniture, and machinery.

Process costing is most often found in such industries as chemicals, oil, textiles, plastics, paints, flour, canneries, rubber, lumber, food processing, glass, mining, cement, and meat packing. In these there is mass production of like units, which usually pass in continuous fashion through a series of uniform production steps called *operations* or *processes*. This is in contrast to the production of tailor-made or unique goods, such as special-purpose machinery or printing.

The distinction between the job-cost and the process-cost methods centers largely on how product costing is accomplished. Unlike process costing, which deals with broad averages and great masses of like units, the essential feature of the job-cost method is the attempt to apply costs to specific jobs, which may consist of either a single physical unit (such as a custom sofa) or a few like units (such as a dozen tables) in a distinct batch or job lot.

The most important point is that product costing is an *averaging* process. The unit cost used for inventory purposes is the result of taking some accumulated cost that has been allocated to production departments and dividing it by some measure of production. The basic distinction between job-order costing and process costing is the breadth of the denominator: In job-order costing, it is small (for example, one painting, one hundred advertising circulars, or one special packaging machine); but in process costing, it is large (for example, thousands of pounds, gallons, or board feet).

ILLUSTRATION OF JOB-ORDER COSTING

☐ Data for Illustration

This section illustrates the principal aspects of a job-costing system, including the basic records and journal entries. Consider the Martinez Electronics Company, which has a job-order cost system with the following inventories on December 31, 19X1:

Direct materials (12 types)	$110,000
Work in process	—
Finished goods (unsold	
units from two jobs)	12,000

The following is a summary of events for the year 19X2:

	MACHINING	ASSEMBLY	TOTAL
1. Direct materials purchased on account	—	—	$1,900,000
2. Direct materials requisitioned	$1,000,000	$890,000	1,890,000
3. Direct-labor costs incurred	200,000	190,000	390,000
4a. Factory overhead **incurred**	290,000	102,000	392,000
4b. Factory overhead **applied**	280,000	95,000	375,000
5. Cost of goods completed and transferred to finished-goods inventory	—	—	2,500,000
6a. Sales on account	—	—	4,000,000
6b. Cost of goods sold	—	—	2,480,000

Job-Costing Systems and Overhead Application

Most of the above data are straightforward and easy to understand. However, the term *factory overhead applied* is being introduced here for the first time. It will be explained later in this chapter.

The accounting for these events will now be explained, step by step.

The bulk of the scorekeeping is a detailed recording and summarization of source documents such as requisitions, work tickets, and invoices. In January 19X2 several jobs were begun. For example, Job 404 was begun and completed. Exhibit 14-1 is the completed job-cost sheet.

As Exhibit 14-1 illustrates, the job-cost sheet is the basic record for product costing. A file of current job-cost sheets becomes the subsidiary ledger for the general ledger account, Work-in-Process Inventory, often simply called Work in Process. As each job begins, a job-cost sheet is prepared. As units are worked on, entries are made on the job-cost sheet. Three classes of costs are applied to the units as they pass through the departments: Material requisitions are used to apply costs of direct material; work tickets are used to apply costs of direct labor; and *predetermined overhead rates* are used to apply factory overhead to products. The computation of these rates will be described in the next major section of this chapter.

EXHIBIT 14-1

Completed Job-Cost Sheet and Sample Source Documents

Job Order No. ____404____

MACHINING DEPARTMENT

Reference	Date	Quantity	Unit Cost	Amount	Summary
Direct materials:					
Type M—					
Various requisitions	Various	900	$2.00	$1,800	
Type N—					
Various requisitions	Various	900	5.00	4,500	$ 6,300
Direct labor:					
Various work tickets	Various	320 hrs	9.00	2,880	2,880
Factory overhead applied		425 mach. hrs	4.00	1,700	1,700
Total machining					$10,880

ASSEMBLY DEPARTMENT

(Entries would be similar to above)					xxx
Total assembly (assumed)					$ 2,000
Total product cost					$12,880

Sample Source Documents

Direct Material Requisition No. XX

Job No. __404__   Date _Jan. 5, 19X2_

Department _Machining_ Account _Work in process_

Description	Quantity	Unit Cost	Amount
	XX	X	XX

Work Ticket No. XX

Job No. __404__   Date _Jan. 7, 19X2_
Department _Machining_ Account _Work in process_
Operation _Drill_

Units: Start _3:00 p.m._ Rate _____
Worked   10
Rejected   —   Stop _4:15 p.m._ Amount _____
Completed 10

The following transaction-by-transaction summary analysis will explain how product costing is achieved.

1. Transaction: Direct materials purchased, $1,900,000

Analysis: The asset Direct-Materials Inventory is increased.
The liability Accounts Payable is increased.

Entry: In the journal (explanation omitted):

Direct-materials inventory	1,900,000	
Accounts payable		1,900,000

Post to the ledger:

Direct-Materials Inventory		Accounts Payable	
Bal. 110,000		1.	1,900,000
1. 1,900,000			

2. Transaction: Direct materials requisitioned, $1,890,000

Analysis: The asset Work in Process (Inventory) is increased.
The asset Direct-Materials Inventory is decreased.

Entry: In the journal:

Work in process	1,890,000	
Direct-materials inventory		1,890,000

Post to the ledger:

Direct-Materials Inventory			Work in Process	
Bal. 110,000	2. 1,890,000	2.	1,890,000	
1. 1,900,000				
Bal. 120,000				

3. Transaction: Direct-labor costs incurred, $390,000

Analysis: The asset Work in Process (Inventory) is increased.
The liability Accrued Payroll is increased.

Entry: In the journal:

Work in process	390,000	
Accrued payroll		390,000

Post to the ledger:

Accrued Payroll			Work in Process	
	3. 390,000	2.	1,890,000	
		3.	390,000	

4a. Transaction: Factory overhead incurred, $392,000

Analysis: The departments are charged with these actual costs, which may be regarded as assets until their amounts are "cleared" or transferred to other accounts. The department managers are charged because they bear responsibility for the *control* of these various costs, item by item. The other accounts affected will be assorted assets and liabilities.

Entry: In the journal:

Factory department overhead control	392,000	
Cash, accounts payable, and various accounts		392,000

Post to the ledger:

Factory Department Overhead Control		Various Accounts	
4a. 392,000		4a.	392,000

4b. Transaction: Factory overhead applied, $95,000 + $280,000 = $375,000

Analysis: The asset Work in Process (Inventory) is increased. The asset Factory Department Overhead Control is decreased. (A fuller explanation occurs later in this chapter.)

Entry: In the journal:

Work in process	375,000	
Factory department overhead control		375,000

Post to the ledger:

Factory Department Overhead Control				Work in Process	
4a.	392,000	4b.	375,000	2.	1,890,000
				3.	390,000
				4b.	375,000

5. Transaction: Cost of goods completed, $2,500,000

Analysis: The asset Finished Goods (Inventory) is increased.
The asset Work in Process (Inventory) is decreased.

Entry: In the journal:

Finished goods	2,500,000	
Work in process		2,500,000

Post to the ledger:

Work in Process				Finished Goods	
2.	1,890,000	5.	2,500,000	Bal.	12,000
3.	390,000			5.	2,500,000
4b.	375,000				
Bal.	155,000				

6a. Transaction: Sales on account, $4,000,000

Analysis: The asset Accounts Receivable is increased.
The revenue Sales is increased.

Entry: In the journal:

Accounts receivable	4,000,000	
Sales		4,000,000

Post to the ledger:

Accounts Receivable			Sales	
6a.	4,000,000		6a.	4,000,000

6b. Transaction: Cost of goods sold, $2,480,000

Analysis: The expense Cost of Goods Sold is increased.
The asset Finished Goods is decreased.

Entry: In the journal:

Cost of goods sold	2,480,000	
Finished goods		2,480,000

Post to the ledger:

Finished Goods				Cost of Goods Sold	
Bal.	12,000	6b.	2,480,000	6b.	2,480,000
5.	2,500,000				
Bal.	32,000				

Exhibit 14-2 summarizes the Martinez transactions for the year. The selected accounts from the general ledger focus on how product costing is accomplished. All the inventory accounts are presented. Work in Process receives central attention. The costs of direct material used, direct labor, and factory overhead applied to product are brought into Work in Process. In turn, the costs of completed goods are transferred to Finished Goods. As goods are sold, their costs become expense in the form of Cost of Goods Sold.

APPLICATION OF OVERHEAD TO PRODUCTS

□ Cost Application

Consider a new term, *cost application*, often called *cost absorption*. Until now the term cost allocation has been used indiscriminately to refer to the identifying or tracing of accumulated costs to *any* cost objective (whether a department or a product). Indeed, *cost allocation* is a general or generic term. However, when costs are allocated *to products,* the process of allocation is frequently called *application* or *absorption*. These latter terms will be used in this chapter. In any event, be alert to obtain the exact meanings of such terms when you encounter them in practice.

□ Predetermined Overhead Application Rates

To show how factory overhead is applied to jobs, let us explore our Martinez illustration in more depth.

The following manufacturing overhead budget has been prepared for the coming year, 19X2:

	MACHINING	ASSEMBLY
Indirect labor	$69,600	$ 28,800
Supplies	14,400	5,400
Utilities	20,000	9,000
Repairs	10,000	6,000
Factory rent	24,000	16,800
Supervision	18,600	20,400
Depreciation on equipment	114,000	14,400
Insurance, property taxes, etc.	7,200	2,400
	$277,800	$103,200

As products are worked on, factory overhead is applied to the jobs. A predetermined overhead rate is used, computed as follows:

$$\text{overhead application rate} = \frac{\text{total budgeted factory overhead}}{\substack{\text{total budgeted amount of application} \\ \text{base (such as direct-labor costs,} \\ \text{direct-labor-hours, or machine-hours)}}}$$

EXHIBIT 14-2 Summary Effects of Job Costing

GENERAL JOURNAL

1. Direct materials inventory	1,900,000	
Accounts payable or cash		1,900,000
Purchases on account		
2. Work in process	1,890,000	
Direct materials inventory		1,890,000
Requisitions applied to jobs for product costing purposes		
3. Work in process	390,000	
Accrued payroll		390,000
Work tickets applied to jobs for product costing purposes		
4a. Factory department overhead control	392,000	
Cash, accounts payable, and various accounts		392,000
Overhead charged to departments as incurred for control purposes		
4b. Work in process	375,000	
Factory department overhead control		375,000
Overhead applied to products, using predetermined application rates		
5. Finished goods	2,500,000	
Work in process		2,500,000
To transfer costs of goods completed		
6a. Accounts receivable	4,000,000	
Sales		4,000,000
6b. Cost of goods sold	2,480,000	
Finished goods		2,480,000

GENERAL LEDGER (Selected accounts)

Direct Materials

Bal.	110,000	2.	1,890,000
1.	1,900,000		

Work in Process

2.	1,890,000	5.	2,500,000
3.	390,000		
4b.	375,000		

Finished Goods

Bal.	12,000	6b.	2,480,000
5.	2,500,000		

Cost of Goods Sold

6b.	2,480,000	

SUBSIDIARY LEDGER (Selected)

Job Cost Sheets

Direct Material

Direct Labor

Applied Overhead

In our illustration, the overhead rates are as follows:

| | YEAR 19X2 | |
	Machining	Assembly
Budgeted manufacturing overhead	$277,800	$103,200
Budgeted machine-hours	69,450	
Budgeted direct-labor cost		$206,400
Predetermined overhead rate, per machine-hour: $277,800 ÷ 69,450 =	$4	
Predetermined overhead rate, per direct-labor dollar: $103,200 ÷ $206,400 =		50%

Factory overhead is a conglomeration of manufacturing costs that, unlike direct material or direct labor, cannot conveniently be applied on an individual basis. But the commonly accepted theory is that such overhead is an integral part of a product's cost. Therefore it is applied in an indirect manner, using a cost-allocation base that is common to all jobs worked on and is the best available index of the product's relative utilization of, or benefits from, the overhead items. In other words, there should be a strong correlation between the factory overhead incurred and the base chosen for its application, such as machine-hours or direct-labor cost.

Two or more machines in the machining department can often be operated simultaneously by a single direct laborer. Because utilization of machines is the major overhead cost in the machining department, machine-hours are the base for application of overhead costs. This necessitates keeping track of the machine-hours used for each job, creating an added clerical cost. Thus, both direct-labor costs and machine-hours must be accumulated for each job.

In contrast, the workers in the assembly department are paid uniform hourly rates, so the cost of direct labor is an accurate reflection of the relative attention and effort devoted to various jobs. No separate job records have to be kept of the labor *hours*. All that is needed is to apply the 50% overhead rate to the cost of direct labor already entered on the job-cost sheets. Of course, if the hourly labor rates differed greatly for individuals performing identical tasks, hours of labor, rather than dollars spent for labor, would have to be used as a base. Otherwise a $9-per-hour worker would cause more overhead to be applied than an $8-per-hour worker, despite the probability that the same time would be taken and the same facilities utilized by each employee to do the same work.

These overhead rates will be used day after day throughout the year to cost the various jobs as they are worked on by each department. All overhead will be applied to all jobs worked on during the year on the appropriate basis of machine-hours or direct-labor costs of each job. If management predictions are accurate, the total overhead applied to the year's jobs on the basis of these predetermined rates should be equal to the total overhead costs actually incurred.

❏ Normalized Overhead Rates

Few companies wait until the *actual* factory overhead is finally known before the costs of products are computed. Instead, a *budgeted* or predetermined overhead rate is commonly used because most managements want a close approximation of the cost of different products before the end of a fiscal period. Essentially this need is for pricing, interim income determination, and inventory valuation.

Basically, our illustration has demonstrated the **normal costing** approach. Why? Because an annual average overhead rate is used consistently throughout the year for product costing, without altering it from day to day and from month to month. The resultant "normal" product costs include an average or normalized chunk of overhead.

As actual overhead costs are incurred by departments from month to month, they are charged, in detail, to the departments. These actual costs are accumulated weekly or monthly and are then compared with budgeted costs to obtain budget variances for performance evaluation. This *control* process is completely divorced from the *product-costing* process of applying overhead to specific jobs.

During the year and at year-end, it is unlikely that the amount incurred and applied will be equal. This variance between incurred and applied cost can be analyzed. The following are usually contributory causes: poor forecasting; inefficient use of overhead items; price changes in individual overhead items; erratic behavior of individual overhead items (e.g., repairs made only during slack time); calendar variations (e.g., 20 workdays in one month, 22 in the next); and, probably most important, operating at a different level of volume than the level used as a denominator in calculating the predetermined overhead rate (e.g., using 100,000 forecasted direct-labor hours as the denominator and then actually working only 80,000 hours).

All these peculiarities of overhead are commingled in an annual overhead pool. Thus an annual rate is predetermined and used regardless of the month-to-month peculiarities of specific overhead costs. Such an approach is more defensible than, say, applying the actual overhead for each month, because a *normal* product cost is more meaningful, and more representative for inventory-costing purposes, than an "actual" product cost that is distorted by month-to-month fluctuations in production volume and by the erratic behavior of many overhead costs. For example, the employees of a gypsum plant had the privilege of buying company-made items "at cost." It was a joke common among employees to buy "at cost" during high-volume months. Unit costs were then lower under the actual overhead application system in use, whereby overhead rates would fall as volume soared, and vice versa, as shown in the box on p. 427.

Another example of the difficulties of product costing was cited by James Lorie, who, after completing a consulting task for Chrysler Corporation, asked some top Chrysler executives if he could buy an Imperial automobile directly from the company "at cost." The response was, "We'll be happy to sell an Imperial to you at cost, which this year happens to be 120% of list price."

	ACTUAL OVERHEAD			DIRECT-LABOR HOURS	ACTUAL OVERHEAD APPLICATION RATE* PER DIRECT-LABOR HOUR
	Variable	Fixed	Total		
Peak-volume month	$60,000	$40,000	$100,000	100,000	$1.00
Low-volume month	30,000	40,000	70,000	50,000	1.40

*Divide total overhead by direct-labor hours. This overall rate can be separated into two rates, one for variable and one for fixed overhead. Note that the presence of fixed overhead causes the fluctuation in unit costs from $1.00 to $1.40. The variable rate is $.60 an hour in both months, but the fixed rate is $.40 in the peak-volume month ($40,000 ÷ 100,000) and $.80 in the low-volume month ($40,000 ÷ 50,000).

❏ Disposition of Underapplied or Overapplied Overhead

Our Martinez illustration contained the following data:

Transaction

4a.	Factory overhead incurred	$392,000
4b.	Factory overhead applied	375,000
	Underapplied factory overhead	$ 17,000

The journal entries led to the following postings:

Factory Department Overhead Control			
4a.	392,000	4b.	375,000
Bal.	17,000		

When predetermined rates are used, the difference between incurred and applied overhead is typically allowed to accumulate during the year. When the amount applied to product exceeds the amount incurred by the departments, the difference is called **overapplied** or *overabsorbed* **overhead;** when the amount applied is less than incurred, the difference is called **underapplied** or *underabsorbed* **overhead.** At year-end, the difference ($17,000 in our illustration) is disposed of in one of two major ways:

Method One: Immediate Write-off. This is the most widely used approach. The $17,000 is regarded as a reduction in current income via adding the underapplied overhead to the cost of goods sold. (The same logic is followed for overapplied overhead except that the result would be an addition to current income because cost of goods sold would be lessened.)

The theory underlying the direct write-off is that most of the goods worked on have been sold, and a more elaborate method of disposition is not worth the extra trouble. Another justification is that the extra overhead costs represented by underapplied overhead do not qualify as part of ending inventory costs because they do not represent assets. They should be written off because they largely represent inefficiency or the underutilization of available facilities.

Job-Costing Systems and Overhead Application

427

The immediate write-off eliminates the $17,000 difference with a simple journal entry:

Cost of goods sold (or a separate charge against revenue)	17,000	
Factory department overhead control		17,000
To close ending underapplied overhead directly to Cost of Goods Sold.		

Method Two: Proration among Inventories. This method prorates underapplied overhead among the accounts where the costs of the 19X2 jobs worked on are now lodged. Theoretically, if the objective is to obtain as accurate a cost allocation as possible, all of the overhead costs of the individual jobs worked on should be recomputed, using the actual rather than the original predetermined rates. This approach is rarely feasible, so the best practical attack is probably to prorate on the basis of the total manufacturing costs of the 19X2 jobs in each of three accounts (Work in Process, $155,000; Finished Goods, $32,000; and Cost of Goods Sold, $2,480,000), assuming that the beginning Finished-Goods Inventory was sold during 19X2:

	(1) UNADJUSTED BALANCE, END OF 19X2*	(2) DEDUCT 19X1 JOBS	(3) (1) − (2) BASIS FOR PRORATION
Work in Process	$ 155,000	$ —	$ 155,000
Finished Goods	32,000	—	32,000
Cost of Goods Sold	2,480,000	12,000	2,468,000
			$2,655,000

	(4) PRORATION OF UNDERAPPLIED OVERHEAD	(1) + (4) ADJUSTED BALANCE END OF 19X2
Work in Process	155/2,655 × 17,000 = $ 992	$ 155,992
Finished Goods	32/2,655 × 17,000 = 205	32,205
Cost of Goods Sold	2,468/2,655 × 17,000 = 15,803	2,495,803
	$17,000	

*See Exhibit 14-2, page 424, for details.

The journal entry for the proration follows:

Work in process	992	
Finished goods	205	
Cost of goods sold	15,803	
Factory department overhead control		17,000
To prorate ending underapplied overhead among the accounts where the costs of the 19X2 jobs worked on are now lodged.		

EXHIBIT 14-3 Disposition of Underapplied Factory Overhead

Method One: Immediate Write-off

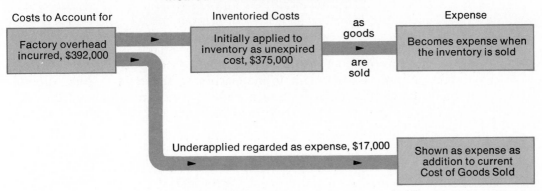

Method Two: Proration Among Inventories

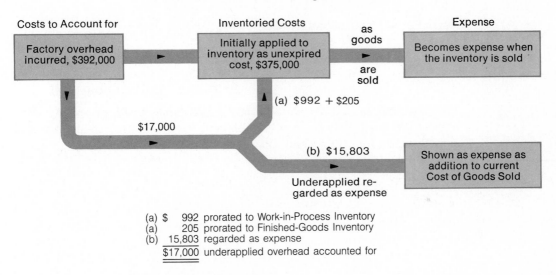

(a) $	992	prorated to Work-in-Process Inventory
(a)	205	prorated to Finished-Goods Inventory
(b)	15,803	regarded as expense
	$17,000	underapplied overhead accounted for

The amounts prorated to inventories here are not significant. In practical situations, prorating is done only when inventory valuations would be materially affected.

Exhibit 14-3 provides a schematic comparison of the two major methods of disposing of underapplied (or overapplied) factory overhead. In sum, overhead application will rarely coincide with overhead incurrence.

☐ The Use of Variable and Fixed Application Rates

As we have seen, overhead application is the most troublesome aspect of product costing. The presence of fixed costs is the biggest single reason for the costing difficulties. Most companies have made no distinction between variable- and fixed-cost behavior in the design of their accounting systems. For instance, reconsider the development of overhead rates in our illustration. The machining department developed the rate as follows:

Job-Costing
Systems and
Overhead
Application

429

$$\text{overhead application rate} = \frac{\text{budgeted total overhead}}{\text{budgeted machine-hours}}$$

$$= \frac{\$277,800}{69,450} = \$4 \text{ per machine-hour}$$

Some companies distinguish between variable overhead and fixed overhead for product costing as well as for control purposes. This distinction could have been made in the machining department. Rent, supervision, depreciation, and insurance would have been considered the fixed portion of the total manufacturing overhead, and two rates could have been developed:

$$\text{variable-overhead application rate} = \frac{\text{budgeted total variable overhead}}{\text{budgeted machine-hours}}$$

$$= \frac{\$114,000}{69,450}$$

$$= \$1.64 \text{ per machine-hour}$$

$$\text{fixed-overhead application rate} = \frac{\text{budgeted total fixed overhead}}{\text{budgeted machine-hours}^1}$$

$$= \frac{\$163,800}{69,450}$$

$$= \$2.36 \text{ per machine-hour}$$

As the next chapter explains, such rates can be used for product costing, and distinctions between variable and fixed overhead incurrence can also be made for control purposes.

❏ Actual Versus Normal Costing

The overall system we have just described is sometimes called an actual costing system because every effort is made to trace the actual costs, as incurred, to the physical units benefited. However, it is only partly an actual system because the overhead, by definition, cannot be definitely assigned to physical products. Instead, overhead is applied on an average or normalized basis, in order to get representative or normal inventory valuations. Hence we shall label the system a *normal* system. The cost of the manufactured product is composed of *actual* direct material, *actual* direct labor, and *normal* applied overhead.

The two job-order costing approaches may be compared as follows:

	ACTUAL COSTING	NORMAL COSTING
Direct materials	Actual	Actual
Direct labor	Actual	Actual
Manufacturing overhead	Actual	Predetermined rates*

*Actual inputs (such as direct-labor hours or direct-labor costs) multiplied by predetermined overhead rates (computed by dividing total budgeted manufacturing overhead by a budgeted application base such as direct-labor hours).

[1] Alternatively, the denominator could be a measure of practical capacity, that is, a measure of the *maximum* feasible number of machine-hours.

Under actual costing no overhead would be applied as jobs were worked on. Instead, overhead would be applied only after all overhead costs for the year were known. Then, using an "actual" average rate(s) instead of a predetermined rate(s), costs would be applied to all jobs that had been worked on throughout the year. All costs incurred would be exactly offset by costs applied to the Work-in-Process Inventory. However, increased accuracy would be obtained at the sacrifice of *timeliness* in reporting costs.

Compare the appropriate journal entries, using the data from our Martinez illustration (in thousands of dollars):

		ACTUAL COSTING		NORMAL COSTING	
4a.	Factory department overhead control	392		392	
	Cash, accounts payable, etc.		392		392
4b.	Work in process	—		375	
	Factory department overhead control		—		375
At end of year:	Work in process	392		—	
	Factory department overhead control		392		—
	Cost of goods sold	—		17	
	Factory department overhead control		—		17

Normal costing has replaced actual costing in many organizations precisely because the latter approach fails to provide costs of products as they are worked on during the year. It is possible to use a normal-costing system plus year-end adjustments to produce final results that closely approximate the results under actual costing. To do so in our illustration, the underapplied overhead is prorated among Work in Process, Finished Goods, and Cost of Goods Sold, as shown earlier in this chapter (Method Two in Exhibit 14-3).

❏ Product Costing in Service and Nonprofit Organizations

This chapter has concentrated on how to apply costs to manufactured products. However, the job-costing approach is used in nonmanufacturing situations too. Examples include appliance repair, auto repair, dentistry, auditing, income tax preparation, and medical care. For example, universities have research "projects," airlines have repair and overhaul "jobs," and public accountants have audit "engagements."

To illustrate, consider service industries, such as repairing, consulting, legal, and accounting services. Each customer order is a different job with a special account or order number. Sometimes only costs are traced directly to the job, sometimes only revenue is traced, and sometimes both. For example, automobile repair shops typically have a repair order for each car worked on, with space for allocating materials and labor. The customer is permitted to see only a copy showing the retail prices of the materials, parts, and labor billed to his or her order. If the repair manager wants cost data, he may also have a system designed so that the "actual" parts and labor costs of each order are traced to a duplicate copy of the job order. That is why you often see auto mechanics "punching in" and "punching out" their starting and stopping times on "work tickets" as each new order is worked on.

The job-order approach occurs in not-for-profit industries too. Costs or revenues may be traced to individual patients, individual social welfare cases, individual doctoral seminars, and individual research projects.

In nonprofit organizations the "product" is usually not called a "job order." Instead, it may be called a program or a class of service. A "program" is an identifiable segment of activities that frequently produce outputs in the form of services rather than goods. Examples include a safety program, an education program, a family counseling program. Often many departments work simultaneously on many programs, so the "job-order" costing challenge is to "apply" the various department costs to the various programs. Then wiser management decisions may be made regarding the allocation of limited resources among competing programs.

Summary

Accounting systems should be designed to satisfy control and product-costing purposes simultaneously. Costs are initially charged to department responsibility centers (cost centers); then they are applied to products in order to get inventory costs for balance sheets and income statements and in order to guide pricing and to evaluate product performance.

Product costing is an averaging process. Process costing deals with broad averages and great masses of like units. Job costing deals with narrow averages and a unique unit or a small batch of like units.

Indirect manufacturing costs (factory overhead) are often applied to products using predetermined overhead rates. The rates are computed by dividing total budgeted overhead by a measure of total activity such as expected labor-hours or machine-hours. These rates are usually annual averages. The resulting product costs are normal costs, consisting of actual direct material plus actual direct labor plus applied overhead using predetermined rates.

Summary Problem for Your Review

❑ Problem

Review the Martinez illustration, especially Exhibits 14-2 and 14-3. Prepare an income statement for 19X2 through the gross profit line.

❑ Solution

Exhibit 14-4 recapitulates the final impact of the Martinez illustration on the financial statements. Note how the immediate write-off means that the $17,000 is added to the cost of goods sold.

As you study Exhibit 14-4, trace the three major elements of cost (direct material, direct labor, and factory overhead) through the accounts.

EXHIBIT 14-4   Relation of Costs to Financial Statements

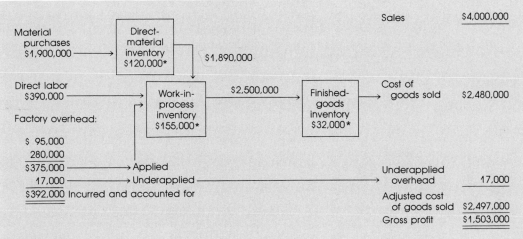

*Ending balance.

Highlights to Remember

1. This chapter emphasized product costing, which may take various forms. However, every accounting system also has a fundamental control purpose:

CONTROL PURPOSE	PRODUCT-COSTING PURPOSE
Accumulate costs by	Apply costs by
a. Responsibility center	Job-order costing
b. Responsibility center	Process costing
c. Responsibility center	Combinations of job-order and process costing

2. Accounting for overhead is frequently the most confusing aspect of job-order costing. If normalized overhead rates are used, underapplied or overapplied overhead usually cumulates from month to month. The final amount of underapplied or overapplied overhead is typically added to or subtracted from the Cost of Goods Sold at the end of the year.

3. If the amount of underapplied or overapplied overhead is significant, it is prorated over the appropriate inventory accounts as well as Cost of Goods Sold.

Accounting Vocabulary

Job order; job-order costing; normal cost system; overapplied factory overhead; process costing; underapplied factory overhead.

Appendix 14: Relationships Among Source Documents, Subsidiary Ledgers, and General Ledger

The source documents, such as material requisitions or work tickets, which were illustrated in Exhibit 14-1, are usually made in multiple copies, each being used for a specific task. For example, a materials requisition could be executed by a foreman in as many as five copies and disposed of as follows:

1. Kept by storekeeper who issues the materials.
2. Used by stores ledger clerk (or a computer) for posting to perpetual inventory cards for materials.
3. Used by job-order cost clerk (or a computer) to post the Job-Cost Sheet (Exhibit 14-1).
4. Used by general ledger clerk as a basis for a summary monthly entry for all of the month's requisitions (Exhibit 14-2).
5. Retained by the foreman. He can use the requisition as a cross check against the performance reports which show his usage of material.

Of course, machine accounting and electronic computer systems can use a single punched card as a requisition. Sorting, re-sorting, classifications, reclassifications, summaries, and re-summaries can easily provide any desired information. Because these source documents are the foundation for data accumulation and reports, the importance of accurate initial recording cannot be overemphasized.

Copies of these source documents are used for direct postings to subsidiary ledgers. Sometimes the subsidiary ledgers will contain summarized postings of daily batches of source documents, rather than individual direct postings. Accounting data are most condensed in the general ledger and most detailed on the source documents, as the following listing shows:

ITEM	
Work in Process	General ledger (usually monthly totals only)
Job-Cost Sheets	Subsidiary ledgers (perhaps daily summaries)
Material Requisitions or Work Tickets	Source documents (minute to minute, hour to hour)

The daily scorekeeping duties are accomplished with source documents and subsidiary ledgers. Copies of the source documents are independently summarized and are usually posted to the general ledger only once a month. See entry 2, Exhibit 14-2, where, for convenience, a year was used, rather than a month.

In order to obtain a bird's-eye view of a system, we have been concentrating on general ledger relationships. However, keep in mind that the general ledger is a very small part of the accountant's daily work. Furthermore, current control is aided by hourly, daily, or weekly flash reports of material, labor, and machine usage. The general ledger itself is a summary device. Reliance on the general ledger for current control is ill-advised because the resulting reports come too late and are often too stale for management control use.

Fundamental Assignment Material

14-1. Basic journal entries. (Alternate is 14–19.) Consider the following data for a printing company (in millions):

Direct-materials inventory, December 31, 19X1	$19
Work-in-process inventory, December 31, 19X1	31
Finished-goods inventory, December 31, 19X1	90

Summarized transactions for 19X2:

a. Purchases of direct materials	88
b. Direct materials used	77
c. Direct labor	90
d. Factory overhead incurred	80
e. Factory overhead applied, 80% of direct labor	?
f. Cost of goods completed and transferred to finished goods	220
g. Cost of goods sold	230
h. Sales on account	400

REQUIRED:

1. Prepare journal entries for 19X2. Omit explanations.
2. Show the T-accounts for all inventories, Cost of Goods Sold, and Factory Department Overhead Control. Compute the ending balances of the inventories. Do not adjust for underapplied or overapplied factory overhead.

14-2. Disposition of overhead. Refer to the preceding problem. Assume that overhead was overapplied by $20 and that the ending inventories were $30, $30, and $70, respectively. Unadjusted cost of goods sold is still $230.

REQUIRED:

1. Assume that the $20 was written off solely as an adjustment to cost of goods sold. Prepare the journal entry.
2. Management has decided to prorate the $20 to the pertinent accounts (using the unadjusted ending balances) instead of writing it off solely as an adjustment of cost of goods sold. Prepare the journal entry. Would gross profit be higher or lower than in Requirement 1? By how much?

Additional Assignment Material

14-3. "The special decision purpose of accounting is difficult to satisfy on a routine basis." Why?

14-4. "Cost application or absorption is terminology related to the product-costing purpose." Why?

14-5. What are some reasons for differences between the amounts of *incurred* and *applied* overhead?

14-6. Sometimes five copies of a stores requisition are needed. What are their uses?

14–7. "The general ledger is an incidental part of the accountant's daily work." Explain.

14–8. "Costs of inefficiency cannot be regarded as assets." Explain.

14–9. "Under actual overhead application, unit costs soar as volume increases, and vice versa." Do you agree? Explain.

14–10. "Overhead application is overhead allocation." Do you agree? Explain.

14–11. Distinguish between job costing and process costing.

14–12. "The basic distinction between job-order costing and process costing is the breadth of the denominator." Explain.

14–13. Describe the subsidiary ledger for work in process in a job-cost system.

14–14. Define *normal costing.*

14–15. What is the best theoretical method of allocating underapplied or overapplied overhead, assuming that the objective is to obtain as accurate a cost application as possible?

14–16. Job-cost sheet. Stanford University uses job-cost sheets for various research projects. A major reason for such records is to justify requests for reimbursement of costs on projects sponsored by the federal government.

Consider the following summarized data regarding Project No. 48 conducted by some physicists:

Jan. 5   Direct materials, various metals, $900
Jan. 7   Direct materials, various chemicals, $800
Jan. 5–12 Direct labor, research associates, 100 hours
Jan. 7–12 Direct labor, research assistants, 200 hours

Research associates receive $30 per hour; assistants, $18. The overhead rate is 90% of direct-labor cost.

REQUIRED:

Sketch a job-cost sheet. Post all the data to the cost sheet. Compute the total cost of the project through January 12.

14–17. Direct materials. Fill in the blanks (in millions of dollars):

	1	2	3	4
Direct-materials inventory, Dec. 31, 19X1	5	9	3	—
Purchased	3	7	—	6
Used	2	—	8	3
Direct-materials inventory, Dec. 31, 19X2	—	4	6	5

14–18. Direct materials. The QP Company had an ending inventory of direct materials of $10 million. During the year the company had acquired $14 million of additional direct materials and had used $8 million. Compute the beginning inventory.

14–19. Normal costing system. (Alternate is 14–1). The following data (in thousands) summarize the factory operations of the Bensmeier Manufacturing Co. for the year 19X1, its first year in business:

a. Direct materials purchased for cash	$230
b. Direct materials issued and used	220
c. Labor used directly on production	100
d1. Indirect labor	80
d2. Depreciation of plant and equipment	40
d3. Miscellaneous factory overhead (ordinarily would be detailed)	30
e. Overhead applied: 180% of direct labor	?
f. Cost of production completed	450
g. Cost of goods sold	300

REQUIRED:

1. Prepare summary journal entries. Omit explanations. For purposes of this problem, combine the items in *d* as "overhead incurred."
2. Show the T-accounts for all inventories, Cost of Goods Sold, and Factory Department Overhead Control. Compute the ending balances of the inventories. Do not adjust for underapplied or overapplied factory overhead.

14–20. Accounting for overhead, predetermined rates. Thomas Allan and Co. uses a predetermined overhead rate in applying overhead to individual job orders on a *machine-hour* basis for Department No. 1 and on a *direct-labor hour* basis for Department No. 2. At the beginning of 19X4, the company's management made the following budget predictions:

	DEPT. NO. 1	DEPT. NO. 2
Direct-labor cost	$1,200,000	$1,000,000
Factory overhead	$1,200,000	$ 800,000
Direct-labor hours	80,000	100,000
Machine-hours	240,000	15,000

Cost records of recent months show the following accumulations for Job Order No. 455:

	DEPT. NO. 1	DEPT. NO. 2
Material placed in production	$10,000	$30,000
Direct-labor cost	$ 9,600	$ 8,000
Direct-labor hours	800	1,000
Machine-hours	3,000	200

REQUIRED:

1. What is the predetermined overhead *rate* that should be applied in Department No. 1? In Department No. 2?
2. What is the *total overhead* cost of Job Order No. 455?
3. If Job Order No. 455 consists of 100 units of product, what is the *unit cost* of this job?
4. At the *end* of 19X4, actual results for the year's operations were as follows:

	DEPT. NO. 1	DEPT. NO. 2
Actual overhead costs incurred	$1,000,000	$950,000
Actual direct-labor hours	800,000	100,000
Actual machine-hours	240,000	17,000

Find the underapplied or overapplied overhead for each department and for the factory as a whole.

14–21. Journal entries for overhead. Consider the following summarized data regarding 19X3:

	BUDGET	ACTUAL
Indirect labor	$300,000	$320,000
Supplies	40,000	35,000
Repairs	90,000	85,000
Utilities	100,000	110,000
Factory rent	120,000	120,000
Supervision	60,000	63,000
Depreciation, equipment	200,000	200,000
Insurance, property taxes, etc.	40,000	41,000
a. Total factory overhead	$950,000	$974,000
b. Direct materials used	$1,500,000	$1,410,000
c. Direct labor	$1,000,000	$1,100,000

REQUIRED:

Omit explanations for journal entries.

1. Prepare a summary journal entry for the actual overhead incurred for 19X3.
2. Prepare summary journal entries for direct materials used and direct labor.
3. Factory overhead was applied by using a budgeted rate based on budgeted direct-labor costs. Compute the rate. Prepare a summary journal entry for the application of overhead to products.
4. Post the journal entries to the T-accounts for Work in Process and Factory Department Overhead Control.
5. Suppose overapplied or underapplied factory overhead is written off as an adjustment to cost of goods sold. Prepare the journal entry. Post the overhead to the overhead T-account.

14–22. Relationships among overhead items. Fill in the unknowns:

	Case A	Case B	Case C
Budgeted factory overhead	$4,000,000	?	$2,000,000
Budgeted application base:			
Direct-labor cost	$2,000,000		
Direct-labor hours		300,000	
Machine-hours			200,000
Overhead application rate	?	$8	?

14–23. Relationship among overhead items. Fill in the unknowns:

	Case 1	Case 2
a. Budgeted factory overhead	$800,000	$420,000
b. Application base, budgeted direct-labor cost	500,000	?
c. Budgeted factory-overhead rate	?	80%
d. Direct-labor cost incurred	550,000	?
e. Factory overhead incurred	860,000	400,000
f. Factory overhead applied	?	?
g. Underapplied (overapplied) factory overhead	?	30,000

14–24. Underapplied and overapplied overhead. Manwell Bandage Corporation applies factory overhead at a rate of $3.50 per direct-labor hour. Selected data for 19X3 operations are (in thousands):

	CASE 1	CASE 2
Direct-labor cost	$120	$210
Direct-labor hours	50	55
Indirect-labor cost	$ 25	$ 35
Sales commissions	$ 15	$ 10
Depreciation, manufacturing equipment	$ 10	$ 15
Direct-material cost	$200	$230
Factory fuel costs	$ 12	$ 18
Depreciation, finished-goods warehouse	$ 4	$ 14
Cost of goods sold	$380	$490
All other factory costs	$119	$138

REQUIRED:

Compute for both cases:

1. Factory overhead applied
2. Total factory overhead incurred
3. Amount of underapplied or overapplied factory overhead

14–25. Disposition of overhead. Assume the following at the end of 19X1 (in thousands):

Cost of goods sold	$300
Direct-materials inventory	80
Work in process	150
Finished goods	50
Factory department overhead control	30 cr.

REQUIRED:

1. Assume that the underapplied or overapplied overhead is regarded as an adjustment to cost of goods sold. Prepare the journal entry.
2. Assume that the underapplied or overapplied overhead is prorated among the pertinent accounts in proportion to their ending unadjusted balances. Show computations and prepare the journal entry.
3. Which adjustment, the one in Requirement 1 or 2, would result in the higher gross profit? Explain, indicating the amount of the difference.

14–26. Disposition of overhead. A company uses a job-order system. At the end of 19X4 the following balances existed (in millions):

Cost of goods sold	$50
Finished goods	20
Work in process	30
Factory overhead (actual)	50
Factory overhead (applied)	40

REQUIRED:

1. Prepare journal entries for two different ways to dispose of the underapplied overhead.
2. Gross profit, before considering the effects in Requirement 1, was $40 million. What is the adjusted gross profit under the two methods demonstrated?

14–27. Disposition of year-end underapplied overhead. A company that uses a normal cost system has the following balances at the end of its first year's operations:

Work-in-process control	$200,000
Finished-goods control	100,000
Cost of goods sold	500,000
Actual factory overhead	360,000
Factory overhead applied	410,000

Prepare journal entries for two different ways to dispose of the year-end overhead balances. By how much would gross profit differ?

14–28. **Relationships of manufacturing costs.** (CMA.) Selected data concerning the past fiscal year's operations (000 omitted) of the Televans Manufacturing Company are presented below:

	INVENTORIES		
	Beginning	Ending	
Raw materials	$75	$85	
Work in process	80	30	
Finished goods	90	110	
Other data:			
Raw materials used			$326
Total manufacturing costs charged to production during the year (includes raw materials, direct labor, and factory overhead applied at a rate of 60% of direct-labor cost)			686
Cost of goods available for sale			826
Selling and general expenses			25

REQUIRED:

Select the best answer for each of the following items:

1. The cost of raw materials purchased during the year amounted to
   a. $411   d. $336
   b. $360   e. None of these
   c. $316

2. Direct-labor costs charged to production during the year amounted to
   a. $135   d. $216
   b. $225   e. None of these
   c. $360

3. The cost of goods manufactured during the year was
   a. $636   d. $716
   b. $766   e. None of these
   c. $736

4. The cost of goods sold during the year was
   a. $736   d. $801
   b. $716   e. None of these
   c. $691

14–29. **Straightforward job costing.** The Dunkel Custom Furniture Company has two departments. Data for 19X5 include the following:
Inventories, January 1, 19X5:

Direct materials (30 types)	$100,000
Work in process (in assembly)	60,000
Finished goods	20,000

Manufacturing overhead budget for 19X5:

	MACHINING	ASSEMBLY
Indirect labor	$200,000	$400,000
Supplies	40,000	50,000
Utilities	100,000	90,000
Repairs	150,000	100,000
Supervision	100,000	200,000
Factory rent	50,000	50,000
Depreciation on equipment	150,000	100,000
Insurance, property taxes, etc.	50,000	60,000
	$840,000	$1,050,000

Budgeted machine-hours were 84,000; budgeted direct-labor cost in Assembly was $2,100,000. Manufacturing overhead was applied using predetermined rates on the basis of machine-hours in Machining and on the basis of direct-labor cost in Assembly.

Following is a summary of actual events for the year:

		MACHINING	ASSEMBLY	TOTAL
a.	Direct materials purchased			$ 1,700,000
b.	Direct materials requisitioned	$1,000,000	$ 600,000	1,600,000
c.	Direct-labor costs incurred	800,000	2,600,000	3,400,000
d1.	Factory overhead incurred	1,000,000	1,000,000	2,000,000
d2.	Factory overhead applied	800,000	?	?
e.	Cost of goods completed	—	—	7,110,000
f1.	Sales	—	—	12,000,000
f2.	Cost of goods sold	—	—	7,100,000

The ending work in process (all in Assembly) was $50,000.

1. Compute the predetermined overhead rates.
2. Compute the amount of the machine-hours actually worked.
3. Compute the amount of factory overhead applied in the assembly department.
4. Prepare general journal entries for transactions *a* through *f*. Work solely with the total amounts, not the details for Machining and Assembly. Explanations are not required. Show data in thousands of dollars. Present T-accounts, including ending inventory balances, for direct materials, work in process, and finished goods.
5. Prepare a partial income statement similar to the one illustrated in Exhibit 14-4. Overapplied or underapplied overhead is written off as an adjustment of current cost of goods sold.

14–30. **Actual versus normal costing.** (Alternate is 14–31.) B Company has the following costs:

Direct materials used	$200,000
Direct labor	300,000
Manufacturing overhead applied, 150% of direct labor	450,000
Actual manufacturing overhead incurred	500,000

There were no beginning inventories. At year-end, one-fourth of the production is unsold and is held as finished-goods inventory. The costs in finished-goods inventory are in the same proportion as the costs in cost of goods sold.

1. Assume normal costing is used and that underapplied overhead is written off as an expense. Compute the finished-goods inventory.
2. Assume actual costing is used. Compute the finished-goods inventory.
3. What is the major difficulty with using actual costing? Do you favor proration of underapplied overhead when normal costing is used? Why?

14–31. **Normal versus actual costing.** (Alternate is 14–30.) Drew Company has compiled the following costs:

Actual manufacturing overhead incurred	$951,000
Direct labor	480,000
Direct materials used	786,000

There were no beginning inventories. At the end of the year, one-third of the production is unsold and is held as finished-goods inventory. The costs in finished-goods inventory are in the same proportion as in cost of goods sold.

REQUIRED:

1. Assume that normal costing is used. Manufacturing overhead is at a rate of 190% of direct labor. Underapplied or overapplied overhead is written off as an expense. Compute the finished-goods inventory.
2. Assume that actual costing is used. Compute the finished-goods inventory.
3. What is the major difficulty with using actual costing? Do you favor proration of underapplied overhead when normal costing is used? Why?

14–32. **Comparison of overhead accounting for control and for product costing.** The Faston Company has an overhead rate of $3 per direct-labor hour, based on expected variable overhead of $100,000 per year, expected fixed overhead of $200,000 per year, and expected direct-labor hours of 100,000 per year.
Data for the year's operations follow:

	DIRECT-LABOR HOURS USED	OVERHEAD COSTS INCURRED*
First six months	60,000	$168,000
Last six months	36,000	136,000

*Fixed costs incurred were exactly equal to budgeted amounts throughout the year.

1. What is the underapplied or overapplied overhead for each six-month period? Label your answer as underapplied or overapplied.
2. Explain *briefly* (not over 50 words for each part) the probable reasons for the exact figures attributable to the causes you cite.

14–33. **Finding unknowns.** (Alternate is 14–34.) The Kroeger Company has the following balances on December 31, 19X7. All amounts are in millions:

Factory overhead applied	$180
Cost of goods sold	400
Factory overhead incurred	200
Direct-materials inventory	40
Finished-goods inventory	140
Work-in-process inventory	80

The cost of goods completed was $380. The cost of direct materials requisitioned for production during 19X7 was $170. The cost of direct materials purchased was $190. Factory overhead was applied to production at a rate of 180% of direct-labor cost.

Compute the beginning inventory balances of direct materials, work in process, and finished goods. These computations can be made without considering any possible adjustments for overapplied or underapplied overhead.

14–34. **Finding unknowns.** (Alternate is 14–33.) The W Company has the following balances (in millions) as of December 31, 19X8:

Work-in-process inventory	$ 7
Finished-goods inventory	150
Direct-materials inventory	70
Factory overhead incurred	150
Factory overhead applied at 150% of direct-labor cost	120
Cost of goods sold	300

The cost of direct materials purchased during 19X8 was $230. The cost of direct materials requisitioned for production during 19X8 was $200. The cost of goods completed was $404, all in millions.

Before considering any year-end adjustments for overapplied or underapplied overhead, compute the beginning inventory balances of direct materials, work in process, and finished goods.

14–35. **Appendix 14 problem: source documents.** Refer to Problem 14–19. For each journal entry, indicate (a) the most likely name for the source documents that would authorize the entry, and (b) how the subsidiary ledgers, if any, would be affected.

14–36. **Appendix 14 problem: source documents.** Refer to Problem 14–1. For each journal entry, indicate (a) the most likely name for the source documents that would authorize the entry, and (b) how the subsidiary ledgers, if any, would be affected.

14–37. **Nonprofit job costing.** Job-order costing is usually identified with manufacturing companies. However, service industries and nonprofit organizations also use the method. Suppose a social service agency has a cost-accounting system that tracks cost by department (for example, family counseling, general welfare, and foster children) and by case. In this way, the manager of the agency is better able to determine how her limited resources (mostly professional social workers) should be allocated. Furthermore, her interchanges with her superiors and various politicians are more fruitful when she can cite the costs of various types of cases.

The condensed line-item budget for the general welfare department of the agency for 19X6 showed:

Professional salaries:		
Level 12	6 @ $32,000 = $192,000	
Level 10	18 @ $24,000 = 432,000	
Level 8	30 @ $16,000 = 480,000	$1,104,000
Other costs		441,600
Total costs		$1,545,600

For costing various cases, the manager favored using a single overhead application rate based on the ratio of total overhead to direct labor. The latter was defined as those professional salaries assigned to specific cases.

The professional workers filled out a weekly "case time" report, which approximated the hours spent for each case.

The instructions on the report were: "Indicate how much time (in hours) you spent on each case. Unassigned time should be listed separately." About 20% of available time was unassigned to specific cases. It was used for professional development (for example, continuing education programs). "Unassigned time" became a part of "overhead," as distinguished from the direct labor.

REQUIRED:

1. Compute the "overhead rate" as a percentage of direct labor (that is, the assignable professional salaries).
2. Suppose that last week a welfare case, Client No. 462, required two hours of Level 12 time, four hours of Level 10 time, and nine hours of Level 8 time. How much job cost should be allocated to Client No. 462 for the week? Assume that all professional employees work a 1,650-hour year.

14-38. Job costing in a consulting firm. AB Engineering Consultants is a firm of professional civil engineers. It mostly has surveying jobs for the heavy construction industry throughout California and Nevada. The firm obtains its jobs by giving fixed-price quotations, so profitability is highly dependent on the ability to predict the time required for the various subtasks on the job. (This situation is similar to that in the auditing profession, where times are budgeted for such audit steps as reconciling cash and confirming accounts receivable.)

A client may be served by various professional staff, who hold positions in the hierarchy from partners to managers to senior engineers to assistants. In addition, there are secretaries and other employees.

AB Engineering has the following budget for 19X4:

Compensation of professional staff	$2,000,000
Other costs	800,000
Total budgeted costs	$2,800,000

Each professional staff member must submit a weekly time report, which is used for charging hours to a client job-order sheet. The time report has seven columns, one for each day of the week. Its rows are as follows:

Chargeable hours:
  Client 234
  Client 262
  Etc.
Nonchargeable hours:
  Attending seminar on new equipment
  Unassigned time
  Etc.

In turn, these time reports are used for charging hours and costs to the client job-order sheets. The managing partner regards these job sheets as absolutely essential for measuring the profitability of various jobs and for providing an "experience base for improving predictions on future jobs."

REQUIRED:

1. This firm applies overhead to jobs at a predetermined percentage of the professional compensation charged directly to the job ("direct labor"). For all categories of professional personnel, chargeable hours average 85% of available hours. The nonchargeable hours are regarded as additional overhead. What is the overhead rate as a percentage of the "direct labor," the chargeable professional compensation cost?

2. A senior engineer works 48 weeks per year, 40 hours per week. His compensation is $36,000. He has worked on two jobs during the past week, devoting 10 hours to Job 234 and 30 hours to Job 262. How much cost should be charged to Job 234 because of his work there?

14–39. Reconstruction of transactions. (This problem is more challenging than the others in this chapter.)

You are asked to bring the following incomplete accounts of a plant in a foreign country up to date through January 31, 19X2. Also consider the data that appear after the T-accounts.

Direct-Materials Inventory		Accrued Factory Payroll	
12/31/X1 Balance 15,000			1/31/X2 Balance 3,000

Work-in-Process		Factory Department Overhead Control	
		Total January charges 57,000	

Finished Goods		Cost of Goods Sold	
12/31/X1 Balance 20,000			

Additional Information

1. The overhead is applied using a predetermined rate that is set every December by forecasting the following year's overhead and relating it to forecast direct-labor costs. The budget for 19X2 called for $400,000 of direct labor and $600,000 of factory overhead.
2. The only job unfinished on January 31, 19X2, was No. 419, on which total labor charges were $2,000 (125 direct-labor hours), and total direct-material charges were $8,000.
3. Total materials placed into production during January totaled $90,000.
4. Cost of goods completed during January was $180,000.
5. January 31 balances of direct materials totaled $20,000.
6. Finished-goods inventory as of January 31 was $15,000.
7. All factory workers earn the same rate of pay. Direct-labor hours for January totaled 2,500. Indirect labor and supervision totaled $10,000.
8. The gross factory payroll paid on January paydays totaled $52,000. Ignore withholdings.
9. All "actual" factory overhead incurred during January has already been posted.

REQUIRED:

a. Direct materials purchased during January
b. Cost of goods sold during January
c. Direct-labor costs incurred during January
d. Overhead applied during January
e. Balance, Accrued Factory Payroll, December 31, 19X1
f. Balance, Work in Process, December 31, 19X1
g. Balance, Work in Process, January 31, 19X2
h. Overapplied or underapplied overhead for January

15

OVERHEAD APPLICATION: DIRECT AND ABSORPTION COSTING

Learning Objectives

When you have finished studying this chapter, you should be able to

1. Identify the basic feature that distinguishes the direct-costing approach from the absorption approach

2. Construct an income statement, using each of the two product-costing approaches

3. Identify the nature of the production volume variance, compute it, and state how it should appear in the income statement

4. Identify the two methods and their rationale for disposing of the standard cost variances at the end of a year

5. Identify the differences among the three alternative cost bases of an absorption-costing system: actual, normal, and standard

6. Analyze and compare all the major variances in a standard cost system (Appendix 15A)

7. Prepare journal entries for a standard cost system (Appendix 15B)

The preceding chapter concentrated on how an accounting system is used to *accumulate* costs by departments and to *apply* costs to the products (or services) that are produced by those departments. This chapter[1] concentrates on two major variations of product costing. We use a standard product-costing system here for illustrative purposes. However, these variations can be used in nonstandard product-costing systems too.

DIRECT VERSUS ABSORPTION COSTING

❑ Accounting for Fixed Manufacturing Overhead

Two major methods of product costing will be compared in this chapter: **direct costing** (the contribution approach) and **absorption costing** (the functional, full-costing, or traditional approach). These methods differ in only one conceptual respect: Fixed manufacturing overhead is excluded from the cost of products under direct costing but included in the cost of products under absorption costing. In other words, direct costing signifies that fixed factory overhead is not inventoried. In contrast, absorption costing signifies that fixed factory overhead is inventoried.

Direct costing is more accurately called **variable** or **marginal costing,** because in substance it applies only the *variable* production costs to the product. As Exhibit 15-1 shows, fixed manufacturing overhead (fixed factory overhead) is regarded as an expired cost to be immediately charged against sales rather than as an unexpired cost to be held back as inventory and charged against sales later as a part of cost of goods sold.

The term "direct" costing is widely used, but "variable" costing is a more accurate description. Why? Because, as Exhibit 15-1 shows, the "direct" costing approach to the inventorying of costs is not confined to only "direct" materials and labor; it also includes an "indirect" cost—the *variable* manufacturing overhead. Such terminological confusion is unfortunate but apparently unavoidable in a field such as management accounting, where new analytical ideas or approaches arise in isolated fashion. Newly coined terms, which may not be accurately descriptive, often become embedded too deeply to be supplanted later.

Take a moment to reflect on Exhibit 15-1. Also, reexamine Exhibit 3-2, page 61, which provides an overview of income statement and balance sheet relationships.

Absorption costing is much more widely used than direct costing, although the growing use of the contribution approach in performance measurement and cost analysis has led to increasing use of direct costing for internal-reporting purposes. Neither the public accounting profession nor the Internal Revenue Service approves of direct costing for external-reporting purposes.

Overhead
Application:
Direct and
Absorption
Costing

447

[1] Chapter 15 may be studied without having studied Chapter 14. However, Chapter 3 (particularly the first half, which is worth reviewing now) and Chapter 7 should be studied before undertaking Chapter 15. This book was written to permit the utmost flexibility. In particular, many instructors may prefer to follow Chapter 3 with Chapter 14 and then follow Chapter 7 with Chapter 15.

EXHIBIT 15-1

Comparison
of Flow of
Costs

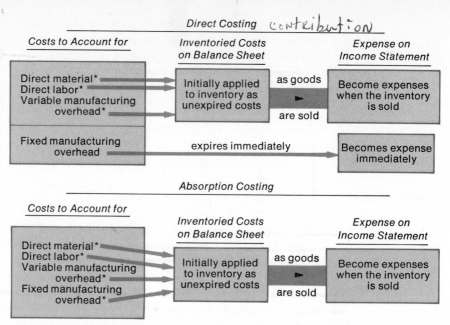

*As goods are manufactured, the costs are "applied" to inventory usually via the use of unit costs.

☐ Facts for Illustration

To make these ideas more concrete, consider the following example. The Tolman Company had the following operating characteristics in 19X4 and 19X5:

BASIC PRODUCTION DATA AT STANDARD COST	
Direct material	$1.30
Direct labor	1.50
Variable manufacturing overhead	.20
Standard variable costs per unit	$3.00

Fixed manufacturing overhead (fixed factory overhead) was $150,000. Expected production in each year was 150,000 units. Sales price, $5 per unit.

Selling and administrative expense is assumed for simplicity as being all fixed at $65,000 yearly, except for sales commissions at 5% of dollar sales.

	19X4	19X5
In units:		
Opening inventory	—	30,000
Production	170,000	140,000
Sales	140,000	160,000
Ending inventory	30,000	10,000

There were no variances from the standard variable manufacturing costs, and fixed manufacturing overhead incurred was exactly $150,000 per year.

REQUIRED:

1. Prepare income statements for 19X4 and 19X5 under direct costing.
2. Prepare income statements for 19X4 and 19X5 under absorption costing.
3. Show a reconciliation of the difference in operating income for 19X4, 19X5, and the two years as a whole.

The solution to this problem will be explained, step by step, in subsequent sections. The solution to Requirement 1 is in Exhibit 15-2, to Requirement 2 in Exhibit 15-3, and to Requirement 3 in Exhibit 15-5.

☐ Direct-Costing Method

The solution to Requirement 1 is shown in Exhibit 15-2. It has a familiar contribution-approach format, the same format introduced in Chapter 3. The only new characteristic of Exhibit 15-2 is the presence of a detailed calculation of cost of goods sold, which is affected by changes in the beginning and ending inventories. (In contrast, the income statements in Chapters 3 through 7 assumed that there were no changes in the beginning and ending inventories.)

The costs of the product are accounted for by applying all variable manufacturing costs to the goods produced at a rate of $3 per unit; thus inventories are valued at standard variable costs. In contrast, fixed manufacturing costs are not applied to any products but are regarded as expenses as actually incurred.

Again, before reading on, please trace the facts from the illustrative problem to the presentation in Exhibit 15-2, step by step.

EXHIBIT 15-2

Direct Costing

TOLMAN COMPANY Comparative Income Statements (in thousands of dollars) For the Years 19X4 and 19X5 (Data are in text)		19X4	19X5
Sales, 140,000 and 160,000 units, respectively	(1)	700	800
Opening inventory—at standard variable cost of $3		—	90*
Add variable cost of goods manufactured at standard, 170,000 and 140,000 units, respectively		510	420
Available for sale, 170,000 units in each year		510	510
Deduct ending inventory—at standard variable cost of $3		90*	30†
Variable manufacturing cost of goods sold		420	480
Variable selling expenses—at 5% of dollar sales		35	40
Total variable expenses	(2)	455	520
Contribution margin	(3) = (1) − (2)	245	280
Fixed factory overhead		150	150
Fixed selling and administrative expenses		65	65
Total fixed expenses	(4)	215	215
Operating income	(3) − (4)	30	65

Overhead Application: Direct and Absorption Costing

449

*30,000 units × $3 = $90,000.
†10,000 units × $3 = $30,000.

Exhibit 15-3 contains the following highlights of **standard absorption costing:**

1. The unit product cost is $4, not $3, because variable manufacturing costs ($3) plus fixed manufacturing overhead ($1) are applied to product.

2. The $1 predetermined application rate for fixed overhead was based on a denominator of 150,000 units ($150,000 ÷ 150,000 = $1). A **production volume variance**[2] appears whenever actual production (140,000 units in 19X5) deviates from the level of activity selected as the denominator for computing the predetermined product-costing rate. As the footnote in Exhibit 15-3 indicates, the measure of the variance is $1 multiplied by the difference between the actual volume of output and the denominator volume.

3. Production volume variances (and other variances) are usually accounted for as expired costs, that is, as expenses of the current period. They are often accounted for as adjustments that convert the gross profit at standard to gross profit at "actual," as shown in Exhibit 15-3.

[2] The term *production volume variance* is not widely used in practice. The equivalent terms, *activity variance, capacity variance,* and especially **volume variance,** are widely used. The term *production volume variance* is favored here because it is a more precise description of the fundamental nature of the variance.

EXHIBIT 15-3

Absorption Costing

TOLMAN COMPANY
Comparative Income Statements (in thousands of dollars)
For the Years 19X4 and 19X5
(Data are in text)

	19X4	19X5
Sales	700	800
Opening inventory—at standard absorption cost of $4*	–	120
Cost of goods manufactured at standard of $4	680	560
Available for sale	680	680
Deduct ending inventory at standard absorption cost of $4	120	40
Cost of goods sold—at standard	560	640
Gross profit at standard	140	160
Production volume variance†	20 F	10 U
Gross margin or gross profit—at "actual"	160	150
Selling and administrative expenses	100	105
Operating income	60	45

*Variable cost $3
Fixed cost ($150,000 ÷ 150,000)   1
Standard absorption cost $4

†Computation of production volume variance based on denominator volume of 150,000 units:

19X4	$20,000 F	(170,000 − 150,000) × $1
19X5	10,000 U	(150,000 − 140,000) × $1
Two years together	$10,000 F	(310,000 − 300,000) × $1

U = Unfavorable; F = Favorable.

The first of these three ideas, overhead application, was explained in the preceding chapter. The production volume variance and the disposition of variances will be discussed in subsequent sections.

FIXED OVERHEAD AND ABSORPTION COSTS OF PRODUCT

❏ Variable and Fixed Unit Costs

A graphical presentation of how an absorption-costing system works for (1) departmental budgeting and control purposes and (2) product-costing purposes may help underscore the assumptions being made. Even though absorption-costing systems rarely split their factory overhead into variable and fixed components, we will do so here to stress the underlying assumptions. For *variable* costs, the graphs are:

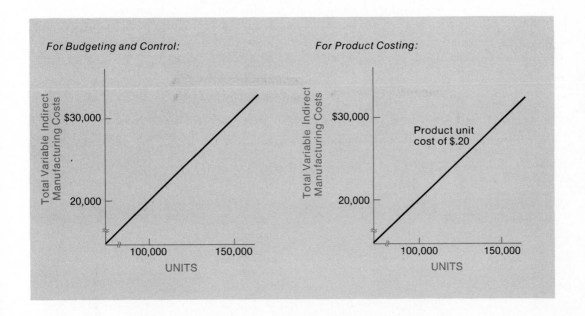

The two graphs are identical, so there is no conflict in the total results if the second graph is used as a basis for predicting how total costs will behave. Variable overhead will increase at a rate of $.20 per unit, as the slope of the graph shows.

Thinking in terms of *total costs* is the most popular way to budget (plan) and control operating activities. In contrast, thinking in terms of *unit costs* is the most popular way to allocate total costs for product-costing purposes.

Under absorption costing, the accounting system for *fixed* manufacturing overhead is shown by the next graphs (which are not to the exact scale of the preceding graphs):

Overhead
Application:
Direct and
Absorption
Costing

451

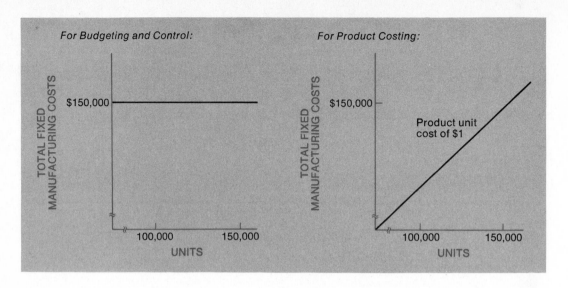

For Budgeting and Control:

For Product Costing:

For product-costing purposes, the accountant takes the total costs in the first graph and chooses a method for applying the costs to the product. The accountant typically accomplishes this application via some unitization, using some predicted volume as a denominator:

$$\text{unit product cost} = \frac{\text{predicted total cost}}{\text{denominator volume}} = \frac{\$150,000}{150,000} = \$1$$

For inventory purposes, as each unit is worked on, a $1 fixed indirect manufacturing cost will be applied to it. Thus the first 100,000 units would bear a total *product cost* of $100,000, the next 100,000 units a total *product cost* of an additional $100,000, as the next graphs demonstrate:

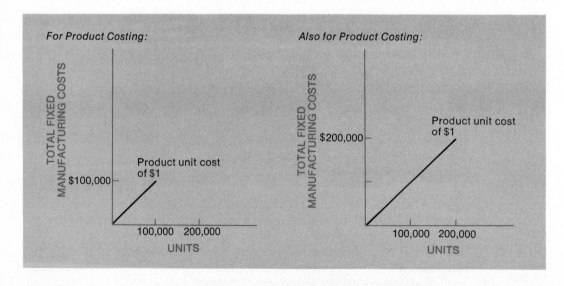

For Product Costing:

Also for Product Costing:

The *total* fixed cost for budgetary planning and control will be unaffected by the specific predicted volume used as a denominator. For instance, when the predicted total fixed cost is $150,000, if the predicted volume were 100,000 instead of 150,000 units, the unit product cost would change:

$$\text{unit product cost} = \frac{\text{predicted total fixed cost}}{\text{denominator volume}} = \frac{\$150,000}{100,000} = \$1.50$$

But the first graph for fixed costs, the one that is of primary concern for planning and control, would not change:

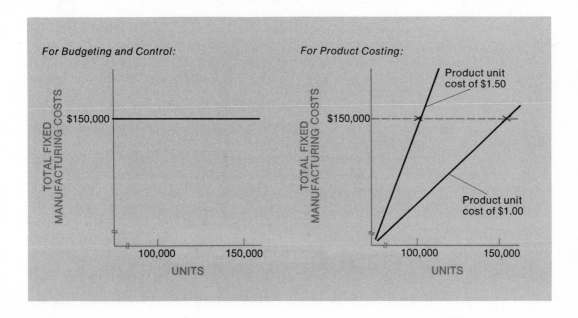

Selecting the Denominator Level

As the immediately preceding graph shows, the unit cost depends on the activity level chosen as the denominator in the computation; the higher the level of activity, the lower the unit cost. The costing difficulty is magnified because management usually desires a single representative standard fixed cost for a unit of product despite month-to-month changes in production volume.

The two graphs dramatize how the two purposes differ. The control-budget purpose regards fixed costs in a straightforward manner, viewing them in accordance with their actual cost behavior pattern. In contrast, as the graphs indicate, the absorption product-costing approach views these fixed costs as though they had a variable cost behavior pattern.

The selection of an appropriate denominator level for the predetermination of fixed-overhead rates is a matter of judgment. Thus the standard product cost would differ, depending on how the rate is set for fixed overhead. Most managers favor using the expected actual activity for the year in question; others favor using some longer-run (three-to-five-year) approximation of "normal" activity; and others favor using maximum or full capacity (often called *practical capacity*) as the denominator.

Although fixed-overhead rates are often important for product costing and long-run pricing, such rates *have limited significance for control pur-*

Overhead
Application:
Direct and
Absorption
Costing

453

poses. At the lower levels of supervision, almost no fixed costs are under direct control; even at higher levels of supervision, few fixed costs are controllable in the short run within wide ranges of anticipated activity.

❏ Nature of Production Volume Variance

A production volume variance arises whenever the actual outputs achieved deviate from the activity level selected as the denominator for computing the predetermined product-costing rate.

The production volume variance is the conventional measure of the cost of departing from the level of activity originally used to set the fixed-overhead rate.[3] Most companies consider production volume variances to be beyond immediate control, although sometimes the top sales executive has to do some explaining or investigating. Sometimes failure to reach the denominator volume is caused by idleness due to poor production scheduling, unusual machine breakdowns, shortages of skilled workers, strikes, storms, and the like.

There is no production volume variance for variable overhead. The concept of production volume variance arises for fixed overhead because of the conflict between accounting for control (by budgets) and accounting for product costing (by application rates). Note again that the fixed-overhead budget serves the control purpose, whereas the development of a product-costing rate results in the treatment of fixed overhead *as if it were* a variable cost. In other words, the applied line in Exhibit 15-4 is artificial in the sense that, for product-costing purposes, it seemingly transforms a fixed cost into a variable cost. This bit of magic forcefully illustrates the distinction between accounting for control and accounting for product costing.

To summarize, the production volume variance arises because the actual production activity level achieved frequently does not coincide with the activity level used as a denominator for selecting a predetermined product-costing rate for fixed factory overhead.

1. When denominator production activity and actual production activity are identical, there is no production volume variance.
2. When actual activity is less than denominator activity, the production volume variance is unfavorable. It is measured in Exhibit 15-4 as follows:

(denominator activity − actual activity) × predetermined fixed-overhead rate = production volume variance

(150,000 hours − 140,000 hours) × $1 = $10,000

or

budget minus applied = production volume variance

$150,000 − $140,000 = $10,000

---

[3] Do not confuse the production volume variance described here with the sales volume variance described in Chapter 7. The production volume variance arises because of the peculiarities of historical-cost accounting for fixed overhead in an absorption-cost system. In contrast, the sales volume variance in Chapter 7 is an entirely separate measure. It aims at estimating the effects on profit of deviating from an original master budget. It is the budgeted unit contribution margin multiplied by the difference between the master budgeted sales in units and the actual sales in units.

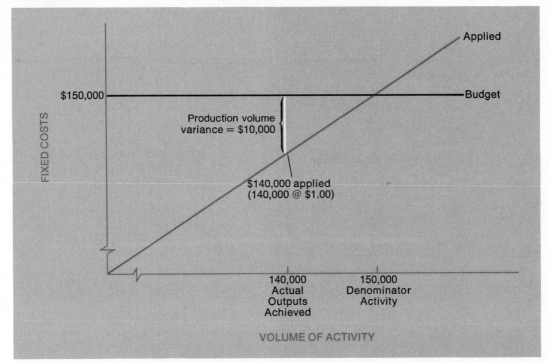

3. Where actual activity exceeds denominator activity, as was the case in 19X4, the production volume variance is favorable because it is an index of better-than-expected utilization of facilities.

Note, too, that the dollar amount of the production volume variance depends on what activity level was selected to determine the application rate. In our example, suppose 200,000 units were selected as the denominator volume level. The predetermined rate would have been $150,000 divided by 200,000, or 75¢. A subsequent volume of 170,000 hours would result in what production volume variance for 19X4? (Compute it before reading on.) The variance would be 30,000 hours multiplied by 75¢, or $22,500, unfavorable, as compared with the $20,000 favorable variance now shown in Exhibit 15-3. This shows how the choice of the volume-level denominator can radically affect the analysis and unit costs for product-costing purposes.

Above all, we should recognize that fixed costs are simply not divisible like variable costs; they come in big chunks and they are related to the provision of big chunks of production or sales capability rather than to the production or sale of a single unit of product.

There are conflicting views on how fixed-overhead variances are best analyzed. Obviously, the "best" way is the one that provides management with the most insight into its company's operations. Consequently, overhead analysis varies from company to company. In many companies production volume variances are most usefully expressed in physical terms only. For instance, a production volume variance could be expressed in machine-hours or kilowatt-hours.

Overhead
Application:
Direct and
Absorption
Costing

455

Exhibit 15-5 contains a reconciliation of the operating incomes shown in Exhibits 15-2 and 15-3. The difference can be explained in a shortcut way by multiplying the fixed-overhead product-costing rate by the *change* in the total units in the beginning and ending inventories. Consider 19X5: The change in units was 20,000, so the difference in net income would be 20,000 units multiplied by $1.00 = $20,000.

Exhibit 15-6 gives a more complete explanation of the difference in results. It traces the $30,000 of fixed costs held over from 19X4 under absorption costing, and it shows how the 19X5 income statement must bear these costs as well as the new costs of 19X5 (except for $10,000 still lodged in the ending inventory of 19X5).

❑ Effect of Other Variances

So far, our example has deliberately ignored the possibility of any variance except the production volume variance, which arises solely because of the desire for an application rate for fixed overhead in an absorption-costing situation (and the resultant likelihood that the chosen denominator level will differ from the actual production level achieved). Now we will introduce other variances that were explained in Chapter 7. Let us assume some additional facts for 19X5 (the second of the two years covered by our example):

Flexible-budget variances:	
Direct material	None
Direct labor	$34,000 U
Variable factory overhead	$ 3,000 U
Fixed factory overhead	$ 7,000 U
Supporting data (used to compute the above variances as	
shown in Appendix 15A):	
Standard direct-labor hours allowed for	
140,000 units of output produced	35,000
Standard direct-labor rate per hour	$6.00
Actual direct-labor hours of input	40,000
Actual direct-labor rate per hour	$6.10
Variable manufacturing overhead actually incurred	$31,000
Fixed manufacturing overhead actually incurred	$157,000

As Chapter 7 explains, flexible-budget variances may arise for both variable overhead and fixed overhead. Consider the following:

	ACTUAL AMOUNTS	FLEXIBLE-BUDGET AMOUNTS	FLEXIBLE-BUDGET VARIANCES
Variable factory overhead	$ 31,000	$ 28,000	$3,000
Fixed factory overhead	157,000	150,000	7,000

EXHIBIT 15-5

Reconciliation of Operating Income under Direct Costing and Absorption Costing			
	19X4	**19X5**	**TOGETHER**
Operating income under:			
Absorption costing (see Exhibit 15-3)	$60,000	$ 45,000	$105,000
Direct costing (see Exhibit 15-2)	30,000	65,000	95,000
Difference to be explained	$30,000	$−20,000	$ 10,000
The difference can be reconciled by multiplying the fixed-overhead rate by the **change** in the total inventory units:			
Fixed-overhead rate	$1	$1	$1
Change in inventory units:			
Opening inventory	—	30,000	—
Ending inventory	30,000	10,000	10,000
Change	30,000	−20,000	10,000
Difference in operating income explained	$30,000	$−20,000	$ 10,000

EXHIBIT 15-6

Tracing Fixed Manufacturing Costs During 19X5 (Data are from Exhibits 15-2 and 15-3)				
			INVENTORY	**EXPENSE**
Direct Costing				
No fixed overhead carried over from 19X4				
Fixed overhead actually incurred in 19X5	$150,000 ─────────────────→			$150,000
		UNITS	**DOLLARS**	
Absorption Costing				
Fixed overhead in beginning inventory	$ 30,000	30,000	$ 30,000	
Fixed overhead incurred in 19X5	150,000			
To account for	$180,000			
Applied to product, 140,000 @ $1		140,000	140,000	
Available for sale		170,000	$170,000	
Contained in standard cost of goods sold	$160,000	160,000	160,000 ──→	$160,000
In ending inventory	10,000	10,000	$ 10,000	
Not applied, so becomes unfavorable production volume variance	10,000 ─────────────────→			10,000
Fixed factory overhead charged against 19X5 operations				$170,000
Accounted for, as above	$180,000			
Difference in operating income occurs because $170,000 expires rather than $150,000				$ 20,000

Flexible-budget variances are the differences between actual amounts and the flexible-budget amounts for the actual output achieved. Such variances will frequently be referred to in this chapter as **flexible-control-budget variances** to emphasize the point that flexible budgets are primarily designed to assist planning and control rather than product costing.

Exhibit 15-7 contains the income statement under absorption costing that incorporates these new facts. These new variances hurt income by $44,000 because, like the production volume variance, they are all charged against income in 19X5. When variances are favorable, they increase operating income.

DISPOSITION OF STANDARD COST VARIANCES

The advocates of standard costing, particularly when the standards are viewed as being currently attainable, contend that variances are by and large subject to current control. Therefore variances are not inventoriable and should be considered as adjustments to the income of the period instead of being prorated over inventories and cost of goods sold. In this way, inventory valuations will be more representative of desirable and attainable costs.

The countervailing view favors a proration of the variances[4] over inventories and cost of goods sold. In this way, inventory valuations will be more representative of the **"actual"** costs incurred to obtain the products.

[4] For example, the Internal Revenue Service advocates proration. Why? Because most variances tend to be unfavorable. Therefore proration of variances causes higher ending inventory values, higher immediate income, and higher income taxes than lack of proration. For instance, if, say, $6,000 of the $54,000 variances in Exhibit 15-7 was prorated to the ending inventory, the income would rise from $1,000 to $7,000.

EXHIBIT 15-7

Absorption Costing
Modification of Exhibit 15-3 for 19X5
(Additional facts are in text)

	(IN THOUSANDS)	
Sales, 160,000 @ $5		$800
Opening inventory at standard, 30,000 @ $4	$120	
Cost of goods manufactured at standard, 140,000 @ $4	560	
Available for sale, 170,000 @ $4	$680	
Deduct ending inventory at standard, 10,000 @ $4	40	
Cost of goods sold at standard, 160,000 @ $4		640
Gross profit at standard		$160
Flexible-budget variances, unfavorable:		
Variable manufacturing costs ($34,000 + 3,000)	$ 37	
Fixed factory overhead	7	
Production volume variance (arises only because of fixed overhead, unfavorable)	10	
Total variances		54
Gross profit at "actual"		$106
Selling and administrative expenses		105
Operating income		$ 1

In practice, unless the variances are deemed significant in amount, they are usually not prorated because the managers who use standard cost systems favor the views in the preceding paragraph.

Therefore, in practice, variances are typically regarded as adjustments to current income. The form of the disposition is unimportant. Exhibit 15-7 shows the variances as a component of the computation of gross profit at "actual." The variances could appear instead as a completely separate section elsewhere in the income statement. This helps to distinguish between product costing (that is, the cost of goods sold, at standard) and loss recognition (unfavorable variances are "lost" or "expired" costs because they represent waste and inefficiency that do not justify them as inventoriable costs. That is, waste is not an asset.)

Summary

Standard cost-accounting systems are usually designed to satisfy **control** and **product-costing** purposes simultaneously. Many varieties of product costing are in use. For years, manufacturing companies have regularly used a version of absorption costing, which includes fixed factory overhead as a part of the cost of product based on some predetermined application rate (variances are not inventoried). In contrast, direct costing, which is more accurately called **variable costing,** charges fixed factory overhead to the period immediately—that is, fixed overhead is altogether excluded from inventories. Absorption costing continues to be much more widely used than direct costing, although the growing use of the contribution approach in performance measurement has led to increasing use of direct costing for internal purposes.

The production volume variance is linked with absorption costing, not direct costing. It arises from the conflict between the control-budget purpose and the product-costing purpose of cost accounting. The production volume variance is measured by the predetermined fixed-overhead rate multiplied by the difference between denominator production volume and actual production volume.

Summary Problems for Your Review

❑ Problems

Overhead Application: Direct and Absorption Costing

459

1. Reconsider Exhibits 15-2 and 15-3. Suppose production in 19X5 was 145,000 units instead of 140,000 units, but sales were 160,000 units. Also assume that the net variances for all variable manufacturing costs were $37,000, unfavorable. Regard these variances as adjustments to standard cost of goods sold. Also assume that actual fixed costs were $157,000. Prepare income statements for 19X5 under direct costing and under absorption costing.

2. Explain why operating income was different under direct costing and absorption costing. Show your calculations.

3. Without regard to Requirement 1, would direct costing or absorption costing give a manager more leeway in influencing short-run operating income through production-scheduling decisions? Why?

❑ Solutions

1. See Exhibits 15-8 and 15-9. Note that the ending inventory will be 15,000 instead of 10,000 units.
2. Decline in inventory levels is 30,000 − 15,000, or 15,000 units. The fixed-overhead rate per unit in absorption costing is $1. Therefore $15,000 more of fixed overhead was charged against operations under absorption costing than under direct costing. Generally, when inventories decline, absorption costing will show less income than direct costing; when inventories rise, absorption costing will show more income than direct costing.
3. Some version of absorption costing will give a manager more leeway in influencing his operating income via production scheduling. Operating income will fluctuate in harmony with changes in net sales under direct costing, but it is influenced by both production and sales under absorption costing. For example, compare the direct costing in Exhibits 15-2 and 15-8. As the second note to Exhibit 15-8 indicates, the operating income may be affected by assorted variances (but not the production volume variance) under direct costing, but production scheduling *per se* will have no effect on operating income. On the other hand, compare the operating income of Exhibits 15-7 and 15-9.

EXHIBIT 15-8

TOLMAN COMPANY
Income Statement (Direct Costing)
For the Year 19X5
(In thousands of dollars)

Sales		$800
Opening inventory—at variable standard cost		
of $3	$ 90	
Add variable cost of goods manufactured	435	
Available for sale	$525	
Deduct ending inventory—at variable standard		
cost of $3	45	
Variable cost of goods sold, at standard	$480	
Net flexible-budget variances for all variable costs,		
unfavorable	37	
Variable cost of goods sold, at actual	$517	
Variable selling expenses—at 5% of dollar sales	40	
Total variable costs charged against sales		557
Contribution margin		$243
Fixed factory overhead	$157*	
Fixed selling and administrative expenses	65	
Total fixed expenses		222
Operating income		$ 21†

*This could be shown in two lines, $150,000 budget plus $7,000 variance.

†The difference between this and the $65,000 operating income in Exhibit 15-2 occurs because of the $37,000 unfavorable variable cost variances and the $7,000 unfavorable fixed-cost control-budget variance.

EXHIBIT
15-9

TOLMAN COMPANY
Income Statement (Absorption Costing)
For the Year 19X5
(In thousands of dollars)

Sales		$800
Opening inventory—at standard cost of $4	$120	
Cost of goods manufactured, at standard	580	
Available for sale	$700	
Deduct ending inventory, at standard	60	
Cost of goods sold, at standard	$640	
Net flexible-budget variances for all variable		
manufacturing costs, unfavorable	$37	
Fixed factory overhead flexible-budget		
variance, unfavorable	7	
Production volume variance, unfavorable	5*	
Total variances	49	
Cost of goods sold, at actual		689†
Gross profit, at "actual"		$111
Selling and administrative expenses		
Variable	$ 40	
Fixed	65	105
Operating income		$ 6‡

*Production volume variance is $1 × (150,000 denominator volume − 145,000 actual production).

†This format differs slightly from Exhibit 15-7, page 458. The difference is deliberate; it illustrates that the formats of income statements are not rigid.

‡Compare this result with the $1,000 operating income in Exhibit 15-7. The *only* difference is traceable to the *production* of 145,000 units instead of 140,000 units, resulting in an unfavorable production volume variance of $5,000 instead of $10,000.

As the third note to Exhibit 15-9 explains, production scheduling as well as sales influence operating income. Production was 145,000 rather than 140,000 units. So $5,000 of fixed overhead became a part of ending inventory (an asset) instead of part of the production volume variance (an expense)—that is, the production volume variance is $5,000 lower and the ending inventory contains $5,000 more fixed overhead in Exhibit 15-9 than in Exhibit 15-7.

Highlights to Remember

1. Standard costing uses fully predetermined product costs for direct material, direct labor, and factory overhead. If the standards are currently attainable, the variances are not inventoried. Instead, they are directly charged or credited to current operations.

2. Readers who study both this and the preceding chapters will readily see that various alternatives of **absorption product costing** are possible:[5]

[5] In addition, the same alternatives are available for *direct product costing*. The *only* change in the above tabulation would be to delete fixed factory overhead entirely because it is not a product cost under direct-costing assumptions.

	ACTUAL COSTING	NORMAL COSTING	STANDARD COSTING
Direct Materials	Actual costs	Actual	Predetermined prices × standard inputs allowed for actual output achieved
Direct labor	Actual	Actual	
Variable factory overhead	Actual	Predetermined rates × actual inputs	
Fixed factory over- head			

3. Exhibit 15-10 summarizes the effects that direct costing and absorption costing have on income.

Accounting Vocabulary

Absorption costing; actual costing; control-budget variance; direct costing; flexi-ble-control-budget variance; marginal costing; normal costing; production volume variance; standard absorption costing; standard direct costing; variable costing; volume variance.

Appendix 15A: Comparisons of Production Volume Variances with Other Variances

PRODUCTION VOLUME VARIANCE IS UNIQUE

The only new variance introduced in this chapter is the production volume vari-ance, which arises because fixed-overhead accounting must serve two masters: the **control-budget** purpose and the product-costing purpose. Let us examine these variances in perspective by using the approach originally demonstrated in Exhibit 7-6, page 187. The results of the approach are in Exhibit 15-11, which deserves your careful study, particularly the two notes. Please ponder the exhibit before read-ing on.

Exhibit 15-12 provides a graphical comparison of the variable and fixed over-head that were analyzed in Exhibit 15-11. Note how the control-budget line and the product-costing line (the applied line) are superimposed in the graph for variable overhead but differ in the graph for fixed overhead.

Underapplied or overapplied overhead is always the difference between the actual overhead incurred and the overhead applied. An analysis may then be made:

underapplied overhead = flexible-control-budget
variance + production volume variance
for variable overhead = $3,000 + 0 = $3,000
for fixed overhead = $7,000 + $10,000 = $17,000

EXHIBIT 15-10

Comparative Income Effects

	DIRECT COSTING	ABSORPTION COSTING	COMMENTS
1. Fixed factory overhead inventoried?	No	Yes	Basic theoretical question of when a cost should become an expense.
2. Production volume variance?	No	Yes	Choice of denominator volume affects measurement of operating income under absorption costing.
3. Treatment of other variances?	Same	Same	Underscores the fact that the basic difference is the accounting for fixed factory overhead, not the accounting for variable factory overhead.
4. Classifications between variable and fixed costs are routinely made?	Yes	No	However, absorption cost can be modified to obtain subclassifications of variable and fixed costs, if desired.
5. Usual effects of changes in inventory levels on operating income: Production = sales Production > sales Production < sales	Equal Lower* Higher	Equal Higher† Lower	Differences are attributable to timing of the transformation of fixed factory overhead into expense.
6. Cost-volume-profit realtionships	Tied to sales	Tied to production *and* sales	Management control benefit: Effects of changes in volume on operating income are easier to understand under variable costing.

*That is, lower than absorption costing.
†That is, higher than direct costing.

EXHIBIT 15-11

Analysis of Variances
(Data are from text)

	(A) COST INCURRED: ACTUAL INPUTS × ACTUAL PRICE	(B) FLEXIBLE CONTROL BUDGET BASED ON ACTUAL INPUTS	(C) FLEXIBLE CONTROL BUDGET BASED ON ACTUAL OUTPUTS ACHIEVED	(D) PRODUCT COSTING: APPLIED TO PRODUCT
Direct labor:	40,000 × $6.10 = $244,000	40,000 × $6 = $240,000	(35,000 × $6 or 140,000 × $1.50) = $210,000*	(35,000 × $6 or 140,000 × $1.50) = $210,000*
		↳ 40,000 × ($6.10 − $6) = Price variance, $4,000 U	↳ 5,000 × $6 = Efficiency variance, $30,000 U	↳ No variance
		↳ Flexible control-budget variance, $34,000 U		↳ No variance
Variable factory overhead:	(given) $31,000	40,000 × $.80 = $32,000	(35,000 × $.80 or 140,000 × $.20) = $28,000*	$28,000*
		↳ Price (spending) variance, $1,000 F	↳ 5,000 × $.80 = Efficiency variance, $4,000 U	↳ No variance
		↳ Flexible control-budget variance, $3,000 U		↳ No variance
		↳ Underapplied overhead, $3,000 U		
Fixed factory overhead:	$157,000	Lump sum $150,000	Lump sum $150,000†	140,000 × $1.00 = $140,000
		↳ Price (spending), $7,000 U	↳ No variance	↳ Production volume variance, $10,000 U
		↳ Flexible control-budget variance, $7,000 U	↳ Production volume variance, $10,000 U	
		↳ Underapplied overhead, $17,000 U		

U = Unfavorable, F = Favorable.

*For emphasis here, the term *flexible control budget* is being used, which is a synonym for flexible budget. Note especially that the control budget for variable costs rises and falls in direct proportion to production. Note also that the control-budget purpose and the product-costing purpose harmonize completely; the total costs in the flexible budget will always agree with the standard variable costs applied to product because they are based on standard costs per unit multiplied by units produced.

†In contrast with variable costs, the control-budget total will always be the same regardless of the units produced. However, the control-budget purpose and the product-costing purpose conflict; whenever actual production differs from denominator production, the standard costs applied to product will differ from the control budget. This difference is the production volume variance. In this case, the production volume variance may be computed by multiplying the $1 rate times the difference between the 150,000 denominator volume and the 140,000 units of output achieved.

EXHIBIT 15-12 Comparison of Control and Product-Costing Purposes, Variable Overhead and Fixed Overhead (not to scale)

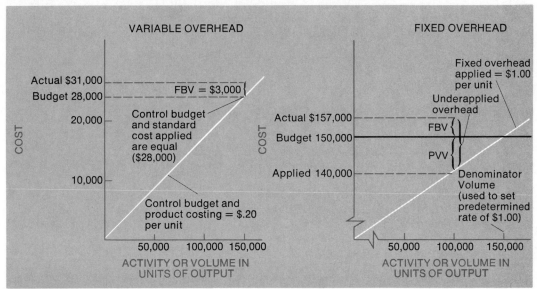

FBV = Flexible-control-budget variance.
PVV = Production volume variance.

LOST-CONTRIBUTION MARGINS

Finally, what is the economic significance of unit fixed costs? Unlike variable costs, total fixed costs do not change in the short run as production or sales fluctuate. Management would obtain a better measure of the cost of underutilization of physical facilities by trying to approximate the related lost-contribution margins instead of the related historical fixed costs.[6] Fixed-cost incurrence often involves lump-sum outlays based on a pattern of expected recoupment. But ineffective utilization of existing facilities has no bearing on the amount of fixed costs currently incurred. The economic effects of the inability to reach target volume levels are often directly measured by lost-contribution margins, even if these have to be approximated. The historical-cost approach fails to emphasize the distinction between *fixed-cost incurrence*, on the one hand, and the objective of *maximizing the total contribution margin*, on the other hand. These are separable management problems, and the utilization of existing capacity is more closely related to the latter.

For instance, the production volume variance in our example was computed at $10,000 by multiplying a unit fixed cost of $1 by the 10,000-unit difference between the 150,000 units of denominator activity and 140,000 units produced. This $10,000 figure may be helpful in the sense that management is alerted in some crude way to the probable costs of failure to produce 150,000 units. But the more relevant information is the lost-contribution margins that pertain to the 10,000 units. This information may not be so easy to obtain. The lost-contribution margins may be zero in those cases where there are no opportunities to obtain any contribution margin from alternative uses of available capacity; in other cases, how-

Overhead
Application:
Direct and
Absorption
Costing

[6] For an expanded discussion, see C. Horngren, "A Contribution Margin Approach to the Analysis of Capacity Utilization," *Accounting Review*, 42, No. 2, 254–64.

ever, the lost-contribution margins may be substantial. For example, if demand is high, the breakdown of key equipment may cost a company many thousands of dollars in lost-contribution margins. Unfortunately, in these cases, existing accounting systems would show production volume variances based on the unitized fixed costs and entirely ignore any lost-contribution margins.

Appendix 15B: Illustration of Standard Absorption-Costing System

This illustration presents the journal entries that would accompany a standard absorption-costing system such as that described in this chapter.

The Delar Company began business on January 2, 19X1. Its executives were experienced in the industry and had a standard cost system installed from the outset.

Overhead rates were established based on an expected activity (volume) level of 25,000 standard direct-labor hours. Note that volume is measured by standard direct-labor hours allowed for any given output of product; it is not measured by the actual direct-labor hours of input. The rates were computed as follows:

$$\text{variable rate} = \frac{\text{budgeted variable factory overhead}}{\text{expected volume}} = \frac{\$50,000}{25,000} = \$2$$

$$\text{fixed rate} = \frac{\text{budgeted fixed factory overhead}}{\text{expected volume}} = \frac{\$150,000}{25,000} = \$6$$

A summary of results follows:

RELATED TO JOURNAL ENTRY NUMBER		
1.	Direct material purchased: 100,000 lbs. @ $1.10, $110,000	
2.	Pounds of direct material used: 90,000	
	Standard allowances per unit of finished output:	
	Direct materials: 1 lb. @ $1	$1.00
3.	Direct labor: .25 hr. @ $12	3.00
4.	Variable factory overhead: .25 hr. @ $2	.50
	Variable factory costs	$4.50
5.	Fixed factory overhead: .25 hr. @ $6	1.50
	Total standard cost per unit	$6.00
3.	Direct labor incurred: 21,250 hours @ $12.20, or $259,250	
4,5.	Factory overhead incurred: variable, $42,000; fixed, $150,000	
6.	Production in units: 80,000	
7.	Sales in units: 60,000	

Purchase price variances for direct materials are measured upon purchase rather than upon withdrawal for production.

Try to prepare your own journal entries before studying those in Exhibit 15-13. Note that all inventories are carried at standard unit costs, not actual unit costs.

EXHIBIT
15-13

Standard Absorption-Costing System
Journal Entries

1. Direct-materials inventory   100,000
   Direct-material purchase price variance   10,000
     Accounts payable   110,000
   ($1.10 − $1.00) × $100,000 lbs. = $10,000

2. Work in process   80,000
   Direct-material efficiency variance   10,000
     Direct-materials inventory   90,000
   (90,000 − 80,000) × $1 = $10,000

3. Work in process   240,000
   Direct-labor price variance   4,250
   Direct-labor efficiency variance   15,000
     Accrued payroll or cash   259,250
   21,250 × ($12.20 − $12.00) = $4,250
   [21,250 − (.25 × 80,000)] × $12 = $15,000

4a. Factory department overhead control   42,000
      Accounts payable and other accounts   42,000

4b. Work in process   40,000
      Factory department overhead control   40,000
    (.25 × 80,000 units) × $2 = $40,000

5a. Factory department overhead control   150,000
      Accounts payable and other accounts   150,000

5b. Work in process   120,000
      Factory department overhead control   120,000
    (.25 × 80,000 units) × $6 = $120,000

6. Finished goods   480,000
     Work in process   480,000
   80,000 units × $6 = $480,000

7. Cost of goods sold   360,000
     Finished goods   360,000
   60,000 units × $6 = $360,000

Variances may be measured at any convenient time. Material efficiency variances and direct-labor variances are usually measured as production occurs. Overhead variances are typically measured monthly. However, they may not be isolated formally in the ledger accounts until the end of the year, as follows:

Variable factory-overhead budget variance   2,000
Fixed factory-overhead production volume variance   30,000
  Factory department overhead control   32,000
Underapplied overhead:
  Variable: $42,000 − $40,000 = $2,000
  Fixed: $150,000 − (.25)(80,000)($6) = $30,000

Note how this entry reduces the balance in Factory Department Overhead Control to zero.

The attained volume of .25 × 80,000 units = 20,000 hours was 5,000 hours below the budgeted hours selected as the denominator volume. This discrepancy caused a production volume variance of $30,000 (5,000 hours × $6), the difference between the *budgeted* and the *applied* fixed factory overhead.

Overhead
Application:
Direct and
Absorption
Costing

467

The journal entry that disposes of all variances as adjustments of Cost of Goods Sold follows:

Cost of goods sold	71,250	
Direct-material purchase price variance		10,000
Direct-material efficiency variance		10,000
Direct-labor price variance		4,250
Direct-labor efficiency variance		15,000
Variable factory-overhead variance		2,000
Fixed factory-overhead variance		30,000
To adjust standard cost of goods sold for all variances.		

Fundamental
Assignment Material

15–1. Comparison of direct costing and absorption costing. (Alternate is 15–13.) From the following information pertaining to a year's operation, answer the questions below:

Units produced	2,400
Units sold	2,000
Selling and administrative expenses (all fixed)	$ 800
Fixed manufacturing overhead	2,400
Variable manufacturing overhead	1,100
Direct labor	3,400
Direct material used	2,700
All beginning inventories	-0-
Gross margin (gross profit)	2,000
Direct-materials inventory, end	300
Work-in-process inventory, end	-0-

REQUIRED:

1. What is the ending finished-goods inventory cost under traditional-costing procedures (absorption costing)?
2. What is the ending finished-goods inventory cost under variable-costing procedures (direct costing)?
3. Would operating income be higher or lower under direct costing? By how much? Why? (Answer: $400 lower, but explain why.)

15–2. Comparison of absorption and direct costing. (Alternate is 15–18.) The next page contains a simplified income statement based on direct costing. Assume that the denominator volume for absorption costing in 19X1 and 19X2 was 1,300 units and that total fixed costs were identical in 19X1 and 19X2. There is no beginning or ending work in process.

REQUIRED:

1. Prepare an income statement based on absorption costing. Assume that actual fixed costs were equal to budgeted fixed costs.
2. Explain the difference in operating income between absorption costing and direct costing. Be specific.

Sales, 1,180 units @ $10		$11,800
Deduct variable costs:		
Beginning inventory, 120 units @ $6	$ 720	
Variable manufacturing cost of goods manufactured, 1,100 units @ $6	6,600	
Variable manufacturing cost of goods available for sale	$7,320	
Ending inventory, 40 units @ $6	240	
Variable manufacturing cost of goods sold	$7,080	
Variable selling and administrative expenses	400	
Total variable costs		7,480
Contribution margin		$ 4,320
Deduct fixed costs:		
Fixed factory overhead at budget	$2,600	
Fixed selling and administrative expenses	500	
Total fixed costs		3,100
Operating income		$ 1,220

Additional Assignment Material

15–3. Why do advocates of currently attainable standard costs as a method for product costing claim that it is conceptually superior to actual costing?

15–4. "Direct costing means that only direct material and direct labor are inventoried." Do you agree? Why?

15–5. "The dollar amount of the production volume variance depends on what activity level was chosen to determine the application rate." Explain.

15–6. Why is it artificial to unitize fixed costs?

15–7. "The fixed cost per unit is directly affected by the denominator selected." Do you agree? Explain.

15–8. "Absorption costing regards more categories of costs as product costs." Explain. Be specific.

15–9. "Direct costing is used in several corporate annual reports." Do you agree? Explain.

15–10. How is fixed overhead applied to product?

15–11. Define the *production volume variance* as conventionally measured.

15–12. **Simple comparison of direct and absorption costing.** B Company began business on January 1, 19X1, with assets of $100,000 cash and equities of $100,000 capital stock. In 19X1 it manufactured some inventory at a cost of $50,000, including $10,000 for factory rent and other fixed factory overhead. In 19X2 it manufactured nothing and sold half of its inventory for $32,000 cash. In 19X3 it manufactured nothing and sold the remaining half for another $32,000 cash. It had no fixed expenses in 19X2 or 19X3.

There are no other transactions of any kind. Ignore income taxes.

Overhead
Application:
Direct and
Absorption
Costing

469

Prepare an ending balance sheet plus an income statement for 19X1, 19X2, and 19X3 under (1) absorption costing and (2) direct costing (variable costing).

15–13. Comparison of direct costing and absorption costing. (Alternate is 15–1.) From the following information pertaining to a year's operations, answer the questions below:

Units sold	1,000
Units produced	1,100
Fixed manufacturing overhead	$2,200
Variable manufacturing overhead	500
Selling and administrative expenses (all fixed)	900
Direct labor	4,000
Direct material used	2,100
Beginning inventories	-0-
Contribution margin	4,000
Direct-material inventory, end	1,000
There are no work-in-process inventories.	

REQUIRED:

1. What is the ending finished-goods inventory cost under traditional costing procedures (absorption costing)?
2. What is the ending finished-goods inventory cost under variable-costing procedures (direct costing)?

15–14. Comparisons over four years. The E Corporation began business on January 1, 19X7, to produce and sell a single product. Reported operating income figures under both absorption and direct (variable) costing for the first four years of operation are:

YEAR	DIRECT COSTING	ABSORPTION COSTING
19X7	$40,000	$40,000
19X8	20,000	50,000
19X9	60,000	40,000
19X0	60,000	50,000

Standard production costs per unit, sales prices, application (absorption) rates, and denominator volume levels were the same in each year. There were no under-applied or overapplied overhead costs, and no variances in any year. All nonmanu-facturing expenses were fixed, and there were no nonmanufacturing cost variances in any year.

REQUIRED:

1. In what year(s) did "units produced" equal "units sold"?
2. In what year(s) did "units produced" exceed "units sold"?
3. What is the dollar amount of the December 31, 19X0, finished-goods inventory? (Give absorption-costing value.)
4. What is the difference between "units produced" and "units sold" in 19X8, if you know that the absorption-costing fixed-manufacturing-overhead application rate is $2 per unit? (Give answer in units.)

15–15. Direct and absorption costing. (H. Schaefer.) Data for 19X2 are on page 471.

REQUIRED:

1. Determine operating income for 19X2, assuming the firm uses the direct-costing approach to product costing. (Do not prepare a statement.)
2. Assume that (a) there is *no* January 1, 19X2, inventory, (b) *no* variances are allocated to inventory, and (c) the firm uses a "full absorption" approach to

Sales: 10,000 units at $12 each	
Actual production	12,000 units
Denominator activity	15,000 units
Manufacturing costs incurred:	
Variable	$60,000
Fixed	30,000
Nonmanufacturing costs incurred:	
Variable	$15,000
Fixed	14,000

product costing. Compute (a) the cost assigned to December 31, 19X2, inventory; and (b) operating income for the year ended December 31, 19X2. (Do not prepare a statement.)

15–16. All-fixed costs. (Suggested by Raymond P. Marple.) The Marple Company has built a massive water-desalting factory next to an ocean. The factory is completely automated. It has its own source of power, light, heat, etc. The salt water costs nothing. All producing and other operating costs are fixed; they do not vary with output because the volume is governed by adjusting a few dials on a control panel. The employees have flat annual salaries.

The desalted water is not sold to household consumers. It has a special taste that appeals to local breweries, distilleries, and soft-drink manufacturers. The price, 10¢ per gallon, is expected to remain unchanged for quite some time.

The following are data regarding the first two years of operations:

	IN GALLONS		COSTS (ALL FIXED)	
	Sales	Production	Manufacturing	Other
19X1	5,000,000	10,000,000	$450,000	$100,000
19X2	5,000,000	0	450,000	100,000

Orders can be processed in four hours, so management decided, in early 19X2, to gear production strictly to sales.

REQUIRED:

1. Prepare three-column income statements for 19X1, for 19X2, and for the two years together using (a) direct costing and (b) absorption costing.
2. What is the break-even point under (a) direct costing and (b) absorption costing?
3. What inventory costs would be carried on the balance sheets on December 31, 19X1 and 19X2, under each method?
4. Comment on your answers in Requirements 1 and 2. Which costing method appears more useful?

15–17. Semifixed costs. The McFarland Company differs from the Marple Company (described in Problem 15–16) in only one respect: It has both variable and fixed manufacturing costs. Its variable costs are $.025 per gallon, and its fixed manufacturing costs are $225,000 per year.

REQUIRED:

Overhead Application: Direct and Absorption Costing

1. Using the same data as in the preceding problem, except for the change in production-cost behavior, prepare three-column income statements for 19X1, for 19X2, and for the two years together using (a) direct costing and (b) absorption costing.
2. Why did McFarland earn a profit for the two-year period while Marple suffered a loss?
3. What inventory costs would be carried on the balance sheets on December 31, 19X1 and 19X2, under each method?

15–18. Extension of chapter illustration. (Alternate is 15–2.) Reconsider Exhibits 15-2 and 15-3. Suppose that in 19X5 production was 156,000 units instead of 140,000 units, and sales were 150,000 units. Also assume that the net variances for all variable manufacturing costs were $24,000, unfavorable. Also assume that actual fixed manufacturing costs were $157,000.

REQUIRED:

1. Prepare income statements for 19X5 under direct costing and under absorption costing. Use a format similar to Exhibits 15-8 and 15-9, pp. 460–461.
2. Explain why operating income was different under direct costing and absorption costing. Show your calculations.

15–19. Absorption and direct costing. The Chavez Company had the following actual data for 19X1 and 19X2:

	19X1	19X2
Units of finished goods:		
Opening inventory	—	3,000
Production	13,000	10,000
Sales	10,000	11,000
Ending inventory	3,000	2,000

The basic production data at standard costs for the two years were:

Direct materials	$20
Direct labor	16
Variable factory overhead	3
Standard variable costs per unit	$39

Fixed factory overhead was budgeted at $96,000 per year. The denominator volume was 12,000 units, so the fixed overhead rate was $96,000 ÷ 12,000 = $8 per unit.
Budgeted sales price was $70 per unit. Selling and administrative expenses were budgeted at variable, $7 *per unit sold,* and fixed, $80,000 per month.
Assume that there were absolutely no variances from any standard variable costs or budgeted selling prices or budgeted fixed costs in 19X1.
There were no beginning or ending inventories of work in process.

REQUIRED:

1. For 19X1, prepare income statements based on standard direct (variable) costing and standard absorption costing. (The next problem deals with 19X2.)
2. Explain why operating income differs between direct costing and absorption costing. Be specific.

15–20. Absorption and direct costing. Assume the same facts as in the preceding problem. In addition, consider the following actual data for 19X2:

Direct materials	$270,000
Direct labor	171,600
Variable factory overhead	32,000
Fixed factory overhead	92,000
Selling and administrative costs:	
Variable	80,800
Fixed	80,000
Sales	790,000

1. For 19X2, prepare income statements based on standard direct (variable) costing and standard absorption costing. Arrange your income statements in the following general format:

Sales (at standard or budgeted prices)
Cost of goods sold (at standard costs)
Gross profit at standard
Selling and administrative costs (at standard)
Operating income before variances
Variances (list in detail)
Operating income

2. Explain why operating income differs between direct costing and absorption costing. Be specific.

15–21. Fundamentals of overhead variances. The Kinnear Company is installing an absorption standard cost system and a flexible overhead budget. Standard costs have recently been developed for its only product and are as follows:

Direct material, 2 pounds @ $15	$30
Direct labor, 6 hours @ $6	36
Variable overhead, 6 hours @ $2	12
Fixed overhead	?
Standard cost per unit of finished product	$?

Denominator activity (expected activity) is expressed as 12,000 standard direct-labor hours per month. Fixed overhead is expected to be $36,000 per month. The predetermined fixed-overhead rate for product costing is not changed from month to month.

1. Calculate the proper fixed-overhead rate per standard direct-labor hour and per unit.
2. Graph the following for activity from zero to 15,000 hours:
   a. Budgeted variable overhead
   b. Variable overhead applied to product
3. Graph the following for activity from zero to 15,000 hours:
   a. Budgeted fixed overhead
   b. Fixed overhead applied to product
4. Assume that 10,000 standard direct-labor hours are allowed for the output achieved during a given month. Actual variable overhead of $20,400 was incurred; actual fixed overhead amounted to $37,000. Calculate the
   a. Fixed-overhead control-budget variance
   b. Fixed-overhead production volume variance
   c. Variable-overhead control-budget variance
5. Assume that 12,500 standard direct-labor hours are allowed for the output achieved during a given month. Actual overhead incurred amounted to $59,800, $37,800 of which was fixed. Calculate the
   a. Fixed-overhead control-budget variance
   b. Fixed-overhead production volume variance
   c. Variable-overhead control-budget variance

15–22. Fixed overhead and practical capacity. The expected activity of the paper-making plant of Scott Paper Company was 36,000 hours per month. Practical capacity was 48,000 hours per month. The standard hours allowed for the actual output achieved in January were 41,000. The budgeted fixed-factory-overhead items were:

Overhead
Application:
Direct and
Absorption
Costing
473

Depreciation, equipment	$260,000
Depreciation, factory building	40,000
Supervision	30,000
Indirect labor	180,000
Insurance	10,000
Property taxes	20,000
Total	$540,000

Because of unanticipated scheduling difficulties and the need for more indirect labor, the actual fixed factory overhead was $565,000.

REQUIRED:

1. Using practical capacity as the denominator for applying fixed factory overhead, prepare a summary analysis of fixed-overhead variances for January.
2. Using expected activity as the denominator for applying fixed factory overhead, prepare a summary analysis of fixed-overhead variances for January.
3. Explain why some of your variances in Requirements 1 and 2 are the same and why some differ.

15–23. **Extension of Appendix 15A illustration.** Study the analysis of variances in Exhibit 15-11. Suppose production is 156,000 units. Also assume:

Standard direct-labor hours allowed per unit produced	.25
Standard direct-labor rate per hour	$6.00
Actual direct-labor hours of input	42,000
Actual direct-labor rate per hour	$6.10
Variable manufacturing overhead actually incurred	$33,000
Fixed manufacturing overhead actually incurred	$157,000

REQUIRED:

Prepare an analysis of variances similar to that shown in Exhibit 15-11, p. 464.

15–24. **Analysis of operating results.** (CMA, adapted.) Sun Company, a wholly owned subsidiary of Guardian, Inc., produces and sells three main product lines. The company employs a standard cost-accounting system for record-keeping purposes.

At the beginning of 19X4, the president of Sun Company presented the budget to the parent company and accepted a commitment to contribute $15,800 to Guardian's consolidated profit in 19X4. The president has been confident that the year's profit would exceed budget target, since the monthly sales reports that he has been receiving have shown that sales for the year will exceed budget by 10%. The president is both disturbed and confused when the controller presents an adjusted forecast as of November 30, 19X4, indicating that profit will be 11% under budget. The two forecasts are presented on the next page.

There have been no sales price changes or product-mix shifts since the 1/1/X4 forecast. The only cost variance on the income statement is the underabsorbed manufacturing overhead. This arose because the company produced only 16,000 standard machine-hours (budgeted machine-hours were 20,000) during 19X4 as a result of a shortage of raw materials while its principal supplier was closed by a strike. Fortunately, Sun Company's finished-goods inventory was large enough to fill all sales orders received.

REQUIRED:

1. Analyze and explain why the profit has declined in spite of increased sales and good control over costs. Show computations.
2. What plan, if any, could Sun Company adopt during December to improve their reported profit at year-end? Explain your answer.

*Includes fixed manufacturing overhead of $30,000.

3. Illustrate and explain how Sun Company could adopt an alternative internal cost-reporting procedure that would avoid the confusing effect of the present procedure. Show the revised forecasts under your alternative.
4. Would the alternative procedure described in Requirement 3 be acceptable to Guardian, Inc., for financial-reporting purposes? Explain.

15–25. **Standard absorption and standard direct costing.** Coleman Company has the following results for a certain year. All variances are written off as additions to (or deductions from) the standard cost of goods sold. Find the unknowns, designated by letters.

Sales: 200,000 units, @ $22	$4,400,000
Net variance for standard variable manufacturing costs	$ 36,000, unfavorable
Variable standard cost of goods manufactured	$ 10 per unit
Variable selling and administrative expenses	$ 2 per unit
Fixed selling and administrative expenses	$1,000,000
Fixed manufacturing overhead	$ 240,000
Maximum capacity per year	240,000 units
Denominator volume for year	200,000 units
Beginning inventory of finished goods	30,000 units
Ending inventory of finished goods	10,000 units
Beginning inventory: direct-costing basis	a
Contribution margin	b
Operating income: direct-costing basis	c
Beginning inventory: absorption-costing basis	d
Gross margin	e
Operating income: absorption-costing basis	f

15–26. **Fill in the blanks.** Study Appendix 15A. Consider these data:

	FACTORY OVERHEAD	
	Fixed	Variable
Actual incurred	$5,500	$10,800
Budget for standard hours allowed for output achieved	5,000	9,000
Applied	4,800	9,000
Budget for actual hours of input	5,000	9,800

Overhead
Application:
Direct and
Absorption
Costing

475

From the above information fill in the blanks below:

The flexible-budget variance is $_____	Fixed $_____
	Variable $_____
The production volume variance is $_____	Fixed $_____
	Variable $_____
The price variance is $_____	Fixed $_____
	Variable $_____
The efficiency variance is $_____	Fixed $_____
	Variable $_____

Mark your variances F for favorable and U for unfavorable.

15–27. Fill in the blanks. Study Appendix 15A. Consider the following data regarding factory overhead:

	VARIABLE	FIXED
Budget for actual hours of input	$40,000	$60,000
Applied	37,000	55,500
Budget for standard hours allowed for actual output achieved	?	?
Actual incurred	44,000	59,000

REQUIRED: | Using the above data, fill in the blanks below. Use F for favorable or U for unfavorable for each variance.

	TOTAL OVERHEAD	VARIABLE	FIXED
1. Price (spending) variance	_____	_____	_____
2. Efficiency variance	_____	_____	_____
3. Production volume variance	_____	_____	_____
4. Flexible-control-budget variance	_____	_____	_____
5. Underapplied overhead	_____	_____	_____

15–28. Straightforward problem on standard cost system. Study Appendix 15A. The Bendex Company uses flexible budgets and a standard cost system. The month's data for a department follow:

Direct-labor costs incurred, 11,000 hours, $125,400
Variable overhead costs incurred, $28,500
Fixed-overhead budget variance, $1,500 favorable
Finished units produced, 2,000
Fixed-overhead costs incurred, $36,000
Variable overhead applied at $2.70 per hour
Standard direct-labor cost, $12 per hour
Denominator production per month, 2,500 units
Standard direct-labor hours per finished unit, 5

REQUIRED: | Prepare an analysis of all variances (similar to Exhibit 15-11, p. 464).

15–29. Straightforward problem on standard cost system. Study Appendix 15A. The Hong Kong Company uses a standard cost system. The month's data regarding its single product follow:

Fixed-overhead costs incurred, $6,150
Variable overhead applied at $.90 per hour
Standard direct-labor cost, $4 per hour
Denominator production per month, 2,500 units

Standard direct-labor hours per finished unit, 5
Direct-labor costs incurred, 11,000 hours, $41,800
Variable overhead costs incurred, $9,500
Fixed-overhead budget variance, $100, favorable
Finished units produced, 2,000

REQUIRED: | Prepare an analysis of all variances (similar to Exhibit 15-11, p. 464).

15–30. Journal entries. Study Appendix 15B. Refer to the data in Problem 15–28. Prepare journal entries for direct labor, variable overhead, and fixed overhead. Include the recognition of all variances in your entries. Omit explanations.

15–31. Journal entries. Study Appendix 15B. Refer to the data in Problem 15–29. Prepare journal entries for direct labor, variable overhead, and fixed overhead. Include the recognition of all variances in your entries. Omit explanations.

15–32. Comparing the performance of two plants. On your first day as assistant to the president of Holland Systems, Inc., your in-box contains the following memo:

To: Assistant to the President
From: The President
Subject: Mickey Mouse Watch Situation

This note is to bring you up-to-date on one of our acquisition problem areas. Market research detected the current nostalgia wave almost a year ago and concluded that HSI should acquire a position in this market. Research data showed that Mickey Mouse Watches could become profitable ($2 contribution margin on a $5 sales price) at a volume of 100,000 units per plant if they became popular again. Consequently, we picked up closed-down facilities on each coast, staffed them, and asked them to keep us posted on operations.

Friday I got preliminary information from accounting that is unclear. I want you to find out why their costs of goods sold are far apart and how we should have them report in the future to avoid confusion. This is particularly important in the Mickey Mouse case, as market projections look bad and we may have to close one plant. I guess we'll close the West Coast plant unless you can show otherwise.

PRELIMINARY ACCOUNTING REPORT		
	EAST	**WEST**
Sales	$500,000	$500,000
Cost of goods sold	300,000	480,000
Gross margin	$200,000	$ 20,000
Administration costs (fixed)	20,000	20,000
Net income	$180,000	$ 0
Production	200,000 units	100,000 units
Variances (included in cost of goods sold)	$180,000, favorable	$ 90,000, unfavorable

REQUIRED:

Reconstruct the given income statements in as much detail as possible. Then explain in detail why the income statements differ, and clarify this situation confronting the president. Assume that there are no price or efficiency variances.

Overhead
Application:
Direct and
Absorption
Costing

15–33. Inventory measures, production scheduling, and evaluating divisional performance. The Dore Company stresses competition between the heads of its various divisions, and it rewards stellar performance with year-end bonuses that vary between 5% and 10% of division net operating income (before considering the bonus or income taxes). The divisional managers have great discretion in setting production schedules.

Division Y produces and sells a product for which there is a longstanding demand but which can have marked seasonal and year-to-year fluctuations. On November 30, 19X2, Robert Smith, the Division Y manager, is preparing a production schedule for December. The following data are available for January 1 through November 30:

Beginning inventory, January 1, in units	10,000
Sales price, per unit	$ 500
Total fixed costs incurred for manufacturing	$11,000,000
Total fixed costs: other (not inventoriable)	$11,000,000
Total variable costs for manufacturing	$22,000,000
Total other variable costs (fluctuate with units sold)	$ 5,000,000
Units produced	110,000
Units sold	100,000
Variances	None

Production in October and November was 10,000 units each month. Practical capacity is 12,000 units per month. Maximum available storage space for inventory is 25,000 units. The sales outlook, for December through February, is 6,000 units monthly. In order to retain a core of key employees, monthly production cannot be scheduled at less than 4,000 units without special permission from the president. Inventory is never to be less than 10,000 units.

The denominator used for applying fixed factory overhead is regarded as 120,000 units annually. The company uses a standard absorption-costing system. All variances are disposed of at year-end as an adjustment to standard cost of goods sold.

1. Given the restrictions as stated, and assuming that the manager wants to maximize the company's net income for 19X2:
   a. How many units should be scheduled for production in December?
   b. What net operating income will be reported for 19X2 as a whole, assuming that the implied cost behavior patterns will continue in December as they did throughout the year, to date? Show your computations.
   c. If December production is scheduled at 4,000 units, what would reported net income be?
2. Assume that standard direct costing is used rather than standard absorption costing:
   a. What would net income for 19X2 be, assuming that the December production schedule is the one in Requirement 1, part *a*?
   b. Assuming that December production was 4,000 units?
   c. Reconcile the net incomes in this requirement with those in Requirement 1.
3. From the viewpoint of the long-run interests of the company as a whole, what production schedule should the division manager set? Explain fully. Include in your explanation a comparison of the motivating influence of absorption and direct costing in this situation.
4. Assume standard absorption costing. The manager wants to maximize his after-income-tax performance over the long run. Given the data at the beginning of the problem, assume that income tax rates will be halved in 19X3. Assume also that year-end write-offs of variances are acceptable for income tax purposes.

   How many units should be scheduled for production in December? Why?

16

INFLUENCES OF QUANTITATIVE TECHNIQUES ON MANAGEMENT ACCOUNTING

Learning Objectives

When you have finished studying this chapter, you should be able to

1. Distinguish between making decisions under certainty and making decisions under uncertainty

2. Construct a decision table involving probabilities and compute the expected value of each action

3. Use standard deviation and expected value to compute the coefficient of variation, and indicate how it can measure the relative degrees of risk among alternatives

4. Compute the expected value of perfect information

5. Construct a graph for a linear-programming solution

6. Develop the equations and inequalities for a linear-programming solution

7. Determine the economic-order quantity (EOQ) by using the formula, and estimate the EOQ by preparing a schedule of the relevant costs of various selected order sizes

8. Determine the safety stock and the reorder point in a simple inventory situation

Because the branches of knowledge overlap, it is always an oversimplification to specify where the field of accounting starts and where it ends. Some accountants take the view that accounting should restrict itself to score-keeping, the compilation of financial history. Others feel that if accountants do not move quickly to assimilate a working knowledge of computer technology and assorted mathematical techniques, their attention-directing and problem-solving functions will be seized by the expanding field of management science.

We need not be concerned with the controversy over what accounting is and what it is not. Regardless of its label, the subject matter of this chapter has a bearing on management planning and control and is therefore important to accountants and to managers. One of the marks of an educated person is his or her ability to recognize and accept changes that promise better ways of accomplishing objectives. The accountant is still the top quantitative expert in nearly all organizations, and few companies employ full-time mathematics specialists. To retain and improve their status, accountants should be aware of how mathematical models can improve planning and control. The alert managers would naturally expect their accountants to keep abreast of the newer quantitative techniques.

This chapter is a survey. Technical competence in any of the areas mentioned can be achieved only by thorough specialized study. We shall explore decision theory and uncertainty, linear-programming models, and inventory-control models.

The accountant often provides many of the data that are included in these decision models. An understanding of the nature of decision models should have a direct effect on how the accountant designs a formal information system.

DECISION THEORY AND UNCERTAINTY

❏ Formal Decision Models

A **model** is a depiction of the interrelationships among the recognized factors in a real situation. Most models spotlight the key interrelationships and de-emphasize the unimportant factors. Models take many forms. Museums contain model rockets and model ships. Automobile companies distribute miniature model cars. Accountants continually work with accounting systems and financial reports, which are models. Operations researchers principally use mathematical equations as models.

Decision models are often expressed in mathematical form. The careful use of mathematical models supplements hunches and implicit rules of thumb with explicit assumptions and criteria. Mathematical models have been criticized because they may oversimplify and ignore important underlying factors. Still, many examples of successful applications can be cited. For example, inventory-control and linear-programming models are widely used. The test of success is not whether mathematical models lead to perfect decisions, but whether such models lead to better decisions than via alternative techniques. How is this test applied? Sometimes it is difficult, but conceptually the test is to compare the net financial impact (after deducting the cost of accumulating the information used in the decision) of the decision generated by the mathematical model versus the net financial impact of the decision generated by other techniques. In other words, the relative attractiveness of using mathematical decision models is again subject to the cost-benefit test.

Decision theory is a complex, somewhat ill-defined body of knowledge developed by statisticians, mathematicians, economists, and psychologists that tries to prescribe how decisions should be made and to describe systematically which variables affect choices. The basic approach of decision theory has the following characteristics:

1. An objective that can be quantified. This objective can take many forms. Most often, it is expressed as a maximization (or minimization) of some form of profit (or cost). This quantification is often called a **choice criterion** or an **objective function.** This objective function is used to evaluate the courses of action and to provide a basis for choosing the best alternative.

2. A set of the alternative courses of action under explicit consideration. This set of *actions* should be collectively exhaustive and mutually exclusive.

3. A set of all relevant **events** (sometimes called **states** or **states of nature**) that can occur. This set should also be collectively exhaustive and mutually exclusive. Therefore only one of the states will actually occur.

4. A set of **probabilities** that describes the likelihood of occurrence for each event.

5. A set of **outcomes** (often called **payoffs**) that measure the consequences of the various possible actions in terms of the objective function. Each outcome is conditionally dependent on a specific course of action and a specific event.

❏ Payoff Tables and Decision Tables

An example may clarify the essential ingredients of a formal model. Suppose a decision maker has two mutually exclusive and exhaustive alternative courses of action regarding the quality-control aspects of a project: accept a unit of product or reject the unit of product. The decision maker also predicts that two mutually exclusive and exhaustive events will affect the outcomes: either the product unit conforms to the quality standards, or it does not conform. The combination of actions, events, and outcomes can be presented in a **decision table** (also called **payoff table**):

ALTERNATIVE ACTIONS	ALTERNATIVE EVENTS AND OUTCOMES	
	Conform	Nonconform
Accept	$12[1]	$2[2]
Reject	$ 7[3]	$7[4]

Note: The number references in this table relate to the corresponding numbers in the list that follows.

The outcomes in this example are the dollar contributions to profit; they are assumed to take the pattern shown here because

1. Acceptance and conformance should produce the normal contribution to profit
2. Acceptance and nonconformance eventually results in expensive rework after the product is processed through later stages, so the contribution is lower
3. Rejection and conformance results in immediate unnecessary rework that reduces the normal contribution
4. Rejection and nonconformance results in the same immediate necessary rework described in item 3

The payoff table includes three of the five ingredients of the formal model: actions, events, and outcomes. The other two ingredients are the probabilities and the choice criterion. Assume that the probability of conform is 0.6 and that of nonconform is 0.4. Assume also that the choice criterion is to maximize the expected value of the outcome, the contribution to profit. The decision table can now be expanded:

Probability of Event	EVENTS		Expected Value of Contribution
	Conform 0.6	Nonconform 0.4	
ACTIONS			
Accept	$12 outcome	$2 outcome	$8
Reject	$ 7 outcome	$7 outcome	$7

Given this model, the decision maker would always accept the product, because the expected value of the outcome is larger for Accept than for Reject. Let $\overline{A}$ = the "average" or expected value;[1] then:

if accept, $\overline{A} = \$12(0.6) + \$2(0.4) = \$7.20 + \$.80 = \$8$

if reject, $\overline{A} = \$7(0.6) + \$7(0.4) = \$4.20 + \$2.80 = \$7$

As you can see, an expected value is simply a weighted average using the probability of each event to weight the outcomes for each action. (Incidentally, $\overline{A}$ is pronounced *A-bar*.)

☐ Decisions Under Certainty

Decisions are frequently classified as those made under certainty and those made under uncertainty. Certainty exists when there is absolutely no doubt about which event will occur and when there is a single outcome for each possible action. The decision table would appear as follows (data assumed):

[1] An expected value is an arithmetic mean, a weighted average using the probabilities as weights. The formula is

where A_x is the outcome or payoff or cost or cash flow for the xth possible event or state of nature, P_x is the probability of occurrence of that outcome, $\overline{A}$ is the expected value of the outcome, x is the identity of each event, and n is the number of events.

	EVENT
	Conform
Probability of Event	1.0
ACTIONS	
Accept	$12 outcome
Reject	$ 7 outcome

Note that there is only one column in the decision table because there is only one possible event. The decision obviously consists of choosing the action that will produce the best outcome. However, decisions under certainty are not *always* obvious. There are often countless alternative actions, each of which may offer certain outcomes. The problem, then, is finding the best one. For example, the problem of allocating 20 different job orders to 20 different machines, any one of which could do the job, can involve literally *billions* of different combinations. Each way of assigning these jobs is another possible action. The payoff table would have only one outcome *column* because the costs of production using the various machines are assumed as known; however, it would have 2½ quintillion *rows*. This demonstrates that decision making under certainty can be more than just a trivial problem.

When an outcome is certain for a particular (or given) action, the prediction is a single point with no dispersion on either side. There is a 100% chance of occurrence if the action is taken; in other words, the probability is 1.0. For example, the expected cash inflow on an action, buying a federal Treasury note, might be, say, $4,000 for next year. This might be graphed as follows:

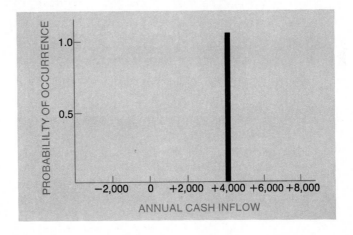

❑ Decisions Under Risk or Uncertainty

Of course, decision makers must frequently contend with uncertainty rather than certainty; they face a number of possible events, given a particular course of action. The distinction among various degrees of uncertainty centers on the degree of objectivity by which probabilities are assigned.

The probabilities may be assigned with a high degree of objectivity.[2] That is, if decision makers know the probability of occurrence of each of a number of events, their assignment of probabilities is "objective" because of mathematical proofs or the compilation of historical evidence. For example, the probability of obtaining a head in the toss of a symmetrical coin is 0.5; that of drawing a particular playing card from a well-shuffled deck, 1/52. In a business, the probability of having a specified percentage of spoiled units may be assigned with great confidence, which is based on production experience with thousands of units.

If decision makers have no basis in past experience or in mathematical proofs for assigning the probabilities of occurrence of the various events, they must resort to the *subjective* assignment of probabilities. For example, the probability of the success or failure of a new product may have to be assessed without the help of any related experience. This assignment is subjective because no two individuals assessing a situation will necessarily assign the same probabilities. Executives may be virtually certain about the *range* of possible events or possible outcomes, but they may differ about the likelihoods of various possibilities within that range.

The concept of uncertainty can be illustrated by considering two investment proposals on new projects.[3] The manager has carefully considered the risks and has subjectively determined the following discrete probability distribution of expected cash flows for the next year (assume that the useful life of the project is one year):

PROPOSAL A		PROPOSAL B	
Probability	Cash Inflow	Probability	Cash Inflow
0.10	$3,000	0.10	$2,000
0.20	3,500	0.25	3,000
0.40	4,000	0.30	4,000
0.20	4,500	0.25	5,000
0.10	5,000	0.10	6,000

❑ Expected Value and Standard Deviation

Exhibit 16-1 shows a graphical comparison of the probability distributions. The usual approach to this problem is to compute an **expected value** for each probability distribution.

The expected value of the cash inflow in Proposal A is

$$\overline{A} = 0.1(3,000) + 0.2(3,500) + 0.4(4,000) + 0.2(4,500) + 0.1(5,000)$$
$$= \$4,000$$

The expected value for the cash inflow in Proposal B is also $4,000:

$$\overline{A} = 0.1(2,000) + 0.25(3,000) + 0.3(4,000) + 0.25(5,000) + 0.1(6,000)$$
$$= \$4,000$$

[2] This is sometimes called decision making under risk, as distinguished from decision making under uncertainty. The distinction between risk and uncertainty in the current literature and in practice is so blurred that the terms are used interchangeably here.

[3] James C. Van Horne, *Fundamentals of Financial Management*, 6th ed. (Englewood Cliffs, N.J.: Prentice-Hall, 1983), Chap. 6.

EXHIBIT
16-1
Comparison
of
Probability
Distributions

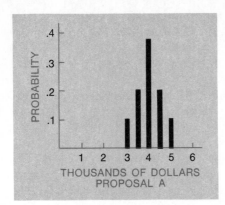

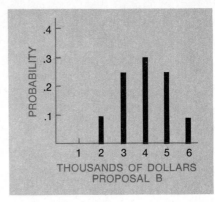

Incidentally, the expected value of the cash inflow in the federal Treasury note is also $4,000:

$$\overline{A} = 1.0(4,000) = \$4,000$$

Note that mere comparison of these $4,000 expected values is an oversimplification. These three single figures are not strictly comparable; one represents certainty, whereas the other two represent the expected values over a range of possible outcomes. Decision makers must explicitly or implicitly (by "feel" or hunch) recognize that they are comparing figures that are really representations of probability distributions; otherwise the reporting of the expected value alone may mislead them.[4]

To give the decision maker more information, the accountant could provide the complete probability distribution for each proposal. However, often that course means flooding the manager with too many data for convenient comprehension. Therefore a middle ground is often used. A summary measure of the underlying dispersion is supplied. The conventional measure of the dispersion of a probability distribution for a single variable is the **standard deviation**—the square root of the mean of the squared deviations from the expected value. The standard deviation is denoted by σ, which is *sigma*, the lowercase Greek letter for *s:*

$$\sigma = \sqrt{\sum_{x=1}^{n} (A_x - \overline{A})^2 P_x}$$

The standard deviation for Proposal A is smaller than that for Proposal B:

$$\begin{aligned}
\text{for A: } \sigma &= [0.1(3,000 - 4,000)^2 + 0.2(3,500 - 4,000)^2 \\
&\quad + 0.4(4,000 - 4,000)^2 + 0.2(4,500 - 4,000)^2 \\
&\quad + 0.1(5,000 - 4,000)^2]^{1/2} \\
&= [300,000]^{1/2} = \$548
\end{aligned}$$

$$\begin{aligned}
\text{for B: } \sigma &= [0.1(2,000 - 4,000)^2 + 0.25(3,000 - 4,000)^2 \\
&\quad + 0.3(4,000 - 4,000)^2 + 0.25(5,000 - 4,000)^2 \\
&\quad + 0.1(6,000 - 4,000)^2]^{1/2} \\
&= [1,300,000]^{1/2} = \$1,140
\end{aligned}$$

$$\text{for the Treasury note: } \sigma = \sqrt{1.0(4,000 - 4,000)^2} = 0$$

Influences of
Quantitative
Techniques on
Management
Accounting

485

[4] For example, how would you feel about choosing between the following two investments? First, invest $10 today with a probability of 1.0 of obtaining $11 in two days. Second, invest $10 today with a probability of 0.5 of obtaining $22 in two days and 0.5 of obtaining $0. The expected value is $11 in both cases.

A measure of relative dispersion is the *coefficient of variation*, which is the standard deviation divided by expected value. The coefficient for Proposal B is 1,140 ÷ 4,000 = 0.29; for A it is 548 ÷ 4,000 = 0.14; and for the Treasury note it is 0 ÷ 4,000 = 0. Therefore, because the coefficient is a relative measure of risk or uncertainty, B is said to have a greater degree of risk than A, which, in turn, has a greater degree of risk than the Treasury note.

❏ The Accountant and Uncertainty

Many accounting practitioners and managers shudder at the notion of using subjective probabilities to quantify things that are supposedly "intangible" or "unmeasurable" or "qualitative" or "unquantifiable." However, their position is weak, simply because decisions *do* have to be made. The attempts by statisticians, mathematicians, and modern accountants to measure the unmeasurable is an old and natural chore that scientists have performed for centuries. The use of subjective probabilities merely formalizes the intuitive judgments and hunches that managers so often use. It forces decision makers to expose and evaluate what they may have done unconsciously for years.

Many statisticians and accountants favor presenting the entire probability distribution directly to the decision maker. Others first divide the information into a threefold classification of optimistic, middle, and pessimistic categories. Still others provide summary measures of dispersion, such as the standard deviation or the coefficient of variation. In any event, we are likely to see the accountants' formal recognition of uncertainty and probability distributions in their reporting. In this way, the information will portray underlying phenomena in a more realistic fashion instead of as if there were only a world of certainty.

❏ Example of General Approach to Uncertainty

An example of the general approach to dealing with uncertainty may clarify some of the preceding ideas.

❏ Problem

Once a day, a retailer stocks units (bags) of fresh pastries; each costs 40¢ and sells for $1. The retailer never reduces his price; leftovers are given to a nearby church. He estimates characteristics as follows:

DEMAND	PROBABILITY
0	0.05
1	0.20
2	0.40
3	0.25
4	0.10
5 or more	0.00
	1.00

The retailer wants to know how many units he should stock in order to maximize profits. Try to solve before consulting the solution that follows.

❑ Solution

The profit, per unit sold, is 60¢; the loss, per unit unsold, is 40¢. All the alternatives may be assessed in the following *decision table*.

	EVENTS: DEMAND OF					
	0	1	2	3	4	Expected
Probability of Event	0.05	0.20	0.40	0.25	0.10	Value
ACTIONS: UNITS PURCHASED:						
0	$ 0	$ 0	$ 0	$ 0	$ 0	$ 0
1	− .40	.60	.60	.60	.60	.55
2	− .80	.20	1.20	1.20	1.20	.90
3	−1.20	−.20	.80	1.80	1.80	.85
4	−1.60	−.60	.40*	1.40	2.40	.55

*Example of computation: $(2 \times \$1.00) - (4 \times \$.40) = \$.40$

As shown in an earlier section, the computation of expected value ($\overline{A}$) for each action is affected by the probability weights and the conditional outcome associated with each combination of actions and events:

$$\overline{A} \text{ (Stock 1)} = 0.05(-.40) + 0.20(.60) + 0.40(.60) + 0.25(.60) + 0.10(.60)$$
$$= \$.55$$

$$\overline{A} \text{ (Stock 2)} = 0.05(-.80) + 0.20(.20) + 0.40(1.20) + 0.25(1.20) + 0.10(1.20)$$
$$= \$.90$$

and so on.

To maximize expected value, the retailer should stock two units ($\overline{A} = \$.90$).

❑ Obtaining Additional Information

Sometimes executives are hesitant about making a particular decision. They want more information before making a final choice. Some additional information is nearly always obtainable—at a price. Consider a popular technique for computing the maximum amount that should be paid for such additional information. The general idea is to compute the expected value under ideal circumstances—that is, circumstances that would permit the retailer to predict, with absolute certainty, the number of units to be sold on any given day.

The basic decision is whether to purchase advance revelation *without knowing what the revelation will be*. Exhibit 16-2 presents a decision table with perfect information. The expected value of the decision *with* perfect information is the sum of the best outcome for each event multiplied by its probability:

$$\overline{A} \text{ (perfect information)} = 0.05(0) + 0.20(.60) + 0.40(1.20)$$
$$+ 0.25(1.80) + 0.10(2.40) = \$1.29$$

In Exhibit 16-2, it is assumed that the retailer will never err in his

Influences of
Quantitative
Techniques on
Management
Accounting

487

EXHIBIT
16-2

Decision Table with Perfect Information						
	EVENT: DEMAND OF					
	0	1	2	3	4	Expected
Probability of Event	0.05	0.20	0.40	0.25	0.10	Value
ACTIONS **UNITS PURCHASED:**						
0	$0					$ 0
1		$.60				.12
2			$1.20			.48
3				$1.80		.45
4					$2.40	.24
Total expected value						$1.29

forecasts and that demand will fluctuate from zero to four exactly as indicated by the probabilities. The maximum day-in, day-out profit is $1.29. Consequently, the most the retailer should be willing to pay for perfect advance information would be the difference between:

Expected value *with* perfect information	$1.29
Expected value *with* existing information	.90
Expected value *of* perfect information	$ .39

In the real world, of course, the retailer would not pay 39¢ because no amount of additional information is likely to provide perfect knowledge. But businesses often obtain additional knowledge through sampling, and sampling costs money. The executive needs a method (a) for assessing the probable benefits, in relation to its cost, of additional information from sampling; and (b) for determining the best sample size. In the present example, no sampling technique would be attractive if its cost allocated to each day's operations equaled or exceeded the 39¢ ceiling price.

❏ Good Decisions and Bad Outcomes

Always distinguish between a good decision and a good outcome. One can exist without the other. By definition, uncertainty rules out guaranteeing that the best outcome will be obtained. Thus it is possible that "bad luck" will produce unfavorable consequences even when "good" decisions have occurred.

Consider the following example. Suppose you are offered a gamble for a mere $1, a fair coin toss where heads you win, tails you lose. You will win $20 if the event is heads, but you will lose $1 if the event is tails. As a rational decision maker, you proceed through the logical phases: gathering information, assessing consequences, and making a choice. You accept the bet. The coin is tossed. You lose. From your viewpoint, this was a bad outcome but a good decision. From your opponent's viewpoint, it was a good outcome but a bad decision.

A decision can only be made on the basis of information available at the time of the decision. Hindsight is often flawless, but a bad outcome does not necessarily mean that it flowed from a bad decision. As D. W. North said, "The best protection we have against a bad outcome is a good decision."[5]

LINEAR-PROGRAMMING MODELS

❑ Characteristics

Linear programming is a potent mathematical approach to a group of management problems that contain many interacting variables and that basically involve the allocation of limited resources in such a way as to increase profit or decrease cost. There are nearly always limiting factors or scarce resources that are restrictions, restraints, or constraints on available alternatives. Linear programming has been applied to a vast number of decisions, such as machine scheduling, product mix, raw-material mix, scheduling flight crews, production routing, shipping schedules, transportation routes, blending gasoline, blending sausage ingredients, and designing transformers. In general, linear programming is the best available technique for combining materials, labor, and facilities to best advantage when all the relationships are approximately linear and many combinations are possible.

Note that linear programming is a decision model under conditions of *certainty*, where constraints affect the allocation of resources among competing uses. That is, the model analyzes a total list of actions whose outcomes are known with certainty and chooses the combination of actions that will maximize profit or minimize cost.

❑ The Techniques, the Accountant, and the Manager

All of us are familiar with linear equations (e.g., $X + 3 = 9$). We also know that simultaneous linear equations with two or three unknowns become progressively more difficult to solve with only pencil and paper. Linear programming essentially involves (1) constructing a set of simultaneous linear equations, which represent the model of the problem and which include many variables; and (2) solving the equations with the help of the digital computer.

The formulation of the equations—that is, the building of the model—is far more challenging than the mechanics of the solution. The model aims at being a valid and accurate portrayal of the problem. Computer programs can then take the equations and process the solution.

As a minimum, accountants and executives should be able to recognize the types of problems in their organizations that are most susceptible to analysis by linear programming. They should be able to help in the

Influences of
Quantitative
Techniques on
Management
Accounting

489

[5] D. W. North, "A Tutorial Introduction to Decision Theory," *IEEE Transactions on Systems Science and Cybernetics,* September 1968, p. 201. Also see Charles A. Holloway, *Decision Making under Uncertainty* (Englewood Cliffs, N.J.: Prentice-Hall, 1979), pp. 7–8.

construction of the model—i.e., in specifying the objectives, the constraints, and the variables. Ideally, they should understand the mathematics and should be able to talk comfortably with the operations researchers who are attempting to express their problem mathematically. However, the position taken here is that the accountant and the manager should concentrate on formulating the model and *analyzing* the solution and not worry too much about the technical intricacies of *obtaining* the solution. The latter may be delegated to the mathematicians; the feasibility and advisability of delegating the former is highly doubtful.

❏ Illustration of Product Mix

Consider the following illustration: Machine 1 is available for 24 hours, and Machine 2 is available for 20 hours, for the processing of two products. Product X has a contribution margin of $2 per unit; Product Y, $1 per unit. These products must be sold in such combination that the quantity of X must be equal to or less than the quantity of Y. X requires 6 hours of time on Machine 1 and 10 hours of time on Machine 2. Product Y requires 4 hours of time on Machine 1 only. What daily production combination will produce the maximum profit?

The linear-programming approach can be divided into four steps, although variations and shortcuts are available in unique situations:

1. Formulate the objectives. The objective is usually to maximize profit or minimize cost.
2. Determine the basic relationships, particularly the constraints.
3. Determine the feasible alternatives.
4. Compute the optimum solution.

Techniques may differ. In the uncomplicated situation in our example, the graphic approach is easiest to understand. In practice, the *simplex method* is used—a step-by-step process that is extremely efficient. Basically, the simplex method begins with one feasible solution and tests it algebraically, by substitution, to see if it can be improved. These substitutions continue until further improvement is impossible, given the constraints. The optimum solution is therefore achieved.

These four steps can be applied to the example.

Step 1. **Formulate the objectives.** In our case, find the product combination that results in the maximum total contribution margin. Maximize:

$$\text{total contribution margin} = \$2X + \$1Y \tag{1}$$

This is called the objective function. *X* represents the number of X product units, and *Y* represents the number of Y units.

Step 2. **Determine the basic relationships.** The relationships may be depicted by the following inequalities:

For Machine 1:	$6X + 4Y \leq 24$
For Machine 2:	$10X \quad\ \leq 20$
Sales of X and Y:	$X - Y \leq 0$
Because negative production is impossible:	$X \quad\ \geq 0$ and $Y \geq 0$

The three solid lines in Exhibit 16-3 will help you to visualize the machine constraints and the product-mix constraint. (To plot a constraint line, assume for Machine 1 that $X = 0$; then $Y = 6$. If $Y = 0$, then $X = 4$. Connect points $(0,6)$ and $(4,0)$ with a straight line.)

EXHIBIT 16-3

Linear Programming: Graphic Solution

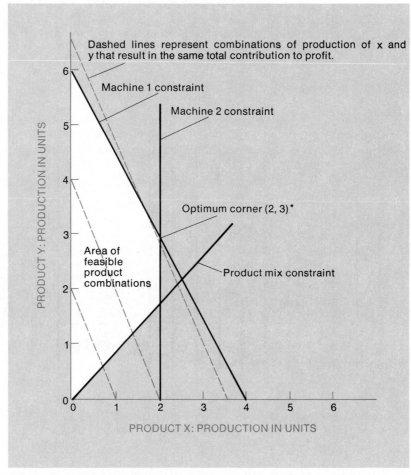

*Here, the coordinates of the corners may be obvious. However, if they are not obvious, they can easily be computed by using simultaneous equations for the constraints that intersect at the corners:

Trial 3:   (1) $6X + 4Y = 24$
          (2) $10X = 20$; $X = 2$
          (1) $(6 \times 2) + 4Y = 24$
          (1) $4Y = 24 - 12 = 12$; $Y = 12 \div 4 = 3$
Thus, coordinates are (2,3).
Trial 4:   (2) $10X = 20$; $X = 2$
          (3) $X - Y = 0$
          (3) $2 - Y = 0$; $Y = 2$
Thus, coordinates are (2,2).

Influences of
Quantitative
Techniques on
Management
Accounting

491

Step 3. **Determine the feasible alternatives.** Alternatives are feasible if they are technically possible. We do not want to bother with computations for impossible solutions. The white area in Exhibit 16-3 shows the boundaries of the feasible product combinations—that is, combinations of X and Y that satisfy all constraining factors.

Step 4. **Compute the optimum solution.** Steps 2 and 3 focused on physical relationships alone. We now return to the economic relationships expressed as the objective in step 1. We test various feasible product combinations to see which one results in a maximum total contribution margin. It so happens that the best solution must lie on one of the corners of the Area of Feasible Product Combinations in Exhibit 16-3. The corners represent the limits of at least two constraints, so those constraints (resources) are being fully utilized. Intuitively, full utilization suggests optimality. The total contribution margin is calculated for each corner. The steps, which are similar to the simplex method, which uses digital computers, are:

a. Start with one possible combination.

b. Compute the profit.

c. Move to another possible combination to see if it will improve the result in step *b*. Keep moving from corner to corner until no further improvement is possible. (The simplex method is more efficient because it does not necessitate testing all possible combinations before finding the best solution.)

These steps are summarized below. They show that the optimum combination is two units of X and three units of Y:

TRIAL	CORNER	COMBINATION PRODUCT X	PRODUCT Y	$2X + $1Y = TOTAL CONTRIBUTION MARGIN
1	0,0	0	0	$2(0) + $1(0) = $0
2	0,6	0	6	2(0) + 1(6) = 6
3	2,3	2	3	2(2) + 1(3) = 7
4	2,2	2	2	2(2) + 1(2) = 6

❑ Substitution of Scarce Resources

Why must the best solution lie on a corner? Consider all possible combinations that will produce a total contribution margin of $1 ($2X + 1Y = $1). This is a straight line through (0,2) and (1,0). Other total contribution margins are represented by the dashed lines parallel to this one. Their associated total contribution margins increase the farther the lines get from the origin. The optimum line is the one farthest from the origin that has a feasible point on it; intuitively, we know that this happens at a corner (2,3). Furthermore, if you put a ruler on the graph and move it parallel with the $1 line, the optimum corner becomes apparent.

As these trials show, the central problem of linear programming is to find the specific combination of variables that satisfies all constraints and achieves the objective sought. Moving from corner to corner (which is really moving from one possible solution to another) implies that the scarce resource, productive capacity, is being transferred between products. Each four-hour period that Machine 1 is productively used to produce one unit of Y may be sacrificed (i.e., given or traded) for one six-hour period re-quired to produce one unit of X. Consider the exchange of twelve hours of time. This means that three units of Y will be traded for two units of X. Will this exchange add to profits? Yes:

Total contribution at corner (0,6)		$6
Additional contribution margin from Product X:		
2 units, @ $2	$4	
Lost contribution margin, Product Y:		
3 units, @ $1	3	
Net additional contribution margin		1
Total contribution margin at corner (2,3)		$7

The problem of substituting of resources is not simply a matter of compar-ing margins per unit of *product* and jumping to the conclusion that the production of Product X, which has the greater margin per unit of product, should be maximized.[6] These substitutions are a matter of trading a given contribution margin per unit of a limiting factor (i.e., a critical resource) for some other contribution margin per unit of a limiting factor.

INVENTORY PLANNING AND CONTROL MODELS

❑ Characteristics

Comprehensive inventory-planning and control systems have been suc-cessfully installed in many companies. The major objective of inventory management is to discover and maintain the optimum level of investment in the inventory. Inventories may be too high or too low. If too high, there are unnecessary carrying costs and risks of obsolescence. If too low, pro-duction may be disrupted or sales permanently lost. The optimum inven-tory level is that which minimizes the total costs associated with inventory.

The purchase costs or the manufacturing costs of the inventory (that is, the acquisition costs) would usually be irrelevant to the inventory-con-trol decisions considered here, because we assume that the total annual quantity required would be the same for the various alternatives. Exhibit 16-4 shows the main relevant costs that must be considered, the costs of ordering plus the costs of carrying.

The two significant cost items tend to offset one another. The total relevant costs of carrying, including interest, rise as orders decrease in frequency and grow in size, but the total costs of ordering, delivery, etc., decrease; and vice versa.

❑ How Much to Order?

The two main questions in inventory control are how much to order at a time and when to order. A key factor in inventory policy is computing the

493

[6] This point is also discussed in Chapter 4, page 95, in the section "Contribution to Profit per Unit of Limiting Factor."

EXHIBIT 16-4

Some Relevant Costs of Inventories

COSTS OF ORDERING

1. Preparing purchase or production orders
2. Receiving (unloading, unpacking, inspecting)
3. Processing all related documents
4. Extra purchasing or transportation costs for frequent orders
5. Extra costs of numerous small production runs, overtime, setups, and training

plus

COSTS OF CARRYING

1. Desired rate of return on investment*
2. Risk of obsolescence and deterioration
3. Storage-space costs
4. Personal property taxes
5. Insurance

*Cost that ordinarily does not explicitly appear on formal accounting records.

optimum size of either a normal purchase order for raw materials or a shop order for a production run. This optimum size is called the **economic order quantity** (EOQ) or **economic lot size**, the size that will result in minimum total annual costs of the item in question. Consider this example:

❏ Problem

A refrigerator manufacturer buys certain steel shelving in sets from outside suppliers at $4 per set. Total annual needs are 5,000 sets at a rate of twenty sets per working day. The following cost data are available:

Desired annual return on inventory investment,		
10% × $4	$.40	
Rent, insurance, taxes, per unit per year	.10	
Carrying costs per unit per year		$ .50
Costs per purchase order:		
Clerical costs, stationery, postage, telephone, etc.		$10.00

What is the economic order quantity?

❏ Solution

Exhibit 16-5 shows a tabulation of total relevant costs under various alternatives. The column with the least cost will indicate the economic order quantity.

Exhibit 16-5 shows minimum costs at two levels, 400 and 500 units. The next step would be to see if costs are lower somewhere between 400 and 500 units—say, at 450 units:

EXHIBIT 16-5

Annualized Relevant Costs of Various Standard Orders (250 working days)

SYMBOLS

E	Order size	50	100	200	400	500	600	800	1,000	5,000
E/2	Average inventory in units*	25	50	100	200	250	300	400	500	2,500
A/E	Number of purchase orders†	100	50	25	12.5	10	8.3	6.3	5	1
S(E/2)	Annual carrying cost @ $.50	$ 13	$ 25	$ 50	$100	$125	$150	$200	$ 250	$1,250
P(A/E)	Annual purchase-order cost @ $10	1,000	500	250	125	100	83	63	50	10
C	Total annual relevant costs	$1,013	$525	$300	$225	$225	$233	$263	$ 300	$1,260

Least cost

E = Order size
A = Annual quantity used in units
S = Annual cost of carrying one unit in stock one year
P = Cost of placing a purchase order
C = Total annual relevant costs

*Assume that stock is zero when each order arrives. (Even if a certain minimum inventory were assumed, it has no bearing on the choice here as long as the minimum is the same for each alternative.) Therefore the average inventory relevant to the problem will be one-half the order quantity. For example, if 600 units are purchased, the inventory on arrival will contain 600. It will gradually diminish until no units are on hand. The average inventory would be 300; the carrying cost, $.50 × 300, or $150.

†Number to meet the total annual need for 5,000 sets.

Average inventory, 225 × $.50	$113 Carrying costs
Number of orders (5,000/450), 11.1 × $10 =	111 Purchase-order costs
	$224 Total relevant costs

The dollar differences here are extremely small, but the approach is important. The same approach can be shown in graphic form. See Exhibit 16-6. Note that in this case, total cost is at a minimum where total purchase-order cost and total carrying cost are equal.

❑ Order-Size Formula

The graphic approach has been expressed as a formula (derived via calculus):

$$E = \sqrt{\frac{2AP}{S}}$$

where E = order size; A = annual quantity used in units; P = cost of placing an order; and S = annual cost of carrying one unit in stock for one year.

Substituting:

$$E = \sqrt{\frac{2(5,000)(\$10)}{\$.50}} = \sqrt{\frac{\$100,000}{\$.50}} = \sqrt{200,000}$$

$$E = 448, \text{ the economic order quantity}$$

EXHIBIT 16-6

Graphic Solution of Economic Order Quantity

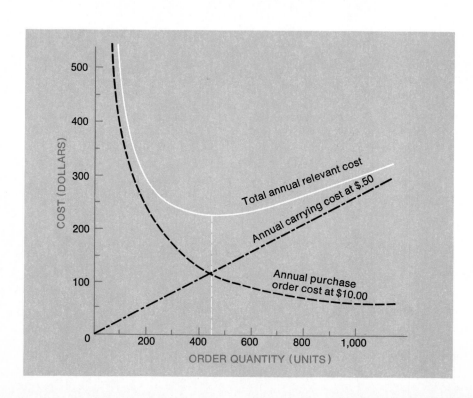

As we may expect, the order size gets larger as *A* or *P* gets larger or as *S* gets smaller.

Note in Exhibit 16-6 that the approach to economic order quantity centers on locating a minimum-cost *range* rather than a minimum-cost *point. The total-cost curve tends to flatten between 400 and 800 units.* In practice, there is a definite tendency to (a) find the range, and (b) select a lot size at the lower end of the range. In our example, there would be a tendency to select a lot size of 400 or slightly more.

❏ When to Order?

Although we have seen how to compute economic order quantity, we have not yet considered another key decision: When to order? This question is easy to answer only if we know the *lead time*, the time interval between placing an order and receiving delivery, know the EOQ, and are *certain* of demand during lead time. The graph in Exhibit 16-7 will clarify the relationships among the following facts:

Economic order quantity	448 sets of steel shelving
Lead time	2 weeks
Average usage	100 sets per week

Exhibit 16-7, Part A, shows that the *reorder point*—the quantity level that automatically triggers a new order—is dependent on expected usage during lead time; that is, if shelving is being used at a rate of 100 sets per week and the lead time is two weeks, a new order will be placed when the inventory level reaches 200 sets.

❏ Minimum Inventory: Safety Allowance

Our previous example assumed that 100 sets would be used per week—a demand pattern that was known with certainty. Businesses are seldom blessed with such accurate forecasting; instead, demand may fluctuate from day to day, from week to week, or from month to month. Thus the company will run out of stock if there are sudden spurts in usage beyond 100 per week, delays in processing orders, or delivery delays. Obviously, then, nearly all companies must provide for some **safety stock**—some minimum or buffer inventory as a cushion against reasonable expected maximum usage. Part B of Exhibit 16-7 is based on the same facts as Part A except that reasonable expected maximum usage is 140 sets per week. The safety stock might be, say, 80 sets (excess usage of 40 sets per week multiplied by two weeks). The reorder point is commonly computed as safety stock plus the average usage during the lead time.

The foregoing discussion of inventory control revolved around the so-called two-bin or constant-order-quantity system: When inventory levels recede to *X*, then order *Y*. Another widely used model is the constant-order-cycle system. For example, every month, review the inventory level on hand and order enough to bring the quantity on hand and on order up to some predetermined level of units. The reorder date is fixed, and the

Influences of
Quantitative
Techniques on
Management
Accounting

497

EXHIBIT 16-7 Demand in Relation to Inventory Levels

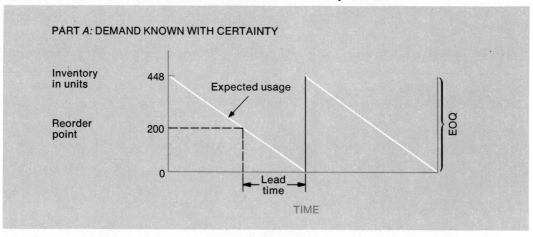

PART *A:* DEMAND KNOWN WITH CERTAINTY

Inventory in units

448 — Expected usage

Reorder point 200

0

Lead time

TIME

EOQ

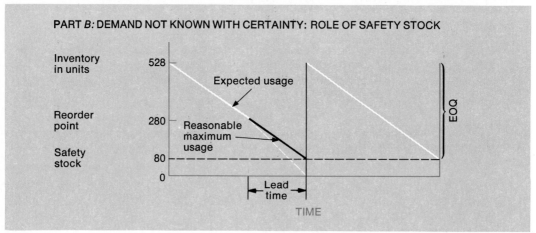

PART *B:* DEMAND NOT KNOWN WITH CERTAINTY: ROLE OF SAFETY STOCK

Inventory in units

528 — Expected usage

Reorder point 280 — Reasonable maximum usage

Safety stock 80

0

Lead time

TIME

EOQ

quantity ordered depends on the usage since the previous order and the outlook during the lead time. Demand forecasts and seasonal patterns should also be considered in specifying the size of orders during the year.

❏ Japanese Influences

The search for increased productivity has focused on many factors, including how inventories are controlled. The high interest rates of the early 1980s have prompted companies to review the levels for safety stocks and the ways of bringing materials to work stations. In particular, Japanese companies have pioneered in developing **just-in-time systems** (also called Kanban systems) to reduce inventory requirements.

The just-in-time system concentrates on the final manufacturing process and then looks backward throughout the preceding processes. The earlier processes produce only enough quantities to replace those withdrawn by the subsequent processes.

The major effects of the just-in-time system have been many more setups and smaller lot sizes. The Japanese have been especially successful in reducing setup times.[7]

Summary

Mathematical decision models are increasingly being used because they replace or supplement hunches with explicit assumptions and criteria. As these decision models become more widely utilized, accounting reports for decision making will tend to give more formal, explicit recognition of uncertainty. For example, the reporting of some measure of probability distributions is more likely.

Accountants often provide inputs to assorted decision models, such as linear-programming models and inventory-control models. Therefore both accountants and managers need to understand the uses and limitations of the models.

Summary Problem for Your Review

❑ Problem

Review this chapter's examples on statistical probability theory, linear programming, and inventory control by trying to solve them before studying their solutions.

Highlights to Remember

1. Accountants generally report and analyze by using single sets of numbers to depict future and past events, as if we were in a world of certainty. The explicit use of probability distributions often helps remind us that we face an uncertain world.

2. Distinguish between good decisions and good outcomes. A good decision can produce either a good or a bad outcome. Similarly, a good outcome can result from a bad decision. However, the best protection against a bad outcome is a good decision. As Damon Runyon observed: "The race is not always to the swift, nor the battle to the strong—but that's the way to bet."

Accounting Vocabulary

Choice criterion; conditional value; decision table; economic lot size; economic order quantity; events; expected value; just-in-time systems; lead time; linear programming; model; objective function; outcomes; payoffs; payoff table; probabilities; safety stock; standard deviation; states; states of nature.

---

[7] Y. Monden, "What Makes the Toyota Production System Really Tick?" *Industrial Engineering*, 13, No. 1 (January 1981), 36–46. Also see *Wall Street Journal*, April 7, 1982, p. 27; and "'Just-in-Time' System Cuts Japan's Auto Costs," *New York Times*, March 25, 1983, pp. 35–37.

Fundamental
Assignment Material

16–1. Influence of uncertainty of forecasts. The figures used in many examples and problems in this and other textbooks are subject to uncertainty. For simplicity, the expected future amounts of sales, direct material, direct labor, and other operating costs are presented as if they were errorless predictions. For instance, this textbook and others might state that a facilities rearrangement "should result in cash operating savings of $X per year." Suppose some industrial engineers have prepared three estimates of savings for next year:

EVENT	PERCENTAGE CHANCE OF OCCURRENCE	SAVINGS
Pessimistic	10%	$1,200
Most likely	60	1,800
Optimistic	30	2,500

REQUIRED: | Using an expected-value table, prepare a single-valued prediction of savings.

16–2. Inventory levels and sales forecasting. Each day an owner of a sidewalk stand stocks toll house cookies, which cost 30¢ and sell for 50¢ each. Leftovers are given to a nearby hospital. Demand characteristics are:

DEMAND	PROBABILITY
Less than 20	0.00
20	0.10
21	0.40
22	0.30
23	0.20
24 or more	0.00

REQUIRED: | How many units should be stocked to maximize expected net income? Show your computations.

16–3. Costs and benefits of perfect information. If the owner of the stand in Problem 16-2 were clairvoyant, so that she could perfectly forecast the demand each day and stock the exact number of cookies needed, what would be her expected profit per day? What is the maximum price that she should be willing to pay for perfect information?

16–4. Fundamental approach of linear programming. A company has two departments, machining and finishing. The company's two products require processing in each of two departments. Data follow:

PRODUCT	CONTRIBUTION MARGIN PER UNIT	DAILY CAPACITY IN UNITS Department 1: Machining	DAILY CAPACITY IN UNITS Department 2: Finishing
A	$2.00	200	120
B	2.50	100	200

Severe shortages of material for Product B will limit its production to a maximum of 90 per day.

REQUIRED: How many units of each product should be produced to obtain the maximum net income? Show the basic relationships as inequalities. Solve by using graphical analysis.

Additional Assignment Material

16–5. "The management accountant must be technically competent in computer technology and modern mathematics." Do you agree? Explain.

16–6. What is a decision table?

16–7. "I'm not certain what uncertainty is." Explain *uncertainty* briefly.

16–8. Consider the following probability distribution:

DAILY SALES EVENT IN UNITS	PROBABILITY
1,000	0.1
1,500	0.5
2,000	0.2
2,500	0.1
3,000	0.1
	1.0

A student commented: "If a manager has perfect information, he will always sell 3,000 units." Do you agree? Explain.

16–9. Which of the following are linear equations?

$$x + y + 4z + 6a = 8c + 4m$$
$$x^2 = y$$
$$x^2 - y = 4$$
$$4c = 27$$

16–10. What is the minimum competence in linear programming that managers should have?

16–11. "Lead time is the interval between placing an order and using the inventory." Do you agree? Explain.

16–12. "The major objective of inventory management is to minimize cash outlays for inventories." Do you agree? Explain.

16–13. What are the principal costs of having too much inventory? Too little inventory?

16–14. "The safety stock is the average amount of inventory used during lead time." Do you agree? Explain.

16–15. "If demand and lead time were known with certainty, no safety stock would be needed." Do you agree? Explain.

16–16. **Money on the table.** The search for oil is a chancy and costly undertaking. For example, in December 1972 the United States government sold a parcel of Louisiana offshore oil leases covering 536,000 acres for $1.6 billion. The previous record was $900 million in the Alaska North Slope in 1969.

Influences of
Quantitative
Techniques on
Management
Accounting

501

The leases are sold on blocks of acreage. Sealed bids are received on various blocks from joint ventures of several oil companies or from a single company. A news item concerning the bidding stated:

☐ The left-on-the-table aggregate this time came to a stunning $660 million or 40% of the winning total. By far, the most open-handed bidder was the group headed by Shell which grabbed fourteen tracts with bids totaling $230 million or more than twice the $93 million sum of the runner-up bids.

REQUIRED: Describe what you think is meant by *money-on-the-table*. Why does it occur? Who collects it?

16–17. Long-distance phone calls. A memorandum from the president of Stanford University contained the following:

☐ As of October 20, 1980, the placement of person-to-person telephone calls from the University extensions will cease; rather, you are asked to place station-to-station calls instead. . . . We anticipate that this change in policy will save over $30,000 per year in toll charges.
☐ You will be interested to know that for the same cost approximately two station-to-station calls can be made for each person-to-person call. Further, a sampling of Stanford users indicates that there is the probability of 66⅔% that a station-to-station call will be successfully completed the first time.

REQUIRED: Using the data given, compute the annual Stanford long-distance phone bill for person-to-person calls before the new policy took effect. In all cases, assume that two station-to-station calls will obtain the desired person.

16–18. Probabilities: automatic or semiautomatic equipment. The Clarion Company is going to produce a new product. Two types of production equipment are being considered. The more costly equipment will result in lower labor and related variable costs:

EQUIPMENT	TOTAL ORIGINAL COST	SALVAGE VALUE	VARIABLE COSTS, PER UNIT OF PRODUCT
Semiautomatic	$40,000	—	$4
Automatic	95,000	—	3

Marketing executives believe that this unique product will be salable only over the next year. The unit selling price is $5. Their best estimate of potential sales follows:

TOTAL UNITS	PROBABILITY
30,000	0.2
50,000	0.4
60,000	0.2
70,000	0.2

Prepare an analysis to indicate the best course of action.

16–19. Probabilities and multiple choice. (CMA.) Select the best answer for each of the accompanying items. Show computations where applicable.

The ARC Radio Company is trying to decide whether or not to introduce as a new product a wrist "radiowatch" designed for shortwave reception of exact time as broadcast by the National Bureau of Standards. The "radiowatch" would be priced at $60, which is exactly twice the variable cost per unit to manufacture and sell it. The incremental fixed costs necessitated by introducing this new product would amount to $240,000 per year. Subjective estimates of the probable demand for the product are shown in the following probability distribution:

ANNUAL DEMAND	PROBABILITY
6,000 units	0.2
8,000 units	0.2
10,000 units	0.2
12,000 units	0.2
14,000 units	0.1
16,000 units	0.1

1. The above probability distribution is a
   a. Normal distribution
   b. Symmetric distribution
   c. Continuous distribution
   d. Binomial distribution
   e. Discrete distribution
2. The expected value of demand for the new product is
   a. 11,000 units
   b. 10,200 units
   c. 9,000 units
   d. 10,600 units
   e. 9,800 units
3. The probability that the introduction of this new product will not increase company's profit is
   a. 0.00
   b. 0.04
   c. 0.40
   d. 0.50
   e. 0.60

16–20. Probability assessment and new product. A new manager, David Fong, has just been hired by the Batten Company. He is considering the market potential for a new toy, Thrillo, which, like many toys, may have great fad appeal.

Fong is experienced in the fad market and is well qualified to assess Thrillo's chances for success. He is certain that sales will not be less than 25,000 units. Plant capacity limits total sales to a maximum of 80,000 units during Thrillo's brief life. Fong thinks that there are two chances in five for a sales volume of 50,000 units. The probability that sales will exceed 50,000 units is four times the probability that they will be less than 50,000.

If sales are less than 50,000, he feels quite certain that they will be 25,000 units. If sales exceed 50,000, unit volumes of 60,000 and 80,000 are equally likely. A 70,000-unit volume is four times as likely as either.

Variable production costs are $3 per unit, selling price is $5, and the special manufacturing equipment (which has no salvage value or alternative use) costs $125,000. Assume, for simplicity, that the above-mentioned are the only possible sales volumes.

REQUIRED:

Should Thrillo be produced? Show detailed computations to support your answer.

16–21. Computation of expected value. (CMA.) The Unimat Company manufactures a unique thermostat which yields dramatic cost savings from effective climatic control of large buildings. The efficiency of the thermostat is dependent upon the quality of a specialized thermocoupler. These thermocouplers are purchased from Cosmic Company for $15 each.

Since early 19X6, an average of 10% of the thermocouplers purchased from Cosmic have not met Unimat's quality requirements. The number of unusable ther-

Influences of
Quantitative
Techniques on
Management
Accounting

503

mocouplers has ranged from 5% to 25% of the total number purchased and has resulted in failures to meet production schedules. In addition, Unimat has incurred additional costs to replace the defective units because the rejection rate of the units is within the range agreed upon in the contract.

Unimat is considering a proposal to manufacture the thermocouplers. The company has the facilities and equipment to produce the components. The engineering department has designed a manufacturing system which will produce the thermocouplers with a defective rate of 4% of the number of units produced. The schedule presents the engineers' estimates of the probabilities that different levels of variable manufacturing cost per thermocoupler will be incurred under this system. The variable manufacturing cost per unit includes a cost adjustment for the defective units at the 4% rate. Additional annual fixed costs incurred by Unimat if it manufactures the thermocoupler will amount to $32,500.

ESTIMATED VARIABLE MANUFACTURING COST PER GOOD THERMOCOUPLER UNIT	PROBABILITY OF OCCURRENCE
$10	10%
12	30
14	40
16	20
	100%

Unimat Company will need 18,000 thermocouplers to meet its annual demand requirements.

REQUIRED:

Prepare an expected value analysis to determine whether Unimat Company should manufacture the thermocouplers.

16–22. Net present values, probabilities, and capital budgeting. At the recent stockholders' meeting of a large utility company, a stockholder raised the question of the profitability of the satellite communications project undertaken by the company. The project was undertaken two years ago. The president stated that $10 million had been invested in the project in each of the previous years and that an equal amount must be invested in each of the next three years. There would be no income from the project until the total investment was completed. At that time the probability of receiving $4 million cash inflow from operations would be 0.8; the probability of receiving $8 million in the second year after completion would be 0.7; the probability of receiving $15 million in the third year after completion would be 0.6; the probability of receiving $30 million for the following seven years would be 0.5.

This company expects a minimum rate of return of 10% on investments.

REQUIRED:

As a stockholder, would you have approved of this project when it was first undertaken? Support your answer with figures, using the net-present-value approach.

16–23. Evaluation of degree of risk: standard deviation and coefficient of variation. Suppose you are the manager of a bottling company. You are trying to choose between two types of equipment, F and G. The following proposals have discrete probability distributions of cash flows in each of the next four years:

PROPOSAL F		PROPOSAL G	
Probability	Net Cash Inflow	Probability	Net Cash Inflow
0.10	$3,000	0.10	$1,000
0.25	4,000	0.25	2,000
0.30	5,000	0.30	3,000
0.25	6,000	0.25	4,000
0.10	7,000	0.10	5,000

REQUIRED:

1. For each proposal, compute (a) the expected value of the cash inflows in each of the next three years, (b) the standard deviation, and (c) the coefficient of variation.
2. Which proposal has the greater degree of risk? Why?

16–24. **Expected value, standard deviation, and risk.** Suppose the Van Horne Company is planning to invest in a common stock for one year. An investigation of the expected dividends and expected market price has been conducted. The probability distribution of expected returns for the year, as a percentage, is:

PROBABILITY OF OCCURRENCE	POSSIBLE RETURN
0.05	.284
0.10	.224
0.20	.160
0.30	.100
0.20	.040
0.10	−.024
0.05	−.084

REQUIRED:

1. Compute the expected value of possible returns, the standard deviation of the probability distribution, and the coefficient of variation.
2. Van Horne could also earn 6% for certain on federal bonds. What are the standard deviation and the coefficient of variation of such an investment?
3. Relate the computations in Requirement 1 with those in Requirement 2. That is, what role does the coefficient of variation play in determining the relative attractiveness of various investments?

16–25. **Probabilities and costs of rework versus costs of setup.** The Schlaifer Company has an automatic machine ready and set to make a production run of 2,000 parts. For simplicity, only four events are assumed possible:

FAULTY PARTS	PROBABILITY
30	0.6
200	0.2
600	0.1
900	0.1

Influences of Quantitative Techniques on Management Accounting

The incremental cost of reworking a faulty part is 20¢. An expert mechanic can check the setting. He can, without fail, bring the faulty parts down to thirty, but this is time-consuming and costs $25 per setting.

Should the setting be checked?

16-26. Cost and value of information. An oil-well driller, Mr. George, is thinking of investing $50,000 in an oil-well lease. He estimates the probability of finding a producing well as 0.4. Such a discovery would result in a net gain of $100,000 ($150,000 revenue − $50,000 cost). There is a 0.6 probability of not getting any oil, resulting in the complete loss of the $50,000.

REQUIRED:

1. What is the net expected value of investing?
2. Mr. George desires more information because of the vast uncertainty and the large costs of making a wrong decision. There will be an unrecoverable $50,000 outlay if no oil is found; there will be a $100,000 opportunity cost if he does not invest and the oil is really there. What is the most he should be willing to pay for perfect information regarding the presence or absence of oil? Explain.

16-27. Decision tables and perfect information. (CMA, adapted.) Vendo, Inc., has been operating the concession stands at a university's football stadium. The university has had successful football teams for many years; as a result the stadium is always full. The university is located in an area that suffers no rain during the football season. From time to time, Vendo has found itself very short of popcorn and at other times it has had many units left. A review of the records of sales of the past nine seasons revealed the following frequency of popcorn sold:

	GAMES
10,000 units	5
20,000 units	10
30,000 units	20
40,000 units	15
	50

Popcorn sells for 50¢ each and costs Vendo 30¢ each. Unsold popcorn is given to a local orphanage without charge.

REQUIRED:

1. Assuming that only the four quantities listed were ever sold and that the occurrences were random events, prepare a decision table (ignore income taxes) to represent the four possible strategies of ordering 10,000, 20,000, 30,000, or 40,000 units.
2. Using the expected value decision rule, determine the best strategy.
3. What is the dollar value of perfect information?

16-28. Production scheduling and linear programming. A factory can produce either Product A or Product B. Machine 1 can produce 15 units of B or 20 units of A per hour. Machine 2 can produce 20 units of B or 12 units of A per hour. Machine 1 has a maximum capacity of 10,000 hours, and Machine 2 a maximum capacity of 8,000 hours.

Product A has a unit contribution margin of 20¢; B, 16¢. There is an unlimited demand for either product; however, both products must be produced together through each machine in a combination such that the quantity of B is at least 20% of the quantity of A.

REQUIRED:

Which combination of products should be produced? Solve by graphic analysis. Express all relationships as inequalities.

16-29. Linear programming and minimum cost. The local agricultural center has advised George Junker to spread at least 4,800 pounds of a special nitrogen fertilizer ingredient and at least 5,000 pounds of a special phosphate fertilizer ingredient in order to increase his crops. Neither ingredient is available in pure form.

A dealer has offered 100-pound bags of VIM @ $1 each. VIM contains the equivalent of 20 pounds of nitrogen and 80 pounds of phosphate. VOOM is available in 100-pound bags @ $3 each; it contains the equivalent of 75 pounds of nitrogen and 25 pounds of phosphate.

REQUIRED: Express the relationships as inequalities. How many bags of VIM and VOOM should Junker buy in order to obtain the required fertilizer at minimum cost? Solve graphically.

16–30. **Change in LP constraints.** (CMA, adapted.) Girth, Inc., makes two kinds of men's suede leather belts. Belt A is a high-quality belt, while Belt B is of somewhat lower quality. The company earns $7 for each unit of Belt A that is sold, and $2 for each unit sold of Belt B. Each unit (belt) of type A requires twice as much manufacturing time as a unit of type B. Further, if only Belt B is made, Girth has the capacity to manufacture 1,000 units per day. A long-term contract makes available to Girth enough suede leather to make 800 belts per day (A and B combined). Belt A requires a fancy buckle, of which only 400 per day are available. Belt B requires a plain buckle, of which 700 per day are available. The demand for the suede leather belts (A or B) is such that Girth can sell all that it produces.

REQUIRED:
1. Prepare a graph of the constraint functions, placing Belt B on the vertical axis.
2. Using the graph, determine how many units of Belt A and Belt B should be produced to maximize daily profits.
3. Assume the same facts as above except that the sole supplier of buckles for Belt A informs Girth, Inc., that it will be unable to supply more than 100 fancy buckles per day. How many units of each of the two belts should be produced each day to maximize profits?
4. Assume the same facts as in Requirement 2 except that Texas Buckles, Inc., could supply Girth Inc., with the additional fancy buckles it needs. The price would be $3.50 more than Girth is paying for such buckles. How many, if any, fancy buckles should Girth buy from Texas Buckles? Explain how you determined your answer.

16–31. **Economic order quantity.** (CMA.) Hermit Company manufactures a line of walnut office products. Hermit executives estimate the demand for the double walnut letter tray, one of the company's products, at 6,000 units. The letter tray sells for $80 per unit. The costs relating to the letter tray are estimated to be as follows for 19X7:

1. Standard manufacturing cost per letter tray unit—$50
2. Costs to initiate a production run—$300
3. Annual cost of carrying the letter tray in inventory—20% of standard manufacturing cost

In prior years, Hermit Company has scheduled the production for the letter tray in two equal production runs. The company is aware that the economic order quantity (EOQ) model can be employed to determine optimum size for production runs. The EOQ formula as it applies to inventories for determining the optimum order quantity is as follows:

Influences of
Quantitative
Techniques on
Management
Accounting

507

$$EOQ = \sqrt{\frac{2(\text{Annual demand})(\text{Cost per order})}{(\text{Cost per unit})(\text{Carrying cost})}}$$

Calculate the expected annual cost savings Hermit Company could experience if it employed the economic order quantity model to determine the number of production runs that should be initiated during the year for the manufacture of the double walnut letter trays.

16–32. Inventory control and television tubes. The Nemmers Company assembles private-brand television sets for a retail chain, under a contract requiring delivery of 100 sets per day for each of 250 business days per year. Each set requires a picture tube, which Nemmers buys outside for $20 each. The tubes are loaded on trucks at the supplier's factory door and are then delivered by a trucking service at a charge of $100 per trip, regardless of the size of the shipment. The cost of storing the tubes (including the desired rate of return on investment) is $2 per tube per year. Because production is stable throughout the year, the average inventory is one-half the size of the truck lot. Tabulate the relevant annual cost of various truck-lot sizes at 5, 10, 15, 25, 50, and 250 trips per year. Show your results graphically. (Note that the $20 unit cost of tubes is common to all alternatives and hence may be ignored.)

16–33. Reorder point. A utility company uses 5,000 tons of coal per year to generate power at one of its plants. The company orders 500 tons at a time. Lead time for the orders is five days, and the safety stock is a three-day supply. Usage is assumed to be constant over a 360-day year. Calculate the reorder point.

16–34. Inventory policy. (CMA.) Breakon, Inc., manufactures and distributes machine tools. The tools are assembled from approximately 2,000 components manufactured by the company. For several years the production schedule called for one production run of each component each month. This schedule has resulted in a high inventory turnover rate of 4.0 times but requires 12 setups for each component every year. (Inventory turnover is cost of goods sold divided by average inventory.) In a normal year $3,500 of cost is incurred for each component to produce the number of units sold. The company has been successful in not letting the year-end inventory drop below $100 for each component.

The production manager recommends that the company gradually switch to a schedule of producing the annual needs of each component in one yearly production run. He believes this would reduce costs because only one setup cost would be incurred each year for every component rather than 12. At the present time the costs for each setup are $36. Estimated annual costs associated with carrying inventory, per $1 of inventory value, are: property tax, 4%; insurance, 2%; and storage cost, 20%. The firm estimates its cost of capital to be 10% after taxes and pays income taxes at 40% of taxable income.

1. If Breakon converts to the "once-a-year" production schedule for its components, calculate the total investment released or additional investment required once the changeover is completed.
2. If Breakon converts to the "once-a-year" production schedule, calculate the after-tax savings or added expenses once the changeover is completed.
3. What factors other than those referred to in Requirements 1 and 2 should be considered in reaching a decision to change the production policy?
4. Do your calculations support a change to the proposed policy? Explain your answer.

Suggested Readings

BIERMAN, HAROLD, and THOMAS R. DYCKMAN, *Managerial Cost Accounting*, 2nd ed. New York: Macmillan, 1976.

DEMSKI, JOEL S., *Information Analysis*, 2nd ed. Reading, Mass.: Addison-Wesley, 1980.

FELTHAM, GERALD A., *Information Evaluation*. Sarasota, Fla.: American Accounting Association, 1972.

HOLLOWAY, CHARLES A., *Decision Making under Uncertainty*. Englewood Cliffs, N.J.: Prentice-Hall, 1979.

HORNGREN, C., *Cost Accounting: A Managerial Emphasis*, 5th ed., Chaps. 14, 24–27. Englewood Cliffs, N.J.: Prentice-Hall, 1982.

Influences of
Quantitative
Techniques on
Management
Accounting

509

17

BASIC ACCOUNTING: CONCEPTS, TECHNIQUES, AND CONVENTIONS

Learning Objectives

When you have finished studying this chapter, you should be able to

1. Identify the meanings and interrelationships of the principal elements of financial statements: assets, liabilities, owners' equity, revenues, expenses, dividends, and others

2. Analyze typical business transactions to determine their effects on the principal elements of financial statements

3. Distinguish between the accrual basis of accounting and the cash basis of accounting

4. Select relevant items from a list of data and assemble them into a balance sheet, an income statement, and a statement of retained income

5. Distinguish between the reporting of corporate owners' equity and the reporting of owners' equity for partnerships and sole proprietorships

6. Identify the generally accepted accounting principles and the main conventions that underlie financial reporting for external purposes

This chapter provides an introduction to the accounting process for individuals with little or no background in accounting and for those who want to review some fundamental ideas.[1] We shall become acquainted with some terminology and with what financial statements say and do not say. Knowing what financial statements do *not* communicate is just as important as knowing what they do communicate. We shall mainly be concerned with how to measure the managers' custodial or stewardship responsibilities for the assets entrusted to them. This is basically a scorekeeping task.

This chapter covers the fundamentals without employing some of the bookkeeping techniques (for example, ledger accounts) and language (for example, debit and credit) that are commonplace in accounting. However, the chapter appendixes probe the ideas of the chapter in greater depth, using a more technical approach.

We consider the essence of profit-making activities and how the accountant portrays them. As we examine what the accountant does, we shall introduce the relevant concepts and conventions. Although the major focus will be on profit-seeking organizations, the main ideas also apply to not-for-profit organizations. Moreover, managers of the latter usually have personal investments in profit-seeking organizations or must interact with businesses in some way.

ENTITIES AND ACCOUNTING TRANSACTIONS

Managers, investors, and other interested groups usually want the answers to two important questions about an organization: How well did the organization perform for a given period of time? and Where does the organization stand at a given point in time? The accountant answers these questions with two major financial statements—an **income statement** and a **balance sheet.** To obtain these statements, accountants continually record the history of an organization. Through the **financial accounting** process, the accountant accumulates, analyzes, quantifies, classifies, summarizes, and reports the seemingly countless events and their effects on the **entity.** An *entity* is a specific area of accountability, a clear-cut boundary for reporting. The entity concept is important because accounting usually focuses on the financial impact of events as they affect a particular entity. An example of an entity is a university, which also encompasses many smaller entities such as the School of Law and the School of Engineering.

In terms of their financial impact on economies throughout the world, **corporations** are the principal form of entity. *Corporations* are organizations created by individual state laws. The owners are identified as stockholders (also called shareholders). When approved by the state, the corporation becomes a separate entity, an "artificial person" that conducts its business completely apart from its owners.

Basic
Accounting:
Concepts,
Techniques,
and
Conventions

511

[1] The aim of this section of the book (Chapters 17–20) is to provide an introduction and overview of an area that has come to be known as financial accounting. Thus, readers of the author's companion volume, *Introduction to Financial Accounting*, will find that these chapters provide a review rather than new material. For expanded coverage, see *Introduction to Financial Accounting*.

The accounting process focuses upon **transactions** as they affect an entity. A *transaction* is any event that affects the financial position of an entity and requires recording. Through the years, many concepts, conventions, and rules have been developed regarding what events are to be recorded as *accounting transactions* and how their financial impact is measured. These concepts will be introduced gradually over the remaining chapters.

FINANCIAL STATEMENTS

Financial statements are summarized reports of accounting transactions. They can apply to any point in time and to any span of time.

An efficient way to learn about accounting is to study a specific illustration. Suppose Retailer No. 1 began business as a corporation on March 1. An opening balance sheet (more accurately called **statement of financial position** or **statement of financial condition**) follows:

RETAILER NO. 1
Balance Sheet (Statement of Financial Position)
As of March 1, 19X1

ASSETS		EQUITIES	
Cash	$100,000	Paid-in capital	$100,000

The balance sheet is a photograph of financial status at an instant of time. It has two counterbalancing sections—assets and equities. **Assets** are economic resources that are expected to benefit future activities. **Equities** are the claims against, or interests in, the assets.

The accountant conceives of the balance sheet as an equation:

$$\text{assets} = \text{equities}$$

The equities side of this fundamental equation is often divided as follows:

$$\text{assets} = \text{liabilities} + \text{owners' equity}$$

The **liabilities** are the economic obligations of the entity. The **owners' equity** is the excess of the assets over the liabilities. For a corporation, the owners' equity is called **stockholders' equity.** In turn, the stockholders' equity is composed of the ownership claim against, or interest in, the total assets arising from any paid-in investment **(paid-in capital),** plus the ownership claim arising as a result of profitable operations (**retained income** or **retained earnings**).

The following is a summary of the *transactions* that occurred in March:

1. Initial investment by owners, $100,000 cash.
2. Acquisition of inventory for $75,000 cash.
3. Acquisition of inventory for $35,000 on open account. A purchase (or a sale) on open account is an agreement whereby the buyer pays cash some time

after the date of sale, often in thirty days. Amounts owed on open accounts are usually called **accounts payable.**

4. Merchandise carried in inventory at a cost of $100,000 was sold on open account for $120,000. These open customer accounts are called **accounts receivable.**

5. Collections of accounts receivable, $30,000.

6. Payments of accounts payable, $10,000.

7. On March 1, $3,000 cash was disbursed for store rent for March, April, and May. Rent is $1,000 per month, payable quarterly in advance, beginning March 1.

Note that these are indeed *summarized* transactions. For example, all the sales will not take place at once, nor will purchases of inventory, collections from customers, or disbursements to suppliers. A vast number of repetitive transactions occur in practice, and specialized data-collection techniques are used to measure their effects on the entity.

The above transactions can be analyzed using the balance sheet equation, as shown in Exhibit 17-1.

Transaction 1 has been explained previously. Note, in this illustration, that paid-in capital represents the claim arising from the owners' total initial investment in the corporation.[2]

Transactions 2 and 3, the purchases of inventory, are steps toward the ultimate goal—the earning of a profit. But stockholders' equity is not affected. That is, no profit is realized until a sale is made.

Transaction 4 is the sale of $100,000 of inventory for $120,000. Two things happen simultaneously: A new asset, Accounts Receivable, is acquired (4a) in exchange for the giving up of Inventory (4b).

Transaction 5, the collection, is an example of an event that has no impact on stockholders' equity. It is merely the transformation of one asset (Accounts Receivable) into another (Cash).

Transaction 6, the payment, also has no effect on stockholders' equity—it affects assets and liabilities only. In general, collections from customers and payments to suppliers of the *principal* amounts of debt have no direct impact on stockholders' equity. Of course, as will be seen in a subsequent section, *interest* on debt does affect stockholders' equity as an item of expense.

Transaction 7, the rent disbursement, is made to acquire the right to use store facilities for the next three months. At March 1, the $3,000 measures the future benefit from these services, so the asset *Prepaid Rent* is created (7a). *Assets* are defined as economic resources. They are not confined to items that you can see or touch, such as cash or inventory. Assets also include legal rights to future services such as the use of facilities.

Transaction 7b recognizes that one-third of the rental services have expired, so the asset is reduced and stockholders' equity is also reduced by $1,000 as rent expense for March. This recognition of rent *expense* means

Basic
Accounting:
Concepts,
Techniques,
and
Conventions

513

[2] Stock certificates usually bear some nominal "par or stated value" that is far below the actual cash invested. For example, the par or stated value of the certificates might be only $10,000; if so, the formal recording of an ownership claim arising from the investment might be split between two subparts, one for $10,000 "capital stock, at par" and another for $90,000 "paid-in capital in excess of par value of capital stock." See the next chapter for additional discussion, p. 566.

EXHIBIT 17-1   *(Put a clip on this page for easy reference.)*

RETAILER NO. 1
Analysis of Transactions (in dollars)
For March 19X1

Transactions	ASSETS				=	EQUITIES		
						Liabilities +	Stockholders' Equity	
	Cash	+ Accounts Receivable	+ Inventory	+ Prepaid Rent	=	Accounts Payable	+ Paid-in Capital	+ Retained Income
1. Initial investment	+100,000				=		+100,000	
2. Acquire inventory for cash	− 75,000		+ 75,000		=			
3. Acquire inventory on credit			+ 35,000		=	+35,000		
4a. Sales on credit		+120,000			=			+120,000 (revenue)
4b. Cost of inventory sold			−100,000		=			−100,000 (expense)
5. Collect from customers	+ 30,000	− 30,000			=			
6. Pay accounts of suppliers	− 10,000				=	−10,000		
7a. Pay rent in advance	− 3,000			+3,000	=			
7b. Recognize expiration of rental services				−1,000	=			− 1,000 (expense)
Balance, 3/31/X1	+ 42,000	+ 90,000	+ 10,000	+2,000	=	+25,000	+100,000	+ 19,000
	144,000						144,000	

that $1,000 of the asset Prepaid Rent has been "used up" (or has flowed out of the entity) in the conduct of operations during March.

For simplicity, we have assumed no expenses other than *cost of goods sold* and *rent*. The accountant would ordinarily prepare at least two financial statements: the balance sheet and the income statement.

RETAILER NO. 1
Income Statement
For the Month Ended March 31, 19X1

Sales (revenue)		$120,000
Expenses:		
Cost of goods sold	$100,000	
Rent	1,000	
Total expenses		101,000
Net income		$ 19,000

RETAILER NO. 1
Balance Sheet
March 31, 19X1

ASSETS		LIABILITIES AND STOCKHOLDERS' EQUITY		
Cash	$ 42,000	Liabilities: Accounts payable		$ 25,000
Accounts				
receivable	90,000	Stockholders' equity:		
Inventory	10,000	Paid-in capital	$100,000	
Prepaid rent	2,000	Retained income	19,000	119,000
Total assets	$144,000	Total equities		$144,000

RELATIONSHIP OF BALANCE SHEET AND INCOME STATEMENT

The income statement has measured the operating performance of the corporation by matching its accomplishments (revenue from customers, which usually is called *sales*) and its efforts (**cost of goods sold** and other expenses). The balance sheet shows the financial position at an instant of time, but the income statement measures performance for a span of time, whether it be a month, a quarter, or longer. The income statement is the major link between balance sheets:

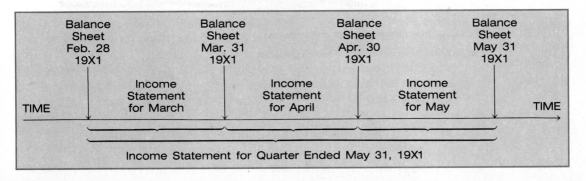

Income Statement for Quarter Ended May 31, 19X1

Examine the changes in stockholders' equity in Exhibit 17-1. The accountant records **revenue** and **expense** so that they represent increases (revenues) and decreases (expenses) in the owners' claims. At the end of a given period, these items are summarized in the form of an income statement.

Each item in a financial statement is frequently called an *account*, so that term will occasionally be used in the rest of this book. In the above example, the outflows of assets are represented by decreases in the Inventory and Prepaid Rent accounts and corresponding decreases in stockholders' equity in the form of Cost of Goods Sold and Rent Expense. Expense accounts are basically negative elements of stockholders' equity. Similarly, the Sales (revenue) account is a positive element of stockholders' equity.

REVENUES AND EXPENSES

Reflect further on transaction 4. As Exhibit 17-1 shows, this transaction has two phases, a revenue phase (4a) and an expense phase (4b) (dollar signs omitted):

DESCRIPTION OF TRANSACTIONS	ASSETS	=	EQUITIES
Balances after Transaction 3 in Exhibit 17-1	135,000 =		135,000
4a. Sales on account (inflow)	Accounts receivable +120,000 =	Stockholders' equity,	+120,000
4b. Cost of inventory sold (outflow)	Inventory −100,000 =	Stockholders' equity,	−100,000
Balances, after Transaction 4	155,000 =		155,000

Transaction 4a illustrates the realization of *revenue*. *Revenues* are generally gross increases in assets from delivering goods or services. To be **realized** (that is, formally recognized in the accounting records as revenue earned during the current period), revenue must ordinarily meet three tests. First, the goods or services must be fully rendered (for example, delivery to customers). Second, an exchange of resources evidenced by a market transaction must occur (for example, the buyer pays or promises to pay cash and the seller delivers merchandise). Third, the collectibility of the asset (for example, an account receivable) must be reasonably assured.

Transaction 4b illustrates the incurrence of an expense. *Expenses* are generally gross decreases in assets from delivering goods or services.

Transactions 4a and 4b also illustrate the fundamental meaning of **profits** or **earnings** or **income,** which can simply be defined as the excess of revenues over expenses.

As the Retained Income column in Exhibit 17-1 shows, increases in revenues increase stockholders' equity. In contrast, increases in expenses decrease stockholders' equity. So expenses are negative stockholders' equity accounts.

Transactions 3 and 4 were purchases of merchandise inventory. They were steps toward the ultimate goal—the earning of a profit. But by themselves purchases earn no profit; remember that stockholders' equity was unaffected by the inventory acquisitions in transactions 2 and 3. That is, no profit is realized until a sale is actually made to customers.

Transaction 4 is the $120,000 sale on open account of inventory that had cost $100,000. Two things happen simultaneously: a $120,000 inflow of assets in the form of accounts receivable (4a) in exchange for a $100,000 outflow of assets in the form of inventory (4b). Liabilities are completely unaffected, so owners' equity rises by $120,000 − $100,000, or $20,000.

Users of financial statements desire an answer to the question, How well did the organization perform for a given period of time? The income statement helps answer this question. For Retailer No. 1, there has been a change in stockholders' equity attributable solely to operations. This change is measured by the revenue and expenses for the specific period.

THE ANALYTICAL POWER OF THE BALANCE SHEET EQUATION

As you study Exhibit 17-1, the following points should become clearer about how accountants use the fundamental balance sheet equation as their framework for analyzing and reporting the effects of transactions:

$$\text{assets (A)} = \text{liabilities (L)} + \text{stockholders' equity (SE)} \qquad (1)$$

SE equals original ownership claim plus the increase in ownership claim due to profitable operations. That is, SE equals the claim arising from paid-in capital plus the claim arising from retained income. Therefore,

$$A = L + \text{paid-in capital} + \text{retained income} \qquad (2)$$

But, in our illustration, Retained Income equals Revenue minus Expenses. Therefore,

$$A = L + \text{paid-in capital} + \text{revenue} - \text{expenses} \qquad (3)$$

Revenue and expense accounts are nothing more than subdivisions of stockholders' equity—temporary stockholders' equity accounts, as it were. Their purpose is to summarize the volume of sales and the various expenses, so that management is kept informed of the reasons for the continual increases and decreases in stockholders' equity in the course of ordinary operations. In this way comparisons can be made, standards or goals can be set, and control can be better exercised.

The entire accounting system is based on the simple balance sheet equation. As you know, equations in general possess enormous analytical potential because of the dual algebraic manipulations that they permit. The equation is always kept in balance because of the duality feature.

Exhibit 17-1 illustrates the dual nature of the accountant's analysis. For each transaction, the equation is *always* kept in balance. If the items affected are confined to one side of the equation, you will find the total amount added equal to the total amount subtracted on that side. If the items affected are on both sides, then equal amounts are simultaneously added or subtracted on each side.

The striking feature of the balance sheet equation is its universal applicability. No transaction has ever been conceived, no matter how simple

Basic
Accounting:
Concepts,
Techniques,
and
Conventions

517

or complex, that cannot be analyzed via the equation. The top technical partners in the world's largest professional accounting firms, when confronted with the most intricate transactions of multinational companies, will inevitably discuss and think about their analyses in terms of the balance sheet equation and its major components: assets, liabilities, and owners' equity (including the explanations of changes in owners' equity that most often take the form of revenues and expenses).

ACCRUAL BASIS AND CASH BASIS

The process of determining income and financial position is anchored to the **accrual basis** of accounting, as distinguished from the **cash basis.** In accrual accounting, the impact of events on assets and equities is recognized in the time periods when services are rendered or utilized instead of when cash is paid or received. That is, revenue is recognized as it is *earned*, and expenses are recognized as they are *incurred*—not when cash changes hands. For example, Transaction 4*a* in Exhibit 17-1, page 514, recognizes revenue when sales are made on credit. Similarly, Transactions 4*b* and 7*b* show that expenses are recognized as efforts are expended or services utilized to obtain the revenue (regardless of when cash is disbursed). Therefore income is affected by measurements of noncash resources and obligations. The accrual basis is the principal conceptual framework for matching accomplishments (revenue) with efforts (expenses).

If the **cash basis** of accounting were used instead of the accrual basis, revenue and expense would depend on the timing of various cash receipts and disbursements. In our Retailer No. 1 example, the March income statement would contain the following:

Revenue (cash collected from customers)		$ 30,000
Expenses:		
Cash disbursed for merchandise ($75,000 in Transaction 2 plus $10,000 in Transaction 6)	$85,000	
Cash disbursement for rent	3,000	
Total expenses		88,000
Net loss		−$58,000

The March 31 balance sheet would have:

Cash	$42,000	Paid-in capital	$100,000
		Retained income	−58,000
		Stockholders' equity	$ 42,000

The major deficiencies of the cash basis of accounting are apparent from this example: It ignores the impact on net income and financial position of the liability for accounts payable and the impact of such very real assets as accounts receivable, inventory, and prepaid rent.

Despite the incompleteness of the cash basis of accounting, it is used widely by individuals when they measure their income for personal income tax purposes. For this limited purpose, the cash basis often gives a good approximation of what might also be reported on the accrual basis. Long ago, however, accountants and managers found cash-basis financial statements, such as those above, to be unsatisfactory as a measure of both performance and position. Now more than 95% of all business is conducted on a credit basis; cash receipts and disbursements are not the critical transactions as far as the recognition of revenue and expense is concerned. Thus the accrual basis evolved in response to a desire for a more complete, and therefore more accurate, report of the financial impact of various events.

ADJUSTMENTS TO THE ACCOUNTS

To measure income under the accrual basis, the accountant uses **adjustments** at the end of each reporting period. *Adjustments* (also called *adjusting the books, adjusting entries, adjusting the accounts*) may be defined as the key final process that ensures the assignment of financial effects of transactions to the appropriate time periods. Thus adjustments are made at periodic intervals, that is, just before the computation of ending balances when the financial statements are about to be prepared.

Earlier a *transaction* was defined as any economic event that should be recorded by the accountant. Note that this definition is *not* confined to market transactions, which are actual exchanges of goods and services between the entity and another party. For instance, the losses of assets from fire or theft are also transactions even though no market exchange occurs.

Adjustments are a special category of transactions. The principal adjustments may be classified into four types:

I. Expiration of Unexpired Costs
II. Realization (Earning) of Previously Deferred Revenues
III. Accrual of Previously Unrecorded Expenses
IV. Accrual of Previously Unrecorded Revenues

As we shall see, all of these adjustments have an important common characteristic. They reflect **implicit transactions,** in contrast to the **explicit transactions** that trigger nearly all day-to-day routine entries.

To illustrate, entries for credit sales, credit purchases, cash received on account, and cash disbursed on account are supported by explicit evidence. This evidence is usually in the form of **source documents** (for example, sales slips, purchase invoices, employee time records). On the other hand, adjustments for wages, prepaid rent, depreciation, and the like, are prepared from special schedules or memorandums that recognize events (like the passage of time) that are temporarily ignored in day-to-day recording procedures.

Adjustments refine the accountant's accuracy and provide a more complete and significant measure of efforts, accomplishments, and financial position. They are an essential part of accrual accounting.

Assets frequently expire because of the passage of time. This first type of adjustment was illustrated in Exhibit 17-1 by the recognition of rent expense in transaction 7b.

Basic
Accounting:
Concepts,
Techniques,
and
Conventions

519

Other examples of adjusting for asset expirations include the write-offs to expense of such assets as Office Supplies Inventory, Advertising Supplies Inventory, and Prepaid Fire Insurance. The other three types of adjustments are discussed later in this chapter.

❑ The Measurement of Expenses: Assets Expire

Transactions 4b and 7b demonstrate how assets may be viewed as bundles of economic services awaiting future use or expiration. It is helpful to think of assets, other than cash and receivables, as prepaid or stored costs (for example, inventories or plant assets) that are carried forward to future periods rather than immediately charged against revenue:

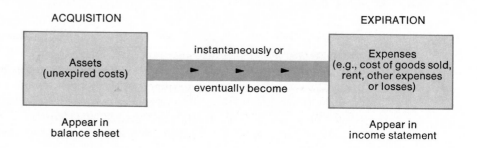

Expenses are used-up assets. Thus assets are **unexpired costs** held back from the expense stream and carried in the balance sheet to await expiration in future periods.

The analysis of the inventory and rent transactions in Exhibit 17-1 maintains this distinction of acquisition and expiration. The unexpired costs of inventory and prepaid rent are assets until they are used up and become expenses.

Sometimes services are acquired and utilized almost instantaneously. Examples are advertising services, interest services (the cost of money, which is a service), miscellaneous supplies, and sales salaries and commissions. Conceptually, these costs should, at least momentarily, be viewed as assets upon acquisition before being written off as expenses. For example, suppose there was an eighth transaction in Exhibit 17-1, whereby newspaper advertising was acquired for $1,000 cash. To abide by the acquisition-expiration sequence, the transaction might be analyzed in two phases:

Trans-action	ASSETS			= LIABILITIES +	STOCKHOLDERS' EQUITY	
	Cash +	Other Assets +	Unexpired Advertising =		Paid-in Capital +	Retained Income
8a.	−1,000		+1,000 =			
8b.			−1,000 =			−1,000 (expense)

Frequently, services are acquired and used up so quickly that accountants do not bother recording an asset such as Unexpired Advertising or Prepaid Rent for them. Instead, a shortcut is taken:

Trans-action	Cash	+ Other Assets	= Liabilities	+ Paid-in Capital	+ Retained Income
8 (a) and (b) together	−1,000		=		−1,000 (expense)

Making the entry in two steps instead of one may seem cumbersome, and it is—from a practical bookkeeping viewpoint. But our purpose is not to learn how to be efficient bookkeepers. We want an orderly way of thinking about what the manager does. The manager acquires goods and services, not expenses *per se*. These goods and services become expenses as they are utilized in obtaining revenue.

Some of the most difficult issues in accounting center on when an unexpired cost expires to become an expense. For example, some accountants believe that research and development costs should be accounted for as unexpired costs (often found on balance sheets as "Deferred Research and Development Costs") and written off (amortized) in some systematic manner over a period of years. But the regulators of financial accounting in the United States have ruled that such costs have vague future benefits that are difficult to measure reliably. Thus, research costs must be written off as expenses immediately; hence, research costs should never be found on balance sheets.

❑ Pause for Reflection

This is an unusually long chapter, so pause. If you have never studied accounting before, or if you studied it long ago, you should not proceed further with your study of this chapter until you have solved the following problem. There are no shortcuts. Pushing a pencil is an absolute necessity for becoming comfortable with accounting concepts. The cost-benefit test will easily be met; your gain in knowledge will exceed your investment of time.

Another suggestion is to do the work on your own. In particular, do not ask for help from any professional accountants if they introduce any new terms beyond those already covered. For example, the technical terms of debits, credits, and ledger accounts will only confuse, not clarify, at this stage. Instead, scrutinize Exhibit 17-1, page 514. Note how the balance sheet equation is affected by each transaction. Then do the review problem that follows.

Summary Problem for Your Review

❑ Problem One

The Retailer No. 1 transactions for March were analyzed early in this chapter. The balance sheet showed the following balances as of March 31, 19X1:

	ASSETS	EQUITIES
Cash	$ 42,000	
Accounts receivable	90,000	
Inventory	10,000	
Prepaid rent	2,000	
Accounts payable		$ 25,000
Paid-in capital		100,000
Retained income		19,000
	$144,000	$144,000

The following is a summary of the transactions that occurred during the next month, April:

1. Collections of accounts receivable, $88,000.
2. Payments of accounts payable, $24,000.
3. Acquisitions of inventory on open account, $80,000.
4. Merchandise carried in inventory at a cost of $70,000 was sold on open account for $85,000.
5. Adjustment for recognition of rent expense for April.
6. Some customers paid $3,000 in advance for merchandise that they ordered but is not expected in inventory until mid-May. (What asset must rise? Does this transaction increase liabilities or stockholders' equity?)
7. Total wages of $6,000 (which were ignored for simplicity in March) were paid on four Fridays in April. These payments for employee services were recognized by increasing Wages Expense and decreasing Cash.
8. Wages of $2,000 were incurred near the end of April, but the employees had not been paid as of April 30. Accordingly, the accountant increased Wages Expense and increased a liability, Accrued Wages Payable.
9. Cash dividends declared by the board of directors and disbursed to stockholders on April 29 equaled $18,000. (What account besides Cash is affected?) As will be explained, Cash and Retained Income are each decreased by $18,000.

REQUIRED:

1. Using the *accrual basis* of accounting, prepare an analysis of transactions, employing the equation approach demonstrated in Exhibit 17-1. To have plenty of room for new accounts, put your analysis sideways.
2. Prepare a balance sheet as of April 30, 19X1, and an income statement for the month of April. Also prepare a new report, the Statement of Retained Income, which should show the beginning balance, followed by a description of any major changes, and end with the balance as of April 30, 19X1.
3. Using the *cash basis* of accounting, prepare an income statement for April. Compare the net income with that computed in Requirement 2. Which net income figure do you prefer as a measure of the economic performance for April? Why?

Entries 6 through 9 and the statement of retained income have not been explained. However, as a learning step, try to respond to the requirements here anyway. Explanations follow almost immediately.

❑ Solution to Problem One

Part 1. *Analysis of transactions.* The answer is in Exhibit 17-2. The first five transactions are straightforward extensions or repetitions of the March transactions. But the rest of the transactions are new. They are discussed in the sections that follow the solutions to the second and third parts of this problem.

EXHIBIT 17-2 *(Place a clip on this page for easy reference.)*

RETAILER NO. 1
Analysis of Transactions (in dollars)
For April 19X1

| | ASSETS | | | | = | EQUITIES | | | | |
| | | | | | | Liabilities | | | Stockholders' Equity | |
Transaction	Cash	+ Accounts Receivable	+ Inventory	+ Prepaid Rent	=	Accounts Payable	+ Accrued Wages Payable	+ Deferred Sales Revenue*	+ Paid-in Capital	+ Retained Income
Bal. 3/31/X1	+42,000	+90,000	+10,000	+2,000	=	+25,000			+100,000	+19,000
1.	+88,000	−88,000			=					
2.	−24,000				=	−24,000				
3.			+80,000		=	+80,000				
4a.		+85,000			=					+85,000 (revenue)
4b.			−70,000		=					−70,000 (expense)
5.				−1,000	=					− 1,000 (expense)
6.	+3,000				=			+ 3,000*		
7.	−6,000				=					− 6,000 (expense)
8.					=		+2,000			− 2,000 (expense)
9.	−18,000				=					−18,000 (dividend)
4/30/X1	+85,000	+87,000	+20,000	+1,000	=	+81,000	+2,000	+3,000	+100,000	+ 7,000
		193,000							193,000	

*Some managers and accountants would call this account "Customer Deposits" or "Advances from Customers."

Part 2. *Preparation of financial statements.* See Exhibits 17-3, 17-4, and 17-5. The first two of these exhibits show financial statements already described in this chapter: the balance sheet and the income statement. Exhibit 17-5 presents a new statement, the *Statement of Retained Income,* which is merely a formal reconciliation of the retained income. It consists of the beginning balance, adds net income for the period in question, and deducts cash dividends to arrive at the ending balance. Fre-

EXHIBIT 17-3

RETAILER NO. 1
Balance Sheet
As of April 30, 19X1

ASSETS		EQUITIES		
Cash	$ 85,000	Liabilities:		
Accounts receivable	87,000	Accounts payable	$ 81,000	
Inventory	20,000	Accrued wages		
Prepaid rent	1,000	payable	2,000	
		Deferred sales		
		revenue	3,000	$ 86,000
		Stockholders' equity:		
		Paid-in capital	$100,000	
		Retained income	7,000	107,000
Total assets	$193,000	Total equities		$193,000

EXHIBIT 17-4

RETAILER NO. 1
Income Statement (Multiple-Step)*
For the Month Ended April 30, 19X1

Sales		$85,000
Cost of goods sold		70,000
Gross profit		$15,000
Operating expenses:		
Rent	$1,000	
Wages	8,000	9,000
Net income		$ 6,000

*A **"single-step" statement** would not draw the gross profit figure but would merely list all the expenses—including cost of goods sold—and deduct the total from sales. **Gross profit** is defined as the excess of sales over the cost of the inventory that was sold. It is sometimes called **gross margin.**

EXHIBIT 17-5

RETAILER NO. 1
Statement of Retained Income
For the Month Ended April 30, 19X1

Retained income, March 31, 19X1	$19,000
Net income for April	6,000
Total	$25,000
Dividends	18,000
Retained income, April 30, 19X1	$ 7,000

quently, this statement is tacked on to the bottom of an income statement. If so, the result is a *combined* statement of income and statement of retained income.

Part 3. *Cash basis income statement.* See Exhibit 17-6. The net income is $61,000 on the cash basis, but only $6,000 on the accrual basis. Accountants prefer the accrual basis because it provides a more complete and precise measurement of economic performance, a better matching of accomplishments with efforts. For example, the timing of disbursements to reduce accounts payable obviously is not as closely related to sales in April as the cost of inventory that was sold.

RETAILER NO. 1 Income Statement (Cash Basis) For the Month Ended April 30, 19X1		
Sales (collections from customers, including advance payments)		$91,000
Expenses:		
Disbursements for merchandise	$24,000	
Wages	6,000	30,000
Net income		$61,000

ACCOUNTING FOR DEFERRED REVENUE

Entry 6 is an example of **deferred revenue,** sometimes called **unearned revenue** or **deferred credit,** which is a liability because the retailer is obligated to deliver the goods ordered or to refund the money if the goods are not delivered. Some managers might prefer to call this account *advances from customers,* or *customer deposits,* instead of *deferred sales revenue,* but it is a deferred revenue account no matter what its label. That is, it is revenue collected in advance that has not been earned as yet. Advance collections of rent and magazine subscriptions are other examples.

Sometimes it is easier to see how accountants analyze transactions by visualizing the financial positions of both parties to a contract. For instance, for the rent transaction of March 1 compare the financial impact on Retailer No. 1 with the impact on the landlord who received the rental payment:

	LANDLORD			RETAILER NO. 1		
	A =	L +	SE	A =	L +	SE
	Cash	Deferred Rent Revenue	Rent Revenue	Cash	Prepaid Rent	Rent Expense
1. Prepayment	+3,000 =	+3,000		−3,000	+3,000 =	
2. March expiration	=	−1,000	+1,000		−1,000 =	−1,000
3. April expiration	=	−1,000	+1,000		−1,000 =	−1,000

You are already familiar with the Retailer No. 1 analysis. The $1,000 monthly entries for Retailer No. 1 are examples of the first type of adjustments, the expiration of unexpired costs.

Study the transactions from the viewpoint of the owner of the rental property. The first transaction recognizes *deferred revenue*, sometimes called *unearned revenue*, which is a *liability* because the lessor is obligated to deliver the rental services (or to refund the money if the services are not delivered).

The first two types of adjustments are often really mirror images of each other. If one party to a contract has a prepaid expense, the other has a deferred revenue. A similar analysis could be conducted for, say, a three-year fire insurance policy or a three-year magazine subscription. The buyer recognizes a prepaid expense (asset) and uses adjustments to spread the initial cost to expense over the useful life of the services. In turn, the seller, such as a magazine publisher, must initially recognize its liability, Deferred Subscription Revenue. The *deferred* revenue is then systematically recognized as *earned* revenue as magazines are delivered throughout the life of the subscription. The diagrams below show that explicit cash transactions in such situations are initially recognized as balance sheet items and are later transformed into income statement items via periodic adjustments:

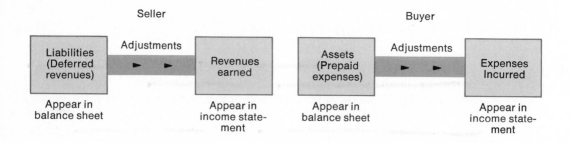

You have now seen how two types of adjustments might occur: (1) expiration of unexpired costs and (2) realization (earning) of previously deferred revenues. Next we consider the third type of adjustment: accrual of previously unrecorded expenses, as illustrated by wages.

ACCRUAL OF PREVIOUSLY UNRECORDED EXPENSES (WAGES)

An entity usually "incurs" an expense and "accrues" a debt or liability during a given period even though no explicit transaction occurs. Examples are wages of employees and interest on borrowed money. The liabilities grow as the clock ticks or as some services are continuously acquired and used, so they are said to **accrue** (accumulate).

It is awkward and unnecessary to make hourly, daily, or even weekly formal recordings in the accounts for many accruals. Consequently, a series of adjustments are made to bring each expense (and corresponding liability) account up to date just before the formal financial statements are prepared.

Accounting for Payment of Wages

Consider wages. Most companies pay their employees at predetermined times. Here is a sample calendar for April:

			APRIL			
S	M	T	W	T	F	S
	1	2	3	4	5	6
7	8	9	10	11	12	13
14	15	16	17	18	19	20
21	22	23	24	25	26	27
28	29	30				

Suppose Retailer No. 1 pays its employees each Friday for services rendered during that week. For example, wages paid on April 26 would be compensation for the week ended April 26. The cumulative total wages paid on the Fridays during April were $6,000. Although day-to-day and week-to-week procedures may differ from entity to entity, a popular way to account for wages expense is the shortcut procedure described earlier for goods and services that are routinely consumed in the period of their purchase:

	ASSETS (A) = LIABILITIES (L) + STOCKHOLDERS' EQUITY (SE)	
	Cash	Wages Expense
7. Routine entry for explicit transactions	−6,000 =	−6,000

Accounting for Accrual of Wages

The company expanded its work force on April 29. Moreover, in addition to the $6,000 already paid, Retailer No. 1 owes $2,000 for employee services rendered during the last two days of April. The employees will not be paid for these services until the next regular weekly payday, May 3. No matter how simple or complex a set of accounting procedures may be in a particular entity, periodic adjustments ensure that the financial statements adhere to accrual accounting. The tabulation that follows repeats entry 7 for convenience and then adds entry 8:

	A	=	L	+	SE
	Cash		Accrued Wages Payable		Wages Expense
7. Routine entry for explicit transactions	−6,000	=			−6,000
8. Adjustment for implicit transaction, the accrual of previously unrecorded wages		=	+2,000		−2,000
Total effects	−6,000	=	+2,000		−8,000

Basic
Accounting:
Concepts,
Techniques,
and
Conventions

527

Entry 8 is the first example in this book of the impact of the analytical shortcut that bypasses the asset account and produces an expense that is offset by an increase in a liability. Conceptually, entries 7 and 8 could each be subdivided into the asset acquisition–asset expiration sequence, but this two-step sequence is not generally used in practice for such expenses that represent the immediate consumption of services.

Other examples of accrued expenses include sales commissions, property taxes, income taxes, and interest on borrowed money. Interest is rent paid for the use of money, just as rent is paid for the use of buildings or automobiles. The interest accumulates (accrues) as time unfolds, regardless of when the actual cash for interest is paid.

ACCRUAL OF PREVIOUSLY UNRECORDED REVENUES

The final type of adjustment, which is not illustrated in the "Summary Problem for Your Review," is the realization of revenues that have been earned but not yet shown in the accounts. It is the mirror image of the accrual of previously unrecorded expenses. Consider a financial institution that lends cash to Retailer No. 1 on a three-month promissory note for $50,000 with interest at 1.5% per month payable at maturity. The following tabulation shows the mirror-image effect of the adjustment for interest at the end of the first month ($.015 \times \$50,000 = \$750$):

FINANCIAL INSTITUTION, AS A LENDER			RETAILER NO. 1 AS A BORROWER		
A	= L +	SE	A =	L +	SE
Accrued Interest Receivable		Interest Revenue		Accrued Interest Payable	Interest Expense
+750	=	+750	=	+750	−750

To recapitulate, you have now seen examples of the four major types of the adjustments needed to implement the accrual basis of accounting:

TYPE	DESCRIPTION	ILLUSTRATION
1	Expiration of unexpired costs	Rent expense (Exhibit 17-2, page 523, entry 5)
2	Realization (earning) of previously deferred revenues	The mirror image of type 1, whereby the landlord recognizes rent revenue and decreases deferred rent revenue (rent collected in advance)
3	Accrual of previously un-recorded expenses	Wage expense (Exhibit 17-2, entry 8)
4	Accrual of previously un-recorded revenues	Interest revenue earned but un-collected by a financial institution

DIVIDENDS AND RETAINED INCOME

☐ Dividends Are Not Expenses

As transaction 9 shows, cash dividends are not expenses like rent and wages. They should not be deducted from revenues because dividends are not directly related to the generation of sales or the conduct of operations. Cash dividends are distributions of assets to stockholders that reduce retained income. The ability to pay dividends is fundamentally caused by profitable operations. Retained income increases as profits accumulate and decreases as dividends occur.

The entire right-hand side of the balance sheet can be thought of as claims against the total assets. The liabilities are the claims of creditors. The stockholders' equity represents the claims of owners arising out of their initial investment (paid-in capital) and subsequent profitable operations (retained income). **Retained income** is also called **retained earnings, undistributed earnings,** or **reinvested earnings.** As a company grows, this account can soar enormously if dividends are not paid. Retained income can easily be the largest stockholders' equity account.

☐ Retained Income Is Not Cash

Retained income is *not* a pot of cash that is awaiting distribution to stockholders. Consider the following illustration:

Step 1. Assume an opening balance sheet of:

Cash	$100	Paid-in capital	$100

Step 2. Purchase inventory for $50 cash. The balance sheet now reads:

Cash	$50	Paid-in capital	$100
Inventory	50		
	$100		

Steps 1 and 2 demonstrate a fundamental point. Ownership equity is an undivided claim against the total assets (in the aggregate). For example, half the shareholders do not have a specific claim on cash, and the other half do not have a specific claim on inventory. Instead, all the shareholders have an undivided claim against (or, if you prefer, an undivided interest in) all the assets.

Step 3. Now sell the inventory for $80:

Cash	$130	Paid-in capital	$100
		Retained income	30
		Total equities	$130

Basic
Accounting:
Concepts,
Techniques,
and
Conventions

529

At this stage, the retained income might be reflected by a $30 increase in cash. But the $30 in retained income connotes only a *general* claim against *total* assets. This may be clarified by the transaction that follows.

Step 4. Purchase equipment and inventory, in the amounts of $40 and $50, respectively. Now:

Cash	$ 40	Paid-in capital	$100
Inventory	50	Retained income	30
Equipment	40		
Total assets	$130	Total equities	$130

Where is the $30 in retained income reflected? Is it reflected in Cash, in Inventory, or in Equipment? The answer is indeterminate. This example helps to explain the nature of the Retained Income account. It is a *claim*, not a pot of gold. Retained income is increased by profitable operations, but the cash inflow from sales is an increment in assets (see step 3). When the cash inflow takes place, management will use the cash, most often to buy more inventory or equipment (step 4). Retained income is a *general* claim against, or undivided interest in, *total* assets, *not* a specific claim against cash or against any other particular asset.

A term that is virtually archaic, **earned surplus,** is sometimes still found in stockholders' equity sections. Fortunately, its use is fading fast. Earned surplus is an interchangeable term for retained income. The trouble with the term is that *surplus* is misleading. It connotes something superfluous or unessential or leftover; therefore, consequent misunderstandings of the term might be expected. As the above example shows, earned surplus (retained income) is not an asset, nor does it represent an unnecessary ownership interest.

As stated above, **dividends** are distributions of assets that reduce ownership claims. The cash assets that are distributed typically arose from profitable operations. Thus dividends or withdrawals are often spoken of as "distributions of profits" or "distributions of retained income." Dividends are often erroneously described as being "paid *out of* retained income." In reality, cash dividends are distributions of assets and liquidate a portion of the ownership claim. The distribution is made possible by profitable operations.

The amount of cash dividends declared by the board of directors of a company depends on many factors, the least important of which is the balance in Retained Income. Although profitable operations are generally essential, dividend policy is also influenced by the company's cash position and future needs for cash to pay debts or to purchase additional assets. It is also influenced by whether the company is committed to a stable dividend policy or to a policy that normally ties dividends to fluctuations in net income. Under a stable policy, dividends may be paid consistently even if a company encounters a few years of little or no net income.

The owners' equity section of the balance sheet can be affected by four basic types of transactions, (1) investments, (2) withdrawals, (3) revenues, and (4) expenses:

ASSETS = LIABILITIES +	OWNERS' EQUITY	
	−Owners' withdrawals (e.g., corporate cash dividends)	+ Owners' investments
	−Expenses	+ Revenues

The basic accounting concepts that underlie the owners' equity are unchanged regardless of whether ownership takes the form of a corporation, sole proprietorship, or partnership. However, in **proprietorships** and **partnerships,** distinctions between contributed capital (that is, the investments by owners) and retained income are rarely made. Compare the possibilities for Retailer No. 1 as of April 30:

OWNERS' EQUITY FOR A CORPORATION

Stockholders' equity:		
Capital stock (paid-in capital)	$100,000	
Retained income	7,000	
Total stockholders' equity		$107,000

OWNERS' EQUITY FOR A SOLE PROPRIETORSHIP

Alice Walsh, capital	$107,000

OWNERS' EQUITY FOR A PARTNERSHIP

Susan Zingler, capital	$ 53,500
John Martin, capital	53,500
Total partners' equity	$107,000

In contrast to corporations, sole proprietorships and partnerships are not legally required to account separately for contributed capital (that is, proceeds from issuances of capital stock) and for retained income. Instead, they typically accumulate a single amount for each owner's original investments, subsequent investments, share of net income, and withdrawals. In the case of a sole proprietorship, then, the owner's equity will consist of a lone capital account.

Other terms for owners' equity are **equity capital** and **net worth.** The latter term is fading (the faster, the better). Net worth is a poor term because it implies that the owners' equity is a measure of the "current value" of the business. The total owners' equity is a measure of the owner-

Basic
Accounting:
Concepts,
Techniques,
and
Conventions

531

ship claim against the total assets, but it does not necessarily yield an accurate approximation of what some outsider is willing to pay for such an ownership interest. The selling price of a business is the subject of independent bargaining that seldom has a direct relationship to the accounting records of the assets or equities of the entity.

NONPROFIT ORGANIZATIONS

The examples in this chapter have focused on profit-seeking organizations, but balance sheets and income statements are also used by not-for-profit organizations. For example, hospitals and universities have income statements, although they are called *statements of revenue and expense*. The "bottom line" is frequently called "excess of revenue over expense" rather than "net income."

The basic concepts of assets, liabilities, revenue, and expense are applicable to all organizations, whether they be utilities, symphony orchestras, private, public, American, Asian, and so forth. However, some nonprofit organizations have been slow to adopt several ideas that are widespread in progressive companies. For example, in many governmental organizations the accrual basis of accounting has not supplanted the cash basis. This has hampered the evaluation of the performance of such organizations.

GENERALLY ACCEPTED ACCOUNTING PRINCIPLES

❏ "Principles" Is a Misnomer

The financial statements of publicly held corporations and many other corporations are subject to an independent **audit** that forms the basis for a professional accounting firm's opinion, typically including the following key phrasing:

> ☐ In our opinion, the accompanying financial statements present fairly the financial position of the ABC Company at December 31, 19X1, and the results of its operations for the year then ended, in conformity with generally accepted accounting principles applied on a basis consistent with that of the preceding year.

We will explore the meaning of such key phrases as "present fairly" and "generally accepted accounting principles." Reflect on the fact that the accounting firm must conduct an audit before it can render the above opinion. An *audit* is an "examination" or in-depth inspection that is made in accordance with generally accepted auditing standards (which have been developed primarily by the American Institute of Certified Public Accountants). Such examination includes miscellaneous tests of the accounting records, internal control systems, and other auditing procedures as deemed necessary. The examination culminates with the rendering of the accountant's **independent opinion.** This opinion (sometimes called **certificate**) is the accountant's stamp of approval on *management's* financial statements.

The auditor's opinion, usually appearing at the end of annual reports prepared for stockholders and other external users, is often mistakenly relied on as an infallible guarantee of financial truth. Somehow accounting is thought to be an exact science, perhaps because of the aura of precision that financial statements possess. But accounting is more art than science. The financial reports may appear accurate because of their neatly integrated numbers, but they are the results of a complex measurement process that rests on a huge bundle of assumptions and conventions called **generally accepted accounting principles (GAAP).**

What are these generally accepted accounting principles? This technical term covers much territory. It includes both broad concepts or guidelines and detailed practices. It includes all conventions, rules, and procedures that together make up accepted accounting practice at any given time.

Accounting principles become "generally accepted" by agreement. Such agreement is not influenced solely by formal logical analysis. Experience, custom, usage, and practical necessity contribute to the set of principles. Accordingly, it might be better to call them *conventions*, because principles connotes that they are the product of airtight logic.

☐ FASB, APB, and SEC

Every technical area seems to have regulatory bodies or professional associations whose names are often abbreviated. Accounting is no exception.

During the 1970s and 1980s, American generally accepted accounting principles have been most heavily influenced by the **Financial Accounting Standards Board (FASB)** and its predecessor body, the **Accounting Principles Board (APB).** The FASB consists of seven qualified individuals who work full time. The board is supported by a large staff and an annual $10 million budget.

The board is an independent creature of the private sector and is financially supported by various professional accounting associations (such as the leading organization of the auditors, the American Institute of Certified Public Accountants, the AICPA).

The FASB was established in 1973 as the replacement for the APB. The APB consisted of a group of eighteen accountants (mostly partners in large accounting firms) who worked part time. The board issued a series of thirty-one opinions during 1962–73, many of which are still the "accounting law of the land." Many of these **APB Opinions** and **FASB Statements** will be referred to in succeeding chapters of this book.

The U.S. Congress has designated the **Securities and Exchange Commission (SEC)** as holding the ultimate responsibility for authorizing the generally accepted accounting principles for companies whose stock is held by the general investing public. However, the SEC has informally delegated much rule-making power to the FASB. This public sector–private sector relationship may be sketched as follows:

Basic
Accounting:
Concepts,
Techniques,
and
Conventions

533

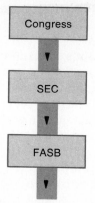

Issues pronouncements on various accounting issues. These pronouncements govern the preparation of typical financial statements.

Independent auditing firms **(Certified Public Accountants)** issue opinions concerning the fairness of financial statements prepared for external use (for example, corporate annual reports). These auditors are required to see that the statements do not depart from the FASB Statements and the APB Opinions.

Reconsider the three-tiered structure above. Note that Congress can overrule both the SEC and the FASB, and the SEC can overrule the FASB. Such undermining of the FASB occurs rarely, but pressure is exerted on all three tiers by corporations if they think an impending pronouncement is "wrong." Hence the setting of accounting principles is a complex process involving heavy interactions among the affected parties: public regulators (Congress and SEC), private regulators (FASB), companies, the public accounting profession, representatives of investors, and other interested groups.[3]

In sum, the public body (the SEC) has informally delegated much rule-making power regarding accounting theory to the private bodies (the APB and FASB). These boards have rendered a series of pronouncements on various accounting issues. Independent auditing firms, which issue opinions concerning the fairness of corporate financial statements prepared for external use, are required to see that corporate statements do not depart from these pronouncements.

THREE MEASUREMENT CONVENTIONS

Three broad measurement or valuation conventions (principles) establish the basis for implementing accrual accounting: realization (when to recognize revenue), matching (when to recognize expense), and the stable dollar (what unit of measure to use).

[3] For a fuller description, see the following in the *Journal of Accountancy* by Charles T Horngren: "The Marketing of Accounting Standards," October 1973, and "Uses and Limitations of a Conceptual Framework," April 1981.

Realization

The first broad measurement or valuation convention, *realization,* was discussed earlier in this chapter in the section "Revenues and Expenses." In general, revenue is realized when the goods or services in question are delivered to customers.

Matching and Cost Recovery

Generally accepted accounting principles are based on the concepts of accrual accounting described earlier in this chapter. You may often encounter a favorite buzzword in accounting: **matching.** The process of matching is the relating of accomplishments or revenues (as measured by the selling prices of goods and services delivered) and efforts or expenses (as measured by the cost of goods and services used) to a *particular period* for which a measurement of income is desired. In short, matching is a short description of the accrual basis for measuring income.

The heart of recognizing expense is the **"cost recovery"** concept. That is, assets such as inventories, prepayments, and equipment are carried forward as assets because their costs are expected to be recovered in the form of cash inflows (or reduced cash outflows) in future periods. At the end of each period, the accountant (especially the outside auditor at the end of each year) carefully examines the evidence to be assured that these assets—these prepaid costs—should not be written off as an expense of the current period. For instance, in our chapter example, prepaid rent of $2,000 was carried forward as an asset as of March 31 because the accountant is virtually certain that it represents a future benefit. Why? Because without the prepayment, cash outflows of $2,000 would have to be made for April and May. So the presence of the prepayment is a benefit in the sense that future cash outflows will be reduced by $2,000. Furthermore, future revenue (sales) will be high enough to ensure the recovery of the $2,000.

Stable Monetary Unit

The monetary unit (the dollar in the United States, Canada, Australia, New Zealand, and elsewhere) is the principal means for measuring assets and equities. It is the common denominator for quantifying the effects of a wide variety of transactions. Accountants record, classify, summarize, and report in terms of the dollar.

Such measurement assumes that the principal counter—the dollar—is an unchanging yardstick. Yet we all know that a 1984 dollar does not have the same purchasing power as a 1974 or 1964 dollar. Therefore accounting statements that include different dollars must be interpreted and compared with full consciousness of the limitations of the basic measurement unit. (For an expanded discussion, see Chapter 20.)

Accountants have been extensively criticized for not making explicit and formal adjustments to remedy the defects of their measuring unit. In the face of this, some accountants maintain that price-level adjustments

Basic
Accounting:
Concepts,
Techniques,
and
Conventions

535

would lessen objectivity and would add to the general confusion. They claim that the price-level problem has been exaggerated, and that the adjustments would not significantly affect the vast bulk of corporate statements because most accounts are in current or nearly current dollars.

On the other hand, inflation has been steady and its effects are sometimes surprisingly pervasive. We can expect to see increasing experimentation with reporting that measures the effects of changes in the general economywide price level and in the prices of specific assets. The most troublesome aspect, however, is how to interpret the results after they are measured. Investors and managers are accustomed to the conventional statements. The intelligent interpretation of statements adjusted for changes in the price level will require extensive changes in the habits of users.

The body of generally accepted accounting principles contains more than just the measurement conventions just discussed. Other major concepts include going concern, objectivity, materiality, and cost-benefit. These are discussed in the first appendix of this chapter.

Summary

An underlying structure of concepts, techniques, and conventions provides a basis for accounting practice. The three major measurement conventions are: realization, matching and cost recovery, and stable monetary unit. The accrual basis is the heart of accounting, whereby revenues are recognized as earned and expenses as incurred rather than as related cash is received or disbursed.

At the end of each accounting period, adjustments must be made so that financial statements may be presented on a full-fledged accrual basis. The major adjustments are for (1) the expiration of unexpired costs, (2) realization (earning) of previously deferred revenues, (3) accrual of previously unrecorded expenses, and (4) accrual of previously unrecorded revenues.

Income statements usually appear in single-step, condensed form in published annual reports and in multiple-step, detailed form in the reports used within an organization.

Summary Problem for Your Review

(Problem One appeared earlier in this chapter, page 521.)

☐ Problem Two

The following interpretations and remarks are sometimes encountered with regard to financial statements. Do you agree or disagree? Explain fully.

1. "If I purchase 100 shares of the outstanding common stock of General Motors Corporation (or Retailer No. 1), I invest my money directly in that corporation. General Motors must record that transaction."

2. "Sales show the cash coming in from customers and the various expenses show the cash going out for goods and services. The difference is net income."

3. Consider the following accounts of Delta, a leading U.S. airline, June 30, 1982:

Paid-in capital	$ 199,371,000
Retained earnings	824,280,000
Total stockholders' equity	$1,023,651,000

A shareholder commented, "Why can't that big airline pay higher wages and dividends too. It can use its hundreds of millions of dollars of retained earnings to do so."

4. "The total Delta stockholders' equity measures the amount that the shareholders would get today if the corporation were liquidated."

5. "Conservatism is desirable because investors will be misled if the financial report is too rosy."

❑ Solution to Problem Two

1. Money is invested directly in a corporation only upon original issuance of the stock by the corporation. For example, 100,000 shares of stock may be issued at $80 per share, bringing in $8 million to the corporation. This is a transaction between the corporation and the stockholders. It affects the corporate financial position:

Cash	$8,000,000	Stockholders' equity	$8,000,000

In turn, 100 shares of that stock may be sold by an original stockholder (A) to another individual (B) for $130 per share. This is a private transaction; no funds come to the corporation. Of course, the corporation records the fact that 100 shares originally owned by A are now owned by B, but the corporate financial position is unchanged. Accounting focuses on the business entity; the private dealings of the owners have no direct effect on the financial position of the entity and hence are unrecorded except for detailed records of the owners' identities.

In sum, B invests her money in the shares of the corporation when she buys them from A. However, individual dealings in shares already issued and held by stockholders have no direct effect on the financial position of the corporation.

2. Cash receipts and disbursements are not the fundamental basis for the accounting recognition of revenues and expenses. Credit, not cash, lubricates the economy. Therefore, if services or goods have been rendered to a customer, a legal claim to cash in the form of a receivable is deemed sufficient justification for recognizing revenue; similarly, if services or goods have been used up, a legal obligation in the form of a payable is justification for recognizing expense.

This approach to the measurement of net income is known as the accrual method. Revenue is recognized as it is earned by (a) goods or services rendered, (b) an exchange in a market transaction, and (c) the assurance of the collectibility of the asset received. Expenses or losses are recognized when goods or services are used up in the obtaining of revenue (or when such goods or services cannot justifiably be carried forward as an asset because they have no potential future benefit). The expenses and losses are deducted from the revenue, and the result of this matching process is net income, the net increase in stockholders' equity from the conduct of operations.

3. As the chapter indicated, retained earnings is not cash. It is a stockholders' equity account that represents the accumulated increase in ownership claims due to profitable operations. This claim or interest may be partially liquidated by the payment of cash dividends, but a growing company will reinvest cash in sustaining the added investments in receivables, inventories, plant, equipment, and other assets so necessary for expansion. As a result, the ownership claims reflected by retained earnings may become "permanent" in the sense that, as a practical matter, they will never be liquidated as long as the company remains a going concern.

Basic
Accounting:
Concepts,
Techniques,
and
Conventions

537

This linking of retained earnings and cash is only one example of fallacious interpretation. As a general rule, there is no direct relationship between the individual items on the two sides of the balance sheet. For example, Delta's cash was less than $46 million on the above balance sheet date when its retained earnings exceeded $800 million.

4. Stockholders' equity is a difference, the excess of assets over liabilities. If the assets were carried in the accounting records at their liquidating value today, and the liabilities were carried at the exact amounts needed for their extinguishment, the remark would be true. But such valuations would be coincidental because assets are customarily carried at *historical cost* expressed in an unchanging monetary unit. Intervening changes in markets and general price levels in inflationary times may mean that the assets are woefully understated. Investors may make a critical error if they think that balance sheets indicate current values.

   Furthermore, the "market values" for publicly owned shares are usually determined by daily trading conducted in the financial marketplaces such as the New York Stock Exchange. These values are affected by numerous factors, including the *expectations* of (a) price appreciation and (b) cash flows in the form of dividends. The focus is on the future; the present and the past are examined as clues to what may be forthcoming. Therefore the present stockholders' equity is usually of only incidental concern.

   For example, the above stockholders' equity was $1,023,651,000 ÷ 39,761,154 shares, or $26 per share. During 1982, a year of low profits, Delta's market price per common share fluctuated between $22 and $36.

5. Conservatism is an entrenched practice among accountants, and it is also favored by many managers and investors. However, it has some ramifications that should be remembered. Conservatism will result in fast write-offs of assets with consequent lower balance sheet values and lower net incomes. But later years may show higher net incomes because of the heavier write-offs in early years.

   So being conservative has some long-run countereffects because, for any asset, early fast write-offs will lighten expenses in later years. This countervailing effect is especially noteworthy when a company is having trouble making any net income. In such cases, the tendency is to wipe the slate clean by massive write-offs that result in an enormous net loss for a particular year. Without such assets to burden future years, the prospects brighten for reporting future net profits rather than net losses.

   Conservatism has another boomerang effect. The understatement of assets and net income may prompt anxious stockholders to sell their shares when they should hold them. A dreary picture may be every bit as misleading as a rosy one.

Highlights to Remember

1. *Balance sheet* is a widely used term, but it is not as descriptive as its newer substitute terms: *statement of financial position* or *statement of financial condition.*

2. Other than cash and receivables, assets may be regarded as unexpired, prepaid, or stored costs (for example, inventory or equipment) that are carried forward to future periods rather than being immediately offset against revenue as expenses of the current period.

3. Revenues and expenses are components of stockholders' equity. Revenues increase stockholders' equity; expenses decrease stockholders' equity.

4. Dividends are not expenses.

5. In accrual accounting, an expense is seldom accompanied by a cash disbursement. That is, *expense* should not be confused with the term *cash disbursement.*

6. In accrual accounting, revenue is seldom accompanied by a cash receipt. That is, *revenue* should not be confused with the term *cash receipt.*

7. Frequently, accounting adjustments are clarified when they are seen as mirror images by looking at both sides of the adjustment simultaneously. For example, (a) the expiration of unexpired costs (the tenant's rent expense) is accompanied by (b) the earning of previously deferred revenues (the landlord's rent revenue).

8. Similarly, (a) the accrual of previously unrecorded expenses (a borrower's interest expense) is accompanied by (b) the accrual of previously unrecorded revenues (a lender's interest revenue).

9. If you have had little or no exposure to accounting, you should solve at least the "Summary Problems for Your Review" before proceeding to the next chapter. To read about basic accounting concepts is not enough. Work some problems too—the more, the better.

Accounting Vocabulary

More new terms were introduced in this chapter (and its appendixes) than in any other, so be sure that you understand the following: *account; Accounting Principles Board (APB); accounts payable; accounts receivable; accrual basis; accrue; adjusting entries; adjustments; APB Opinions; assets; audit; balance sheet; capital; cash basis; certificate; Certified Public Accountant; continuity convention; corporation; cost-benefit criterion; cost of goods sold; credit; debit; deferred credit; deferred income; deferred revenue; dividends; earned surplus; earnings; entity; equities; expense; expired costs; explicit transactions; FASB Statements; financial accounting; Financial Accounting Standards Board (FASB); generally accepted accounting principles (GAAP); going concern convention; gross margin; gross profit; implicit transactions; income; income statement; independent opinion; ledger; liabilities; matching and cost recovery; materiality; net worth; objectivity; owners' equity; paid-in capital; partnership; profits; proprietorship; realization; reinvested earnings; retained earnings; retained income; revenue; Securities and Exchange Commission (SEC); single-step income statement; source documents; statement of financial condition; statement of financial position; stockholders' equity; transaction; undistributed earnings; unearned revenue; unexpired costs; verifiability.*

Appendix 17A: Additional Accounting Concepts

This appendix describes the following concepts, which are prominent parts of the body of generally accepted accounting principles: going concern or continuity, objectivity or verifiability, materiality, and cost-benefit.

THE GOING CONCERN OR CONTINUITY CONVENTION

Many accountants would regard **going concern** as a fact of life rather than as a convention or assumption. To view an entity as a going concern is to assume that it will continue indefinitely or at least that it will not be liquidated in the near future. This notion implies that existing *resources,* such as plant assets, *will be used* to fulfill the general purposes of a continuing entity *rather than sold* in tomorrow's real estate or equipment markets. It also implies that existing liabilities will be paid at maturity in an orderly manner.

Suppose some old specialized equipment has a depreciated cost of $10,000, a replacement cost of $12,000, and a realizable value of $7,000 in the used-equipment

Basic
Accounting:
Concepts,
Techniques,
and
Conventions

539

market. The going concern convention is often cited as the justification for adhering to acquisition cost (or acquisition cost less depreciation, $10,000 in this example) as the primary basis for valuing assets such as inventories, land, buildings, and equipment. Some critics of these accounting practices believe that such valuations are not as informative as their replacement cost ($12,000) or their realizable values upon liquidation ($7,000). Defenders of using $10,000 as an appropriate asset valuation argue that a going concern will generally use the asset as originally intended. Therefore the recorded cost (the acquisition cost less depreciation) is the preferable basis for accountability and evaluation of performance. Hence other values are not germane because replacement or disposal will not occur en masse as of the balance sheet date.

The opposite view to this going concern or **continuity convention** is an immediate-liquidation assumption, whereby all items on a balance sheet are valued at the amounts appropriate if the entity were to be liquidated in piecemeal fashion within a few days or months. This liquidation approach to valuation is usually used only when the entity is in severe, near-bankrupt straits.

OBJECTIVITY OR VERIFIABILITY

Users want assurance that the numbers in the financial statements are not fabricated by management or by accountants in order to mislead or to falsify the financial position and performance. Consequently, accountants seek and prize **objectivity** as one of their principal strengths and regard it as an essential characteristic of measurement. Objectivity results in accuracy that is supported by convincing evidence that can be verified by independent accountants. It is a relative rather than an absolute concept. Some measurements can be extremely objective (such as cash in a cash register) in the sense that the same measurement would be produced by each of a dozen CPAs. But there are gradations of objectivity. A dozen CPAs are less likely to arrive at the same balances for receivables, inventories, plant and equipment, and miscellaneous assets. Yet they strive for measurement rules that will produce results that are subject to independent check. That is why accountants are generally satisfied with existing tests of realization: requiring an exchange to occur before revenue is realized helps ensure **verifiability.**

Many critics of existing accounting practices want to trade objectivity (accuracy) for what they conceive as more relevant or valid information. For example, the accounting literature is peppered with suggestions that accounting should attempt to measure "economic income," even though objectivity may be lessened. This particular suggestion often involves introducing asset valuations at replacement costs when these are higher than historical costs. The accounting profession has generally rejected these suggestions, even when reliable replacement price quotations are available, because no evidence short of a bona fide sale is regarded as sufficient to justify income recognition. However, inflation during the past decade has led to experimentation with the use of replacement costs and other versions of current values for external purposes. (See Chapter 20 for a fuller discussion.)

MATERIALITY

Because accounting is a practical art, the practitioner often tempers accounting reports by applying the convention of materiality. Many outlays that theoretically should be recorded as assets are immediately written off as expenses because of their lack of significance. For example, many corporations have a rule that requires the immediate write-off to expense of all outlays under a specified minimum of, say, $100, regardless of the useful life of the asset acquired. In such a case, coat hangers may be acquired that may last indefinitely but may never appear in the balance sheet as assets. The resulting $100 understatement of assets and stockholders' equity would be too trivial to worry about.

When is an item material? There will probably never be a universal clear-cut answer. What is trivial to General Motors may be material to Joe's Tavern. An item is material if it is sufficiently large so that its omission or misstatement would tend to mislead the user of the financial statements under consideration. A working rule is that an item is material if its proper accounting would probably affect the decision of a knowledgeable user. In sum, materiality is an important convention. But it is difficult to use anything other than prudent judgment to tell whether an item is material.

COST-BENEFIT

Accounting systems vary in complexity from the minimum crude records kept to satisfy governmental authorities to the sophisticated budgeting and feedback schemes that are at the heart of management planning and controlling. As a system is changed, its potential benefits usually must exceed its additional costs. Often the benefits are difficult to measure, but this **cost-benefit criterion** at least implicitly underlies the decisions about the design of accounting systems. The reluctance to adopt suggestions for new ways of measuring financial position and performance is frequently because of inertia, but it is often because the apparent benefits do not exceed the obvious costs of gathering and interpreting the information.

ROOM FOR JUDGMENT

Accounting is commonly misunderstood as being a precise discipline that produces exact measurements of a company's financial position and performance. As a result, many individuals regard accountants as little more than mechanical tabulators who grind out financial reports after processing an imposing amount of detail in accordance with stringent predetermined rules. Although accountants take methodical steps with masses of data, their rules of measurement allow much room for judgment. Managers and accountants who exercise this judgment have more influence on financial reporting than is commonly believed. These judgments are guided by the basic concepts, techniques, and conventions called generally accepted accounting principles (GAAP). Examples of the latter include the basic concepts just discussed. Their meaning will become clearer as these concepts are applied in future chapters.

Appendix 17B: Using Ledger Accounts

This chapter offered some insight into the overall approach of the accountant to the measuring of economic activity. This appendix focuses on some of the main techniques that the accountant would use to analyze the illustration in the chapter.

To begin, consider how the accountant would record the Retailer No. 1 transactions that were introduced in the chapter. Recall their effects on the elements of the balance sheet equation:

	A		=	L	+	SE
	Cash	Inventory	=	Accounts Payable		Paid-in Capital
1. Initial investment by owners	+100,000		=			+100,000
2. Acquire inventory for cash	−75,000	+75,000	=			
3. Acquire inventory on credit		+35,000	=	+35,000		

This balance sheet equation approach emphasizes the concepts, but it can obviously become unwieldy if many transactions occur. You can readily see that changes in the balance sheet equation can occur many times daily. In large businesses, such as in a department store, hundreds or thousands of repetitive transactions occur hourly. In practice, **ledger accounts** must be used to keep track of how these multitudes of transactions affect each particular asset, liability, revenue, expense, and so forth. The accounts used here are simplified versions of those used in practice. They are called T-accounts because they take the form of the capital letter *T*. The above transactions would be shown in T-accounts as follows:

ASSETS = EQUITIES

or

ASSETS = LIABILITIES + STOCKHOLDERS' EQUITY

Cash			
Increases		Decreases	
(1)	100,000	(2)	75,000
Bal.	25,000		

Accounts Payable			
Decreases		Increases	
		(3)	35,000

Inventory			
Increases		Decreases	
(2)	75,000		
(3)	35,000		
Bal.	110,000		

Paid-in Capital			
Decreases		Increases	
		(1)	100,000

The above entries were made in accordance with the rules of a *double-entry system*, whereby at least two accounts are affected by each transaction. Asset accounts have left-hand balances. They are increased by entries on the left-hand side and decreased by entries on the right-hand side.

Liabilities and stockholders' equity accounts have right-hand balances. They are increased by entries on the right-hand side and decreased by entries on the left-hand side.

Each T-account summarizes the changes in a particular asset or equity. Each transaction is keyed in some way, such as by the numbering used in this illustration or by date or both. This keying facilitates the rechecking (auditing) process by aiding the tracing of transactions to original sources. A balance of an account is computed by deducting the smaller total amount from the larger. Accounts exist to keep an up-to-date summary of the changes in specific assets and equities.

A balance sheet can be prepared at any instant if the accounts are up to date.

The necessary information is tabulated in the accounts. For example, the balance sheet after the first three transactions would contain:

ASSETS		EQUITIES	
Cash	$ 25,000	Liabilities:	
Inventory	110,000	Accounts payable	$ 35,000
		Stockholders' equity:	
		Paid-in capital	100,000
Total assets	$135,000	Total equities	$135,000

GENERAL LEDGER

Exhibit 17-7 is the *general ledger* of Retailer No. 1. The *general ledger* is defined as the group of accounts that supports the accounts shown in the major financial state-

EXHIBIT 17-7

General Ledger of RETAILER NO. 1

1. Initial investment
2. Acquire inventory for cash
3. Acquire inventory on credit
4a. Sales on credit
4b. Cost of inventory sold

5. Collect from customers
6. Pay accounts of suppliers
7a. Pay rent in advance
7b. Recognize expiration of rental services

ASSETS
(INCREASES ON LEFT, DECREASES ON RIGHT)

EQUITIES
(DECREASES ON LEFT, INCREASES ON RIGHT)

Cash

(1)	100,000	(2)	75,000
(5)	30,000	(6)	10,000
		(7a)	3,000
3/31 Bal.			
	42,000		

Accounts Payable

| (6) | 10,000 | (3) | 35,000 |

Paid-in Capital

| | | (1) | 100,000 |

Accounts Receivable

| (4a) | 120,000 | (5) | 30,000 |

Retained Income

| | | 3/31 Bal. | |
| | | | 19,000 |

EXPENSE AND REVENUE ACCOUNTS

Inventory

(2)	75,000	(4b)	100,000
(3)	35,000		
3/31 Bal.			
	10,000		

Cost of Goods Sold

| (4b) | 100,000 | | |

Sales

| | | (4a) | 120,000 |

Prepaid Rent

| (7a) | 3,000 | (7b) | 1,000 |

Rent Expense

| (7b) | 1,000 | | |

*The details of the revenue and expense accounts appear in the income statement. Their net effect is then transferred to a single account, Retained Income, in the balance sheet. Note: An ending balance should be drawn for each account, but all balances are not shown here because some can be computed easily by inspection.

ments.[4] Exhibit 17-7 is merely a recasting of the facts that were analyzed in Exhibit 17-1. Study Exhibit 17-7 by comparing its analysis of each transaction against its corresponding analysis in Exhibit 17-1, page 514.

DEBITS AND CREDITS

The balance sheet equation has often been mentioned in this chapter. Recall:

$$A = L + \text{paid-in capital} \tag{1}$$

$$A = L + \text{paid-in capital} + \text{retained income} \tag{2}$$

$$A = L + \text{paid-in capital} + \text{revenue} - \text{expense} \tag{3}$$

The accountant often talks about entries in a technical way:

Transposing, $A + \text{expenses} = L + \text{paid-in capital} + \text{revenue}$ (4)

Finally,   left = right   (5)
                        debit = credit

Debit means one thing and one thing only—"left side" (not "bad," "something coming," etc.). **Credit** means one thing and one thing only—"right side" (not "good," "something owed," etc.) The word *charge* is often used instead of *debit*, but no single word is used as a synonym for *credit*.

For example, if you asked an accountant what entry to make for transaction 4*b*, the answer would be: "I would debit (or charge) Cost of Goods Sold for $100,000; and I would credit Inventory for $100,000." Note that the total dollar amount of the debits (entries on the left side of the account(s) affected) will *always* equal the total dollar amount of the credits (entries on the right side of the account(s) affected) because the whole accounting system is based on an equation. The symmetry and power of this analytical debit-credit technique is indeed impressive.

Assets are traditionally carried as left-side balances. Why do assets and expenses both carry debit balances? They carry left-side balances for different reasons. *Expenses* are temporary stockholders' equity accounts. Decreases in stockholders' equity are entered on the left side of the accounts because they offset the normal (i.e., right-side) stockholders' equity balances. Because expenses decrease stockholders' equity, they are carried as left-side balances.

To recapitulate:

ASSETS		=	LIABILITIES		+ STOCKHOLDERS' EQUITY	
Increase	Decrease	Decrease	Increase	Decrease	Increase
+	−	−	+	−	+
debit	credit	debit	credit	debit	credit
left	right	left	right	left	right

[4] The general ledger is usually supported by various *subsidiary ledgers,* which provide details for several accounts in the general ledger. For instance, an accounts receivable subsidiary ledger would contain a separate account for each credit customer. The accounts receivable balance that appears in the Sears balance sheet is in a single account in the Sears general ledger. However, that lone balance is buttressed by detailed individual accounts receivable with millions of credit customers. You can readily visualize how some accounts in general ledgers might have subsidiary ledgers supported by subsubsidiary ledgers, and so on. Thus a subsidiary accounts receivable ledger might be subdivided alphabetically into Customers A–D, E–H, and so forth.

Because revenues increase stockholders' equity, they are recorded as credits. Because expenses decrease stockholders' equity, they are recorded as debits.

You have just seen an example of *double-entry* accounting, so named because at least two accounts are *always* affected in each transaction.

THE STRANGE DEBIT-CREDIT LANGUAGE

Beginners in the study of accounting are frequently confused by the words *debit* and *credit*. Perhaps the best way to minimize confusion is to ask what words would be used as substitutes? *Left* would be used instead of debit, and *right* would be used instead of credit.

The words *debit* and *credit* have a Latin origin. They were used centuries ago when double-entry bookkeeping was introduced by Paciolo, an Italian monk. Even though *left* and *right* are more descriptive words, *debit* and *credit* are too deeply entrenched to avoid.

Debit and credit are used as verbs, adjectives, or nouns. That is, "debit $1,000 to cash and credit $1,000 to accounts receivable" are examples of uses as verbs, meaning that $1,000 should be placed on the left side of the cash account and on the right side of the accounts receivable account. Similarly, if "a debit is made to cash" or "cash has a debit balance of $12,000," the *debit* is a noun or adjective that describes the status of a particular account. Thus debit and credit are short words that are packed with meaning.

In our everyday conversation we sometimes use the words *debits* and *credits* in a general sense that may completely diverge from their technical accounting uses. For instance, we may give praise by saying "She deserves plenty of credit for her good deed" or "That misplay is a debit on his ledger." When you study accounting, forget these general uses and misuses of the words. Merely think right (or left).

Assignment Material

The assignment material for each remaining chapter is divided as follows:
  Fundamental Assignment Material
    General Coverage
    Understanding Published Financial Reports
  Additional Assignment Material
    General Coverage
    Understanding Published Financial Reports

The "General Coverage" subgroups focus on concepts and procedures that are applicable to a wide variety of specific settings. Many instructors believe that these "traditional" types of questions, exercises, and problems have proved their educational value over many years of use in introductory textbooks.

The "Understanding Published Financial Reports" subgroups focus on real-life situations. They have the same basic aims as the "General Coverage" subgroups. Indeed, some instructors may confine their assignments to the "Understanding Published Financial Reports" subgroups. The distinctive characteristic of the latter subgroups is the use of actual companies and news events to enhance the student's interest in accounting. Many students and instructors get more satisfaction out of a course that frequently uses actual situations as a means of learning accounting methods and concepts.

Basic
Accounting:
Concepts,
Techniques,
and
Conventions

545

Fundamental
Assignment Material _____

❏ General Coverage

17–1. Balance sheet equation. (Alternate is 17–4.) For each of the following independent cases, compute the amounts (in thousands) for the items indicated by letters, and show your supporting computations:

	CASE		
	1	2	3
Revenues	$130	$ K	$310
Expenses	110	170	270
Dividends declared	-0-	5	Q
Additional investment by stockholders	-0-	30	35
Net income	E	20	P
Retained income:			
Beginning of year	30	60	100
End of year	D	J	110
Paid-in capital:			
Beginning of year	15	10	N
End of year	C	H	85
Total assets:			
Beginning of year	85	F	L
End of year	95	280	M
Total liabilities:			
Beginning of year	A	90	105
End of year	B	G	95

17–2. Analysis of transactions, preparation of statements. (Alternates are 17–5 and 17–29.) The Boone Company was incorporated on April 1, 19X2. Boone had ten holders of common stock. Ella Boone, who was the president and chief executive officer, held 51% of the shares. The company rented space in chain discount stores and specialized in selling ladies' shoes. Boone's first location was in a store of Century Market Centers, Inc.

The following events occurred during April:

1. The company was incorporated. Common stockholders invested $100,000 cash.
2. Purchased merchandise inventory for cash, $45,000.
3. Purchased merchandise inventory on open account, $25,000.
4. Merchandise carried in inventory at a cost of $37,000 was sold for cash for $25,000 and on open account for $65,000, a grand total of $90,000. Boone (not Century) carries and collects these accounts receivable.
5. Collection of the above accounts receivable, $15,000.
6. Payments of accounts payable, $18,000. See transaction 3.
7. Special display equipment and fixtures were acquired on April 1 for $36,000. Their expected useful life was thirty-six months with no terminal scrap value. Straight-line depreciation was adopted. This equipment was removable. Boone paid $12,000 as a down payment and signed a promissory note for $24,000.
8. On April 1, Boone signed a rental agreement with Century. The agreement called for a flat $2,000 per month, payable quarterly in advance. Therefore, Boone paid $6,000 cash on April 1.
9. The rental agreement also called for a payment of 10% of all sales. This payment was in addition to the flat $2,000 per month. In this way, Century would share in any success of the venture and be compensated for general services such as cleaning and utilities.

This payment was to be made in cash on the last day of each month as soon as the sales for the month were tabulated. Therefore, Boone made the payment on April 30.

10. Wages, salaries, and sales commissions were all paid in cash for all earnings by employees. The amount was $39,000.

11. Depreciation expense was recognized. See transaction 7.

12. The expiration of an appropriate amount of prepaid rental services was recognized. See transaction 8.

REQUIRED:

1. Prepare an analysis of Boone Company's transactions, employing the equation approach demonstrated in Exhibit 17-1. Show all amounts in thousands.

2. Prepare a balance sheet as of April 30, 19X2, and an income statement for the month of April. Ignore income taxes.

3. Given these sparse facts, analyze Boone's performance for April and its financial position as of April 30, 19X2.

17–3. **Comparison of cash basis versus accrual basis.** Refer to the preceding problem. Prepare an income statement on the cash basis for April. Compare it with the income statement on the accrual basis. Which basis provides a better measure of economic performance? Why?

☐ Understanding Published Financial Reports

17–4. **Balance sheet equation.** (Alternate is 17–1.) General Foods Corporation is a large processor and marketer of food products, including Maxwell House Coffee, Jell-O, Birds Eye, and Oscar Mayer brands. Its actual terminology and actual data (in millions of dollars) follow for its fiscal year ended March 31, 1982:

Assets, beginning of period	$3,130
Assets, end of period	E
Liabilities, beginning of period	A
Liabilities, end of period	2,158
Paid-in capital, beginning of period	148
Paid-in capital, end of period	D
Retained earnings, beginning of period	1,463
Retained earnings, end of period	C
Revenues	8,411
Costs and expenses	B
Net earnings	200
Dividends	109
Additional investments by stockholders	1

REQUIRED:

Find the unknowns (in millions), showing computations to support your answers.

17–5. **Analysis of transactions, preparation of statements.** (Alternates are 17–2 and 17–29.) Ohio-Sealy Mattress Company manufactures and sells Sealy-brand bedding. The company's actual condensed balance sheet data, December 31, 1981, follow (in millions):

Basic
Accounting:
Concepts,
Techniques,
and
Conventions

547

Cash	$ 9		Accounts payable	$ 2
Accounts receivable	8		Other liabilities	7
Inventories	7		Paid-in capital	6
Prepaid expenses	1			
Property, plant, and equipment	20		Retained earnings	30
Total	$45		Total	$45

The following summarizes some major transactions during January 1982 (in millions):

1. Mattresses carried in inventory at a cost of $3 were sold for cash of $2 and on open account of $5, a grand total of $7.
2. Acquired inventory on account, $5.
3. Collected receivables, $3.
4. On January 2, used $3 cash to prepay some rent and insurance for 1982.
5. Payments on accounts payable (for inventories), $2.
6. Paid selling and administrative expenses in cash, $1.
7. The $1 of prepaid expenses, December 31, 1981, for rent and insurance expired in January 1982.
8. Depreciation expense of $1 was recognized for January.

REQUIRED:

1. Prepare an analysis of Ohio-Sealy's transactions, employing the equation approach demonstrated in Exhibit 17-1, p. 514. Show all amounts in millions. (For simplicity, only a few major transactions are illustrated here.)
2. Prepare a statement of earnings for the month ended January 31, 1982, and a balance sheet, January 31, 1982. Ignore income taxes.

17-6. **Cash basis versus accrual basis.** Refer to the preceding problem. Prepare a statement of earnings on the cash basis for January. Compare it with the earnings statement on the accrual basis. Which basis provides a better measure of economic performance? Why?

Additional Assignment Material

❏ General Coverage

17-7. Give five examples of accounting entities.

17-8. Define *going concern.*

17-9. What is the major criticism of the dollar as the principal accounting measure?

17-10. What does the accountant mean by *objectivity?*

17-11. Criticize: "Assets are things of value owned by the entity."

17-12. Criticize: "Net income is the difference in the ownership capital account balances at two points in time."

17-13. Distinguish between the accrual basis and the cash basis.

17-14. How do adjusting entries differ from routine entries?

17-15. Why is it better to refer to the *costs,* rather than *values,* of assets such as plant or inventories?

17-16. Give at least two synonymous terms for each of the following: *balance sheet; income statement; assets.*

17-17. Give at least three other terms for *retained earnings.*

17-18. Criticize: "As a stockholder, I have a right to more dividends. You have millions stashed away in retained earnings. It's about time that you let the true owners get their hands on that pot of gold."

17-19. Criticize: "Dividends are distributions of profits."

17-20. Explain why advertising should be viewed as an asset upon acquisition.

17-21. What is the role of cost-benefit (economic feasibility) in the development of accounting principles?

17-22. If gross profit is 60%, express the relationship of cost of goods sold to gross profit in percentage terms.

17-23. **Income statement.** Here is a statement of an automobile dealer:

MARVEL CARS, INC.
Statement of Profit and Loss
December 31, 19X3

Revenues:		
Sales	$1,000,000	
Increase in market value of land and building	200,000	$1,200,000
Deduct expenses:		
Advertising	$ 100,000	
Sales commissions	50,000	
Utilities	20,000	
Wages	150,000	
Dividends	100,000	
Cost of cars purchased	700,000	1,120,000
Net profit		$ 80,000

REQUIRED:

| List and describe any shortcomings of this statement.

17-24. **Nature of retained income.** This is an exercise on the relationships between assets, liabilities, and ownership equities. The numbers are small, but the underlying concepts are large.

1. Assume an opening balance sheet of:

Cash	$1,000	Paid-in capital	$1,000

2. Purchase inventory for $600 cash. Prepare a balance sheet. A heading is unnecessary in this and subsequent requirements.
3. Sell the entire inventory for $850 cash. Prepare a balance sheet. Where is the retained income in terms of relationships within the balance sheet? That is, what is the meaning of the retained income? Explain in your own words.
4. Buy inventory for $400 cash and equipment for $700 cash. Prepare a balance sheet. Where is the retained income in terms of relationships within the balance sheet? That is, what is the meaning of the retained income? Explain in your own words.
5. Buy inventory for $300 on open account. Prepare a balance sheet. Where is the retained income and account payable in terms of the relationships within the balance sheet? That is, what is the meaning of the account payable and the retained income? Explain in your own words.

17-25. **Find unknowns.** The following data pertain to the Bunce Corporation. Total assets at January 1, 19X1, were $100,000; at December 31, 19X1, $120,000. During 19X1, sales were $200,000, cash dividends were $4,000, and operating expenses (exclusive of cost of goods sold) were $50,000. Total liabilities at December 31, 19X1, were $55,000; at January 1, 19X1, $40,000. There was no additional capital paid in during 19X1.

REQUIRED:

| (These need not be computed in any particular order.)

1. Net income for 19X1
2. Cost of goods sold for 19X1
3. Stockholders' equity, January 1, 19X1

17–26. **Tenant and landlord.** The Marshall Company, a retail furniture store, pays quarterly rent on its store at the beginning of each quarter. The rent per quarter is $6,000. The owner of the building in which the store is located is the Owen Corporation.

REQUIRED:

Using the balance sheet equation format, analyze the effects of the following on the tenant's and the landlord's financial position:

1. Marshall pays $6,000 rent on October 1.
2. Adjustment for October.
3. Adjustment for November.
4. Adjustment for December.

17–27. **Customer and airline.** Genuine Elements Company decided to hold a managers' meeting in Bermuda in January. To take advantage of special fares, Genuine purchased airline tickets in advance from Universal Airlines at a total cost of $60,000. These were acquired on November 1 for cash.

REQUIRED:

Using the balance sheet equation format, analyze the impact of the November payment and the January travel on the financial position of both Genuine and Universal.

17–28. **Balance sheet equation; solving for unknowns.** Compute the unknowns (V, W, X, Y, and Z) in each of the individual cases, Columns A through G.

GIVEN	A	B	C	D	E	F	G
Assets at beginning of period		$10,000				Z	$ 8,200
Assets at end of period		11,000					9,600
Liabilities at beginning of period		6,000				$12,000	4,000
Liabilities at end of period		Y					6,000
Stockholders' equity at beginning of period	$5,000	Z				V	X
Stockholders' equity at end of period	X	5,000				10,000	W
Sales			$15,000		X	14,000	20,000
Inventory at beginning of period			6,000	$ 8,000		Y	
Inventory at end of period			7,000	6,000		7,000	
Purchases of inventory			10,000	10,000		6,000	
Gross profit		Y			2,000	6,000	V
Cost of goods sold*			X	X	4,500	X	Z
Other expenses			4,000			4,000	5,000
Net profit	3,000	X	Z			W	Y
Dividends	1,000	-0-				1,500	400
Additional investments by stockholders						5,000	-0-

*Note that Cost of goods sold = Beginning inventory + Purchases − Ending inventory.

17–29. Fundamental transaction analysis and preparation of statements. (Alternates are 17–2 and 17–5, but this is longer.) Three women who were college classmates have decided to pool a variety of work experiences by opening a women's clothing store. The business has been incorporated as Sartorial Choice, Inc. The following transactions occurred during April.

1. On April 1, 19X1, each woman invested $9,000 in cash in exchange for 1,000 shares of stock each.

2. The corporation quickly acquired $50,000 in inventory, half of which had to be paid for in cash. The other half was acquired on open accounts that were payable after thirty days.

3. A store was rented for $500 monthly. A lease was signed for one year on April 1. The first two months' rent were paid in advance. Other payments were to be made on the second of each month.

4. Advertising during April was purchased on open account for $3,000 from a newspaper owned by one of the stockholders. Additional advertising services of $6,000 were acquired for cash.

5. Sales were $65,000. The average markup above the cost of the merchandise was two-thirds of cost. Eighty percent of the sales were on open account.

6. Wages and salaries incurred in April amounted to $11,000, of which $5,000 was paid.

7. Miscellaneous services paid for in cash were $1,410.

8. On April 1, fixtures and equipment were purchased for $6,000 with a down payment of $1,000 plus a $5,000 note payable in one year.

9. See transaction 8 and make the April 30 adjustment for interest expense *accrued* at 9.6%. (The interest is not *due* until the note matures.)

10. See transaction 8 and make the April 30 adjustment for depreciation expense on a straight-line basis. The estimated life of the fixtures and equipment is ten years with no expected terminal scrap value. Depreciation is the allocation as expense of the acquisition cost of plant and equipment to the particular periods that benefit from the use of the assets. Straight-line depreciation here would be $6,000 ÷ 10 years = $600 per year, or $50 per month.

11. Cash dividends of $300 were declared and disbursed to stockholders on April 29.

REQUIRED:

1. Using the accrual basis of accounting, prepare an analysis of transactions, employing the equation approach demonstrated in Exhibit 17-1. Place your analysis sideways; to save space, use abbreviated headings. Work slowly. Use the following headings: Cash, Accounts Receivable, Inventory, Prepaid Rent, Fixtures and Equipment, Accounts Payable, Notes Payable, Accrued Wages Payable, Accrued Interest Payable, Paid-in Capital, and Retained Income. Exhibit 17-1 is on p. 514.

2. Prepare a balance sheet and a multiple-step income statement. Also prepare a statement of retained income.

3. What advice would you give the owners based on the information compiled in the financial statements?

17–30. Debits and credits. Study Appendix 17B. For the following transactions, indicate whether the accounts *in parentheses* are to be debited or credited. The accrual basis is used. Use *DR* or *CR*:

1. A county government received property taxes in advance (Deferred Tax Revenue).
2. A three-year fire insurance policy was acquired (Prepaid Expenses).
3. Wages were earned by employees but had not yet been paid (Accrued Wages Payable).
4. A magazine company delivered magazines that had been paid for in advance (Deferred Subscription Revenue).
5. Interest was earned but had not been collected (Accrued Interest Receivable).
6. Dividends were declared and paid in cash (Retained Income).

17–31. True or false. Study Appendix 17B. Use *T* or *F* to indicate whether each of the following statements is true or false:

Basic
Accounting:
Concepts,
Techniques,
and
Conventions

551

1. In general, entries on the right side of asset accounts represent decreases in the account balances.
2. Increases in liability and revenue accounts should be recorded on the left side of the accounts.
3. Decreases in retained income are recorded as debits.
4. In general, all credit entries are recorded on the right side of accounts and represent decreases in the account balances.
5. Both increases in assets and decreases in liabilities are recorded on the debit sides of accounts.
6. In some cases, increases in account balances are recorded on the right sides of accounts.
7. Cash collections of accounts receivable should be recorded as debits to Cash and credits to Accounts Receivable.
8. Credit purchases of equipment should be debited to Equipment and charged to Accounts Payable.
9. Repayments of bank loans should be charged to Notes Payable and credited to Cash.
10. Asset debits should be on the left and liability debits should be on the right.
11. Inventory purchases on account should be credited to Accounts Payable and debited to an expense account.

17–32. **Using T-accounts.** Study Appendix 17B. Refer to Problem 17–2. Make entries for March in T-accounts. Key your entries and check to see that the ending balances agree with the financial statements.

17–33. **Using T-accounts.** Study Appendix 17B. Refer to Problem One of the "Summary Problems for Your Review." The transactions are analyzed in Exhibit 17-2. Make entries in T-accounts and check to see that the ending balances agree with the financial statements in Exhibits 17-3, 17-4, 17-5 on page 524.

17–34. **T-accounts.** Study Appendix 17B. Refer to Problem 17-29. Use T-accounts to present an analysis of April transactions. Key your entries and check to see that the ending balances agree with the financial statements.

☐ Understanding Published Financial Reports

17–35. **Balance sheet effects.** The Wells Fargo Bank showed the following items (among others) on its balance sheet at December 31, 19X1:

Cash	$ 947,000,000
Total deposits	$6,383,000,000

REQUIRED:

1. Suppose you made a deposit of $1,000 in the Wells Fargo Bank. How would each of the bank's assets and equities be affected? How much would each of your personal assets and equities be affected? Be specific.
2. Suppose a savings and loan association makes an $800,000 loan to a local hospital for remodeling. What would be the effect on each of the association's assets and equities immediately after the loan is made? Be specific.
3. Suppose you borrowed $10,000 from the Household Finance Company on a personal loan. How would such a transaction affect each of your personal assets and equities?

17–36. **Statement of income and retained income.** Westinghouse Electric Corporation is a huge international manufacturer of power systems and communication equipment. The following information has been condensed from its 1981 annual report (in millions of dollars):

Revenues	$9,522
Cash	68
Depreciation	219
Inventories	1,141
Interest expense	143
Accounts payable	575
Retained income at beginning of year	1,830
Distribution, administration, and general expenses	1,501
Dividends declared	154
Cost of sales	7,090
Income taxes	131

Depreciation, which is explained more thoroughly in the next chapter, is the allocation as expense of the acquisition cost of plant and equipment to the particular periods that benefit from the use of the assets. Its pertinent amount for the year is given here.

REQUIRED:

Select the relevant data and prepare (1) the income statement for 1981, and (2) the statement of retained income for 1981.

17–37. **Net income and retained income.** McDonald's Corporation is a well-known fast-foods restaurant company. The following data are from its 1981 annual report (in thousands):

McDonald's Corporation

Retained earnings, end of year	$1,289,662	Dividends paid on common stock	$ 38,252
Revenues	2,515,836	General, administrative, and selling expenses	268,323
Interest expense	91,317	Depreciation	126,375
Income tax expense	216,800		
Food and paper	720,293	Retained earnings, beginning of year	1,063,080
Wages and salaries	431,031		
Rent	54,942	Other operating expenses	341,921

Depreciation, which is explained more thoroughly in the next chapter, is the allocation as expense of the acquisition cost of plant and equipment to the particular periods that benefit from the use of the assets. Its pertinent amount for the year is given here.

REQUIRED:

1. Prepare the following for the year: (a) income statement and (b) statement of retained income.
2. Comment briefly on the relative size of the cash dividend.

17–38. **The case of the president's wealth.** From the *Chicago Tribune*, August 20, 1964:

☐ Accountants acting on President Johnson's orders today reported his family wealth totaled $3,484,098.

☐ The statement of capital, arrived at through conservative procedures of evaluation, contrasted with a recent estimate published by *Life* magazine, which put the total at 14 million dollars.

☐ The family fortune, which is held in trust while the Johnsons are in the White House, was set forth in terms of book values. The figures represent original cost rather than current market values on what the holdings would be worth if sold now.

Basic
Accounting:
Concepts,
Techniques,
and
Conventions

553

☐ Announced by the White House press office, but turned over to reporters by a national accounting firm at their Washington branch office, the financial statement apparently was intended to still a flow of quasi-official and unofficial estimates of the Johnson fortune. . . .

ASSETS	
Cash	$ 132,547
Bonds	398,540
Interest in Texas Broadcasting Corp.	2,543,838
Ranch properties and other real estate	525,791
Other assets, including insurance policies	82,054
Total assets	$3,682,770
LIABILITIES	
Note payable on real estate holding, 5% due 1971	$ 150,000
Accounts payable, accrued interest, and income taxes	48,672
Total liabilities	$ 198,672
Capital	$3,484,098

☐ The report apportions the capital among the family, with $378,081 credited to the President; $2,126,298 to his wife Claudia T., who uses the name Lady Bird; $490,141 to their daughter Lynda Bird; and $489,578 to their daughter Luci Baines.

☐ The statement said the family holdings—under the names of the President, his wife, and his two daughters, Lynda Bird and Luci Baines—had increased from $737,730 on January 1, 1954, a year after Johnson became Democratic leader of the Senate, to $3,484,098 on July 31 this year, a gain of $2,746,368. . . .

☐ A covering letter addressed to Johnson said the statement was made "in conformity with generally accepted accounting principles applied on a consistent basis."

☐ By far the largest part of the fortune was listed as the Johnsons' interest in the Texas Broadcasting Corporation, carried on the books as worth $2,543,838.

☐ The accountants stated that this valuation was arrived at on the basis of the cost of the stock when the Johnsons bought control of the debt-ridden radio station between 1943 and 1947, plus accumulated earnings ploughed back as equity, less 25 percent capital gains tax.[5]

Editorial, *Chicago Tribune*, August 22, 1964:

☐ An accounting firm acting on Mr. Johnson's instructions and employing what it termed "generally accepted auditing standards" has released a statement putting the current worth of the Lyndon Johnson family at a little less than 3 1/2 million dollars. . . .

☐ Dean Burch, chairman of the Republican National Committee, has remarked that the method used to list the Johnson assets was comparable to placing the value of Manhattan Island at $24, the price at which it was purchased from the Indians. The Johnson accounting firm conceded that its report was "not intended to indicate the values that might be realized if the investment were sold."

☐ In fact, it would be interesting to observe the response of the Johnson family if a syndicate of investors were to offer to take Texas Broadcasting off the family's hands at double the publicly reported worth of the operation. . . .

[5] You need not be concerned about the details of this method of accounting until you study Chapter 19. In brief, when an investor holds a large enough stake in a corporation, such investment is accounted for at its acquisition cost plus the investor's pro-rata share of the investee's net income (or net loss) minus the investor's share of dividends. For example, suppose the Texas Broadcasting Company earned $100,000 in a given year and Johnson owned 100% of the company. In this situation, the Johnson financial statements would show an increase in Interest in Texas Broadcasting Corp. of $100,000 less the $25,000 income tax that would become payable upon disposition of the investment. (Today's accountants would prefer to increase the Investment account by the full $100,000 and the liabilities by $25,000. See the Carter financial statements.)

1. Evaluate the criticisms, making special reference to fundamental accounting concepts or "principles."

2. The financial statements of President and Mrs. Carter are shown in an accompanying exhibit. Do you prefer the approach taken by the Carter statements as compared with the Johnson statements? Explain.

Perry, Chambliss, Sheppard and Thompson
Certified Public Accountants
Americus, Georgia

JAMES EARL CARTER, JR. AND ROSALYNN CARTER
STATEMENT OF ASSETS AND LIABILITIES
DECEMBER 31, 1977
(UNAUDITED)

ASSETS

	COST BASIS	ESTIMATED CURRENT VALUE
Cash	$204,979.04	$204,979.04
Cash Value of Life Insurance	45,506.88	45,506.88
U.S. Savings Bonds, Series E	1,425.00	1,550.94
Loan Receivable	50,000.00	50,000.00
Overpayment of 1977 Income Taxes	51,121.27	51,121.27
Personal Assets Trust—Note 3	151,097.87	557,717.11
Residence, Plains, Georgia	45,000.00	54,090.00
Lots in Plains, Georgia	1,100.00	3,155.00
Automobile	4,550.75	2,737.50
Total Assets	$554,780.81	$970,857.74

LIABILITIES

	COST BASIS	ESTIMATED CURRENT VALUE
Miscellaneous Accounts Payable, Estimated	$ 1,500.00	$ 1,500.00
Provision for Possible Income Taxes on Unrealized Asset Appreciation—Note 4	0	174,000.00
Total Liabilities	$ 1,500.00	$175,500.00
Excess of Assets Over Liabilities	$553,280.81	$795,357.74

NOTES TO FINANCIAL STATEMENTS
DECEMBER 31, 1977

NOTE 1: Estimated market values of real estate are 100% of the fair market values as determined by county tax assessors except as to certain assets held in the personal assets trust, which are stated at book value.

NOTE 2: This statement excludes campaign fund assets and liabilities.

NOTE 3: The interest in Carter's Warehouse partnership, the capital stock of Carter's Farms, Inc., the remainder interest in certain real estate and securities and a commercial lot in Plains, Georgia, were transferred to a personal assets trust in January, 1977. The primary purpose of the trust is to isolate the President from those of his assets which are most likely to be affected by actions of the federal government. The President was responsible as a general partner for obligations of the partnership before his partnership interest was transferred to the trust. The transfer to the trust did not affect such responsibility.

NOTE 4: If the market values of the assets were realized, income taxes would be payable at an uncertain rate. A provision for such income taxes has been made at rates in effect for 1977.

NOTE 5: The amounts in the accompanying statements are based principally upon the accrual basis method of accounting.

18

UNDERSTANDING CORPORATE ANNUAL REPORTS— PART ONE

Learning Objectives

When you have finished studying this chapter, you should be able to

1. Identify the meanings and inter-relationships of the main types of items in the classified balance sheet of a corporation
2. Measure the financial effects of various transactions.
3. Distinguish between reserves and funds in the financial statements
4. Identify the meanings and inter-relationships of the principal elements in the income statement of a corporation
5. Identify the meanings and inter-relationships of the elements in the retained income statement
6. Prepare the statement of changes in financial position
7. Identify the relationship of depreciation to the statement of changes in financial position and indicate the effects of depreciation on income taxes, cash, and working capital

Accounting has often been called the language of business. But it is a language with a special vocabulary aimed at conveying the financial story of organizations. To understand corporate annual reports, a reader must learn at least the fundamentals of the language. This chapter presents the basic meanings of the terms and relationships used in the financial statements found in annual reports.

Accounting is commonly misunderstood as being a precise discipline that produces exact measurements of a company's financial position and performance. As a result, many individuals regard accountants as little more than mechanical tabulators who grind out financial reports after processing an imposing amount of detail in accordance with stringent predetermined rules. Although accountants take methodical steps with masses of data, their rules of measurement allow much room for judgment. Managers and accountants who exercise this judgment have more influence on financial reporting than is commonly believed.

This chapter extends the discussion of the financial statements in the preceding chapter. It also introduces the Statement of Changes in Financial Position. Additional coverage (including investments in subsidiaries, consolidated statements, financial ratios, accounting for inventories, and accounting for inflation) will be found in the final two chapters of this book.

CLASSIFIED BALANCE SHEET

❏ Current Assets

Assets are usually grouped in the manner shown in Exhibit 18-1. The *current assets* are cash plus assets that are reasonably expected to be converted to cash or sold or consumed during the normal operating cycle. They are the assets directly involved in the operating cycle, including cash; temporary investments in marketable securities; receivables of nearly all kinds, including installment accounts and notes receivable if they conform to normal industry practice and terms; inventories; and prepaid expenses.

Most organizations exist to serve a desire for some type of goods or services. Whether they are profit seeking or not, they typically follow a similar, somewhat rhythmic, pattern of economic activity. An **operating cycle** (also called a *cash cycle* or *working-capital cycle* or *earnings cycle*) is the time span during which cash is used to acquire goods and services, which in turn are sold to customers, who in turn pay for their purchases with cash. Consider the following example. A retail business usually engages in some version of the operating cycle in order to earn profits. See the diagram on the top of the next page (figures assumed).

The box for Accounts Receivable (amounts owed to the business by customers) is larger than the other two boxes because the objective is to sell goods at a price higher than acquisition cost. Retailers and nearly all other businesses buy goods and services and perform acts (such as placing them in a convenient location or changing their form) that merit selling prices that hopefully will yield a profit. The total amount of profit earned during a particular period heavily depends on the excess of the selling prices over the costs of the goods and additional expenses and on the speed of the operating cycle.

Understanding
Corporate
Annual
Reports—
Part One

557

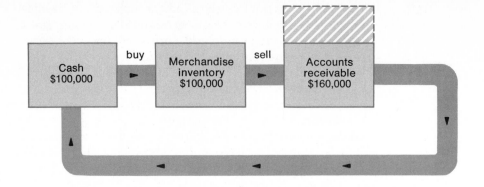

EXHIBIT
18-1

(Place a clip on this page for easy reference.)

THE GREEN CO.
Balance Sheet
(In thousands of dollars)

ASSETS	DECEMBER 31 19X1	19X0
Current assets:		
Cash	$ 2,600	$ 2,200
Temporary investments in marketable securities	600	600
Receivables, net of allowance for doubtful accounts	5,300	5,100
Inventories at cost	14,600	14,400
Prepaid expenses	600	600
Total current assets	$23,700	$22,900
Plant assets:		
Land	$ 300	$ 300
Buildings and equipment, net of accumulated depreciation	7,000	5,800
Total plant assets	$ 7,300	$ 6,100
Total assets	$31,000	$29,000
EQUITIES		
Current liabilities:		
Accounts payable	$ 7,100	$ 5,200
Accrued expenses payable	1,600	1,700
Accrued income taxes payable	500	400
Total current liabilities	$ 9,200	$ 7,300
Mortgage bonds payable	$16,000	$16,000
Total liabilities	$25,200	$23,300
Stockholders' equity:		
Preferred stock, 6%, $100 par value, $100 liquidating value	$ 1,600	$ 1,600
Common stock, $10 par value	2,000	2,000
Additional paid-in capital	1,000	1,000
Retained income	1,200	1,100
Total stockholders' equity	$ 5,800	$ 5,700
Total equities	$31,000	$29,000

Several operating cycles may occur during one year. But some businesses need more than one year to complete a single cycle. The distillery, tobacco, and lumber industries are examples. Inventories in such industries are nevertheless regarded as current assets. Similarly, installment accounts and notes receivable are typically classified as current assets even though they will not be fully collected within one year.

Some comments on specific kinds of current assets follow:

Cash consists of bank deposits in checking accounts plus money on hand. Incidentally, visualize how a deposit would be accounted for by a bank. Its cash will increase and its liabilities increase in the form of "Deposits," which are really "Deposits Payable."

Marketable securities is a misnomer, although the expression is encountered frequently. Strictly speaking, marketable securities may be held for either a short-term or a long-term purpose. A better expression would be *temporary or short-term investments* (as distinguished from *long-term investments* in capital stock or bonds of other companies, which are not current assets). They represent an investment of excess cash not needed immediately. The idea is to get earnings on otherwise idle cash. The money is typically invested in securities that are highly liquid (easily convertible into cash) and that have relatively stable prices, such as short-term notes or government bonds. These securities are usually shown at cost or market price, whichever is lower. The market price is disclosed parenthetically if it is above cost.

Accounts receivable is the total amount owed to the company by its customers. Because some accounts will ultimately be uncollectible, the total is reduced by an allowance or provision for doubtful accounts (that is, possible "bad debts" arising from credit extended to customers who do not pay). The difference represents the net amount that will probably be collected.

Inventories consist of merchandise, finished products of manufacturers, goods in the process of being manufactured, and raw materials. These are frequently carried at cost or market (defined as replacement cost), whichever is lower. Cost of manufactured products normally is composed of raw material plus the costs of its conversion (direct labor and manufacturing overhead) into a finished product.

Once the total cost of goods purchased or produced by a company is measured, how should it be allocated between the goods sold (an expense) and the goods still on hand (an asset)? This is easy to do if the products are readily identifiable, like the cars of an automobile dealer or the expensive merchandise of a jewelry store. But it is infeasible to have an elaborate identification system for goods that are purchased and sold in vast numbers and variety. Therefore one of the following assumptions regarding cost flows is typically used: average cost; first-in, first-out; or last-in, first-out.[1]

Prepaid expenses are usually unimportant in relation to other assets. They are short-term prepayments or advance payments to suppliers. Ex-

Understanding
Corporate
Annual
Reports—
Part One

559

---

[1] Accounting for manufacturing costs is discussed in Chapters 13, 14, and 15. Incidentally, recent progress in data-processing capabilities at lower and lower costs has made specific identification more and more economical. Inventory methods are discussed at length in the final chapter of this book.

amples are short-term prepaid expenses such as rent, operating supplies, and insurance that will be used up within the current operating cycle. They belong in current assets because if they were not present, more cash would be needed to conduct current operations.[2]

❏ Plant Assets

Plant assets are sometimes called **fixed assets** or *property, plant, and equipment*. Because they are physical items that can be seen and touched, they are often called *tangible assets.*

Land is typically accounted for as a separate item and is carried indefinitely at its original cost.

Plant and equipment are initially recorded at cost: the invoice amount, plus freight and installation, less cash discounts. The major difficulties of measurement center on the choice of a pattern of depreciation—that is, the allocation of the original cost to the particular periods or products that benefit from the utilization of the assets.

Accountants often stress that depreciation is a process of allocation of the original cost of acquisition; it is not a process of valuation in the ordinary sense of the term. The usual balance sheet presentation does *not* show replacement cost, resale value, or the price changes since acquisition. The accounting for the latter is discussed in the final chapter.

The amount of original cost to be allocated over the total useful life of the asset as depreciation is the difference between the total acquisition cost and the estimated **terminal disposal value.** The depreciation allocation to each year may be made on the basis of time or service. The estimate of useful life, which is an important factor in determining the yearly allocation of depreciation, is influenced by estimates of physical wear and tear, technological change, and economic obsolescence.

For example, suppose equipment with an estimated useful life of four years is acquired for $41,000. Its estimated scrap value is $1,000. Exhibit 18-2 shows how the asset would be displayed in the balance sheet if a straight-line method of depreciation were used. The annual depreciation expense that would appear on the income statement would be:

$$\frac{\text{original cost} - \text{estimated terminal value}}{\text{years of useful life}}$$

or

$$\frac{\$41,000 - \$1,000}{4} = \$10,000 \text{ per year}$$

❏ Depreciation Is Not Cash

An understanding of how the accountant reports plant assets and depreciation will highlight the limitations of financial statements. Professor Wil-

---

[2] Sometimes prepaid expenses are lumped with **deferred charges** as a single amount, *prepaid expenses and deferred charges,* that appears at the bottom of the current asset classification or at the bottom of all the assets as an "other asset." Deferred charges are like prepaid expenses, but they have longer-term benefits. For example, the costs of relocating a mass of employees to a different geographical area or the costs of rearranging an assembly line may be carried forward as deferred charges and written off as expense over a three- to five-year period.

EXHIBIT 18-2

Straight-Line Depreciation* (figures assumed)				
	BALANCES AT END OF YEAR			
	1	**2**	**3**	**4**
Plant and equipment (at original acquisition cost)	$41,000	$41,000	$41,000	$41,000
Less: Accumulated depreciation (the portion of original cost that has already been charged to operations as expense)	10,000	20,000	30,000	40,000
Net book value (the portion of original cost that will be charged to future operations as expense)	$31,000	$21,000	$11,000	$ 1,000

*Other patterns of depreciation are discussed later in this chapter.

liam A. Paton, a leading scholar in accounting for more than sixty years, once compared accounting for fixed assets with a boy's acquisition of a jelly-filled doughnut (the original cost, $41,000). The boy is so eager to taste the jelly that he licks it and creates a hole in the center of the doughnut (the accumulated depreciation of $10,000 at the end of Year 1). He continues his attack on the doughnut, and the hole enlarges. The hole is the **accumulated depreciation.** The *net book value* or *carrying amount* of the asset diminishes as the hole gradually becomes larger throughout the useful life of the doughnut. At the end of the useful life, the **book value** consists of the original doughnut ($41,000) less its gaping hole ($40,000), leaving a crumbly $1,000.

If you remember that accumulated depreciation is like a hole in a doughnut, you will be less likely to fall into the trap of those who think that accumulated depreciation is a sum of cash being accumulated for the replacement of plant assets.

Some accountants despise the likening of accumulated depreciation to the hole in the doughnut. Regardless of your degree of fondness for the doughnut analogy, remember that accumulated depreciation is not cash. If a company does actually decide to accumulate specific cash for the replacement of assets, such cash would be an asset that should be specifically labeled as a cash fund for replacement and expansion or a fund of marketable securities for replacement and expansion. Holiday Inns, Inc., has such a fund, calling it a *capital construction fund.* Such funds are quite rare because most companies can earn better returns by investing any available cash in ordinary operations rather than in special funds. Typically, companies will use or acquire cash for the replacement and expansion of plant assets only as specific needs arise.

Leasehold improvements are not illustrated in the Exhibit 18-1 balance sheet, but they are often grouped with plant assets. Such improvements may be made by a lessee (tenant) who invests in painting, decorating, fixtures, and air-conditioning equipment that cannot be removed from the premises when a lease expires. The costs of leasehold improvements are written off in the same manner as depreciation; however, their periodic write-off is called **amortization.**

Natural resources such as mineral deposits are not illustrated here, but they are typically grouped with plant assets. Their original cost is written off in the form of *depletion* as the resources are used. For example, a coal mine may cost $10 million and originally contain an estimated 5 million tons. The depletion rate would be $2 per ton. If 500,000 tons were mined during the first year, depletion would be $1 million for that year; if 300,000 tons were mined the second year, depletion would be $600,000; and so forth.

☐ Intangible Assets

Intangible assets are a class of **long-lived assets** that are not physical in nature. They are rights to expected future benefits deriving from their acquisition and continued possession. They are not illustrated in the Exhibit 18-1 balance sheet, but examples are goodwill, franchises, patents, trademarks, and copyrights.

Goodwill, which is discussed in more detail in the next chapter, is defined as the excess of the cost of an acquired company over the sum of the fair market value of its identifiable individual assets less the liabilities. For example, suppose Company A acquires Company B at a cost to A of $10 million and can assign only $9 million to various identifiable assets such as receivables, plant, and patents less liabilities assumed by the buyer; the remainder, $1 million, is goodwill. Identifiable intangible assets, such as franchises and patents, may be acquired singly, but goodwill cannot be acquired separately from a related business. This excess of the purchase price over the fair market value is called "goodwill" or "purchased goodwill" or, more accurately, "excess of cost over fair value of net identifiable assets of businesses acquired."

The accounting for goodwill illustrates how an *exchange* transaction is a basic concept of accounting. After all, there are many owners who could obtain a premium price for their companies. But such goodwill is never recorded. Only the goodwill arising from an *actual acquisition* with arm's-length bargaining should be shown as an asset on the purchaser's records.

For shareholder-reporting purposes, goodwill must be amortized, generally in a straight-line manner, over the periods benefited. The maximum amortization period should not be longer than forty years. The minimum amortization period was not specified by the Accounting Principles Board (APB *Opinion No. 17*), but a lump-sum write-off on acquisition is forbidden.

Research and development costs are those resulting from planned search or critical investigation aimed at obtaining new products or processes or significant improvements in existing products or processes. The Financial Accounting Standards Board (*Statement No. 2*) has required that all such costs be charged to expense when incurred. The FASB recognized that research and development costs may generate many long-term benefits, but the general high degree of uncertainty about the extent and measurement of future benefits led to conservative accounting in the form of immediate write-off.

❑ Historical Thrust Toward Conservatism

Many managers and accountants insist that some intangible assets have unlimited lives. But the Accounting Principles Board ruled that the values of all intangible assets eventually disappear. The attitudes of the regulatory bodies toward accounting for intangible assets became increasingly conservative during the 1970s. For example, before October 31, 1970, the amortization of goodwill, trademarks, and franchises with indefinite useful lives was not mandatory. The new requirement for amortization was not imposed retroactively. Consequently, many companies *are* currently amortizing goodwill acquired after October 31, 1970, but *are not* amortizing goodwill acquired before that date.

Before 1975, many companies regarded research and development costs as assets. Research costs were treated as deferred charges to future operations and amortized over the years of expected benefit, usually three to six years. But, as already mentioned, the FASB banned deferral and required write-off of these costs as incurred.

❑ Income Tax Reporting and Shareholder Reporting

Throughout this discussion of long-lived assets, please distinguish between reporting to stockholders and reporting to the income tax authorities. Reports to stockholders must abide by "generally accepted accounting principles." In contrast, reports to income tax authorities must abide by the income tax rules and regulations. These rules are in accordance with GAAP in many respects, but they frequently diverge.

Keep in mind that the income tax laws are patchworks that often are designed to give taxpayers special incentives for making investments. For example, England permits a taxpayer to write off the full cost of new equipment as expense in the year acquired. Although a total write-off may be permitted for income tax purposes, it is not permitted for shareholder-reporting purposes.

American companies are generally not required to follow the same valuations or depreciation schedules for both shareholder-reporting and income tax purposes. Therefore there is nothing immoral or unethical about "keeping two sets of records." For example, consider how the accounting for perpetual franchises, trademarks, and goodwill differs. Their acquisition costs *must* be amortized for shareholder reporting but *must not* be amortized for income tax purposes; the Internal Revenue Service will not allow amortization because of the indefinite duration of their usefulness.

The following table summarizes how accounting for two purposes can conflict:

Understanding
Corporate
Annual
Reports—
Part One

563

TYPE OF INTANGIBLE ASSET	MAXIMUM* USEFUL LIVES IN YEARS FOR MEASURING ANNUAL AMORTIZATION IN REPORTS	
	To Shareholders	To Internal Revenue Service
Patents	17	Same as first column
Copyrights	40	Same
Sports player contracts	Length of contract	Same
Franchise and licenses	Length of contract or 40 if length is unlimited	Same or no amortization permitted†
Trademarks	40	No amortization permitted†
Goodwill	40	No amortization permitted†
Research and development	Full write-off as incurred	Same
Covenants not to compete‡	Length of contract	Same

*These maximums are frequently far in excess of the economic lives. Thus patents and copyrights are often written off in two or three years because the related products have short lives.
†The Internal Revenue Service does not permit amortization of intangible assets with indefinite useful lives. Examples are franchises of unlimited duration, such as a football franchise, goodwill, and trademarks.
‡For example, the seller of a pest control business promises not to open a competing business within 100 miles for five years.

☐ Liabilities

Current liabilities are those that fall due within the coming year or within the normal operating cycle if longer than a year. *Accounts payable* are amounts owed to suppliers who extended credit for purchases on open account. These open account purchases from trade creditors are ordinarily supported by signatures on purchase orders or similar business documents. *Notes payable* are backed by formal promissory notes held by a bank or business creditors.

Accrued expenses payable are recognized for wages, salaries, interest, and similar items. The accountant tries to recognize expenses as they occur in relation to the operations of a given time period regardless of when they are paid for in cash. *Accrued income taxes payable* is a special accrued expense of enough magnitude to warrant a separate classification.

Long-term liabilities are those that fall due beyond one year. Bonds payable are formal certificates of indebtedness that are accompanied by a promise to pay interest at a specified annual rate.

Mortgage bonds are supposed to provide some additional safety for the bondholders in case the company is unable to meet its regular obligations on the bonds. If such an undesirable event occurs, the bondholders will have a prior lien on a specific asset(s). This means that such an asset may be sold and the proceeds used to liquidate the obligations to the bondholders. If no such lien exists, the bondholders have no special claims against the assets beyond the general claim against the *total* assets by the general creditors such as trade creditors.

Subordinated debentures (not illustrated in Exhibit 18-1) are like any long-term debt except that *subordinated* means such bondholders are junior to the other general creditors in exercising claims against assets, and *debenture* means a general claim against all unencumbered assets rather than a specific claim against particular assets.

The following example should clarify these ideas. Suppose a company is liquidated. *Liquidation* means converting assets to cash and terminating outside claims. The company had miscellaneous assets, including a building, that were converted into $110,000 cash.

ASSETS		EQUITIES	
Cash	$110,000	Accounts payable	$ 30,000
		First-mortgage bonds payable	90,000
		Subordinated debentures payable	40,000
		Total liabilities	$160,000
		Stockholders' equity (negative)	(50,000)
Total assets	$110,000	Total equities	$110,000

The mortgage bonds would be paid in full, the trade creditors would get paid two-thirds on the dollar ($20,000 for a $30,000 claim), and the other claimants would get nothing. If the debentures were *unsubordinated*, the $20,000 of cash remaining after paying $90,000 to the mortgage holders would be used to settle the $70,000 claims of the unsecured creditors as follows:

To trade creditors	$3/7 \times $20,000 =$	$ 8,571
To debenture holders	$4/7 \times $20,000 =$	11,429
Total cash distributed		$20,000

Deferred income taxes, which arise because the timing of income tax payments is delayed beyond the current operating cycle, are not shown in Exhibit 18-1 but are commonly found in the annual reports of American companies.

☐ Stockholders' Equity

Stockholders' equity (also called *owners' equity* or *capital* or *net worth*) as an overall class is the total residual interest in the business. It is a balance sheet difference, the excess of total assets over total liabilities. There may be many subclasses. It arises from two main sources: (1) contributed or paid-in capital and (2) retained income.

Paid-in capital typically comes from owners who invest in the business in exchange for stock certificates, which are issued as evidence of shareholder rights. It is often composed of a number of classes of capital stock with a variety of different attributes. *Preferred stock* typically has some priority over other shares regarding dividends or the distribution of assets upon liquidation. A *cumulative* preferred stock means that if a specified

Understanding
Corporate
Annual
Reports—
Part One

565

annual dividend of, say, $5 per share is not paid, this preferred claim accumulates and must be paid in full before any dividends are paid to any other classes of stock. Preferred shareholders do not ordinarily have voting privileges regarding the management of the corporation.

Stock frequently has a designated **par** or **legal** or **stated** value that is printed on the face of the certificate. For preferred stock (and bonds), par is a basis for designating the amount of dividends or interest. Many preferred stocks have $100 par values; therefore a 9%, $100-par preferred stock would carry a $9 annual dividend. Similarly, an 8% bond usually means that the investor is entitled to annual interest of $80 because most bonds have par values of $1,000. Par value of common stock has no practical importance. Historically, it was used for establishing the maximum legal liability of the stockholder in case the corporation could not pay its debts. Currently, it is set at a nominal amount (for example, $5) in relation to the market value of the stock upon issuance (for example, $70). It is generally illegal for a corporation to sell an original issue of its common stock below par. Common shareholders typically have *limited liability*, which means that creditors cannot resort to them as individuals if the corporation itself cannot pay its debts.

Common stock has no predetermined rate of dividends and is the last to obtain a share in the assets when the corporation is dissolved. Common shares usually have voting power in the management of the corporation. Common stock is usually the riskiest investment in a corporation, being unattractive in dire times but attractive in prosperous times because, unlike other stocks, there is no limit to the stockholder's potential participation in earnings.

Paid-in capital in excess of par (formerly called *capital surplus* or *paid-in surplus*) is the excess received over the par or stated or legal value of the shares issued. This amount is also frequently called *additional paid-in capital*. Common shares are often issued at a price substantially greater than par. The balance sheet effects of selling 100,000 shares of $5 par common at $80 per share would be:

Cash	$8,000,000	Common stock	$ 500,000
		Paid-in capital in excess of par	7,500,000
		Stockholders' equity	$8,000,000

Retained income, also called *retained earnings* or *reinvested earnings*, is the increase in stockholders' equity due to profitable operations. It was explained more fully in Chapter 17. Retained income is the dominant item of stockholders' equity for most companies. For instance, as of January 1, 1982, Eastman Kodak Co. had a stockholders' equity of $6,770 million, of which $6,027 million was retained income.

Treasury stock is a corporation's issued stock that has subsequently been repurchased by the company. Such repurchase is a liquidation of an ownership claim. It should therefore appear on a balance sheet as a deduction from total stockholders' equity. The stock is not retired; it is only held temporarily "in the treasury" to be distributed later as a part of an employee stock purchase plan or as an executive bonus or for use in an acquisition of another company. Cash dividends are not paid on shares held in the treasury; cash dividends are distributed only to the shares outstanding (in the hands of stockholders), and treasury stock is not outstanding stock. Treasury stock is usually of minor significance in the financial picture of a corporation.

☐ Reserves and Funds

Accountants frequently use the term **reserve** in their reports. To a lay-person, reserve normally means setting aside a specific amount of cash or securities for a special purpose such as vacations, illness, and birthday gifts. Accountants *never* use the word *reserve* to describe such an amount; instead they call such assets a **fund.** For example, a *pension fund* is cash or other highly liquid assets segregated for meeting the pension obligations. Similarly, a *sinking fund* is usually cash or securities segregated for meeting obligations on bonded debt. Holiday Inns, Inc., has a *construction fund* for building new hotels.

The word *reserve* is on the wane, but it is used frequently enough to warrant an acquaintance with its three broad meanings in accounting:

1. *Retained income reserve.* A restriction of intent or authority to *declare* dividends, denoted by a specific subdivision of retained income. The term *appropriated* or *restricted* is better terminology than reserve. Examples are reserves for contingencies (which can refer to any possible *future* losses from such miscellany as foreign devaluations of currency, lawsuits, and natural disasters) and reserves for self-insurance (which refer to possible *future* losses from fires or other casualty losses). This reserve is *not* a reduction of total retained income; it is merely an earmarking or subdividing of part of retained income. The 1982 annual report of R. J. Reynolds Industries (Winston, Camel, Del Monte brands) provides an illustration in the stockholders' equity section:

   > Earnings retained (of which $1.36 billion
   > is restricted as to dividend payments) $3.45 billion

2. *Asset valuation.* An offset to an asset. Examples: reserves for depreciation, depletion, uncollectible accounts, or reduction of inventory or investments to market value. "Allowance for . . ." is much better terminology.

3. *Liability.* An estimate of a definite liability of indefinite or uncertain amount. Examples: reserves for income taxes, warranties, pensions, and vacation pay. "Estimated liability for . . ." is much better terminology. An example of a liability reserve is provided by the annual report of Pitney-Bowes, Inc. (the major manufacturer of postage meters). It contains the following liability account: Reserve for Future Windup Costs of Discontinued Operations.

INCOME STATEMENT

☐ Use of Subtotals

Most investors are vitally concerned about the company's ability to produce long-run earnings and dividends. In this regard, income statements are much more important than balance sheets. The income statement is

EXHIBIT
18-3

THE GREEN CO.
Statement of Income
For the Year Ended December 31, 19X1
(In thousands of dollars)

Sales		$55,000
Cost of goods sold		40,000
Gross profit on sales		$15,000
Operating expenses:		
Selling expenses	$8,900	
Administrative expenses	2,000	
Depreciation expense	1,000	11,900
Operating income		$ 3,100
Interest expense		800
Income before income taxes		$ 2,300
Income taxes		1,150
Net income		$ 1,150
Earnings per share of common stock		$5.27*

*Computation of earnings per share:

Net income	$1,150,000
Deduct preferred dividends	96,000
Net income for holders of common stock	$1,054,000
Divide by common shares	200,000
Earnings per share of common stock	$5.27

straightforward and, for the most part, is stated in terms of current dollars. Revenue is shown first; this represents the total sales value of products delivered and services rendered to customers. Expenses are then listed and deducted. The statement can take two major forms: single-step and multiple-step. The single-step statement merely lists all expenses without drawing subtotals, whereas the multiple-step statement contains one or more subtotals, as illustrated in Exhibit 18-3.

Subtotals often highlight significant relationships. As explained in the preceding chapter, sometimes cost of goods sold is deducted from sales to show gross profit or gross margin. This indicates the size of the margin above merchandise costs—an important statistic for many managers and analysts.

Depreciation expense, various selling expenses, and various administrative expenses are often grouped as "operating expenses" and deducted from the gross profit to obtain *operating income*, which is also called *operating profit*. (Of course, cost of goods sold can actually be viewed as an operating expense because it is also deducted from sales revenue to obtain "operating income.")

❑ Operating and Financial Management

Operating income is a popular subtotal because of the oft-made distinction between operating management and financial management. *Operating management* is mainly concerned with the major day-to-day activities that generate sales revenue (that is, utilizing a given set of resources). In contrast, *financial management* is mainly concerned with where to get cash and how to use cash for the benefit of the entity (that is, obtaining and investing the needed capital). Examples of questions of financial management include: How much cash should be held in checking accounts? Should we pay a dividend? Should we borrow or issue common stock? The best managements perform both operating management and financial management superbly. However, many managers are superior operating managers and inferior financial managers, or vice versa.

Because interest expense is usually a result of financial rather than operating decisions, it appears as a separate item after operating income. In this way, comparisons of operating income between years and between companies are facilitated. Some companies make heavy use of debt, which causes high interest expenses, whereas other companies incur little debt and interest expenses.

❏ Income, Earnings, Profits

Although this book does tend to use *income* most often, the terms *income, earnings,* and *profits* are often used as synonyms. The income statement is also called the *statement of earnings,* the *statement of profit and loss,* and the *P & L statement.* For some strange reason, many companies, as illustrated in Exhibits 18-3 and 18-4, will use net *income* on their income statements but will refer to retained income as retained *earnings.*

The term *net income* is the residual after deducting income taxes. The term "net" is seldom used for any subtotals that precede the calculation of net income; instead, the subtotals are called "income." Thus the appropriate term is "operating income" or "income from operations," not "net operating income."

Income taxes are often a prominent expense and are not merely listed with operating expenses. Instead, income taxes are often deducted as a separate item immediately before net income.

STATEMENT OF RETAINED EARNINGS

The analysis of the changes in retained earnings is frequently placed in a separate statement, the **statement of retained earnings,** also called **statement of retained income.** As Exhibit 18-4 demonstrates, the

EXHIBIT
18-4

Understanding
Corporate
Annual
Reports—
Part One

569

THE GREEN CO.
Statement of Retained Earnings
For the Year Ended December 31, 19X1
(In thousands of dollars)

Retained earnings, December 31, 19X0		$ 900
Net income (Exhibit 18-3)		1,150
Total		$2,050
Deduct dividends:		
On preferred stock	$ 96	
On common stock	954	1,050
Retained earnings, December 31, 19X1		$1,000

major reasons for changes in retained income are dividends and net income. Note especially that dividends are *not* expenses. They are not deductions in computing net income, as Chapter 17 explained in more detail. (This is a long chapter. Solve problems one through five, p. 583, before proceeding.)

STATEMENT OF CHANGES IN FINANCIAL POSITION

❑ Concept of Changes Statement

In 1971, in *Opinion No. 19*, the Accounting Principles Board added another financial report to its requirements. A **statement of changes in financial position** must be presented as a basic financial statement in corporate annual reports. Before 1971, the statement was most widely known as a **statement of sources and applications of funds.** For brevity in the ensuing discussion, the statement will frequently be called a **changes statement.** Many accountants call it a *funds statement;* the term is convenient, but not descriptive.

The major purpose of the statement of changes in financial position is to provide a detailed presentation of the results of financial management, as distinguished from operating management. The changes statement summarizes the financing and investing activities of the enterprise. The statement shows directly information that readers of financial reports could otherwise obtain only by makeshift analysis and interpretation of published balance sheets and statements of income and retained income.

Balance sheets are statements of financial position, whereas changes statements are obviously statements of *changes* in financial position. Balance sheets show the status at a day in time. In contrast, changes statements, income statements, and retained income statements cover periods of time; they provide the explanations of why the balance sheet items have changed. This linkage may be depicted as shown in the accompanying diagram:

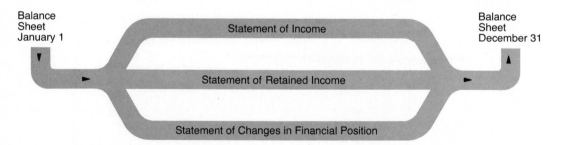

Balance Sheet January 1 — Statement of Income — Statement of Retained Income — Statement of Changes in Financial Position — Balance Sheet December 31

The overall idea of the statement of changes in financial position may be most easily summarized by calling it a *where got, where gone statement*, a term used to describe the statement in its early stages of development. It was devised to provide the reader with a glimpse of where the resources came from during the year and where they have gone.

Focus on Working Capital

The statement of changes in financial position is still in its infancy as a required major financial report. It is undergoing experimentation as more experience is being gained with it. There has been longstanding disagreement on the concept and format of the changes statement. By far the most popular approach has been to view it as an explanation of why **working capital** has changed for a given period. The probable reason that the changes statement has focused on working capital is the perspective it provides on the entire natural operating cycle rather than just one part thereof (such as cash or cash plus receivables).

Accountants define *working capital* as the excess of current assets over current liabilities. Pure, unrestricted cash is working capital in its finest sense. However, *working capital* is broader than *cash* alone. It is a "net" concept; that is, it is the *difference* between a particular category of assets and the related category of liabilities.

As used in a statement of changes in financial position, working capital is a residual concept, a relatively abstract idea. You cannot borrow it or spend it. Working capital, sometimes called net current assets, is akin to net assets (which equals stockholders' equity). The only difference is that working capital is confined to current assets minus current liabilities, whereas stockholders' equity encompasses all assets minus all liabilities.

Typical Sources and Uses

Most changes statements have displayed the sources and uses of working capital, as follows:

Sources of working capital (or working capital provided):
   Operations (excess of revenue over charges against revenue requiring working capital)
   Sale of noncurrent assets (plant, equipment, long-term investments in securities)
   Issuance of long-term debt
   Issuance of capital stock

Uses of working capital (or working capital applied):
   Declaration of cash dividends
   Purchase of noncurrent assets (plant, equipment, long-term investments in securities)
   Reduction of long-term debt
   Repurchase of outstanding capital stock

Financial analysts have cited the following useful information as being revealed by a changes statement: the major sources from which working capital has been obtained (that is, profitable operations, borrowing, sale of capital stock); clues as to the financial management habits of the executives (that is, management attitudes toward spending and financing); the proportion of working capital applied to plant, dividends, debt retirement, and so forth; indications of the impact of working capital flows upon

Understanding
Corporate
Annual
Reports—
Part One

571

future dividend-paying probabilities; and an indication of the company's trend toward general financial strength or weakness.

❑ Example of Changes Statement

The preparation of a changes statement can become complex in some instances, but the basic ideas are straightforward. Generally, as the example will show, a changes statement can simply be prepared from a visual inspection of the changes in balance sheet items, the use of a few additional facts, and a familiarity with the typical sources and uses of working capital listed above.

Consider the example of the B Company, which had the following condensed income statement for 19X2:

B COMPANY
Statement of income
For the Year Ended December 31, 19X2
(In thousands)

Sales		$200
Deduct expenses:		
Expenses requiring working capital	$140	
Depreciation	17	157
Net income		$ 43

[handwritten: haven't collected all Receivables during the yr]

The B Company had the following condensed balance sheets (in thousands of dollars):

[handwritten: bought more INV]

	DECEMBER 31 19X2	DECEMBER 31 19X1	CHANGE		DECEMBER 31 19X2	DECEMBER 31 19X1	CHANGE
Current assets:				Current			
Cash	$ 5	$ 25	$ (20)	liabilities	$100	$ 10	+$ 90
Net receivables	45	25	20	Long-term debt	105	5	100
Inventories	100	60	40	Total liabilities	$205	$ 15	$190
Total current assets	$150	$110	$ 40	Stockholders' equity	425	315	110
Plant assets, net of accumulated depreciation	480	220	260				
Total assets	$630	$330	$300	Total equities	$630	$330	$300

Additional information: In 19X2 the company issued long-term debt and capital stock for cash of $100,000 and $87,000, respectively. Cash dividends were $20,000. New equipment was acquired for $277,000 cash.

Because the changes statement explains the *causes* for the change in working capital, the first step is to compute the amount of the change (which represents the net *effect*):

	DECEMBER 31	
	19X2	19X1
Current assets	$150	$110
Current liabilities	100	10
Working capital	$ 50	$100
Net decrease in working capital		$50

Exhibit 18-5 illustrates how this computation is usually shown in detail in the second part of the changes statement in the section called *changes in components of working capital*.

When business expansion occurs, as in this case where there is a strong working-capital position at the outset, working capital will probably decline. Why? Because the managers tend to postpone paying short-term payables as long as seems prudent. Cash balances will also tend to fall to a bare minimum because the cash is usually needed for investment in various business assets required for expansion.

The statement in Exhibit 18-5 gives a direct picture of where the working capital came from and where it has gone. In this instance, the excess of uses over sources reduced working capital by $50,000. Without the statement of changes, the readers of the annual report would have to conduct their own analysis of the balance sheets, income statement, and statement of retained income to get a grasp of the impact of financial management decisions.

Changes in Balance Sheet Equation

The balance sheet equation is again useful because it can provide the conceptual framework underlying the statement of changes in financial position. Consider the following:

$$\text{assets} = \text{liabilities} + \text{stockholders' equity}$$

$$\begin{aligned}\text{current assets (CA)} + \\ \text{noncurrent assets (NCA)} = \ &\text{current liabilities (CL)} + \\ &\text{noncurrent liabilities (NCL)} + \\ &\text{paid-in capital (PC)} + \text{retained} \\ &\text{income (RI)}\end{aligned}$$

$$CA - CL = NCL + PC + RI - NCA$$

therefore, working capital (WC),
which is $CA - CL = NCL + PC + RI - NCA$

Change (Δ) in working capital between balance sheet dates:

$$\Delta WC = \Delta NCL + \Delta PC + \Delta RI - \Delta NCA$$

or

change in working capital = change in all nonworking capital accounts

EXHIBIT 18-5

B COMPANY
Statement of Changes in Financial Position
For the Year Ended December 31, 19X2
(In thousands of dollars)

SOURCES AND USES OF WORKING CAPITAL

[handwritten: Dep NI NI 17+43]

Sources:
Working capital provided by operations (Schedule A)	$ 60
Issuance of long-term debt	100
Issuance of additional capital stock	87
Total sources	$247

Uses:
Payment of cash dividends	$ 20	
Acquisition of plant and equipment	277	
Total uses		297
Decrease in working capital		$ (50)

CHANGES IN COMPONENTS OF WORKING CAPITAL

	DECEMBER 31 19X2	DECEMBER 31 19X1	INCREASE (DECREASE) IN WORKING CAPITAL
Current assets:			
Cash	$ 5	$ 25	$(20)
Net receivables	45	25	20
Inventories	100	60	40
Total current assets	$150	$110	$ 40
Current liabilities (detailed)	100	10	(90)
Working capital	$ 50	$100	
Decrease in working capital			$(50)

SCHEDULE A
WORKING CAPITAL PROVIDED BY OPERATIONS

First Alternative Presentation (Using the Addback Method):
Net income (from income statement)	$ 43
Add: Charges against income not requiring working capital:	
Depreciation	17
Working capital provided by operations	$ 60

Second Alternative Presentation* (Using the Straightforward Method):
Sales	$200
Deduct: All expenses requiring working capital (detailed)	140
Working capital provided by operations	$ 60

*Although the straightforward method is frequently easier to understand, the addback method is used almost exclusively in annual reports. Be sure you see why each method produces the same figure, $60.

or

what happened to working capital = why it happened

The statement of changes in financial position focuses on the *changes in the nonworking capital accounts* (that is, the *noncurrent accounts*) as a way of explaining how and *why* the level of working capital has gone up or down during a given period. Thus the major changes in the accounts on the right-hand side of the above equation appear in the statement of changes in financial position as *causes* of the change in working capital. The left side of the equation measures the *net effect* of the change in working capital.

Applying the equation to our data, we can see, step by step, how the changes statement in Exhibit 18-5 is based on the same theoretical foundation that underlies the other financial statements (in thousands of dollars):

	ΔWC	=	ΔNCL	+	ΔPC	+	ΔRI	−	ΔNCA
Sales	+200	=					+200		
Expenses requiring working capital	−140	=					−140		
Working capital provided by operations	+60	=					+60		
Expense not requiring working capital: depreciation	0	=					−17	−	(−17)
Net income, a subtotal							+43		
Issuance of long-term debt	+100	=	+100						
Issuance of capital stock	+87	=			+87				
Cash dividends	−20	=					−20		
Acquisition of new equipment	−277	=						−	(+277)
Net changes	−50	=	+100		+87		+23	−	(+260)

$$-50$$

When statements become complicated, accountants prefer to use work sheets or T-accounts to help their analysis. In any event, the totals shown in the tabulation indicate that all transactions affecting working capital have been accounted for. The $50,000 *change* in working capital is explained by the *changes* in the nonworking capital accounts. Each noncurrent account can be analyzed in detail if desired.

☐ Steps in Preparation

Although balance sheet equations, T-accounts, or work sheets are frequently helpful, the statement of changes in financial position can also be prepared in a less-formal way:

1. Prepare a schedule of changes in the components of working capital. (See the second section of Exhibit 18-5.)
2. Prepare the sources section, which customarily starts with working capital provided by operations. (See the top part of Exhibit 18-5.)
3. Determine other sources and uses of working capital by gathering additional information (given in this illustration). In an actual case, the keys to this approach are (a) to know the typical sources and uses and (b) to search systematically for them through the annual report.
4. If all the necessary information is not directly available, the changes should be analyzed for all balance sheet items *except* current assets and current liabilities. To illustrate such analysis, consider the B Company balance sheets on page 572:

a. The change in long-term debt is an increase of $105,000 − $5,000 = $100,000. The indication is that additional long-term debt was issued, a source of working capital.
b. The change in stockholders' equity was an increase of $425,000 − $315,000 = $110,000, to be explained. What are the typical explanations for

Understanding
Corporate
Annual
Reports—
Part One

575

changes in stockholders' equity? Issuances of capital stock, net income (or loss), and dividends. Thus:

$$\text{net increase} = \text{new issuance} + \text{net income} - \text{dividends}$$
$$\$110,000 = \text{new issuance} + \$43,000 - \$20,000$$
$$\text{new issuance} = \$110,000 - \$43,000 + \$20,000$$
$$\text{new issuance} = \$87,000, \text{ a source of working capital}[3]$$

c. Turning to uses, the only other noncurrent account not fully explained is net plant assets. The net change is an increase of $480,000 - $220,000 = $260,000. Changes therein are usually explained by assets acquired, asset disposals (none in this example), and depreciation expense for the period:

$$\text{net increase} = \text{acquisitions} - \text{disposals} - \text{depreciation expense}$$
$$\$260,000 = \text{acquisitions} - 0 - \$17,000$$
$$\text{acquisitions} = \$260,000 + \$17,000$$
$$\text{acquisitions} = \$277,000, \text{ a use or application of working capital}[4]$$

5. The difference between the total sources and uses of working capital is the net change in working capital, which must agree with the amount computed in step 1, a $50,000 decrease in this illustration.

6. APB *Opinion No. 19* requires that major financing and investing activities be included in the changes statement even though working capital is unaffected. For example, the statement would show the acquisition of a building (a use) in exchange for the issuance of capital stock (a source). Other examples are the exchanging of one type of long-term debt for another, the conversion of long-term debt into common stock, and the swapping of plant assets. Our illustration does not include such transactions.

❏ Working Capital Provided by Operations

The first major item in the sources section is **working capital provided by operations.** There are two ways to compute the amount of this item: the **addback method** and the **straightforward method,** shown in Schedule A of Exhibit 18-5. Because it is easier to understand, please initially consider the *straightforward method.* Sales to customers are almost always *the* major source of working capital. Correspondingly, outlays for cost of goods sold and operating expenses are almost always *the* major uses of working capital. The excess of sales over all the expenses requiring working capital is, by definition, the working capital provided by operations. The direct way to compute this figure is shown as the second alternative presentation in Schedule A, sales of $200,000 minus expenses of $140,000 equals working capital provided by operations, $60,000.

An alternative, often convenient, way to compute working capital

---

[3] The $87,000 new issuance was disclosed in the given data. Even if the $87,000 were not specifically revealed, it could be deduced from the other known amounts, as shown above in the equation approach.

[4] Here again, the amount was included in the given data, but if it were not, it could be computed in the manner demonstrated above in the equation approach.

provided by operations is to begin with net income. Then adjust for those items that entered the computation of net income but did *not* affect working capital. This can be called the *addback method.* Using the balance sheet equation, compare the two methods:

EFFECTS OF OPERATIONS	ΔWC	$= \Delta$NCL $+ \Delta$PC $+ \Delta$RI	$- \Delta$NCA
Straightforward method:			
Sales	+200,000 =	+200,000	
Expenses requiring working capital	−140,000 =	−140,000	
Expenses not requiring working capital:			
depreciation	0 =	−17,000 − (−17,000)	
Working capital provided by operations	+60,000 =	+43,000 − (−17,000)	
Addback method:			
Begin with net income	+43,000 =	+43,000	
Add charges to income not requiring			
working capital: depreciation*	+17,000 =	− (−17,000)	
Working capital provided by operations	+60,000 =	+43,000 − (−17,000)	

*The depreciation of $17,000 was *deducted* in computing the net income of $43,000. Its effect on the equation was to decrease RI and decrease NCA, so it had *no effect* on working capital. Therefore, unless the $17,000 is added back to net income, working capital provided by operations would be understated as being $43,000 instead of $60,000. Note that both methods have the same final effects on net changes in the equation.

As the footnote to Schedule A indicates, the first alternative presentation, here called the *addback method,* is used almost exclusively in annual reports even though it may require a bit more effort to understand. The usual presentation would omit Schedule A and include its content in the body of the changes statement as follows:

Sources:	
Net income	$ 43,000
Add charges not requiring working capital:	
Depreciation	17,000
Working capital provided by operations	$ 60,000
Other sources:	
Issuance of long-term debt	100,000
Issuance of additional capital stock	87,000
Total sources	$247,000

If the addback method is somewhat more difficult to fathom, why is it used so heavily? There are two main reasons besides the unsatisfying reason: "Because we've always done it that way." First, beginning with net income shows the important link with the income statement. Second, the straightforward method (which begins with sales) can require a detailed listing of expenses that is cumbersome and duplicates much of what is already contained in the income statement. The addback method is really a short-cut computation of the target number, working capital provided by operations.

Understanding
Corporate
Annual
Reports—
Part One

577

❏ Role of Depreciation

The most crucial aspect of a changes statement is how **depreciation** and other expenses that do not require working capital relate to the flow of working capital. There is widespread misunderstanding of the role of depreciation in financial reporting, so let us examine this point in detail.

Accountants view depreciation as an allocation of historical cost to expense. Therefore depreciation expense does not entail a current outflow of resources in the form of cash, which is the prime form of working capital. Exhibit 18-6 shows the typical relationship of current operations to the production of working capital. Net income is a residual; by itself, it provides no working capital. Instead of beginning with the Sales total and working down, accountants usually start with Net Income and work up (E + D = $60,000 in Exhibit 18-6) by adding back all charges not requiring working capital, as previously explained.

Unfortunately, the use of this shortcut method may at first glance create an erroneous impression that depreciation is, by itself, a source of working capital. If that were really true, a corporation could merely double or triple its bookkeeping entry for depreciation expense when working capital was badly needed! What would happen? Working capital provided by operations would be unaffected. Suppose that depreciation in Exhibit 18-6 is doubled:

Sales	$200,000
Less: All expenses requiring working capital (detailed)	140,000
Working capital provided by operations	$ 60,000
Less: Depreciation	34,000
Net income	$ 26,000

The doubling affects depreciation *and* net income, but it has no direct influence on working capital provided by operations, which, of course, still amounts to $60,000, the sum of net income and depreciation.

FOCUS ON CASH

❏ Computing Cash Provided by Operations

Although the focus on working capital is favored by the vast majority of reporting companies, there is a definite trend toward changing the focus to cash or cash plus short-term investments. For instance, a sample of 170 annual reports for 1981 revealed that 55 focused on the latter, using a variety of formats. This change in focus represented an increase of 34 companies in one year; it was in response to the FASB's and SEC's emphasis on cash information. Among the companies that now focus on cash are Westinghouse, Xerox, and Nabisco Brands.

There are many possible ways for the changes statement to focus on cash rather than working capital. Probably the easiest format is shown in Exhibit 18-7. The steps are identical to the working capital focus. However,

EXHIBIT
18-6

Analysis of Income Statement to Show Effects of Operations on Working Capital	
Sales	$200,000 (A)
Less: All expenses requiring working capital (detailed)	140,000 (B)
Working capital provided by operations	$ 60,000 (C)
Less: Depreciation	17,000 (D)
Net income	$ 43,000 (E)

Note: Figures are from the preceding example. In this example, depreciation is the only expense not requiring working capital.

the increases (or decreases) in noncash working capital items are deducted from (or added to) the working capital from operations to obtain cash provided by operations. In Exhibit 18-7, $30 is added to $60 to obtain the $90 cash provided by operations.

EXHIBIT
18-7

B COMPANY
Statement of Changes in Financial Position (Cash)
For the Year Ended December 31, 19X2
(In thousands of dollars)

SOURCES AND USES OF CASH

Sources:		
Net income	$ 43	
Add charges not requiring working capital: Depreciation or amortization	17	
Working capital provided by operations	$ 60	
Add net decrease in noncash working capital (see components)	30	
Cash provided by operations*		$ 90
Issuance of long-term debt		100
Issuance of additional capital stock		87
Total sources		$277
Uses:		
Payment of cash dividends	$ 20	
Acquisition of plant and equipment	277	
Total uses		297
Decrease in cash		$ (20)
Cash, December 31, 19X1		25
Cash, December 31, 19X2		$ 5

CHANGES IN COMPONENTS OF NONCASH WORKING CAPITAL

	DECEMBER 31		INCREASE (DECREASE) IN NONCASH WORKING CAPITAL
	19X2	19X1	
Net receivables	$ 45	$ 25	$ 20
Inventories	100	60	40
Current liabilities (detailed)	100	10	(90)
Decrease in noncash working capital			$(30)

*Frequently called *cash flow from operations* or just plain *cash flow*.

Compare Exhibits 18-7 and 18-5 (p. 574):

1. Working capital provided by operations is converted to *cash provided by operations*. As the schedule of changes in components of noncash working capital indicates, increases in receivables and inventories mean that operating cash has been invested therein, so the resulting cash provided by operations would decline. For example, cash provided by operations is diminished by the immediate reinvestment of cash collections in the expansion of inventory.

On the other hand, increases in current liabilities such as trade accounts payable, short-term bank loans, and various accruals have favorable effects on operating cash. For example, cash provided by operations is increased by a ninety-day bank loan, and drains on cash are postponed when suppliers give credit instead of demanding immediate payment.

In a nutshell, when cash is tied up in inventories, it cannot be used to pay creditors. Therefore, when inventories go up, cash provided by operations goes down. In contrast, when a company has less receivables and more payables, it has more cash.

Some typical adjustments to convert from working capital provided by operations to cash provided by operations are:

Add
    Increases in current liabilities
    Decreases in noncash current assets
Deduct
    Decreases in current liabilities
    Increases in noncash current assets

2. The schedule of components of noncash working capital is similar to the schedule of components of working capital. The only difference is that cash is excluded and moved to the upper section of the changes statement, which ends with a summary of the changes in cash.

❏ Cash Flow

Rampant inflation in recent years has engendered many criticisms of the historical cost/nominal dollar accrual measures of income and financial position. One response, as Chapter 20 describes, has been supplementary disclosures using constant dollars and current costs. Another response has been a more intense focus on cash provided by operations and a trend toward focusing on cash rather than working capital in the statement of changes in financial position. Synonyms have arisen for *cash provided by operations,* most notably *cash flow,* which is shortened nomenclature for *cash flow from operations.* These terms are used interchangeably, but *cash flow* is used most frequently. The importance of cash flow was stressed by Harold Williams, the former chairman of the Securities and Exchange Commission: "If I had to make a forced choice between having earnings information and having cash flow information, today I would take cash flow information.''[5]

Some companies like to stress a **cash-flow-per-share** figure (or a working-capital-generated-per-share figure) and provide it in addition to the required earnings-per-share figure. Cash flow per share and working capital provided by operations per share are sometimes erroneously used as synonyms. Net income is an attempt to summarize management performance. Cash flow or working capital provided by operations gives an incomplete picture of that performance because it ignores noncash expenses that are just as important as cash expenses for judging overall company performance. Moreover, such reported cash flows per share say nothing about the funds needed for replacement and expansion of facilities, thus seeming to imply that the entire per-share cash flows from operations may be available for cash dividends. Because they give an incomplete picture, cash-flow-per-share figures can be quite misleading. They should be interpreted cautiously.

DEPRECIATION, INCOME TAXES, AND WORKING CAPITAL

A major objective of this chapter is to pinpoint the relationships between depreciation expense, income tax expense, cash as a major item of working capital, and accumulated depreciation. Too often, these relationships are confused. For instance, the business press frequently contains misleading quotations such as the following: ''. . . we're looking for financing $3.75 billion. Of that, about 60% will be recovered in depreciation and amortization.'' Accountants quarrel with such phrasing because depreciation itself is not a direct source of cash, as we saw earlier in this chapter.

To encourage investment in plant and equipment, federal income tax laws permit faster write-offs for depreciation than straight-line. These faster write-offs, called **accelerated depreciation,** take a variety of forms. For example, for most plant and equipment placed in service after 1980, the United States income tax laws specify an Accelerated Cost Recovery System (ACRS). In essence, ACRS bases depreciation deductions on arbitrary ''recovery'' periods rather than on estimated useful lives. Terminal values are ignored. Moreover, ACRS spreads the depreciation deductions so that higher amounts are taken in the earlier years than in the later years of the prescribed lives.

Depreciation is a deductible noncash expense for income tax purposes. Hence the higher the depreciation allowed to be deducted in any given year, the lower the taxable income and the cash disbursements for income taxes. In short, if depreciation expense is higher, more cash is conserved and kept for various uses. Therefore, compared with the straight-line method, accelerated depreciation methods result in a higher cash balance *after* income tax. Compare an accelerated method with the straight-line method, using assumed numbers. In this case, assume that the ACRS

Understanding
Corporate
Annual
Reports—
Part One

581

[5] *Forbes*, February 2, 1981, p. 69. Also see ''A Better Yardstick,'' *Forbes*, September 27, 1982, p. 66.

schedules provide a $28,000 deduction instead of the $17,000 deduction under straight-line depreciation:

	STRAIGHT-LINE DEPRECIATION	ACCELERATED DEPRECIATION
(C) Income before depreciation	$60,000	$60,000
Depreciation deduction on income tax return	17,000	28,000
Income before income taxes	$43,000	$32,000
(T) Income taxes @ 40%	17,200	12,800
Net income	$25,800	$19,200
Net after-tax working capital provided by operations:		
C − T = $60,000 − $17,200 =	$42,800	
= $60,000 − $12,800 =		$47,200

Some strange results occur here. The reported net income is *lower* under accelerated depreciation than under straight-line depreciation, but the cash balance is *higher*. Thus, suppose managers were forced to use one depreciation method for all purposes. Managers who are concerned about reported net income to shareholders may prefer straight-line to accelerated depreciation. This dilemma is not faced by managers in the United States, where straight-line depreciation is often used for shareholder purposes while accelerated depreciation is used for income tax purposes. (See page 563 for additional explanation.)

There is only one source of working capital provided by operations: *sales to customers*. As our example shows, the effect of more depreciation on cash or working capital is *indirect*: it reduces income taxes by 40% of the extra depreciation deduction of $11,000, or $4,400. Therefore accelerated depreciation keeps more cash in the business for a longer span of time because of the postponement of disbursements for income taxes.

Consider the account for accumulated depreciation. No cash is there. It is a negative asset, a hole in the doughnut regardless of whether income tax rates are zero, 20%, or 90%.

Summary

This chapter explained the meaning of the account titles most often found in the major financial statements. Accountants have narrow meanings for many of their terms, including **funds, reserves, working capital, depreciation,** and others. In particular, the term **depreciation** is misunderstood. Unless these terms are clear, the user is likely to misinterpret financial reports.

Statements of changes in financial position, also (less accurately) called **funds statements,** are increasing in importance because they yield direct insights into the financial management policies of a company. They also directly explain why a company with high net income may nevertheless be unable to pay dividends because of the weight of other financial commitments to plant expansion or retirement of debt.

Summary
Problems for Your Review _____

Problem One

"The book value of plant assets is the amount that would be spent today for their replacement." Do you agree? Explain.

Problem Two

On December 31, 19X1, a magazine publishing company receives $300,000 in cash for three-year subscriptions. This is regarded as deferred revenue. Show the balances in that account at December 31, 19X2, 19X3, and 19X4. How much revenue would be earned in each of those three years?

Problem Three

"A reserve for depreciation provides cash for the replacement of fixed assets." Do you agree? Explain.

Problem Four

"A reserve for taxes is cash set aside in a special bank account so that the cash is readily available when taxes are due." Do you agree? Explain.

Problem Five

"A reserve for contingencies is cash earmarked for use in case of losses on lawsuits or fires." Do you agree? Explain.

Problem Six

1. Using Exhibits 18-1, 18-3, and 18-4, prepare a statement of changes in financial position for the Green Company. Focus on working capital. See pp. 558, 568–9.
2. In your own words, explain why working capital declined. What other sources of funds are likely to be available?

Solution to Problem One

Net book value of the plant assets is the result of deducting accumulated depreciation from original cost. This process does not attempt to capture all the technological and economic events that may affect replacement value. Consequently, there is little likelihood that net book value will approximate replacement cost.

❑ Solution to Problem Two

The balance in Deferred Revenue would decline at the rate of $100,000 yearly; $100,000 would be recognized as earned revenue in each of three years.

❑ Solution to Problem Three

Reserve for depreciation is a synonym for *accumulated depreciation.* It is a negative asset, an offset to or deduction from original cost. It is a "hole in a doughnut" and in no way represents a direct stockpile of cash for replacement.

❑ Solution to Problem Four

Reserve for taxes is a liability reserve, not a fund gathered for a particular purpose. It is a misleading label because it means "estimated income taxes payable." This does not preclude the establishment of a special *fund* if one is desired, although this is seldom done in practice.

❑ Solution to Problem Five

Reserve for contingencies is a retained income reserve, a formal restriction of intent or authority to *declare* dividends, often made voluntarily by a board of directors. Its purpose is to warn stockholders that future dividend possibilities are constrained by future possible events that might bear sad economic consequences.

Often restrictions of authority to *declare* dividends are the result of legal agreements with bondholders or other creditors who do not want resources paid to shareholders in the form of dividends until creditor claims are met.

❑ Solution to Problem Six

1.

GREEN CO.
Statement of Changes in Financial Position
For the Year Ended December 31, 19X1

Sources:		
Net income	$ 1,150,000	
Add charges against income not requiring working capital: depreciation	1,000,000	
Working capital provided by operations		$2,150,000
Other sources		—
Total sources		$ 2,150,000
Applications:		
Purchases of plant and equipment	$ 2,200,000*	
Cash dividends:		
On preferred stock	96,000	
On common stock	954,000	
Total applications		3,250,000
Decrease in working capital (see schedule)		$(1,100,000)

*($7,000,000 − $5,800,000) + depreciation of $1,000,000 = $2,200,000.

CHANGES IN COMPONENTS OF WORKING CAPITAL		
	19X1	19X0
Current assets:		
Cash	$ 2,600,000	$ 2,200,000
Temporary investments in marketable securities	600,000	600,000
Receivables, net	5,300,000	5,100,000
Inventories	14,600,000	14,400,000
Prepaid expenses	600,000	600,000
Total current assets	$23,700,000	$22,900,000
Current liabilities:		
Notes payable	$ 3,900,000	$ 2,800,000
Accounts payable	3,200,000	2,400,000
Accrued expenses payable	1,600,000	1,700,000
Accrued income taxes payable	500,000	400,000
Total current liabilities	$ 9,200,000	$ 7,300,000
Working capital	$14,500,000	$15,600,000
Decrease in working capital (explained above)		($1,100,000)

2. The decline in working capital came from the inability to generate enough working capital from operations to cover expenditures for plant and equipment and dividends. In view of the pressure on working capital, we may question the wisdom of paying a $954,000 cash dividend to common shareholders. Other sources of working capital might be sales of long-term investments, if any; sales of plant and equipment; issuance of long-term debt; or sale of capital stock.

Highlights to Remember

1. Traditionally, accountants have accounted for *costs* (measured by historical outlays) rather than *values* (measured by what might be paid or received for individual assets at the current date).
2. For a given year, the accrual basis of accounting will produce different measures of income than the cash basis.
3. Most controversies in accounting center on when revenue is earned or when costs expire and become expenses. In particular, many disputes arise over how and when the costs of inventories and equipment should be released as expenses.
4. Pinpoint the relationships of depreciation to cash. Moreover, "generally accepted accounting principles" pertain mainly to reports to shareholders. In contrast, reports to income tax authorities must be in accord with laws and regulations.

Accounting Vocabulary

Accelerated Cost Recovery System (ACRS); accelerated depreciation; accumulated depreciation; addback method; amortization; book value; changes statement; common stock; deferred charges; depreciation; fixed assets; funds provided by operations; funds statement; goodwill; intangible assets; legal value; long-lived assets; marketable securities; operating cycle; par value; preferred stock; prepaid expenses; reserve; residual value; scrap value; stated value; statement of changes in financial position; statement of retained earnings; statement of retained income; statement of sources and applications of funds; straightforward method; tangible assets; terminal value; trademarks; working capital; working capital provided by operations.

Fundamental Assignment Material

❏ General Coverage

Note: Instructors who prefer to focus on cash rather than working capital may wish to assign one or more of Problems 18–49, 18–50, and 18–51.

18–1. Changes statement. (Alternate is 18–47.) The R Company has the following balance sheets (in millions of dollars):

	AS OF DECEMBER 31			AS OF DECEMBER 31	
	19X4	19X3		19X4	19X3
Current assets (detailed)	$ 95	$ 80	Current liabilities (detailed)	$ 50	$ 45
Fixed assets (net of depreciation)	60	40	Long-term debt	5	—
Goodwill	5	10	Stockholders' equity	105	85
	$160	$130		$160	$130

Net income was $25 million. Cash dividends paid were $5 million. Depreciation was $7 million. Half the goodwill was amortized. Fixed assets of $27 million were purchased.

REQUIRED: Prepare a statement of changes in financial position (sources and applications of working capital).

18–2. Prepare statement. (Alternate is 18–48.) G Company had a net income of $80,000 in 19X3. Sales were $990,000; expenses requiring working capital, $790,000; and depreciation, $120,000. G Company had the following balance sheets (in thousands):

	DECEMBER 31			DECEMBER 31	
	19X3	19X2		19X3	19X2
Current assets:			Current liabilities:		
Cash	$ 20	$ 60	Accounts payable	$ 560	$ 300
Net receivables	240	150	Accrued payables	100	10
Inventories	450	350	Total current liabilities	$660	$310
Total current assets	$710	$560	Long-term debt	—	400
Plant assets, net of accumulated depreciation	850	670	Stockholders' equity	900	520
Total assets	$1,560	$1,230	Total equities	$1,560	$1,230

In 19X3 the company issued additional capital stock for $400,000 cash. The long-term debt was retired for cash. Cash dividends declared and paid were $100,000. New equipment was acquired for $300,000 cash.

REQUIRED:

1. Prepare a statement of changes in financial position including two alternative presentations of a supporting schedule of working capital provided by operations.
2. Write a short memorandum summarizing the information contained in the statement.
3. Refer to Requirement 1. Support your financial statement by using a form of the balance sheet equation. Step by step, show in equation form how each item in the changes statement affects working capital.

18–3. **Depreciation and working capital.** Dale Company has the following data for 19X5: All expenses requiring working capital, $610,000; depreciation, $70,000; sales, $880,000. Ignore income taxes.

REQUIRED:

1. Compute working capital provided by operations and net income.
2. Assume that depreciation is tripled. Compute working capital provided by operations and net income.

❑ Understanding Published Financial Reports

18–4. **Cash and working capital provided by operations.** Inland Steel's 1981 annual report included the following items in its "consolidated statement of funds flow" (in thousands):

Net increase in noncash working capital	$ 76,476
Increase (decrease) in cash	(12,709)
Cash provided by operations	161,572
Dividends paid to stockholders	42,837

REQUIRED: | Compute the working capital provided by operations.

Additional
Assignment Material

❑ General Coverage

18–5. "The schedule of changes in components of working capital is an integral part of the statement of changes in financial position." Do you agree? Explain.

18–6. Demonstrate how the fundamental balance sheet equation can be recast to focus on working capital.

18–7. "Cash flow per share (or working capital provided by operations per share) can be downright misleading." Why?

18–8. What are the major sources of working capital? Applications?

18–9. What type of insights are provided by a changes statement?

18–10. Define *funds statement*.

18–11. What is working capital?

18–12. What are some examples of expenses and losses not affecting working capital?

Understanding
Corporate
Annual
Reports—
Part One

587

18–13. What are the two major ways of computing working capital provided by operations?

18–14. "The ordinary purchase of inventory has no effect on working capital." Why?

18–15. "Net losses mean drains on working capital." Do you agree? Explain.

18–16. "Depreciation is usually a big source of working capital." Do you agree? Explain.

18–17. What are some weaknesses of the idea that funds are working capital?

18–18. Give other definitions of *funds*.

18–19. What is the major difference between a statement of changes in financial position that focuses on cash and a statement that focuses on working capital?

18–20. Criticize the following presentation of part of a changes statement:

Sources:	
Sales	$100,000
Less expenses requiring working capital	70,000
Funds provided by operations	$ 30,000

18–21. The gain on the sale of a fixed asset represents part of the working capital received by the X Company. How should this item be presented on a changes statement? Why?

18–22. What are the effects on working capital flows of the following transaction: The purchase of fixed assets at a cost of $100,000, of inventories at a cost of $200,000, and of receivables at a cost of $50,000, paid for by the assumption of a $70,000 mortgage on the fixed assets and the giving of a ninety-day promissory note for $280,000.

18–23. The net income of the Lear Company was $1.5 million. Included on the income statement are the following:

Uninsured loss of inventory, by flood (classified as a part of operating expenses)	$100,000
Gain on the sale of equipment	200,000
Dividend income	10,000
Interest income, including $5,000 not yet received	20,000
Amortization of patents	50,000
Depreciation	400,000

Compute the working capital provided by operations, assuming that interest and dividend income are a part of operating income.

18–24. "Asset valuation reserves are created by charges to stockholders' equity." Do you agree? Explain.

18–25. Why is the term *marketable securities* a misnomer?

18–26. "Accumulated depreciation is a hole in a doughnut." Explain.

18–27. "Accumulated depreciation is a sum of cash being accumulated for the replacement of fixed assets." Do you agree? Explain.

18–28. "Goodwill may have nothing to do with the personality of the manager or employees." Do you agree? Explain.

18–29.   Why should short-term prepaid expenses be classified as current assets?

18–30.   Why are intangible assets and deferred charges usually swiftly amortized?

18–31.   What is a subordinated debenture?

18–32.   "Mortgage bonds are always safer investments than debentures." Do you agree? Explain.

18–33.   What is the role of a par value of stock or bonds?

18–34.   "Common shareholders have limited liability." Explain.

18–35.   "Treasury stock is negative stockholders' equity." Do you agree? Explain.

18–36.   "ACRS helps conserve cash." Do you agree? Explain.

18–37.   What are the three major types of reserves?

18–38.   Enumerate the items most commonly classified as current assets.

18–39.   "Sometimes 100 shares of stock should be classified as current assets and sometimes not." Explain.

18–40.   What is the proper measure for an asset newly acquired through an exchange (e.g., an exchange of land for securities)? Explain.

18–41.   Criticize: "Depreciation is the loss in value of a fixed asset over a given span of time."

18–42.   What factors influence the estimate of useful life in depreciation accounting?

18–43.   "Accountants sometimes are too concerned with physical objects or contractual rights." Explain.

18–44.   How may the distinction between contributed and accumulated capital be blurred by traditional accounting?

18–45.   **Balance sheet classification of reserves and funds.**   Designate whether each of the following is essentially an asset account *(A)*; asset valuation account *(AV)*; liability account *(L)*; or retained earnings acount *(R)*:

1. Reserve for sinking fund
2. Reserve for vacation pay
3. Reserve for possible future losses in foreign operations
4. Sinking fund for retirement of bonds
5. Reserve for employees' bonuses
6. Reserve for purchases of other companies
7. Construction fund
8. Reserve for impending economic recession
9. Reserve for replacement of facilities at higher price levels
10. Reserve to reduce investments from cost to market value

18–46.   **Meaning of book value.**   Y Company purchased an office building twenty years ago for $1 million, $200,000 of which was attributable to land. The mortgage has been fully paid. The current balance sheet follows:

Cash		$400,000	Stockholders'
Land		200,000	equity	$750,000
Building at cost	$800,000		
Accumulated depreciation	650,000		
Book value		150,000	
Total assets		$750,000	

Understanding
Corporate
Annual
Reports—
Part One
589

The company is about to borrow $1.8 million on a first mortgage to modernize and expand the building. This amounts to 60% of the combined appraised value of the land and building before the modernization and expansion.

REQUIRED: Prepare a balance sheet after the loan is made and the building is expanded and modernized. Comment on its significance.

18–47. Changes statement and analysis of growth. (Alternate is 18–1.) The Alvarez Company has the following balance sheets (in millions):

	DECEMBER 31			DECEMBER 31	
	19X7	19X6		19X7	19X6
Current assets:			Current liabilities		
Cash	$ 3	$ 10	(detailed)	$105	$ 30
Receivables, net	60	30	Long-term debt	150	—
Inventories	100	50	Stockholders' equity	208	160
Total current assets	$163	$ 90			
Plant assets (net of accumulated depreciation)	300	100			
Total assets	$463	$190	Total equities	$463	$190

Net income was $54 million. Cash dividends paid were $6 million. Depreciation was $20 million. Fixed assets were purchased for $220 million, $150 million of which was financed via the issuance of long-term debt outright for cash.

Raul Alvarez, the president and majority stockholder, was a superb operating executive. He was an imaginative, aggressive marketing man and an ingenious, creative production man. But he had little patience with financial matters. After examining the most recent balance sheet and income statement he muttered, "We've enjoyed ten years of steady growth; 19X7 was our most profitable ever. Despite such profitability, we're in the worst cash position in our history. Just look at those current liabilities in relation to our available cash! This whole picture of the more you make, the poorer you get just does not make sense. These statements must be cockeyed."

REQUIRED:
1. Prepare a statement of changes in financial position (sources and applications of working capital).
2. Using the changes statement and other information, write a short memorandum to Mr. Alvarez, explaining why there is such a squeeze on cash.

18–48. Prepare changes statement. (Alternate is 18–2.) The Weinberg Co. has assembled the accompanying (a) trial balance and (b) income statement and reconciliation of retained earnings.

Trial Balance, December 31 (in millions)			
	19X2	19X1	CHANGE
debits:			
Cash	$ 10	$ 25	$(15)
Accounts receivable	40	28	12
Inventory	70	50	20
Prepaid general expenses	4	3	1
Plant assets, net	202	150	52
	$326	$256	$ 70

credits:

Accounts payable for merchandise	$ 74	$ 60	$ 14
Accrued property tax payable	3	2	1
Mortgage payable in 19X9	50	—	50
Capital stock	100	100	—
Retained earnings	99	94	5
	$326	$256	$ 70

WEINBERG CO.
Income Statement and Reconciliation of Retained Earnings
For the Year Ended December 31, 19X2 (in millions)

Sales		$250
Less cost of goods sold:		
Inventory, Dec. 31, 19X1	$ 50	
Purchases	160	
Cost of goods available for sale	$210	
Inventory, Dec. 31, 19X2	70	140
Gross profit		$110
Less other expenses:		
General expense	$ 51	
Depreciation	40	
Property taxes	10	101
Net income		$ 9
Dividends		4
Net income of the period retained		$ 5
Retained earnings, Dec. 31, 19X1		94
Retained earnings, Dec. 31, 19X2		$ 99

On December 30, 19X2, Weinberg paid $42 million in cash and signed a $50 million mortgage on a new plant acquired to expand operations. Because net income was $9 million, the highest in the company's history, Ms. Weinberg, the chief executive officer, was distressed by the company's extremely low cash balance.

REQUIRED:

1. Prepare a statement of changes in financial position that focuses on working capital. You may wish to use Exhibit 18-5 as a guide. However, incorporate the First Alternative Presentation (as illustrated there in Schedule A) in the body of your changes statement. That is, the sources section will begin with net income.
2. Redo the sources section (only) in Requirement 1 by incorporating the Second Alternative Presentation (as illustrated in Schedule A of Exhibit 18-5) in the body of your changes statement. That is, the body of the sources section will begin with sales.
3. What is revealed by the statement of changes in financial position? Does it help you reduce Ms. Weinberg's distress? Why?
4. Briefly explain to Ms. Weinberg why cash has decreased even though working capital has increased and net income was $9 million.
5. Refer to Requirement 1. Support your financial statement by using a form of the balance sheet equation. Step by step, show in equation form how each item in the changes statement affects working capital.

18–49. **Focus on cash.** Refer to the facts in Problem 18–2. Prepare a statement of changes in financial position (cash). Then write a short memorandum summarizing the information contained in the statement.

18–50. Focus on cash. Refer to the facts in Problem 18–47. Prepare a statement of changes in financial position (cash). Then briefly explain to Mr. Alvarez why cash has decreased even though net income was $54 million.

18–51. Focus on cash. Refer to the facts in Problem 18–48. Prepare a statement of changes in financial position (cash). Then briefly explain to Ms. Weinberg why cash has decreased even though working capital has risen by $3 million and net income was $9 million.

❑ Understanding Published Financial Reports

18–52. Various intangible assets. Consider the following:

1. (a) Dow Chemical Company's annual report indicated that research and development expenditures were $404 million during 1981. How did this amount affect operating income, which was $916 million? (b) Suppose the entire $404 million arose from outlays for patents acquired from various outside parties on December 30, 1981. What would be the operating income for 1981? (c) How would the Dow balance sheet, December 31, 1981, be affected by *b*?

2. On December 30, 1983, CBS Inc. acquired some new patents on some communications equipment for $10 million. Technology changes quickly. The equipment's useful life is expected to be five years rather than the seventeen-year life of the patent. What will be the amortization for 1984?

3. MGM Grand Hotels has an account classified under *other assets* in its balance sheet called *preoperating costs, net.* Its balance on December 31, 1981, was $2,386,000; 1980, $1,810,000. A footnote said that these costs "are amortized over a five-year period commencing with the opening of the particular hotel." Expenditures for preopening costs in 1981 were $2,000,000. What amount was amortized for 1981?

4. The Times Mirror Company, publisher of many newspapers, such as the *Los Angeles Times,* purchased the *Denver Post* on December 31, 1980, for $95 million. A footnote in the annual report stated that goodwill is "amortized over a period of 40 years." Assume that the Times Mirror could assign only $83 million to identifiable individual assets. What is the minimum amount of amortization of goodwill for 1981? Could the entire amount be written off in 1981? Explain.

18–53. Various liabilities. For each of the following items, indicate how the financial statements will be affected. Identify the affected accounts specifically.

1. Whirlpool Corporation sells electric appliances; including automatic washing machines. Experience in recent years has indicated that warranty costs average 3.2% of sales. Sales of washing machines for October were $3 million. Cash disbursements and obligations for warranty service on washing machines during October totaled $81,000.

2. Pepsi-Cola Company of New York gets cash deposits for its returnable bottles. In August it received $100,000 cash and disbursed $89,000 for bottles returned.

3. The Chase Manhattan Bank received a $1,200 savings deposit on April 1. On June 30 it recognized interest thereon at an annual rate of 5%. On July 1 the depositor closed her account with the bank.

4. The Schubert Theater sold for $100,000 cash a "season's series" of tickets in advance of December 31 for four plays, each to be held in successive months beginning in January. (a) What is the effect on the balance sheet, December 31? (b) What is the effect on the balance sheet, January 31?

18–54. Airplane crash. A DC-10 airplane owned by American Airlines crashed in May 1979. It had been purchased for $18 million but was carried on American's books at $10.8 million. The plane's replacement cost, reflected in the insurance payment, was $37 million.

A news story reported: "American Airlines reported yesterday second-quarter earnings jumped 117.1 percent over those a year earlier. The quarter's profits included a $24.3 million after-tax gain from the proceeds of insurance . . ."

1. Prepare an analysis of the above facts, including the acquisition of a new airplane. Use the format of the balance sheet equation. Because of various complications, the applicable income tax was relatively small.
2. Do you think a casualty should generate a reported gain? Why?

18–55. Depreciation, income taxes, and cash flow. The annual report of Alaska Airlines showed some balances, December 31, 1981, in the following way:

Flight equipment	$108,985,000
Other property and equipment	28,678,000
	$137,663,000
Less accumulated depreciation	29,580,000
	$108,083,000

The cash balance was $1,325,000.

Depreciation expense during 1981 was $7,419,000. The condensed income statement follows:

Revenues	$181,960,000
Expenses	167,853,000
Operating income	$ 14,107,000

For purposes of this problem, assume that all revenues and expenses, excluding depreciation, are for cash.

1. Alaska used straight-line depreciation. Suppose accelerated depreciation had been $10,419,000 instead of $7,419,000. (Operating income would be decreased by $3,000,000.) Assume zero income taxes. Fill in the blanks in the accompanying table (in thousands of dollars).
2. Repeat Requirement 1, but assume an income tax rate of 40%. Assume also that Alaska uses the same depreciation method for reporting to shareholders and to the income tax authorities.
3. Compare your answers in Requirements 1 and 2. Does depreciation provide cash? Explain as precisely as possible.
4. Assume that Alaska had used straight-line depreciation for reporting to shareholders and to income tax authorities. Indicate the change (increase or decrease and amount) in the following balances if Alaska had used accelerated depreciation instead of straight-line: cash, accumulated depreciation, operating income, retained income. What would be the new balances in cash and accumulated depreciation?
5. Refer to Requirement 1. Suppose depreciation were increased by an extra $2 million under both the straight-line and the accelerated method. How would cash be affected? Be specific.

18–56. Valuation of intangible assets of football team. New owners acquired the Los Angeles Rams football team in 19X2 for $7.2 million. They valued the contracts of their forty players at a total of $3.5 million, the franchise at $3.6 million, and other assets at $100,000. For income tax purposes, the Rams amortized the $3.5 million over five years; therefore they took a tax deduction of $700,000 annually.

The Internal Revenue Service challenged the deductions. It maintained that only $300,000 of the $7.2 million purchase price was attributable to the player contracts, and that the $3.2 million of the $3.5 million in dispute should be attributed to the league franchise rights. Such franchise rights are regarded by the Internal Revenue Service as a valuable asset with an indefinite future life; therefore no amortization is permitted for tax-reporting purposes.

Understanding
Corporate
Annual
Reports—
Part One

593

Table for Problem 18–55

	1. ZERO INCOME TAXES		2. 40% INCOME TAXES	
	Straight-line Depreciation	Accelerated Depreciation	Straight-line Depreciation	Accelerated Depreciation
Revenues	$?	$?	$?	$?
Cash operating expenses	?	?	?	?
Cash provided by operations before income taxes	?	?	?	?
Depreciation expense	?	?	?	?
Operating income	?	?	?	?
Income tax expense	?	?	?	?
Net income	?	?	?	?
Supplementary analysis:				
Cash provided by operations before income taxes	?	?	?	?
Income tax expense	?	?	?	?
Net cash provided by operations	$?	$?	$?	$?

Suppose the operating income for each of the five years (before any amortization) was $1 million.

1. Consider the reporting to the Internal Revenue Service. Tabulate a comparison of annual operating income (after amortization) according to two approaches: (a) the Rams and (b) the IRS. What is the difference in annual operating income?

2. Consider the reporting to shareholders. Reports to shareholders by American companies do not have to adhere to the same basis used for income tax purposes. The Rams had been using a five-year life for player contracts and a forty-year life for the league franchise rights. Tabulate a comparison of operating income (after amortization) using (a) this initial approach and (b) the approach whereby only $300,000 would have been attributed to player contracts. What is the difference in annual operating income?

3. Comment on the results in Requirements 1 and 2. Which alternative do you think provides the most informative report of operating results? Why? Prior to 1970, many companies did not amortize intangible assets.

Understanding
Corporate
Annual
Reports—
Part One

595

19

UNDERSTANDING CORPORATE ANNUAL REPORTS— PART TWO

Learning Objectives

After studying this chapter, you should be able to

1. Contrast accounting for investments using the equity method and the cost method
2. Explain the basic ideas and methods used in the preparation of consolidated financial statements
3. Describe how goodwill arises and is accounted for
4. Explain and illustrate a variety of popular financial ratios
5. Identify the major implications that "efficient" stock markets have for accounting

This chapter continues the discussion of corporate annual reporting begun in the preceding chapter. Part One covers intercorporate investments, including consolidated statements and goodwill. Part Two covers the analysis of financial statements. *Either part may be studied independently, depending on your specific interest.*

☐ PART ONE   Intercorporate Investments, Including Consolidations

EQUITY METHOD FOR INTERCORPORATE INVESTMENTS

Investments in the equity securities of one company by another company are accounted for in different ways, depending on the type of the relationship between the "investor" and the "investee." For example, the ordinary stockholder is a passive investor who follows the *cost method* whereby the initial investment is recorded at cost and dividends are recorded as income when received.

Beginning in 1970 (APB *Opinion No. 18*), U.S. companies were required to use the *equity method* instead of the cost method if the investor exerts a "significant influence" over the operating and financial policies of an investee, even though the investor holds 50% or less of the outstanding voting stock. The **equity method** is defined as the cost at date of acquisition adjusted for the investor's share of dividends and earnings or losses of the investee subsequent to the date of investment. Accordingly, the carrying amount of the investment is reduced by dividends received from the investee and by the investor's share of investee's losses. The carrying amount of the investment is increased by the investor's share of investee's earnings. The equity method is generally used for a 20% through 50% interest because such a level of ownership is regarded as a presumption that the owner has the ability to exert significant influence, whereas the cost method is generally used to account for interests of less than 20%. The treatment of an interest in excess of 50% is explained in the following section, "Consolidated Financial Statements."

The equity method is relatively new. Long-term investments in equity securities were carried at acquisition cost for many years by U.S. companies and are still carried at cost by parent companies in many countries.

Compare the cost and equity methods. Suppose Company A acquires 40% of the voting stock of Company B for $80 million. In Year 1, B has a net income of $30 million and pays cash dividends of $10 million. A's 40% shares would be $12 million and $4 million, respectively. The balance sheet equation of A would be affected as tabulated on the top of the next page.

Under the equity method, income is recognized by A as it is earned by B rather than when dividends are received. Cash dividends do not affect net income; they increase Cash and decrease the Investment balance. In a sense, the dividend is a partial liquidation of the investor's "claim" against the investee. The receipt of a dividend is similar to the collection of an account receivable. The revenue from a sale of merchandise on account

Understanding
Corporate
Annual
Reports—
Part Two

597

	EQUITY METHOD				COST METHOD			
	ASSETS		=	EQUITIES	ASSETS		=	EQUITIES
	Cash	Investments		Liab.	Stk. Eq.	Cash	Investments	Liab.	Stk. Eq.
1. Acquisition	−80	+80	=			−80	+80	=	
2. Net income of B		+12	=		+12	No entry and no effect			
3. Dividends from B	+4	−4	=		___	+4		=	+4
Effects for year	−76	+88	=		+12	−76	+80	=	+4

The investment account will have a net increase of $8 million for the year. The dividend will increase the cash account by $4 million.

The investment account will be unaffected. The dividend will increase the cash account by $4 million.

is recognized when the receivable is created; to include the collection also as revenue would be double-counting. Similarly, it would be double-counting to include the $1 million of dividends as income after the $12 million of income is already recognized as it is earned.

The major justification for requiring the use of the equity method is that it is more appropriate than the cost method for recognizing increases or decreases in the economic resources underlying the investments. The most striking difference between the two methods is that the cost method allows management to influence reported net income. Under the cost method, the reported net income of the investor could be directly affected by the dividend policies of the investee, over whom the investor might have significant influence. Under the equity method, the reported net income could not be influenced by the manipulation of dividend policies.

Sears, the world's largest retailer of general merchandise, holds ownership in several companies. An example is Sears's 40.2% interest in Roper Corporation, a manufacturer of household appliances. Sears must use the equity method in accounting for such investments because an ownership interest in excess of 20% is presumed to be evidence of ability to exert significant influence.

CONSOLIDATED FINANCIAL STATEMENTS

United States companies having substantial ownership of other companies must issue consolidated financial statements, which are explained in this section. A reader cannot hope to understand a corporate annual report without understanding the assumptions underlying consolidations. Furthermore, the 1970s were marked by a worldwide movement toward requiring consolidated financial statements instead of parent-company-only statements.[1]

A publicly held business is typically composed of two or more separate legal entities that constitute a single overall economic unit. This is almost always a parent-subsidiary relationship where one corporation (the parent) owns more than 50% of the outstanding voting shares of another corporation (the subsidiary).

[1] For example, in 1977 Japanese companies were required to use consolidated statements. See "Japan's Accounting Shake-up," *Business Week*, April 25, 1977, pp. 112–14.

Why have subsidiaries? Why not have the corporation take the form of a single legal entity? The reasons include limiting the liabilities in a risky venture, saving income taxes, conforming with government regulations with respect to a part of the business, doing business in a foreign country, and expanding in an orderly way. For example, there are often tax advantages in acquiring the capital stock of a going concern rather than its individual assets.

Consolidated statements combine the financial positions and earnings reports of the parent company with those of various subsidiaries into an overall report as if they were a single entity. The aim is to give the readers better perspective than could be obtained by their examining a large number of separate reports of individual companies.

❑ The Acquisition

When parent and subsidiary financial statements are consolidated, double-counting of assets and equities must be avoided via "intercompany eliminations." Suppose Company P acquired a 100% voting interest in S for $213 million cash at the beginning of the year. Their balance sheet accounts are analyzed in the equation form below. Investment in S is presented in the first column because it is a focal point in this chapter, not because it appears first in actual balance sheets. Figures in this and subsequent tables are in millions of dollars and are assumed:

	ASSETS		= LIABILITIES +	STOCKHOLDERS' EQUITY
	Investment + in S	Cash and Other Assets	= Accounts Payable, + Etc.	Stockholders' Equity
P's accounts, Jan. 1:				
Before acquisition		650	= 200 +	450
Acquisition of S	+213	−213	=	
S's accounts, Jan. 1		400	= 187 +	213
Intercompany				
eliminations	−213		=	−213
Consolidated, Jan. 1	0	+ 837	= 387 +	450

Note that the $213 million is paid to the *former owners* of S as private investors. The $213 million is *not* an addition to the existing assets and stockholders' equity of S. *That is, the books of S are completely unaffected by P's initial investment and P's subsequent accounting thereof.* S is not dissolved; it lives on as a separate legal entity.

Each legal entity has its individual set of books, but the consolidated entity does not keep a day-to-day set of books. Instead, working papers are used to perform the consolidation, which reports *all* assets and liabilities of *both* the parent and the subsidiary.

Suppose a consolidated balance sheet were prepared immediately after the acquisition. The consolidated entity shows the details of *all* assets and liabilities of *both* the parent and the subsidiary. The Investment in S

Understanding
Corporate
Annual
Reports—
Part Two

599

account is the evidence of an ownership interest, which is held by P but is really composed of all of the S assets and the S liabilities. The consolidated statements cannot show both the evidence of interest *plus* the detailed underlying assets and liabilities. So this double-counting is avoided by eliminating the reciprocal evidence of ownership present in two places: (a) the Investment in S on P's books, and (b) the Stockholders' Equity on S's books.

In summary, if the $213 million elimination of the reciprocal accounts did not occur, there would be a double-counting in the consolidated statement:

ENTITY	TYPES OF RECORDS
P	Parent books
+ S	Subsidiary books
= Consolidated report to investors	No separate books, but periodically P and S assets and liabilities are added together via work sheets, where "eliminating entries" remove double-counting

❑ After Acquisition

Long-term investments in equity securities, such as this investment in S, are carried in the investor's balance sheet by the equity method, the same method of accounting for an unconsolidated ownership interest of 20% through 50%, as previously described. Suppose S has a net income of $50 million for the year. If the parent company were reporting alone, it would have to account for the net income of its subsidiary by increasing its Investment in S account and its Stockholders' Equity account (in the form of Retained Income) by 100% of $50 million.

The income statements for the year would contain (numbers in millions assumed):

	P	S	CONSOLIDATED
Sales	$900	$300	$1,200
Expenses	800	250	1,050
Operating income	$100	$ 50	$ 150
Pro-rata share (100%) of subsidiary net income	50	—	
Net income	$150	$ 50	

P's parent-company-only income statement would show its own sales and expenses plus its pro-rata share of S's net income (as the equity method requires).

Reflect on the changes in P's accounts, S's accounts, and the consolidated accounts (in millions of dollars):

	ASSETS			= LIABILITIES +		STOCKHOLDERS' EQUITY
	Investment + In S		Cash and Other Assets	= Accounts Payable, Etc.	+	Stockholders' Equity
P's accounts:						
Beginning of year	213	+	437	= 200	+	450
Operating income			+100	=		+100 in retained income
Share of S income	+50			=		+50 in retained income
End of year	263	+	537	= 200	+	600
S's accounts:						
Beginning of year			400	= 187	+	213
Net income			+50	=		+50 in retained income
End of year			450	= 187	+	263
Intercompany eliminations	−263			=		−263
Consolidated, end of year	0	+	987	= 387	+	600

Review at this point to see that consolidated statements are the summation of the individual accounts of two or more separate legal entities. They are prepared periodically via work sheets. The consolidated entity does not have a separate continuous set of books like the legal entities. Moreover, a consolidated income statement is merely the summation of the revenue and expenses of the separate legal entities being consolidated after eliminating double-counting. The income statement for P shows a $150 million net income; for S, a $50 million net income; for consolidated, a $150 million net income.

☐ Minority Interests

A consolidated balance sheet usually includes an account on the equities side called **Outside Stockholders' Interest in Subsidiaries,** often also termed simply **Minority Interests.** It arises because the consolidated balance sheet is a combination of all the assets and liabilities of a subsidiary. If the parent owns, for example, 90% of the subsidiary stock, then outsiders to the consolidated group own the other 10%. The account Outside Stockholders' Interest in Subsidiaries is a measure of this minority interest. The diagram on the next page shows the area encompassed by the consolidated statements; it includes all the subsidiary assets, item by item. The creation of an account for minority interests, in effect, corrects this overstatement.

The next table, using the basic figures of the previous example, shows the overall approach to a consolidated balance sheet immediately after the acquisition. P owns 90% of the stock of S for a cost of .90 × $213, or $192 million. The minority interest is 10%, or $21 million. (All dollars amounts are rounded to the nearest million.)

Understanding
Corporate
Annual
Reports—
Part Two

601

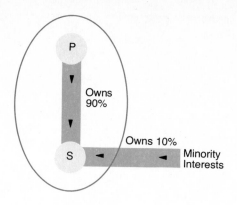

	ASSETS		=	LIABILITIES	+ STOCKHOLDERS' EQUITY		
	Investment + In S	Cash and Other Assets	=	Accounts Payable, Etc.	+ Minority Interest	+ Stockholders' Equity
P's accounts, Jan. 1: Before acquisition		650	=	200		+	450
Acquisition of 90% of S	+192	−192	=				
S's accounts, Jan. 1		400	=	187		+	213
Intercompany eliminations	−192		=		+21		−213
Consolidated, Jan. 1	0	+ 858	=	387	+ 21	+	450

Again, suppose S has a net income of $50 million for the year. The same basic procedures are followed by P and by S regardless of whether S is 100% owned or 90% owned. However, the presence of a minority interest changes the *consolidated* statements slightly. The income statements would include:

	P	S	CONSOLIDATED
Sales	$900	$300	$1,200
Expenses	800	250	1,050
Operating income	$100	$ 50	$ 150
Pro-rata share (90%) of subsidiary net income	45	—	
Net income	$145	$ 50	
Outside Interest (10%) in subsidiaries' net income (minority interest in income)			5
Net income to consolidated entity			$ 145

Consolidated balance sheets at the end of the year would be prepared as follows:

	ASSETS		=	LIABILITIES + STOCKHOLDERS' EQUITY		
	Investment + In S	Cash and Other Assets	=	Accounts Payable, Etc.	+ Minority Interest	+ Stockholders' Equity
P's accounts:						
Beginning of year	192 +	458*	=	200	+	450
Operating income		+100	=			+100
Share of S income	+45		=			+45
End of year	237 +	558	=	200	+	595
S's accounts:						
Beginning of year		400	=	187	+	213
Net income		+50	=			+50
End of year	+	450	=	187	+	263
Intercompany eliminations	−237		=		+26†	−263
Consolidated, end of year	0 +	1,008	=	387	+ 26 +	595

*650 beginning of year − 192 for acquisition = 458.
†21 beginning of year + .10(50) = 21 + 5 = 26.

As indicated in the table, the eliminating entry on the work sheet used for consolidating the balance sheet would offset the $263 of stockholders' equity (on S books) against the $237 of investment in S (on P books). The $26 difference is the minority interest (on consolidated statements). Thus the minority interest can be regarded as identifying those shareholders who own the 10% of the **subsidiary** stockholders' equity that is not eliminated by consolidation.

PERSPECTIVE ON CONSOLIDATED STATEMENTS

☐ Consolidated Subsidiaries

Exhibits 19-1 through 19-3 on pages 604–05 provide an overall look at how financial statements appear in corporate annual reports. The circled items 1 and 2 in the exhibits deserve special mention:

1. The headings indicate that these are *consolidated* financial statements.
2. On balance sheets, the minority interest typically appears just above the stockholders' equity section, as Exhibit 19-1 shows. On income statements, the minority interest in net income is deducted as if it were an expense of the consolidated entity, as Exhibit 19-2 demonstrates. Note that minority interest is a claim of outside stockholders' interest in a *consolidated subsidiary* company. Note also that minority interests arise only in conjunction with *consolidated* financial statements.

EXHIBIT 19-1 *(Place a clip on this page for easy reference.)*

GOLIATH CORPORATION
Consolidated Balance Sheets
As of December 31
(In millions of dollars)

ASSETS	19X3	19X2	CHANGE
Current assets:			
Cash	$ 90	$ 56	
Short-term investments in debt securities at cost (which approximates market value)	—	28	
Accounts receivable (less allowance for doubtful accounts of $2,000,000 and $2,100,000 at their respective dates)	91	95	
Inventories at average cost	120	130	
Total current assets	301	309	(8)
Investments in unconsolidated subsidiaries	63	55	8
Investments in affiliated companies	10	9	1
Property, plant, and equipment:			
Land at original cost	50	39	11
Plant and equipment	**19X3**	**19X2**	
Original cost	$192	$135	
Accumulated depreciation	126	112	
Net plant and equipment	66	23	57
Total property, plant, and equipment	116	62	(14)
Other assets:			
Franchises and trademarks	15	16	
Deferred charges and prepayments	3	4	
Total other assets	18	20	(2)
Total assets	$508	$455	53

EQUITIES	19X3	19X2	CHANGE
Current liabilities:			
Accounts payable	$100	$ 84	
Notes payable	10	—	
Accrued expenses payable	32	22	
Accrued income taxes payable	34	38	
Total current liabilities	176	144	32
Long-term liabilities:			
First mortgage bonds, 5% interest, due Dec. 31, 19X6	25	25	
Subordinated debentures, 6% interest, due Dec. 31, 19X9	30	20	10
Total long-term liabilities	55	45	
Deferred income*	12	9.3	2.7
Outside stockholders' interest in consolidated subsidiaries (minority interests)	6	5.7	0.3
Total liabilities	249	204	
Stockholders' equity:			
Preferred stock, 100,000 shares, $30 par†	3	3	
Common stock, 1,000,000 shares, $1 par	1	1	
Paid-in capital in excess of par	55	55	
Retained income	200	192	8
Total stockholders' equity	259	251	
Total equities	$508	$455	53

* Advances from customers on long-term contracts. Other examples are collections for rent and subscriptions, which often are classified as current liabilities.

† Dividend rate is $5 per share; each share is convertible into two shares of common stock. The shares were originally issued for $100. The excess over par is included in "paid-in capital in excess of par." Liquidating value is $100 per share.

EXHIBIT
19-2

GOLIATH CORPORATION
Consolidated Income Statements
① For the year ended December 31
(000's omitted)

	19X3	19X2
Net sales and other operating revenue	$499,000	$599,100
Cost of goods sold and operating expenses, exclusive of depreciation	468,750	554,550
Depreciation	14,000	11,000
Total operating expenses	482,750	565,550
Operating Income	16,250	33,550
④ Equity in earnings of affiliates	1,000	900
③ Equity in earnings of unconsolidated subsidiary	8,000	10,000
Total income before interest expense and income taxes	25,250	44,450
Interest expense	2,450	2,450
Income before income taxes	22,800	42,000
Income taxes	12,000	21,900
Income before minority interests	10,800	20,100
② Outside stockholders' interest (minority interests) in consolidated subsidiaries' net income	300	600
Net consolidated income to Goliath Corporation*	10,500	19,500
Preferred dividends	500	500
Net income to Goliath Corporation common stock	$ 10,000	$ 19,000
Earnings per share of common stock: On shares outstanding (1,000,000 shares)	$10.00†	$19.00
Assuming full dilution, reflecting conversion of all convertible securities (1,200,000 shares)	$8.75‡	$16.25

*This is the total figure in dollars that the accountant traditionally labels net income. It is reported accordingly in the financial press.

†This is the figure most widely quoted by the investment community: $10,000,000 ÷ 1,000,000 = $10.00; $19,000,000 ÷ 1,000,000 = $19.00.

‡Computed, respectively: $10,500,000 ÷ 1,200,000 = $8.75; $19,500,000 ÷ 1,200,000 = $16.25.

EXHIBIT
19-3

GOLIATH CORPORATION
Consolidated Statement of Retained Income
For the Year Ended December 31
(000's omitted)

	19X3	19X2
Balance beginning of year	$192,000	$176,000
Add: Net income to Goliath Corporation	10,500	19,500
Total	202,500	195,500
Deduct:		
Cash dividends on preferred stock (also shown in Exhibit 19-2)	500	500
Cash dividends on common stock	2,000	3,000
Total dividends	2,500	3,500
Balance, end of year	$200,000	$192,000

Understanding
Corporate
Annual
Reports—
Part Two

605

To help understanding, consider the following hypothetical relationships that exist for Goliath Corporation, which for more realism could be viewed as a simplified version of General Motors:

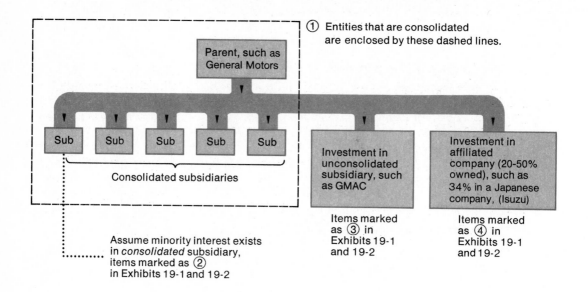

❑ Unconsolidated Subsidiaries

We have already seen how the equity method is used on a parent company's books to account for its investment in subsidiaries. Most often, such investment accounts are eliminated when consolidated statements are prepared, as was just illustrated. Sometimes there is justification for not consolidating one or two subsidiaries with businesses totally different from the parent and other subsidiaries. Examples are a manufacturer's subsidiary finance companies and insurance companies. For instance, a consolidated statement of General Motors (GM) and its finance company subsidiary, General Motors Acceptance Corporation (GMAC), would produce a meaningless hodgepodge, so the interest in GMAC is shown as an Investment on the GM consolidated balance sheet, even though the GM interest is 100%. A separate set of GMAC statements is included in the GM annual report.

Investments in domestic unconsolidated subsidiaries are carried via the equity method. The use of the equity method necessitates recognition of the parent's share of unconsolidated subsidiary net income. Exhibit 19-2 is an example of how this income usually appears as a separate item in the consolidated income statement. Note also that the beginning balance of the Investment account in Exhibit 19-1 was $55 million. It has risen by $8 million for the year because of the consolidated enterprise's share in the unconsolidated subsidiary net income.

Exhibits 19-1 and 19-2 indicate that the unconsolidated subsidiary did not declare dividends during 19X3. But suppose the parent received $6 million in dividends. The equity method would have the following effects:

Original investment	$55	
Share of subsidiary net income	8	→Same as now appears in the
Balance	$63	income statement in
Dividends received	6	Exhibit 19-2
Balance, December 31, 19X3	$57	

The $6 million dividend would not appear in the income statement because it would represent a double-counting. Instead, it is regarded as a partial liquidation of the $63 million ownership "claim" as measured in the Investment account. Thus net income of the subsidiary increases this claim and dividends reduce this claim.

Investments in foreign subsidiaries are sometimes carried at cost because of a longstanding reluctance to recognize gains prior to the receipt of a corresponding amount of funds from the foreign subsidiaries. This conservative approach is an outgrowth of many unhappy experiences with wars, expropriations of assets, devaluations of currencies, and currency restrictions.

☐ Investments in Affiliates

As described earlier in the chapter, investments in equity securities that represent 20% to 50% ownership are usually accounted for under the equity method. These investments are frequently called **Investments in Affiliates** or **Investments in Associates.** For example, see the items marked as 4 in Exhibits 19-1 and 19-2. General Motors would account for its 34% investment in Isuzu in this manner. Exhibit 19-1 shows how the Investment account in the balance sheet has risen by the pro-rata share of the current earnings of affiliates, the $1 million shown in the income statement in Exhibit 19-2.

RECAPITULATION OF INVESTMENTS IN EQUITY SECURITIES

Exhibit 19-4 summarizes all the relationships depicted in the preceding exhibits. Take a few moments to review Exhibits 19-1 and 19-2 in conjunction with Exhibit 19-4. In particular, note that minority interests arise only in conjunction with *consolidated* subsidiaries. Why? Because consolidated balance sheets and income statements aggregate 100% of the detailed assets, liabilities, sales, and expenses of the subsidiary companies. Thus, if a minority interest were not recognized, the stockholders' equity and net income of the consolidated enterprise would be overstated.

In contrast, minority interests do not arise in connection with the accounting for investments in *unconsolidated* subsidiaries or investments in affiliated companies. Why? Because no detailed assets, liabilities, revenues, and expenses of the unconsolidated subsidiaries or affiliated companies are included in the consolidated statements. The investor's interests in these companies have been recognized on a pro-rata basis only.

Understanding
Corporate
Annual
Reports—
Part Two

607

EXHIBIT 19-4

Summary of Equity Method and Consolidations

ITEM IN EXHIBITS 19-1 AND 19-2	PERCENTAGE OF OWNERSHIP	TYPE OF ACCOUNTING	BALANCE SHEET EFFECTS	INCOME STATEMENT EFFECTS
①	100%	Consolidation	Individual assets, individual liabilities added together	Individual revenues, individual expenses added together
②	Greater than 50% and less than 100%	Consolidation	Same as 1, but recognition given to minority interest in liability section	Same as 1, but recognition given to minority interest near bottom of statement when consolidated net income is computed
③	Greater than 50% up to 100%, but subsidiary in totally different business, so not consolidated	Equity method	Investment carried at cost plus pro-rata share of subsidiary earnings less dividends received	Equity in earnings of **unconsolidated subsidiary** shown on one line as addition to income
④	20% to and including 50%	Equity method	Same as 3	Same as 3, often called equity in earnings of **affiliated** or **associated** companies

As we have seen, the accounting for investments *in voting stock* depends on the nature of the investment:

1. Except for those subsidiaries in insurance and finance activities, nearly all investments that represent more than a 50% ownership interest are usually consolidated. A subsidiary is a corporation controlled by another corporation. The usual condition for control is ownership of a majority (more than 50%) of the outstanding voting stock.

2. **a.** If the subsidiary is not consolidated, it is carried by the parent under the equity method, which is cost at date of acquisition adjusted for the investor's share of the earnings or losses of the investee subsequent to the date of investment. Dividends received from the investee reduce the carrying amount of the investment.

   b. The equity method is also generally used for a 20% through 50% interest because such a level of ownership is regarded as a presumption that the owner has the ability to exert significant influence.

   c. Investments in corporate joint ventures should also be accounted for under the equity method. "Corporate joint ventures" are corporations owned and operated by a small group of businesses (the "joint venturers") as a separate business or project for the mutual benefit of the members of the group. Joint ventures are common in the petroleum and construction industries.

3. Marketable *equity* securities held as **short-term investments** are generally carried at the lower of cost or market value.[2] These investments are typically passive in the sense that the investor exerts no significant influence on the investee.

ACCOUNTING FOR GOODWILL

❑ Purchased Goodwill

The major example on intercorporate investments assumed that the acquisition cost of Company S by Company P was equal to the *book values* of Company S. However, the total purchase price paid by P often exceeds the book values of the assets acquired. In fact, the purchase price also often exceeds the sum of the fair market values (current values) of the identifiable individual assets less the liabilities. Such excess of purchase price over fair market value is called "goodwill" or "purchased goodwill" or, more accurately, "excess of cost over fair value of net identifiable assets of businesses acquired." Recall that Chapter 18 discusses the nature of goodwill.

To see the impact on the consolidated statements, refer to our initial example on consolidations, where there was an acquisition of a 100% interest in S by P for $213 million. Suppose the price were $40 million higher, or

Understanding
Corporate
Annual
Reports—
Part Two

609

[2] FASB *Statement No. 12*, "Accounting for Certain Marketable Securities," requires that a portfolio of securities (rather than each security as an individual investment) should be stated at the lower of cost or market. If the investment is classified as a current asset, any write-downs to market should affect current net income. If the investment is a noncurrent asset, the write-down shall be recorded directly in the stockholders' equity section of the balance sheet as a separate valuation account and not as a component of the determination of net income.

a total of $253 million. For simplicity, assume that all other assets and liabilities in P and S were unaffected by paying $253 million. Also assume that the fair values of the individual assets of S are equal to their book values. The balance sheets immediately after the acquisition are:

| | ASSETS | | = LIABILITIES + | STOCKHOLDERS' EQUITY |
	Investment In S	+ Cash and Other Assets =	Accounts Payable, Etc. +	Stockholders' Equity
P's accounts:				
Before acquisition		650 =	200 +	450
Acquisition	+253	−253 =		
S's accounts		400 =	187 +	213
Intercompany eliminations	−213	=		−213
Consolidated	40*	+ 797 =	387 +	450

*The $40 million "goodwill" would appear in the consolidated balance sheet as a separate intangible asset account. It often is shown as the final item in a listing of assets. It is usually amortized in a straight-line manner as an expense in the consolidated income statement over a span of no greater than forty years.

☐ Fair Values of Individual Assets

If the book values of the S individual assets are not equal to their fair values, the usual procedures are:

1. S continues as a going concern and keeps its accounts on the same basis as before.
2. P records its investment at its acquisition cost (the agreed purchase price).
3. For consolidated reporting purposes, the excess of the acquisition cost over the book values of S is identified with the individual assets, item by item. (In effect, they are revalued at the current market prices prevailing when P acquired S.) Any *remaining excess* that cannot be identified is labeled as purchased goodwill.

Suppose that in our example the fair value of the other assets of S (e.g., machinery and equipment) exceeded their book value by $30 million. The balance sheets immediately after acquisition would be the same as above, with a single exception. The $40 million goodwill would now be only $10 million. The remaining $30 million would appear in the consolidated balance sheet as an integral part of the "other assets." That is, the S equipment would be shown at $30 million higher in the consolidated balance sheet than the carrying amount on the S books. Similarly, the depreciation expense on the consolidated income statement would be higher. For instance, if the equipment had five years of useful life remaining, the straight-line depreciation would be $30 ÷ 5, or $6 million higher per year.

As in the preceding tabulation, the $10 million "goodwill" would appear in the consolidated balance sheet as a separate intangible asset account.

Goodwill is frequently misunderstood. The layperson often thinks of goodwill as being the friendly attitude of the neighborhood store manager. But goodwill has many aspects that some observers have divided into causes (sources) and effects (fruits). A purchaser may be willing to pay more than the current values of the individual assets received because the acquired company is able to generate abnormally high earnings (the effects, or fruits). The causes of this excess earning power may be traceable to personalities, skills, locations, operating methods, and so forth. For example, a purchaser may be willing to pay extra (the fruits) because excess earnings can be forthcoming from

1. Saving in time and costs by purchasing a corporation having a share of the market in a type of business or in a geographical area where the acquiring corporation planned expansion
2. Excellent general management skills or a unique product line
3. Potential efficiency by combination, rearrangement, or elimination of duplicate facilities and administration

Of course, "goodwill" is originally generated internally. For example, a happy combination of advertising, research, management talent, and timing may give a particular company a dominant market position (the cause) for which another company is willing to pay dearly (the fruit). This ability to command a premium price for the total business is goodwill. Nevertheless, such goodwill should never be recorded by the selling company. Therefore the *only* goodwill generally recognized as an asset is that identified when one company is purchased by another. The consolidated company must then show in its financial statements the purchased goodwill.

Summary

Nearly all corporate annual reports contain consolidated financial statements, as well as "investment" accounts of various sorts. Acquiring a fundamental understanding of accounting for intercorporate investments is therefore essential for intelligent usage of financial reports.

Summary Problem for Your Review

❑ **Problem One**

1. Review the section on minority interests. Suppose P owns 60% of the stock of S for a cost of .60 × $213, or $128 million. The total assets of P consist of this $128 million plus $522 million of other assets, a total of $650 million. The S

assets and equities are unchanged from the amount given in the example on page 599. Prepare an analysis showing what amounts would appear in a consolidated balance sheet immediately after the acquisition.

2. Suppose S has a net income of $50 million for the year, and P has an operating income of $100 million. Other details are described in the example on page 600. Prepare an analysis showing what amounts would appear in a consolidated income statement and year-end balance sheet.

❑ Solution to Problem One

1.

| | ASSETS | | = LIABILITIES | + STOCKHOLDERS' EQUITY | |
	Investment In S	+ Cash and Other Assets =	Accounts Payable, Etc.	+ Minority Interest +	Stockholders' Equity
P's accounts, Jan. 1: Before acquisition		650 =	200	+	450
Acquisition of 60% of S	+128	−128 =			
S's accounts, Jan. 1:		400 =	187	+	213
Intercompany eliminations	−128	=		+85	−213
Consolidated, Jan. 1	0 +	922 =	387	+ 85 +	450

2.

	P	S	CONSOLIDATED
Sales	$900	$300	$1,200
Expenses	800	250	1,050
Operating income	$100	$ 50	$ 150
Pro-rata share (60%) of unconsolidated subsidiary net income	30	—	
Net income	$130	$ 50	
Outside interest (40%) in consolidated subsidiary net income (minority interest in income)			20
Net income to consolidated entity			$ 130

3.

| | ASSETS | | = LIABILITIES + | | STOCKHOLDERS' EQUITY |
	Investment In S	+ Cash and Other Assets =	Accounts Payable, Etc.	+ Minority Interest +	Stockholders' Equity
P's accounts:					
Beginning of year	128 +	522* =	200	+	450
Operating income		+100 =			+100
Share of S income	+ 30	=			+ 30
End of year	158 +	622 =	200	+	580
S's accounts:					
Beginning of year		400 =	187	+	213
Net income		+ 50 =			+ 50
End of year		450 =	187	+	263
Intercompany eliminations	−158	=		+105†	−263
Consolidated, end of year	0 +	1,072 =	387	+ 105 +	580

*650 beginning of year − 128 for acquisition = 522.
†85 beginning of year + .40(50) = 85 + 20 = 105.

Highlights to Remember

1. Exhibits 19-1 and 19-2 summarize how intercorporate investments are accounted for. Note how the equity method is applied. The $8 million increase in the Investments account is attributable to the pro-rata share of the **unconsolidated** subsidiary net income shown in Exhibit 19-2. See pages 604 and 605.

2. Minority interests are also displayed in Exhibits 19-1 and 19-2. Consider the $300,000 increase (Exhibit 19-1) in Outside Stockholders' Interest in Consolidated Subsidiaries. It is attributable to the minority interests' share of the income of **consolidated** subsidiaries, as indicated in the income statement in Exhibit 19-2.

3. Exhibit 19-4, page 608, summarizes the accounting for long-term investments in equity securities. Please review it before you try to solve any problems in these categories.

Accounting Vocabulary

Consolidated statements; cost method for investments; equity method; goodwill; investments in affiliates; investments in associates; minority interests; outside stockholders' interest in subsidiaries; short-term investment; subsidiary.

❑ PART TWO Analysis of Financial Statements

OBJECTIVE OF ANALYSIS

The primary uses of financial statements are evaluating past performance and predicting future performance. Both of these uses are facilitated by comparisons. The ultimate effect of analyzing statements is usually some financial *decision*. After conducting *comparisons* (usually between periods, similar organizations, and organizations in relation to their industry averages), the analyst will *predict* how the organization will fare. The analyst will then *decide* to buy, sell, or hold the common stock (or lend or not lend).

The financial statements in Exhibits 19-5 through 19-7 will be the focus of our extended illustration of the computation of financial ratios. Both managers and investors find ratios helpful for comparing and predicting. The managers and the financial community (such as bank officers and stockholders) want clues to help evaluate the operating and financial outlook for an entity. For example, extenders of credit want assurance of being paid in full and on time. Where feasible and where the amounts lent are significant, the creditor will ask the debtor for a set of budgeted financial statements. A **budget** is a carefully formulated expression of predicted results, including a schedule of the amounts and timings of cash repayments. For example, the holder of the Oxley note payable may have insisted on getting a budget from Oxley before granting the loan. As a result, the creditor may have no misgivings whatsoever about how the $80,000 short-term portion (see Exhibit 19-5, December 31, 19X2) will be paid in 19X3.

Understanding
Corporate
Annual
Reports—
Part Two

613

EXHIBIT
19-5

(Place a clip
on this page
for easy
reference.)

Oxley Company
Balance Sheet
(In thousands)

	DECEMBER 31 19X2	19X1
assets		
Current assets:		
Cash	$150	$ 57
Accounts receivable	95	70
Accrued interest receivable	15	15
Inventory of merchandise	20	60
Prepaid rent	10	–
Total current assets	$290	$202
Long-term assets*:		
Long-term note receivable	288	288

	DECEMBER 31 19X2	19X1		
Equipment, at original cost	$200	$200		
Deduct: Accumulated depreciation	120	80		
Equipment, net			80	120
Total assets			$658	$610
liabilities and stockholders' equity				
Current liabilities:				
Accounts payable			$ 90	$ 65
Accrued wages payable			24	10
Accrued income taxes payable			16	12
Accrued interest payable			9	9
Deferred sales revenue			–	5
Note payable—current portion			80	–
Total current liabilities			$219	$101
Long-term note payable			40	120
Total liabilities			$259	$221
Stockholders' equity:				
Paid-in capital†			$102	$102
Retained income			297	287
Total stockholders' equity			$399	$389
Total liabilities and stockholders' equity			$658	$610

*This caption is frequently omitted. Instead, the long-term note receivable, the equipment, and other categories are merely listed as separate items following the current assets.
†Details are often shown in a supplementary statement or in footnotes. In this case, there are 200,000 common shares outstanding; $.25 par per share, or 200,000 × $.25 = $50,000. Additional paid-in capital is $52,000.

USES OF RATIOS

In addition to obtaining a budget, the supplier of large amounts of credit will inevitably conduct further analysis. Moreover, many lenders do not extend large amounts of credit to a single entity, so they do not probe

EXHIBIT
19-6

OXLEY COMPANY
Statement of Income
(In thousands except earnings per share)

	FOR THE YEAR ENDED DECEMBER 31, 19X2		FOR THE YEAR ENDED DECEMBER 31, 19X1	
Sales		$999		$800
Cost of goods sold		399		336
Gross profit (or gross margin)		$600		$464
Operating expenses:				
Wages	$214		$150	
Rent	120		120	
Miscellaneous	100		50	
Depreciation	40	474	40	360
Operating income (or operating profit)		$126		$104
Other revenue and expense:				
Interest revenue	$ 36		$ 36	
Deduct: Interest expense	12	24	12	24
Income before income taxes		$150		$128
Income tax expense		60		48
Net income		$ 90		$ 80
Earnings per common share*		$ .45		$ .40

*Dividends per share, $.40 and $.20, respectively. For publicly held companies, there is a requirement to show earnings per share on the face of the income statement, but it is not necessary to show dividends per share.

EXHIBIT
19-7

OXLEY COMPANY
Statement of Retained Income
(In thousands)

	FOR THE YEAR ENDED DECEMBER 31	
	19X2	19X1
Retained income, beginning of year	$287	$247
Add: Net income	90	80
Total	$377	$327
Deduct: Dividends declared	80	40
Retained income, end of year	$297	$287

deeply enough to obtain budgets. There are many indirect ways to make judgments. History is examined. Performances are compared. Industry standards or rules of thumb are employed.

Our illustrative analysis focuses on one company and one or two years. This is sufficient as a start, but other firms in the industry and a series of years should be examined to get a better perspective. That is why annual reports typically contain a table of comparative statistics for five or ten years.

Above all, recognize that by itself a ratio is of limited use. There must

Understanding
Corporate
Annual
Reports—
Part Two

615

be a standard for comparison—a history, a similar entity, an industry, a budget (or similar target).

COMPONENT PERCENTAGES

The income statement and the balance sheet are often analyzed by **component percentages** (see Exhibit 19-8). In this way, the statements are made comparable through time and among companies inside and outside an industry.

The income statement percentages are usually based on sales = 100%. Oxley seems very profitable, but such percentages have more meaning when compared with the budgeted performance for the current year 19X2

EXHIBIT 19-8

Component Percentages

OXLEY COMPANY
(In thousands except percentages)

Statement of Income

FOR THE YEAR ENDED	DECEMBER 31			
	19X2		19X1	
Sales	$999*	100%	$800	100%
Cost of goods sold	399	40	336	42
Gross profit (or gross margin)	$600	60	$464	58
Wages	$214	21	$150	19
Rent	120	12	120	15
Miscellaneous	100	10	50	6
Depreciation	40	4	40	5
Operating expenses	$474	47	$360	45
Operating income	$126	13	$104	13
Other revenue and expense	24	2	24	3
Income before income taxes	$150	15	$128	16
Income tax expense	60	6	48	6
Net income	$ 90	9%	$ 80	10%

Balance Sheet

DECEMBER 31	19X2		19X1	
Current assets	$290	44%	$202	33%
Long-term note receivable	288	44	288	47
Equipment, net	80	12	120	20
Total assets	$658	100%	$610	100%
Current liabilities	$219	33%	$101	16%
Long-term note	40	6	120	20
Total liabilities	$259	39%	$221	36%
Stockholders' equity	399	61	389	64
Total equities	$658	100%	$610	100%
Working capital	$ 71		$101	

*Note the use of dollar signs in columns of numbers. Frequently, they are used at the top and bottom only and not for every subtotal. Their use by companies depends on the preference of management.

(not shown here). The gross margin rate seems high; Oxley may be vulnerable to price competition. The behavior of each expense in relation to changes in total revenue is often revealing. That is, which expenses go up or down as sales fluctuate? For example, during these two years rent, depreciation, and interest have been fixed in total but have decreased in relation to changes in sales. In contrast, the wages have increased in total and as a percentage of sales. The latter is not a welcome sign. Exhibit 19-8 indicates that wages in 19X1 were $150 ÷ $800 = 19% of sales, whereas wages in 19X2 were $214 ÷ $999 = 21% of sales.

Corporate annual reports to the public must contain a section that is usually labeled *management's discussion and analysis.* This section concentrates on explaining the major changes in the income statement, changes in liquidity and capital resources, and the impact of inflation. The focus is on a comparison of one year with the next. For example, the 1982 annual report of General Foods Corporation contained five pages of detailed comparisons, such as the following: "Interest expense increased to $141.6 million from $46.7 million in fiscal 1981 as a result of a higher level of borrowings principally related to the financing of the acquisition of Oscar Mayer."

The balance sheet percentages are usually based on total assets = 100%. See Exhibit 19-8. The most notable feature of the balance sheet percentages is that both current assets and current liabilities are more prominent at the end of 19X2. Moreover, the working capital has declined largely because $80,000 of the long-term debt has become a current liability (because it is now less than one year from maturity). Some careful planning for 19X3 should provide for the orderly payment of this $80,000 and the probable increase of inventory levels.

The ratios of current liabilities (current debt) to stockholders' equity and of total liabilities (total debt) to stockholders' equity seem respectable, as is shown more clearly in the next section, "Industry Statistics and Typical Ratios." Both creditors and shareholders watch these ratios to judge the degree of risk of insolvency and of stability of profits. Typically, companies with heavy debt in relation to ownership capital are in greater danger of suffering net losses or even insolvency when business conditions sour. Why? Because revenue and many expenses decline, but interest expenses and maturity dates do not change.

INDUSTRY STATISTICS AND TYPICAL RATIOS

Exhibit 19-9 shows how some typical ratios are computed. As you can readily imagine, various combinations of financial ratios are possible. In any event, one of the most popular uses of such ratios is comparison with similar companies.

Dun and Bradstreet, a financial services firm, informs its subscribers of the credit-worthiness of thousands of companies. The firm also regularly compiles many ratios of the companies it monitors. Consider each ratio in Exhibit 19-9 in relation to the industry statistics. For example, some of the 1983 Dun-Bradstreet ratios for seventy-nine retail nurseries, lawn, and garden and farm supplies companies are tabulated on page 619.

Understanding
Corporate
Annual
Reports—
Part Two

617

EXHIBIT 19-9   Some Typical Financial Ratios

TYPICAL NAME OF RATIO	NUMERATOR	DENOMINATOR	USING APPROPRIATE OXLEY NUMBERS APPLIED TO DECEMBER 31 OF YEAR	
			19X2	19X1
Short-term ratios:				
Current ratio	Current assets	Current liabilities	290 ÷ 219 = 1.3	202 ÷ 101 = 2.0
Inventory turnover	Cost of goods sold	Average inventory at cost	399 ÷ ½(20 + 60) = 10	Unknown*
Average collection period in days	Average accounts receivable × 365	Sales on account	[½(95 + 70) × 365] ÷ 999 = 30†	Unknown*
Debt-to-equity ratios:				
Current debt to equity	Current liabilities	Stockholders' equity	219 ÷ 399 = 54.9%	101 ÷ 389 = 26.0%
Total debt to equity	Total liabilities	Stockholders' equity	259 ÷ 399 = 64.9%	221 ÷ 389 = 56.8%
Profitability ratios:				
Gross profit rate or percentage	Gross profit or gross margin	Sales	600 ÷ 999 = 60%	464 ÷ 800 = 58%
Return on sales	Net income	Sales	90 ÷ 999 = 9%	80 ÷ 800 = 10%
Return on stockholders' equity	Net income	Average stockholders' equity	90 ÷ ½(399 + 389) = 22.8%	Unknown*
Earnings per share	Net income less dividends on preferred stock, if any	Average common shares outstanding	90 ÷ 200 = $.45	80 ÷ 200 = $.40
Price-earnings	Market price of common share (assume $3 and $2)	Earnings per share	3 ÷ .45 = 6.667 = 7	2 ÷ .40 = 5
Dividend ratios:				
Dividend-yield	Dividends per common share	Market price of common share (assume $3 and $2)	.40 ÷ 3 = 13.3%	.20 ÷ 2 = 10%
Dividend-payout	Dividends per common share	Earnings per share	.40 ÷ .45 = 89%	.20 ÷ .40 = 50%

*Insufficient data available because the *beginning* balance sheet balances for 19X1 are not provided. Without them the *average* investment during 19X1 cannot be computed.

†This may be easier to see as follows:
Average receivables = ½(95 + 70) = 82.5
Average receivables as a percentage of annual sales = 82.5 ÷ 999 = 8.25%
Average collection period = 8.25% × 365 days = 30 days

	CURRENT RATIO (times)	CURRENT DEBT TO STOCK-HOLDERS' EQUITY (percent)	TOTAL DEBT TO STOCK-HOLDERS' EQUITY (percent)	RETURN ON SALES (percent)	RETURN ON STOCK-HOLDERS' EQUITY (percent)
Seventy-nine companies:					
Upper quartile*	3.2	28.6	47.8	6.1	17.3
Median	1.8	60.4	82.0	3.2	10.1
Lower quartile	1.3	125.9	161.2	1.1	2.0
Oxley†	1.3	54.9	64.9	9.0	22.8

*The individual ratios are ranked from best to worst. The middle figure is the median. The figure halfway between the median and the best is the upper quartile. Similarly, the figure halfway between the median and the worst is the lower quartile.

†Ratios are from Exhibit 19-9. Please consult that exhibit for an explanation of the components of each ratio.

DISCUSSION OF INDIVIDUAL RATIOS

The current ratio is a widely used statistic. Other things being equal, the higher the current ratio, the more assurance the creditor has about being paid in full and on time. As Exhibit 19-9 shows, Oxley's current ratio of 1.3 has declined from 2.0 and is unimpressive in relation to the industry median of 1.8.

The next two ratios in Exhibit 19-9 are not available from Dun and Bradstreet on an industry-comparable basis. Still, the inventory turnover and the average collection period are closely watched signals. Deteriorations through time in these ratios help alert managers to problem areas. For example, a decrease in inventory turnover may suggest slower-moving (or even unsalable) merchandise or a worsening coordination of the buying and selling functions. An increase in the average collection period of receivables may indicate increasing acceptance of poor credit risks or less-energetic collection efforts. Whether the inventory turnover of 10 and the average collection period of thirty days are "fast" or "slow" depends on past performance and the performance of similar companies.

Note how the average collection period is affected by sales *on account.* The computation in Exhibit 19-9 assumes that all sales are credit sales. However, if we relax our assumption, the thirty-day period would rise markedly. For example, if half the sales were for cash, the average collection period for accounts receivable would change from thirty to sixty days:

$$\frac{\frac{1}{2}(95 + 70) \times 365}{\frac{1}{2}(999)} = 60 \text{ days}$$

Ratios of debt to equity are shown in the second and third columns of the Dun and Bradstreet tabulation. As mentioned in the preceding section, the debt management is watched as an indication of its effects on future profitability and solvency. Oxley's ratios of 54.9% and 64.9% are better than their medians for the industry because they reflect greater stability of profits and lower risk or uncertainty concerning the company's ability to pay its debts on time.

Understanding
Corporate
Annual
Reports—
Part Two

619

The final two columns in the Dun and Bradstreet tabulation are examples of profitability ratios. Managers and investors study the ratios of net income to sales and gross profit to sales as indicators of *operating success*. To owners, however, the ultimate measure of *overall accomplishment* is the rate of return on their invested capital. Hence the final column displays the ratio of net income to stockholders' equity. Oxley's rate of return is splendid. The opportunities to make more handsome returns than 22% after income taxes are rare.

To summarize, in comparison with the Dun and Bradstreet ratios, Oxley's current ratio is unimpressive, but its profit ratios are outstanding. Its debt management ratios are better than the medians. All in all, Oxley's operating and financial performance seems excellent. The only serious question is whether Oxley can meet the current portion of its long-term debt without disrupting its normal operations. Oxley's large cash balance will help in the meeting of its short-term commitments.

EARNINGS AND DIVIDENDS

Every analyst has a favorite set of ratios, but one is so popular that it dwarfs all others: *earnings per share of common stock (EPS)*. This is the only ratio that is required as a part of the body of financial statements of publicly held corporations. The EPS must be presented on the face of the income statement.

Exhibit 19-9 shows how EPS is computed, as well as how three other popular ratios are calculated: price-earnings, dividend-yield, and dividend-payout.

OPERATING PERFORMANCE

An important measure of overall accomplishment is the rate of return on invested capital:

$$\text{rate of return on investment} = \frac{\text{income}}{\text{invested capital}} \qquad (1)$$

On the surface, this measure is straightforward, but its ingredients may differ according to the purpose it is to serve. What is Invested Capital, the denominator of the ratio? What income figure is appropriate?

The measurement of operating performance (i.e., how profitably assets are employed) should not be influenced by the management's financial decisions (i.e., how assets are obtained). Operating performance is best measured by operating rate of return on average total assets:

$$\frac{\text{pretax operating rate}}{\text{of return on total assets}} = \frac{\text{operating income}}{\text{average total assets available}} \qquad (2)$$

The right-hand side of Equation 2 consists, in turn, of two important ratios:

$$\frac{\text{operating income}}{\text{average total assets available}}$$

$$= \frac{\text{operating income}}{\text{sales}} \times \frac{\text{sales}}{\text{average total assets available}} \quad (3)$$

Using Exhibits 19-5 and 19-6, we can compute the following 19X2 results for Oxley Company:

$$\frac{\$126}{\frac{1}{2}(\$658 + \$610)} = \frac{\$126}{\$999} \times \frac{\$999}{\$634}$$

The right-hand terms in Equation 3 are often called the *operating margin percentage on sales* and the *total asset turnover*, respectively. Equation 3 may be reexpressed:

pretax operating rate of return on total assets
$$= \text{operating margin percentage on sales}$$
$$\times \text{total asset turnover}$$
$$= 12.6 \times 1.576 \text{ times} = 19.9\% \quad (4)$$

If ratios are used to evaluate operating performance, they should exclude extraordinary items because they are regarded as nonrecurring items that do not reflect normal performance.

A scrutiny of Equation 4 shows that there are two basic factors in profit making: operating margin percentages and turnover. An improvement in either will, by itself, increase the rate of return on total assets.

The ratios used can also be computed on the basis of figures after taxes. However, the peculiarities of the income tax laws may sometimes distort results—for example, the tax rate may change, or losses carried back or forward might eliminate the tax in certain years.

Many more ratios could be computed. For example, Standard and Poor's Corporation sells a COMPUSTAT service, which via computer can provide financial and statistical information for thousands of companies. The information includes twenty-two income statement items, nineteen balance sheet items, and a variety of financial ratios for up to twenty past years.

EFFICIENT MARKETS AND INVESTOR DECISIONS

Much recent research in accounting and finance has concentrated on whether the stock markets are "efficient." An **efficient capital market** is one in which market prices "fully reflect" all information available at a given time. Therefore, searching for "underpriced" securities in such a market would be fruitless. If the real-world markets are indeed efficient, a relatively inactive portfolio approach would be an appropriate investment strategy. The hallmarks of the approach are risk control, high diversification, and low turnover of securities. The role of accounting information would mainly be in identifying the different degrees of risk among various stocks.

Understanding
Corporate
Annual
Reports—
Part Two

621

Research in finance and accounting during the 1970s reinforced the idea that financial ratios and other data such as reported earnings provide inputs to predictions of such economic phenomena as financial failure or earnings growth. Furthermore, many ratios are used simultaneously rather than one at a time for such predictions. Above all, the research showed that accounting reports are only one source of information and that in the aggregate the market is not fooled by companies that choose the least-conservative accounting policies. In sum, the market as a whole sees through any attempts by companies to gain favor through the choice of accounting policies that tend to boost immediate income. Thus there is evidence that the stock markets may indeed be "efficient," at least in their reflection of accounting data.

Suppose you are the chief executive officer of Company A. Reported earnings are $4 per share and the stock price is $40. You are contemplating changing your method of depreciation for investor-reporting purposes from accelerated to straight-line. Your competitors use straight-line. You think the Company A stock price unjustifiably suffers in comparison to other companies in the same industry.

If straight-line depreciation is adopted by Company A, reported earnings will be $5 instead of $4 per share. Would the stock price rise accordingly from $40 to $50? No, the empirical research on these issues indicates that the stock price would remain at $40.

The chief executive's beliefs as shown in the above example are shared by many managers, who essentially adhere to an extremely narrow view of the role of an income statement. Such a "bottom-line" mentality is slowly, surely, and sensibly falling into disrepute. At the risk of unfair exaggeration, the view is summarized as follows:

1. The income statement is the sole (or at least the primary) source of information about a company.
2. Lenders and shareholders invest in a company because of its reported earnings. For instance, the higher the reported earnings per share, the higher the stock price, and the easier it is to raise capital.

Basically, these arguments assume that investors can be misled by how reported earnings are measured. But there is considerable evidence that securities markets are not fooled with respect to accounting changes that are devoid of economic substance (that have no effect on cash flows). Why? Because the change generally reveals no new information, so no significant change in stock price is likely.

The research described above concentrates on the effects of accounting on investors **in the aggregate.** Individual investors vary in how they analyze financial statements. One by one, individual users must either incur the costs of conducting careful analyses or delegate that chore to professional analysts. In any event, intelligent analysis cannot be accomplished without an understanding of the assumptions and limitations of financial statements, including the presence of various alternative accounting methods.

Summary

Financial ratios aid the intelligent analysis of statements. They are used as a basis of evaluation, comparison, and prediction. The rate of return on invested capital is a very popular means of comparing performance.

Summary
Problem for Your Review

(Problem One appeared earlier in this chapter.)

❑ Problem Two

Examine Exhibits 19-5 and 19-6, pages 614–615. Assume some new data in place of certain old data for the December 31, 19X2, balance sheet (in thousands):

	OLD DATA	NEW DATA
Accounts receivable	$ 95	$130
Inventory	20	40
Total current assets	290	345
Paid-in capital	102	157
Total stockholders' equity	399	454

REQUIRED:

Compute the following ratios applicable to December 31, 19X2, or to the year 19X2, as appropriate: current ratio, inventory turnover, average collection period, working capital, and return on stockholders' equity. Compare this new set of ratios with the old set of ratios. Are the new ratios more desirable? Explain.

❑ Solution to Problem Two

All the ratios would be affected except that the net profit on sales would be unchanged.

$$\text{current ratio} = \frac{\text{current assets}}{\text{current liabilities}}$$

$$= \frac{345}{219} = 1.6 \text{ to 1 instead of 1.3 to 1.}$$

$$\text{inventory turnover} = \frac{\text{cost of goods sold}}{\text{average inventory}}$$

$$= \frac{399}{\frac{1}{2}(40 + 60)}$$

$$= \frac{399}{50} = 8 \text{ times instead of 10 times.}$$

Understanding
Corporate
Annual
Reports—
Part Two

623

$$\text{average collection period} = \frac{\text{average accounts receivable}}{\text{sales on account}} \times 365$$

$$= \frac{\frac{1}{2}(130 + 70)}{999} \times 365$$

$$= \frac{100 \times 365}{999} = 37 \text{ days instead of 30 days.}$$

Working capital is current assets minus current liabilities, which is $345 - 219 = 126$ instead of 71.

$$\text{return on stockholders' equity} = \frac{\text{net income}}{\text{average stockholders' equity}}$$

$$= \frac{90}{\frac{1}{2}(389 + 454)}$$

$$= 21.4\% \text{ instead of } 22.8\%.$$

The new set of ratios has good news and bad news. The good news is that the company would appear to be slightly more liquid (a current ratio of 1.6 instead of 1.3) and to have more working capital ($126 instead of $71). The bad news is that the inventory turnover, the average collection period, and the rate of return on stockholders' equity are less attractive.

Highlights to Remember

1. Earnings per share is the only financial ratio that is required to be shown in the financial reports of publicly held corporations.
2. Recent research has indicated that capital markets are "efficient" in the sense that investors in the aggregate are not fooled by companies that try to look good by choosing less-conservative accounting policies. Accounting is a major source of information, but it is not the sole source.

Accounting Vocabulary

For various financial ratios, see Exhibit 19-9. Also become familiar with *budget; component percentages;* and *efficient capital market.*

Fundamental Assignment Material

Special Note: Problems relating to Part One of the chapter are presented first in each subgrouping of the assignment material.

19–1. Cost or equity method. (Alternate is 19–6.) Company G acquired 25% of the voting stock of Company H for $40 million cash. In Year 1, H had a net income of $36 million and paid a cash dividend of $20 million.

REQUIRED:

Using the equity and the cost methods, show the effects of the three transactions on the accounts of G. Use the balance sheet equation format. Also show the accompanying journal entries.

19–2. Consolidated financial statements. (Alternate is 19–7.) Company P acquired a 100% voting interest in Company S for $100 million cash at the start of the year. Immediately before the business combination, each company had the following condensed balance sheet accounts (in millions):

	P	S
Cash and other assets	$500	$140
Accounts payable, etc.	$200	$ 40
Stockholders' equity	300	100
Total equities	$500	$140

REQUIRED:

1. Prepare a tabulation of the consolidated balance sheet accounts immediately after the acquisition. Use the balance sheet equation format.
2. Suppose P and S have the following results for the year:

	P	S
Sales	$600	$200
Expenses	450	180

Prepare income statements for the year for P, S, and the consolidated entity.
3. Present the effects of the operations for the year on P's accounts and on S's accounts, using the balance sheet equation. Also tabulate the consolidated balance sheet accounts at the end of the year. Assume that liabilities are unchanged.
4. Suppose S paid a cash dividend of $15 million. What accounts in Requirement 3 would be affected and by how much?

19–3. Minority interests. This extends the preceding problem. However, this problem is self-contained because all the facts are reproduced below. Company P acquired an 80% voting interest in Company S for $80 million cash at the start of the year. Immediately before the business combination, each company had the following condensed balance sheet accounts (in millions):

	P	S
Cash and other assets	$500	$140
Accounts payable, etc.	$200	$ 40
Stockholders' equity	300	100
Total equities	$500	$140

Understanding
Corporate
Annual
Reports—
Part Two

625

1. Prepare a tabulation of the consolidated balance sheet accounts immediately after the acquisition. Use the balance sheet equation format.
2. Suppose P and S have the following results for the year:

	P	S
Sales	$600	$200
Expenses	450	180

Prepare income statements for the year for P, S, and the consolidated entity.
3. Using the balance sheet equation format, present the effects of the operations for the year on P's accounts and S's accounts. Also tabulate consolidated balance sheet accounts at the end of the year. Assume that liabilities are unchanged.
4. Suppose S paid a cash dividend of $15 million. What accounts in Requirement 3 would be affected and by how much?

19–4. Goodwill and consolidations. This extends Problem 19–2. However, this problem is self-contained because all the facts are reproduced below. Company P acquired a 100% voting interest in Company S for $150 million cash at the start of the year. Immediately before the business combination, each company had the following condensed balance sheet accounts (in millions):

	P	S
Cash and other assets	$500	$140
Accounts payable, etc.	200	$ 40
Stockholders' equity	300	100
Total equities	$500	$140

Assume that the fair values of the individual assets of S were equal to their book values.

1. Prepare a tabulation of the consolidated balance sheet accounts immediately after the acquisition. Use the balance sheet equation format.
2. If goodwill is going to be amortized over forty years, how much was amortized for the first year? If over five years, how much was amortized for the first year?
3. Suppose the book values of the S individual assets are equal to their fair market values except for equipment. The net book value of equipment is $30 million and its fair market value is $50 million. The equipment has a remaining useful life of four years. Straight-line depreciation is used.
   a. Describe how the consolidated balance sheet accounts immediately after the acquisition would differ from those in Requirement 1. Be specific as to accounts and amounts.
   b. By how much will consolidated income differ in comparison with the consolidated income that would be reported in Requirement 2? Assume amortization of goodwill over a forty-year period.

19–5. Rate-of-return computations.

1. Almagam Company reported a 5% operating margin on sales, an 8% pretax operating return on total assets, and $400 million of total assets. Compute the (a) operating income, (b) total sales, and (c) total asset turnover.

2. MacIver Corporation reported $600 million of sales, $24 million of operating income, and a total asset turnover of 5 times. Compute the (a) total assets, (b) operating margin percentage on sales, and (c) pretax operating return on total assets.

☐ Understanding Published Financial Reports

19–6. Equity method. (Alternate is 19–1.) Sears acquired one-third of the voting stock of Whirlpool Company for $25 million cash. In Year 1, Whirlpool had a net income of $21 million and paid cash dividends of $12 million.

REQUIRED:

Prepare a tabulation that compares the equity method and the cost method of accounting for Sears's investment in Whirlpool. Show the effects on the balance sheet equation under each method. What is the year-end balance in the Investment in Whirlpool account under the equity method? Under the cost method?

19–7. Consolidated financial statements. (Alternate is 19–2.) Consider Company P, which could be a large soft-drink company such as PepsiCo. Suppose P acquired a 100% voting interest in Company S for $300 million at the beginning of the year. Company S could be a snack-food company such as Frito-Lay, which is now owned by PepsiCo.

The balance sheet accounts immediately after the acquisition were (in millions):

	P	S
Investment in S	$300	$ –
Cash and other assets	600	550
Total assets	$900	$550
Accounts payable, etc.	$200	$250
Stockholders' equity	700	300
Total equities	$900	$550

REQUIRED:

1. Using the balance sheet equation format, prepare a tabulation of the consolidated balance sheet accounts immediately after the acquisition.
2. Suppose S had sales of $500 million and expenses of $450 million for the year. P had sales of $990 million and expenses of $840 million. Prepare income statements for P, for S, and for the consolidated company.
3. Using the balance sheet equation, present the effects of the operations for the year on P's accounts and S's accounts. Also tabulate the consolidated balance sheet accounts at the end of the year. Assume that liabilities are unchanged.
4. Suppose S paid a cash dividend of $18 million. What accounts in Requirement 3 would be affected and by how much?

19–8. Investments in equity securities. Clark Equipment Company is a multinational corporation with subsidiaries and affiliations throughout the world. Its annual report for 1981 showed total assets of $1,036.2 million. Investments in companies in which Clark owned 20% or more minority interest were $33.3 million. The remaining investments in companies in which Clark owned less than 20% amounted to $3.0 million.

REQUIRED:

How did Clark report the investments in which it owned more than 50% interest? Indicate briefly how the following three classes of investments should be accounted for: (a) greater than 50% interest; (b) 20% through 50% interest; and (c) less than 20% interest.

19–9. Equity method of accounting for unconsolidated subsidiaries. Trans World Airlines owns 100% of Hilton International Company. The airline and hotel operations are now being reported on a consolidated basis. However, in past years the hotel operations have not been consolidated with the airline operations for financial-reporting purposes. The following data are extracted from the TWA 1972 annual report (in millions):

	12/31/72	12/31/71
From statement of income:		
Income from airline operations (detailed)	(5.3)	
Income from hotel operations (on one line)	8.8	
Net income for the year	$ 3.5	
From balance sheet:		
Investments: equity in Hilton International	$47.0	$38.2

REQUIRED:

If Hilton International had paid cash dividends of $4.1 million in 1972, how would the payment have affected TWA net income for the year? How would it have affected the investment balance at December 31, 1972?

19–10. Income ratios and asset turnover. A semiannual report to the stockholders of Texaco included the following comments on earnings:

☐ On an annualized basis, net income represented an 8.9% return on average total assets of approximately $27.3 billion and an 18.9% return on average stockholders' equity. . . . Net income per gallon on all petroleum products sold worldwide averaged 3.6 cents. Net income was 4 cents on each dollar of revenue.

REQUIRED:

Using only this information, compute the (1) total asset turnover, (2) net income, (3) total revenues, (4) average stockholders' equity, and (5) gallons of petroleum products sold.

Additional Assignment Material

❑ General Coverage

19–11. Why is *marketable securities* an ill chosen term to describe short-term investments?

19–12. "The equity method is usually used for long-term investments." Do you think this is appropriate? Explain.

19–13. "A consolidated balance sheet can contain an asset, Investment in Unconsolidated Subsidiary." Do you agree that this is appropriate? Explain.

19–14. Distinguish between control of a company and significant influence over a company.

19–15. "Goodwill is the excess of purchase price over the book values of the individual assets acquired." Do you agree? Explain.

19–16. What criterion is used to determine whether a parent-subsidiary relationship exists?

19–17. Why have subsidiaries? Why not have the corporation take the form of a single legal entity?

19–18. What is a minority interest?

19–19. When is there justification for not consolidating subsidiaries in accounting reports?

19–20. What is the equity method?

19–21. Contrast the cost method and the equity method.

19–22. "The lower-of-cost-or-market rule is applied to investments in short-term securities." Do you agree? Explain.

19–23. "A company can carry some investments in unconsolidated subsidiaries at cost." Under what circumstances is this a correct statement?

19–24. **Purchased goodwill.** Consider the following balance sheets (in millions of dollars):

	COMPANY X	COMPANY Y
Cash	150	20
Inventories	60	30
Plant assets, net	60	30
Total assets	270	80
Common stock and paid-in surplus	70	30
Retained income	200	50
Total equities	270	80

X paid $120 million to Y stockholders for all their stock. The "fair value" of the plant assets of Y is $70 million. The fair value of cash and inventories is equal to their carrying amounts. X and Y continued to keep separate books.

REQUIRED:

1. Prepare a tabulation showing the balance sheets of X, of Y, Intercompany Eliminations, and Consolidated immediately after the acquisition.
2. Suppose that only $60 million rather than $70 million of the total purchase price of $120 million could be logically assigned to the plant assets. How would the consolidated accounts be affected?
3. Refer to the facts in Requirement 1. Suppose X had paid $144 million rather than $120 million. State how your tabulation in Requirement 1 would change.

19–25. **Amortization and depreciation.** Refer to the preceding problem, Requirement 3. Suppose a year passes, and X and Y generate individual net incomes of $20 million and $13 million, respectively. The latter is after a deduction by Y of $6 million of straight-line depreciation. Compute the consolidated net income if goodwill is amortized (1) over forty years and (2) over ten years. Ignore income taxes.

19–26. **Allocating total purchase price to assets.** Two entities had the following balance sheet accounts as of December 31, 19X1 (in millions):

Understanding
Corporate
Annual
Reports—
Part Two

629

	GREYMONT	PARADELT		GREYMONT	PARADELT
Cash and			Current liabilities	$ 50	$ 20
receivables	$ 30	$ 22	Common stock	100	10
Inventories	120	3	Retained income	150	90
Plant assets, net	150	95	Total equities	$300	$120
Total assets	$300	$120			
Net income for					
19X1	$ 19	$ 4			

On January 4, 19X2, these entities combined. Greymont issued $180 million of its shares (at market value) in exchange for all the shares of Paradelt, a motion picture division of a large company. The inventory of films acquired through the combination had been fully amortized on Paradelt's books.

During 19X2, Greymont entered into many television distribution contracts that called for $21 million in film rentals over a prolonged span of years. These rentals were to be collected over this period of time, but the contracts were used as support for immediate recognition of revenue (and consequent net income).

Greymont earned $20 million on its other operations during 19X2. Paradelt broke even on its other operations during 19X2.

REQUIRED:

1. Prepare a consolidated balance sheet for the combined company immediately after the combination on a purchase basis. Assume that on a purchase basis $80 million would be assigned to the inventory of films.
2. Prepare a comparison of net income between 19X1 and 19X2 where 25% of the cost of the film inventories would be properly matched against the revenue from the television contracts. What would be the net income for 19X2 if the $80 million were assigned to goodwill rather than to the library of films, and goodwill were amortized over forty years?

19–27. **Consolidated financial statements.** The Parent Company owns 90% of the common stock of Company S-1 and 60% of the common stock of Company S-2. The balances as of December 31, 19X4, in the condensed accounts follow (in thousands):

	PARENT	S-1	S-2
Sales	300,000	80,000	100,000
Investment in subsidiaries*	72,000	—	—
Other assets	128,000	90,000	20,000
Liabilities to creditors	100,000	20,000	5,000
Expenses	280,000	90,000	95,000
Stockholders' equity, including current net income	100,000	70,000	15,000

*Carried at equity in subsidiaries.

REQUIRED:

Prepare a consolidated balance sheet as of December 31, 19X4, and a consolidated income statement for 19X4.

19–28. **Prepare consolidated financial statements.** From the following data, prepare a consolidated balance sheet and an income statement of the Schiff Corporation. All data are in millions and pertain to December 31, 19X2 or to operations for 19X2:

Paid-in capital in excess of par	$ 82
Interest expense	25
Retained income	218
Accrued income taxes payable	30
Investments in unconsolidated subsidiaries (which are two insurance companies)	70
Cost of goods sold and operating expenses, exclusive of depreciation and amortization	700
Subordinated debentures, 11% interest, due December 31, 19X9	100
Outside stockholders' interest in consolidated subsidiaries' net income	20
Goodwill	100
Net sales and other operating revenue	950
Investments in affiliated companies	30
Common stock, 10,000,000 shares, $1 par	10
Depreciation and amortization	20
Accounts payable	200
Equity in earnings of unconsolidated subsidiary	17
Cash	50
First-mortgage bonds, 10% interest, due December 31, 19X8	80
Property, plant, and equipment, net	120
Preferred stock, 2,000,000 shares, $50 par, dividend rate is $5 per share, each share is convertible into one share of common stock	100
Short-term investments at cost, which approximates current market	40
Income tax expense	90
Accounts receivable, net	100
Outside stockholders' interest in subsidiaries (minority interests)	90
Inventories at average cost	400
Dividends declared and paid on preferred stock	10
Equity in earnings of affiliated companies	3

19-29. **Financial ratios.** The annual reports of Top-Ranking Corporation included the following selected data (in millions):

	19X6	19X5	19X4
Annual Amounts:			
Net income	$100	$ 60	$ 25
Gross margin on sales	525	380	200
Cost of goods sold	975	620	300
Operating expenses	380	295	165
Income tax expense	45	25	10
Dividends declared	30	15	5
End-of-Year Amounts:			
Long-term assets	$250	$220	$180
Long-term debt	80	65	40
Current liabilities	70	55	35
Cash	10	5	10
Accounts receivable	95	70	40
Merchandise inventory	125	85	60
Paid-in capital	205	205	205
Retained income	125	55	10

Understanding
Corporate
Annual
Reports—
Part Two

631

During each of the three years, there were outstanding 10 million shares of capital stock, all common. Assume that all sales were on account and that the applicable market prices per share of stock were $30 for 19X5 and $40 for 19X6.

REQUIRED:

1. Compute each of the following for each of the last two years, 19X5 and 19X6:
   a. Rate of return on sales
   b. Rate of return on stockholders' equity
   c. Inventory turnover
   d. Current ratio
   e. Ratio of total debt to stockholders' equity
   f. Ratio of current debt to stockholders' equity
   g. Gross profit rate
   h. Average collection period for accounts receivable
   i. Price-earnings ratio
   j. Dividend-payout percentage
   k. Dividend yield
2. Answer yes or no to each of these questions and indicate which of the above computations support your answer:
   a. Has the merchandise become more salable?
   b. Is there a decrease in the effectiveness of collection efforts?
   c. Has gross margin improved?
   d. Has the rate of return on sales deteriorated?
   e. Has the rate of return on owners' investment increased?
   f. Are dividends relatively more generous?
   g. Have the risks of insolvency changed significantly?
   h. Has the market price of the stock become cheaper relative to earnings?
   i. Have business operations improved?
   j. Has there been a worsening of the company's ability to pay current debts on time?
   k. Has there been a decline in the cash return on the market value of the capital stock?
   l. Did the collectibility of the receivables improve?
3. Basing your observations on only the available data and the ratios you computed, prepare some brief comments on the company's operations and financial changes during the three years.

❑ Understanding Published Financial Reports

19–30. Classification on balance sheet.   The following accounts appeared in the annual report of the Jewel Companies, Inc.:

1. Accumulated earnings—reserved for self-insured losses and general contingencies
2. Long-term indebtedness, due within one year
3. Investments: minority interest in foreign affiliates (at cost)
4. Prepaid expenses and supplies
5. Dividends payable
6. Treasury stock at cost

REQUIRED:

Indicate in detail in what section of the balance sheet each account should appear.

19–31. Meaning of account descriptions.   The following account descriptions were found in two annual reports:

Du Pont: Minority interests in earnings of consolidated subsidiaries; Minority interests in consolidated subsidiaries

Philip Morris: Investments in unconsolidated subsidiaries and affiliates;
Equity in net earnings of unconsolidated subsidiaries and affiliates

In your own words, explain what each type of account represents. Indicate whether the item appears on the balance sheet or the income statement.

19–32. Meaning of account descriptions. The following account descriptions were found in various annual reports:

Montgomery Ward: Net earnings of subsidiaries not consolidated
Tenneco: Equity in undistributed earnings of 50% owned companies
St. Regis Paper: Equity in net earnings of subsidiaries not consolidated and associated companies

In your own words, explain what each type of account represents. Also indicate whether the item appears on the balance sheet or the income statement.

19–33. Consolidations in Japan. *Business Week* (April 25, 1977, p. 112) reported that Japan's finance ministry issued a directive requiring the six hundred largest Japanese companies to produce consolidated financial statements after April 1, 1977. The story said: "Financial observers hope that the move will help end the tradition-honored Japanese practice of 'window dressing' the parent company financial results by shoving losses onto hapless subsidiaries, whose red ink was seldom revealed. . . . When companies needed to show a bigger profit, they would sell their product to subsidiaries at an inflated price. . . . Or the parent company charged a higher rent to a subsidiary company using its building."

REQUIRED:

Could a parent company follow the quoted practices and achieve window dressing in its parent-only financial statements if it used the equity method of accounting for its intercorporate investments? The cost method? Explain.

19–34. Effect of transactions under the equity method. (J. Patell, adapted and updated.) Koppers Company Inc. is a diversified manufacturer. Its balance sheets showed (in thousands):

	DECEMBER 31	
	1981	1980
Investments, affiliated companies, at equity	$83,804	$50,780

These affiliated companies were owned by Koppers in various proportions from 20% to 50%. Dividends received from these companies during 1981 totaled $8,304,000.
The income statement for 1981 showed (in thousands):

Equity in earnings of affiliates	5,369

REQUIRED:

1. Did Koppers purchase more shares in affiliated companies during 1981 or sell off part of its holdings (in aggregate)? Give the dollar amount of the transaction, and label it as a purchase or sale. *Hint:* Use a balance sheet equation or a T-account to aid your analysis.
2. Income before taxes in 1981 was $85,528,000. What would Koppers's 1981 income before taxes have been if it had accounted for its Investment in Affiliated Companies by the cost method?

19-35. Income ratios and asset turnover. Dun and Bradstreet Corporation's 1981 annual report to stockholders included the following data:

Net income	$121,474,000
Total assets:	
Beginning of year	770,137,000
End of year	905,694,000
Net income as a percent of:	
Total revenue	9.1%
Average stockholders' equity	29.9%

REQUIRED:

Using only the above data, compute the (1) net income percent of average assets, (2) total revenues, (3) average stockholders' equity, and (4) asset turnover, using two different approaches.

20

DIFFICULTIES IN MEASURING NET INCOME

Learning Objectives

After studying this chapter, you should be able to

1. Explain the differences between various inventory methods, especially FIFO and LIFO, and their effects on the measurements of assets and net income
2. Describe the major differences between financial capital and physical capital
3. Explain and illustrate four different ways of measuring income: (a) historical cost/nominal dollars, (b) current cost/nominal dollars, (c) historical cost/constant dollars, and (d) current cost/constant dollars
4. Explain the difference between monetary and nonmonetary items (Appendix 20)
5. Compute general purchasing-power gains and losses (Appendix 20)

The income statement summarizes the performance of an entity. This chapter focuses on how income is affected by choices among alternative accounting methods. The focus is on the assumptions and limitations of generally accepted accounting methods.

The two major parts of this chapter examine the controversial effects on income of (1) the principal inventory methods and (2) various measurements of changes in price levels. Each major part may be studied independently. There are, of course, many other controversial topics in accounting, including, for example, accounting for long-term leases, pensions, deferred income taxes, and foreign currency translation. However, space limitations preclude our coverage of these accounting controversies.

Above all, recognize that all these controversial topics illustrate a central question that managers and accountants worry about: How should income be measured?

☐ PART ONE   Principal Inventory Methods

FOUR MAJOR METHODS

There are various ways to measure the cost of goods sold and inventories. If unit prices did not fluctuate, all inventory methods would show identical results. But prices change, and these changes raise central issues regarding cost of goods sold (income measurement) and inventories (asset measurement). Four principal methods have been generally accepted in the United States: specific identification, weighted average, FIFO, and LIFO. Each will be explained and compared.

As a preview of the remainder of this section, consider the following simple example of the choices facing management. A new vendor of a cola drink at the fairgrounds bought one can on Monday for 30 cents; a second can on Tuesday for 40 cents; and two more cans on Wednesday for 53 cents each. He then sold one can on Thursday for 90 cents. What was his gross profit? His ending inventory? Answer these questions in your own mind before reading on.

Exhibit 20-1 provides a quick glimpse of the nature of the generally accepted methods. Their underlying assumptions will be explained shortly. As you can readily see, the vendor's choice of an inventory method can often significantly affect his gross profit (and hence net income) and his ending inventory valuation for balance sheet purposes.

1. SPECIFIC IDENTIFICATION (COLUMN 1). This method concentrates on the *physical* linking of the *particular* items sold. If the vendor reached for the Monday can instead of the Wednesday can, the *same inventory method* would show different results. Thus Exhibit 20-1 indicates that gross profit for operations of Monday through Thursday could be 60¢, 50¢, or 37¢. Obviously, this method permits great latitude for measuring results in any given period. The next three methods do not trace the actual physical flow of goods except by coincidence.

EXHIBIT 20-1

Comparison of Inventory Methods for Cola Vendor
(all monetary amounts are in cents)

	(1A)	(1B)	(1C)	(2) FIFO	(3) LIFO	(4) WEIGHTED AVERAGE
		(1) SPECIFIC IDENTIFICATION				
Sales, 1 unit on Thursday @ 90	90	90	90	90	90	90
Deduct cost of goods sold, 1 unit	30	40	53	30	53	44
Gross profit for Monday through Thursday	60	50	37	60	37	46
Computation of cost of goods sold:						
Beginning inventory	0	0	0	0	0	0
Purchase (4 units):						
1 @ 30 = 30						
1 @ 40 = 40						
2 @ 53 = 106						
4 176	176	176	176	176	176	176
Cost of goods available for sale	176	176	176	176	176	176
Ending Inventory, Thursday						
(3 units)						
1 @ 40 = 40						
2 @ 53 = 106	146					
or						
1 @ 30 = 30						
2 @ 53 = 106		136				
or						
1 @ 30 = 30						
1 @ 40 = 40						
1 @ 53 = 53			123			
or						
1 @ 40 = 40						
2 @ 53 = 106				146		
or						
1 @ 30 = 30						
1 @ 40 = 40						
1 @ 53 = 53					123	
or						
Weighted average is						
176 ÷ 4 = 44 per unit,						
so 3 units × 44 = 132	—	—	—	—	—	132
Cost of goods sold on Thursday (to second line above)	30	40	53	30	53	44
Sales, 3 units on the following Monday @ 90	270	270	270	270	270	270
Cost of goods sold on Monday (Thurs. ending Inventory from above)	146	136	123	146	123	132
Gross profit for Friday through Monday	124	134	147	124	147	138
Gross profit for life of entity	184	184	184	184	184	184

2. FIRST-IN, FIRST-OUT (FIFO) (COLUMN 2). This method assumes that the stock acquired earliest is sold (used up) first. Thus the Monday unit is deemed to have been sold regardless of the actual physical unit sold. In times of rising prices, FIFO shows the largest gross profit (60¢ in Exhibit 20-1).

3. LAST-IN, FIRST-OUT (LIFO) (COLUMN 3). This method assumes that the stock acquired most recently is sold (used up) first. Thus one of the Wednesday units is deemed to have been sold regardless of the actual physical unit sold. In times of rising prices, LIFO generally shows the lowest gross profit (37¢ in Exhibit 20-1).

4. WEIGHTED-AVERAGE COST (COLUMN 4). This method assumes that all items available for sale during the period are best represented by a weighted average. Exhibit 20-1 shows the calculations and also shows that the weighted-average method produces a gross profit somewhere between that obtained under FIFO and LIFO (46¢ as compared with 60¢ and 37¢ in Exhibit 20-1).

INVENTORIES AND MATCHING

This illustration shows why theoretical and practical disputes can easily arise regarding the "best" inventory method. As Exhibit 20-2 demonstrates, the four inventory methods are based on four separate cost-flow assumptions. When identical goods are purchased at different times and at different prices, the accountant faces a "matching" problem. The choice of an inventory method is an attempt to adhere to the basic concept of matching and cost recovery, which was introduced in Chapter 17. The difficulty is not with "matching" as an *abstract* idea; instead, disputes arise regarding how to *apply* it. Thus more than one inventory method has evolved, and

EXHIBIT
20-2

Diagram of Inventory Methods
(Data are from preceding exhibit)

Beginning inventory	+	Merchandise purchases	=	Cost of goods available for sale
0	+	176	=	176

Cost of goods available for sale	−	Cost of goods sold	=	Ending inventory

1 @ 30
1 @ 40
1 @ 53
1 @ 53

176	−	30 or 40 or 53	=	146 or 136 or 123	Specific identification
	−	30	=	146	FIFO
	−	53	=	123	LIFO
	−	44	=	132	Weighted average

the four methods illustrated in Exhibits 20-1 and 20-2 have all become accepted as a part of the body of generally accepted accounting principles.

ESSENCE OF FIFO

Accountants and managers tend to develop strong feelings regarding the comparative merits of FIFO and LIFO. Adherents of FIFO maintain that it is the most practical way to reflect what operating managers actually do. That is, most managers deliberately attempt to move their merchandise on a first-in, first-out basis. This approach avoids spoilage, obsolescence, and the like. Thus the inventory flow assumption underlying FIFO corresponds most closely with the actual physical flows of inventory items in most businesses. Furthermore, the asset balance for inventories is a close approximation of the "actual" dollars invested, because the inventory is carried at the most recent purchase prices paid. Such prices are not likely to be very different from current prices at the balance sheet date. Consequently, its proponents maintain that FIFO properly meets the objectives of both the income statement and the balance sheet.

ESSENCE OF LIFO

In 1982, LIFO was used by 65% of a sample of six hundred large companies that are surveyed annually by the American Institute of CPAs. Adherents of LIFO are usually critical of FIFO because of the latter's effects on income when prices are rising. They claim that FIFO-based income is deceiving in the sense that some of the corresponding increase in net assets is merely an "inventory profit." That is, an "inventory profit" is fictitious because for a going concern, part of it is needed for replenishing the inventory. Consequently, it is not profit in the layperson's sense of the term; it does not indicate an amount that is entirely available to pay dividends. For instance, consider our cola vendor:

	FIFO	LIFO
Sales, one unit on Thursday	90¢	90¢
Cost of goods sold	30	53
Gross profit	60¢	37¢

The proponent of LIFO would claim that FIFO "overstates" profits (the "inventory profit") by 60¢ − 37¢ = 23¢. Unless replacement prices have fallen, the vendor will need not merely the 30¢ reported as cost of goods sold, but 30¢ + 23¢ = 53¢ for the replacement of the unit sold.

Advocates of LIFO also stress that in times of rising prices, there may be greater pressure from stockholders to pay unjustified higher cash dividends under FIFO than LIFO. In the above example, the payment of a cash dividend of 60¢ by a vendor using FIFO would result in his not having enough cash to replenish his inventory. He would have only

Difficulties in
Measuring Net
Income

639

90¢ − 60¢ = 30¢. In contrast, LIFO would be more likely to conserve cash to the extent that less cash dividends would be paid if less income is reported. The vendor would have 90¢ − 37¢ = 53¢ available for replenishing inventory (if he paid a cash dividend of 37¢, ignoring the effects of other expenses).

CRITICISMS OF LIFO

Critics of LIFO point to absurd balance sheet valuations. Under LIFO, older and older prices, and hence less-useful inventory values, are reported, especially if physical stocks grow through the years. In contrast, under FIFO, the balance sheet tends to reflect current prices and values.

Another criticism of LIFO is that, unlike FIFO, it permits management to influence immediate net income by the *timing of purchases*. For instance, if prices are rising and a company desires, for income tax or other reasons, to report less income in a given year, managers may be inclined to buy a large amount of inventory near the end of the year. That is, managers may accelerate the replacement of inventory that would normally not occur until early in the next year.

Consider an example. Suppose in our illustration that acquisition prices had increased from 53¢ on Wednesday to 61¢ on Thursday, the day of the sale of the one unit. Suppose one more unit was acquired on Thursday for 61¢. How would net income be affected under FIFO? Under LIFO?

There would be no effect on cost of goods sold or gross profit under FIFO, although the balance sheet would show ending inventory as 61¢ higher. In contrast, LIFO would show an 8¢ higher cost of goods sold and an 8¢ lower gross profit:

	LIFO			
	As in Exhibit 20-1		If One More Unit Acquired	
Sales	90¢		90¢	
Cost of goods sold	53		61	
Gross profit	37¢		29¢	
Ending inventory:				
First layer, Monday	1 @ 30¢ =	30¢	1 @ 30¢ =	30¢
Second layer, Tuesday	1 @ 40¢ =	40¢	1 @ 40¢ =	40¢
Third layer, Wednesday	1 @ 53¢ =	53¢	2 @ 53¢ =	106¢
		123¢		176¢

Thus a 37¢ gross profit may be transformed into a 29¢ gross profit merely because of a change in the timing and amount of merchandise *acquired*, not because of any change in *sales*.

The second part of the above tabulation uses the word *layer*. As the term implies, a **LIFO layer** (also called LIFO **increment** or LIFO **pool**) is an identifiable addition to inventory. As a company grows, the LIFO layers tend to pile on one another as the years go by. Thus many LIFO companies will show inventories that may have ancient layers (going back to 1940 in some instances). The reported LIFO values may therefore be far below what FIFO values might otherwise show.

IMPORTANCE OF INCOME TAXES

The accounting literature is full of fancy theoretical arguments that support LIFO. For example, LIFO shows the "real" impact of inflation on cost of goods sold more clearly than FIFO. But there is one—and only one—dominant reason why more and more U.S. companies have adopted LIFO. *Income taxes!* LIFO is acceptable for income tax purposes. Furthermore, the Internal Revenue Code requires that if LIFO is used for income tax purposes, it must also be used for financial-reporting purposes. If prices persistently rise, and if inventory quantities are maintained so that LIFO layers bearing "old" prices are not used up, current taxable income will be less under LIFO than FIFO. Consequently, income taxes will be postponed. Intelligent financial management would therefore be tempted to adopt LIFO. Indeed, some observers maintain that executives are guilty of serious mismanagement by not adopting LIFO when FIFO produces significantly higher taxable income.

General management often faces some significant choices between accounting methods. The impact of these choices on the cash position can be enormous.

TYRANNY OF REPORTED EARNINGS

The accrual accounting model has survived many tests through time. It is here to stay. Nevertheless, as valuable as it is for evaluating performance, its limitations should never be overlooked. For example, net income (or earnings per share) is *only one* measure of performance. Even though this "bottom line" is important, it is sometimes overemphasized in the minds of management. It may lead to decisions that boost current reported net income but may not be in the best long-run interests of the stockholders. Thus managers may slash advertising, maintenance, and research expenses to bolster 19X1 earnings. But such "economy measures" can produce some unfavorable results: reduction in share of the customer market, poorer condition of equipment, and lack of new products, all of which may have devastating effects on earnings in 19X2, 19X3, and thereafter.

Similarly, managers may be reluctant to switch to LIFO from FIFO because reported income will be less. There is widespread but mistaken belief that the stock market can be fooled by the reported net income numbers. In the long run, the wealth of the shareholders is usually enhanced by decisions that postpone income tax disbursements even though reported net income may be lower.

Difficulties in Measuring Net Income

The accompanying table summarizes the choices faced by many top managers:

641

INVENTORY METHOD	ACTUAL CASH POSITION	REPORTED NET INCOME
FIFO	Lower	Higher
LIFO	Higher	Lower

The dilemma should often be solved in favor of LIFO. Then the company would have a greater ability to meet the dividend expectations of stockholders or of other demands. Why? Because the company will have a better cash position despite lower reported net income.

Summary

Four major inventory methods are in use: specific identification, average, FIFO, and LIFO. When prices are rising, less income is shown by LIFO than FIFO.

LIFO is popular in the United States because it offers income tax advantages that become most pronounced during times of steady or rising inventories combined with rising prices. Note that even when inventories are declining, *cumulative* taxable income is always less under LIFO than FIFO because the inventory valuation is less and the cumulative cost of goods sold is higher.

Summary Problems for Your Review

❏ Problem One

Refer to Exhibit 20-1, page 637. Suppose one more can had been acquired on early Thursday for 58¢. All other data are unchanged. Compute (1) the ending inventory value on Thursday and (2) the gross profit through Thursday under FIFO and under LIFO.

❏ Problem Two

"When prices are rising, FIFO results in fool's profits because more resources are needed to maintain operations than previously." Do you agree? Explain.

❏ Solution to Problem One

Note how the late purchase affects gross profit under LIFO but not under FIFO:

	FIFO	LIFO
1. Cost of goods available for sale: 176 + 58	234¢	234¢
2. Ending inventory:		
Increase by 58¢: 146 + 58 =	204	
Increase by 53¢: 123 + 58 + 53* − 58* =		176
3. Cost of goods sold:		
Before purchase of 58¢	30	53
After purchase of 58¢: 234 − 204 =	30	
234 − 176 =		58
4. Gross profit:		
Before purchase of 58¢	60	37
After purchase of 58¢: 90 − 30 =	60	
90 − 58 =		32

*Substitution in inventory of a 53¢ Wednesday purchase. The 58¢ purchase comes into and out of inventory on Thursday.

☐ Solution to Problem Two

The merit of this position is directly dependent on the concept of income favored. As Exhibit 20-1 shows, LIFO does give a better measure of "distributable" income than FIFO. Recall the cola example in the chapter. The gross profit under FIFO was sixty cents and under LIFO was thirty-seven cents. The 60¢ − 37¢ = 23¢ difference is a fool's profit because it must be reinvested to maintain the same inventory level as previously. Therefore the twenty-three cents cannot be distributed as a cash dividend without reducing the current level of operations.

Highlights to Remember

The following table may be helpful:

INVENTORY METHOD	INCOME STATEMENT: MEASUREMENT OF COST OF GOODS SOLD	BALANCE SHEET: MEASUREMENT OF INVENTORY ASSET
FIFO	Distant from current replacement cost	Near current replacement cost
LIFO	Near current replacement cost	Distant from current replacement cost

Accounting Vocabulary

First-in, first-out (FIFO); last-in, first-out (LIFO); LIFO increment; LIFO layer; LIFO pool; LIFO reserve; specific identification; weighted-average cost.

The measurement of income is easily the most controversial subject in accounting. The remainder of this chapter focuses on how inflation is portrayed by the income statement. An appendix explores the problems of accounting for inflation in more depth, although still at an introductory level.

COMPLAINTS ABOUT HISTORICAL COST

Since the early 1970s a pet theme of politicians and others has been the "unconscionable" or "obscene" profits reported by American companies. In turn, business executives maintain that our well-known historical-cost basis for measuring income produces misleading results, especially during a time of rising prices. Some managers have complained that the reported profits are so badly overstated that income taxes have been unfairly levied. In many cases, invested capital, rather than earned income, has been taxed. We now concentrate on these issues, which will help to clarify the various concepts of income and capital.

The industries with huge investments in plant and equipment claim that their profits are badly misstated by generally accepted accounting principles. For instance, Bethlehem Steel reported 1981 net income of $211 million, which would have been a net loss of $108 million if depreciation had been computed on a replacement-cost basis.

Suggestions for change led to regulatory actions that departed from the historical-cost measures which had almost exclusively dominated financial reporting throughout the century. These departures will now be described. In essence, the controversies center on how income and capital should be defined. Different sets of concepts of income and capital will lead to different measurement methods.

INCOME OR CAPITAL

At first glance, the concept of income seems straightforward. Income is increase in wealth. But what is wealth? It is capital. But what is capital? An endless chain of similar questions can be constructed. The heart of the issue is the distinction between invested capital and income. The time-honored interpretation is that invested capital is a *financial* concept (rather than a *physical* concept). The focus is on the potential profitability of the money invested, no matter what types of inventory, equipment, or other resources have been acquired.

Financial resources (capital) are invested with the expectation of a return *of* that capital together with an additional amount representing the return *on* that capital. Controversies have arisen regarding whether the financial resources generated by the invested capital qualify as returns *of* or *on* capital.

The Financial Accounting Standards Board distinguishes between financial and physical capital maintenance concepts, as follows:

□ Capital is maintained when revenues are at least equal to all costs and expenses. The appropriate measurement of costs and expenses depends on the concept of capital maintenance adopted. The capital maintenance concepts . . . may be described as follows:

a. *Financial capital maintenance.* If capital is regarded as a quantity of financial resources, costs and expenses should be measured in terms of the financial resources (usually historical costs) used up in earning the revenues. Suppose, for example, that an enterprise is established with a capital of $1,000 in cash; that sum is used immediately to purchase inventory; the inventory is sold a year later for $1,500. Cost of goods sold would be measured at $1,000, the amount required to maintain the original money amount of capital invested in the inventory, and income would be measured at $500. Suppose, as an alternative, that the inventory is held and measured at its current cost ($1,200) at the end of the year. Those who believe in financial capital maintenance would recognize the increase in current cost ($200) as part of income: $1,000 is deducted from the current cost of $1,200 at the end of the year to maintain the amount of financial capital invested.

b. *Physical capital maintenance* (the maintenance of physical operating capability). According to this view, costs and expenses are measured at an amount sufficient to preserve the capacity of the enterprise to maintain previous levels of output of goods and services. Consider again the numerical example given in subparagraph (a) above. If the inventory is sold for $1,500, and if the current cost of the inventory is $1,200 at the date of sale, income would be measured at $300 ($1,500 less $1,200); $1,200 must be retained to maintain the physical operating capability of the enterprise.[1]

The G Company situation described below is used to compare various concepts of income and capital. Four basic methods of income measurement are presented, two using nominal dollars and two using constant dollars. **Nominal dollars** are dollar measurements that are not restated for fluctuations in the general purchasing power of the monetary unit, whereas **constant dollars** are nominal dollars restated in terms of current purchasing power.

G Company has the following comparative balance sheets at December 31 (based on historical costs in nominal dollars):

	19X1	19X2
Cash	$ 0	$10,500
Inventory, 400 and 100 units, respectively	8,000	2,000
Total assets	$8,000	$12,500
Original paid-in capital	$8,000	$ 8,000
Retained income	—	4,500
Stockholders' equity	$8,000	$12,500

The company had acquired all of its four hundred units of inventory at $20 per unit (total of $8,000) on December 31, 19X1, and had held the units until December 31, 19X2. Three hundred units were sold for $35 per unit (total of $10,500 cash) on December 31, 19X2. The replacement cost of the inventory at that date was $30 per unit. The general-price-level index was 100 on December 31, 19X1, and 110 on December 31, 19X2. Assume that these are the only transactions. Ignore income taxes.

[1] Financial Accounting Standards *Statement No. 33,* "Financial Reporting and Changing Prices" (Stamford, Conn.: FASB, 1979), paragraph 100.

Exhibit 20-3 is the basis for the explanations that follow in the next several pages. The first set of financial statements in Exhibit 20-3 shows the time-honored method that uses historical cost/nominal dollars (Method 1). Basically, this method measures invested capital in nominal dollars. It is the most popular approach to income measurement and is commonly called the historical-cost method. Operating income (equals net income in this case) is the excess of realized revenue ($10,500 in 19X2) over the "not restated" historical costs of assets used in obtaining that revenue. As we have already seen, when the conventional accrual basis of accounting is used, an exchange transaction is ordinarily necessary before revenues (and

EXHIBIT 20-3   (Put a clip on this page for easy reference)

Four Major Methods to Measure Income and Capital

	NOMINAL DOLLARS*				CONSTANT DOLLARS*			
	(METHOD 1)		(METHOD 2)		(METHOD 3)		(METHOD 4)	
	Historical Cost		Current Cost		Historical Cost		Current Cost	
	19X1	19X2	19X1	19X2	19X1	19X2	19X1	19X2
Balance sheets as of December 31								
Cash	—	10,500	—	10,500	—	10,500	—	10,500
Inventory, 400 and 100 units, respectively	8,000	2,000[b]	8,000	3,000[c]	8,800[e]	2,200[e]	8,800[e]	3,000[c]
Total assets	8,000	12,500	8,000	13,500	8,800	12,700	8,800	13,500
Original paid-in capital	8,000	8,000	8,000	8,000	8,800[f]	8,800[f]	8,800[f]	8,800[f]
Retained income (confined to income from continuing operations)		4,500		1,500		3,900		1,500
Revaluation equity (accumulated holding gains)				4,000				3,200
Total equities	8,000	12,500	8,000	13,500	8,800	12,700	8,800	13,500
Income Statement for 19X2								
Sales, 300 units @ $35		10,500		10,500		10,500		10,500
Cost of goods sold, 300 units		6,000[b]		9,000[c]		6,600[c]		9,000[c]
Income from continuing operations (to retained income)		4,500		1,500		3,900		1,500
Holding gains:[a]								
on 300 units sold				3,000[d]				2,400[g]
on 100 units unsold				1,000[d]				800[g]
Total holding gains[a] (to revaluation equity)				4,000				3,200

*Nominal dollars are not restated for a general price index, whereas constant dollars are restated.

[a]Many advocates of this current cost method favor showing these gains in a completely separate statement of holding gains rather than as a part of the income statement. Moreover, many favor including some or all of these gains as a part of income for the year; see Appendix 20 for further discussion.

[b]$100 \times \$20$ [c]$100 \times \$30$ [d]$300 \times (\$30 - \$20)$ [e]$110/100 \times \$8,000$ [f]$110/100 \times \$8,000$
    $300 \times \$20$ $300 \times \$30$ $100 \times (\$30 - \$20)$ $110/100 \times \$2,000$
                                                       $110/100 \times \$6,000$

[g]$\$9,000 -$ Restated cost of $\$6,600 = \$2,400$ $\$3,000 -$ Restated cost of $\$2,200 = \$800$
or   or
   $300 \times (\$30 - 110\%$ of $\$20) = \$2,400$ $100 \times (\$30 - 110\%$ of $\$20) = \$800$

resulting incomes) are deemed to be realized. Thus, no income generally appears until the asset is sold; intervening price fluctuations are ignored.

CURRENT COST/NOMINAL DOLLARS

The second set of financial statements in Exhibit 20-3 illustrates a **current-cost** method that has especially strong advocates in the United Kingdom and Australia (Method 2). This method uses current cost/ nominal dollars. In general, the current cost of an asset is the cost to replace it. The focus is on income from continuing operations. As shown in the column for the income statements, this model emphasizes that operating income should be "distributable" income. That is, G Company could pay dividends in an amount of only $1,500, leaving enough assets to allow for replacement of the inventory that has just been sold.

Critics of the historical-cost approach claim that the $4,500 measure of income from continuing operations is misleading because it inaccurately reflects (it overstates) the net increment in distributable assets. If a $4,500 dividend were paid, the company would be less able to continue operations at the same level as before. The $3,000 difference between the two operating incomes ($4,500 − $1,500 = $3,000) is frequently referred to as an "inventory profit" or an "inflated profit." Why? Because $9,000 instead of $6,000 is now necessary to replace the 300 units sold (300 × the increase in price from $20 to $30 equals the $3,000 difference).

HOLDING GAINS AND PHYSICAL CAPITAL

The current-cost method stresses a separation between *income from continuing operations*, which is defined as the excess of revenue over the current costs of the assets consumed in obtaining that revenue, and *holding gains* (or *losses*), which are increases (or decreases) in the replacement costs of the assets held during the current period. Accountants differ sharply on how to account for holding gains. The "correct" accounting depends on distinctions between capital and income. That is, income cannot occur until invested capital is "recovered" or "maintained." The issue of capital versus income is concretely illustrated in Exhibit 20-3. The advocates of a physical concept of capital maintenance claim that *all* holding gains (both those gains related to the units sold and the gains related to the units unsold) should be excluded from income and become a part of revalued capital, called **revaluation equity.** That is, for a going concern no income can result unless the physical capital devoted to operations during the current period can be replaced.

For simplicity, income taxes are ignored in Exhibit 20-3. The historical cost/nominal dollar method *(Method 1)* is the only acceptable method for reporting on income tax returns in English-speaking countries. As Appendix 20 discusses in more detail, many managers of heavy industries like steel and aluminum claim that their capital is being taxed under the historical cost/nominal dollar method. These managers maintain that taxes should be levied only on *income from continuing operations*, as computed under the current cost/nominal dollar method (Method 2).

During the late 1970s, accountants in many countries struggled with the problem of measuring the current cost of assets. For example, in 1976 the U.S. Securities and Exchange Commission issued a revolutionary requirement for supplementary footnote disclosure (as distinguished from a full-fledged balance sheet and income statement) of the replacement cost of inventories; replacement cost of productive capacity of plant and equipment; cost of goods sold based on replacement cost as of time of sale; and depreciation based on average replacement cost for the period.

After extensive public hearings, the Financial Accounting Standards Board issued similar but more extensive disclosure requirements in 1979. Its *Statement No. 33*, "Financial Reporting and Changing Prices," applies to public companies that have either (1) inventories and property, plant, and equipment (before deducting accumulated depreciation) amounting to more than $125 million or (2) total assets amounting to more than $1 billion (after deducting accumulated depreciation). No changes must be made in the *primary* financial statements. All information required by *Statement No. 33* is to be presented as *supplementary* schedules in published annual reports. Appendix 20 has a fuller description of the FASB requirements.

HISTORICAL COST/CONSTANT DOLLARS

Method 3 of Exhibit 20-3 shows the results of applying general index numbers to historical costs. Essentially, the income measurements in each year are restated in terms of *constant dollars* (possessing the same general purchasing power of the current year) instead of the *nominal dollars* (possessing different general purchasing power of various years).

The fundamental reasoning underlying the Method 3 approach goes to the heart of the measurement theory itself. Additions or subtractions must use a *common measuring unit,* be it dollars, francs, meters, ounces, or any chosen measure.

Consider the objections to Method 1. Deducting 6,000 19X1 dollars from 10,500 19X2 dollars to obtain $4,500 is akin to deducting 60 *centimeters* from 105 *meters* and calling the result 45. Grade-school tests are marked wrong when such nonsensical arithmetic is discovered, but accountants have been paid well for years for performing similar arithmetic.

Method 3, historical cost/constant dollars, shows how general indexes may be used to restate the amounts of historical cost/nominal dollar Method 1 and thereby remedy the foregoing objections. Examples of such indexes are the Gross National Product Implicit Price Deflator and the Consumer Price Index for All Urban Consumers (CPI). Anyone who has lived long enough to be able to read this book is aware that the purchasing power of the dollar is unstable. Index numbers are used to gauge the relationship between current conditions and some norm or base condition (which is assigned the index number of 100). For our purpose, a general price index compares the average price of a group of goods and services at one date with the average price of a similar group at another date. A price index is an average. It does not measure the behavior of the individual component prices. Some individual prices may move in one direction and some in another. The general consumer price level may soar while the prices of eggs and chickens decline.

Do not confuse *general* indexes, which are used in constant-dollar accounting, with *specific* indexes. The two have entirely different purposes. Sometimes specific price indexes are used as a means of approximating the *current costs* of particular assets or types of assets. That is, companies have found specialized indexes to be good enough to get approximations of current costs. This avoids the hiring of professional appraisers or the employing of other expensive means of valuation. For example, Inland Steel uses the Engineering News Record Construction Cost Index to value most of its property, plant, and equipment for purposes of using the current-cost method.

MAINTAINING INVESTED CAPITAL

The historical cost/constant dollar approach (Method 3) is *not* a fundamental departure from historical costs. Instead, it maintains that all historical costs to be matched against revenue should be restated on some constant-dollar basis so that all revenue and all expenses can be expressed in dollars of the same (usually current) purchasing power. The restated figures *are historical costs* expressed in constant dollars via the use of a general price index.

The current dollar is typically employed because users of financial statements tend to think in such terms instead of in terms of old dollars with significantly different purchasing power. The original units in inventory would be updated on each year's balance sheet along with their effect on stockholders' equity. For example, the December 31, 19X1, balance sheet would be restated for comparative purposes on December 31, 19X2:

	NOT RESTATED COST	MULTIPLIER	RESTATED COST
Inventory	$8,000	110/100	$8,800
Original paid-in capital	8,000	110/100	8,800

Difficulties in Measuring Net Income

To extend the illustration, suppose all the inventory was held for two full years. The general price index rose from 110 to 132 during 19X3. The December 31, 19X2, balance sheet items would be restated for comparative purposes on December 31, 19X3:

	RESTATED COST 12/31/X2	MULTIPLIER	RESTATED COST 12/31/X3
Inventory	$8,800	132/110	$10,560*
Original paid-in capital	8,800	132/110	10,560*

*The same result could be tied to the year of acquisition:
Inventory $8,000 × 132/100 = $10,560
Original paid-in capital $8,000 × 132/100 = $10,560

The restated amount is just that—a restatement of original *cost* in terms of current dollars—not a gain in any sense. Therefore this approach should *not* be labeled as an adoption of "current-cost" accounting. Thus, under this approach, if the specific current cost of the inventory goes up or down, the restated cost is unaffected.

The restated historical-cost approach harmonizes with the concept of maintaining the general purchasing power of the invested capital (a financial concept of capital maintenance) in total rather than maintaining "specific invested capital," item by item. More will be said about this distinction after we examine Method 4.

CURRENT COST/CONSTANT DOLLARS

Method 4 of Exhibit 20-3 shows the results of applying general index numbers to current costs. As the footnotes of the exhibit explain in more detail, the nominal gains reported under Method 2 are adjusted so that only gains in constant dollars are reported. For example, suppose you buy 100 units on December 31, 19X1, for $2,000 cash. If the current replacement cost of your inventory at December 31, 19X2, is $3,000 but the general price index has risen from 100 to 110, your nominal gain is $1,000 but your "real" gain in constant dollars in 19X2 is only $800: the $3,000 current cost minus the restated historical cost of $2,000 × 1.10 = $2,200.

Suppose the 100 units are held throughout 19X3. The general price index rises from 110 to 132. The replacement cost rises from $30 to $34, a nominal holding gain for 19X3 of $4 × 100 = $400. However, the current cost/constant dollar approach (Method 4) would report a real holding loss:

Current cost, restated, December 31, 19X2:	
$3,000 × 132/110	$3,600
Current cost, December 31, 19X3, 100 × $34	3,400
Holding loss	$ 200

Many theorists disagree on the relative merits of historical-cost approaches versus miscellaneous versions of current-cost approaches to income measurement. But there is general agreement among the theorists that restatements in constant dollars would be an improvement (ignoring practical barriers), because otherwise income includes illusory gains caused by using an unstable measuring unit.

EXHIBIT 20-4

Recasting of Preceding Exhibit
(To reflect FASB preferences per *FAS 33*)
Statement of Income from Continuing Operations Adjusted for Changing Prices
For the Year Ended December 31, 19X2

	AS REPORTED IN THE PRIMARY STATEMENTS	ADJUSTED FOR GENERAL INFLATION	ADJUSTED FOR CHANGES IN SPECIFIC PRICES (CURRENT COSTS)
Sales, 300 units @ $35	$10,500	$10,500	$10,500
Cost of goods sold, 300 units	6,000	6,600	9,000
Income from continuing operations	$ 4,500	$ 3,900	$ 1,500
Increase in specific prices (current cost) of inventories held during the year: 400 units × ($30 − $20)			$ 4,000
Less effect of increase in general price level: 10% × 400 × $20			800
Excess of increase in specific prices over increase in the general price level			$ 3,200

FASB PRESENTATION

FASB *Statement No. 33* contains illustrations of formats and language for presenting the information required by the statement. Exhibit 20-4 recasts the income statement in Exhibit 20-3 in accordance with the FASB preferences. Compare the two exhibits:

1. The FASB avoids using the term *holding gain.* Instead, it uses verbose descriptions of the final three numbers in Exhibit 20-4. Why? Probably because accountants and managers continue to disagree about whether all, some, or none of the holding gains are really "net income." Note too that in both exhibits these numbers are reported but are not added to income from continuing operations.

2. The middle column in Exhibit 20-4 is similar to the Method 3 format used in Exhibit 20-3, historical cost/constant dollar. The final column is similar to the Method 4, current cost/constant dollar. There is no separate column similar to the Method 2 format, current cost/nominal dollar. However, the final column does double duty. It provides the same data that were shown for Method 2 in Exhibit 20-3 ($10,500, $9,000, $1,500, and $4,000), and then it subtracts the $800 (originally shown in Method 4 in Exhibit 20-3) from the $4,000 to get the holding gain on the basis of current cost/constant dollars.

Business Week (May 2, 1983) reported that the average 1982 income from continuing operations of four hundred of the largest U.S. industrial corporations on the historical cost/constant dollar basis was 22% of the historical cost/nominal dollar income. The current cost/nominal dollar basis was 27% of the historical cost/nominal dollar income.

Summary

The matching of historical costs with revenue is the generally accepted means of measuring net income. But basing such computations on some version of current costs has been proposed as a better gauge of the distinctions between income (the return *on* capital) and capital maintenance (the return *of* capital).

General price indexes are used to adjust historical costs so that all expenses are measured in current dollars of the same purchasing power. Such adjustments do not represent a departure from historical cost. In contrast, specific price indexes are often used to implement the current-cost approach to measuring income and capital.

Summary Problem for Your Review

(Problems One and Two appeared earlier in this chapter.)

❑ Problem Three

In 1930 a parcel of land was purchased for $1,200. An identical parcel was purchased today for $3,600. The general-price-level index has risen from 100 in 1930 to 300 now. Fill in the blanks.

PARCEL	(1) HISTORICAL COST MEASURED IN 1930 PURCHASING POWER	(2) HISTORICAL COST MEASURED IN CURRENT PURCHASING POWER	(3) HISTORICAL COST AS ORIGINALLY MEASURED
1			
2			
Total	————	————	————

1. Compare the figures in the three columns. Which total presents a nonsense result. Why?
2. Does the write-up of parcel 1 in column 2 result in a gain? Why? Assume that these parcels are the only assets of the business. There are no liabilities. Prepare a complete balance sheet for each of the three columns.

❑ Solution to Problem Three

1.

PARCEL	(1) HISTORICAL COST MEASURED IN 1930 PURCHASING POWER	(2) HISTORICAL COST MEASURED IN CURRENT PURCHASING POWER	(3) HISTORICAL COST AS ORIGINALLY MEASURED
1	$1,200	$3,600	$1,200
2	1,200	3,600	3,600
Total	$2,400	$7,200	$4,800

The addition in column 3 produces a nonsense result. In contrast, the other sums are the results of applying a standard unit of measure. The computations in columns 1 and 2 are illustrations of a restatement of historical cost in terms of a common dollar, a standard unit of measure. Such computations have been frequently termed as adjustments for changes in the general price level. Whether the restatement is made using the 1930 dollar or the current dollar is a matter of personal preference; columns 1 and 2 yield equivalent results. The preponderance of opinion seems to favor restatement in terms of the current dollar (column 2) because the current dollar has more meaning than the old dollar to the reader of the financial statements.

The mere restatement of identical assets in terms of different but equivalent measuring units cannot be regarded as a gain. Expressing parcel 1 as $1,200 in column 1 and $3,600 in column 2 is like expressing parcel 1 in terms of, say, either 1,200 square yards or $9 \times 1,200 = 10,800$ square feet. Surely, the "write-up" from 1,200 square yards to 10,800 square feet is not a gain; it is merely another way of measuring the same asset. The 1,200 square yards and the 10,800 square feet are equivalent; they are different ways of describing the same asset. That is basically what general-price-level accounting is all about. It says you cannot measure one plot of land in square yards and another in square feet and add them together before converting to some common measure. Unfortunately, column 3 fails to perform such a conversion before adding the two parcels together; hence the total is internally inconsistent.

2. Note especially that write-ups under general-price-level accounting do not result in the recognition of gains. They are *restatements* of costs in dollars of equivalent purchasing power. The balance sheets would be:

	(1)	(2)	(3)
Land	$2,400	$7,200	$4,800
Paid-in capital	$2,400	$7,200	$4,800

Highlights to Remember

Restatements in constant dollars can be applied to both the historical-cost and the current-cost basis of income measurement, as Methods 3 and 4 illustrate. Avoid the misconception that the choices are among the first three methods only. In fact, many advocates of the current cost/constant dollar method insist it provides the most useful approximation of net income. In any event, any measurement of income should be based on constant dollars.

When inflation accounting is discussed, accountants and managers frequently confuse and blur the various concepts of income just covered. Highlights of Exhibit 20-3, page 646, include:

1. The choice among accounting measures is often expressed as either historical-cost accounting or general-price-level accounting or current-cost (specific-price-level) accounting. But this is an inaccurate statement of choices.

2. A correct statement would be that there are four major concepts. Nominal dollars may be combined with either historical cost (Method 1) or current cost (Method 2). In addition, general-price-level (constant dollar) accounting may be combined with either historical-cost accounting (Method 3) or current-cost accounting (Method 4).

3. Method 3, the historical cost/constant dollar method, is *not* concerned with current-cost concepts of income, whatever their strengths and weaknesses.

4. The current-cost Methods 2 and 4 are based on *physical* rather than *financial* concepts of maintenance of invested capital.

5. Write-ups of nonmonetary assets (inventory in this example) under Method 3 do *not* result in the recognition of gains. They are restatements of *costs* in dollars of equivalent purchasing power. See Appendix 20 for a discussion of the distinction between monetary and nonmonetary assets, as well as other aspects of inflation accounting.

Appendix 20: More on Inflation Accounting

This appendix extends the discussion in the body of the chapter, emphasizing current-cost depreciation and monetary items. Special attention is given to the FASB requirements regarding these topics.

MEANING OF CURRENT COST

Current cost is the most popular term for describing the fundamental basis for valuing the inventory as shown for Method 2 in Exhibit 20-3. However, it is a general term having several variations. Be on guard as to its meaning in a particular situation. As illustrated in Exhibit 20-3, the current-cost method stresses that income cannot emerge until deducting the current (or reproduction) cost of replenishing the item at today's prices. The regulatory authorities in most of the English-speaking countries have proposed that the current-cost approach be based on replacement costs. In most instances, *replacement cost* means today's cost of obtaining a similar asset that *would produce the same expected cash flows as the existing asset.* For a particular company, these replacement costs would be obtained via price quotations, specific appraisals, or specific indexes for material or construction.

The FASB uses current replacement cost as its dominant requirement for measuring current cost. However, sometimes the replacement cost of a particular asset exceeds its *recoverable amount.* For example, some equipment or inventory may be obsolete. *Recoverable amount* is defined as (1) the net realizable value of an asset that is about to be sold or (2) the net present value of expected cash flows (called *value in use*) of an asset that is not about to be sold. *Net realizable value* is the amount of cash (or its equivalent) expected to be derived from sale of an asset, net of costs required to be incurred as a result of the sale. In sum, the FASB rule is current cost or lower recoverable amount.

PROPERTY, PLANT, AND EQUIPMENT

The general idea of current cost is the same for equipment as for inventories. Nevertheless, the application of the idea is more difficult. An illustration will help to clarify the issues. Extending the example in Exhibit 20-3, suppose that on January 2, 19X3, $5,000 of the $10,500 cash was used to buy sales equipment. The equipment was being fully depreciated over a five-year life on a straight-line basis. The replacement cost of the equipment (new) at the end of 19X3 was $8,000. The general price index was 110 at the end of 19X2 and 132 at the end of 19X3. Exhibit 20-5 shows the

EXHIBIT 20-5

	NOMINAL DOLLARS				CONSTANT DOLLARS			
Relation of Depreciation to Four Methods of Measuring Income	(METHOD 1)		(METHOD 2)		(METHOD 3)		(METHOD 4)	
	Historical Cost		Current Cost		Historical Cost		Current Cost	
	19X2	19X3	19X2	19X3	19X2	19X3	19X2	19X3
Balance Sheet Accounts as of December 31								
Equipment	5,000	5,000	5,000	8,000	6,000^d	6,000	6,000	8,000
Accumulated depreciation	—	1,000	—	1,600	—	1,200	—	1,600
Net carrying amount	5,000	4,000	5,000	6,400	6,000	4,800	6,000	6,400
Income Statement Effects for 19X3								
Depreciation expense		1,000^a		1,600^b		1,200^e		1,600
Holding gain, equipment		—		3,000^c		—		2,000^f

^{a}.20 × 5,000 ^{c}.60 × 5,000 ^{e}.20 × 6,000
^{b}.20 × 8,000 ^{d}132/110 × 5,000 ^{f}8,000 − 6,000

effects and why manufacturers of heavy goods favor the current-cost approach. That is, the manufacturers would want depreciation expense of $1,600 to be deductible for income tax purposes. At the same time, the "holding gain" of $3,000 should not be subject to tax because it represents capital maintenance rather than income.

Current-cost depreciation is computed by multiplying the depreciation percentage based on useful life (1 ÷ 5 years = 20%) by the new *gross* carrying amount at current cost: .20 × $8,000 = $1,600.

The holding gain in Method 2 (current cost/nominal dollars) is computed by multiplying the percentage increase in gross carrying amount for the year (from $5,000 to $8,000 is a 60% increase) by the beginning *net* carrying amount at current cost: .60 × $5,000 = $3,000.

Pursuing the example for one more year, suppose the replacement cost of the equipment (new) at the end of 19X4 was $12,000. The percentage increase in gross carrying amount would be 50% (from $8,000 to $12,000). Method 2 (current cost/nominal dollars) would show the following effects on the 19X4 income statement:

Depreciation expense, .20 × gross carrying amount at current cost, .20 × $12,000	$2,400
Holding gain, equipment, .50 × the beginning *net* carrying amount at current cost, .50 × $6,400	$3,200

Computations of holding gains can rapidly become complex. For instance, this introductory explanation has avoided such intricacies as (1) using average current cost as a basis for depreciation and (2) restating current costs through a series of years in constant dollars. The basic concepts are unchanged, but the arithmetic is tedious.

Difficulties in Measuring Net Income

Income tax laws in the English-speaking countries have been changed to permit accelerated write-offs of the historical costs of depreciable assets. However, no departures from historical-cost methods have been permitted. Managers of companies having large investments in inventories and property, plant, and equipment generally favor the adoption of a current-cost approach to measuring taxable income. Why? Because in times of rising prices, cost of goods sold and depreciation are higher based on current costs than on historical costs. Therefore, taxable income would be less and income tax outflows would be less—as long as no holding gains are subject to taxes.[2]

Annual reports frequently contain complaints about high income tax rates. Comparative effective income tax rates are often tabulated to demonstrate striking differences. For example, Du Pont showed effective income tax rates of 49%, 62%, and 70% on income from continuing operations based on historical cost/nominal dollars, historical cost/constant dollars, and current cost, respectively.

GENERAL PURCHASING-POWER GAINS AND LOSSES

We now return to constant dollar/historical cost accounting, the comparison of Methods 1 and 3 in Exhibit 20-3, page 646, that was introduced in the body of this chapter.

❏ Monetary Items

A *monetary item* is a claim receivable or payable in a specified number of dollars; the claim remains fixed regardless of changes in either specific or general price levels. Examples are cash, accounts receivable, accounts payable, and bonds payable. In contrast, nonmonetary items have prices that can vary. Examples are inventory, land, equipment, and liabilities for product warranties.

The distinction between monetary and nonmonetary assets is the key to understanding the impact of constant-dollar accounting on income measurement and stockholders' equity. Reconsider the facts depicted in Exhibit 20-3 except that we extend matters throughout 19X3. Suppose the inventory was not replaced. Instead, the $10,500 cash received on December 31, 19X2, was held throughout 19X3 in a non-interest-bearing checking account. Furthermore, assume that the 100 units of inventory on December 31, 19X2, were held throughout 19X3 and remained unsold on December 31, 19X3. The general-price-level index rose from 110 to 132 during 19X3. The familiar historical cost/nominal dollar (Method 1) statement would be:

	19X2	19X3
Balance Sheets as of December 31		
Cash	$10,500	$10,500
Inventory	2,000	2,000
Total assets	$12,500	$12,500
Original paid-in capital	$ 8,000	$ 8,000
Retained income	4,500	4,500
Total stockholders' equity	$12,500	$12,500
Income Statement for 19X3		
None (no revenue or expenses)		

[2] If taxes were levied as indicated, the capital-goods industries would have relatively lower incomes subject to tax than other industries. However, keep in mind that a country usually has the same target *total* income taxes to be generated by the corporate sector. If the taxable income of all corporations declined, all income tax *rates* would undoubtedly be raised so as to produce the same *total* tax collections as before. Thus a replacement-cost basis may redistribute the tax burden among companies so that capital-goods industries pay less total tax. But the chances are high that the overall percentage rate would increase, so that the tax savings would not be as large as indicated.

Before reading on, reflect on the intuitive meaning of holding cash during a time of inflation. The holder of cash or claims to cash gets burned by inflation. In contrast, the debtor benefits from inflation because the debtor can pay his or her creditors with a fixed amount of dollars that have less current purchasing power than when the debt was originally contracted.

How do we measure the economic effects of holding cash during inflation? Using the basic historical cost/constant dollar method in Exhibit 20-3, let us restate in constant dollars, using 19X3 dollars. Because the general-price-level index rose from 110 to 132, the restatements would be as follows:

	19X2	19X3
Balance Sheets as of December 31		
Cash: 132/110 × 10,500 19X2 dollars	$12,600	$10,500
Inventory: 132/100 × 2,000 19X1 dollars	2,640	2,640
Total assets	$15,240	$13,140
Original paid-in capital:		
132/100 × 8,000 19X1 dollars	$10,560	$10,560
Retained income	4,680[a]	4,680
Revaluation equity	–	(2,100)[b]
Total stockholders' equity	$15,240	$13,140
Income Statement for 19X3		
Holding gain (loss) on monetary item		$ (2,100)

[a]$15,240 − $10,560   [b]$12,600 − $10,500

The cash balance is not restated in 19X3 because it is already measured in 19X3 dollars. The formal constant-dollar income statement, assuming no operating activities, would consist of the lone item as in the above table: holding loss on monetary item, $2,100. The monetary item in this case is cash; its loss of purchasing power is $12,600 − $10,500 = $2,100. In turn, stockholders' equity would be reduced by $2,100, as shown by the amount of the revaluation equity.

The label "holding loss" on the monetary item is not used by FASB *No. 33*. Instead, the following nomenclature is favored: gain (loss) from decline in purchasing power of net monetary items. By using such labels, the FASB tries to dampen the controversy regarding whether holding gains are really a part of net income. For this reason, the accompanying tables here include holding gains and losses in revaluation equity rather than in retained income.

☐ Nonmonetary Items

Before reading on, reflect on the intuitive meaning of holding a nonmonetary asset during a time of inflation. Assets in the form of physical things have prices that can fluctuate and thus, unlike cash, offer more protection against the risks of inflation.

As of the end of 19X2, the $10,500 cash balance represented the equivalent of $12,600 in terms of 19X3 purchasing power, but at the end of 19X3 it is worth only $10,500. In contrast, the $2,000 historical investment in inventory, which does not represent a fixed monetary claim, represented $2,640 in terms of *19X3 purchasing power;* its purchasing power has not been eroded. The inventory is *restated* to an amount of $2,640. But the $2,640 investment in inventory is unaffected by changes in the general-price-level index during 19X3.

Two difficulties and subtleties of constant-dollar accounting deserve emphasis here. First, all past balance sheets are restated in today's dollars. Second, the balance sheet changes are computed among the *monetary* items to produce purchasing-power gains or losses. No such gains or losses will ever appear for nonmonetary items. For example, suppose the $10,500 cash had been immediately reinvested in 300 more units of inventory. How would the constant-dollar statements be affected? No purchasing-power loss or gain would have occurred in 19X3:

	DECEMBER 31, 19X2	DECEMBER 31, 19X3
Inventory (instead of cash)		
132/110 × $10,500	$12,600	$12,600
Inventory (as before)	2,640	2,640
Total assets	$15,240	$15,240
Original capital	$10,560	$10,560
Retained income	4,680	4,680
Total stockholders' equity	$15,240	$15,240

Many accountants and managers confuse these restatements of *historical-cost* statements with current-cost notions of income. However, these constant-dollar statements (Method 3 in Exhibit 20-3) adhere to historical cost. The aim is to see whether the *general* purchasing power of the original invested capital has been maintained. Hence, whether *specific* inventory prices have gone up, down, or sideways is of no concern.

In sum, constant-dollar accounting will modify historical-cost statements in two major ways. First, historical costs are restated in constant dollars. Second, purchasing-power gains and losses arising from holding monetary assets and monetary liabilities will be recognized.

Note that holding gains on monetary items are linked with constant-dollar accounting. They do not exist under nominal-dollar accounting. Holding gains on nonmonetary items are associated exclusively with "current-cost" accounting and are not an integral part of "historical-cost" accounting.

Finally, constant-dollar accounting may be linked with *either* historical-cost statements or current-cost statements. Thus the $2,100 holding loss on the monetary item computed above would also appear under the current cost/constant dollar method as well as the historical cost/constant dollar method of Exhibit 20-3.

Summary Problem for Your Review _____

(The first three problems appeared earlier in this chapter.)

❑ Problem Four

You purchased a parcel of land ten years ago for $40,000 when the general-price-level index was 90. You also placed $40,000 cash in a safety deposit box. The general-price-level index is now 180. A local real estate appraiser maintains that you could obtain $220,000 for the land today.

REQUIRED:

1. Prepare a four-column tabulation of the holding gain (loss) on the monetary item and holding gain (loss) on the nonmonetary item for the ten-year period. The four methods of measurement to be shown are historical cost/nominal dollar, current cost/nominal dollar, historical cost/constant dollar, and current cost/constant dollar.

2. Prepare a summary of the four methods. For each method:

    a. Specify whether a financial or a physical concept of capital maintenance is used for determining income from continuing operations.

    b. Does the method explicitly identify holding gains (losses) on monetary items, frequently called gains (losses) in general purchasing power? Answer *yes* or *no* here and in Requirements *c*, *d*, and *e*.

    c. Does the method explicitly identify holding gains (losses) on nonmonetary items?

    d. Does the method use general price indexes such as the Consumer Price Index?

    e. Does the method use specific price indexes such as a construction index?

3. Of the four methods, which do you prefer as the most accurate measure of income? Why?

❑ Solution to Problem Four

1. All amounts are in thousands of dollars.

	MEASUREMENT METHOD			
	(1) Historical Cost/ Nominal Dollar	(2) Current Cost/ Nominal Dollar	(3) Historical Cost/ Constant Dollar	(4) Current Cost/ Constant Dollar
Holding loss on monetary item, commonly called loss in general purchasing power	–	–	(40)[a]	(40)[a]
Holding gain on nonmonetary item	–	180[b]	–	140[c]
Total	–	180	(40)	100

[a]Cash held today, expressed in current purchasing power   = 40
Cash held ten years ago, expressed in current purchasing power

$$40 \times \frac{180}{90} = \underline{\underline{\frac{80}{(40)}}}$$

Holding loss
[b]Current value of 220 − Historical cost of 40 = 180.
[c]Current value of 220 −

$$\left(\text{Restated historical cost of } 40 \times \frac{180}{90}, \text{ or } 80 \right) = 140.$$

2. The relationships among the four methods are shown in the following table:

	MEASUREMENT METHOD			
	(1) Historical Cost/ Nominal Dollar	(2) Current Cost/ Nominal Dollar	(3) Historical Cost/ Constant Dollar	(4) Current Cost/ Constant Dollar
a. Concept of capital maintenance for determining income from continuing operations	Financial	Physical	Financial	Physical
Explicit identification of holding gains:				
b. On monetary items	No	No	Yes	Yes
c. On nonmonetary items	No*	Yes	No	Yes
d. Use of general price indexes	No	No	Yes	Yes
e. Use of specific price indexes	No	Yes	No	Yes

*Recognizes losses, not gains, under lower-of-cost-market valuations, which are most often applicable in accounting for inventories and marketable equity securities.

3. Accountants and others have been unable to agree on which method (or model) provides the "most accurate" measure of income. Those who favor Method 1 maintain that no income emerges until an actual sale occurs. Those who favor Method 2 assert that there has been an overall increase in wealth of $180,000 and that the actual sale of land is an incidental factor. Those who favor Method 3 essentially favor the historical-cost approach to measuring income but believe that gains or losses on monetary items are actually realized by mere holding.

Economists tend to favor Method 4 as the most comprehensive way of calibrating an entity's income because it aims at measuring changes in overall command over goods and services, measured in constant purchasing power.

Economists have frequently distinguished between "real" and "nominal" income and capital. The historical-cost method has been severely criticized because it uses a "nominal" measure in the form of unrestated dollars rather than a "real" measure in the form of restated dollars with constant purchasing power. Adherents of the current cost/constant dollar model insist that no income can emerge without the maintenance of real capital, that is, nominal capital restated in terms of constant purchasing power.

Essentially, the FASB has avoided answering the tough question that professors and others have debated for years: If you must pick a single number as a measure of net income, which would you choose? As mentioned earlier, the FASB requires disclosures in accordance with Method 4. However, the holding gains are merely reported; they are *not* added to income from continuing operations. In short, the FASB has decided to provide an array of income measurements that may be useful. The user of financial statements can then select the numbers that seem most helpful

As an example of different views as to what really constitutes income, some accountants maintain that a holding gain on a monetary liability is really an adjustment to interest expense. Why? Because lenders raise interest rates to compensate for expected inflation. Therefore the interest expense component of income from continuing operations should be reduced by the holding gain. Du Pont has followed this theory, which often boosts income considerably. For instance, Du Pont's supplementary disclosures for 1981 included the following current cost/constant dollar tabulation (in millions):

Income from continuing operations	$475
Gain attributable to holding net monetary liabilities	215
Income including gain attributable to holding net monetary liabilities	$690

The $690 is 45% higher than the $475 income from continuing operations.

Fundamental Assignment Material

Special Note: Problems relating to Part One of the chapter are presented first in each subgrouping of the assignment material. For coverage of the basic ideas of inflation accounting, Problem 20-2 is especially recommended; for a closer but still fundamental look, Problem 20-39 is especially recommended.

20–1. LIFO, FIFO, cash effects. Schmidlein Company had sales revenue of $360,000 in 19X2 for a line of hardware supplies. The company uses a periodic inventory system. Pertinent data for 19X2 included:

Inventory, December 31, 19X1	14,000 units @ $6	$ 84,000
January purchases	20,000 units @ $7	140,000
July purchases	32,000 units @ $8	256,000
Sales for the year	30,000 units	

REQUIRED:

1. Prepare a statement of gross margin for 19X2. Use columns, one assuming LIFO and one assuming FIFO.
2. Assume a 40% income tax rate. Suppose all transactions are for cash. Which inventory method results in more cash for Schmidlein Company? By how much?

20–2. Four versions of income and capital. Z Company has the following comparative balance sheets as of December 31 (based on historical costs in nominal dollars):

	19X4	19X5
Cash	$ —	$4,500
Inventory, 50 and 20 units, respectively	5,000	2,000
Total assets	$5,000	$6,500
Paid-in capital	$5,000	$5,000
Retained income	—	1,500
Stockholders' equity	$5,000	$6,500

The general-price-level index was 140 on December 31, 19X4, and 161 on December 31, 19X5. The company had acquired fifty units of inventory on December 31, 19X4, for $100 each and had held them throughout 19X5. Thirty units were sold on December 31, 19X5, for $150 cash each. The replacement cost of the inventory at that date was $120 per unit. Assume that these are the only transactions. Ignore income taxes.

REQUIRED:

Use four sets of columns to prepare comparative balance sheets as of December 31, 19X4 and 19X5, and income statements for 19X5 under (1) historical cost/nominal dollars, (2) current cost/nominal dollars, (3) historical cost/constant dollars, and (4) current cost/constant dollars.

☐ Understanding Published Financial Reports

20–3. Comparison of inventory methods. Sperry Corporation is a producer of electronic systems for information processing, aerospace, and defense. The following actual data and descriptions are from the company's fiscal 1982 annual report (in millions):

Difficulties in
Measuring Net
Income

	MARCH 31	
	1982	1981
Inventories	$1,331.2	$1,461.7

A footnote states: "Inventories are valued at the lower of cost or market, cost generally representing average cost."

The income statement for the fiscal year ended March 31, 1982, included:

Net sales of products	$4,195.0
Cost of sales of products	2,687.5

Assume that Sperry used the periodic inventory system. Suppose its Univac division had the accompanying data regarding the use of its computer parts that it acquires and resells to customers for maintaining equipment:

Data for Problem 20-3 (dollars are *not* in millions)	UNITS	TOTAL
Inventory (March 31, 1981)	100	$ 400
Purchase (May 20, 1981)	200	1,000
Sales, June 17 (at $9 per unit)	150	
Purchase (September 25, 1981)	140	840
Sales, February 7, 1982 (at $10 per unit)	160	

REQUIRED:

1. For these computer parts only, prepare a tabulation of the cost-of-goods-sold section of the income statement for the year ended March 31, 1982. Support your computations. Round totals to the nearest dollar. Show your tabulation for four different inventory methods: (a) FIFO, (b) LIFO, (c) weighted-average, and (d) specific identification.

   For Requirement *d*, assume that the purchase of May 20 was identified with the sale of June 17. Also assume that the purchase of September 25 was identified with the sale of February 7; the additional units sold were identified with the beginning inventory.

2. By how much would income taxes differ if Sperry used (a) LIFO instead of FIFO for this inventory item? (b) LIFO instead of weighted-average? Assume a 40% tax rate.

20–4. **Effects of late purchases.** Refer to the preceding problem. Suppose Sperry acquired 60 extra units @ $7 each on March 29, 1982, a total of $420. How would gross margin and income taxes be affected under FIFO? That is, compare FIFO results before and after the purchase of 60 extra units. Under LIFO? That is, compare LIFO results before and after the purchase of 60 extra units. Show computations and explain.

20–5. **FASB format.** Reconsider Problem 20-2. Recast the income statement data to fit the FASB format as illustrated by Exhibit 20-4, page 651. This is the format most often found in published annual reports.

Additional
Assignment Material

❏ General Coverage

20–6. "An inventory profit is a fictitious profit." Do you agree? Explain.

20–7. LIFO produces absurd inventory valuations. Why?

20–8. "There is a single dominant reason why more and more companies have adopted LIFO." What is the reason?

20–9. "Purchases of inventory at the end of a fiscal period can have a direct effect on income under LIFO." Do you agree? Explain.

20–10. What are the two polar approaches to income measurement?

20–11. Explain how net income is measured under the current-cost approach.

20–12. What is *distributable income?*

20–13. Explain what a general price index represents.

20–14. Distinguish between general indexes and specific indexes.

20–15. Enumerate four ways to measure income.

20–16. "Specific indexes are used in nominal-dollar accounting but not in constant-dollar accounting." Do you agree? Explain.

20–17. "The choice among accounting measures of income is often expressed as either historical-cost accounting or general-price-level accounting or current-cost accounting." Do you agree? Explain.

20–18. "A holding gain may simultaneously be a holding loss." Do you agree? Explain.

20–19. "General-price-level accounting is a loose way of achieving replacement-cost income accounting." Do you agree? Explain.

20–20. Distinguish between the physical and the financial concepts of maintenance of invested capital.

20–21. "Holding gains on nonmonetary items are not recognized in historical cost/constant dollar accounting." Do you agree? Explain.

20–22. What is the common meaning of *current cost?*

20–23. "Net realizable value and replacement cost are generally equal." Do you agree? Explain.

20–24. "All holding gains should be excluded from income." What is the major logic behind this statement?

20–25. What are three basic positions regarding whether holding gains are income?

20–26. "A holding gain can be recognized but unrealized." Do you agree? Explain.

20–27. Why do managers in heavy industries like steel favor the current-cost concept for income tax purposes?

20–28. "The debtor benefits from inflation." Why?

20–29. "Constant-dollar accounting modifies historical-cost accounting in two major ways." Describe the two ways.

20–30. Net monetary position is the relationship of current assets to current liabilities." Do you agree? Explain.

20–31. What is the argument for departing from the use of historical cost as a basis of recording depreciation of fixed assets?

20–32. **LIFO and FIFO.** The inventory of the Corey Gravel Company on June 30 shows 1,000 tons at $9 per ton. A physical inventory on July 31 shows a total of 1,200 tons on hand. Revenue from sales of gravel for July totals $42,000. The following purchases were made during July:

July 8	2,000 tons @ $10 per ton
July 13	500 tons @ $11 per ton
July 22	600 tons @ $12 per ton

1. Compute the inventory cost, as of July 31, using (a) LIFO and (b) FIFO.
2. Compute the gross profit, using each method.

20–33. LIFO, FIFO, purchase decisions, and earnings per share. Suppose a company with one million shares of common stock outstanding has had the following transactions during 19X1, its first year in business:

Sales:	1,000,000 units @ $5
Purchases:	800,000 units @ $2
	300,000 units @ $3

The current income tax rate is a flat 50%; the rate next year is expected to be 40%. Prices on inventory are not expected to decline next year.

It is December 20, and as the president, you are trying to decide whether you should buy the 600,000 units you need for inventory now or early next year. The current price is $4 per unit. Prices on inventory are expected to remain stable; in any event, no decline in prices is anticipated.

You have not chosen an inventory method as yet, but you will pick either LIFO or FIFO.

Other expenses for the year will be $1.4 million.

1. Using LIFO, prepare a comparative income statement assuming the 600,000 units (a) are not purchased, (b) are purchased. The statement should end with reported earnings per share.
2. Repeat Requirement 1, using FIFO.
3. Comment on the above results. Which method would you choose? Why? Be specific.
4. Suppose that in Year 2 the tax rate drops to 40%, prices remain stable, 1 million units are sold @ $5, enough units are purchased at $4 so that the ending inventory will be 700,000 units, and other expenses are reduced to $800,000.
   a. Prepare a comparative income statement for the second year showing the impact of each of the four alternatives on net income and earnings per share for the second year.
   b. Explain any difference in net income that you encounter among the four alternatives.
   c. Why is there a difference in ending inventory values under LIFO even though the same amount of physical inventory is in stock?
   d. What is the total cash outflow for income taxes for the two years together under the four alternatives?
   e. Would you change your answer in Requirement 3 now that you have completed Requirement 4? Why?

20–34. LIFO, FIFO, prices rising and falling. The Romero Company has a periodic inventory system. Inventory on December 31, 19X1, consisted of 10,000 units @ $10 = $100,000. Purchases during 19X2 were 13,000 units. Sales were 12,000 units for sales revenue of $20 per unit.

Prepare a four-column comparative statement of gross margin for 19X2:

1. Assume purchases were at $12 per unit. Assume FIFO and then LIFO.
2. Assume purchases were at $8 per unit. Assume FIFO and then LIFO.
3. Assume an income tax rate of 30%. Suppose all transactions are for cash. Which inventory method in Requirement 1 results in more cash for Romero Company? By how much?

4. Repeat the preceding requirement. Which inventory method in Requirement 2 results in more cash for Romero Company? By how much?

20–35. FIFO and LIFO. Two companies, the Lifo Company and the Fifo Company, are in the scrap metal warehousing business as archcompetitors. They are about the same size and in 19X1 coincidentally encountered seemingly identical operating situations.

Their beginning inventory was 10,000 tons; it cost $50 per ton. During the year, each company purchased 50,000 tons at the following prices:

$$\boxed{\begin{array}{l} 20{,}000 \ @ \ \$70 \\ 30{,}000 \ @ \ \$90 \end{array}}$$

Each company sold 45,000 tons at average prices of $100 per ton. Other expenses in addition to cost of goods sold but excluding income taxes were $700,000. The income tax rate is 60%.

REQUIRED:

1. Compute net income for the year for both companies. Show your calculations.
2. As a manager, which method would you prefer? Why? Explain fully. Include your estimate of the overall effect of these events on the cash balances of each company, assuming that all transactions during 19X1 were direct receipts or disbursements of cash.

20–36. Effects of LIFO and FIFO. (Adapted from a problem originated by George H. Sorter.) The Cado Company is starting in business on December 31, 19X0. In each *half year*, from 19X1 through 19X4, it expects to purchase 1,000 units and sell 500 units for the amounts listed below. In 19X5, it expects to purchase no units and sell 4,000 units for the amount indicated below.

	19X1	19X2	19X3	19X4	19X5
Purchases:					
First 6 months	$ 2,000	$ 4,000	$ 6,000	$ 6,000	0
Second 6 months	4,000	9,000	6,000	8,000	0
Total	$ 6,000	$13,000	$12,000	$14,000	0
Sales (at selling price)	$10,000	$10,000	$10,000	$10,000	$40,000

Assume that there are no costs or expenses other than those shown above. The tax rate is 60%, and taxes for each year are payable on December 31 of each year. Cado Company is trying to decide whether to use FIFO or LIFO throughout the five-year period.

REQUIRED:

1. What was net income under FIFO for each of the five years? Under LIFO? Show calculations.
2. Explain briefly which method, LIFO or FIFO, seems more advantageous, and why.

Difficulties in
Measuring Net
Income

20–37. Meaning of general index applications and choice of base year. Mears Company acquired land in mid-1964 for $3 million. In mid-1984 it acquired a substantially identical parcel of land for $6 million. The general-price-level index annual averages were:

REQUIRED:

1. In four columns, show the computations of the total cost of the two parcels of land expressed in (a) costs as traditionally recorded, (b) dollars of 1984 purchasing power, (c) 1974 purchasing power, and (d) 1964 purchasing power.
2. Explain the meaning of the figures that you computed in Requirement 1.

20–38. Concepts of income. Suppose you are in the business of investing in land and holding it for resale. On December 31, 19X2, a parcel of land has a historical cost of $100,000 and a current value (measured via use of a specific price index) of $300,000; the general price level had doubled since the land was acquired. Suppose also that the land is sold on December 31, 19X3, for $360,000. The general price level rose by 5% during 19X3.

REQUIRED:

1. Prepare a tabulation of income from continuing operations and holding gains for 19X3, using the four methods illustrated in Exhibit 20-3.
2. In your own words, explain the meaning of the results, giving special attention to what income represents.

Assignment Material for Appendix 20

20–39. Monetary and nonmonetary items. R Company began business on December 31, 19X1, with the following balance sheet. The assets were held throughout 19X2, when the general-price-level index rose from 120 to 144. The familiar historical cost/nominal dollar statements would be:

	19X1	19X2
Balance sheets as of December 31:		
Cash	$100,000	$100,000
Land	70,000	70,000
Total assets	$170,000	$170,000
Paid-in capital	$170,000	$170,000

REQUIRED:

1. Using the historical cost/constant dollar approach, prepare comparative balance sheets and an income statement. Ignore interest and income taxes.
2. Repeat Requirement 1. However, assume that a long-term note payable was issued for $60,000 on December 31, 19X1, and that paid-in capital was therefore $170,000 − $60,000 = $110,000.

20–40. Monetary items. Suppose H Company has $150,000 cash, which it had acquired at the end of 19X3. It held the cash in a safety deposit box through the end of 19X4. The general-price-level index was 200 on December 31, 19X3, and 236 on December 31, 19X4.

1. Fill in the blanks for the cash held in the safety box:

	(1) MEASURED IN 12/31/X3 PURCHASING POWER	(2) MEASURED IN 12/31/X4 PURCHASING POWER	(3) AS CONVENTIONALLY MEASURED
Cash balance, December 31, 19X3			
Cash balance, December 31, 19X4	____	____	____
Purchasing-power loss from holding monetary item	====	====	====

2. Suppose the company had purchased land for $150,000 cash on December 31, 19X3, and held the land throughout 19X4. Prepare a similar tabulation for the land balance except that the final line would refer to a "nonmonetary" rather than a "monetary" item.

20–41. Monetary versus nonmonetary assets. Sloan Company owns land acquired for $100,000 one year ago when the general price index was 100. It also owns $100,000 of government bonds acquired at the same time. The index today is 110. Operating expenses and operating revenue, including interest income, resulted in net income (and an increase of cash) of $4,000 measured in historical-dollar terms. Assume that all income and expense transactions occurred yesterday. The Sloan Company has no other assets and no liabilities. Its cash balance one year ago was zero.

1. Prepare comparative balance sheets for the two instants of time plus an income statement summary based on the historical cost/nominal dollar method. Then prepare such statements using the historical cost/constant dollar method.
2. This is a more important requirement. In your own words, explain the meaning of the historical cost/constant dollar statements. Why should the holding of a monetary asset generate a monetary loss while the holding of land causes neither a loss nor a gain?

20–42. Comprehensive review of appendix. A company has the following comparative balance sheets at December 31 (based on historical cost in nominal dollars):

	19X1	19X2
Cash	$2,000	$3,400
Inventory, 20 units and 10 units, respectively	2,000	1,000
Total assets	$4,000	$4,400
Original capital	$4,000	$4,000
Retained income	—	400
Stockholders' equity	$4,000	$4,400
General-price-level index	160	176

Difficulties in Measuring Net Income

The company had acquired all the inventory at $100 per unit on December 31, 19X1, and had held the inventory throughout 19X2; ten units were sold for $140 cash each on December 31, 19X2. The replacement cost of the inventory at that date was $125 per unit.

Note: If you are going to solve the next problem too, ignore the requirements of this problem and proceed directly to the more comprehensive problem that follows.

Prepare a four-column tabulation of income statements: (1) historical cost/nominal dollars; (2) current cost/nominal dollars; (3) historical cost/constant dollars, and (4) current cost/constant dollars. Also show beginning and ending balance sheet accounts for each of the four columns. For example, the above accounts accompany column 1.

20–43. **Extension of appendix problem.** Suppose in the preceding problem that sales equipment had been purchased on December 31, 19X1, for $1,000 cash provided by an extra $1,000 of capital. The equipment was being fully depreciated over a ten-year life on a straight-line basis. The replacement cost of the equipment (new) at the end of 19X2 was $1,500.

Prepare a four-column tabulation in the same manner described in the requirement to the preceding problem.

Understanding Published Financial Reports

20–44. **Switch from LIFO to FIFO.** Effective January 1, 1970, Chrysler Corporation adopted the FIFO method for inventories previously valued by the LIFO method. The 1970 annual report stated: "This . . . makes the financial statements with respect to inventory valuation comparable with those of the other United States automobile manufacturers."

The Wall Street Journal reported:

☐ The change improved Chrysler's 1970 financial results several ways. Besides narrowing the 1970 loss by $20 million it improved Chrysler's working capital. The change also made the comparison with 1969 earnings look somewhat more favorable because, upon restatement, Chrysler's 1969 profit was raised only $10.2 million from the original figures.

☐ Finally, the change helped Chrysler's balance sheet by boosting inventories, and thus current assets, by $150 million at the end of 1970 over what they would have been under LIFO. As Chrysler's profit has collapsed over the last two years and its financial position tightened, auto analysts have eyed warily Chrysler's shrinking ratio of current assets to current liabilities.

☐ Chrysler's current liabilities shrank last year because it was able to pay off sizable amounts of short-term debt with the help of a $200 million long-term financing last winter. Chrysler's short-term debt stood at $374 million at year-end, down from $477 million a year earlier but up slightly from $370 million on Sept. 30. Chrysler's cash and marketable securities shrank during the year to $156.4 million at year-end, down from $309.3 million a year earlier and $220 million on Sept. 30.

☐ To get the improvements in its balance sheet and results, however, Chrysler paid a price. Roger Helder, vice president and comptroller, said Chrysler owed the government $53 million in tax savings it accumulated by using the LIFO method since it switched from FIFO in 1957. The major advantage of LIFO is that it holds down profit and thus tax liabilities. The other three major auto makers stayed on the FIFO method. Mr. Helder said Chrysler now has to pay back that $53 million to the government over 20 years, which will boost Chrysler's tax bills about $3 million a year.

Given the content of this text chapter, do you think the Chrysler decision to switch from LIFO to FIFO was beneficial to its stockholders? Explain, being as specific and using as many data as you can.

20–45. Year-end purchases and LIFO. A company engaged in the manufacture and sale of jewelry maintained an inventory of gold for use in its business. The company used LIFO for the gold content of its products.

On the final day of its fiscal year, the company bought 10,000 ounces of gold at $800 per ounce. Had the purchase not been made, the company would have penetrated its LIFO layers for 8,000 ounces of gold acquired at $660 per ounce. The applicable income tax rate is 40%.

REQUIRED:

1. Compute the effect of the year-end purchase on the income taxes of the fiscal year.
2. On the second day of the next fiscal year, the company resold the 10,000 ounces of gold to its suppliers. What do you think the Internal Revenue Service should do if it discovers this resale, if anything? Explain.

20–46. Replacement costs (P. Griffin). This problem does not require knowledge of Appendix 20. Accompanying this problem are excerpts from the 1974 annual report of Barber-Ellis Limited of Canada. Note 1 to the financial report includes the following passage:

☐ The current replacement costs of inventories and of property, plant and equipment are shown on the balance sheet and earnings are determined by matching current costs with current revenues. Adjustments of the historical cost of physical assets to their current replacement cost are considered as restatements of shareholders' equity and are shown on the balance sheet under "Revaluation Surplus."

☐ Since 1974 is the first year that the company has prepared current replacement cost financial statements, comparative figures are not available.

REQUIRED:

From information in the balance sheet, statement of earnings and retained earnings, and statement of revaluation surplus, determine, as of December 31, 1974:

1. Current replacement cost "Inventories"
2. Current replacement cost "Property, Plant and Equipment"
3. Current replacement cost "Accumulated Depreciation"
4. Current replacement cost "Total Assets"
5. Current replacement cost "Retained Earnings"

Also, for the year ended December 31, 1974, determine

6. Current replacement cost "Cost of Products Sold"
7. Current replacement cost "Net Earnings"

Finally, explain in words the nature of

8. The difference between the current-replacement-cost "Net Earnings" and the historical-cost "Net Earnings" for the year ended December 31, 1974

20–47. Holding gains on monetary and nonmonetary items. (Study Appendix 20. This problem is more difficult than the other problems.) Refer to the data in the preceding problem. The following information is available.

Items from the historical-cost balance sheet of Barber-Ellis dated December 31, 1973:

Cash: $25,200
Long-term debt: $4,133,650
General-price-level index:
    December 31, 1973: 140
    December 31, 1974: 154
    Average for the year 1974: 147

For all constant dollar calculations, use the 12/31/74 dollar.

BARBER-ELLIS OF CANADA, LIMITED

CURRENT REPLACEMENT COST BALANCE SHEET
AS AT DECEMBER 31, 1974

assets

	CURRENT REPLACEMENT COST	HISTORICAL COST
Current:		
Cash	$ 29,783	$ 29,783
Accounts receivable	12,074,945	12,074,945
Inventories	(1)	10,117,804
Prepaid expenses	249,545	249,545
Current assets	$22,721,077	$22,472,077
Property, plant and equipment	(2)	11,261,927
Accumulated depreciation	(3)	(5,817,772)
Unamortized excess of purchase price of subsidiaries over fair value of net assets acquired	—	816,067
Total assets	$ (4)	$28,732,299

liabilities

	CURRENT REPLACEMENT COST	HISTORICAL COST
Current:		
Bank indebtedness	$ 7,573,983	$ 7,573,983
Accounts payable and accrued liabilities	4,109,189	4,109,189
Income taxes	1,296,693	1,296,693
Dividends—preference shares	700	700
Current portion of long-term debt	486,650	486,650
Current liabilities	$13,467,215	$13,467,215
Deferred income taxes	278,362	278,362
Long-term debt (Note 1)	4,133,650	4,133,650
Total liabilities	$17,879,227	$17,879,227
shareholders' equity		
Capital Stock	$ 565,705	$ 565,705
Contributed surplus	45,000	45,000
Retained earnings	(5)	10,242,367
Revaluation surplus	4,319,204	—
Total equities	$ (4)	$28,732,299

CURRENT REPLACEMENT COST STATEMENT OF EARNINGS AND RETAINED EARNINGS FOR THE YEAR ENDED DECEMBER 31, 1974

	CURRENT REPLACEMENT COST	HISTORICAL COST
Net sales	$69,058,300	$69,058,300
Cost of products sold	$ (6)	$50,389,580
Selling, general and administration	10,705,281	10,705,281
Depreciation and amortization	1,095,567	786,969
Interest—long-term debt	381,884	381,884
Interest—current	590,284	590,284
Cost and expenses	$	$62,853,998
Earnings before income taxes	$	$ 6,204,302
Provision for income taxes	2,927,442	2,927,442
Net Earnings	$ (7)	$ 3,276,860
Retained earnings, beginning of year	7,939,344	7,939,344
Sub-total	$	$11,216,204
Adjustment of prior years' depreciation on current replacement cost of plant and equipment	$ 1,948,116	—
Dividends	973,837	$ 973,837
Retained Earnings, End of Year	$	$10,242,367
Earnings Per Share		
Basic	$ 4.30	$ 7.09
Fully diluted	4.22	6.96

STATEMENT OF REVALUATION SURPLUS FOR THE YEAR ENDED DECEMBER 31, 1974

Revaluation of physical assets to reflect current replacement cost as at December 31, 1974

Inventories	$ 249,000
Property, plant and equipment	3,902,271
Excess of purchase price over fair value of assets acquired	(816,067)

Revaluation of cost of products sold during the year ended December 31, 1974

Portion of 1974 earnings determined on historical cost basis which are required to replace inventory sold at the current cost in effect at the date of sale	984,000
Revaluation surplus December 31, 1974	$4,319,204

Report on Supplementary Financial Statements

To the Shareholders,
Barber-Ellis of Canada, Limited

In conjunction with our examination of and report on the financial statements of Barber-Ellis of Canada, Limited for 1974 we have also examined the accompanying supplementary financial statements which have been prepared on a current replacement cost basis.

Uniform criteria for the preparation and presentation of such supplementary financial information have not yet been established and accordingly, acceptable alternatives are available as to their nature and content. In our opinion, however, the accounting basis described in the notes to the supplementary financial statements has been applied as stated and is appropriate in these circumstances.

Touche Ross & Co.
Chartered Accountants

Toronto, Ontario
February 21, 1975

1. Assume that long-term debt did not change during 1974. Calculate the purchasing-power gain or loss associated with long-term debt (a monetary item). Label it as a gain or loss.

2. Calculate the purchasing-power gain or loss associated with cash and label it as a gain or loss. You may assume that a $4,583 increase in cash occurred uniformly throughout 1974.

3. Assume that Barber-Ellis purchased *all* of its inventory on December 31, 1973 (no other purchases prior to or subsequent to that date). Also assume that goods were sold continuously throughout the year. What are the following numbers?

   a. Holding gain on inventory in 1974, using the current cost/ nominal dollar model

   b. Holding gain on inventory in 1974 *net* of inflation (that is, based on the current cost/constant dollar model)

APPENDIX A:
Recommended Readings

The following readings are suggested as an aid to those readers who want to pursue some topics in more depth than is possible in this book. Of course, many of the chapters have footnotes or suggested readings on a particular topic. Therefore the specific chapters should be consulted for direct references.

There is a hazard in compiling a group of recommended readings. Inevitably, some worthwhile books or periodicals are overlooked. Moreover, such a list cannot include books published subsequent to the compilation here.

Professional journals are typically available in university libraries. *Management Accounting* and the *Financial Executive* tend to stress articles on management accounting. The *Journal of Accountancy* emphasizes financial accounting and is directed at the practicing CPA. The *Harvard Business Review* and *Fortune,* which are aimed at general managers, contain many articles on planning and control.

The *Accounting Review* and the *Journal of Accounting Research* cover all phases of accounting at a more theoretical level than the preceding publications.

The *Opinions* of the Accounting Principles Board are available from the American Institute of CPAs, 1211 Avenue of the Americas, New York, N.Y. 10036. The institute also has a series of research studies on a variety of topics. The pronouncements of the Financial Accounting Standards Board are available from the board's offices, High Ridge Park, Stamford, Conn. 06905.

The Financial Executives Institute, 633 Third Ave., New York, N.Y. 10017, and the National Association of Accountants, 919 Third Avenue, New York, N.Y. 10022, have long lists of accounting research publications.

There are many books on elementary management accounting. Also, many books entitled *Cost Accounting* stress a management approach, including that published by Charles Horngren (Prentice-Hall).

The following books on planning and control should be helpful:

ANTHONY, R. N., and JOHN DEARDEN, *Management Control Systems,* 5th ed. Homewood, Ill.: Richard D. Irwin, 1984.

BARRETT, M., and W. BRUNS, *Case Problems in Management Accounting.* Homewood, Ill.: Richard D. Irwin, 1981.

BEYER, ROBERT, and DONALD TRAWICKI, *Profitability Accounting for Planning and Control,* 2nd ed. New York: Ronald Press, 1972.

DEMSKI, J., *Information Analysis*. Reading, Mass.: Addison-Wesley, 1980. This book is more rigorous than the others in this list.

DERMER, J., *Management Planning and Control Systems*. Homewood, Ill.: Richard D. Irwin, 1977.

KAPLAN, R., *Advanced Management Accounting*. Englewood Cliffs, N.J.: Prentice-Hall, 1982.

LORANGE, P., *Corporate Planning: An Executive Viewpoint*. Englewood Cliffs, N.J.: Prentice-Hall, 1980.

LORANGE, P., and R. VANCIL, *Strategic Planning Systems*. Englewood Cliffs, N.J.: Prentice-Hall, 1977.

ROTCH, W., and B. ALLEN, *Cases in Management Accounting and Control Systems*. Richmond, Va.: Robert F. Dame, 1982.

SHANK, J., *Contemporary Managerial Accounting: A Casebook*. Englewood Cliffs, N.J.: Prentice-Hall, 1981.

VANCIL, RICHARD, *Decentralization: Managerial Ambiguity by Design*. New York: Financial Executives Research Foundation, 1979.

WILLSON, J., and J. CAMPBELL, *Controllership: The Work of the Managerial Accountant*, 3rd ed. New York: John Wiley, 1981.

For a book-length study of management accounting in not-for-profit organizations, see

ANTHONY, R. N., and R. HERZLINGER, *Management Control in Nonprofit Organizations*, rev. ed. Homewood, Ill.: Richard D. Irwin, 1980.

Several books of readings and handbooks are published each year. The following is a list of those published in 1978 and later:

ANTON, HECTOR R., PETER A. FIRMIN, and HUGH D. GROVE, eds., *Contemporary Issues in Cost and Managerial Accounting*, 3rd ed. Boston: Houghton Mifflin, 1978.

BLACK, H., and J. EDWARDS, eds., *Managerial and Cost Accountant's Handbook*. Homewood, Ill.: Dow Jones-Irwin, 1979.

BULLOCH, J., D. KELLER and L. VLASHO, eds., *Accountants' Cost Handbook*, 3rd ed., New York: John Wiley, 1983.

CHENALL, R., G. HARRISON, and D. WATSON, eds., *Organizational Context of Management Accounting*. Boston: Pitman, 1981.

DAVIDSON, S., and R. L. WEIL, eds., *Handbook of Cost Accounting*. New York: McGraw-Hill, 1978.

DECOSTER, D., K. RAMANTHAN, and G. SUNDEM, eds., *Accounting for Managerial Decision Making*, 2nd ed. Los Angeles: Melville, 1978.

GELLER, L., and J. SHIM, eds., *Readings in Cost and Managerial Accounting*. Dubuque, Iowa: Kendall/Hunt, 1980.

GOODMAN, S., and J. REECE, eds., *Controllers' Handbook*. Homewood, Ill.: Dow Jones-Irwin, 1978.

HOLZER, H. P., ed., *Management Accounting 1980: Proceedings of the University of Illinois Management Accounting Symposium*. Urbana: University of Illinois, 1980.

RAPPAPORT, ALFRED, ed., *Information for Decision Making*, 3rd ed. Englewood Cliffs, N.J.: Prentice-Hall, 1982.

SCHIFF, J., ed., *Readings in Managerial Accounting*. Princeton, N.J.: Dow Jones/Arno Press, 1980.

THOMAS, W., ed., *Readings in Cost Accounting, Budgeting and Control*. 6th ed. Cincinnati: South-Western Publishing, 1983.

Fundamentals of Compound Interest and the Use of Present-Value Tables

NATURE OF INTEREST

Interest is the cost of using money. It is the rental charge for cash, just as rental charges are often made for the use of automobiles or boats.

Interest does not always entail an outlay of cash. The concept of interest applies to ownership funds as well as to borrowed funds. The reason why interest must be considered on *all* funds in use, regardless of their source, is that the selection of one alternative necessarily commits funds that could otherwise be invested in some other opportunity. The measure of the interest in such cases is the return forgone by rejecting the alternative use. For instance, a wholly owned home or business asset is not cost-free. The funds so invested could alternatively be invested in government bonds or in some other venture. The measure of this opportunity cost depends on what alternative incomes are available.

Newspapers often contain advertisements of financial institutions citing interest rates that are "compounded." This appendix explains compound interest, including the use of present-value tables.

Simple interest is calculated by multiplying an interest rate times an unchanging principal amount. In contrast, *compound interest* is calculated by multiplying an interest rate times a principal amount that is changed each interest period by the previously accumulated (unpaid) interest. The accumulated interest is added to the principal to become the principal for the new period. For example, suppose you deposited $10,000 in a financial institution that promised to pay 10% interest per annum. You would let the amount accumulate for three years before withdrawing the full balance of the deposit. The *simple-interest* deposit would accumulate to $13,000 at the end of three years:

	PRINCIPAL	SIMPLE INTEREST	BALANCE, END OF YEAR
Year 1	$10,000	$10,000 × .10 = $1,000	$11,000
Year 2	10,000	10,000 × .10 = 1,000	12,000
Year 3	10,000	10,000 × .10 = 1,000	13,000

Compound interest provides interest on interest. That is, the principal changes from period to period. The deposit would accumulate to $10,000 \times (1.10)^3 = \$10,000 \times 1.331 = \$13,310$:

	PRINCIPAL	COMPOUND INTEREST	BALANCE, END OF YEAR
Year 1	$10,000	$10,000 × .10 = $1,000	$11,000
Year 2	11,000	11,000 × .10 = 1,100	12,100
Year 3	12,100	12,100 × .10 = 1,210	13,310

The "force" of compound interest can be staggering. For example, the same deposit would accumulate as follows:

	AT END OF		
	10 Years	20 Years	40 Years
Simple interest:			
$10,000 + 10 ($1,000) =	$20,000		
10,000 + 20 ($1,000) =		$30,000	
10,000 + 40 ($1,000) =			$ 50,000
Compound interest:			
$10,000 × (1.10)^{10} = $10,000 × 2.594 =	$25,940		
$10,000 × (1.10)^{20} = $10,000 × 6.728 =		$67,280	
$10,000 × (1.10)^{40} = $10,000 × 45.260 =			$452,600

Hand calculations of compound interest quickly become burdensome. Therefore, compound interest tables have been constructed to ease computations. (Indeed, many hand calculators contain programs that provide speedy answers.) Hundreds of tables are available, but only two widely used basic tables should suffice for this introduction.

TABLE 1: PRESENT VALUE OF $1

Two basic tables are used in capital budgeting. The first table (Table 1, p. 680), the Present Value of $1, deals with a single lump-sum cash inflow or outflow at a given instant of time, the *end* of the period in question. An example should clarify the reasoning underlying the construction and use of the table.

Illustration: Assume that a prominent city is issuing a three-year non-interest-bearing note payable that promises to pay a lump sum of $1,000 exactly three years from now. You desire a rate of return of exactly 6%, compounded annually. How much would you be willing to pay now for the three-year note? The situation is sketched as follows:

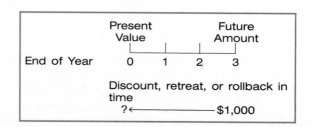

Let us examine the chart, period by period. First, let us assume that you are to purchase the $1,000 note at the end of Year 2 instead of at time zero. How much would you be willing to pay? If you wish to earn 6¢ annually on every $1 invested, you would want to receive $1.06 after one year for every $1 you invest today. Therefore, at the end of Year 2 you would be willing to pay $1.00/$1.06 × $1,000 for the right to receive $1,000 at the end of Year 3, or .943 × $1,000 = $943. Let us enter this in a tabular calculation:

END OF YEAR	INTEREST PER YEAR	CUMULATIVE DISCOUNT, CALLED COMPOUND DISCOUNT	PRESENT VALUE AT THE END OF YEAR
3	$57	$ 57	$1,000
2	53	110	943
1	50	160	890
0	—	—	840

Note that what is really being done in the tabulation is a series of computations that could be formulated as follows:

$$PV_2 = \$1,000\left[\frac{1.00}{1.06}\right] = \$943$$

$$PV_1 = \$1,000\left[\frac{1.00}{(1.06)^2}\right] = \$890$$

$$PV_0 = \$1,000\left[\frac{1.00}{(1.06)^3}\right] = \$840$$

This can be written as a formula for the present value of $1:

$$PV = \frac{S}{(1 + i)^n}$$

where PV = Present value at time zero; S = Future amount; i = Interest rate; and n = Number of periods.

Check the answers in the tabulation by using Table 1 (p. 680). For example, the Period 3 row and the 6% column show a factor of .840. Multiply this factor by the future cash flow, $1,000, to obtain its present value, $840.

As a further check on your understanding, review the earlier example of compound interest. Suppose the financial institution promised to pay $13,310 at the end of three years. How much would you be willing to deposit at time zero if you desired a 10% rate of return compounded annually? Using Table 1, the Period 3 row and the 10% column shows a factor of .751. Multiply this factor by the future amount:

$$PV = .75131^* \times \$13,310 = \$10,000$$

* This factor has five decimal places, which produces the $10,000 answer here. In contrast, the factors in the tables in this book are rounded to three decimal places. Therefore, small rounding errors are common. For instance, this calculation would be .751 × $13,310 = $9,996 instead of $10,000.

A diagram of this computation follows:

End of Year	0	1	2	3
10% PV FACTOR		PRESENT VALUE		FUTURE AMOUNT
.75131		$10,000 ⟵——— $13,310		

Pause for a moment. Use Table 1 to obtain the present values of

1. $1,600, @ 20%, at the end of 20 years
2. $8,300, @ 10%, at the end of 12 years
3. $8,000, @ 4%, at the end of 4 years

Answers:

1. $1,600 (.026) = $41.60
2. $8,300 (.319) = $2,648
3. $8,000 (.855) = $6,840

TABLE 2: PRESENT VALUE
OF AN ORDINARY ANNUITY OF $1

An ordinary annuity is a series of equal cash flows to take place at the *end* of successive periods of equal length. Assume that you buy a non-interest-bearing serial note from a municipality that promises to pay $1,000 at the end of *each* of three years. How much should you be willing to pay if you desire a rate of return of 6%, compounded annually?

The tabulation in Exhibit B-1 shows how the formula for PV_A, *the present value of an ordinary annuity,* is developed.

$$PV_A = \text{sum of present values of each item} \qquad (1)^*$$

This formula is the basis for Table 2 (p. 681). Check the answer in the table. Minor differences are due to rounding.

---

*Pursuing the first step, the details of the general formula are developed below.

$$PV_A = \frac{1}{1+i} + \frac{1}{(1+i)^2} + \frac{1}{(1+i)^3} \qquad (2)$$

Substituting values from our illustration:

$$PV_A = \frac{1}{1.06} + \frac{1}{(1.06)^2} + \frac{1}{(1.06)^3} \qquad (3)$$

Multiply by 1/1.06:

$$PV_A\left(\frac{1}{1.06}\right) = \frac{1}{(1.06)^2} + \frac{1}{(1.06)^3} + \frac{1}{(1.06)^4} \qquad (4)$$

Subtract Equation 4 from Equation 3:

$$PV_A - PV_A\left(\frac{1}{1.06}\right) = \frac{1}{1.06} - \frac{1}{(1.06)^4} \qquad (5)$$

Factor:

$$PV_A\left(1 - \frac{1}{1.06}\right) = \frac{1}{1.06}\left[1 - \frac{1}{(1.06)^3}\right] \qquad (6)$$

or

$$PV_A\left(\frac{.06}{1.06}\right) = \frac{1}{1.06}\left[1 - \frac{1}{(1.06)^3}\right] \qquad (7)$$

Multiply by 1.06/.06:

$$PV_A = \frac{1}{.06}\left[1 - \frac{1}{(1.06)^3}\right] \qquad (8)$$

The general formula for the present value of an annuity of $1 is:

$$PV_A = \frac{1}{i}\left[1 - \frac{1}{(1+i)^n}\right] \qquad (9)$$

Applied to our illustration:

$$PV_A = \frac{1}{.06}(1 - .840) = \frac{.160}{.06} = 2.673 \qquad (10)$$

EXHIBIT B-1

END OF YEAR		0	1	2	3
		PRESENT VALUE			
1st payment:	$\dfrac{1,000}{1.06}$	\$ 943 ⟵ \$1,000			
2nd payment:	$\dfrac{1,000}{(1.06)^2}$	\$ 890 ⟵——————— \$1,000			
3rd payment:	$\dfrac{1,000}{(1.06)^3}$	\$ 840 ⟵————————————— \$1,000			
		$2,673			

Table 2 lists the present values of ordinary annuities of \$1. Table 2 is convenient, but it is really a compilation of the basic data in Table 1. For example, the present value of each of the three payments could be computed individually, using Table 1:

PV FACTOR	
.943 × \$1,000 =	\$ 943
.890 × \$1,000 =	890
.840 × \$1,000 =	840
	$2,673

Alternatively, a shortcut computation would use the present-value factor from Table 2, which is merely the sum of the three individual factors = .943 + .890 + .840 = 2.673. Therefore the shortcut computation would be 2.673 × \$1,000 = \$2,673. If you were marooned on a desert island with one table, Table 1 would be preferable to Table 2.[1]

Use Table 2 to obtain the present values of the following ordinary annuities.

1. \$1,600 at 20% for 20 years
2. \$8,300 at 10% for 12 years
3. \$8,000 at 4% for 4 years

Answers:

1. \$1,600 (4.870) = \$7,792
2. \$8,300 (6.814) = \$56,556
3. \$8,000 (3.630) = \$29,040

In particular, note that the higher the interest rate, the lower the present value.

Fundamentals
of Compound
Interest and
the Use of
Present-
Value Tables

679

[1] For additional tables, see R. Vichas, *Handbook of Financial Mathematics, Formulas and Tables* (Englewood Cliffs, N.J.: Prentice-Hall, 1979).

TABLE 1 (Put a clip on this page for easy reference.)

Present Value of $1

$$PV = \frac{S}{(1 + i)^n}$$

PERIODS	3%	4%	5%	6%	7%	8%	10%	12%	14%	16%	18%	20%	22%	24%	26%	28%	30%	40%
1	0.971	0.962	0.952	0.943	0.935	0.926	0.909	0.893	0.877	0.862	0.847	0.833	0.820	0.806	0.794	0.781	0.769	0.714
2	0.943	0.925	0.907	0.890	0.873	0.857	0.826	0.797	0.769	0.743	0.718	0.694	0.672	0.650	0.630	0.610	0.592	0.510
3	0.915	0.889	0.864	0.840	0.816	0.794	0.751	0.712	0.675	0.641	0.609	0.579	0.551	0.524	0.500	0.477	0.455	0.364
4	0.888	0.855	0.823	0.792	0.763	0.735	0.683	0.636	0.592	0.552	0.516	0.482	0.451	0.423	0.397	0.373	0.350	0.260
5	0.863	0.822	0.784	0.747	0.713	0.681	0.621	0.567	0.519	0.476	0.437	0.402	0.370	0.341	0.315	0.291	0.269	0.186
6	0.837	0.790	0.746	0.705	0.666	0.630	0.564	0.507	0.456	0.410	0.370	0.335	0.303	0.275	0.250	0.227	0.207	0.133
7	0.813	0.760	0.711	0.665	0.623	0.583	0.513	0.452	0.400	0.354	0.314	0.279	0.249	0.222	0.198	0.178	0.159	0.095
8	0.789	0.731	0.677	0.627	0.582	0.540	0.467	0.404	0.351	0.305	0.266	0.233	0.204	0.179	0.157	0.139	0.123	0.068
9	0.766	0.703	0.645	0.592	0.544	0.500	0.424	0.361	0.308	0.263	0.225	0.194	0.167	0.144	0.125	0.108	0.094	0.048
10	0.744	0.676	0.614	0.558	0.508	0.463	0.386	0.322	0.270	0.227	0.191	0.162	0.137	0.116	0.099	0.085	0.073	0.035
11	0.722	0.650	0.585	0.527	0.475	0.429	0.350	0.287	0.237	0.195	0.162	0.135	0.112	0.094	0.079	0.066	0.056	0.025
12	0.701	0.625	0.557	0.497	0.444	0.397	0.319	0.257	0.208	0.168	0.137	0.112	0.092	0.076	0.062	0.052	0.043	0.018
13	0.681	0.601	0.530	0.469	0.415	0.368	0.290	0.229	0.182	0.145	0.116	0.093	0.075	0.061	0.050	0.040	0.033	0.013
14	0.661	0.577	0.505	0.442	0.388	0.340	0.263	0.205	0.160	0.125	0.099	0.078	0.062	0.049	0.039	0.032	0.025	0.009
15	0.642	0.555	0.481	0.417	0.362	0.315	0.239	0.183	0.140	0.108	0.084	0.065	0.051	0.040	0.031	0.025	0.020	0.006
16	0.623	0.534	0.458	0.394	0.339	0.292	0.218	0.163	0.123	0.093	0.071	0.054	0.042	0.032	0.025	0.019	0.015	0.005
17	0.605	0.513	0.436	0.371	0.317	0.270	0.198	0.146	0.108	0.080	0.060	0.045	0.034	0.026	0.020	0.015	0.012	0.003
18	0.587	0.494	0.416	0.350	0.296	0.250	0.180	0.130	0.095	0.069	0.051	0.038	0.028	0.021	0.016	0.012	0.009	0.002
19	0.570	0.475	0.396	0.331	0.277	0.232	0.164	0.116	0.083	0.060	0.043	0.031	0.023	0.017	0.012	0.009	0.007	0.002
20	0.554	0.456	0.377	0.312	0.258	0.215	0.149	0.104	0.073	0.051	0.037	0.026	0.019	0.014	0.010	0.007	0.005	0.001
21	0.538	0.439	0.359	0.294	0.242	0.199	0.135	0.093	0.064	0.044	0.031	0.022	0.015	0.011	0.008	0.006	0.004	0.001
22	0.522	0.422	0.342	0.278	0.226	0.184	0.123	0.083	0.056	0.038	0.026	0.018	0.013	0.009	0.006	0.004	0.003	0.001
23	0.507	0.406	0.326	0.262	0.211	0.170	0.112	0.074	0.049	0.033	0.022	0.015	0.010	0.007	0.005	0.003	0.002	
24	0.492	0.390	0.310	0.247	0.197	0.158	0.102	0.066	0.043	0.028	0.019	0.013	0.008	0.006	0.004	0.003	0.002	
25	0.478	0.375	0.295	0.233	0.184	0.146	0.092	0.059	0.038	0.024	0.016	0.010	0.007	0.005	0.003	0.002	0.001	
26	0.464	0.361	0.281	0.220	0.172	0.135	0.084	0.053	0.033	0.021	0.014	0.009	0.006	0.004	0.002	0.002	0.001	
27	0.450	0.347	0.268	0.207	0.161	0.125	0.076	0.047	0.029	0.018	0.011	0.007	0.005	0.003	0.002	0.001	0.001	
28	0.437	0.333	0.255	0.196	0.150	0.116	0.069	0.042	0.026	0.016	0.010	0.006	0.004	0.002	0.002	0.001	0.001	
29	0.424	0.321	0.243	0.185	0.141	0.107	0.063	0.037	0.022	0.014	0.008	0.005	0.003	0.002	0.001	0.001	0.001	
30	0.412	0.308	0.231	0.174	0.131	0.099	0.057	0.033	0.020	0.012	0.007	0.004	0.003	0.002	0.001	0.001	0.001	
40	0.307	0.208	0.142	0.097	0.067	0.046	0.022	0.011	0.005	0.003	0.001	0.001						

Table 2

Present Value of Ordinary Annuity of $1

$$PV_A = \frac{1}{i}\left[1 - \frac{1}{(1+i)^n}\right]$$

PERIODS	3%	4%	5%	6%	7%	8%	10%	12%	14%	16%	18%	20%	22%	24%	25%	26%	28%	30%	40%
1	0.971	0.962	0.952	0.943	0.935	0.926	0.909	0.893	0.877	0.862	0.847	0.833	0.820	0.806	0.800	0.794	0.781	0.769	0.714
2	1.913	1.886	1.859	1.833	1.808	1.783	1.736	1.690	1.647	1.605	1.566	1.528	1.492	1.457	1.440	1.424	1.392	1.361	1.224
3	2.827	2.775	2.723	2.673	2.624	2.577	2.487	2.402	2.322	2.246	2.174	2.106	2.042	1.981	1.952	1.923	1.868	1.816	1.589
4	3.717	3.630	3.546	3.465	3.387	3.312	3.170	3.037	2.914	2.798	2.690	2.589	2.494	2.404	2.362	2.320	2.241	2.166	1.849
5	4.580	4.452	4.329	4.212	4.100	3.993	3.791	3.605	3.433	3.274	3.127	2.991	2.864	2.745	2.689	2.635	2.532	2.436	2.035
6	5.417	5.242	5.076	4.917	4.767	4.623	4.355	4.111	3.889	3.685	3.498	3.326	3.167	3.020	2.951	2.885	2.759	2.643	2.168
7	6.230	6.002	5.786	5.582	5.389	5.206	4.868	4.564	4.288	4.039	3.812	3.605	3.416	3.242	3.161	3.083	2.937	2.802	2.263
8	7.020	6.733	6.463	6.210	5.971	5.747	5.335	4.968	4.639	4.344	4.078	3.837	3.619	3.421	3.329	3.241	3.076	2.925	2.331
9	7.786	7.435	7.108	6.802	6.515	6.247	5.759	5.328	4.946	4.607	4.303	4.031	3.786	3.566	3.463	3.366	3.184	3.019	2.379
10	8.530	8.111	7.722	7.360	7.024	6.710	6.145	5.650	5.216	4.833	4.494	4.192	3.923	3.682	3.571	3.465	3.269	3.092	2.414
11	9.253	8.760	8.306	7.887	7.499	7.139	6.495	5.938	5.453	5.029	4.656	4.327	4.035	3.776	3.656	3.544	3.335	3.147	2.438
12	9.954	9.385	8.863	8.384	7.943	7.536	6.814	6.194	5.660	5.197	4.793	4.439	4.127	3.851	3.725	3.606	3.387	3.190	2.456
13	10.635	9.986	9.394	8.853	8.358	7.904	7.103	6.424	5.842	5.342	4.910	4.533	4.203	3.912	3.780	3.656	3.427	3.223	2.468
14	11.296	10.563	9.899	9.295	8.745	8.244	7.367	6.628	6.002	5.468	5.008	4.611	4.265	3.962	3.824	3.695	3.459	3.249	2.477
15	11.938	11.118	10.380	9.712	9.108	8.559	7.606	6.811	6.142	5.575	5.092	4.675	4.315	4.001	3.859	3.726	3.483	3.268	2.484
16	12.561	11.652	10.838	10.106	9.447	8.851	7.824	6.974	6.265	5.669	5.162	4.730	4.357	4.033	3.887	3.751	3.503	3.283	2.489
17	13.166	12.166	11.274	10.477	9.763	9.122	8.022	7.120	6.373	5.749	5.222	4.775	4.391	4.059	3.910	3.771	3.518	3.295	2.492
18	13.754	12.659	11.690	10.828	10.059	9.372	8.201	7.250	6.467	5.818	5.273	4.812	4.419	4.080	3.928	3.786	3.529	3.304	2.494
19	14.324	13.134	12.085	11.158	10.336	9.604	8.365	7.366	6.550	5.877	5.316	4.844	4.442	4.097	3.942	3.799	3.539	3.311	2.496
20	14.877	13.590	12.462	11.470	10.594	9.818	8.514	7.469	6.623	5.929	5.353	4.870	4.460	4.110	3.954	3.808	3.546	3.316	2.497
21	15.415	14.029	12.821	11.764	10.836	10.017	8.649	7.562	6.687	5.973	5.384	4.891	4.476	4.121	3.963	3.816	3.551	3.320	2.498
22	15.937	14.451	13.163	12.042	11.061	10.201	8.772	7.645	6.743	6.001	5.410	4.909	4.488	4.130	3.970	3.822	3.556	3.323	2.498
23	16.444	14.857	13.489	12.303	11.272	10.371	8.883	7.718	6.792	6.044	5.432	4.925	4.499	4.137	3.976	3.827	3.559	3.325	2.499
24	16.936	15.247	13.799	12.550	11.469	10.529	8.985	7.784	6.835	6.073	5.451	4.937	4.507	4.143	3.981	3.831	3.562	3.327	2.499
25	17.413	15.622	14.094	12.783	11.654	10.675	9.077	7.843	6.873	6.097	5.467	4.948	4.514	4.147	3.985	3.834	3.564	3.329	2.499
26	17.877	15.983	14.375	13.003	11.826	10.810	9.161	7.896	6.906	6.118	5.480	4.956	4.520	4.151	3.988	3.837	3.566	3.330	2.500
27	18.327	16.330	14.643	13.211	11.987	10.935	9.237	7.943	6.935	6.136	5.492	4.964	4.524	4.154	3.990	3.839	3.567	3.331	2.500
28	18.764	16.663	14.898	13.406	12.137	11.051	9.307	7.984	6.961	6.152	5.502	4.970	4.528	4.157	3.992	3.840	3.568	3.331	2.500
29	19.188	16.984	15.141	13.591	12.278	11.158	9.370	8.022	6.983	6.166	5.510	4.975	4.531	4.159	3.994	3.841	3.569	3.332	2.500
30	19.600	17.292	15.372	13.765	12.409	11.258	9.427	8.055	7.003	6.177	5.517	4.979	4.534	4.160	3.995	3.842	3.569	3.332	2.500
40	23.115	19.793	17.159	15.046	13.332	11.925	9.779	8.244	7.105	6.234	5.548	4.997	4.544	4.166	3.999	3.846	3.571	3.333	2.500

APPENDIX C:
Glossary

The italicized words within the definitions or explanations are also described in the glossary.

ABSORPTION COSTING. That type of product costing that assigns fixed *manufacturing overhead* to the units produced as a product cost. Contrast with *direct costing*.

ACCELERATED COST RECOVERY SYSTEM (ACRS). A system of the Internal Revenue Service that requires *depreciation* deductions to be based on arbitrary "recovery periods" instead of useful lives.

ACCELERATED DEPRECIATION. Any pattern of *depreciation* that systematically writes off depreciable costs more quickly than the ordinary straight-line method based on expected useful life.

ACCOUNT. Summary of the changes in a particular *asset* or *equity*.

ACCOUNTING METHOD. See *Accounting rate of return*.

ACCOUNTING PRINCIPLES BOARD (APB). The top private-sector regulatory body, which existed from 1959 to 1973, when it was succeeded by the *Financial Accounting Standards Board*.

ACCOUNTING RATE OF RETURN. An expression of the utility of a given project as the ratio of the increase in future average annual *net income* to the initial increase in required investment. Also called *book value rate* and *unadjusted rate*.

ACCOUNTS PAYABLE. The debts shown on the buyer's balance sheet when the buyer has bought goods or services on open account. Usually a *current liability*.

ACCOUNTS RECEIVABLE. The claims against debtors generally arising from sales of goods or services on open account. Usually a *current asset*.

ACCRUAL BASIS. A matching process whereby *revenue* is recognized as services are rendered and *expenses* are recognized as efforts are expended or services utilized to obtain the revenue, regardless of when cash is received or disbursed.

ACCRUE. Accumulation of a receivable or payable during a given period even though no explicit *transaction* occurs.

ACCUMULATED DEPRECIATION. The cumulative sum of all *depreciation* recognized since the date of acquisition of the particular *assets* described.

ACQUISITION COST. The original *historical cost* of an *asset* acquired. Usually includes directly associated *costs* such as freight and installation.

ACRS. See *Accelerated Cost Recovery System*.

ACTIVITY ACCOUNTING. See *Responsibility accounting*.

ACTUAL COSTING. The method of allocating *costs* to products using actual *direct materials, direct labor,* and *overhead.*

ADDBACK METHOD. The practice of beginning a statement of changes in financial position with *net income* and then adding or deducting income statement items not affecting *working capital.*

ADJUSTING ENTRIES. The records made of an accounting transaction giving effect to the correction of an error, an accrual, a write-off, a prepayment, a provision for bad debts or *depreciation,* or the like.

ADJUSTMENTS. The key final process (before the computation of ending *account* balances) that assures the accountant that the financial effects of transactions are assigned to the appropriate time periods.

ALLOCATION. Assigning one or more items of *cost* or *revenue* to one or more segments of an organization according to cause, benefits received, responsibilities, or other logical measure of use.

AMORTIZATION. The systematic reduction of a lump-sum amount.

APB. See *Accounting Principles Board.*

APB OPINIONS. A series of thirty-one Opinions of the Accounting Principles Board issued during 1962–73, many of which are still the accounting law of the land.

APPROPRIATION. An authorization to spend up to a specified dollar ceiling.

ASSETS. Economic resources that are expected to benefit future activities.

ASSET TURNOVER. The ratio of sales to total *assets* available.

ATTENTION DIRECTING. That function of the accountant's information-supplying task which focuses on problems in the operation of the firm or which points out imperfections or inefficiencies in certain areas of the firm's operation.

AUDIT. An examination that is made in accordance with generally accepted auditing standards. Its aim is to give credibility to financial statements.

AUDITOR'S REPORT. The written description of an auditor's findings together with the auditor's professional opinion regarding the credibility of management's financial statements.

AVOIDABLE COST. Those *costs* that will not continue if an ongoing operation is changed or deleted.

BALANCE. The difference between the total *debits* and the total *credits* in an *account* at any particular time.

BALANCE SHEET. A statement of financial status at an instant of time.

BILL OF MATERIALS. A specification of the quantities of *direct material* allowed for manufacturing a given quantity of output.

BOOK VALUE. The carrying amount in the *accounts,* net of any *contra accounts.* For example, the book value of equipment is its *acquisition cost* minus its *accumulated depreciation.*

BOOK VALUE METHOD. See *Accounting rate of return.*

BUDGET. A plan of action expressed in figures.

BUDGET APPROPRIATION. An authority to spend, usually up to a ceiling amount.

BUDGET VARIANCE. The difference between an actual and a *budget* amount. Also see *Control-budget variance.*

CAPACITY COSTS. An alternate term for *fixed costs,* emphasizing the fact that fixed costs are needed in order to provide operating facilities and an organization ready to produce and sell at a planned volume of activity.

CAPITAL. In accounting, this word is too general by itself. In most cases, capital implies owners' equity. Money generated by long-term debt is also often called capital.

CAPITAL BUDGETING. Long-term planning for proposed capital outlays and their financing.

CAPITAL SURPLUS. The excess received over the par or stated or legal value of the shares issued.

CAPITAL TURNOVER. *Revenue* divided by invested capital.

CASH BASIS. A process of accounting whereby *revenue* and *expense* recognition depend solely on the timing of various cash receipts and disbursements.

CASH BUDGET. A schedule of expected cash receipts and disbursements.

CASH FLOW. A general term that must be interpreted carefully. Most strictly, cash flow means inflows or outflows of cash. Frequently, the term is used loosely to represent funds provided by operations.

CERTIFIED MANAGEMENT ACCOUNTANT. A designation given by the Institute of Management Accounting of the National Association of Accountants to those who pass a set of examinations and meet specified experience and continuing education requirements.

CERTIFIED PUBLIC ACCOUNTANT. In the U.S., an accountant earns this designation by a combination of education, qualifying experience, and the passing of a three and one-half day written national examination.

CHANGES STATEMENT. A *statement of changes in financial position.*

CHOICE CRITERION. Often used as a synonym for *objective function.*

CMA. See *Certified Management Accountant.*

COMMITTED COSTS. Those *fixed costs* arising from the possession of plant and equipment and a basic organization and thus are affected primarily by long-run decisions as to the desired level of capacity.

COMMON COST. A *cost* that is common to all the segments in question and is not clearly or practically allocable except by some questionable allocation base.

COMMON STOCK. Stock representing the class of owners having a "residual" ownership of a corporation.

COMPONENT PERCENTAGES. Analysis and presentation of financial statements in percentage form to aid comparability.

COMPTROLLER. See *Controller.*

CONDITIONAL VALUE. The value that will ensue if a particular *event* occurs.

CONSERVATISM. Selecting that method of measurement which yields the gloomiest immediate results.

CONSOLIDATED STATEMENTS. Statements that combine legally separate companies as though they were a single fused *entity.*

CONSTANT DOLLARS. Those monetary units restated so as to represent the same general purchasing power.

CONTINUITY CONVENTION. See *Going concern convention.*

CONTINUOUS BUDGET. A *budget* that perpetually adds a month in the future as the month just ended is dropped.

CONTRA ACCOUNT. A separate offsetting *account.* Examples are allowance for uncollectible accounts and *accumulated depreciation.*

CONTRIBUTED CAPITAL. The total amounts invested by owners at the inception of a business or subsequently. Usually distinguished from capital arising from *retained income.*

CONTRIBUTION APPROACH. A method of preparing *income statements* that separates *variable costs* from *fixed costs* in order to emphasize the importance of cost behavior patterns for purposes of planning and control.

CONTRIBUTION MARGIN. Excess of sales price over variable expenses. Also called marginal income. May be expressed as a total, as a ratio, or on a per-unit basis.

CONTROL-BUDGET VARIANCE. See *flexible-budget variance.*

CONTROL FACTOR UNIT. A measure of workload. Examples are lines per hour and pieces mailed per hour.

CONTROLLABLE COST. A *cost* that may be directly regulated at a given level of managerial authority, either in the short run or in the long run.

CONTROLLER. The chief management accounting executive. Also spelled *comptroller.*

CONTROLLING. Obtaining conformity to plans through action and evaluation.

CONVERSION COSTS. *Direct labor* plus *factory overhead.*

COPYRIGHT. Exclusive right conveyed by federal statute to reproduce and sell a book, design, pamphlet, drawing, or other creations, and to forbid the publication of excerpts or other imitations.

CORPORATION. Organizations that are "artificial beings" created by individual state laws.

COST. Sacrifice made for goods or services. May take the form of an *outlay cost* or an *opportunity cost*.

COST ACCUMULATION. Gathering of *costs* in some organized way via an accounting system.

COST ALLOCATION. Assignment of and reassignment of a *cost* or group of costs to one or more *cost objectives*.

COST-ALLOCATION BASE. A common denominator used to trace the *cost* or costs in question to the *cost objectives*. Examples are direct-labor-hours and machine-hours.

COST APPLICATION. Also called *cost absorption*. The allocation to products rather than to departments.

COST APPROXIMATION. See *Cost estimation*.

COST BEHAVIOR PATTERN. See *Cost function*.

COST-BENEFIT CRITERION. As a system is changed, its expected additional benefits usually must exceed its expected additional *costs*.

COST-BENEFIT THEME. See *Cost-benefit criterion*.

COST CENTER. An area of responsibility for *costs*.

COST ESTIMATION. An attempt to specify some underlying relationship between x and y over a stipulated *relevant range* of x that may be of interest. An approximation of how a *cost* truly behaves. The approximation is in linear rather than nonlinear form.

COST FUNCTION. A relationship between a *cost* and one or more variables such as the total cost of repairs in relation to miles driven.

COST METHOD FOR INVESTMENTS. The method whereby the initial investment is recorded at cost and *dividends* are recorded as income.

COST OBJECTIVE. Any activity for which a separate measurement of *costs* is desired. Examples include departments, products, territories, etc.

COST OF CAPITAL. As used in this book, and in many finance books, a synonym for *required rate of return*.

COST OF GOODS SOLD. Cost of the merchandise that is acquired and resold.

COST OF SALES. See *Cost of goods sold*.

COST POOL. A group of individual *costs* that is allocated as a group to *cost objectives* in some plausible way.

CREDIT. In accounting, means one thing and one thing only—"right," as distinguished from "left." It typically refers to an entry in an *account* or the *balance* of an account.

CURRENT ASSETS. Cash plus those *assets* that are reasonably expected to be converted to cash or sold or consumed during the normal operating cycle.

CURRENT COST. *Cost* stated in terms of current market prices instead of *historical cost*.

CURRENT-COST METHOD. See *Current cost*.

CURRENT LIABILITIES. *Liabilities* that fall due within the coming year or within the normal *operating cycle* if longer than a year.

CURRENT RATIO. The ratio of *current assets* to *current liabilities*.

CURRENTLY ATTAINABLE STANDARDS. Standards expressing a level of economic efficiency that can be reached with skilled, diligent, superior effort.

CUTOFF RATE. Minimum desired rate of return.

DDB. See *double-declining-balance depreciation*.

DEBENTURE. A security with a general claim against all unencumbered *assets* rather than a specific claim against particular assets.

DEBIT. An entry on the left side of an *account*.

DECENTRALIZATION. The relative freedom to make decisions. The lower the level in the organization that decisions are made, the greater the decentralization.

DECISION MODEL. A formal method for making a choice that often involves quantitative analysis.

DECISION TABLE. A convenient technique for showing the total *expected value* of each of a number of contemplated acts in the light of the varying *probabilities* of the *events* that may take place and the varying values of each act under each of the events.

DEFERRED CHARGE. An *expenditure* not recognized as a *cost* of operations of the period in which incurred but carried forward to be written off in one or more future periods.

DEFERRED CREDIT. Often used as a synonym for *deferred revenue* or as a description for *deferred income tax*. In its bookkeeping application, the term refers to an amount that is classified as a *liability* that will eventually be transferred as a *credit* to *revenue* or a credit to *expense*.

DEFERRED INCOME. See *Deferred revenue*.

DEFERRED INCOME TAX (LIABILITY). A *liability* in the *balance sheet* that represents the additional federal income taxes that would have been due if a company had not been allowed to deduct greater amounts for *expenses* for income-tax-reporting purposes than are recorded for financial-reporting purposes. Also see *Interperiod tax allocation*.

DEFERRED REVENUE. Income received or recorded before it is earned.

DENOMINATOR VARIANCE. Same as *production volume variance*.

DEPRECIATION. The allocation of the *acquisition cost* of plant, property, and equipment to the particular periods or products that benefit from the utilization of the *assets*.

DIFFERENTIAL COST. See *Incremental cost*.

DIRECT COSTING. That type of product costing which charges fixed *manufacturing overhead* immediately against the *revenue* of the period in which it was incurred, without assigning it to specific units produced. Also called *variable costing* or *marginal costing*.

DIRECT LABOR. All labor that is obviously related to and specifically and conveniently traceable to specific products.

DIRECT MATERIAL. All raw material that is an integral part of the finished good and can be conveniently assigned to specific physical units.

DIRECT METHOD. A method that ignores other service departments when any given service department's *costs* are allocated to revenue-producing or production departments.

DISCOUNT RATE. As used in *capital budgeting*, the minimum desired rate of return.

DISCRETIONARY COSTS. Fixed costs arising from periodic, usually yearly, appropriation decisions that directly reflect top-management policies. Also called *programmed costs* or *managed costs*.

DIVIDENDS. Ordinarily distributions of *assets* that liquidate a portion of the ownership claim.

DOUBLE-DECLINING-BALANCE DEPRECIATION (DDB). A form of *accelerated depreciation* that results in first-year *depreciation* being twice the amount of *straight-line depreciation* when zero terminal disposal value is assumed.

DYSFUNCTIONAL BEHAVIOR. Actions taken in conflict with top-management goals.

EARNED SURPLUS. A virtually archaic term for *retained income*.

EARNINGS. The excess of *revenues* over *expenses*.

EARNINGS PER SHARE. *Net income* divided by the number of common shares outstanding. However, where preferred stock exists, the preferred dividends must be deducted in order to compute the net income applicable to common stock.

ECONOMIC LOT SIZE. Synonym for *economic order quantity*.

ECONOMIC ORDER QUANTITY. The amount of inventory that should be ordered at one time so that the associated annual costs of the inventory can be minimized.

EFFECTIVENESS. Attainment of a predetermined goal.

EFFICIENCY. Optimal relationship between inputs and outputs.

EFFICIENCY VARIANCE. The standard price for a given resource, multiplied by the difference between the actual quantity of inputs used and the total standard quantity of inputs allowed for the number of good outputs achieved.

EFFICIENT CAPITAL MARKET. One in which market prices "fully reflect" all information available at a given time.

ENGINEERED COST. Any *cost* that has an explicit, specified physical relationship with a selected measure of activity.

ENTITY. A specific area of accountability that is the focus of the accounting process. It may be a single corporation, a tax district, a department, a papermaking machine, or a consolidated group of many interrelated corporations.

EQUITIES. The claims against or interests in the *assets*. The creditors' claims are *liabilities* and the owners' claims are *owners' equity* or, in the case of corporations, *stockholders' equity*.

EQUITY METHOD. A basis for carrying long-term investments at *cost* plus a pro-rata share of accumulated *retained income* since acquisition.

EQUIVALENT UNITS. The expression of output in terms of doses or amount of work applied thereto.

EVENTS. Set of all relevant occurrences that can happen. Synonym for *states of nature*.

EXCESS MATERIAL REQUISITIONS. A form to be filled out by the production staff to secure any materials needed in excess of the standard amount allotted for output.

EXPECTED VALUE. A weighted average of all the conditional values of an act. Each conditional value is weighted by its probability.

EXPENDITURE. Cash or other resources paid, or to be paid, for an *asset* purchased or service acquired.

EXPENSES. Generally a gross decrease in *assets* from delivering goods or services.

EXPIRED COSTS. *Expenditures* from which no further benefit is anticipated; an *expense*; a *cost* absorbed over the period during which benefits were enjoyed or a *loss* incurred.

EXPLICIT TRANSACTIONS. Events such as cash receipts and disbursements that trigger nearly all day-to-day routine entries.

FACTORY BURDEN. See *Factory overhead*.

FACTORY OVERHEAD. All factory costs other than direct labor and direct material. Also called *factory burden, indirect manufacturing costs, manufacturing overhead*, and *manufacturing expense*.

FASB STATEMENTS. Official rules and regulations regarding external financial reporting issued in a numbered series by the *Financial Accounting Standards Board*.

FINANCIAL ACCOUNTING. Is concerned mainly with how accounting can serve external decision makers, as distinguished from *management accounting*.

FINANCIAL ACCOUNTING STANDARDS BOARD (FASB). The primary regulatory body over accounting principles and practices. It is an independent creature of the private sector.

FINANCIAL BUDGET. That part of the *master budget* that is composed of the capital budget, cash budget, budgeted balance sheet, and budgeted statement of changes in financial position.

FINANCIAL CAPITAL MAINTENANCE. The quantity of financial resources (usually historical costs), as distinguished from physical resources or operating capability, to be recovered before *income* emerges.

FIRST-IN, FIRST-OUT. The stock of merchandise or material that is acquired earliest is assumed to be used first; the stock acquired latest is assumed to be still on hand.

FIXED ASSETS. Tangible *assets* or physical items that can be seen and touched, often called property, plant, and equipment or plant assets.

FIXED COST. A *cost* that, for a given period of time and range of activity called the *relevant range*, does not change in total but becomes progressively smaller on a *per-unit* basis as volume increases.

FLEXIBLE BUDGET. A budget, often referring to overhead costs only, that is prepared for a range, rather than for a single level, of activity—one that can be automatically geared to changes in the level of volume. Also called *variable budget*. *Direct material* and *direct labor* are sometimes included in the flexible budget.

FLEXIBLE-BUDGET VARIANCES. Difference between actual amounts and the *flexible-budget* amounts for the actual output achieved.

FLEXIBLE-CONTROL-BUDGET VARIANCES. Same as *flexible-budget variances*.

FOREIGN CORRUPT PRACTICES ACT. A federal law that requires adequate *internal controls*, among other requirements.

FRANCHISE. A privilege granted by a government, manufacturer, or distributor to sell a product or service in accordance with specified conditions.

FULL COST. Has two commonly used meanings. First, it is often a synonym for *absorption cost*. Second, it often means absorption cost *plus* an allocation of nonmanufacturing cost.

FULL COSTING. See *Full cost*.

FUNCTIONAL APPROACH. See *Functional costing*.

FUNCTIONAL COSTING. Classifying *costs* by allocating them to the various functions performed, such as manufacturing, warehousing, delivery, and billing.

FUND. A specific amount of cash or securities earmarked for a special purpose.

FUNDS PROVIDED BY OPERATIONS. The excess of *revenue* over all *expenses* requiring *working capital*.

FUNDS STATEMENT. A statement of sources and applications of *working capital* or cash.

GENERALLY ACCEPTED ACCOUNTING PRINCIPLES (GAAP). A technical term including both broad concepts or guidelines and detailed practices. It includes all conventions, rules, and procedures that together make up accepted accounting practice at a given time.

GOAL CONGRUENCE. Sharing of the same goals by top managers and their subordinates.

GOING CONCERN CONVENTION. An *entity* that it is assumed will continue indefinitely or at least will not be liquidated in the near future.

GOODWILL. The total purchase price of *assets* acquired in a lump-sum purchase that exceeds the total of the amounts that can be justifiably assigned to the individual assets.

GROSS BOOK VALUE. Carrying amount of an *asset* before deducting any related amounts (such as *accumulated depreciation*).

GROSS MARGIN. Also called *gross profit*. Excess of sales over the *cost of goods sold*, that is, over the cost of the merchandise inventory that is acquired and resold.

GROSS PROFIT. The difference between sales revenue and the cost of inventories sold.

HALF-YEAR CONVENTION. A widely used custom of regarding all depreciable *assets* placed in service during the year as if they had been placed in service at the year's midpoint.

HISTORICAL COST. See *Sunk cost*.

HOLDING GAINS. Increases (or decreases) in the *replacement cost* (or other appropriate measure of current value) of the *assets* held during the current period.

HURDLE RATE. Minimum desired rate of return. Also called *required rate of return*.

IDEAL CAPACITY. The absolute maximum number of units that could be produced in a given operating situation, with no allowance for work stoppages or repairs. Also called theoretical capacity.

IDLE TIME. A classification of *indirect labor* that constitutes wages paid for unproductive time due to circumstances beyond the worker's control.

IMPLICIT TRANSACTIONS. Events (like the passage of time) that are temporarily ignored in day-to-day recording procedures and that are recognized via end-of-period *adjustments*.

INCENTIVE. Those informal and formal performance measures and rewards that enhance *goal congruence* and *managerial effort*.

INCOME. The excess of *revenues* over *expenses*.

INCOME PERCENTAGE OF REVENUE. *Income* divided by *revenue*.

INCOME STATEMENT. A statement that evaluates the operating performance of the corporation by matching its accomplishments (*revenue* from customers, which usually is called sales) and efforts (*cost of goods sold* and other *expenses*).

INCREMENT. See *Incremental*.

INCREMENTAL. The change in total results (such as *revenue, expenses,* or *income*) under a new condition in comparison with some given or known condition.

INCREMENTAL APPROACH. A method of determining which of two alternative courses of action is preferable by calculating the present value of the difference in net cash inflow between one alternative and the other.

INCREMENTAL COST. The difference in total *cost* between two alternatives. Also called *differential cost*.

INDEPENDENT OPINION. See *Auditor's report*.

INDIRECT LABOR. All factory labor that is not *direct labor*.

INDIRECT MANUFACTURING COSTS. All manufacturing *costs* other than *direct material* and *direct labor*.

INTANGIBLE ASSETS. Rights or economic benefits that are not physical in nature. Examples are *franchises, patents, trademarks, copyrights,* and *goodwill.*

INTERNAL ACCOUNTING CONTROL. Methods and procedures that are mainly concerned with the authorization of transactions, safeguarding of *assets,* and accuracy of the financial records.

INTERNAL RATE OF RETURN. The rate of interest at which the present value of expected cash inflows from a particular project equals the present value of expected cash outflows of the same project. Also called *time-adjusted rate.*

INTERPERIOD TAX ALLOCATION. Accounting procedures that account for *timing differences* between *revenues* and *expenses* reported to income tax authorities and to others.

INVESTMENT CENTER. An area of responsibility for *costs, revenues,* and related investment.

INVESTMENTS IN AFFILIATES. Often used to describe investments in voting stock that represents 20% to 50% ownership.

INVESTMENTS IN ASSOCIATES. Often used as synonym for *investments in affiliates.*

INVESTMENT TAX CREDIT. Direct reductions of income taxes arising from the acquisition of depreciable *assets.*

JOB ORDER. A document that shows the *costs* allocated to a specific batch of product.

JOB-ORDER COSTING. The method of allocating *costs* to products that receive varying attention and effort.

JOINT PRODUCT COSTS. *Costs* of two or more manufactured goods, of significant sales values, that are produced by a single process and that are not identifiable as individual products up to a certain stage of production, known as the *split-off point.*

JUST-IN-TIME. A system of inventory control that concentrates on the final manufacturing process and then looks backward throughout the preceding processes. The earlier processes produce only enough quantities to replace those withdrawn by the subsequent processes.

LAST-IN, FIRST-OUT. A cost-flow assumption that the stock acquired earliest is still on hand; the stock of merchandise or material acquired latest is used first.

LEAD TIME. The time interval between placing an order and receiving delivery.

LEDGER. A group of *accounts.*

LEGAL VALUE. *Par* or *stated value* that is almost always far below the actual cash invested by a stockholder.

LIABILITIES. Probable future sacrifices of economic benefits stemming from present legal, equitable, or constructive obligations of a particular enterprise to transfer *assets* or provide services to other entities in the future as a result of past *transactions* or events affecting the enterprise.

LIFO. See *Last-in, First-out.*

LIFO INCREMENT. See *LIFO layer.*

LIFO LAYER. A separately identifiable additional segment of LIFO inventory.

LIFO POOL. See *LIFO layer.*

LIFO RESERVE. The amount of "cushion" or "understatement" of current inventory values that the LIFO method produces in relation to FIFO.

LIMITED LIABILITY. Corporate creditors ordinarily have claims against the corporate *assets* only. Therefore the stockholders as individuals have no liability beyond their original investment in the corporation.

LIMITING FACTOR. The item that restricts or constrains the production or sale of a product or service.

LINEAR PROGRAMMING. A mathematical approach to a group of business problems that contains many interacting variables and basically involves combining limited resources to maximize *profits* or minimize *costs.*

LINE AUTHORITY. Authority that is exerted downward over subordinates.

LONG-LIVED ASSETS. Resources that are held for an extended time, such as land, buildings, equipment, natural resources, and *patents.*

LOSSES. Losses (or other appropriately descriptive terms) are decreases in *owners' equity* (net assets) from peripheral or incidental *transactions* of an enterprise and from all other transactions and other events and circumstances affecting the enterprise during the period except those that result from *expenses* or distributions by the enterprise to owners.

LOWER OF COST OR MARKET. The superimposition of a market-price test on an inventory cost method.

MANAGED COSTS. See *Discretionary costs.*

MANAGEMENT ACCOUNTING. Concerned mainly with how accounting can serve internal decision makers. Defined as the process of identification, measurement, accumulation, analysis, preparation, interpretation, and communication of information that assists executives in fulfilling organizational objectives.

MANAGEMENT AUDIT. A review to determine whether the policies and procedures specified by top management have been implemented.

MANAGEMENT BY EXCEPTION. The practice by the executive of focusing his or her attention mainly on significant deviations from expected results. It might also be called management by variance.

MANAGEMENT BY OBJECTIVES (MBO). Joint formulation by a manager and his or her superior of a set of goals and of plans for achieving the goals for a forthcoming period.

MANAGERIAL EFFORT. Exertion toward a goal. Includes all actions (such as watching or thinking) that result in more *efficiency* and *effectiveness.*

MANUFACTURING EXPENSES. See *Factory overhead.*

MANUFACTURING OVERHEAD. See *Factory overhead.*

MARGINAL COSTING. See *Direct costing.*

MARGINAL INCOME. See *Contribution margin.*

MARKETABLE SECURITIES. Any notes, bonds, or stocks that can readily be sold via public markets. The term is often used as a synonym for *short-term investments.*

MARKETING VARIANCE. Synonym for *sales volume variance.*

MASTER BUDGET. The *budget* that consolidates the organization's overall plans.

MASTER BUDGETED SALES. The expected sales employed in formulating the master budget for the period.

MATCHING. Establishing a relationship between efforts *(expenses)* and accomplishments *(revenues).*

MATCHING AND COST RECOVERY. The procedure of accrual accounting whereby *expenses* are either directly attributed to related *revenues* (matching) of a given period or are otherwise regarded as *costs* that will not be recovered from revenue in future periods. In short, cost recovery is the justification for carrying *unexpired costs* as *assets* rather than writing them off as expenses.

MATERIALITY. The accounting convention that justifies the exclusion of insignificant information from financial reports. Whether an item is material (significant) is a matter of professional judgment.

MBO. Symbol for *management by objectives.*

MINORITY INTEREST. The total shareholder interest (other than the parent's) in a *subsidiary corporation.*

MIXED COST. A *cost* that has both fixed and variable elements.

MODEL. A depiction of interrelationships of recognized factors in a real situation.

MONETARY ITEMS. A claim receivable or payable in a specified number of dollars; the claim remains fixed regardless of changes in either specific or general price levels.

NAA. See *National Association of Accountants.*

NATIONAL ASSOCIATION OF ACCOUNTANTS. The largest U.S. professional organization of accountants whose major interest is management accounting.

NEGOTIATED MARKET PRICE. A transfer price negotiated by the buying and selling segments when there is no market mechanism to fix a price clearly relevant to the situation.

NET BOOK VALUE. Carrying amount of an *asset*, net of any related *accounts* (such as *accumulated depreciation*).

NET INCOME. The excess of all *revenues* and gains for a period over all *expenses* and *losses*.

NET MONETARY POSITION. Total monetary *assets* minus total monetary *liabilities*.

NET-PRESENT-VALUE METHOD. A method of calculating the expected utility of a given project by discounting all expected future cash flows to the present, using some predetermined minimum desired rate of return.

NET REALIZABLE VALUE. Estimated selling price of a product in the ordinary course of business, less reasonably predictable *costs* of completion and disposal.

NET WORTH. A synonym for *owners' equity*; no longer widely used.

NOMINAL DOLLARS. Those that are not restated for fluctuations in the general purchasing power of the monetary unit.

NORMAL ACTIVITY. The rate of activity needed to meet average sales demand over a period long enough to encompass seasonal and cyclical fluctuations.

NORMAL COSTING. The method of allocating *costs* to products using actual *direct materials*, actual *direct labor*, and predetermined overhead rates.

NORMAL COST SYSTEM. See *Normal costing.*

NOTES PAYABLE. Promissory notes that are evidence of a debt and state the terms of payment.

OBJECTIVE FUNCTION. Goal that can be quantified, often expressed as a maximization (or minimization) of some form of *profit* (or *cost*).

OBJECTIVITY. Accuracy supported by convincing evidence that can be verified by independent accountants.

OBJECT OF COSTING. See *Cost objective.*

OPEN ACCOUNT. Buying or selling on credit usually by just an "authorized signature" of the buyer.

OPERATING BUDGET. *Budget* of the *income statement* together with supporting schedules.

OPERATING CYCLE. The time span during which cash is used to acquire goods and services, which in turn are sold to customers, who in turn pay for their purchases with cash.

OPERATION COSTING. System where distinctions are made between batches of product. Materials and *conversion costs* are computed for each operation undergone during production.

OPERATIONS RESEARCH. A diffused collection of mathematical and statistical models applied to decision making.

OPPORTUNITY COST. The maximum alternative earning that might have been obtained if the productive good, service, or capacity had been applied to some alternative use.

ORDER-FILLING COST. A marketing *cost* incurred in the storing, packing, shipping, billing, credit and collection, and in other similar aspects of selling merchandise.

ORDER-GETTING COST. A marketing *cost* incurred in the effort to attain a desired sales volume and mix.

ORDINARY INCREMENTAL BUDGET. *Budget* that usually considers the previous period's *budget* and actual results as a given. The budget amount is then changed in accordance with experience during the previous period and expectations for the next period.

ORGANIZATION STRUCTURE. The formal relationships among the individuals and segments within an organization.

OUTCOMES. Consequences of the various possible combinations of actions and *events*.

OUTLAY COST. A cash disbursement, as distinguished from an *opportunity cost*.

OUTSIDE STOCKHOLDERS' INTEREST IN SUBSIDIARIES. Synonym for *minority interest*.

OVERABSORBED OVERHEAD. See *Overapplied factory overhead.*

OVERAPPLIED FACTORY OVERHEAD. The excess of *overhead* applied to products over actual overhead incurred.

OVERHEAD. *Costs* that are not directly traced to a given *cost objective*. These indirect costs are usually divided into manufacturing, selling, and administrative categories.

OVERTIME PREMIUM. A classification of *indirect labor costs*, consisting of the wages paid to *all* factory workers in excess of their straight-time wage rates.

OWNERS' EQUITY. The interest of stockholders or other owners in the *assets* of an enterprise and, at any time, the cumulative net result of past *transactions* and other events and circumstances affecting the enterprise.

PAID-IN CAPITAL. The *owners' equity* measured by the total amounts invested at the inception of a business and subsequently.

PAID-IN SURPLUS. See *Capital surplus.*

PARAMETER. A constant, such as *a*, or a coefficient, such as *b*, in a model or system of equations, such as $y = a + bx$.

PARTNERSHIP. A special form of organization that joins two or more individuals together as co-owners.

PAR VALUE. The value printed on the face of the security certificate.

PATENTS. Grants by the federal government to inventors, giving them the exclusive right to produce and sell their inventions for a period of seventeen years.

PAYBACK. The measure of the time needed to recoup, in the form of cash inflow from operations, the initial dollars invested. Also called *payout* and *payoff.*

PAYOFFS. Synonym for *outcomes.*

PAYOFF TABLE. See *Decision table.*

PAYOUT. See *Payback.*

PERFORMANCE REPORT. The comparison of actual results with the *budget.*

PERIOD COSTS. Those costs being deducted as *expenses* during the current period without having been previously classified as *product costs.*

PHYSICAL CAPITAL MAINTENANCE. The capacity to maintain previous levels of output of goods and services.

PLANNING. Selecting objectives and the means for their attainment.

PRACTICAL CAPACITY. The maximum level at which the plant or department can realistically operate most efficiently, i.e., ideal capacity less allowances for unavoidable operating interruptions. Also called practical attainable capacity.

PREFERRED STOCK. Stock that has some priority over other shares regarding *dividends* or the distribution of *assets* upon liquidation.

PREPAID EXPENSES. *Assets* that exist because operating supplies and rights to services have been acquired in advance of use.

PREVIOUS-DEPARTMENT COSTS. See *Transferred-in Costs.*

PRICE VARIANCE. The difference between the actual price and the standard price, multiplied by the total number of items acquired. The term "price variance" is usually linked with *direct material;* the term "rate variance," which is conceptually similar to the price variance, is usually linked with *direct labor.*

PRIME COSTS. *Direct material* plus *direct labor.*

PRIORITY INCREMENTAL BUDGET. Similar to *ordinary incremental budget.* However, the budget request must be accompanied by a statement of what incremental activities or changes would occur if the budget were increased or decreased by a given amount or percentage.

PROBABILITIES. Likelihoods of occurrence of *events.*

PROBLEM SOLVING. That function of the accountant's information-supplying task which expresses in concise, quantified terms the relative advantages and disadvantages to the firm of pursuing a possible future course of action, or the relative advantages of any one of several alternative methods of operation.

PROCESS. A series of actions or operations leading to a definite end.

PROCESS COSTING. The method of allocating *costs* to the products resulting from the mass production of like units.

PRODUCT COSTS. *Costs* that are identified with goods produced or purchased for resale.

PRODUCTION VOLUME VARIANCE. Difference between *budgeted* fixed factory overhead and the fixed factory overhead *applied* to products.

PROFITABILITY ACCOUNTING. See *Responsibility accounting*.

PROFIT CENTER. A segment of a business that is responsible for both *revenue* and *expense*.

PROFITS. The excess of *revenues* over *expenses*.

PRO-FORMA STATEMENTS. Forecasted financial statements.

PROGRAMMED COSTS. See *Discretionary costs*.

PROPRIETORSHIP. A separate *entity* with a single owner.

P/V CHART. A graph showing volume on the horizontal axis and net income on the vertical axis.

QUALITATIVE FACTOR. A factor that is of consequence but cannot be measured precisely and easily in dollars.

QUANTITY VARIANCE. *Efficiency variance* pertaining to materials or direct labor.

QUOTE SHEET. An analysis of *costs* used as a basis for determining selling prices.

RATE VARIANCE. The difference between actual wages paid and the standard wage rate, multiplied by the total actual hours of *direct labor* used. See *Price variance*.

REALIZATION. The recognition of *revenue*. Generally three tests must be met. First, the earning process must be virtually complete in that the goods or services must be fully rendered. Second, an exchange of resources evidenced by a market transaction must occur. Third, the *asset* received must be cash or convertible into cash with reasonable certainty.

REALLOCATION. Allocation of the *costs* of operating the service departments to the various production departments in proportion to the relative benefits or services received by each production department.

REAPPORTIONMENT. See *Reallocation*.

REGRESSION ANALYSIS. The measurement of the average amount of change in one variable (e.g., shipping cost) that is associated with unit increases in the amounts of one or more other variables.

REINVESTED EARNINGS. See *Retained income*.

RELEVANT DATA FOR DECISION MAKING. Expected future data that will differ among alternatives.

RELEVANT INFORMATION. See *Relevant data for decision making*.

RELEVANT RANGE. The band of activity in which budgeted sales and expense relationships will be valid.

REPLACEMENT COST. *Cost* to replenish a given amount of an *asset*.

REQUIRED RATE OF RETURN. Minimum desired rate of return.

RESERVE. Has one of three meanings: (1) a restriction of dividend-declaring power as denoted by a specific subdivision of *retained income*; (2) an offset to an *asset*; and (3) an estimate of a definite *liability* of indefinite or uncertain amount.

RESIDUAL INCOME (RI). The *net income* of a *profit center* or investment center, less the "imputed" interest on the net *assets* used by the center.

RESIDUAL INTEREST. The *owners' equity* in the entity's *assets* after deducting *liabilities* and any other claims with a higher priority.

RESIDUAL VALUE. The predicted disposal value of a *long-lived asset*.

RESPONSIBILITY ACCOUNTING. A system of accounting that recognizes various responsibility centers throughout the organization and reflects the plans and actions of each of these centers by allocating particular *revenues* and *costs* to those having the pertinent responsibilities. Also called *profitability accounting* and *activity accounting*.

RETAINED EARNINGS. See *Retained income*.

RETAINED INCOME. Additional *owners' equity* generated by *profits*.

RETURN ON INVESTMENT (ROI). A measure of *income* or *profit* divided by the investment required to help obtain the *income* or *profit*.

RETURN ON STOCKHOLDERS' EQUITY. The rate of return on the invested capital of the shareholders.

REVALUATION EQUITY. That portion of *stockholders' equity* that shows all accumulated *holding gains* not otherwise shown in *retained income*.

REVENUES. Generally, a gross increase in net *assets* from delivering goods or services. More specifically, revenues are inflows or other enhancements of *assets* of an enterprise or settlements of its *liabilities* (or a combination of both) during a period from delivering or producing goods, rendering services, or other activities that constitute the enterprise's ongoing major or central operations.

RI. Symbol for *residual income.*

ROI. Symbol for *return on investment.*

SAFETY STOCK. A minimum inventory that provides a cushion against reasonably expected maximum demand and against variations in *lead time.*

SALES MIX. The relative combination of the quantities of a variety of company products that compose total sales.

SALES VOLUME VARIANCES. Difference between the *flexible budget* amounts and the *static budget* amounts.

SCOREKEEPING. That data accumulation function of the accountant's information-supplying task which enables both internal and external parties to evaluate the financial performance of the firm.

SCRAP VALUE. See *Residual value.*

SECURITIES AND EXCHANGE COMMISSION (SEC). The federal agency designated by the U.S. Congress as holding the ultimate responsibility for authorizing the generally accepted accounting principles for companies whose stock is held by the general investing public.

SEGMENT. Any line of activity or part of an organization for which separate determination of costs and sales is wanted.

SEGMENT MARGIN. The contribution margin for each segment less all separable fixed *costs,* both discretionary and committed. A measure of long-run profitability.

SENSITIVITY ANALYSIS. Measuring how the basic predicted results will be affected by variations in the critical data inputs that will influence those results.

SEPARABLE COST. A *cost* directly identifiable with a particular segment.

SERVICE DEPARTMENTS. Those departments that exist solely to aid the production departments by rendering specialized assistance with certain phases of the work.

SHORT-RUN PERFORMANCE MARGIN. The contribution margin for each segment, less separable discretionary *costs.*

SHORT-TERM INVESTMENT. A temporary investment in *marketable securities* of otherwise idle cash.

SINGLE-STEP INCOME STATEMENT. One that groups all *revenue* together (sales plus interest and rent revenues) and then lists and deducts all *expenses* together without drawing any intermediate subtotals.

SOURCE DOCUMENTS. The original records of any *transaction,* internal or external, that occurs in the *entity's* operation.

SPECIFIC IDENTIFICATION. This inventory method concentrates on the physical tracing of the particular items sold.

SPENDING VARIANCE. Basically, a *price variance* applied to variable overhead. However, other factors besides price may influence the amount of the *variance.*

SPLIT-OFF POINT. The juncture of the production where the *joint products* become individually identifiable.

STAFF AUTHORITY. The authority to *advise* but not to command; it may be exerted laterally or upward.

STANDARD ABSORPTION COSTING. That type of product costing in which the cost of the finished unit is calculated as the sum of the *costs* of the standard allowances for factors of production, *including* fixed factory overhead, without reference to the costs actually incurred.

STANDARD COST. A carefully predetermined *cost* that should be attained, usually expressed per unit.

STANDARD DEVIATION. Square root of the mean of the squared deviations from the *expected value.*

STANDARD DIRECT COSTING. That type of product costing in which the *cost* of the finished unit is calculated as the sum of the costs of the standard allowances for the factors of production, *excluding* fixed factory overhead, which is treated as a *period cost,* and without reference to costs actually incurred.

STATED VALUE. A nominal value of a stock certificate that is usually far below the actual cash invested. See *Par value.*

STATEMENT OF CHANGES IN FINANCIAL POSITION. A formal explanation of the sources and uses of resources, usually sources and uses of *working capital.*

STATEMENT OF FINANCIAL CONDITION. A synonym for *balance sheet.*

STATEMENT OF FINANCIAL POSITION. A substitute term for *balance sheet.*

STATEMENT OF PROFIT AND LOSS. The *income statement.*

STATEMENT OF RETAINED EARNINGS. A financial statement that analyzes changes in the *retained earnings* or *retained income* account for a given period.

STATEMENT OF RETAINED INCOME. Synonym for *statement of retained earnings.*

STATEMENT OF SOURCES AND APPLICATIONS OF FUNDS. See *Statement of changes in financial position.*

STATES. Synonym for *events.*

STATES OF NATURE. Synonym for *events.*

STATIC BUDGET. A *budget* prepared for only one level of activity and, consequently, one that does not adjust automatically to changes in the level of volume.

STEP-DOWN METHOD. Allocation of service department *costs* to other service departments as well as production departments. Once a department's costs are allocated to other departments, no subsequent department costs are allocated back to it.

STEP-VARIABLE COSTS. Those *variable costs* that change abruptly at intervals of activity because their acquisition comes in indivisible chunks.

STOCK DIVIDEND. A distribution to stockholders of additional shares of any class of the distributing company's stock, without any payment to the company by the stockholders.

STOCKHOLDERS' EQUITY. The excess of *assets* over *liabilities* of a corporation.

STOCK SPLIT. The issuance of additional shares for no consideration and under conditions indicating that the objective is to increase the number of outstanding shares for the purpose of reducing their unit market price.

STRAIGHT-LINE DEPRECIATION. A method of allocating the *cost* of plant assets to periods or products based on units of time (years). The result is an equal amount of *depreciation* per period.

SUBORDINATED. A creditor claim that is junior to other creditor claims.

SUBORDINATED DEBENTURE. See *Subordinated* and *Debenture.*

SUBSIDIARY. A corporation owned or controlled by a parent company, through the ownership of more than 50% of the voting stock.

SUBUNIT AUTONOMY. Possession of decision-making power by managers of subunits of an organization.

SUM-OF-THE-YEARS'-DIGITS DEPRECIATION (SYD). A popular form of *accelerated depreciation* where the sum of the digits is the total of the numbers representing the years of life.

SUNK COST. A *cost* that has already been incurred and, therefore, is irrelevant to the decision-making process. Also called *historical cost.*

SYSTEM. A formal means of gathering data to aid and coordinate the process of making decisions.

TANGIBLE ASSETS. See *Fixed assets.*

TARGET RATE. Often used in *capital budgeting* as either the minimum desired rate of return or the budgeted rate of return.

TAX ALLOCATION. See *Interperiod tax allocation.*

TAX SHIELD. Usually defined as noncash items (e.g., *depreciation*) charged against income, thus protecting that amount from tax.

TERMINAL VALUE. See *Residual value.*

TIME-ADJUSTED RATE OF RETURN. See *Internal rate of return.*

TIMING DIFFERENCES. Differences between the periods in which *transactions* affect pretax income for reporting to income tax authorities and the periods in which they enter into the determination of pretax income for reporting to shareholders.

TOTAL PROJECT APPROACH. A method of comparing two or more alternative courses of action by computing the total expected inflows and outflows of each alternative and then converting these flows to their present value by applying some predetermined minimum rate of return.

TRADEMARKS. Distinctive identifications of a manufactured product or of a service taking the form of a name, a sign, a slogan, or an emblem.

TRADING ON THE EQUITY. Using borrowed money at a fixed interest rate and/or using funds provided by preferred stockholders with the aim of enhancing the rate of return on common stockholders' equity.

TRADITIONAL COSTING. See *Absorption costing.*

TRANSACTION. Any event that affects the financial position of an *entity* and requires recording.

TRANSFER PRICE. The amounts charged by one subunit of an organization for a product or service that it supplies to another subunit of the same organization.

TRANSFERRED-IN COSTS. In *process costing, costs* incurred in a previous department that have been received by a subsequent department.

TREASURY STOCK. Outstanding stock that has subsequently been repurchased and not canceled by the company.

UNADJUSTED RATE OF RETURN. See *Accounting rate of return.*

UNAVOIDABLE COST. The opposite of *avoidable cost.*

UNBILLED REVENUE. Fees earned in a given period but for which no bills have been sent to the customer.

UNDERAPPLIED FACTORY OVERHEAD. The excess of actual *factory overhead* over the factory overhead applied to products.

UNDISTRIBUTED EARNINGS. See *Retained income.*

UNEARNED REVENUE. See *Deferred revenue.*

UNEXPIRED COSTS. Any *expenditures* benefiting the future; any asset, including *prepaid expenses,* normally appearing on a *balance sheet.*

USAGE VARIANCE. *Efficiency variance* pertaining to materials or *direct labor.*

VARIABLE BUDGET. See *Flexible budget.*

VARIABLE COST. A *cost* that is uniform *per unit* but fluctuates in total in direct proportion to changes in the related total activity or volume.

VARIABLE COST PERCENTAGE. The *variable expense ratio* expressed as a percentage.

VARIABLE COSTING. See *Direct costing.*

VARIABLE COST RATIO. See *Variable expense ratio.*

VARIABLE EXPENSE RATIO. All variable *expenses* divided by *revenues.*

VARIANCE. The deviation of actual results from the expected or budgeted result.

VERIFIABILITY. See *Objectivity.*

VOLUME VARIANCE. See *Production volume variance* and *Sales volume variances.*

WEIGHTED-AVERAGE COST. This inventory method assumes that all items available for sale during the period are best represented by their weighted-average cost prices.

WORKING CAPITAL. The excess of *current assets* over *current liabilities.*

WORKING-CAPITAL CYCLE. See *Operating cycle.*

WORKING CAPITAL PROVIDED BY OPERATIONS. *Revenues* less all operating *expenses* requiring *working capital.*

WORK MEASUREMENT. The careful analysis of a task, its size, the methods used in its performance, and its efficiency.

ZBB. Symbol for *zero-base budgeting.*

ZERO-BASE BUDGETING (ZBB). Budgeting from the ground up as though the *budget* were being initiated for the first time.

INDEX

Verifiability, 540
Visual-fit method, 224–25

W

Wages:
  accounting for accrual of, 527–28
  accounting for payment of, 527
Weighted-average inventory method,
    397–401, 406, 636–38
Weight unit, 389
Working capital:
  defined, 571
  depreciation and, 578, 581–82

Working capital *(cont.)*
  in example of changes statement, 572–73
  preparation of changes statement and,
    575–76
  provided by operations, 576–77
  typical sources and uses of, 571–72
Working-capital cycle, 557, 559
Work-in-process inventory, 62
Work measurement, 213–15

Z

Zero-base budgeting, 218–19